Mastering

VMware® Infrastructure 3

Mastering

VMware® Infrastructure 3

Chris McCain

WILEY

Wiley Publishing, Inc.

Acquisitions Editor: Tom Cirtin
Development Editor: Lisa Bishop
Technical Editor: Chris Huss
Production Editor: Christine O'Connor
Copy Editor: Liz Welch
Production Manager: Tim Tate
Vice President and Executive Group Publisher: Richard Swadley
Vice President and Executive Publisher: Joseph B. Wikert
Vice President and Publisher: Neil Edde
Proofreader: Ian Golder and David Fine, Word One
Indexer: Robert Swanson
Cover designe: Ryan Sneed
Cover image: © Pete Gardner/Digital Vision/gettyimages

Library of Congress Cataloging-in-Publication Data
McCain, Chris.
    Mastering VMware Infrastructure 3 / Chris McCain, Rawlinson Rivera. — 1st ed.
        p. cm.
    ISBN 978-0-470-18313-7 (pbk. : website)
    1.   VMware.   2.   Operating systems (Computers)   3.   Virtual computer systems.
I. Rivera, Rawlinson, 1976- II. Title.
    QA76.76.O63M37483 2008
    005.4'3—dc22
                                        2007045713

10 9 8 7 6 5 4 3

Dear Reader

Thank you for choosing *Mastering VMware Infrastructure 3*. This book is part of a family of premium quality Sybex books, all written by outstanding authors who combine practical experience with a gift for teaching.

Sybex was founded in 1976. More than thirty years later, we're still committed to producing consistently exceptional books. With each of our titles we're working hard to set a new standard for the industry. From the paper we print on, to the authors we work with, our goal is to bring you the best books available.

I hope you see all that reflected in these pages. I'd be very interested to hear your comments and get your feedback on how we're doing. Feel free to let me know what you think about this or any other Sybex book by sending me an email at nedde@wiley.com, or if you think you've found a technical error in this book, please visit http://sybex.custhelp.com. Customer feedback is critical to our efforts at Sybex.

Best regards,

Neil Edde
Vice President and Publisher
Sybex, an Imprint of Wiley

This book is dedicated to the support group that surrounds me and makes each day an enjoyable step in the architecture of my life. To my wife and sons — who remind me each day why everything I do has so much value and meaning. To my mom and brothers — who have helped me develop the tools to be successful in life. To my good friends Shawn and Rawlinson — who assure me each day that being a nerd is one of the best things I can be. Without all these folks work would be work — not an enjoyable experience to look forward to. It is all those close to me who help me face and overcome the many challenges that I face. I am certain that without their support I would not thrive for a moment.

Acknowledgments

Although I am content knowing that books like this don't hit the top of the best sellers list, I know that this one has been written as a labor of love. There are many people to credit for keeping the dream alive.

First, a quick thanks to VMware directly. They have constructed a product that has altered the layout of information systems and that is unrivaled in today's market. While the VMware engineers have been great at producing the software, the employees of VMware education have been instrumental in bringing the product to the world. Thanks to VMware Education Services for their support.

To all of the folks at Sybex, including Tom Cirtin, Pete Gaughan, Lisa Bishop, Christine O'Connor, and Neil Edde — thank you. I have written for several publishers and without a doubt this group of folks works as hard as any I have seen. Tom and Pete, thanks for believing in this book even when the technologies changed so quickly that the scope seemed to go out of focus. Lisa and Christine, I don't know what to say except for a humongous *thanks* for putting up with my ever-so-frequent revisions and my repetitious queries regarding file locations. Thanks also to copy editor Liz Welch, proofreaders Ian Golder and David Fine of Word One, and indexer Robert Swanson. The organization and professionalism of the Sybex team was a cornerstone in making this book happen.

A special thanks to Andrew Ellwood, my longtime friend and colleague, who contributed some incredible intellectual property to this book. I can trace my success in training and IT back to a few people and without a doubt Andrew is one of those few. You are a great mentor and friend, and I know we will continue to work together in as many ways as the IT world will let us.

To Brian Perry, who, like Andrew, lent his great virtualization mind to the creation of this book. Undoubtedly you have one of the brightest minds in the business, and I am lucky to have had your expertise reflected in the final product. Certainly our paths will lead us to more endeavors where we can pool our brainpower for the greater good of the virtualization community.

And what would a good book be without an amazing technical editor? Thank you to Chris Huss, who like me, saw this project as a labor of love and a way to spread that virtual love to the rest of the virtualization community. It was clear from the beginning that we shared a vision of what we wanted to offer through this book. I believe your work and efforts cemented our ability to deliver exactly what we set out to do. Thanks Chris.

To Rawlinson, my partner in crime, who may have gotten lost in the mix, you can rest assured that you keep me motivated to stay on top of my game. You are constantly pushing me to be a better nerd. But more so thanks for being a great friend who makes what I do for a living the best job on the planet. You may have been dancing on stage with Madonna at the MTV Movie Awards but that just makes your transition to IT professional (aka Nerd#1) even more impressive than anyone can imagine. Who would have thought you would go from X Games rollerblading competitor to one of the best and brightest minds in the world of information technology?

Last, but certainly not least, to Shawn Long, thank you for an unquantifiable amount of support in completing this book. The hardware, software, and time you supplied are nothing in comparison to the uncompromising faith you had in my finishing the book. If the world could see the way we work, there would be no better picture of teamwork. What I don't know, you certainly do know. What you don't know, I try to learn. While our work is built around something virtual, our friendship is anything but. A lifetime of thanks for the energy you supply in helping me succeed.

I almost forgot: Thank you to Red Bull and Smarties for giving me the sugar high needed to push through the nights.

About the Author

Chris McCain is an author, consultant, and trainer who focuses on VMware and Microsoft products. As an owner in the National IT Training & Certification Institute (NITTCI) and a partner at viLogics, he has been instrumental in providing training to thousands of IT professionals and consulting to some of the largest companies in the world. Chris has provided support in the form of training and consulting to companies such as Microsoft, VMware, IBM, Dell, Credit Suisse, Intel, and others.

In addition to virtualization, Chris offers expertise across a variety of technologies, including Active Directory, public key infrastructure, SQL Server 2005, IPSec, SharePoint, and more.

Chris holds a long list of industry certifications, including VCP, VCI, MCT, MCITP, MCSE: Security, and CISSP, to name a few. His other book credits include contributing to the *Microsoft Office SharePoint Server 2007 Administrator's Companion* by Microsoft Press, the *MCITP Self-Paced Training Kit (Exam 70-647)* by Microsoft Press, and the *Mike Meyers Passport Certification Series: Exam 70-293* by McGraw-Hill.

As an IT professional, Chris is dedicated to providing value to the community as a whole through his personal blogs at `http://www.GetYourNerdOn.com`. Visit the site to find a growing library of videos and commentary on IT technologies across Microsoft, VMware, and more.

Contents at a Glance

Contents

Introduction

For the past several years, the buzzword exciting the information technology community has been security: network security, host security, application security, just about any type of security imaginable. There is a new buzzword around the information technology world and it's rapidly becoming the most talked about technology since the advent of the client/server network. That buzzword is virtualization.

Virtualization is the process of implementing multiple operating systems on the same set of physical hardware to better utilize the hardware. Companies with strong plans to implement virtualized computing environments look to gain many benefits, including easier systems management, increased server utilization, and reduced datacenter overhead. Traditional IT management has incorporated a one-to-one relationship between the physical servers implemented and the roles they play on the network. When a new database is to be implemented, we call our hardware vendor of choice and order a new server with specifications to meet the needs of the database. Days later we may order yet another server to play the role of a file server. This process of ordering servers to fill the needs of new network services is oftentimes consuming and unnecessary given the existing hardware in the datacenter. To ensure stronger security, we separate services across hosts to facilitate the process of hardening the operating system. We have learned over time that the fewer the functions performed by a server, the fewer the services that are required to be installed, and, in turn, the easier it is to lock down the host to mitigate vulnerabilities. The byproduct of this separation of services has been the exponential growth of our datacenters into large numbers of racks filled with servers, which in most cases are barely using the hardware within them.

Virtualization involves the installation of software commonly called a hypervisor. The hypervisor is the virtualization layer that allows multiple operating systems to run on top of the same set of physical hardware. Figure I.1 shows the technological structure of a virtualized computing environment. Virtual machines that run on top of the hypervisor can run almost any operating system, including the most common Windows and Linux operating systems found today as well as legacy operating systems from the past.

FIGURE I.1
The process of virtualization involves a virtualization layer called a hypervisor that separates the physical hardware from the virtual machines. This hypervisor manages the virtual machines' access to the underlying hardware components.

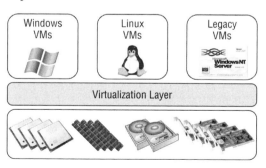

For those just beginning the journey to a virtual server environment and for those who have already established their virtual infrastructures, the reasons for using virtualization can vary. Virtualization offers many significant benefits, including server consolidation, rapid server provisioning, new options in disaster recovery, and better opportunities to maintain service-level agreements (SLAs), to name a few. Perhaps the most common reason is server consolidation.

Most servers in a datacenter are performing at less than 10 percent CPU utilization. This leaves an overwhelming amount of processing power available but not accessible because of the separation of services. By virtualizing servers into virtual machines running on a hypervisor, we can better use our processors while reducing rack space needs and power consumption in the datacenter.

Depending on the product used to virtualize a server environment, there are many more benefits to virtualization. Think of the struggles IT professionals have had throughout the years and you'll gain a terrific insight into why virtualization has become such a popular solution. The simple process of moving a server from a datacenter in Tampa, Florida, to a datacenter in Atlanta, Georgia, is a good example of a common pain point for IT pros. The overhead of removing an 80-pound server from a rack, boxing it, shipping it, unboxing it, and placing it back into another rack is enough to make you want to virtualize. With virtual machines this same relocation process can be reduced to simply copying a directory to an external media device, shipping the external media device, and copying the directory back to another ESX implementation. Other methods, such as virtual machine replication and full and delta images of virtual machines, can be taken with third-party tools.

Although a handful of products have emerged for enterprise-level virtualization, this book provides all of the details an IT professional needs to design, deploy, manage, and monitor an environment built on the leading virtualization product, VMware Infrastructure 3.

What Is Covered in This Book

This book is written with a start-to-finish approach to installing, configuring, managing, and monitoring a virtual environment using the VMware Infrastructure 3 (VI3) product suite. The book begins by introducing the VI3 product suite and all of its great features. After introducing all of the bells and whistles, this book details an installation of the product and then moves into configuration. Upon completion of the installation and configuration, we move into virtual machine creation and management, and then into monitoring and troubleshooting. This book can be read from cover to cover to gain an understanding of the VI3 product in preparation for a new virtual environment. Or it can also be used as a reference for IT professionals who have begun their virtualization and want to complement their skills with real-world tips, tricks, and best practices as found in each chapter.

This book, geared toward the aspiring and the practicing virtualization professional, provides information to help implement, manage, maintain, and troubleshoot an enterprise virtualization scenario. As an added benefit we have included four appendices: one offering solutions to Master It problems, another detailing common Linux and ESX commands, another discussing some of the more popular tools and third-party products that can be used to facilitate virtual infrastructure management, and another describing best practices for VI3.

Here is a glance at what's in each chapter:

Chapter 1: Introducing VMware Infrastructure 3   begins with a general overview of all the products that make up the VI3 product suite. VMware has created a suite with components to allow for granular licensing and customization of features for each unique deployment.

Chapter 2: Planning and Installing ESX Server   looks at planning the physical hardware, calculating the return on investment, and installing ESX Server 3.5 both manually and in an unattended fashion.

Chapter 3: Creating and Managing Virtual Networks   dives deep into the design, management, and optimization of virtual networks. In addition, it initiates discussions and provides solutions on how to integrate the virtual networking architecture with the physical network architecture while maintaining network security.

Chapter 4: Creating and Managing Storage Devices   provides an in-depth overview of the various storage architectures available for ESX Server 3.5. This chapter discusses fibre channel, iSCSI, and NAS storage design and optimization techniques as well as the new advanced storage features like round-robin load balancing, NPIV, and Storage VMotion.

Chapter 5: Installing and Configuring VirtualCenter 2.0   offers an all-encompassing look at VirtualCenter 2.5 as the brains behind the management and operations of a virtual infrastructure built on the VI3 product suite. From planning, installing, and configuring, this chapter covers all aspects of VirtualCenter 2.5.

Chapter 6: Creating and Managing Virtual Machines   introduces the practices and procedures involved in provisioning virtual machines through VirtualCenter 2.5. In addition, you'll be introduced to timesaving techniques, virtual machine optimization, and best practices that will ensure simplified management as the number of virtual machines grows larger over time.

Chapter 7: Migrating and Importing Virtual Machines   continues with more information about virtual machines but with an emphasis on performing physical-to-virtual (P2V) and virtual-to-virtual (V2V) migrations in the VI3 environment. This chapter provides a solid, working understanding of the VMware Converter Enterprise tool and offers real-world hints at easing the pains of transitioning physical environments into virtual realities.

Chapter 8: Configuring and Managing Virtual Infrastructure Access Controls   covers the security model of VI3 and shows you how to manage user access for environments with multiple levels of system administration. The chapter shows you how to use Windows users and groups in conjunction with the VI3 security model to ease the administrative delegation that comes with enterprise-level VI3 deployments.

Chapter 9: Managing and Monitoring Resource Access   provides a comprehensive look at managing resource utilization. From individual virtual machines to resource pools to clusters of ESX Server hosts, this chapter explores how resources are consumed in VI3. In addition, you'll get details on the configuration, management, and operation of VMotion and Distributed Resource Scheduler (DRS).

Chapter 10: High Availability and Business Continuity   covers all of the hot topics regarding business continuity and disaster recovery. You'll get details on building highly available server clusters in virtual machines as well as multiple suggestions on how to design a backup strategy using VMware Consolidated Backup and other backup tools. In addition, this chapter discusses the use of VMware High Availability (HA) as a means of providing failover for virtual machines running on a failed ESX Server host.

Chapter 11: Monitoring Virtual Infrastructure Performance   takes a look at some of the native tools in VI3 that allow virtual infrastructure administrators the ability to track and troubleshoot performance issues. The chapter focuses on monitoring CPU, memory, disk, and network adapter performance across ESX Server 3.5 hosts, resource pools, and clusters in VirtualCenter 2.5.

Chapter 12: Securing a Virtual Infrastructure   covers different security management aspects, including managing direct ESX Server access and integrating ESX Servers with Active Directory.

Chapter 13: Configuring and Managing ESXi   finishes the book by looking at the future of the hypervisor in ESXi. This chapter covers the different versions of ESXi and how they are managed.

Appendix A: Solutions to the Master It Problems   offers solutions to the Master It problems in each chapter.

Appendix B: Common Linux and ESX Commands   focuses on navigating through the Service Console command line and performing management, configuration, and trouble-shooting tasks.

Appendix C: Third-Party Virtualization Tools   discusses some of the virtualization tools available from third-party vendors.

Appendix D: Virtual Infrastructure 3 Best Practices   serves as an overview of the design, deployment, management, and monitoring concepts discussed throughout the book. It is designed as a quick reference for any of the phases of a virtual infrastructure deployment.

The Mastering Series

The *Mastering* series from Sybex provides outstanding instruction for readers with intermediate and advanced skills, in the form of top-notch training and development for those already working in their field and clear, serious education for those aspiring to become pros. Every *Mastering* book includes:

◆   Real-World Scenarios, ranging from case studies to interviews, that show how the tool, technique, or knowledge presented is applied in actual practice

◆   Skill-based instruction, with chapters organized around real tasks rather than abstract concepts or subjects

◆   Self-review test questions, so you can be certain you're equipped to do the job right

The Hardware Behind the Book

Due to the specificity of the hardware for installing VMware Infrastructure 3, it might be difficult to build an environment in which you can learn by implementing the exercises and practices detailed in this book. It is possible to build a practice lab to follow along with the book; however, the lab will require very specific hardware and can be quite costly. Be sure to read Chapter 2 before attempting to construct any type of environment for development purposes.

For the purpose of writing this book, we used the following hardware configuration:

◆   Three Dell PowerEdge 2850 servers for ESX

    ◆   Two Intel Xeon 2.8GHz processors

    ◆   4GB of RAM

    ◆   Two hard drives in RAID-1 Array (Mirror)

    ◆   QLogic 23xx iSCSI HBA

    ◆   Four Gigabit Ethernet adapters: two on-board, two and two in a dual-port expansion card

    ◆   QLogic 40xx iSCSI HBA

- EMC CX-300 storage device

- Two Brocade fibre channel switches

- LeftHand Networks iSCSI virtual storage appliance

As we move through the book, we'll provide diagrams to outline the infrastructure as it progresses.

Who Should Buy This Book

This book is for IT professionals looking to strengthen their knowledge of constructing and managing a virtual infrastructure on VMware Infrastructure 3. While the book can be helpful for those new to IT, there is a strong set of assumptions made about the target reader:

- A basic understanding of networking architecture

- Experience working in a Microsoft Windows environment

- Experience managing DNS and DHCP

- A basic understanding of how virtualization differs from traditional physical infrastructures

- A basic understanding of hardware and software components in standard x86 and x64 computing

How to Contact the Author

I welcome feedback from you about this book or about books you'd like to see from me in the future. You can reach me by writing to chris.mccain@nittci.com or by visiting my blog at http://www.getyournerdon.com.

Chapter 1

Introducing VMware Infrastructure 3

VMware Infrastructure 3 (VI3) is the most widely used virtualization platform available today. The lineup of products included in VI3 makes it the most robust, scalable, and reliable server virtualization product on the market. With dynamic resource controls, high availability, distributed resource management, and backup tools included as part of the suite, IT administrators have all the tools they need to run an enterprise environment consisting of anywhere from ten to thousands of servers.

In this chapter you will learn to:

Identify the role of each product in the VI3 suite

Discriminate between the different products in the V13 suite

Understand how V13 differs from other virtualization products

Exploring VMware Infrastructure 3

The VI3 product suite includes several products that make up the full feature set of enterprise virtualization. The products in the VI3 suite include:

◆ VMware ESX Server

◆ VMware Virtual SMP

◆ VMware VirtualCenter

◆ Virtual Infrastructure Client

◆ VMware VMotion

◆ VMware Distributed Resource Scheduler (DRS)

◆ VMware High Availability (HA)

◆ VMware Consolidated Backup (VCB)

Rather than wait to introduce the individual products in their own chapters, I'll introduce each product so I can refer to the products and explain how they affect each piece of the design, installation, and configuration of your virtual infrastructure. Once you understand the basic functions and features of each product in the suite, you'll have a better grasp of how that product fits into the big picture of virtualization, and you'll more clearly understand how each of the products fits into the design.

VMware ESX Server

VMware ESX Server 3.5 and ESXi are the core of the VI3 product suite. They function as the hypervisor, or virtualization layer, that serves as the foundation for the whole VI3 package. Unlike some virtualization products that require a host operating system, ESX Server is a bare metal installation, which means no host operating system (Windows or Linux) is required. ESX Server is a leaner installation than products requiring a host operating system, which allows more of its hardware resources to be utilized by virtual machines rather than by processes required to run the host. The installation process for ESX Server installs two components that interact with each other to provide a dynamic and robust virtualization environment: the Service Console and the VMkernel.

The Service Console, for all intents and purposes, is the operating system used to manage ESX Server and the virtual machines that run on the server. The console includes services found in other operating systems, such as a firewall, Simple Network Management Protocol (SNMP) agents, and a web server. At the same time, the Service Console lacks many of the features and benefits that other operating systems offer. This deficiency, however, serves as a true advantage in making the Service Console a lean, mean, virtualization machine.

The other installed component is the VMkernel. While the Service Console gives you access to the VMkernel, it is the VMkernel that is the real foundation of the virtualization process. The VMkernel manages the virtual machines' access to the underlying physical hardware by providing CPU scheduling, memory management, and virtual switch data processing. Figure 1.1 shows the structure of ESX Server.

FIGURE 1.1
Installing ESX Server installs two interoperable components: 1) the Linux-derived Service Console, and 2) the virtual machine–managing VMkernel.

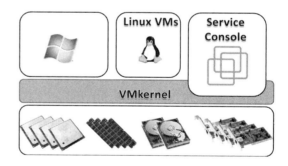

ESXi is the next generation of the VMware virtualization foundation in that it lightens the load to a 32MB footprint as installation of a hypervisor only. ESXi is *only* a hypervisor and does not have any reliance on an accompanying Service Console.

I'll go into much more detail about the installation of ESX Server in Chapter 2. The installation procedure of ESX Server also allows for the configuration of VMware File System (VMFS) datastores. Chapter 4 will provide an in-depth look at the various storage technologies. Once your core product, ESX Server, is installed, you can build off this product with the rest of the product suite.

VMware Virtual SMP

The VMware Virtual Symmetric Multi-Processing (SMP) product allows virtual infrastructure administrators to construct virtual machines with multiple virtual processors. VMware Virtual

SMP is *not* the licensing product that allows ESX Server to be installed on servers with multiple processors; it is the configuration of multiple processors *inside* a virtual machine. Figure 1.2 identifies the differences between multiple processors in the ESX Server host system and multiple virtual processors.

FIGURE 1.2
VMware Virtual SMP allows virtual machines to be created with two or four processors.

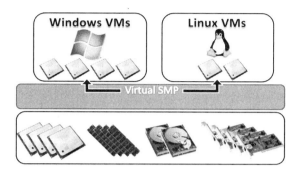

In Chapter 6 we'll look at how, why, and when to build virtual machines with multiple virtual processors.

ESX Server includes a host of new features and support for additional hardware and storage devices. At the urging of the virtualization community, ESX Server now boasts support for Internet Small Computer Systems Interface (iSCSI) storage and network attached storage (NAS) in addition to Fibre Channel storage technologies. Chapter 4 describes the selection, configuration, and management of all three storage technologies supported by ESX Server.

VMware VirtualCenter

Stop for a moment and think about your current Windows network. Does it include Active Directory? There is a good chance it does. Now imagine your Windows network without Active Directory, without the ease of a centralized management database, without the single sign-on capabilities, and without the simplicity of groups. That is what managing ESX Server computers would be like without using VMware VirtualCenter 2.0. Now calm yourself down, take a deep breath, and know that VirtualCenter, like Active Directory, is meant to provide a centralized management utility for all ESX Server hosts and their respective virtual machines. VirtualCenter is a Windows-based, database-driven application that allows IT administrators to deploy, manage, monitor, automate, and secure a virtual infrastructure in an almost effortless fashion. The back-end database (SQL or Oracle) used by VirtualCenter stores all the data about the hosts and virtual machines. In addition to its configuration and management capabilities, VirtualCenter provides the tools for the more advanced features of VMware VMotion, VMware DRS, and VMware HA. Figure 1.3 details the VirtualCenter features provided for the ESX Server hosts it manages.

In Chapter 5, you'll learn the details of the VirtualCenter implementation, configuration, and management, as well as look at ways to ensure its availability.

Virtual Infrastructure Client

The Virtual Infrastructure (VI) Client is a Windows-based application that allows you to connect to and manage an ESX Server or a VirtualCenter Server. You can install the VI Client by browsing to the URL of an ESX Server or VirtualCenter and selecting the appropriate installation link. The VI Client is a graphical user interface (GUI) used for all the day-to-day management tasks and for the advanced configuration of a virtual infrastructure. Using the client to connect directly to an ESX Server requires that you use a user account residing in the Service Console (a Linux account), while using the client to connect to a VirtualCenter Server requires you to use a Windows account. Figure 1.4 shows the account authentication for each connection type.

FIGURE 1.3
VirtualCenter 2.0 is a Windows-based application used for the centralization of authentication, accounting, and management of ESX Server hosts and their corresponding virtual machines.

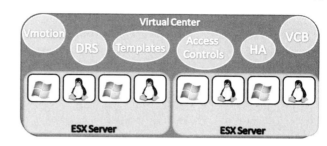

FIGURE 1.4
The Virtual Infrastructure Client can be used to manage an individual ESX Server by authenticating with a Linux account that resides in the Service Console; however, it can also be used to manage an entire enterprise by authenticating to a VirtualCenter Server using a Windows account.

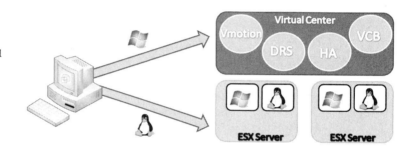

Almost all the management tasks available when you're connected directly to an ESX Server are available when you're connected to a VirtualCenter Server, but the opposite is not true. The management capabilities available through VirtualCenter Server are more significant and outnumber the capabilities of connecting directly to an ESX Server.

VMware VMotion and Storage VMotion

If you have read anything about VMware, you have most likely read about the extremely unique and innovative feature called VMotion. VMotion is a feature of ESX Server and VirtualCenter that allows a running virtual machine to be moved from one ESX Server host to another without having to power off the virtual machine. Figure 1.5 illustrates the VMotion feature of VirtualCenter.

FIGURE 1.5
The VMotion feature of VirtualCenter allows a running virtual machine to be transitioned from one ESX Server host to another.

VMotion satisfies an organization's need for maintaining service-level agreements (SLAs) that guarantee server availability. Administrators can easily instantiate a VMotion to remove all virtual machines from an ESX Server host that is to undergo scheduled maintenance. Once the maintenance is complete and the server is brought back online, VMotion can once again be utilized to return the virtual machines to the original server.

Even in a normal day-to-day operation, VMotion can be used when multiple virtual machines on the same host are in contention for the same resource (which ultimately is causing poor performance across all the virtual machines). VMotion can solve the problem by allowing an administrator to migrate any of the running virtual machines that are facing contention to another ESX host with greater availability for the resource in demand. For example, when two virtual machines are in contention with each other for CPU power, an administrator can eliminate the contention by performing a VMotion of one of the virtual machines to an ESX host that has more available CPU. More details on the VMware VMotion feature and its requirements will be provided in Chapter 9.

Storage VMotion builds on the idea and principle of VMotion in that downtime can be reduced when running virtual machines can be migrated to different physical environments. Storage VMotion, however, allows running virtual machines to be moved between datastores. This feature ensures that outgrowing datastores or moving to a new SAN does not force an outage for the effected virtual machines.

VMware Distributed Resource Scheduler (DRS)

Now that I've piqued your interest with the introduction of VMotion, let me introduce VMware Distributed Resource Scheduler (DRS). If you think that VMotion sounds exciting, your anticipation will only grow after learning about DRS. DRS, simply put, is a feature that aims to provide automatic distribution of resource utilization across multiple ESX hosts that are configured in a cluster. An ESX Server cluster is a new feature in VMware Infrastructure 3. The use of the term *cluster* often draws IT professionals into thoughts of Microsoft Windows Server clusters. However, ESX Server clusters are not the same. The underlying concept of aggregating physical hardware to serve a common goal is the same, but the technology, configuration, and feature sets are very different between ESX Server clusters and Windows Server clusters.

An ESX Server cluster is an implicit aggregation of the CPU power and memory of all hosts involved in the cluster. Once two or more hosts have been assigned to a cluster, they work in unison to provide CPU and memory to the virtual machines assigned to the cluster. The goal of DRS is to provide virtual machines with the required hardware resources while minimizing the amount of contention for those resources in an effort to maintain good performance levels.

DRS has the ability to move running virtual machines from one ESX Server host to another when resources from another host can enhance a virtual machine's performance. Does that sound familiar? It should, because the behind-the-scenes technology for DRS is VMware VMotion. DRS can be configured to automate the placement of each virtual machine as it is powered on as well as to manage the virtual machine's location once it is running. For example, let's say three servers have been configured in an ESX Server cluster with DRS enabled. When one of those servers begins to experience a high contention for CPU utilization, DRS will use an internal algorithm to determine which virtual machine(s) will experience the greatest performance boost by being moved to another server with less CPU contention. Figure 1.6 outlines the automated feature of DRS.

FIGURE 1.6
VMware Distributed
Resource Scheduler
(DRS) aims to maintain
balance and fairness
of resource utilization
for virtual machines
running within an ESX
Server cluster.

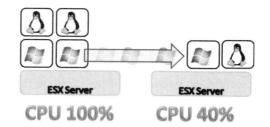

Chapter 9 dives deeper into the configuration and management of DRS on an ESX Server cluster.

VMware High Availability (HA)

With the introduction of the ESX Server cluster, VMware has also introduced a new feature called VMware High Availability (HA). Once again, by nature of the naming conventions (clusters, high availability), many traditional Windows administrators will have preconceived notions about this feature. Those notions, however, are premature in that VMware HA does not function like a high-availability configuration in Windows. The VMware HA feature provides an automated process for restarting virtual machines that were running on an ESX Server at a time of complete server failure. Figure 1.7 depicts the virtual machine migration that occurs when an ESX Server that is part of an HA-enabled cluster experiences failure.

FIGURE 1.7
The VMware High
Availability (HA) fea-
ture will power on any
virtual machines that
were previously running
on an ESX Server that
has experienced server
failure.

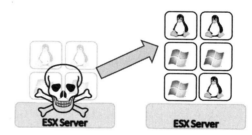

The VMware HA feature, unlike DRS, does not use the VMotion technology as a means of migrating servers to another host. In a VMware HA failover situation, there is no anticipation of failure; it is not a planned outage and therefore there is no time to perform a VMotion. VMware HA does not provide failover in the event of a single virtual machine failure. It provides an automated restart of virtual machines during an ESX Server failure.

Chapter 10 will explore the configuration and working details of VMware High Availability.

VMware Consolidated Backup (VCB)

One of the most critical aspects to any network, not just a virtualized infrastructure, is a solid backup strategy as defined by a company's disaster recovery and business continuity plan. VMware Consolidated Backup (VCB) is a Windows application that provides a LAN-free Fibre Channel or iSCSI-based backup solution that offloads the backup processing to a dedicated physical server. VCB takes advantage of the snapshot functionality in ESX Server to mount the snapshots into the file system of the dedicated VCB server. Once the respective virtual machine files are mounted, entire virtual machines or individual files can be backed up using third-party backup tools. VCB scripts integrate with several major third-party backup solutions to provide a means of automating the backup process. Figure 1.8 details a VCB implementation.

FIGURE 1.8
VMware Consolidated Backup (VCB) is a LAN-free online backup solution that uses a Fibre Channel or iSCSI connection to expedite and simplify the backup process.

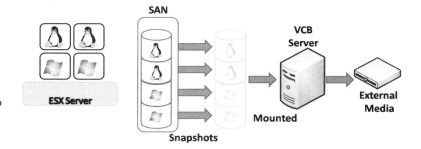

In Chapter 10 you'll learn how to use VCB to provide a solid backup and restore practice for your virtual infrastructure.

Real World Scenario

VIRTUAL INFRASTRUCTURE 3 VS. VMWARE SERVER (AND THE OTHERS)

The Virtual Infrastructure 3 (VI3) product holds a significant advantage over most other virtualization products because virtualization on VI3 does not require a host operating system. Products like VMware Server and Microsoft Virtual Server 2005 both require an underlying operating system to host the hypervisor.

The lack of the host operating system in VI3 offers additional stability and security. Without an underlying operating system like Windows, there is less concern for viruses, spyware, and unnecessary exposure to vulnerabilities.

With products like VMware Server (which require a host operating system), limitations from the host operating systems spill into the virtualization deployment. For example, installing VMware Server on Windows Server 2003 Web edition would establish two processors and 2GB of RAM limitations on VMware Server, despite its ability to use up to 16 processors and 64GB of RAM. At the same time, however, there's the advantage that hosted products have over the bare metal install of ESX Server. The existence of the host operating system greatly extends the level of hardware support on which the hypervisor will run. If the host operating system offers support, then the virtual machine will too. A great example of this hardware support is to look at the use of USB. ESX Server does not support USB, while VMware Server (and Workstation) includes support. Since the underlying host understands the USB technology, the virtual machines will also offer support.

In all, each of the virtualization products has its place in a network infrastructure. The Virtual Infrastructure 3 product is more suited to the mission-critical enterprise data center virtualization scenario, while the VMware Server product is best for noncritical test or branch office scenarios. And of course you cannot forget the best part of VMware Server: it's *free*!

The Bottom Line

Identify the role of each product in the VI3 suite. Now that you've been introduced to the products included in the VMware Infrastructure 3 suite, we can begin discussing the technical details, best practices, and how-tos that will make your life as a virtual infrastructure administrator a whole lot easier. This chapter has shown that each of the products in the VI3 suite plays an integral part in the overall process of creating, managing, and maintaining a virtual enterprise. Figure 1.9 highlights the VI3 product suite and how it integrates and interoperates to provide a robust set of tools upon which a scalable, reliable, and redundant virtual enterprise can be built.

FIGURE 1.9
The products in the VMware Infrastructure suite work together to provide a scalable, robust, and reliable framework for creating, managing, and monitoring a virtual enterprise.

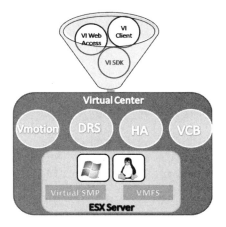

The next chapter will begin a start-to-finish look at designing, implementing, managing, monitoring, and troubleshooting a virtual enterprise built on VI3. I'll dive into much greater detail on each of the products I introduced in this chapter. This introduction should provide you with a solid foundation so we can discuss the different products beginning with the next chapter. You can use this introduction as a reference throughout the remaining chapters if you want to refresh your base knowledge for each of the products in the suite.

Master It You want to centralize the management of ESX Server hosts and all virtual machines.

Master It You want to minimize the occurrence of system downtime during periods of planned maintenance.

Master It You want to provide an automated method of maintaining fairness and balance of resource utilization.

Master It You want to provide an automated restart of virtual machines when an ESX Server fails.

Master It You want to institute a method of providing disaster recovery and business continuity in the event of virtual machine failure.

Chapter 2

Planning and Installing ESX Server

Now that you've been introduced to VMware Infrastructure 3 (VI3) and its suite of applications in Chapter 1, you're aware that ESX Server 3 is the foundation of VI3. The deployment, installation, and configuration of the ESX Server requires adequate planning for a VMware-supported installation.

In this chapter you will learn to:

◆ Understand ESX Server compatibility requirements

◆ Plan an ESX Server deployment

◆ Install ESX Server

◆ Perform postinstallation configuration

◆ Install the Virtual Infrastructure Client (VI Client)

Planning a VMware Infrastructure 3 Deployment

In the world of information technology management, there are many models that reflect the project management lifecycle. In each of the various models, it is almost guaranteed that you'll find a step that involves planning. Though these models might stress this stage of the lifecycle, the reality is that planning is often passed over very quickly if not avoided altogether. However, a VI3 project requires careful planning due to hardware constraints for the ESX Server software. In addition, the server planning can have a significant financial impact when calculating the return on investment for a VI3 deployment.

VMware ESX Server includes stringent hardware restrictions. Though these hardware restrictions provide a limited environment for deploying a supported virtual infrastructure, they also ensure the hardware has been tested and will function as expected as a platform for VMware's VMkernel hypervisor. Although not every vendor or whitebox configuration can play host to ESX Server, the list of supported hardware platforms will continue to change as newer models and more vendors are tested by VMware. The official VMware Systems Compatibility guide can be found on VMware's website at `http://www.vmware.com/pdf/vi3_systems_guide.pdf`. With a quick glance at the systems compatibility guide, you will notice Dell, HP, and IBM among a dozen or so lesser-known vendors. Within the big three, you will find different server models that provide a tested and supported platform for ESX Server.

THE RIGHT SERVER FOR THE JOB

Selecting the appropriate server is undoubtedly the first step in ensuring a successful Vl3 deployment. In addition, it is the only way to ensure VMware will provide any needed support.

A deeper look into a specific vendor, like Dell, will reveal that the compatibility guide identifies server models of all sizes (see Figure 2.1) as valid ESX Server hosts, including:

- The 1U PowerEdge 1950
- The 2U PowerEdge 2950 and 2970
- The 4U PowerEdge R900
- The 6U PowerEdge 6850 and 6950
- The PowerEdge 1955 Blade Server

FIGURE 2.1
Servers on the compatibility list come in various sizes and models.

The model selected as the platform has a direct effect on server configuration and scalability, which will in turn influence the return on investment for a virtual infrastructure.

Calculating the Return on Investment

In today's world, every company is anxious and hoping for the opportunity for growth. Expansion is often a sign that a company is fiscally successful and in a position to take on the new challenges that come with an increasing product line or customer base. For the IT managers, expansion means planning and budgeting for human capital, computing power, and spatial constraints.

As many organizations are figuring out, virtualization is a means of reducing the costs and overall headaches involved with either consistent or rapid growth. Virtualization offers solutions that help IT managers address the human, computer, and spatial challenges that accompany corporate demands.

Let's look at a common scenario facing many successful medium-to-large business environments. Take the fictitious company Learn2Virtualize (L2V) Inc. L2V currently has 40 physical servers and an EMC fibre channel storage device in a datacenter in St. Petersburg, Florida. During the coming fiscal year, through acquisitions, new products, and new markets L2V expects to grow to more than 100 servers. If L2V continues to grow using the traditional information systems model, they will buy close to 100 physical servers during their rapid expansion. This will allow them to continue minimizing services on hosts in an effort to harden the operating systems. This practice is not uncommon for many IT shops. As a proven security technique, it is best to minimize the number of services provided by a given server to reduce the exposure to vulnerability across different services. Using physical server deployment will force L2V to look at their existing and future power and datacenter space consumption. In addition, they will need to consider the additional personnel that might be required. With physical server implementations, L2V might be looking at expenses of more than $150,000 in hardware costs alone. And while that might be on the low side, consider that power costs will rise and that server CPU utilization, if it is consistent with industry norms, might sit somewhere between 5 and 10 percent. The return on investment just doesn't seem worth it.

Now let's consider the path to virtualization. Let's look at several options L2V might have if they move in the direction of server consolidation using the VI3 platform. Since L2V already owns a storage device, we'll refrain from including that as part of the return on investment (ROI) calculation for their virtual infrastructure. L2V is interested in the enterprise features of VMotion, DRS, and HA, and therefore they are included in each of the ROI calculations.

THE PRICE OF HARDWARE

The prices provided in the ROI calculations were abstracted from the small and medium business section of Dell's website, at http://www.dell.com. The prices should be used only as a sample for showing how to determine the ROI. It is expected that you will work with your preferred hardware vendor on server make, model, and pricing while using the information given here as a guide for establishing the right hardware for your environment and budget.

Each of the following three ROI calculations identifies various levels of availability, including single server failure, two-server failure, or no consideration for failover. All of the required software licenses have been included as part of the calculation; however, annual licensing fees have not been included since there are several options and they are recurring annual charges.

Scenario 1: Quad Core 3 Server Cluster

3 Dell 2950 III Energy Smart 2U Servers	**$35,000 ($7,000 × 5)**
Two Quad-Core Intel CPUs	
16GB of RAM	
Two 73GB 10K RPM SAS hard drives in RAID1	
Two QLogic 2460 4Gbps fibre channel HBAs	
Dell Remote Access Controller (DRAC)	
Six network adapters (two onboard, one quad-port card)	
3-Year Gold 7 × 24, 4-hour response support	
VMware Midsize Acceleration Kit	$21,824
3 VMware Infrastructure 3 Enterprise licenses (6 procs)	
Virtual SMP	
VirtualCenter Agent	
VMFS	
VMotion and Storage VMotion	
DRS	
HA	
Update Manager	
VCB	
1 VirtualCenter 2.5 Foundation license	
10 CPU Windows Server 2003 Datacenter Licenses	$25,000 ($2,500 × 10)
Hardware and licensing total	$71,824
Per virtual machine costs	
One server HA failover capacity: Average 10, 1GB VMs per host (30 VMs)	$2,394 per VM
Maximum capacity: Average 14, 1GB VMs per host (42 VMs)	$1,710 per VM

Scenario 2: Quad Core Four Server Cluster

4 Dell R900 Servers	**$164,000 ($41,000 × 4)**
Four Quad-Core Intel processors	
128GB of RAM	
Two 73GB 10K RPM SAS hard drives in RAID1	
Two QLogic 2460 4Gbps fiber channel HBAs	
Dell Remote Access Controller (DRAC)	

4 Dell R900 Servers	**$164,000 ($41,000 × 4)**
Six network adapters (two onboard, one quad port card)	
3-Year Gold 7 × 24, 4-hour response support	
8 CPU VI3 Enterprise licenses	$75,328 ($9,416 × 8)
8 VMware Infrastructure 3 Enterprise licenses (16 processors)	
Virtual SMP	
VirtualCenter Agent	
VMFS	
VMotion and Storage VMotion	
DRS	
HA	
Update Manager	
VCB	
1 VMware Virtual Center 2.0 License	$8,180
16 CPU Windows Server 2003 Datacenter Licenses	$40,000 ($2,500 × 16)
Hardware and licensing totals	$287,508
Per virtual machine costs	
One server HA failover capacity: Average 80, 1GB VMs per host (320 VMs)	$898 per VM
Two server HA failover capacity: Average 60, 1GB VMs per host (240 VMs)	$1,197 per VM

Although both scenarios present a different deployment, the consistent theme is that using VI3 reduces the cost per server by introducing them as virtual machines. At the lowest cost, virtual machines would each cost $898, and even at the highest cost, they would run $2,394 per machine. These cost savings do not include the intrinsic savings on power consumption, space requirements, and additional employees required to manage the infrastructure.

Though your environment may certainly differ from the L2V Inc. example, the concepts and processes of identifying the ROI will be similar. Use these examples to identify the sweet spot for your company based on your existing and future goals.

THE BEST SERVER FOR THE JOB

With several vendors and even more models to choose from, it is not difficult to choose the right server for a VI3 deployment. However, choosing the best server for the job means understanding the scalability and fiscal implications while meeting current and future needs. The samples provided are simply guidelines that can be used. They do not take into consideration virtual machines with high CPU utilization. The assumption in the previous examples is that memory will be the resource with greater contention. You may adjust the values as needed to determine what the ROI would be for your individualized virtual infrastructure.

No matter the vendor or model selected, ESX Server 3.5 has a set of CPU and memory maximums, as shown in Table 2.1.

ESX SERVER MAXIMUMS

Where appropriate, each chapter will include additional values for ESX Server 3.5 maximums for NICS, storage configuration, virtual machines, and so forth.

TABLE 2.1: ESX Server 3.5 Maximums

COMPONENT	MAXIMUM
No. of virtual CPUs per host	128
No. of cores per host	32
No. of logical CPU (hyperthreading enabled)	32
No. of virtual CPUs per core	8
Amount of RAM per host	256GB

ESX Server Installation

In addition to the choice of server vendor, model, and hardware specification, the planning process involves a decision between using ESX Server 3.5 versus ESXi 3.5. This chapter will cover the installation of ESX Server 3.5, while Chapter 13 will examine the specifics of ESXi 3.5.

Installing ESX Server 3.5 can be done in a graphical mode or a text-based installation, which limits the intricacy of the screen configuration during the installation. The graphical mode is the more common of the two installation modes. The text mode is reserved for remote installation scenarios where the wide area network is not strong enough to support the graphical nature of the graphical installation mode.

ESX Server Disk Partitioning

Before we offer step-by-step instructions for installing ESX Server, it is important to review some of the functional components of the disk architecture upon which ESX Server will be installed. Because of its roots in Red Hat Linux, ESX Server does not use drive letters to represent the partitioning of the physical disks. Instead, like Linux, ESX Server uses mount points to represent the various partitions. Mount points involve the association of a directory with a partition on the physical disk. Using mount points for various directories under the root file system protects the root file system by not allowing a directory to consume so much space that the root becomes full. Since most folks are familiar with the Microsoft Windows operating system, think of the following example. Suppose you have a server that runs Windows using a standard C: system volume label. What happens when the C drive runs out of space? Without going into detail let s just leave the answer as a simple one: bad things. Yes, bad things happen when the C drive of a Windows computer runs out of space. In ESX Server, as noted, there is no C drive. The root of the operating system file structure is called exactly that: the root. The root is noted with the / character. Like Windows, if the / (root) runs out of space, bad things happen. Figure 2.2 compares Windows disk partitioning and notation against the Linux disk partitioning and notation methods.

FIGURE 2.2
Windows and Linux represent disk partitions in different ways. Windows, by default uses drive letters, while Linux uses mount points.

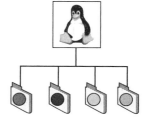

C:
D:
E:
F:

In addition, because of the standard x86 architecture, the disk partitioning strategy for ESX Server involves creating three primary partitions and an extended partition that contains multiple logical partitions. The standard x86 disk partitioning strategy does not allow for more than three primary partitions to be created.

ALLOW ME

It is important to understand the disk architecture for ESX Server; however, as you will soon see, the installation wizard provides a selection that creates all the proper partitions automatically.

With that said, the partitions created are enough for ESX Server 3.5 to run properly, but there is room for customizing the defaults. The default partitioning strategy for ESX Server 3.5 is shown in Table 2.2.

TABLE 2.2:   Default ESX Partition Scheme

MOUNT POINT NAME	TYPE	SIZE
/boot	Ext3	100MB
/	Ext3	5000MB (5GB)
(none)	VMFS 3	Varies
(none)	Swap	544MB
/var/log	Ext3	2000MB (2GB)
(none)	vmkcore	100MB

THE /BOOT PARTITION

The /boot partition, as its name suggests, stores all the files necessary to boot and ESX Server. The default size of 100MB is ample space for the necessary files. This 100MB size, however, is twice the size of the default boot partition created during the installation of the ESX 2 product. It is not uncommon to find recommendations of doubling this to 200MB in anticipation of a future increase. By no means is this a requirement — it is just a suggestion. The assumption is that an existing installation is already configured for support of the next version of ESX, presumably ESX 4.0.

THE / PARTITION

The / partition is the root of the Service Console operating system. We have already alluded to the importance of the / (root) of the file system, but now we should detail the implications of its configuration. Is 5GB enough for the / of the console operating system? The obvious answer is that 5GB must be enough if that is what VMware chose as the default. The minimum size of the / partition is 2.5GB, so the default is twice the size of the minimum. So why change the size of the / partition? Keep in mind that the / partition is where any third-party applications would install by default. This means that six months, eight months, or a year from now when there are dozens of third-party applications available for ESX Server, all of these applications will likely be installed into the / partition. As you can imagine, 5GB can be used rather quickly. One of the last things on any administrator's list of things to do is reinstallations of each of their ESX Servers. Planning for future growth and the opportunity to install third-party programs into the Service Console means creating a / partition with plenty of space to grow. I, as well as many other consultants, often recommend that the / partition be given more than the default 5GB of space. It is not uncommon for virtualization architects to suggest root partition sizes of 20GB to 25GB. However, the most important factor is to choose a size that fits your comfort for growth.

THE SWAP PARTITION

The swap partition, as the name suggests, is the location of the Service Console swap file. This partition defaults to 544MB. As a general rule, swap files are created with a size equal to two times the memory allocated to the operating system. The same holds true for ESX Server. The swap partition is 544MB in size by default because the Service Console is allocated 272MB of RAM by default. By today's standards, 272MB of RAM seems low, but only because we are used to Windows servers requiring more memory for better performance. The Service Console is not as memory intensive as Windows operating systems can be. This is not to say that 272MB is always enough. Continuing with ideas from the previous section, if the future of the ESX Server deployment includes the installation of third-party products into the Service Console, then additional RAM will certainly be warranted. Unlike Windows or Linux, the Service Console is limited to only 800MB of RAM. The Post-Installation Configuration section of this chapter will show exactly how to make this change, but it is important to plan for this change during the installation so that the swap partition can be increased accordingly. If the Service Console is to be adjusted up to the 800MB maximum, then the swap partition should be increased to 1600MB (2 × 800MB).

THE /VAR/LOG PARTITION

The /var/log partition is created with a default size of 2000MB, or 2GB of space. This is typically a safe value for this partition. However, I recommend that you make a change to this default configuration. ESX Server uses /var directory during patch management tasks. Since the default partition is /var/log, this means that the /var partition is still under the / (root) partition. Therefore, space consumed in /var is space consumed in / (root). For this reason I recommend that you change the mount point to /var instead of /var/log and that you increase the space to a larger value like 10GB or 15GB. This alteration provides ample space for patch management without jeopardizing the / (root) file system and still providing a dedicated partition to store log data.

THE VMKCORE PARTITION

The vmkcore partition is the dump partition where ESX Server writes information about a system halt. We are all familiar with the infamous Windows blue screen of death (BSOD) either from experience or the multitude of jokes that arose from the ever-so-frequent occurrences. When an ESX Server crashes, it, like Windows, writes detailed information about the system crash. This information is written to the vmkcore type partition. Unlike Windows, an ESX Server system crash results in a purple screen of death (PSOD) that many administrators have never seen. The size of this partition does not need to be altered.

THE VMFS3 PARTITION

You might have noticed that I skipped over the VMFS3 partition. I did so for a reason. The VMFS3 partition is created, by default, with a size equal to the disk size minus the default sizes of all other partitions. In other words, ESX Server creates all the other partition types and then uses the remaining free space as the local VMFS3 storage. In most VI3 infrastructures, the local VMFS3 storage device will be negligible in light of the dedicated storage devices that will be in place. Fibre channel and iSCSI storage devices that provide the proper infrastructure for VMotion, DRS, and HA reduce the need for large amounts of local VMFS3 storage.

ALL THAT SPACE AND NOTHING TO DO

Although local disk space is useless in the face of a dedicated storage network, there are ways to take advantage of local storage rather than let it go to waste. LeftHand Networks (http://www .lefthandnetworks.com) has developed a virtual storage appliance (VSA) that presents local ESX Server storage space as an iSCSI target. In addition, this space can be combined with other local storage on other servers to provide data redundancy. And the best part of being able to present local storage as virtual shared storage units is the availability of VMotion, DRS, and HA.

Table 2.3 provides a customized partitioning strategy that offers strong support for any future needs in an ESX Server installation.

TABLE 2.3:   Custom ESX Partition Scheme

MOUNT POINT NAME	TYPE	SIZE
/boot	Ext3	200MB
/	Ext3	25,000MB (25GB)
(none)	VMFS 3	Varies
(none)	Swap	1,600MB(1.6GB)
/var	Ext3	12,000MB (12GB)
(none)	vmkcore	100MB

LOCAL DISKS, REDUNDANT DISKS

Just because local VMFS 3 storage might not hold much significance in an ESX Server deployment does not mean that all local storage is irrelevant. The availability of the /(root) file system, vmkcore, Service Console swap, and so forth is critical to a functioning ESX Server. For the safety of the installed Service Console always install ESX Server on a hardware-based RAID array. Unless you intend to use a product like LeftHand Networks' VSA, there is little need to build a RAID 5 array with three or more large hard drives. A RAID1 (mirrored) array provides the needed reliability while minimizing the disk requirements.

ESX Server 3.5 offers a CD-based installation and an unattended installation that uses the same kickstart file technology commonly used for unattended Linux installations. We'll begin by looking at a standard CD installation and then transition into the automated ESX Server installation method.

CD-ROM-Based Installation

Readers who have already done ESX Server installs are probably wondering what we could be talking about in this section given that the installation can be completed by simply clicking Next until the Finish button shows up. And though this is true, there are some significant decisions to be made through the installation — decisions that affect the future of the ESX Server deployment as well as decisions that could cause severe damage to company data. For this reason, it is important for the experienced administrator and the installation newbie to read this section carefully and understand how best to install ESX Server to support the current and future demands of the VI3 deployment.

Perform the following steps to install ESX Server 3.5 from a CD:

1. Configure the server to boot from the CD, insert the VMware ESX Server 3.5 CD, and reboot the computer.

2. Select the graphical installation mode by pressing the Enter key at the boot options screen, shown in Figure 2.3.

FIGURE 2.3
ESX Server 3.5 includes a graphical installation mode, which includes an enhanced GUI and a text-based installation mode better suited for installing over a wide area network.

3. At the CD Media Test screen, shown in Figure 2.4, click the Skip button to continue with the installation. Click the Test button to identify any errors in the installation media.

FIGURE 2.4
To prevent installation errors due to bad media, the CD can be tested early in the install procedure.

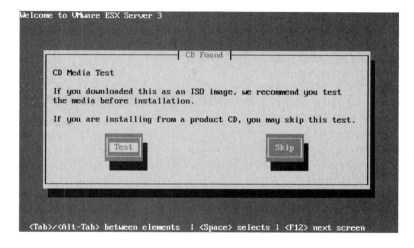

4. Click the Next button on the Welcome to the ESX Server 3.5 Installer screen.

5. Select the U.S. English keyboard layout, or whichever is appropriate for your installation, as shown in Figure 2.5. Then click the Next button.

FIGURE 2.5
ESX Server 3.5 offers support for numerous keyboard layouts.

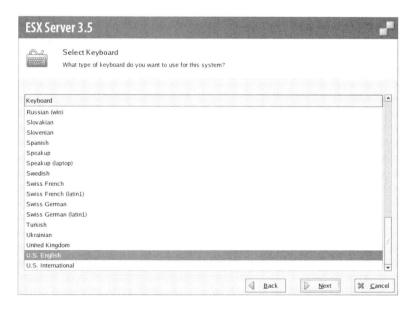

6. Select the Wheel Mouse (PS/2), shown in Figure 2.6. Or if you choose to match your mouse model exactly, select the appropriate option.

FIGURE 2.6
ESX Server 3.5 offers support for numerous models of mouse devices.

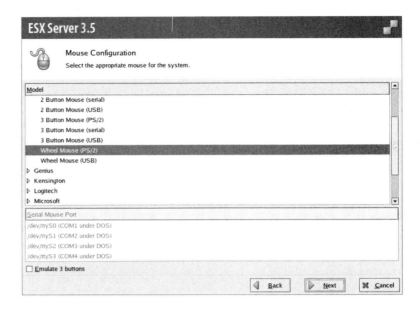

7. Select the Yes button to initialize any device to be used for storing the ESX Server 3.5 installation partitions, shown in Figure 2.7.

FIGURE 2.7
Unknown devices must be initialized for ESX Server 3.5 to be installed.

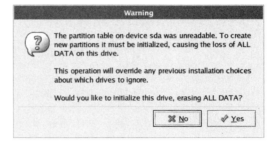

WARNING! YOU COULD LOSE DATA IF YOU DON'T READ THIS...

If SAN storage has already been presented to the server being installed, it could be possible to initialize SAN LUNs with production data. As a precaution, it is an excellent idea to disconnect the server from the SAN or ensure LUN masking has been performed to prevent the server from accessing LUNs.

Access to the SAN is only required during installation if a boot from SAN configuration is required.

8. As shown in Figure 2.8, select the check box labeled I Accept the Terms of the License Agreement and click the Next button.

FIGURE 2.8
The ESX Server 3.5
license agreement must
be accepted; however
no licenses are con-
figured during the
installation wizard.

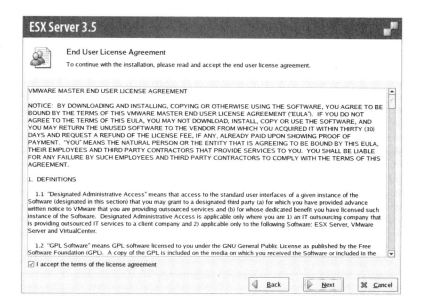

9. As shown in Figure 2.9, select the Recommended radio button option to allow the installation wizard to automatically partition the local disk. Ensure that the local disk option is
   selected in the Install ESX Server on the drop-down list. To protect any existing VMFS data,
   ensure that the Keep Virtual Machines and the VMFS (Virtual Machine File System) That
   Contains Them option is selected.

FIGURE 2.9
The ESX Server 3.5
installation wizard offers
automatic partitioning
of the selected disk and
protection for any exist-
ing data that resides
in a VMFS-formatted
partition.

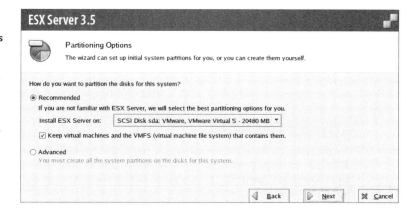

10. Click the Yes button on the partition removal warning, shown in Figure 2.10.

11. Review the partitioning strategy, as shown in Figure 2.11, and click the Next button to con-
    tinue the installation.

FIGURE 2.10
The ESX Server 3.5 installation wizard offers a warning before removing all partitions on the selected disk.

FIGURE 2.11
ESX Server 3.5 default partitioning provides a configuration that offers successful installation and system operation.

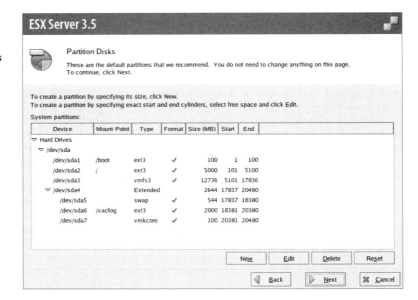

STRAY FROM THE NORM

As discussed in the previous section, it might be necessary to alter the default partitioning strategy. This does not mean that all partitions must be built from scratch. To change the default partition strategy, select the partition to change and click the Edit button.

Start the partition customization by reducing the space allocated to the local partition with a type of VMFS 3. Once this partition is reduced, the other partitions — /boot, /swap, and /var/log — can be edited. After these partitions have been reconfigured, any leftover space can be given back to the local VMFS 3 partition and the installation can proceed.

---

12. Ensure that the ESX Server 3.5 installation wizard has selected to boot from the same drive that was selected for partitioning. By default, the selection should be correct and should not be configurable without selecting the option to allow editing. As shown in Figure 2.12, this screen provides a default configuration consistent with the previous installation configuration. This avoids misconfiguration in which the installation is performed on a local disk but the server is booted from a SAN LUN, or vice versa.

FIGURE 2.12
An ESX Server 3.5 host should be booted from the same device where the installation partitions have been configured.

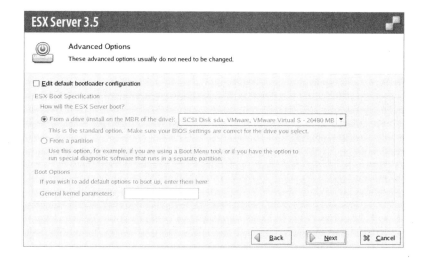

13. As shown in Figure 2.13, select the network interface card (NIC) through which the Service Console should communicate. Assign a valid IP address, as well as subnet mask, default gateway, DNS servers, and host name for the ESX Server 3.5 host.

FIGURE 2.13
A NIC must be selected and configured for Service Console communication over the appropriate physical network.

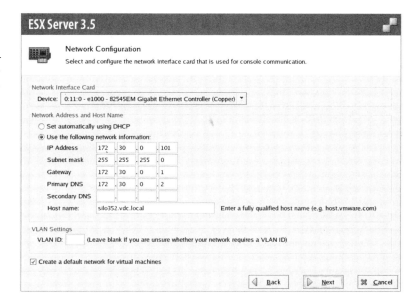

If the Service Console must communicate over a virtual LAN (VLAN), enter the appropriate VLAN ID in the VLAN Settings text box.

If virtual machines must communicate over the same physical subnet as the Service Console, leave the Create a Default Network for Virtual Machines option selected. The outcome of this option can always be modified during postinstallation configuration.

Once the Network Configuration page is configured correctly, click the Next button.

DO I HAVE TO MEMORIZE THE PCI ADDRESSES OF MY NICs?

Although the configuration screen for the Service Console is not very user friendly with respect to identifying the physical NICs in the computer, it is not a big deal to fix the NIC association should the wrong NIC be selected during the installation wizard. As part of the PostInstallation Configuration section of this chapter, we will detail how to recover if the wrong NIC is selected during the installation wizard.

The bright side is that if your hardware remains consistent, then the PCI addresses would also remain consistent. Therefore, company policy could document the PCI address to be selected during any new ESX Server deployments.

Keep in mind that since the NIC was incorrect, access to the server via SSH, web page, or VI Client will fail. The fix to be detailed later in the chapter requires direct access to the console or an out-of-band management tool like Dell's Remote Access Controller, which provides console access from a dedicated Ethernet port.

---

14. Select the appropriate time zone for the ESX Server host and then click the Next button, as shown in Figure 2.14.

FIGURE 2.14
ESX Server 3.5 can be configured with one of many time zones from around the world.

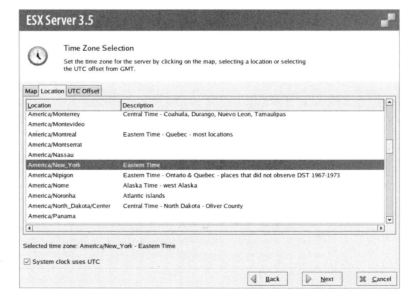

15. Set and confirm a root password, as shown in Figure 2.15.

FIGURE 2.15
FIGURE 2.15
Each ESX Server 3.5
host maintains its own
root user and password
configuration. The pass-
word must be at least
six characters.

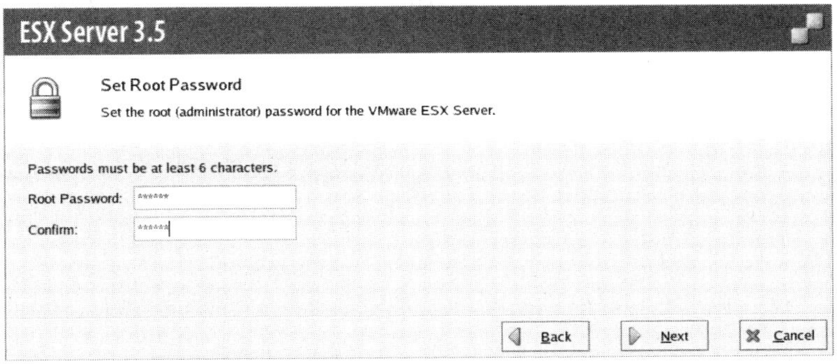

16. Review the installation configuration parameters, as shown in Figure 2.16.

FIGURE 2.16
The installation review
offers a final chance
to double-check the
server configuration.

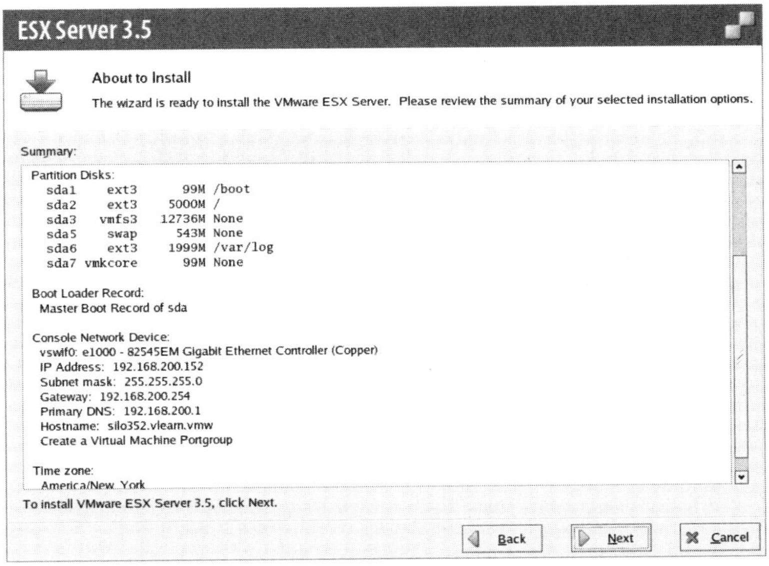

If everything looks correct, click the Next button to begin the installation procedure.

17. As shown in Figure 2.17, the installation will begin.

18. As shown in Figure 2.18, click the Finish button to reboot the computer once the installation is complete.

19. During the reboot, the GRUB boot loader will show the boot options, as shown in Figure 2.19.
Ensure that the VMware ESX Server option is selected and press the Enter key (or select nothing and the option will be selected by default).

20. Upon completion of the server reboot, the console session will display the information for accessing the server from a remote computer, as shown in Figure 2.20.

FIGURE 2.17
Installing ESX Server 3.5

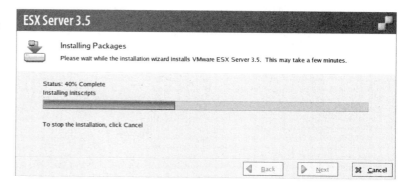

FIGURE 2.18
The new ESX Server 3.5 host must be rebooted to finalize the installation.

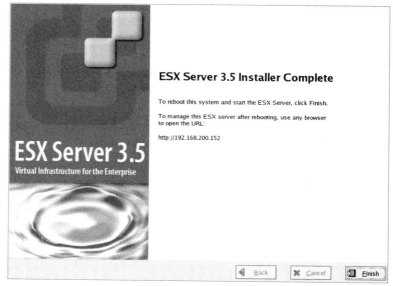

Despite the ease with which ESX Server 3.5 can be installed, it is still not preferable to perform manual, attended installations of a bulk number of servers. Nor is it preferable to perform manual, attended installation in environments that are rapidly deploying new ESX Server hosts. To support large numbers or rapid-deployment scenarios, ESX Server 3.5 can be installed in an unattended fashion.

Unattended ESX Server Installation

Installing an ESX Server 3.5 host in an unattended fashion can be done using third-party imaging tools or using the native VMware tools. Using the native tools requires several network-accessible components, including:

◆ An existing ESX Server 3.5 installation

◆ An NFS server accessible by the host to be installed

FIGURE 2.19
ESX Server 3.5 uses the
GRUB boot loader.

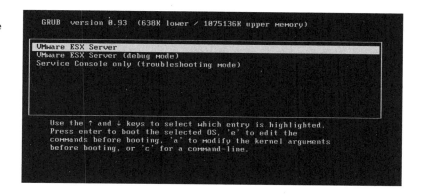

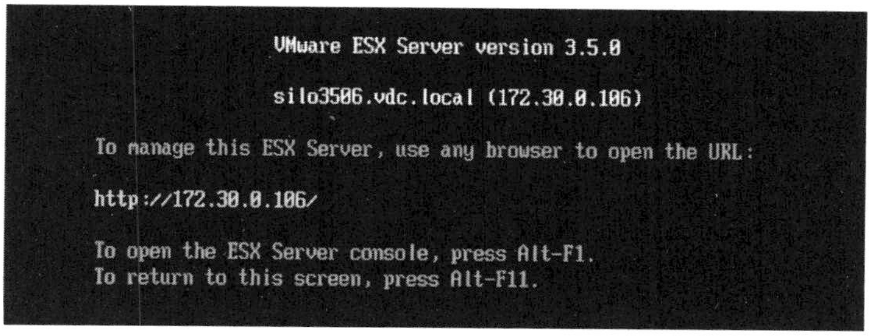

FIGURE 2.20
After a reboot, the con-
sole offers the data
necessary for access-
ing the server from a
remote computer.

- ◆ A copy of the ESX Server 3.5 installation media

- ◆ An installation script with the appropriate configuration parameters

Figure 2.21 details the infrastructure components needed to complete an unattended ESX Server 3.5 installation using the tools built into ESX Server 3.5.

The unattended installation procedure involves booting the computer and reading the installation files, and reading the unattended installation script. The destination host can be booted from CD, floppy, or PXE boot and then directed to the location of the installation files and answer files. The installation files and/or answer script can be stored and accessed from any of the following locations:

- ◆ An HTTP URL

- ◆ A shared NFS directory

- ◆ An FTP directory

- ◆ A CD (install files only)

- ◆ A floppy disk (answer files only)

Table 2.4 outlines the various methods and the boot options required for each option set. The boot option is typed at the boot prompt on ESX Server 3.5 graphical versus text mode selection screen.

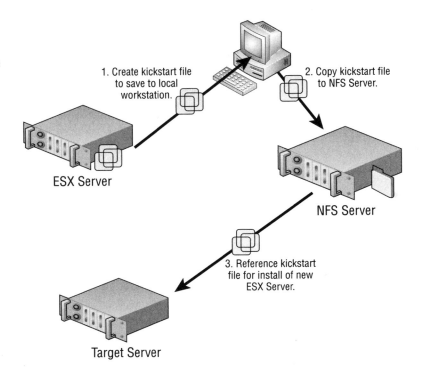

FIGURE 2.21
Performing an unattended ESX Server 3.5 installation requires the proper network servers and services.

TABLE 2.4: Unattended Installation Methods

IF THE COMPUTER BOOTS FROM	AND THE MEDIA IS STORED ON A	AND THE ANSWER FILE IS STORED ON A	THEN THE BOOT OPTION IS
PXE	(Media) URL	(Answer) URL	esx ks=<answer URL> method=<media URL> ksdevice=<NIC>
CD	CD	URL	esx ks=<answer URL> ksdevice=<NIC>
CD	CD	Floppy	esx ks=<floppy drive>
Floppy	URL	Floppy	esx ks=<floppy drive>

The kickstart answer file is created from a web-based wizard accessible from the default home page of an ESX Server host, as shown in Figure 2.22.

By default, an ESX Server 3.5 host is not configured to allow access to the scripted installer. An error, shown in Figure 2.23, identifies clearly that a given host has not been configured.

FIGURE 2.22
The home page for an ESX Server host provides access to the Scripted Installer, which generates an answer file through a web-based wizard.

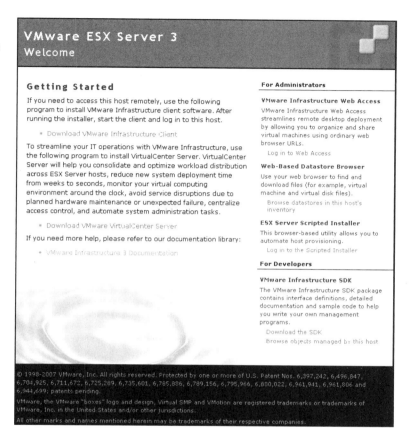

FIGURE 2.23
Access to the scripted installer must be enabled on an ESX Server 3.5 host.

Perform the following steps to enable the Scripted Installer on an ESX Server 3.5 host and to create a kickstart file:

1. Establish a console session with an ESX Server 3.5 host.

2. Type the following command:

   ```
   cd /usr/lib/vmware/webAccess/tomcat/apache-tomcat-5.5.17/webapps/ui/WEB-INF
   ```

3. Type the following command to get a list of all files and folders in the current directory:

   ```
   ls
   ```

4. Type the following command:

```
nano -w struts-config.xml
```

5. Comment out the following line by adding `<!--` to the front of the line and `-->` to the end of the line, as shown here and in Figure 2.24:

```
<!-- action path ="/scriptedInstall" type="org.apache.struts.actions.
ForwardAction" parameter="/WEB-INF/jsp/scriptedInstall/disabled.jsp" -->
```

FIGURE 2.24
Enabling the Scripted Installer requires minor editing of the `struts-config.xml` file.

6. Uncomment the following lines by removing the `<!--` and `-->` that precede and conclude the series of lines, as shown here and in Figure 2.24:

```
<action path="scriptedInstall" type="com.vmware.webcenter.scripted.
ProcessAction">
<forward name="scriptedInstall.form1" path="/Web-INF/jsp/scriptedInstall/
form1.jsp" />
<forward name="scriptedInstall.form2" path="/Web-INF/jsp/scriptedInstall/
form2.jsp" />
<forward name="scriptedInstall.form3" path="/Web-INF/jsp/scriptedInstall/
form3.jsp" />
<forward name="scriptedInstall.form4" path="/Web-INF/jsp/scriptedInstall/
form4.jsp" />
<forward name="scriptedInstall.form5" path="/Web-INF/jsp/scriptedInstall/
form5.jsp" />
<forward name="scriptedInstall.form6" path="/Web-INF/jsp/scriptedInstall/
form6.jsp" />
<forward name="scriptedInstall.form7" path="/Web-INF/jsp/scriptedInstall/
form7.jsp" />
</action>
```

7. Type the following command:

```
service vmware-webAccess restart
```

8. Return to the ESX Server 3.5 home page and click the link labeled Log In to the Scripted Installer.

9. The Scripted Install web-based wizard will begin. Select the appropriate options for the unattended installation, as shown in Figure 2.25, and then click the Next button. The options include:

   ◆ Installation Type: Initial Installation | Upgrade

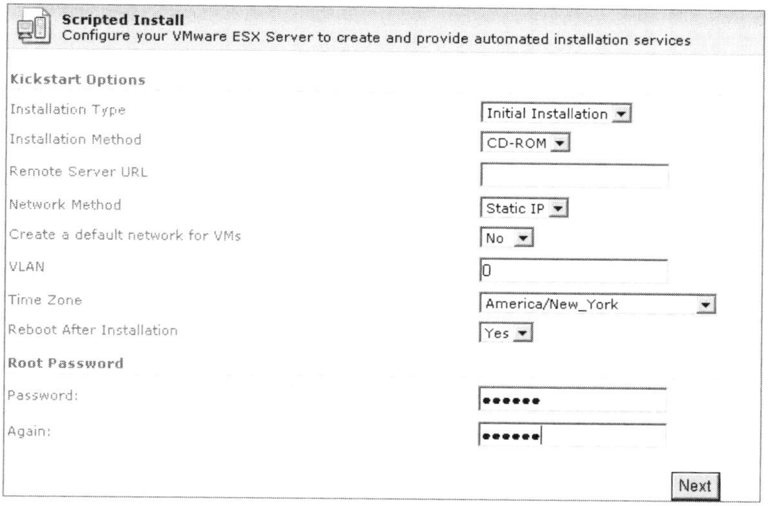

FIGURE 2.25
The Scripted Installer wizard defines the installation type and method as well as the Service Console configuration information.

Scripted Install
Configure your VMware ESX Server to create and provide automated installation services

Kickstart Options

Installation Type	Initial Installation ▾
Installation Method	CD-ROM ▾
Remote Server URL	
Network Method	Static IP ▾
Create a default network for VMs	No ▾
VLAN	0
Time Zone	America/New_York ▾
Reboot After Installation	Yes ▾

Root Password

Password:	●●●●●●
Again:	●●●●●●

Next

◆ Installation Method: CD-ROM | Remote | NFS
  ◆ This selection identifies where the installation files are located.

◆ Remote Server URL:<URL of remote server when installation method is set to Remote>

◆ Network Method: DHCP | Static IP
  ◆ Static will be the more common selection.

◆ Create a default network for VMs: Yes | No
  ◆ This option is negligible. If Yes is selected, the VM network can be deleted later. If No is selected, the VM network can be created later.

◆ VLAN:<VLAN ID if Service Console should be on a VLAN>
  ◆ Provide a VLAN ID for Service Console only if you know that a VLAN is configured on the physical switch to which the network adapter is connected.

◆ Time Zone

◆ Reboot After Installation: Yes | No

◆ Root password

10. As shown in Figure 2.26, set the hostname and IP address information of the server to be installed with the answer file and then click the Next button.

11. Select the check box labeled I Have Read and Accept the Terms of the License Agreement and then click the Next button.

12. As shown in Figure 2.27, configure the disk partitioning strategy and licensing mode for the target server and then click the Next button. Apply any necessary customizations to the partitions. Licensing options include: Post Install | Use License Server | Use Host License File.

13. Configure the licensing options, as shown in Figure 2.28, and then click the Next button.

FIGURE 2.26
The Scripted Installer defines the hostname and IP address configuration for the target ESX Server.

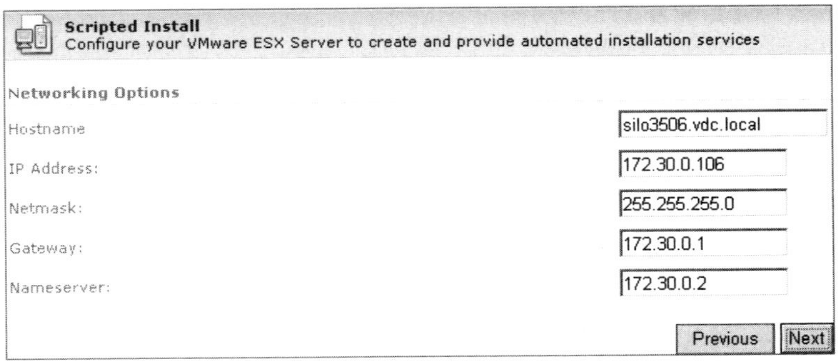

FIGURE 2.27
The Scripted Installer allows disk partitioning customizations and licensing mode.

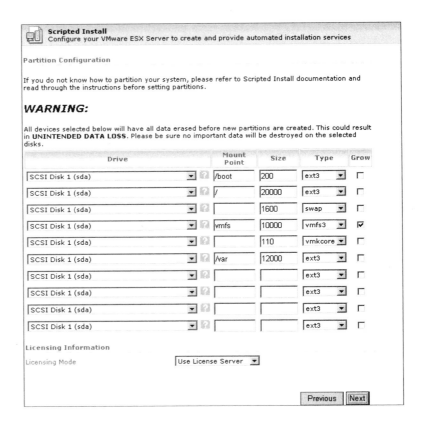

14. Click the Download Kickstart File from the final page of the Scripted Installer, as shown in Figure 2.29.

Since a Windows file share is not an option for the location of a kickstart file, the file must be copied to an appropriate location, which is most commonly an NFS directory. Use WordPad to review the kickstart file created by the Scripted Installer wizard. A sample default file is shown in Figure 2.30.

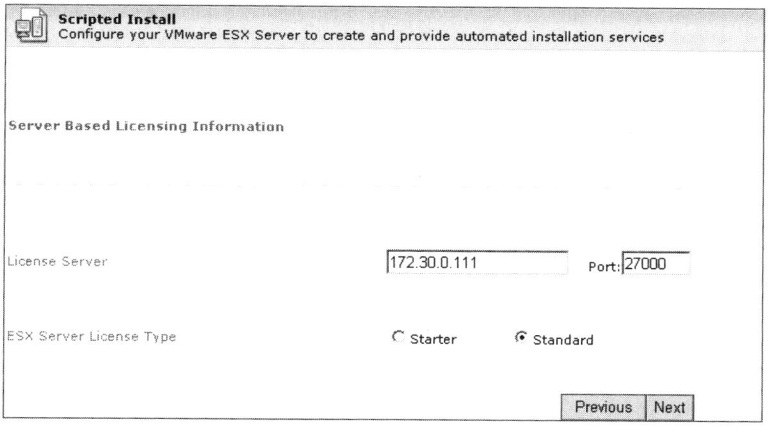

FIGURE 2.28
The Scripted Installer
automates the con-
figuration of pointing
an ESX Server to a
license server.

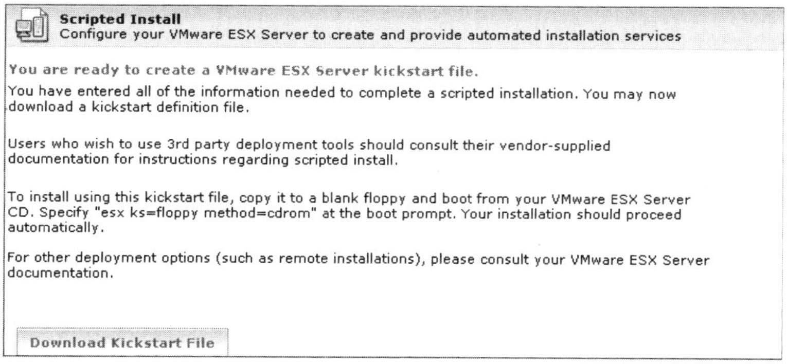

Scripted Install
Configure your VMware ESX Server to create and provide automated installation services

Server Based Licensing Information

License Server   172.30.0.111   Port: 27000

ESX Server License Type   ○ Starter   ● Standard

Previous | Next

FIGURE 2.29
The finished kickstart
file can be saved to the
local computer accessing
the Scripted Installer
web-based wizard.

Scripted Install
Configure your VMware ESX Server to create and provide automated installation services

You are ready to create a VMware ESX Server kickstart file.

You have entered all of the information needed to complete a scripted installation. You may now download a kickstart definition file.

Users who wish to use 3rd party deployment tools should consult their vendor-supplied documentation for instructions regarding scripted install.

To install using this kickstart file, copy it to a blank floppy and boot from your VMware ESX Server CD. Specify "esx ks=floppy method=cdrom" at the boot prompt. Your installation should proceed automatically.

For other deployment options (such as remote installations), please consult your VMware ESX Server documentation.

Download Kickstart File

Using free tools like Veeam FastSCP (`http://www.veeam.com`) or WinSCP (`http://www.winscp.com`), the kickstart file can be copied to an NFS directory that is accessible to the target ESX Server. Once the file is in place on the NFS directory, the unattended installation can be launched from the target server.

Perform the following steps to perform an unattended installation using a CD for the installation files and a remote NFS directory for the kickstart file:

1. Boot the target computer from the ESX Server 3.5 CD.

2. At the installation mode selection screen, type the following command, as shown in Figure 2.31:

    ```
    esx ks=nfs:<IP address or name of NFS server>:<path to kickstart file>
    ksdevice=<NIC to use>
    ```

3. The installation will begin and continue until the final reboot.

Kickstart files can be edited directly through WordPad so that the wizard does not have to be executed for each new installation. Unfortunately, the kickstart file does not provide a way of generating unique information for each installation and therefore each install will require a manually created (or adjusted) kickstart file that is specific to that installation — particularly configuration of static information that must be unique like IP address and hostname.

FIGURE 2.30

A sample kickstart file created by the Scripted Installer wizard, viewed through WordPad

```
# Auto-Generated Scripted Install Configuration file.
# This file is used for VMware ESX Server Scripted Install Deployment

# Installation Method
cdrom
# root Password
rootpw --iscrypted  $1$Eia8g0Ga$ItB/IHMck4JHCDcFSXNwZ/
# Authconfig
auth --enableshadow --enablemd5
# BootLoader ( The user has to use grub by default )
bootloader --location=mbr
# Timezone
timezone America/New_York
# X windowing System
skipx
# Install or Upgrade
install
# Text Mode
text
# Network install type
network --bootproto static --ip 172.30.0.106 --setmask 255.255.255.0 --gateway 172.30.0.1 --nameserver 172.30.0.2 --hostname silo3506.vdc.local
# Language
lang en_US
# Language Support
langsupport --default en_US
# Keyboard
keyboard us
# Mouse
mouse none
# Reboot after install ?
reboot
# Firewall settings
firewall --disabled
# Clear Partitions
clearpart --all --initlabel --drives=sda
# Partitioning
part /boot --fstype ext3 --size 200 --ondisk sda
part / --fstype ext3 --size 20000 --ondisk sda
part swap --size 1600 --ondisk sda
part None --fstype vmfs3 --size 10000 --grow --ondisk sda
part None --fstype vmkcore --size 110 --ondisk sda
part /var --fstype ext3 --size 12000 --ondisk sda
# VMware Specific Commands
vmaccepteula
vmlicense --mode=server --server=27000@172.30.0.111 --edition=esxFull
%packages
@base
%post
%vmlicense text
```

FIGURE 2.31

Using a local installation media with a kickstart file on an NFS directory

KICKSTART CUSTOMIZATIONS

You may have noticed the kickstart file creation wizard did not allow for configuration of Service Console NIC or any virtual networking or storage configuration. That's because by default it doesn't. The lack of Service Console NIC configuration can cause access problems because the kickstart installation automatically selects the NIC with the lowest PCI address. If your Service Console is not to be associated with the NIC that has the lowest PCI address, a postinstallation configuration will be required to unlink the current NIC and link the correct NIC. We will cover how to do this in the next section of this chapter.

Kickstart files can be edited to configure postinstallation configuration. These configurations can include Service Console NIC corrections, creation of virtual switches and port groups, storage configuration, and even customizations of Service Console config files for setting up external time servers.

The command-line syntax for virtual networking and storage will be covered in Chapters 3 and 4. The following kickstart file makes many postinstallation changes:

```
# Advanced Kickstart file with postinstallation configuration.
# Installation Method
cdrom
# root Password
rootpw --iscrypted a6fh$/hkQQrCaeucOmAe38$.captvmyeT4
# Authconfig
auth --enableshadow --enablemd5
# BootLoader (Grub has to be the default boot loader for ESX Server 3)
bootloader --driveorder=sda --location=mbr
# Timezone (set this time zone to fit your company policy)
timezone --utc UTC
# Do not install the X windowing System
skipx
# Clean Installation or upgrade an existing installation
install
# Text Mode
text
# Network install type (this server will have a static IP address of  172.30.0.105
with a subnet mask of 2555.255.255.0, a gateway of 172.30.0.1, a DNS server
# of 172.30.0.2 and a hostname of silo3505.vdc.local. It will not be configured
 on a vlan
network --bootproto static --ip 172.30.0.105 --netmask 255.255.255.0 --gateway
172.30.0.1 --nameserver 172.30.0.2 --hostname silo3505.vdc.local --vlanid=0
# Language
lang en_US
# Langauge Support
langsupport --default en_US
# Keyboard
keyboard us
# Mouse
mouse none
# Force a reboot after the install
reboot
# Firewall settings
firewall --disabled
# Clear all Partitions on the local disk sda
clearpart --all --initlabel --drives=sda
# Partitioning strategy for ESX Server host
part /boot --fstype ext3 --size 200 --ondisk sda
part / --fstype ext3 --size 25000 --ondisk sda
part swap --size 1600 --ondisk sda
part None --fstype vmfs3 --size 1 --grow --ondisk sda
part None --fstype vmkcore --size 100 --ondisk sda
```

```
part /var --fstype ext3 --size 12000 --ondisk sda
part /tmp --fstype ext3 --size 2000 --ondisk sda
# VMware Specific Commands for accepting the license agreement, configuring a
license server at 172.30.0.2 on port 270000, and a full license
vmaccepteula
vmlicense --mode=server --server=27000@172.30.0.2 --edition=esxFull
%packages
@base
@ everything
%post
# Create a new file named S11Post_Install_Config that will become an executable
that is run during the first reboot of the ESX Server
cat > /etc/rc.d/rc3.d/S11Post_Install_Config << EOF
#!/bin/bash
# Overwrite the resolv.conf file to create primary and secondary DNS entries
cat > /etc/resolv.conf << DNS
nameserver 172.30.0.2
nameserver 172.30.0.3
DNS
# Link vSwitch0 used for Service Console communication to vmnic2 if the vmnic0
 was not correct
/usr/sbin/esxcfg-vswitch -U vmnic0 vSwitch0
/usr/sbin/esxcfg-vswitch -L vmnic1 vSwitch0
# Add a vmkernel port for NAS access named NFSPort, with IP address of 172.30.0.101,
 and a default gateway of 172.30.0.1 (if required for routing)
/usr/sbin/esxcfg-vswitch -A NFSAccess vSwitch0
/usr/sbin/esxcfg-vmknic -a -i 172.30.0.101 -n 255.255.255.0 NFSport
/usr/sbin/esxcfg-route 172.30.0.1
# Add an NFS datastore named NFSDatastore01 with an NFS server at 172.30.0.100
 and a shared directory of ISOImages
/usr/sbin/esxcfg-nas -a -o 172.30.0.100 -s /ISOImages NFSDatastore01
# Enable the Service Console firewall to allow ntp and iSCSI client firewall ports
/usr/sbin/esxcfg-firewall -e ntpClient
/usr/sbin/esxcfg-firewall -e swISCSIClient
# Add a vmkernel port named VMotion on a virtual switch named vSwitch1. The VMkernel
 port will have an IP address of 172.29.0.105
# and a subnet mask of 255.255.255.0
/usr/sbin/esxcfg-vswitch -a vSwitch1
/usr/sbin/esxcfg-vswitch -A VMotion vSwitch1
/usr/sbin/esxcfg-vswitch -L vmnic0 vSwitch1
/usr/sbin/esxcfg-vmknic -a -i 172.29.0.105 -n 255.255.255.0 VMotion
# Add a vswitch named vSwitch2 with a virtual machine port group named ProductionLAN
/usr/sbin/esxcfg-vswitch -a vSwitch2
/usr/sbin/esxcfg-vswitch -L vmnic2 vSwitch2
/usr/sbin/esxcfg-vswitch -A ProductionLAN vSwitch2
# Set up time synchronization for ESX Server
cat > /etc/ntp.conf << NTP
```

```
restrict default kod nomodify notap noquery nopeer
restrict 173.30.0.111
172.30.0.111
fudge 127.127.1.0 stratum 10
driftfile /etc/ntp/drift
broadcastdelay 0.008
authenticate yes
keys /etc/ntp/keys
NTP
cat > /etc/ntp/step-tickers << STEP
172.30.0.111
STEP
/sbin/service ntpd start
/sbin/chkconfig --level 3 ntpd on
# Update system clock
/sbin/hwclock --systohc --utc
# The --utc setting in the "timezone" command above eliminates the need for updating
the clock file
#cat > /etc/sysconfig/clock << CLOCK
#ZONE="UTC"
#UTC=true
#ARC=false
#CLOCK
# Allow incoming/outgoing communications on the Service Console via SSH.
esxcfg-firewall -e sshServer
esxcfg-firewall -e sshClient
# Rename the S11Post_Install_Config file to S11Post_Install_Complete after first
 execution. Since file name will now be incorrect it will
# not be triggerd in subsequent ESX Server boot sequences. EOF dictates end of file.
mv /etc/rc.d/rc3.d/S11Post_Install_Config /etc/rc.d/rc3.d/S11Post_Install_complete
EOF
# Make the S11servercfg file an executable
/bin/chmod +x /etc/rc.d/rc3.d/S11Post_Install_Config
```

Postinstallation Configuration

Once the installation of ESX Server is complete, there are several postinstallation changes that either must be set or are just strongly recommended. Among these configurations are adjusting the amount of RAM allocated to the Service Console, changing the physical NIC used by the Service Console, and configuring the ESX Server host to synchronize with an external Network Time Protocol (NTP) server.

Service Console NIC

During the installation of ESX Server, the NIC selection screen creates a virtual switch bound to the selected physical NIC. The tricky part, as noted earlier, is choosing the correct PCI address that corresponds to the physical NIC connected to the physical switch that makes up the logical

IP subnet from which the ESX Server will be managed. The problem often arises when the wrong PCI address is selected, resulting in the inability to access the Service Console. Figure 2.32 shows the structure of the virtual networking when the wrong NIC is selected and when the correct NIC is selected.

FIGURE 2.32
The virtual switch used by the Service Console must be associated with the physical switch that makes up the logical subnet from which the Service Console will be managed.

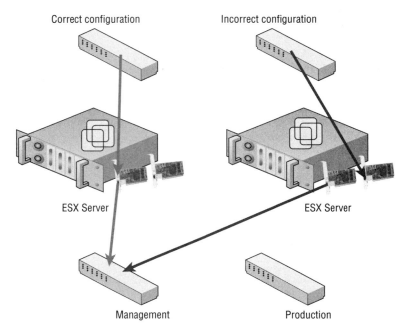

Correct configuration   Incorrect configuration

ESX Server   ESX Server

Management   Production

Should the incorrect PCI address be selected, the result is an inability to reach the ESX Server Web Access page after the installation is complete. The simplest fix for this problem is to unplug the network cable from the current Ethernet port and continue trying the remaining ports until the web page is accessible. The problem with this solution is that it puts a quick end to any type of documented standard that dictates the physical connectivity of the ESX Server hosts in a virtual environment.

So what then is the better fix? Is a reinstallation in order? If you like installations, go for it, but there is something much better. A quick visit to the command line and this problem is solved:

SOMETIMES IT'S ALL ABOUT THE CASE

Remember that ESX Server holds its roots in Linux and therefore any type of command-line management or configuration will always be case sensitive.

---

1. Log in to the console of the ESX Server using the root user account.

2. Review the PCI addresses of the physical NICs in the server by typing the following command:

   ```
   esxcfg-nics -l
   ```

3. The results, as shown in Figure 2.33, will list identifying information for each NIC. Note the PCI addresses and names of each adapter.

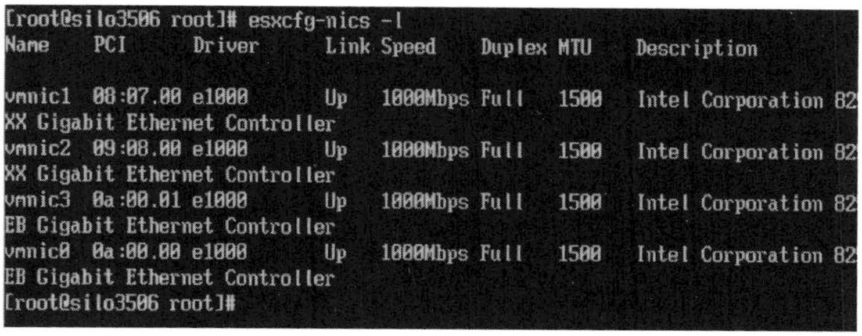

FIGURE 2.33
The `esxcfg-nics` command provides detailed information about each adapter in an ESX Server host.

```
[root@silo3506 root]# esxcfg-nics -l
Name    PCI      Driver     Link  Speed     Duplex MTU    Description

vmnic1  08:07.00 e1000      Up    1000Mbps  Full   1500   Intel Corporation 82
XX Gigabit Ethernet Controller
vmnic2  09:08.00 e1000      Up    1000Mbps  Full   1500   Intel Corporation 82
XX Gigabit Ethernet Controller
vmnic3  0a:00.01 e1000      Up    1000Mbps  Full   1500   Intel Corporation 82
EB Gigabit Ethernet Controller
vmnic0  0a:00.00 e1000      Up    1000Mbps  Full   1500   Intel Corporation 82
EB Gigabit Ethernet Controller
[root@silo3506 root]#
```

4. Review the existing Service Console configuration by typing the following command:

   `esxcfg-vswitch -l`

5. The results, as shown in Figure 2.34, will display the current configuration of the Service Console port association.

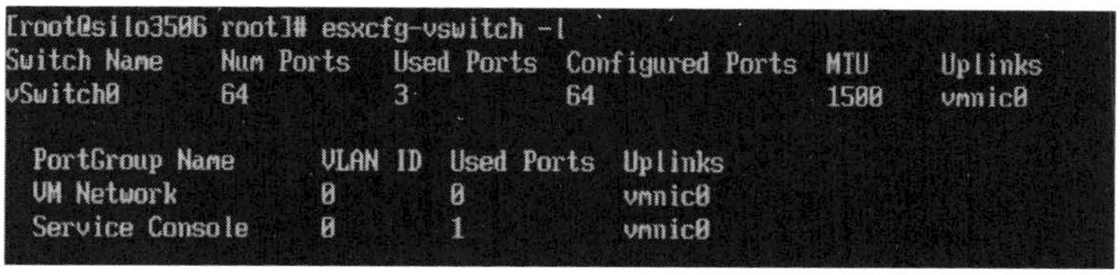

FIGURE 2.34
The `esxcfg-vswitch` command provides information about the current Service Console configuration.

```
[root@silo3506 root]# esxcfg-vswitch -l
Switch Name   Num Ports   Used Ports   Configured Ports   MTU    Uplinks
vSwitch0      64          3            64                 1500   vmnic0

   PortGroup Name     VLAN ID   Used Ports   Uplinks
   VM Network         0         0            vmnic0
   Service Console    0         1            vmnic0
```

6. To change the NIC association, the existing NIC must be unlinked by typing the following command:

   `esxcfg-vswitch -U vmnic# vSwitch#`

   In this example the appropriate command would be:

   `esxcfg-vswitch -U vmnic0 vSwitch0`

7. Use the following command to associate a new NIC with the vSwitch0 used by the Service Console:

   `esxcfg-vswitch -L vmnic# vSwitch#`

   If still unsure of the correct NIC, try each NIC listed in the output from step 2. For this example, to associate vmnic1 with a PCI address of 08:07:00, the appropriate command would be:

   `esxcfg-vswitch -L vmnic1 vSwitch0`

8. Repeat steps 6 and 7 until a successful connection is made to the Web Access page of the ESX Server host.

Service Console Memory

Adjusting the amount of memory given to the Service Console is not mandatory but is strongly recommended if you have to install third-party applications into the console operating system. These third-party applications will consume memory available to the Service Console. As noted earlier, the Service Console is only granted 272MB of RAM by default, as shown in Figure 2.35, with a hard-coded maximum of 800MB.

FIGURE 2.35
The Service Console is allocated 272 MB of RAM by default.

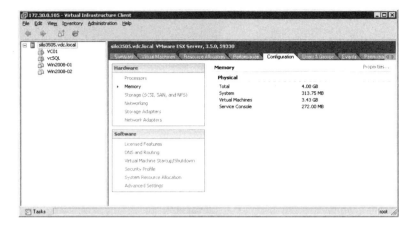

The difference of 528MB is, and should be, negligible in relation to the amount of memory in the ESX Server host. Certainly an ESX Server host in a production network would not have less than 8GB of memory. Even that would be the low end. So adding 528MB of memory for use by the Service Console does not place a significant restriction on the number of virtual machines a host is capable of running due to lack of available memory.

Perform the following steps to increase the amount of memory allocated to the Service Console:

1. Use the VI Client to connect to an ESX Server host or VirtualCenter Server installation.

2. Select the appropriate host from the inventory tree on the left and then select the Configuration tab from the details pane on the right.

3. Select Memory from the Hardware menu.

4. Click the Properties link.

5. As shown in Figure 2.36, enter the amount of memory to be allocated to the Service Console in the text box and then click the OK button. The value entered must be between 256 and 800.

FIGURE 2.36
The amount of memory allocated to the Service Console can be increased to a maximum of 800 MB.

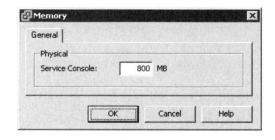

6. Reboot the ESX Server host. As shown in Figure 2.37, the Configuration tab now reflects the current memory allocated and the new amount of memory to be allocated after a reboot.

FIGURE 2.37
Altering the amount
of memory allocated
to the Service Console
requires a reboot of the
ESX Server host.

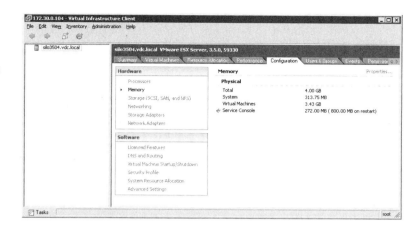

Time Synchronization

Time synchronization in ESX Server is an important configuration because the ramifications of incorrect time run deep. Time synchronization issues can affect things like performance charting, SSH key expirations, NFS access, backup jobs, authentication, and more. After the installation of ESX Server (or in a kickstart script), the host should be configured to perform time synchronization with a reliable time source. This source could be another server on your network or an Internet time source. For the sake of managing time synchronization, it is easiest to synchronize all your servers against one reliable internal time server and then synchronize the internal time server with a reliable Internet time server.

Configuring time synchronization for an ESX Server requires several steps, including Service Console firewall configuration and edits to several configuration files.

Perform the following steps to enable the NTP Client in the Service Console firewall:

1. Use the VI Client to connect directly to the ESX Server host or to a VirtualCenter installation.

2. Select the hostname from the inventory tree on the left and then click the Configuration tab in the details pane on the right.

3. Select Security Profile from the Software menu.

4. As shown in Figure 2.38, enable the NTP Client option in the Firewall Properties dialog box.

5. Alternatively the NTP client could be enabled using the following command:

   ```
   esxcfg-firewall -e ntpClient
   ```

   Type the following command to apply the changes made to the Service Console Firewall:

   ```
   service mgmt-vmware restart
   ```

Perform the following steps to configure the `ntp.conf` and step-tickers files for NTP time synchronization on an ESX Server host:

1. Log in to a console or SSH session with root privileges. If SSH has not been enabled for the host, log in with a standard user account and use the `su -` command to elevate to the root user privileges and environment.

FIGURE 2.38
The NTP Client can be enabled through the Security Profile of an ESX Server host configuration.

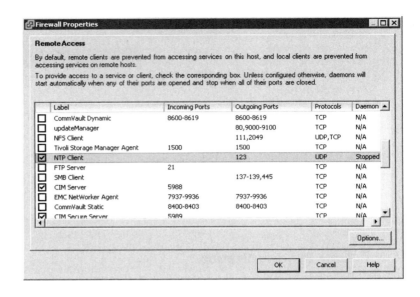

2. Create a copy of the `ntp.conf` file by typing the following command:

   `cp /etc/ntp.conf /etc/old.ntpconf`

3. Type the following command to use the `nano` editor to open the `ntp.conf` file:

   `nano -w /etc/ntp.conf`

4. Replace the following line:

   `restrict default ignore`

   with this line:

   `restrict default kod nomodify notrap noquery nopeer`

5. Uncomment the following line:

   `#restrict mytrustedtimeserverip mask 255.255.255.255 nomodify notrap noquery`
   Edit the line to include the IP address of the new time server. For example, if the time server's IP address is 172.30.0.111, the line would read:

   `restrict 172.30.0.111 mask 255.255.255.255 nomodify notrap noquery`

6. Uncomment the following line:

   `#server mytrustedtimeserverip`
   Edit the line to include the IP address of the new time server. For example, if the time server's IP address is 172.30.0.111, the line would read:

   `server 172.30.0.111`

   Save the file by pressing Ctrl+X. Click Y to accept.

7. Create a backup of the step-tickers file by typing the following command:

   ```
   cp /etc/ntp/step-tickers /etc/ntp/backup.step-tickers
   ```

8. Type the following command to open the step-tickers file:

   ```
   nano -w /etc/ntp/step-tickers
   ```

9. Type the IP address of the new time server. For example, if the time server's IP address is 172.30.0.111, the single entry in the step-tickers would read:

   ```
   172.30.0111
   ```

   Save the file by pressing Ctrl+X. Click Y to accept.

WINDOWS AS A RELIABLE TIME SERVER

An existing Windows Server can be configured as a reliable time server by performing these steps:

1. Use the Group Policy Object editor to navigate to Administrative Templates ➤ System ➤ Windows Time Service ➤ Time Providers.

2. Enable the Enable Windows NTP Server Group Policy option.

3. Navigate to Administrative Templates ➤ System ➤ Windows Time Service.

4. Double-click on the Global Configuration Settings option and select the Enabled radio button.

5. Set the AnnounceFlags option to 4.

6. Click the OK button.

Installing the Virtual Infrastructure Client

The VI Client is a Windows-only application that allows for connecting directly to an ESX Server host or to a VirtualCenter installation. The only difference in the tools used is that connecting directly to an ESX Server requires authentication with a user account that exists within the Service Console, while connecting to a VirtualCenter installation relies on Windows users for authentication. The VI Client can be installed as part of a VirtualCenter installation or with the VirtualCenter installation media. However, the easiest installation method is to simply connect to the Web Access page of an ESX Server or VirtualCenter and choose to install the application right from the web page.

Perform the following steps to install the VI Client from an ESX Server Web Access home page:

1. Open an Internet browser (Internet Explorer or Firefox).

2. Type in the IP address or fully qualified domain name of the ESX Server host from which the VI Client should be installed.

3. From the ESX Server host or VirtualCenter home page, click the link labeled Download the Virtual Infrastructure Client.

4. The application can be saved to the local system by clicking the Save button, or if the remote computer is trusted, it can be run directly from the remote computer by clicking the Run button.

5. Click the Run button in the Security Warning box that identifies an unverified publisher, as shown in Figure 2.39.

FIGURE 2.39
The VI Client might issue a warning about an unverified publisher.

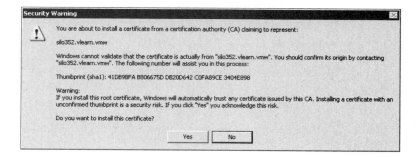

6. Click the Next button on the welcome page of the Virtual Infrastructure Client installation wizard.

7. Click the radio button labeled I Accept the Terms in the License Agreement and then click the Next button.

8. Specify a username and organization name and then click the Next button.

9. Configure the destination folder and then click the Next button.

10. Click the Install button to begin the installation.

11. Click the Finish button to complete the installation.

NO BITS FOR 64 BITS

As of the writing of this book, the latest VI Client (version 2.5) could not be installed on 64-bit operating systems.

The Bottom Line

Understand ESX Server compatibility requirements. ESX Server has tight restrictions with regard to supported hardware. VMware is the only company that provides hardware drivers for the VMware-supported hardware. The compatibility lists provided by VMware are living documents that will continue to change as new hardware is approved.

Master It   You want to reconfigure an existing physical server as an ESX Server host.

Plan an ESX Server deployment.   A great deal of detailed planning and projecting is required to deploy a scalable virtual infrastructure.

Master It   Your company wants to achieve the greatest ROI while maintaining high performance and availability levels. You need to produce a report that details the virtual infrastructure hardware specifications and costs.

Install ESX Server.   ESX Server is a fairly straightforward installation process with only one or two details to pay close attention to.

Master It   You need to reinstall ESX Server and want to be sure that inadvertent data loss cannot occur. The ESX Server will boot from local disks.

Perform postinstallation configuration.   Once the installation of ESX Server is complete the configuration can be tweaked to meet the needs of the organization.

Master It   After installing ESX Server, the web-based management page is returning a "page not found" error.

Master It   Your department heads have defined a company policy mandating the installation of antivirus software into the Service Console. Additional software might be installed at a later date.

Install the Virtual Infrastructure Client (VI Client).   The Virtual Infrastructure Client is a flexible management tool that allows management of an ESX Server host directly or by connecting to a VirtualCenter installation.

Master It   You want to manage the ESX Server hosts from your administrative workstation.

Chapter 3

Creating and Managing Virtual Networks

The goal of this chapter is to arm you with the most critical tools required for designing, managing, and troubleshooting a virtual infrastructure. Fluency in storage management, virtual machine provisioning, security, and backup are pointless if virtual machines cannot talk to the rest of the network. Server consolidation, simplified management, and greater return on investment are wasted efforts if production systems are not available.

In this chapter you will learn to:

◆ Identify the components of virtual networking

◆ Create virtual switches and virtual switch port groups

◆ Create and manage NIC teams

◆ Create and manage virtual LANs (vLANs)

◆ Configure virtual switch security policies

Virtual Networking Components

When it comes to constructing the virtual networking infrastructure of your ESX Server hosts, you will notice some similar components and some not-so-similar components. The following list defines the various components involved in a virtual network architecture:

Virtual switch   A switch that resides in the VMkernel and provides traffic management for virtual machines.

Port/port group   A logical object on a virtual switch that provides specialized services for the Service Console, VMkernel, or hosted virtual machines. A virtual switch can contain a Service Console port, a VMkernel port, or a virtual machine port group.

Service Console port   A specialized virtual switch port type that is configured with an IP address to allow access to the Service Console at the respective address. A Service Console port is also referred to as a vswif.

VMkernel port   A specialized virtual switch port type that is configured with an IP address to allow VMotion, iSCSI storage access, or NAS/NFS storage access. A VMkernel port is also referred to as a vmknic.

Virtual Machine port group   A specialized virtual switch port that is representative of a switch-to-switch connection and that allows virtual machines to access physical networks.

Virtual LAN (vLAN)   A logical LAN configured on a virtual or physical switch that provides efficient traffic segmentation, security, and efficient bandwidth utilization by providing traffic only to the ports configured for a respective vLAN.

Trunk port (trunking)   A trunk port on a switch is a port that listens for and knows how to pass traffic for all vLANs configured on the switch.

NIC team   The aggregation of physical ports to form a single logical communication channel.

vmxnet adapter   A virtualized network adapter operating inside a guest operating system. The vmxnet adapter is a high-performance virtual network adapter that operates only if VMware Tools have been installed. The vmxnet adapter is identified as "flexible" in the virtual machine properties.

vlance adapter   A virtualized network adapter operating inside a guest operating system. The vlance adapter is the default adapter used until the VMware Tools installation has been completed.

e1000 adapter   A virtualized network adapter that emulates the Intel e1000 network adapter. The e1000 network adapter is most common in 64-bit virtual machines.

FIGURE 3.1
Successful virtual net-
working is a blend of
virtual and physical
network adapters and
switches.

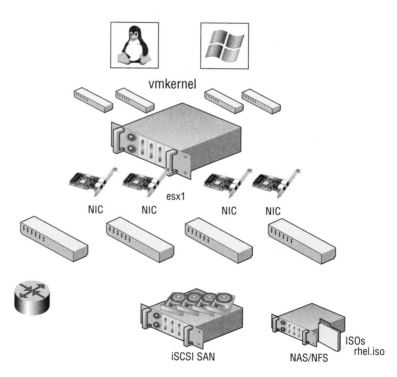

The networking architecture of ESX revolves around the creation and configuration of virtual switches. Virtual switches are created and managed through the Service Console, but they operate within the VMkernel. Virtual switches provide the connectivity to provide communication:

◆ between virtual machines within an ESX Server host

◆ between virtual machines on different ESX Server hosts

◆   between virtual machines and physical machines on the network

◆   for Service Console access

◆   for VMkernel access to networks for VMotion, iSCSI, or NFS

Figure 3.1 details the various communication channels provided by virtual network adapters through virtual switches created in the VMkernel. The VMkernel then manages the virtual switch communication through a physical network adapter to connect the virtual and physical networking components.

As the virtual network implementation makes virtual machines accessible, it is essential that virtual switches be configured in a manner that supports reliable and efficient communication around the different network infrastructure components.

Creating Virtual Switches and Port Groups

The answers to the following questions are an integral part of the design of your virtual networking:

◆   Do you have a dedicated network for Service Console management?

◆   Do you have a dedicated network for VMotion traffic?

◆   Do you have an IP storage network? iSCSI? NAS/NFS?

◆   How many NICs are standard in your ESX Server host design?

◆   Is the existing physical network comprised of vLANs?

◆   Do you want to extend the use of vLANs into the virtual switches?

As a precursor to the setup of a virtual networking architecture, the physical network components and the security needs of the network will need to be identified and documented.

Virtual switches in ESX Server are constructed and operated in the VMkernel. Virtual switches (also known as vSwitches) are not managed switches and do not provide all the advanced features that many new physical switches provide. These vSwitches operate like a physical switch in some ways, but in other ways they are quite different. Like their physical counterparts, vSwitches operate at Layer 2, support vLAN configurations, prevent overdelivery, forward frames to other switch ports, and maintain MAC address tables. Despite the similarities to physical switches, vSwitches do have some differences. A vSwitch created in the VMkernel cannot be connected to another vSwitch, thereby eliminating a potential loop configuration and the need to offer support for Spanning Tree Protocol (STP). In physical switches, STP offers redundancy for paths and prevents loops in the network topology by locking redundant paths in a standby state. Only when a path is no longer available will STP activate the standby path.

---

vSWITCH LOOPING

Though the VMkernel does not allow looping because it does not allow vSwitches to be interconnected, it would be possible to manually create looping by connecting a virtual machine with two network adapters to two different vSwitches and then bridging the virtual network adapters. Since looping is a common network problem, it is a benefit for network administrators that vSwitches don't allow looping and prevent it from happening.

ESX Server allows for the configuration of three types of virtual switches. The type of switch is dependent on the association of a physical network adapter with the virtual switch. The three types of vSwitches, as shown in Figure 3.2 and Figure 3.3, include:

◆ Internal-only virtual switch

◆ Virtual switch bound to a single network adapter

◆ Virtual switch bound to two or more network adapters

FIGURE 3.2
Virtual switches provide the cornerstone of virtual machine, VMkernel, and Service Console communication.

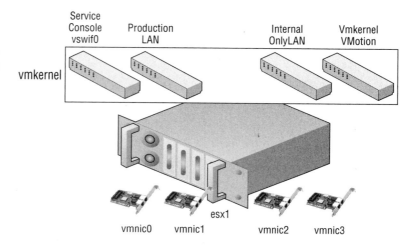

FIGURE 3.3
Virtual switches created on an ESX Server host manage all the different forms of communication required in a virtual infrastructure.

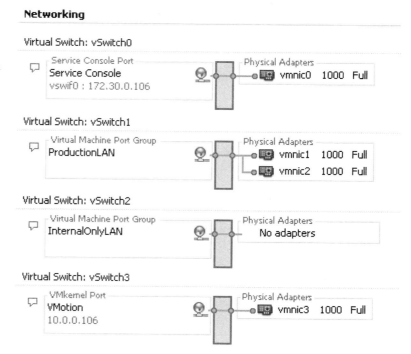

VIRTUAL SWITCH CONFIGURATION MAXIMUMS

The maximum number of vSwitches for an ESX Server host is 127. Virtual switches created through the VI Client will be provided default names of vSwitch#, where # begins with 0 and increases sequentially to 127.

CREATING AND CONFIGURING VIRTUAL SWITCHES

By default every virtual switch is created with 64 ports. However, only 56 of the ports are available and only 56 are displayed when looking at a vSwitch configuration through the Virtual Infrastructure client. Reviewing a vSwitch configuration via the esxcfg-vswitch command shows the entire 64 ports. The 8 port difference is attributed to the fact that the VMkernel reserves these 8 ports for its own use.

Once a virtual switch has been created the number of ports can be adjusted to 8, 24, 56, 120, 248, 504, or 1016. These are the values that are reflected in the Virtual Infrastructure client. But, as noted, there are 8 ports reserved and therefore the command line will show 32, 64, 128, 256, 512, and 1,024 ports for virtual switches.

Changing the number of ports in a virtual switch requires reboot of the ESX Server 3.5 host on which the virtual switch was altered.

Without an uplink, the internal-only vSwitch allows communication only between virtual machines that exist on the same ESX Server host. Virtual machines that communicate through an internal-only vSwitch do not pass any traffic through a physical adapter on the ESX Server host. As shown in Figure 3.4, communication between virtual machines connected to an internal-only switch takes place entirely in software and happens at whatever speed the VMkernel can perform the task.

FIGURE 3.4
Virtual machines communicating through an internal-only vSwitch do not pass any traffic through a physical adapter.

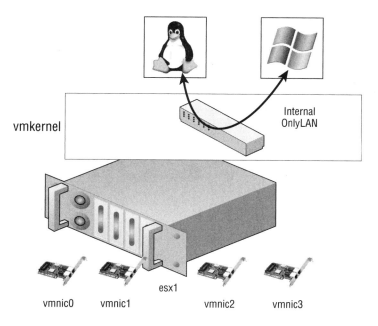

NO UPLINK, NO VMOTION

Virtual machines connected to an internal-only vSwitch are not VMotion capable. However, if the virtual machine is disconnected from the internal-only vSwitch, a warning will be provided but VMotion will succeed if all other requirements have been met. The requirements for VMotion will be covered in Chapter 9.

For virtual machines to communicate with resources beyond the virtual machines hosted on the local ESX server, a vSwitch must be configured to use a physical network adapter, or uplink. A vSwitch bound to a single physical adapter allows virtual machines to establish communication with physical servers on the network, or with virtual machines on other ESX Server hosts that are also connected to a vSwitch bound to a physical adapter. The vSwitch associated with a physical network adapter provides virtual machines with the amount of bandwidth the physical adapter is configured to support. For example, a vSwitch bound to a network adapter with a 1Gbps maximum speed will provide up to 1Gbps worth of bandwidth for the virtual machines connected to it. Figure 3.5 displays the communication path for virtual machines connected to a vSwitch bound to a single network adapter. In the diagram, when VM01 on silo104 needs to communicate with VM02 on silo105, the traffic from the virtual machine is passed through the ProductionLAN virtual switch (port group) in the VMkernel on silo104 to the physical network adapter to which the virtual switch is bound. From the physical network adapter, the traffic will reach the physical switch (PhySw1). The physical switch (PhySw1) passes the traffic to the second physical switch (PhySw2), which will pass the traffic through the physical network adapter associated with the ProductionLAN virtual switch on silo105. In the last stage of the communication, the virtual switch will pass the traffic to the destination virtual machine VM02.

FIGURE 3.5
The vSwitch with a single network adapter allows virtual machines to communicate with physical servers and other virtual machines on the network.

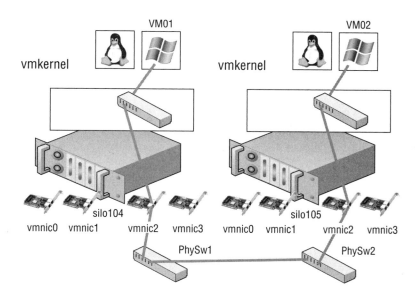

NETWORK ADAPTERS AND NETWORK DISCOVERY

Discovering the network adapters, and even the networks they are connected to, is easy with the VI Client. While connected to a VirtualCenter server or an individual ESX Server host, the Network Adapters node of the Configuration tab of a host will display all the available adapters. The following image shows how each adapter will be listed with information about the model of the adapter, the vmnic# label, the speed and duplex setting, its association to a vSwitch, and a discovery of the IP addresses it has found on the network:

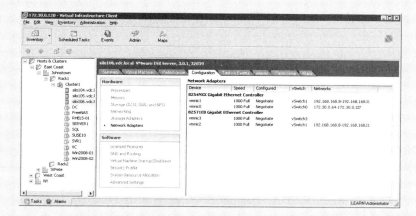

The network IP addresses listed under the Networks column are a result of a discovery across that network. The IP address range may change as new addresses are added and removed. For those NICs without a range, no IP addresses have been discovered. The network IP addresses should be used for information only and should be verified since they can be inaccurate.

The last type of virtual switch is referred to as a NIC team. As shown in Figure 3.6 and Figure 3.7, a NIC team involves the association of multiple physical network adapters with a single vSwitch. A vSwitch configured as a NIC team can consist of a maximum of 32 uplinks. In other words, a single vSwitch can use up to 32 physical network adapters to send and receive traffic from the physical switches. NIC teams offer the advantage of redundancy and load distribution. Later in this chapter, we will dig deeper into the configuration and workings of the NIC team.

UPLINK LIMITS

Although a single vSwitch can be associated with multiple physical adapters as in a NIC team, a single physical adapter cannot be associated with multiple vSwitches. Pending the expansion capability, ESX Server 3.0.1 hosts can have up to 26 e100 network adapters, 32 e1000 network adapters, or 20 Broadcom network adapters. The maximum number of Ethernet ports on an ESX Server host is 32, regardless of the expansion slots or the number of adapters used to reach the maximum. For example, using eight quad-port NICs would achieve the 32-port maximum. All 32 ports could be configured for use by a single vSwitch or could be spread across multiple vSwitches.

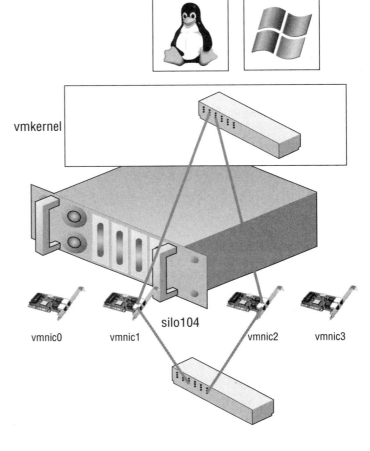

FIGURE 3.6
A vSwitch with a NIC team has multiple available adapters for data transfer. A NIC team offers redundancy and load distribution.

FIGURE 3.7
Virtual switches with a NIC team are identified by the multiple physical network adapters assigned to the vSwitch.

The vSwitch, as introduced in the first section of the chapter, allows several different types of communication, including communication to and from the Service Console, to and from the VMkernel, and between virtual machines. The type of communication provided by a vSwitch is dependent on the port (group), or connection type that is created on the switch. ESX Server hosts can have a maximum of 512 port groups, while the maximum number of ports (port groups) across all virtual switches is 4096.

ROOM TO GROW

During the virtual network design I am often asked why virtual switches should not be created with the largest number of ports to leave room to grow. To answer this question let's look at some calculations against the network maximums of an ESX Server 3.5 host.

The maximum number of ports in a virtual switch is 1016. The maximum number of ports across all switches on a host is 4096. This means that if virtual switches are created with the 1016 port maximum only 4 virtual switches can be created. If you're doing a quick calculation of 1016 x 4 and realizing it is not 4096, don't forget that virtual switches actually have 8 reserved ports. Therefore, the 1016 port switch actually has 1,024 ports. Calculate 1,024 x 4 and you will arrive at the 4096 port maximum for an ESX Server 3.5 host.

Create virtual switches with a number of ports to meet your goals. If you can anticipate growth it will save you from a seemingly needless reboot in the future should you have to alter the virtual switch, but if it comes to it, that is why we are thankful for VMotion. Virtual machines can be moved to another host in order to satisfy the rebooting needs of tasks like editing the number of ports on a virtual switch.

Port groups operate as a boundary for communication and/or security policy configuration. Each port group includes functionality for a specific type of traffic but can also be used to provide more or less security to the traffic passing through the respective port group. There are three different connection types or port (groups), shown in Figure 3.8 and Figure 3.9, that can be configured on a vSwitch:

- Service Console port
- VMkernel port
- Virtual Machine port group

A Service Console port on a vSwitch, shown in Figure 3.10 and Figure 3.11, acts as a passage into the management and monitoring capabilities of the console operating system. The Service Console port, also called a vswif, requires that an IP address be assigned. The vSwitch with a Service Console port must be bound to the physical network adapter connected to the physical switch on the network from which management tasks will be performed. In Chapter 2, we covered how the ESX Server installer creates the first vSwitch with a Service Console port to allow postinstallation access.

SERVICE CONSOLE FIREWALL

The console operating system (COS), or Service Console, includes a firewall that, by default, blocks all incoming and outgoing traffic except that required for basic server management. In Chapter 12 we will detail how to manage the firewall.

FIGURE 3.8
Virtual switches can contain three different connection types: Service Console, VMkernel, and virtual machine.

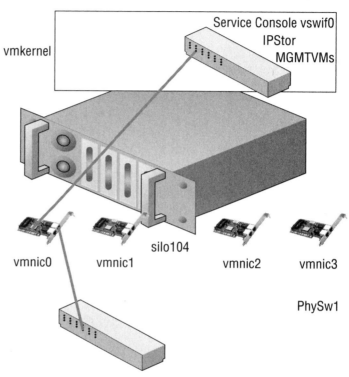

FIGURE 3.9
Virtual switches can be created with all three connection types on the same switch.

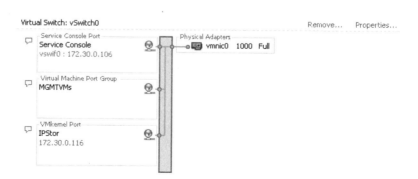

FIGURE 3.10
The Service Console port type on a vSwitch is assigned an IP address that can be used for access to the console operating system.

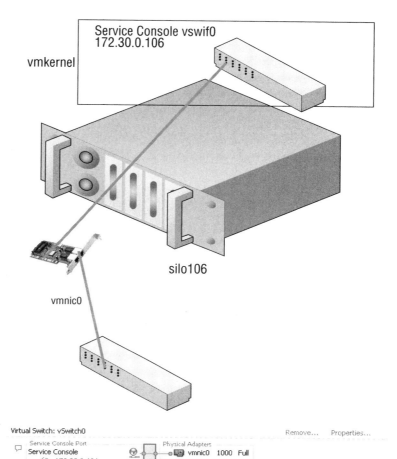

FIGURE 3.11
The Service Console port, known as a vswif, provides access to the console operating system.

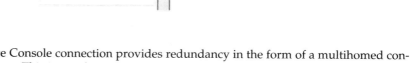

A second Service Console connection provides redundancy in the form of a multihomed console operating system. This is not the same as a NIC team since this configuration will actually provide Service Console access on two different IP addresses. Perform the following steps to create a vSwitch with a Service Console connection using the VI Client:

1. Use the VI Client to establish a connection to a VirtualCenter server or an ESX Server host.

2. Click the hostname in the inventory panel on the left, select the Configuration tab from the details pane on the right, and then choose Networking from the Hardware menu list.

3. Click Add Networking to start the Add Network Wizard.

4. Select the Service Console radio button and click Next.

5. Select the checkbox that corresponds to the network adapter to be assigned to the vSwitch for Service Console communication, as shown in Figure 3.12.

FIGURE 3.12
Adding a second vSwitch
with a Service Console
port creates a multi-
homed Service Console
with multiple entry
points.

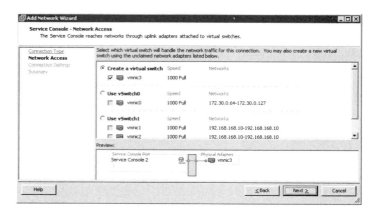

6. Type a name for the port in the Network Label text box.

7. Enter an IP address for the Service Console port. Ensure the IP address is a valid IP
   address for the network to which the physical NIC from step 5 is connected. You do
   not need a default gateway for the new Service Console port if a functioning gateway
   has already been assigned on the Service Console port created during the ESX Server
   installation process.

8. Click Next to review the configuration summary and then click Finish.

Perform the following steps to create a vSwitch with a Service Console port using the
command line:

1. Use `putty.exe` or a console session to log in to an ESX Server and establish root-level
   permissions. Use `su -` to elevate to root or log in as root if permitted.

2. Use the following command to create a vSwitch named vSwitch:

   ```
   esxcfg-vswitch -a vSwitchX
   ```

3. Use the following command to create a port group named SCX to a vSwitch
   named vSwitchX:

   ```
   esxcfg-vswitch -A SCX vSwitchX
   ```

4. Use the following command to add a Service Console NIC named vswif99 with an IP
   address of 172.30.0.204 and a subnet mask of 255.255.255.0 to the SCX port group created
   in step 3:

   ```
   esxcfg-vswif --add --ip=172.30.0.204 --netmask=255.255.255.0
   --portgroup=SCX vswif99
   ```

5. Use the following command to assign the physical adapter vmnic3 to the new vSwitch:

   ```
   esxcfg-vswitch -L vmnic3 vSwitchX
   ```

6. Use the following command to restart the VMware management service:

   ```
   service mgmt-vmware restart
   ```

The VMkernel port, shown in Figure 3.13 and Figure 3.14, is used for VMotion, iSCSI, and NAS/NFS access. Like the Service Console port, the VMkernel port requires the assignment of an IP address and subnet mask. The IP addresses assigned to VMkernel ports are needed to support the source-to-destination type IP traffic of VMotion, iSCSI, and NAS. Unlike with the Service Console, there is no need for administrative access to the IP addresses assigned to the VMkernel. In later chapters we will detail the iSCSI and NAS/NFS configurations, as well as the details of the VMotion process. These discussions will provide insight into the traffic flow between VMkernel and storage devices (iSCSI/NFS) or other VMkernels (for VMotion).

FIGURE 3.13

A VMkernel port created on a vSwitch is assigned an IP address that can be used for accessing iSCSI or NFS storage devices or for performing VMotion with another ESX Server host.

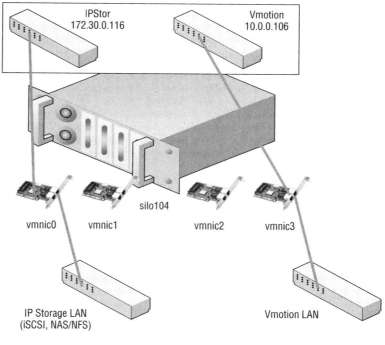

FIGURE 3.14

A VMkernel port is assigned an IP address and a port label. The label should identify the use of the VMkernel port.

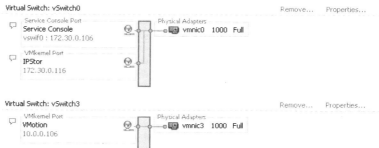

Perform these steps to add a VMkernel port using the VI Client:

1. Use the VI Client to establish a connection to a VirtualCenter server or an ESX Server host.

2. Click the hostname in the inventory panel on the left, select the Configuration tab from the details pane on the right, and then choose Networking from the Hardware menu list.

3. Click Properties for the virtual switch to host the new VMkernel port.

4. Click the Add button, select the VMkernel radio button option, and click Next.

5. Type the name of the port in the Network Label text box.

6. Select Use This Port Group for VMotion if this VMkernel port will host VMotion traffic; otherwise, leave the checkbox unselected.

7. Enter an IP address for the VMkernel port. Ensure the IP address is a valid IP address for the network to which the physical NIC is connected. You do not need to provide a default gateway if the VMkernel does not need to reach remote subnets.

8. Click Next to review the configuration summary and then click Finish.

Follow these steps to create a vSwitch with a VMkernel port using the command line:

1. Use the following command to add a port group named VMkernel to a virtual switch named vSwitch0:

```
esxcfg-vswitch -A VMkernel vSwitch0
```

2. Use the following command to assign an IP address and subnet mask to the VMkernel port group:

```
esxcfg-vmknic -a -i 172.30.0.114 -n 255.255.255.0 VMkernel
```

3. Use the following command to assign a default gateway of 172.30.0.1 to the VMkernel port group:

```
esxcfg-route 172.30.0.1
```

4. Use the following command to restart the VMware management service:

```
service mgmt-vmware restart
```

The last connection type (or port group) to discuss is the Virtual Machine port group. The Virtual Machine port group is much different than the Service Console or VMkernel. Whereas both of the other port types require IP addresses for the source-to-destination communication that they are involved in, the Virtual Machine port group does not require an IP address. For a moment, forget about vSwitches and consider standard physical switches. Let's look at an example, shown in Figure 3.15, with a standard 16-port physical switch that has 16 computers connected and configured as part of the 192.168.250.0/24 IP network. The IP network provides for 254 valid IP addresses, but only 16 IP addresses are being used because the switch only has 16 ports. To increase the number of hosts that can communicate on the same logical IP subnet, a second switch could be introduced. To accommodate the second switch, one of the existing computers would have to be unplugged from the first switch. The open port on the first switch could then be connected to a second 16-port physical switch. Once the unplugged computer is reconnected to a port on the new switch, all 16 computers will once again communicate. In addition, there will be 15 open ports on the second switch to which new computers could be added.

A vSwitch created with a virtual machine port group bound to a physical network adapter that is connected to a physical switch acts just as the second switch did in the previous example. As in the physical switch to physical switch example, an IP address does not need to be configured for a virtual machine port group to combine the ports of a vSwitch with those of a physical switch. Figure 3.16 shows the switch-to-switch connection between a vSwitch and a physical switch.

FIGURE 3.15
Two physical switches can be connected to increase the number of available hosts on the IP network.

FIGURE 3.16
A vSwitch with a virtual machine port group uses an associated physical network adapter to establish a switch-to-switch connection with a physical switch.

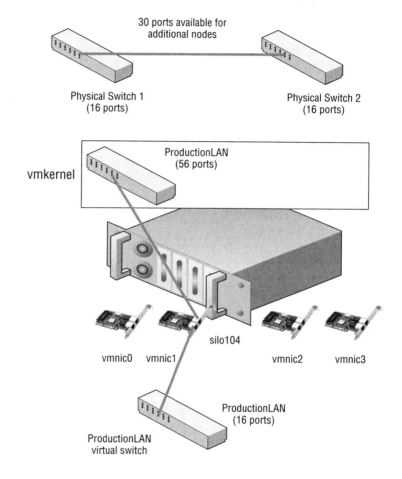

FASTER COMMUNICATION THROUGH THE VMKERNEL

The virtual network adapter inside a guest operating system is not always susceptible to the maximum transmission speeds of the physical network cards to which the vSwitch is bound. Take, for example, two virtual machines, VM01 and VM02, both connected to the same vSwitch on an ESX Server host. When these two virtual machines communicate with each other, there is no need for the vSwitch to pass the communication traffic to the physical adapter to which it is bound. However, for VM01 to communicate with VM03 residing on a second ESX Server host, the communication must pass into the physical networking elements. The requirement of reaching into the physical network places a limit on the communication speed between the virtual machines. In this case, VM01 and VM03 would be limited to the 1Gbps bandwidth of the physical network adapter.

This image details how virtual machines communicating with one another through the same vSwitch are not susceptible to the bandwidth limits of a physical network adapter because there is no need for traffic to pass from the vSwitch to the physical adapter.

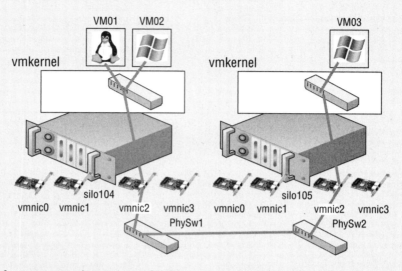

Although the guest operating systems of VM01 and VM02 will identify the virtual network adapters with speed and duplex settings, these settings are not apparent when VM01 and VM02 communicate with one another. This communication will take place at whatever speed the VMkernel can perform the operation. In other words, the communication is occurring in the host system's RAM and happens almost instantaneously as long as the VMkernel can allocate the necessary resources to make it happen. Even though uplinks might be associated with the vSwitch, the VMkernel neglects using the uplink to process the local traffic between virtual machines connected to the same vSwitch. Given that, there are advantages to ensuring that two virtual machines with a strong networking relationship remain on the same ESX Server host. Web servers or application servers that use back-end databases hosted on another server are prime examples of the type of networking relationship that can gain tremendous advantage from the efficient networking capability of the VMkernel.

Perform the following steps to create a vSwitch with a virtual machine port group using the VI Client:

1. Use the VI Client to establish a connection to a VirtualCenter server or an ESX Server host.

2. Click the hostname in the inventory panel on the left, select the Configuration tab from the details pane on the right, and then select Networking from the Hardware menu list.

3. Click Add Networking to start the Add Network Wizard.

4. Select the Virtual Machine radio button option and click Next.

5. Select the checkbox that corresponds to the network adapter to be assigned to the vSwitch. Select the NIC connected to the switch where production traffic will take place.

6. Type the name of the virtual machine port group in the Network Label text box.

7. Click Next to review the virtual switch configuration and then click Finish.

Follow these steps to create a vSwitch with a virtual machine port group using the command line:

1. Use the following command to add a virtual switch named vSwitch1:

```
esxcfg-vswitch -a vSwitch1
```

2. Use the following command to assign vSwitch1 to vmnic1:

```
esxcfg-vswitch -L vmnic1 vSwitch1
```

3. Use the following command to create a virtual machine port group named ProductionLAN on vSwitch1:

```
esxcfg-vswitch -A ProductionLAN vSwitch1
```

4. Use the following command to restart the VMware management service:

```
service mgmt-vmware restart
```

PORTS AND PORT GROUPS ON A VIRTUAL SWITCH

A vSwitch can consist of multiple connection types, or each connection type can be created in its own vSwitch.

The creation of vSwitches and port groups and the relationship between vSwitches and uplinks is dependent on several factors, including the number of network adapters in the ESX Server host, the number of IP subnets to connect to, the existence of vLANs, and the number of physical networks to connect to. With respect to the configuration of the vSwitches and virtual machine port groups, there is no single correct configuration that will satisfy every scenario. It is true, however, to say that the greater the number of physical network adapters in an ESX Server host, the more flexibility you will have in your virtual networking architecture.

Later in the chapter we will discuss some advanced design factors, but for now let's stick with some basic design considerations. If the vSwitches created in the VMkernel are not going to be configured with multiple port groups or vLANs, you will be required to create a separate vSwitch for every IP subnet that you need to connect to. In Figure 3.17, there are five IP subnets that our virtual infrastructure components need to reach. The virtual machines in the production environment must reach the production LAN, the virtual machines in the test environment must reach the test LAN, the VMkernel needs to access the IP storage and VMotion LANs, and finally the Service Console must be on the management LAN. Notice that the physical network is configured with vLANs for the test and production LANs. They share the same physical network but are still separate IP subnets. Figure 3.17 displays a virtual network architecture that does not include the use of vLANs in the vSwitches and as a result requires one vSwitch for every IP subnet; five IP subnets means five vSwitches. In this case, each vSwitch consists of a specific connection type.

In this example, each connection type could be split because there were enough physical network adapters to meet our needs. Let's look at another example where an ESX Server host has only two network adapters to work with. Figure 3.18 shows a network environment with five IP subnets: management, production, test, IP storage, and VMotion, where the production, test, and IP storage networks are configured as vLANs on the same physical network. Figure 3.18 displays a virtual network architecture that includes the use of vLANs and that combines multiple connection types into a single vSwitch.

FIGURE 3.17
Without the use of port groups and vLANs in the vSwitches, each IP subnet will require a separate vSwitch with the appropriate connection type.

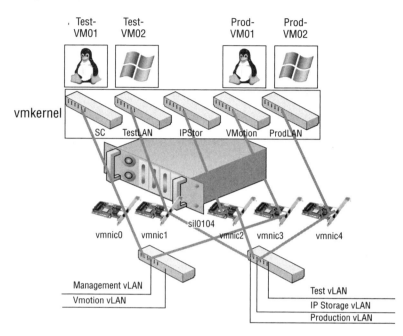

FIGURE 3.18
With a limited number of physical network adapters available in an ESX Server host, vSwitches will need multiple connection types to support the network architecture.

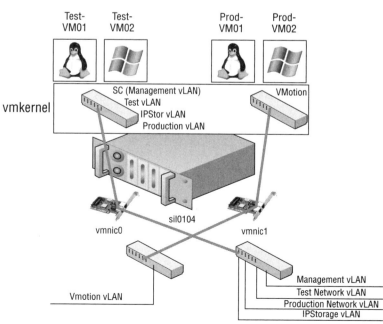

The vSwitch and connection type architecture of ESX Server, though robust and customizable, is subject to all of the following limits:

◆ An ESX Server host cannot have more than 4,096 ports.

◆ An ESX Server host cannot have more than 1,016 ports per vSwitch.

◆ An ESX Server host cannot have more than 127 vSwitches.

◆ An ESX Server host cannot have more than 512 virtual switch port groups.

VIRTUAL SWITCH CONFIGURATIONS . . . DON'T GO TOO BIG!

Although a vSwitch can be created with a maximum of 1,016 ports (really 1,024), it is not recommended if growth is anticipated. Because ESX Server hosts cannot have more than 4,096 ports (1,024 × 4), if vSwitches are created with 1,016 ports then only four vSwitches would be possible. Virtual switches should be created with just enough ports to cover existing needs and projected growth.

By default, all virtual network adapters connected to a vSwitch have access to the full amount of bandwidth on the physical network adapter with which the vSwitch is associated. In other words, if a vSwitch is assigned a 1Gbps network adapter, then each virtual machine configured to use the vSwitch has access to 1Gbps of bandwidth. Naturally, if contention becomes a bottleneck hindering virtual machine performance, a NIC team would be the best option. However, as a complement to the introduction of a NIC team, it is also possible to enable and to configure traffic shaping. Traffic shaping involves the establishment of hard-coded limits for a peak bandwidth, average bandwidth, and burst size to reduce a virtual machine's outbound bandwidth capability.

As shown in Figure 3.19, the peak bandwidth value and the average bandwidth value are specified in Kbps, and the burst size is configured in units of KB. The value entered for the average bandwidth dictates the data transfer per second across the virtual vSwitch. The peak bandwidth value identifies the maximum amount of bandwidth a vSwitch can pass without dropping packets. Finally, the burst size defines the maximum amount of data included in a burst. The burst size is a calculation of bandwidth multiplied by time. During periods of high utilization, if a burst exceeds the configured value packets will be dropped in favor of other traffic; however, if the queue for network traffic processing is not full, the packets will be retained for transmission at a later time.

TRAFFIC SHAPING AS A LAST RESORT

Use the traffic shaping feature sparingly. Traffic shaping should be reserved for situations where virtual machines are competing for bandwidth and the opportunity to add network adapters is removed by limitations in the expansion slots on the physical chassis. With the low cost of network adapters, it is more worthwhile to spend time building vSwitch devices with NIC teams as opposed to cutting the bandwidth available to a set of virtual machines.

Perform the following steps to configure traffic shaping:

1. Use the VI Client to establish a connection to a VirtualCenter server or an ESX Server host.

2. Click the hostname in the inventory panel on the left, select the Configuration tab from the details pane on the right, and then select Networking from the Hardware menu list.

3. Click the Properties for the virtual switch, select the name of the virtual switch or port group from the Configuration list, and then click the Edit button.

4. Select the Traffic Shaping tab.

5. Select the Enabled option from the Status drop-down list.

6. Adjust the Average Bandwidth value to the desired number of Kbps.

7. Adjust the Peak Bandwidth value to the desired number of Kbps.

8. Adjust the Burst Size value to the desired number of KB.

FIGURE 3.19
Traffic shaping reduces the outbound bandwidth available to a port group.

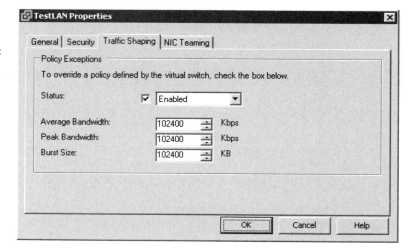

With all the flexibility provided by the different virtual networking components, you can be assured that whatever the physical network configuration may hold in store, there will be several ways to integrate the virtual networking. What you configure today may change as the infrastructure changes or as the hardware changes. Ultimately the tools provided by ESX Server are enough to ensure a successful communication scheme between the virtual and physical networks.

Creating and Managing NIC Teams

In the previous section, we looked at some good examples of virtual network architectures needed to support the physical networking components. Now that you have some design and configuration basics under your belt, let's move on to extending the virtual networking beyond just establishing communication. A NIC team can support any of the connection types discussed in the previous section. Using NIC teams provides redundancy and load balancing of network communications to Service Console, VMkernel, and virtual machines.

A NIC team, shown in Figure 3.20 and Figure 3.21, is defined as a vSwitch configured with an association to multiple physical network adapters (uplinks). As mentioned in the previous section, the ESX Server host can either have a maximum of 32 uplinks spread across multiple vSwitches or be configured as a NIC team on one vSwitch.

Successful NIC teaming requires that all uplinks be connected to physical switches that belong to the same broadcast domain. As shown in Figure 3.22, all of the physical network adapters in the NIC team should be connected to the same physical switch or to physical network adapters connected to physical switches that are connected to one another.

FIGURE 3.20
Virtual switches, like vSwitch1, with multiple uplinks offer redundancy and load balancing.

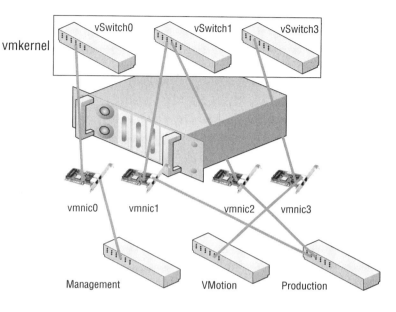

FIGURE 3.21
A NIC team is identified by the association of multiple physical network adapters assigned to a vSwitch.

FIGURE 3.22
All of the physical network adapters that make up a NIC team must belong to same Layer 2 broadcast domain.

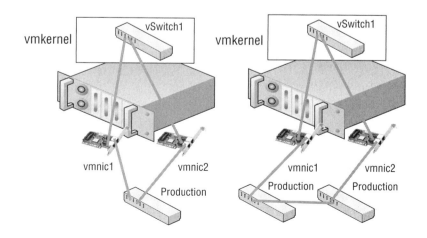

CONSTRUCTING NIC TEAMS

NIC teams should be built on physical network adapters located on separate bus architectures. For example, if an ESX Server host contains two on-board network adapters and a PCI-based quad-port network adapter, a NIC team should be constructed using one on-board network adapter and one network adapter on the PCI bus. This design eliminates a single point of failure.

Perform the following steps to create a NIC team using the VI Client:

1. Use the VI Client to establish a connection to a VirtualCenter server or an ESX Server host.

2. Click the hostname in the inventory panel on the left, select the Configuration tab from the details pane on the right, and then select Networking from the Hardware menu list.

3. Click the Properties for the virtual switch that will be assigned a NIC team and select the Network Adapters tab.

4. Click Add and select the appropriate adapter from the Unclaimed Adapters list, as shown in Figure 3.23.

FIGURE 3.23
Create a NIC team using unclaimed network adapters that belong to the same Layer 2 broadcast domain as the original adapter.

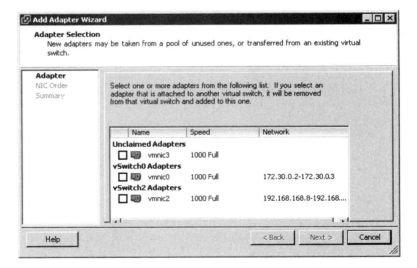

5. Adjust the Policy Failover Order as needed to support an Active/Standby configuration.

6. Review the summary of the virtual switch configuration, click Next, and then click Finish.

The load-balancing feature of NIC teaming does not function like the load-balancing feature of advanced routing protocols. Load balancing across a NIC team is not a product of identifying the amount of traffic transmitted through a network adapter and shifting traffic to equalize data flow through all available adapters. The load-balancing algorithm for NIC teams in a vSwitch is a balance of the number of connections — not the amount of traffic. NIC teams on a VI vSwitch can be configured with one of the following three load-balancing policies:

- ◆ vSwitch port-based load balancing (default)
- ◆ Source MAC-based load balancing
- ◆ IP hash-based load balancing

OUTBOUND LOAD BALANCING

The load-balancing feature of NIC teams on a vSwitch only applies to the outbound traffic.

Virtual Switch Port Load Balancing

The vSwitch port-based load-balancing policy that is used by default uses an algorithm that ties each virtual switch port to a specific uplink associated with the vSwitch. The algorithm will maintain an equal number of port-to-uplink assignments across all uplinks to achieve load balancing. As shown in Figure 3.24, this policy setting ensures that traffic from a specific virtual network adapter connected to a virtual switch port will consistently use the same physical network adapter. In the event that one of the uplinks fails, the traffic from the failed uplink will failover to another physical network adapter.

FIGURE 3.24
The vSwitch port-based load-balancing policy assigns each virtual switch port to a specific uplink. Failover to another uplink occurs when one of the physical network adapters experiences failure.

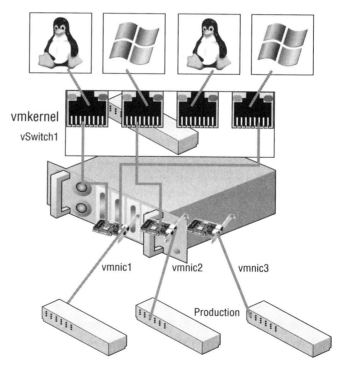

You can see how this policy does not provide load balancing of the amount of traffic because each virtual machine can access only one physical network adapter at any given time. Since the port to which a virtual machine is connected does not change, each virtual machine is tied to a physical network adapter until failover occurs. Looking at Figure 3.24, imagine that the Linux virtual machine and the Windows virtual machine on the far left and far right are the two most network-intensive virtual machines. In this case, the vSwitch port-based policy has assigned both of the ports used by these virtual machines to the same physical network adapter. Meanwhile, the Linux and Windows virtual machines in the middle, which both might be processing very little traffic, are connected to ports assigned to individual physical network adapters.

The physical switch passing the traffic learns the port association and therefore sends replies back through the same physical network adapter from which the request initiated. The vSwitch port-based policy is best used when the number of virtual network adapters is greater than the number of physical network adapters. In the case where there are fewer virtual network adapters than physical adapters, some physical adapters will not be used. For example, if five virtual machines are connected to a vSwitch with six uplinks, only five used vSwitch ports will be assigned to exactly five uplinks, leaving one uplink with no traffic to process.

Source MAC Load Balancing

The second load-balancing policy available for a NIC team is the source MAC-based policy, shown in Figure 3.25. This policy is susceptible to the same pitfalls as the vSwitch port-based policy simply because the static nature of the source MAC address is the same as the static nature of a vSwitch port assignment. Like the vSwitch port-based policy, the source MAC-based policy is best used when the number of virtual network adapters exceeds the number of physical network adapters. In addition, virtual machines are still not capable of using multiple physical adapters unless configured with multiple virtual network adapters. Multiple virtual network adapters inside the guest operating system of a virtual machine will provide multiple source MAC addresses and therefore offer an opportunity to use multiple physical network adapters.

VIRTUAL SWITCH TO PHYSICAL SWITCH

To eliminate a single point of failure, the physical network adapters in NIC teams set to use the vSwitch port-based or source MAC-based load-balancing policies can be connected to different physical switches; however, the physical switches must belong to the same Layer 2 broadcast domain. Link aggregation using 802.3ad teaming is not supported with either of these load-balancing policies.

IP Hash Load Balancing

The third load-balancing policy available for NIC teams is the IP hash-based policy, also called the out-IP policy. This policy, shown in Figure 3.26, addresses the limitation of the other two policies that prevents a virtual machine from accessing two physical network adapters without having two virtual network adapters. The IP hash-based policy uses the source and destination IP addresses to determine the physical network adapter for communication. This algorithm then allows a single virtual machine to communicate over different physical network adapters when communicating with different destinations.

FIGURE 3.25
The source MAC-based load-balancing policy, as the name suggests, ties a virtual network adapter to a physical network adapter based on the MAC address.

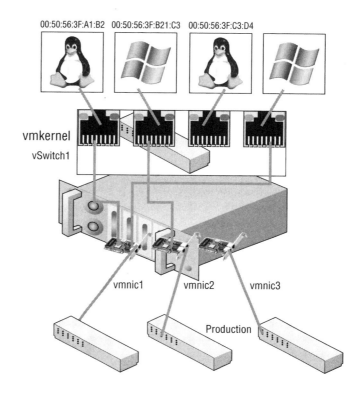

BALANCING FOR LARGE DATA TRANSFERS

Although the IP hash-based load-balancing policy can more evenly spread the transfer traffic for a single virtual machine, it does not provide a benefit for large data transfers occurring between the same source and destination systems. Since the source-destination hash will be the same for the duration of the data load, it will only flow through a single physical network adapter.

A vSwitch with a NIC team set to use the IP hash-based load-balancing policy should have all physical network adapters connected to the same physical switch to support link aggregation. ESX Server supports standard 802.3ad teaming in static (manual) mode, but does not support the Link Aggregation Control Protocol (LACP) or Port Aggregation Protocol (PAgP) commonly found on switch devices. Link aggregation will increase throughput by combining the bandwidth of multiple physical network adapters for use by a single virtual network adapter of a virtual machine.

Follow these steps to alter the load-balancing policy of a vSwitch with a NIC team:

1. Use the VI Client to establish a connection to a VirtualCenter server or an ESX Server host.

2. Click the hostname in the inventory panel on the left, select the Configuration tab from the details pane on the right, and then select Networking from the Hardware menu list.

3. Click the Properties for the virtual switch, select the name of virtual switch from the Configuration list, and then click the Edit button.

4. Select the NIC Teaming tab and then select the desired load-balancing strategy from the Load Balancing drop-down list.

5. Click OK and then click Close.

FIGURE 3.26
The IP hash-based policy is a more scalable load-balancing policy that allows virtual machines to use more than one physical network adapter when communicating with multiple destination hosts.

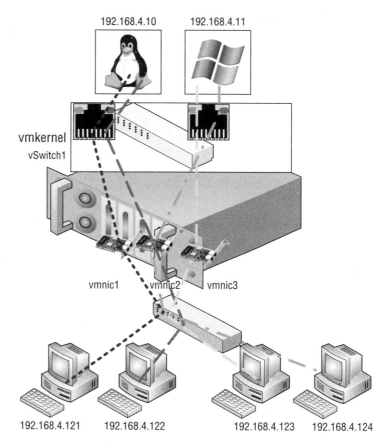

Now that the load-balancing policies are explained, let's take a deeper look at the failover and failback of uplinks in a NIC team. Failover detection in a NIC team can be configured to use either a link status method or a link status and beacon probing method.

The link status failover detection method works just as the name suggests. Failure of an uplink is identified by the link status provided by the physical network adapter. In this case, failure is identified for events like removed cables or power failures on a physical switch. The downside to the link status failover detection setting is its inability to identify misconfigurations or pulled cables that connect the switch to other networking devices (i.e., a cable connecting one switch to another switch.)

The beacon probing failover detection setting, which includes link status as well, sends Ethernet broadcast frames across all physical network adapters in the NIC team. These broadcast frames allow the vSwitch to detect upstream network connection failures and will force failover when ports are blocked by a spanning tree, are configured with the wrong vLAN, or a switch-to-switch connection has failed. When a beacon is not returned on a physical network adapter, the vSwitch triggers the failover notice and reroutes the traffic from the failed network adapter through another available network adapter based on the failover policy. Consider a vSwitch with a NIC team consisting of four physical network adapters, where each adapter is connected to a different physical switch and each physical switch is connected to a single physical switch, which is then connected to a router, as shown in Figure 3.27. When the NIC team is set to the beacon probing failover detection method, a beacon will be sent out over all four uplinks.

FIGURE 3.27
The beacon probing failover detection policy sends beacons out across the physical network adapters of a NIC team to identify upstream network failures or switch misconfigurations.

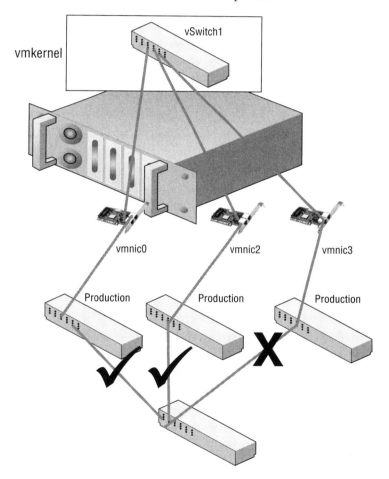

Once a failure has been detected, the vSwitch will use either a Rolling Failover or a Failover Order policy setting to continue passing traffic through another physical network adapter. By default, a NIC team is set to use a Rolling Failover policy of No, as shown in Figure 3.28. When the Rolling Failover policy is set to No, the NIC team not only provides a failover policy but also applies a fail-back policy. This means that if a failed physical network adapter is repaired and brought back online, the NIC team will reroute the traffic back to the adapter and relieve the standby adapter that assumed its role during failover. When the Rolling Failover policy is set to Yes, the NIC team will not perform a failback. In this case, the physical network adapter that assumed responsibility for the failed adapter will continue to process the traffic. Meanwhile, the failed adapter that is not back online will function as a standby until another adapter experiences failure.

FIGURE 3.28
By default, a NIC team is configured with a Rolling Failover policy setting of No.

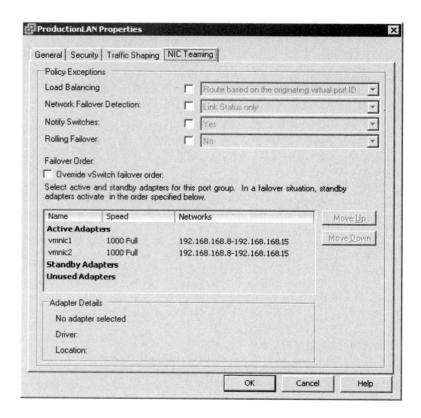

As an alternative to the Rolling Failover policy, a Failover Order policy can be manually configured. The Failover Order policy involves an administrative assignment of priority to each of the physical network adapters in the NIC team. As shown in Figure 3.29, a vSwitch with a NIC team set to use a Failover Order policy can have physical network adapters designated as active and standby.

Perform the following steps to configure the Failover Order policy for a NIC team:

1. Use the VI Client to establish a connection to a VirtualCenter server or an ESX Server host.

2. Click the hostname in the inventory panel on the left, select the Configuration tab from the details pane on the right, and then select Networking from the Hardware menu list.

3. Click the Properties for the virtual switch, select the name of virtual switch from the Configuration list, and then click the Edit button.

4. Select the NIC Teaming tab.

5. Use the Move Up and Move Down buttons to adjust the order of the network adapters and their location within the Active Adapters, Standby Adapters, and Unused Adapters lists, as shown in Figure 3.30.

6. Click OK and then click Close.

FIGURE 3.29
The Failover Order policy allows for the designation of active, standby, and unused network adapters for a NIC team.

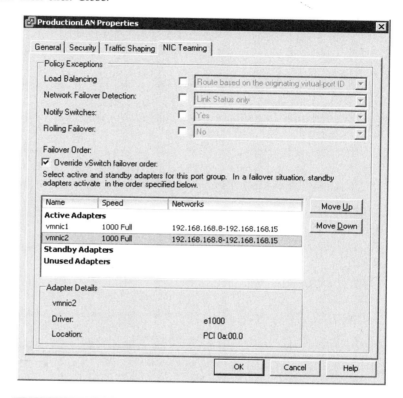

FIGURE 3.30
Failover order for a NIC team is determined by the order of network adapters as listed in the Active Adapters, Standby Adapters, and Unused Adapters lists.

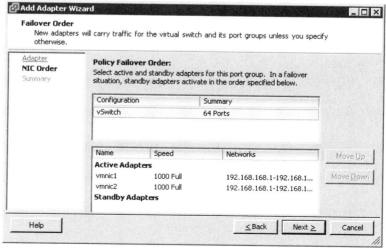

When a failover event occurs on a vSwitch with a NIC team, the vSwitch is obviously aware of the event. The physical switch that the vSwitch is connected to, however, will not know immediately. As shown in Figure 3.31, a NIC Team includes a Notify Switches configuration setting which, when set to Yes, will allow the physical switch to immediately learn of any of the following changes:

◆ A virtual machine is powered on (or any other time a client registers itself with the vSwitch)

◆ A VMotion occurs

◆ A MAC address is changed

◆ A NIC team failover or failback has occurred

FIGURE 3.31
The Notify Switches option allows physical switches to be notified of changes in NIC teaming configurations.

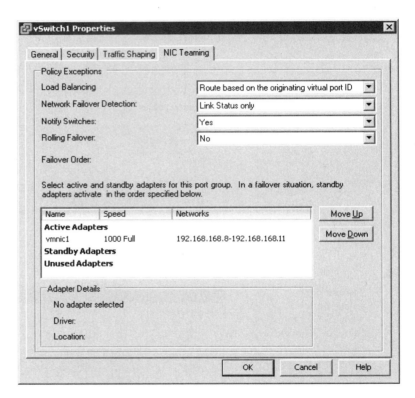

In any of these events, the physical switch is notified of the change using the Reverse Address Resolution Protocol (RARP). RARP updates the lookup tables on the physical switches and offers the shortest latency when a failover event occurs.

Although the VMkernel works proactively to keep traffic flowing from the virtual networking components to the physical networking components, VMware recommends taking the following actions to minimize networking delays:

◆ Disable Port Aggregation Protocol (PAgP) and Link Aggregation Control Protocol (LACP) on the physical switches

◆ Disable Dynamic Trunking Protocol (DTP) or trunk negotiation

◆ Disable Spanning Tree Protocol (STP)

VIRTUAL SWITCHES WITH CISCO SWITCHES

VMware recommends configuring Cisco devices to use PortFast mode for access interfaces or PortFast trunk mode for trunking interfaces.

Creating and Managing VLANs

To vLAN or not to vLAN? That is the question. As defined in the first section, a virtual LAN (vLAN) is a logical LAN configured on a virtual or physical switch port that provides efficient traffic segmentation, security, and efficient bandwidth utilization by providing traffic only to the ports configured for a respective vLAN. In addition to the security and segmentation advantages, vLANs allow network administrators to exceed the physical distance limitations of standard cabling. Using vLANs is advantageous when an ESX Server host has a limited number of physical network adapters.

Figure 3.32 shows a typical vLAN configuration across physical switches.

FIGURE 3.32
Virtual LANs provide secure traffic segmentation without the cost of additional hardware.

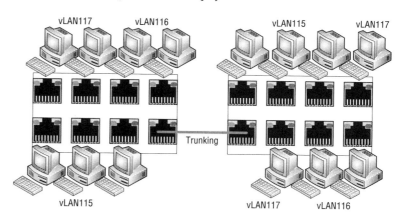

NO VLAN NEEDED

Virtual switches in the VMkernel do not need vLANs if an ESX Server host has enough physical network adapters to connect to each of the vLAN subnets.

Blade servers provide an excellent example of when vLANs offer tremendous benefit, because the blade servers offer limited expansion slots for physical network adapters due to the small form factor of the blade casing. Figure 3.33 shows a vSwitch architecture with vLANs as it integrates with a physical architecture also using vLANs. For a vSwitch to successfully send and receive packets tagged as one vLAN or another, a trunk port must be configured on the physical switch port to which the physical network adapter assigned to the vSwitch is connected.

FIGURE 3.33
The physical switch port to which a vSwitch's assigned physical network adapter is connected must be configured as a trunk port for vLAN tagging to work between virtual and physical switches.

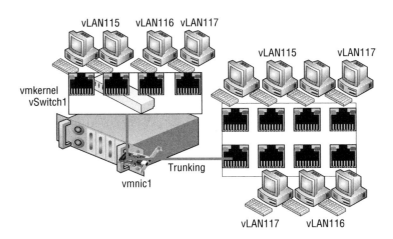

Follow these steps to configure a vSwitch with a virtual machine port group with a vLAN using an ID of VLAN 117:

1. Use the VI Client to establish a connection to a VirtualCenter server or an ESX Server host.

2. Click the hostname in the inventory panel on the left, select the Configuration tab from the details pane on the right, and then select Networking from the Hardware menu list.

3. Click the Properties link for the vSwitch where the new vLAN should be created.

4. Click the Add button, select the Virtual Machine radio button option, and then click Next.

5. Type the name of the virtual machine port group in the Network Label text box. In this case, **vLAN117** would be appropriate.

6. Type **117** in the VLAN ID (Optional) text box, as shown in Figure 3.34.

FIGURE 3.34
The vLAN tagging support of vSwitches simplifies integration with existing physical hardware configured with vLANs.

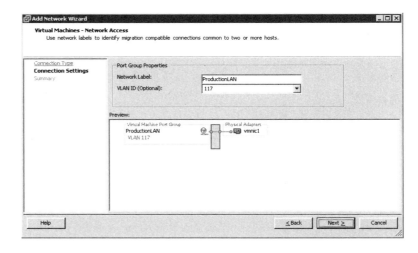

7. Click Next to review the vSwitch configuration and then click Finish.

Although vLANs reduce the costs of constructing multiple logical subnets, keep in mind that the contention through physical switches and network adapters is still present. For bandwidth-intensive network operations, the disadvantage of the shared physical network might outweigh the scalability and cost savings of the vLAN.

Configuring Virtual Switch Security

Even though the vSwitches created in the VMkernel are considered to be "dumb switches," they can be configured with vSwitch security policies to enhance or ensure Layer 2 security. Security policies can be applied at the vSwitch or at the lower-level connection types configured on a vSwitch and include the following three security options:

◆ Promiscuous Mode

◆ MAC Address Changes

◆ Forged Transmits

Applying a security policy to the vSwitch is effective, by default, for all connection types within the switch. However, if a connection type, or port group, is configured with a competing security policy, it will override the policy set at the vSwitch. As in the example in Figure 3.35, if a vSwitch is configured with a security policy that rejects the use of MAC address changes but a virtual machine port group on the switch is configured to accept MAC address changes, then any virtual machines connected to that port group will be allowed to communicate even though it is using a MAC address that differs from what is configured in its VMX file.

FIGURE 3.35
Security policies at the switch level are effective by default for all connection types on the switch. Security policies at the connection type (port group) level override the policy set at the virtual switch.

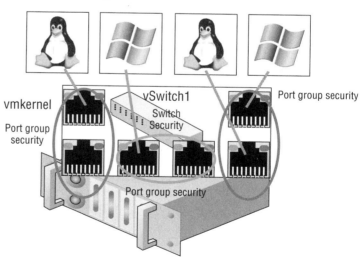

The default security profile for a vSwitch, shown in Figure 3.36, is set to reject Promiscuous mode and to accept MAC address changes and Forged transmits.

Promiscuous Mode

The Promiscuous Mode option is set to Reject by default to prevent virtual network adapters from observing any of the traffic submitted through the vSwitch. For enhanced security, allowing

Promiscuous mode is not recommended because it is an insecure mode of operation that allows virtual adapters to access traffic other than its own. Despite the security concerns, there are valid reasons for permitting a switch to operate in Promiscuous mode. An intrusion detection system (IDS) requires the ability to identify all traffic to scan for anomalies and malicious patterns of traffic. To support the use of the IDS without overextending the reduced security of Promiscuous mode, you can create a dedicated virtual machine port group for use with the IDS. As shown in Figure 3.37, the virtual switch security policy will remain at the default setting of Reject for the Promiscuous Mode option, while the virtual machine port group for the IDS will be set to Accept. This setting will override the virtual switch, allowing the IDS to monitor all switch traffic.

FIGURE 3.36
The default security pro-
file for a virtual switch
prevents Promiscuous
Mode but allows MAC
Address Changes and
Forged transmits.

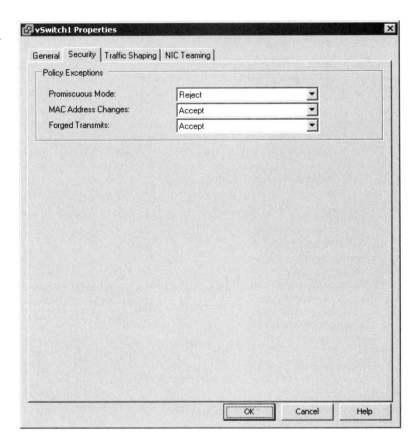

MAC Address Changes and Forged Transmits

When a virtual machine is created with one or more virtual network adapters, a MAC address is generated for each virtual adapter. Just as Intel, Broadcom, and others manufacture network adapters and include unique MAC address strings, VMware is also a network adapter manufacturer that has its own MAC prefix to ensure uniqueness. Of course, VMware doesn't actually manufacture anything, since the product exists as a virtual NIC in a virtual machine. The six-byte, randomly generated MAC addresses for a virtual machine can be seen in the configuration file

(.vmx) of the virtual machine, as shown in Figure 3.38. A VMware-assigned MAC address begins with the prefix 00:50:56 or 00:0C:29. The value of the fourth set (XX) cannot exceed 3F to prevent conflicts with other VMware products, while the fifth and sixth sets (YY:ZZ) are generated randomly based on the Universally Unique Identifier (UUID) of the virtual machine that is tied to the location of the virtual machine. For this reason, when a virtual machine location is changed a prompt will appear prior to successful boot. The prompt will inquire about keeping the UUID or generating a new UUID, which helps prevent MAC address conflicts.

FIGURE 3.37
Promiscuous mode, though a reduction in security, is required when using an intrusion detection system.

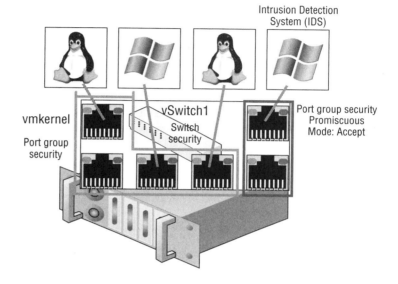

FIGURE 3.38
A virtual machine's initial MAC address is automatically generated and listed in the configuration file for the virtual machine.

```
displayName = "Win2008-01"
extendedConfigFile = "Win2008-01.vmxf"

scsi0.present = "true"
scsi0.sharedBus = "none"
scsi0.virtualDev = "lsilogic"
memsize = "1476"
scsi0:0.present = "true"
scsi0:0.fileName = "Win2008-01.vmdk"
scsi0:0.deviceType = "scsi-hardDisk"
ide0:0.present = "true"
ide0:0.clientDevice = "FALSE"
ide0:0.deviceType = "cdrom-image"
ide0:0.startConnected = "true"
floppy0.startConnected = "false"
floppy0.clientDevice = "FALSE"
ethernet0.present = "true"
ethernet0.allowGuestConnectionControl = "false"
ethernet0.networkName = "SvrMgmt"
ethernet0.addressType = "vpx"
ethernet0.generatedAddress = "00:50:56:a4:24:5d"
guestOS = "longhorn"
uuid.bios = "50 24 6b f4 9f 2c f7 b8-23 3b 19 a5 67 dc 22 37"
```

MANUALLY SETTING A MAC

Manually configuring a MAC address in the configuration file of a virtual machine will not work unless the first three bytes are VMware-provided prefixes and the last three bytes are unique. If a non-VMware MAC prefix is entered in the configuration file, the virtual machine will not power on.

All virtual machines have two MAC addresses: the initial MAC and the effective MAC. The initial MAC address is the MAC discussed in the previous paragraph that is generated automatically and that resides in the configuration file. The guest operating system has no control over the initial MAC address. The effective MAC address is the MAC address configured by the guest operating system that is used during communication with other systems. The effective MAC address is included in network communication as the source MAC of the virtual machine. By default, these two addresses are identical. To force a non-VMware-assigned MAC address to a guest operating system, change the effective MAC address from within the guest operating system, as shown in Figure 3.39.

FIGURE 3.39
A virtual machine's source MAC address is the effective MAC address, which by default matches the initial MAC address configured in the VMX file. The effective MAC, however, can be changed in the guest operating system.

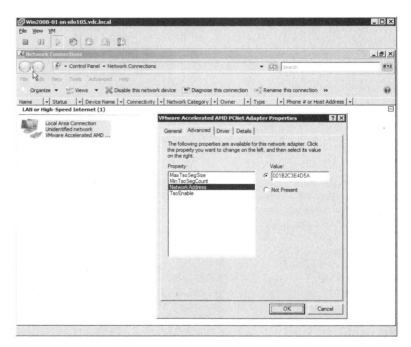

The ability to alter the effective MAC address cannot be removed from the guest operating system. However, the ability to let the system function with this altered MAC address is easily addressable through the security policy of a vSwitch. The remaining two settings of a virtual switch security policy are MAC Address Changes and Forged Transmits. Both of these security policies are concerned with allowing or denying differences between the initial MAC address in the configuration file and the effective MAC address in the guest operating system.

As noted earlier, the default virtual switch security is to accept the differences and process traffic as needed.

The difference between the MAC Address Changes and Forged Transmits security settings involves the direction of the traffic. MAC Address Changes is concerned with the integrity of incoming traffic, while Forged Transmits oversees the integrity of outgoing traffic. If the MAC Address Changes option is set to Reject, traffic will not be passed through the vSwitch to the virtual machine (incoming) if the initial and the effective MAC addresses do not match. If the Forged Transmits option is set to Reject, traffic will not be passed from the virtual machine to the vSwitch (outgoing) if the initial and the effective MAC addresses do not match. Figure 3.40 highlights the security restrictions implemented when MAC Address Changes and Forged Transmits are set to Reject.

FIGURE 3.40

The MAC Address Changes and Forged Transmits security options deal with incoming and outgoing traffic respectively.

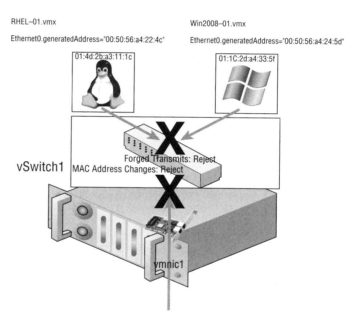

For the highest level of security, VMware recommends setting MAC Address Changes, Forged Transmits, and Promiscuous Mode on each vSwitch to Reject. When warranted or necessary, use port groups to loosen the security for a subset of virtual machines to connect to the port group.

 **Real World Scenario**

VIRTUAL SWITCH POLICIES FOR MICROSOFT NETWORK LOAD BALANCING

As with anything, there are, of course, exceptions. For virtual machines that will be configured as part of a Microsoft network load balancing (NLB) cluster set in Unicast mode, the virtual machine port group must allow MAC Address Changes and Forged Transmits. Systems that are part of an NLB cluster will share a common IP address and virtual MAC address, as shown here:

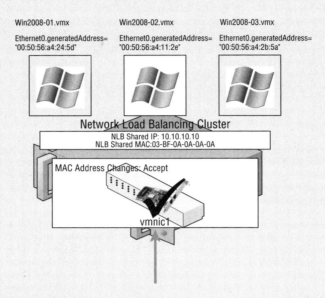

The shared virtual MAC address is generated by using an algorithm that includes a static component based on the NLB cluster's configuration of Unicast or Multicast mode plus a hexadecimal representation of the four octets that make up the IP address. This shared MAC address will certainly differ from the MAC address defined in the VMX file of the virtual machine. If the virtual machine port group does not allow for differences between the MAC addresses in the VMX and guest operating system, NLB will not function as expected. VMware recommends running NLB clusters in Multicast mode due to these issues with NLB clusters in Unicast mode.

Perform the following steps to edit the security profile of a vSwitch:

1. Use the VI Client to establish a connection to a VirtualCenter server or an ESX Server host.

2. Click the hostname in the inventory panel on the left, select the Configuration tab from the details pane on the right, and then select Networking from the Hardware menu list.

3. Click the Properties link for the virtual switch.

4. Click the name of the virtual switch under the Configuration list and then click the Edit button.

5. Click the Security tab and make the necessary adjustments.

6. Click OK and then click Close.

Follow these steps to edit the security profile of a port group:

1. Use the VI Client to establish a connection to a VirtualCenter server or an ESX Server host.

2. Click the hostname in the inventory panel on the left, select the Configuration tab from the details pane on the right, and then select Networking from the Hardware menu list.

3. Click the Properties link for the virtual switch.

4. Click the name of the port group under the Configuration list and then click the Edit button.

5. Click the Security tab and make the necessary adjustments.

6. Click OK and then click Close.

Managing the security of a virtual network architecture is much the same as managing the security for any other portion of your information systems. Security policy should dictate that settings be configured as secure as possible to err on the side of caution. Only with proper authorization, documentation, and change management processes should security be reduced. In addition, the reduction in security should be as controlled as possible to affect the least number of systems if not just the systems requiring the adjustments.

The Bottom Line

Identify the components of virtual networking.   Virtual networking is made up of a combination of relationships that exist between the logical networking components created in the VMkernel of ESX Server and the physical network devices. The virtual machines are configured on vSwitches bound to physical network adapters that are connected to physical switches.

Create virtual switches and virtual switch port groups.   Virtual switches, ports, and port groups are the cornerstone of the virtual networking architecture. These virtual components provide the tools for connecting to the physical network components to allow communication between the virtual and physical environments.

Master It   Virtual machines need to communicate with physical servers on the production network.

Master It   Service console communication must occur on a dedicated management network.

Master It   A dedicated network has been implemented to support VMotion.

Master It   A dedicated storage network has been implemented to support communication to iSCSI and NFS storage devices.

Create and manage NIC teams.   NIC teams offer the opportunity for redundancy and load balancing of network traffic. NIC teams offer three load-balancing policies: port-based, source MAC-based, and IP hash-based load balancing.

Master It   Virtual machines with one virtual network adapter must be capable of using multiple physical network adapters when connecting to multiple network destinations.

Master It   A vSwitch configured with a NIC team needs to experience failback when a physical network adapter is repaired after failover.

Master It   Bandwidth available on multiple physical network adapters must be accessible to a single virtual network adapter on a virtual machine.

Master It   Discovery time after a failover event on a NIC team needs to be minimized to prevent unnecessary delays.

Create and manage virtual LANs (VLANs).   The use of vLANs in a virtual networking architecture offers security, scalability, and communication efficiency.

Master It   A vSwitch needs to be configured with two vLANs named VLAN101 and VLAN102.

Master It   A vSwitch is configured with vLANs identical to those configured on the physical switch to which it is connected; however, traffic between the two switches is not functioning.

Configure virtual switch security policies.   Virtual switch security comes in a tight little package that includes three specific security settings that deal with identifying and processing traffic through a virtual switch. Promiscuous Mode, MAC Address Changes, and Forged Transmits each provides a securable vSwitch architecture, which ensures that only the right systems are sending and receiving traffic as expected.

Master It   A virtual machine with an installed intrusion detection system (IDS) needs to "sniff" the traffic passing through a vSwitch but the vSwitch is not configured to allow virtual machines to identify all traffic on the switch. You need to allow the functionality of the IDS while minimizing the security impact on the network.

Master It   An administrator of a Windows Server 2003 computer has changed the IP address of the guest operating system from the properties of the network adapter. The administrator now states that the Windows Server 2003 computer cannot communicate with requesting clients. You identify that the virtual machine port group to which the virtual machine is connected does not permit the vSwitch to send traffic when the effective and initial MAC addresses do not match.

Chapter 4

Creating and Managing Storage Devices

Fibre channel? iSCSI? NAS? Should you use all three? Is one better than the others? Should you create a few large LUNs? Should you create smaller LUNs? Where do you put your ISO files? Answers to all these common questions lie ahead as we dive into the vast array of storage options, architectures, and configuration settings for ESX Server.

In this chapter you will learn to:

◆ Differentiate among the various storage options available to VI3

◆ Design a storage area network for VI3

◆ Configure and manage Fibre Channel and iSCSI storage networks

◆ Configure and manage NAS storage

◆ Create and manage VMFS volumes

Understanding VI3 Storage Options

VMware Infrastructure 3 (VI3) offers several options for deploying a storage configuration as the back-end to an ESX Server implementation. These options include storage for virtual machines, ISO images, or templates for server provisioning. An ESX Server can have one or more storage options available to it, including:

◆ Fibre Channel storage

◆ iSCSI software-initiated storage

◆ iSCSI hardware-initiated storage

◆ Network Attached Storage (NAS)

◆ Local storage

ESX Server can take advantage of multiple storage architectures within the same host or even for the same virtual machine. ESX Server uses a proprietary file system called VMware File System (VMFS) that provides significant benefits for storing and managing virtual machine files. The virtual machines hosted by an ESX Server can have the associated virtual machine disk files (.vmdk) or mounted CD/DVD-ROM images (.iso) stored in different locations on different storage devices. Figure 4.1 shows an ESX Server host with multiple storage architectures. A Windows virtual machine has the virtual machine disk and CD-ROM image file stored on two different Fibre Channel storage area network (SAN) logical unit numbers (LUNs) on the same storage device. At the same time, a Linux virtual machine stores its virtual disk files on an iSCSI SAN LUN and its CD-ROM images on an NAS device.

FIGURE 4.1
An ESX Server host can be configured with multiple storage options for hosting files used by virtual machines, ISO images, or templates.

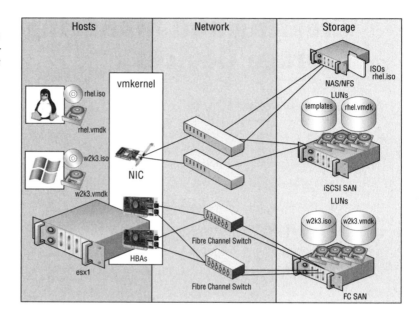

THE ROLE OF LOCAL STORAGE

During installation, an ESX Server host is configured by default with a local VMFS storage location, named Storage1 by default. The value of this local storage, however, is severely diminished because of the inability to support VMotion, DRS, or HA, and therefore should only be used for non-mission-critical virtual machines or templates and ISO images that are not required by other ESX hosts.

For this reason, when you're sizing a new ESX host, it is not important to dedicate time and money to large storage pools connected to the internal controllers of the host. Investing in large RAID 5, RAID 1+0, or RAID 0+1 volumes for ESX hosts is extremely unnecessary. In order for you to gain the full benefits of virtualization, the virtual machine disk files must reside on a shared storage device that is accessible by multiple ESX hosts. Direct any fiscal and administrative attention to memory and CPU sizing, or even network adapters, but not to locally attached hard drives.

The purpose of this chapter is to answer all your questions about deploying, configuring, and managing a back-end storage solution for your virtualized environment. Ultimately, each implementation will differ, and therefore the various storage architectures available might be the proper solution in one scenario but not in another. As you'll see, each of the storage solutions available to VI3 provides its own set of advantages and disadvantages.

Choosing the right storage technology for your infrastructure begins with a strong understanding of each technology and an intimate knowledge of the systems that will be virtualized as part of the VI3 deployment. Table 4.1 outlines the features of the three shared storage technologies.

TABLE 4.1:   Features of Shared Storage Technologies

FEATURE	FIBRE CHANNEL	ISCSI	NAS/NFS
Ability to format VMFS	Yes	Yes	No
Ability to hold VM files	Yes	Yes	Yes
Ability to boot ESX	Yes	Yes	No
VMotion, DRS, HA	Yes	Yes	Yes
Microsoft clustering	Yes	No	No
VCB	Yes	Yes	No
Templates, ISOs	Yes	Yes	Yes
Raw device mapping	Yes	Yes	No

MICROSOFT CLUSTER SERVICES

As of the writing of this book, VMware had not yet approved support for building Microsoft server clusters with virtual machines running on ESX Server 3.5. All previous versions up to 3.5 offered support, and once VMware has performed due diligence in testing server clusters on the latest version, it is assumed that the support will continue.

Once you have mastered the differences among the various architectures and identified the features of each that are most relevant to your data and virtual machines, you can feel confident in your decision. Equipped with the right information, you will be able to identify a solid storage platform on which your virtual infrastructure will be scalable, efficient, and secure.

The storage adapters in ESX Server will be identified automatically during the boot process and are available for configuration through the VI client or by using a set of command-line tools. The storage adapters in your server must be compatible. Remember to check the VI3 I/O Compatibility Guide before adding any new hardware to your server. You can find this guide at VMware's website (http://www.vmware.com/pdf/vi3_io_guide.pdf).

In the following sections, we'll cover both sets of tools, command line and GUI, and explore how to use them to create and manage the various storage types. Figure 4.2 and Figure 4.3 show the Virtual Infrastructure (VI) Client's configuration options for storage adapters and storage, respectively.

FIGURE 4.2
Storage adapters in
ESX Server are found
automatically because
only adapters certified
to work with VMware
products should be used.
Consult the appropriate
guides before adding
new hardware.

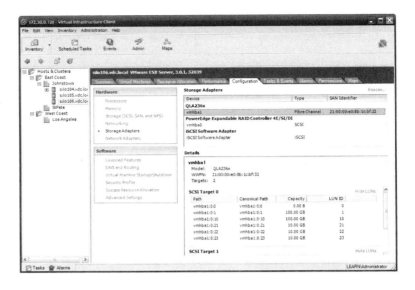

FIGURE 4.3
The VI Client provides
an easy-to-use interface
for adding new datas-
tores located on fibre
channel, iSCSI, or NAS
storage devices.

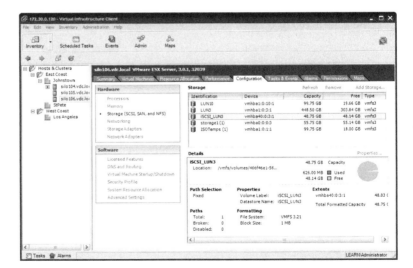

Understanding a Storage Area Network

A storage area network (SAN) is a communication network designed to handle the block-level transfer of data between a storage device and the requesting servers or hosts. The block-level transfer of data makes for highly efficient and highly specialized network communication that enables the reliable, low-latency transfer of large amounts of data with minimal server overhead.

A SAN consists of several components that direct and manage the flow of data across the dedicated network. These components reside in one of three segments on the SAN:

◆ The hosts accessing the storage

◆ The network across which traffic runs

◆ The storage

The concepts of a storage area network have long revolved around using a Fibre Channel protocol for communication among nodes connected to the network. However, recently the quick adoption of iSCSI storage area networks has introduced a strong competitor to its fibre channel predecessor. Whereas fibre channel storage networks use the Fibre Channel Protocol (FCP) for communication among nodes, iSCSI provides a similar block-level data transfer over standard IP networks.

As your virtualization career moves forward, you will, at some point, most certainly be in a position where you must understand and differentiate between the two most popular SAN architectures today: Fibre Channel and iSCSI. Both architectures offer significant benefits in the areas of reliability, redundancy, scalability, performance, and security. Incorporating a shared storage back-end helps eliminate many of the network failure issues that administrators find themselves constantly fixing. ESX Server with a back-end SAN offers:

◆ Automatic failover and multipathing at the host bus adapter (HBA) and storage port

◆ A high-performance file system in VMFS-3

◆ VMotion, Distributed Resource Scheduler (DRS), and High Availability (HA)

◆ Support for Microsoft Cluster Services (MSCS)

◆ VMware Consolidate Backup (VCB)

SAN devices offer additional benefits in the areas of storage replication and mirroring. Using third-party software, you can replicate or mirror the data on your LUNs to other LUNs on the same or even different storage devices. This feature offers administrators great possibilities in the areas of disaster recovery and business continuity.

Creating and Managing LUNs

After you finish your debate on fibre channel versus iSCSI and you purchase one or the other, you will then have to spend some time devising the proper procedure for managing and implementing LUNs. We are discussing LUN creation and management separately from the fibre channel and iSCSI sections because of its independence from the actual storage architecture. Details on the configuration of fibre channel and iSCSI will follow.

A logical unit number (LUN) is a logical configuration of disk space carved from an underlying set of physical disks. The physical disks on which LUNs are configured are most often arranged as a Redundant Array of Independent Disks (RAID) to support performance and/or redundancy for the data to be stored on the LUN. This section will look at RAID architectures, LUN addressing, and the age-old question of many little LUNs versus fewer big LUNs.

No matter your storage device, fibre channel or iSCSI, you will need to create LUNs, or at least work closely with someone who will create LUNs for you. Virtual machine performance can, in some cases, come down to a matter of having a solid LUN strategy in place for the activity level of that VM. Choosing the right RAID level for a LUN is therefore an integral part of your VI3 implementation. The most common types of RAID configurations are:

RAID 0   Disks configured in RAID 0 do not offer any type of redundancy or protection against drive failure. RAID 0 does, however, provide the fastest performance times because data is written simultaneously to all drives involved. A RAID 0 volume, also commonly referred to as a stripe, can have two or more disks as part of the array. Figure 4.4 outlines the structure of a RAID 0 configuration.

FIGURE 4.4
A RAID 0 disk
configuration provides
high-speed performance
for data stored across
a series of disks.

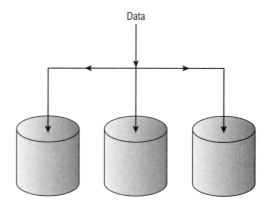

Data

RAID 1   A RAID 1 configuration puts two identically sized allocations of space from two drives together for the provisioning of a backup strategy that allows for either of the drives to fail and still maintain data. A RAID 1 volume, also commonly referred to as a mirrored array, loses 50 percent of the available drive space. For example, two 500GB LUNs configured as a RAID 1 array will only provide 500GB of storage. Figure 4.5 outlines the structure of a RAID 1 configuration.

FIGURE 4.5
A RAID 1 disk array, or
mirrored volume, pro-
vides redundancy in the
event of a single drive
failure. A RAID 1 array is
the most expensive disk
type because it incurs
a 50 percent loss in the
amount of storage.

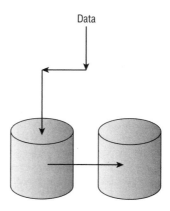

Data

RAID 5   A RAID 5 array writes data and parity simultaneously to all drives involved in the array. RAID 5 arrays provide redundancy in the event of a single drive failure by writing parity in equal increments across all drives. Parity is a mathematical calculation that allows N-1 drives the ability to make up the data on any other drive. A RAID 5 is the most efficient array when looking at disk space loss. The RAID 5 array only loses one drive's worth of space. For example, a RAID 5 array made up of four 250GB hard drives will have approximately 750GB of storage space available. Figure 4.6 outlines the structure of a RAID 5 configuration.

FIGURE 4.6
A RAID 5 array is commonly used because of its data protection and limited loss of space. Both data and parity are written equally across all drives in the array.

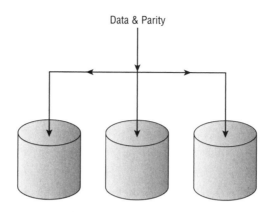

Data & Parity

RAID 1+0/RAID 0+1   For a more advanced disk array configuration, a RAID 1+0 or RAID 0+1 might be used. These structures combine the use of RAID 0 and RAID 1 technologies. RAID 1+0 involves mirroring a stripe, while RAID 0+1 involves striping several mirrors.

One of the most common challenges facing VI3 administrators is the process of sizing LUNs. Administrators can quite easily determine the RAID levels of a LUN (as explained in the preceding paragraphs), but sizing the LUN is an entirely different challenge. To determine the size of a LUN, administrators must have a game plan for testing virtual machine performance or have a solid understanding of the functions of the virtual machine(s) to be located on a LUN.

HOW MUCH SPACE DOES A VIRTUAL MACHINE CONSUME?

There is no definitive answer to this question, simply because administrators can choose to build virtual machines with virtual hard drives of varying sizes. There is, however, a generic but effective way of determining size requirements for a virtual machine. For each virtual machine, there is a set of associated files that have a direct influence on storage requirements, including the virtual machine hard disk, the suspended state, and the virtual machine swap file. Use the following formula to calculate the storage requirements for a virtual machine:

<size of the virtual machine hard disks> + *<size of suspended state for virtual machine>* + *<memory limit – memory reservation>* = minimum storage requirement for a virtual machine

For example, if a virtual machine consisted of a 25GB Virtual Machine Disk Format (VMDK) file, a memory limit of 4GB, and a memory reservation of 2GB, the minimum storage requirement could be calculated as follows:

25GB (virtual machine) + 25GB (suspended state) + 2GB (limit – reservation) = 52GB

In this case, a 55GB LUN would suffice for the virtual machine. However, keep in mind that if you decide to increase the RAM limit to 8GB or to reduce the RAM reservation to 0, you will then be jeopardizing the accuracy of the minimum storage requirement calculation.

Storage space for snapshots should also be considered, even if only for the temporary duration of the snapshot process (see Chapter 6). Luckily for SAN and VI3 administrators, the placement of a virtual machine's files is not a permanent decision. Moving a virtual machine to different storage locations is a simple but offline process.

When it comes to LUN design and management, VMware defines two common philosophies:

◆ The adaptive scheme

◆ The predictive scheme

Each scheme offers its own set of advantages and disadvantages to VI3 administrators. Undoubtedly, you will find that neither option is the appropriate solution in every situation. It is safe to say that most administrators will find themselves incorporating a blend of both philosophies as a means of compromise and earning the best of both worlds.

Adaptive Scheme

We'll start by introducing the adaptive scheme because of its simplicity. The adaptive scheme involves creating a small number of larger LUNs for the storage of virtual machines. The adaptive scheme results in fewer requirements on the part of the SAN administrator, less effort when performing LUN masking, fewer datastores to manage, and better opportunities for virtual disk resizing.

The downside to the adaptive scheme is the increased contention for LUN access across all of the virtual machines in the datastore. For example, if a 500GB LUN holds the virtual machine disk files for 10 virtual machines, then there will be contention among all of the virtual machines for access to the LUN. This might not be an issue, as the virtual machines' disk files residing on the LUN may be for virtual machines that are not disk intensive — that is, they do not rely heavily on hard disk input/output (I/O). For the adaptive scheme to be a plausible and manageable solution, VI3 administrators must be proactive in monitoring the virtual machines stored together on a LUN. When the performance of the virtual machines begins to reach unacceptable levels, administrators must look to creating more LUNs to be made available for new or existing virtual machines. Figure 4.7 shows an implementation of the adaptive scheme for storing virtual machines.

Predictive Scheme

The predictive scheme overcomes the limitations of the adaptive scheme but introduces administrative challenges of its own. The predictive involves the additional administrative effort of customizing LUNs to be specific for individual virtual machines. Take the following example: When administrators deploy a new server to play host to a database application, it is a common practice to enhance database performance by implementing multiple disks with characteristics specific to the data stored on the disk. On a database server, this often means a RAID 1 (mirror) volume for the operating system, a RAID 5 volume for the database files, and another RAID 1 volume for the database logs. Using the predictive scheme to architect a LUN solution for this database server would result in three SAN LUNs built on RAID arrays as needed by the database server. The sizes of the LUNs would depend on the estimated sizes of the operating system, database, and log files. Figure 4.8 shows this type of predictive approach to LUN design.

Table 4.2 outlines all of the pros and cons for each of the LUN design strategies.

FIGURE 4.7
The adaptive scheme involves creating a small number of LUNs that are larger in size and play host to virtual machine disk files for multiple virtual machines.

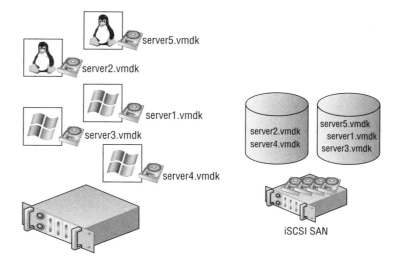

FIGURE 4.8
The predictive scheme, though administratively more involved, offers better performance measures for critical virtual machines.

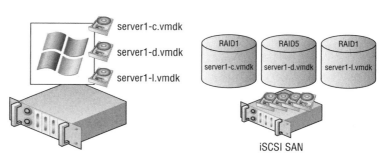

TABLE 4.2: Adaptive and Predictive Scheme Comparisons

TYPE OF SCHEME	PROS	CONS
Adaptive	Less need for SAN administrator Easy resizing of virtual disks Easy snapshot management Less volume management	Possible undersizing of LUN, resulting in greater administrative effort to create new LUNs Possible oversizing of LUN, resulting in wasted storage space
Predictive	Less contention on each VMFS More flexible share allocation and management Less wasted space on SAN storage RAID specificity for VMs Greater multipathing capability Support for Microsoft clusters Greater backup policy flexibility	Greater administrative overhead for LUN masking Greater administrative effort involved in VMotion, DRS, and HA planning

As we noted earlier in this section, the most appropriate solution will most likely involve a combination of the two design schemes. You may find a handful of virtual machines where performance is unaffected by storing all the virtual machine disk files on the same LUN, and at the same time you will find those virtual machines that require a strict nonsharing approach for the virtual machine disk files. But in between the two extremes, you will find the virtual machines that require specific RAID characteristics but, at the same time, can share LUN access with multiple virtual machines. Figure 4.9 shows a LUN design strategy that incorporates both the adaptive and predictive schemes as well as a hybrid approach.

FIGURE 4.9
Neither the adaptive nor the predictive scheme will be the most appropriate solution in all cases, which means most environments will be built on a hybrid solution that involves both philosophies.

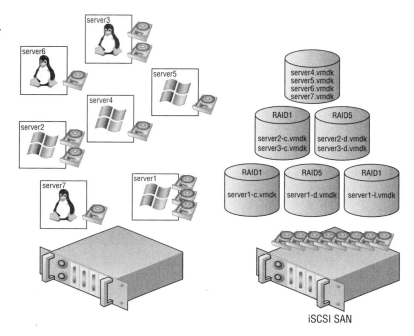

With all of the effort that will be put into designing the appropriate LUN structures, you will undoubtedly run into situations in which the design will require change. Luckily for the VI3 administrative community, the product is very flexible in the way virtual machine disk files are managed. In just a few short steps, a virtual machine's disk files can be moved from one LUN to another. The simplified nature of relocating disk files means that if you begin with one approach and discover it does not fit your environment, you can easily transition to a more suitable LUN structure. In Chapter 6, we'll detail the steps required to move a virtual machine from one datastore to another.

ESX Network Storage Architectures: Fibre Channel, iSCSI, and NAS

VMware Infrastructure 3 offers three shared storage options for locating virtual disk files, ISO files, and templates. Each storage technology presents its own benefits and challenges and requires careful attention. Despite their differences, there is often room for two or even all three of the technologies within a single virtualized environment.

Fibre Channel Storage

Despite its high cost, many companies rely on fibre channel storage as the backbone for critical data storage and management. The speed and security of the dedicated fibre channel storage network are attractive assets to companies looking for reliable and efficient storage solutions.

UNDERSTANDING FIBRE CHANNEL STORAGE NETWORKS

Fibre channel SANs can run at either 2GFC or 4GFC speeds and can be constructed in three different topologies: point-to-point, arbitrated loop, or switched fabric. The point-to-point fibre channel architecture involves a direct connection between the server and the fibre channel storage device. The arbitrated loop, as the name suggests, involves a loop created between the storage device and the connected servers. In either of these cases, a fibre channel switch is not required. Each of these topologies places limitations on the scalability of the fibre channel architecture by limiting the number of nodes that can connect to the storage device. The switched fabric architecture is the most common and offers the most functionality, so we will focus on it for the duration of this chapter and throughout the book. The fibre channel switched fabric includes a fibre channel switch that manages the flow of the SCSI communication over fibre channel traffic between servers and the storage device. Figure 4.10 displays the point-to-point and arbitrated loop architectures.

FIGURE 4.10
Fibre channel SANs can be constructed as point-to-point or arbitrated loop architectures.

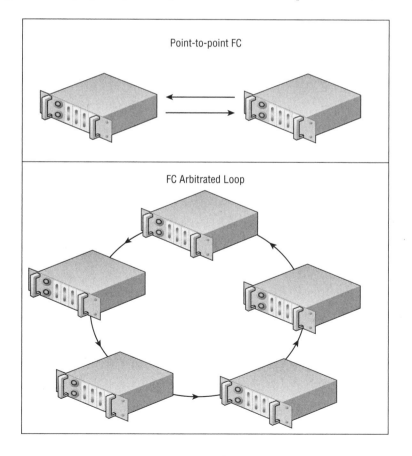

Point-to-point FC

FC Arbitrated Loop

The switched fabric architecture is more common because of its scalability and increased reliability. A fibre channel SAN is made up of several different components, including:

Logical unit numbers (LUNs)   A logical configuration of disk space created from one or more underlying physical disks. LUNs are most commonly created on multiple disks in a RAID configuration appropriate for the disk usage. LUN design considerations and methodologies will be covered later in this chapter.

Storage device   The storage device houses the disk subsystem from which the storage pools or LUNs are created.

Storage Processor (SP)   One or more storage processors (SPs) provide connectivity between the storage device and the host bus adapters in the hosts. SPs can be connected directly or through a fibre channel switch.

Fibre channel switch   A hardware device that manages the storage traffic between servers and the storage device. Although devices can be directly connected over fibre channel networks, it is more common to use a fibre channel switched network. The term *fibre channel fabric* refers to the network created by using fibre-optic cables to connect the fibre channel switches to the HBAs and SPs on the hosts and storage devices, respectively.

Host bus adapters (HBAs)   A hardware device that resides inside a server that provides connectivity to the fibre channel network through a fibre-optic cable.

These SAN components make up the infrastructure that processes storage requests and manages the flow of traffic among the nodes on the network. Figure 4.11 shows a commonly configured fibre channel storage area network with two ESX Servers, redundant fibre channel switches, and a storage device.

FIGURE 4.11
Most storage area networks consist of hosts, switches, and a storage device interconnected to provide servers with reliable and redundant access to storage pools residing in the storage device.

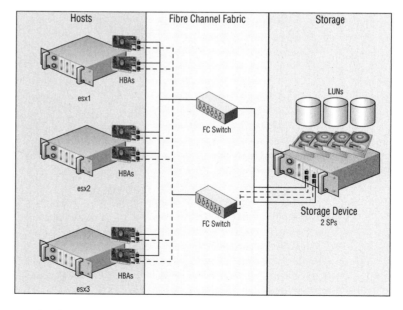

A SAN can be an expensive investment, predominantly because of the redundant hardware built into each of the segments of the SAN architecture. As shown in Figure 4.11, the hosts were outfitted with multiple HBAs connected to the fibre channel fabric, which consisted of multiple fibre channel switches connected to multiple storage processors in the storage device. The trade-off for the higher cost is less downtime in the event of a single piece of hardware failing in the SAN structure.

Now that we have covered the hardware components of the storage area network, it is important that, before moving into ESX specifics, we discuss how the different SAN components communicate with one another.

Each node in a SAN is identified by a globally unique 64-bit hexadecimal World Wide Name (WWN) or World Wide Port Name (WWPN) assigned to it. A WWN will look something like this:

```
22:00:00:60:01:B9:A7:D2
```

The WWN for a fibre channel node is discovered by the switch and is then assigned a port address upon login to the fabric. The WWN assigned to a fibre channel node is the equivalent of the globally unique Media Access Control (MAC) address assigned to network adapters on Ethernet networks.

Once the nodes are logged in and have been provided addresses they are free to begin communication across the fibre channel network as determined by the zoning configuration on the fibre channel switches. The process of zoning involves the configuration of a set of access control parameters that determine which nodes in the SAN architecture can communicate with other nodes on the network. Zoning establishes a definition of communication between storage processors in the storage device and HBAs installed on the ESX Server hosts. Figure 4.12 shows a fibre channel zoning configuration.

FIGURE 4.12
Zoning a fibre channel network at the switch level provides a security boundary that ensures that host devices do not see specific storage devices.

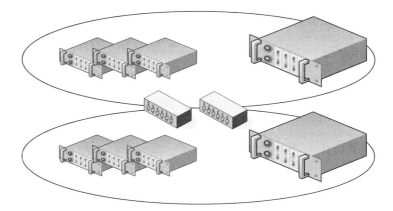

Zoning is a highly effective means of preventing non-ESX hosts from discovering storage volumes that are formatted as VMFS. This process effectively creates a security boundary between fibre channel nodes that simplifies management in large SAN environments. The nodes within a zone, or segment, of the network can communicate with one another but not with other nodes outside their zone. The zoning configuration on the fibre channel switches dictates the number of targets available to an ESX Server host. By controlling and isolating the paths within the switch fabric, the switch zoning can establish strong boundaries of fibre channel communication.

In most VI3 deployments, only one zone will be created since the VMotion, DRS, and HA features require all nodes to have access to the same storage. That is not to say that larger, enterprise VI3 deployments cannot realize a security and management advantage by configuring multiple zones to establish a segregation of departments, projects, or roles among the nodes. For example, a large enterprise with a storage area network that supports multiple corporate departments (i.e., marketing, sales, finance, and research) might have ESX Server hosts and LUNs for each respective department. In an effort to prevent any kind of cross-departmental LUN access, the switches can establish a zone for each department ensuring only the appropriate LUN access. Proper fibre channel switch zoning is a critical tool for separating a test or development environment from a production environment.

In addition to configuring zoning at the fibre channel switches, LUNs must be presented, or not presented, to an ESX Server. This process of LUN masking, or hiding LUNs from a fibre channel node, is another means of ensuring that a server does not have access to a LUN. As the name implies, this is done at the LUN level inside the storage device and not on the fibre channel switch. More specifically, the storage processor (SP) on the storage device allows for LUNs to be made visible or invisible to the fibre channel nodes that are available based on the zoning configuration. The hosts with LUNs that have been masked are not allowed to store or retrieve data from those LUNs.

Zoning provides security at a higher, more global level, whereas LUN masking is a more granular approach to LUN security and access control. The zoning and LUN masking strategies of your fibre channel network will have a significant impact on the functionality of your virtual infrastructure. You will learn in Chapter 9 that LUN access is critical to the advanced VMotion, DRS, and HA features of VirtualCenter.

Figure 4.13 shows a fibre channel switch fabric with multiple storage devices and LUNs configured on each storage device. Table 4.3 describes a LUN access matrix that could help a storage administrator and VI3 administrator work collaboratively on planning the zoning and LUN masking strategies.

FIGURE 4.13
A fibre channel network consists of multiple hosts, multiple storage devices, and LUNs across each storage device. Every host does not always need access to every storage device or every LUN, so zoning and masking are a critical part of SAN design and configuration.

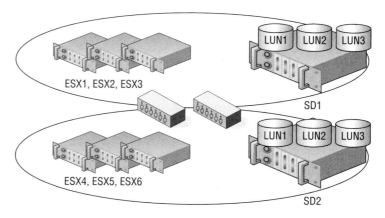

Fibre channel storage networks are synonymous with "high performance" storage systems. Arguably, this is in large part due to the efficient manner in which communication is managed by the fibre channel switches. Fibre channel switches work intelligently to reduce, if not eliminate, oversubscription problems in which multiple links are funneled into a single link. Oversubscription results in information being dropped. With less loss of data on fibre channel networks, there is reduced need for retransmission of data and, in turn, processing power becomes available to process new storage requests instead of retransmitting old requests.

CONFIGURING ESX FOR FIBRE CHANNEL STORAGE

Since fibre channel storage is currently the most efficient SAN technology, it is a common back-end to a VI3 environment. ESX has native support for connecting to fibre channel networks through the host bus adapter. However, ESX Server has limited support for the available storage devices and host bus adapters. Before investing in a SAN, make sure it is compatible and supported by VMware. Even if the SAN is capable of "working" with ESX, it does not mean VMware is going to provide support. VMware is very stringent with the hardware support for VI3; therefore, you should always implement hardware that has been tested by VMware.

TABLE 4.3:   LUN Access Matrix

Host	SD1	SD2	LUN1	LUN2	LUN3
ESX1	Yes	No	Yes	Yes	No
ESX2	Yes	No	No	Yes	Yes
ESX3	Yes	No	Yes	Yes	Yes
ESX4	No	Yes	Yes	Yes	Yes
ESX5	No	Yes	Yes	No	Yes
ESX6	No	Yes	Yes	No	Yes

Note: The processes of zoning and masking can be facilitated by generating a matrix that defines which hosts should have access to which storage devices and which LUNs.

Always check the compatibility guides before adding new servers, new hardware, or new storage devices to your virtual infrastructure.

Since VMware is the only company (at this time) that provides drivers for hardware supported by ESX, you must be cautious when adding new hardware like host bus adapters. The bright side, however, is that so long as you opt for a VMware-supported HBA, you can be certain it will work without incurring any of the driver conflicts or misconfiguration common in other operating systems.

VMWARE FIBRE CHANNEL SAN COMPATIBILITY

You can find a complete list of compatible SAN devices online on VMware's website at http://www.vmware.com/pdf/vi3_san_guide.pdf. Be sure to check the guides regularly as they are consistently updated. When testing a fibre channel SAN against ESX, VMware identifies compatibility in all of the following areas:

◆ Basic connectivity to the device.

◆ Multipathing capability for allowing access to storage via different paths.

◆ Host bus adapter (HBA) failover support for eliminating single point of failure at the HBA.

◆ Storage port failover capability for eliminating single point of failure on the storage device.

◆ Support for Microsoft Clustering Services (MSCS) for building server clusters when the guest operating system is Windows 2000 Service Pack 4 or Windows 2003.

◆ Boot-from-SAN capability for booting an ESX server from a SAN LUN.

◆ Point-to-point connectivity support for nonswitch-based fibre channel network configurations.

Naturally, since VMware is owned by EMC Corporation you can find a great deal of compatibility between ESX Server and the EMC line of fibre channel storage products (also sold by Dell). Each of the following vendors provides storage products that have been tested by VMware:

- 3PAR: http://www.3par.com
- Bull: http://www.bull.com
- Compellent: http://www.compellent.com
- Dell: http://www.dell.com
- EMC: http://www.emc.com
- Fujitsu/Fujitsu Siemens: http://www.fujitsu.com and http://www.fujitsu-siemens.com
- HP: http://www.hp.com
- Hitachi/Hitachi Data Systems (HDS): http://www.hitachi.com and http://www.hds.com
- IBM: http://www.ibm.com
- NEC: http://www.nec.com
- Network Appliance (NetApp): http://www.netapp.com
- Nihon Unisys: http://www.unisys.com
- Pillar Data: http://www.pillardata.com
- Sun Microsystems: http://www.sun.com
- Xiotech: http://www.xiotech.com

Although the nuances, software, and practices for managing storage devices across different vendors will most certainly differ, the concepts of SAN storage covered in this book transcend the vendor boundaries and can be used across various platforms.

Currently, ESX Server supports many different QLogic 236x and 246x fibre channel HBAs for connecting to fibre channel storage devices. However, because the list can change over time, you should always check the compatibility guides before purchasing and installing a new HBA.

It certainly does not make sense to make a significant financial investment in a fibre channel storage device and still have a single point of failure at each server in the infrastructure. We recommend that you build redundancy into the infrastructure at each point of potential failure. As shown in the diagrams earlier in the chapter, each ESX Server host should be equipped with a minimum of two fibre channel HBAs to provide redundant path capabilities in the event of HBA failure. ESX Server 3 supports a maximum of 16 HBAs per system and a maximum of 15 targets per HBA. The 16-HBA maximum can be achieved with four quad-port HBAs or eight dual-port HBAs provided that the server casing has the expansion capability.

Adding a new HBA requires that the physical server be turned off since ESX Server does not support adding hardware while the server is running, otherwise known as a "hot add" of hardware. Figure 4.14 displays the redundant HBA and storage processor (SP) configuration of a VI3 environment.

FIGURE 4.14

An ESX Server configured through VirtualCenter with two QLogic 236x fibre channel HBAs and multiple SCSI targets or storage processors (SPs) in the storage device.

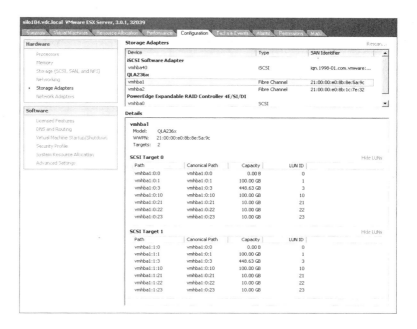

Once fibre channel storage is presented to a server and the server recognizes the pools of storage, then the administrator can create datastores. A datastore is a storage pool on an ESX Server host that can be a local disk, fibre channel LUN, iSCSI LUN, or NFS share. A datastore provides a location for placing virtual machine files, ISO images, and templates.

For the VI3 administrator, the configuration of datastores on fibre channel storage is straightforward. It is the LUN masking, LUN design, and LUN management that incur significant administrative overhead (or more to the point, brainpower!). For VI3 administrators who are not responsible for SAN management and configuration, it is essential to work closely with the storage personnel to ensure performance and security of the storage pools used by the ESX Server hosts.

Later in this chapter we'll discuss LUN design in greater detail, but for now let's assume that LUNs have been created and masking has been performed. With those assumptions in place, the work required by the VI3 administrator is quick and easy. Figure 4.15 identifies five LUNs that are available to silo105.vdc.local through its redundant connection to the storage device. The ESX Server silo105.vdc.local has two HBAs connecting to a storage device, with two SPs creating redundant paths to the available LUNs. Although there are six LUNs in the targets list, the LUN with ID 0 is disregarded since it is not available to the ESX Server for storage.

A portion of the ESX Server boot process includes LUN discovery. An ESX Server, at boot-up and by default, will attempt to enumerate LUNs with LUN IDs between 1 and 255.

Even though silo105.vdc.local is presented with five LUNs, it does not mean that all five LUNs are currently being used to store data for the server. Figure 4.16 shows that silo105.vdc.local has three datastores, only two of which are LUNs presented by the fibre channel storage device. With two fibre channel SAN LUNs already in use, silo105.vdc.local has three more LUNs available when needed. Later in this chapter you'll learn how to use the LUNs as VMFS volumes.

FIGURE 4.15
An ESX Server discovers its available LUNs and displays them under each available SCSI target. Here, five LUNs are available to the ESX Server for storage.

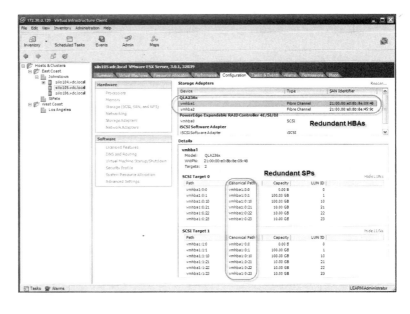

FIGURE 4.16
An ESX Server host with a local datastore named storage1 (2) and two datastores ISOTemps (1) and LUN10 on a fibre channel storage device.

Storage Refresh Remove Add Storage...

Identification	Device	Capacity	Free	Type
ISOTemps (1)	vmhba1:0:1:1	99.75 GB	8.91 GB	vmfs3
LUN10	vmhba1:0:10:1	99.75 GB	19.66 GB	vmfs3
storage1 (2)	vmhba0:0:0:3	124.00 GB	123.39 GB	vmfs3

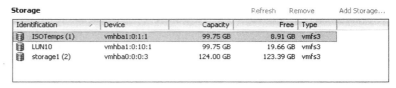

When an ESX Server host is powered on, it will process the first 256 LUNs (LUN 0 through LUN 255) on the storage devices to which it is given access. ESX will perform this enumeration at every boot, even if many of the LUNs have been masked out from the storage processor side. You can configure individual ESX Server hosts not to scan all the way up to LUN 255 by editing the Disk.MaxLUN configuration setting. Figure 4.17 shows the default configuration of the Disk.MaxLUN value that results in accessibility to the first 256 LUNs.

LUN MASKING AT THE ESX SERVER

Despite the potential benefit of performing LUN masking at the ESX Server (to speed up the boot process), the work necessary to consistently manage LUNs on each ESX Server may offset that benefit. I suggest that you perform LUN masking at the SAN.

To change the Disk.MaxLUN setting, perform the following steps:

1. Use the VI client to connect to a VirtualCenter Server or an individual ESX Server host.
2. Select the hostname in the inventory tree and select the Configuration tab in the details pane on the right.

3. In the Software section, click the Advanced Settings link.

4. In the Advanced Settings for <hostname> window, select the Disk option from the selection tree.

5. In the Disk.MaxLUN text box, enter the desired integer value for the number of LUNs to scan.

FIGURE 4.17
Altering the Disk.MaxLUN value can result in a faster boot or rescan process for an ESX Server host. However, it may also require attention when new LUNs must be made available that exceed the custom configuration.

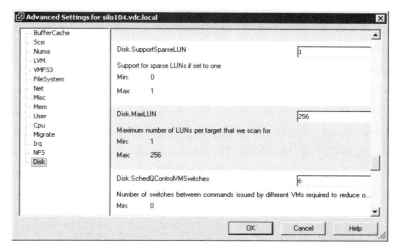

You should alter the Disk.MaxLUN parameter only when you are certain that LUN IDs will never exceed the custom value. Otherwise, though a performance benefit might result, you will have to revisit the setting each time available LUN IDs must exceed the custom value.

Although LUN masking is most commonly performed at the storage processor, as it should be, it is also possible to configure LUN masking on each individual ESX Server host to speed up the boot process.

Let's take an example where an administrator configures LUN masking at the storage processor. Once the masking at the storage processor is complete, the LUNs that have been presented to the hosts are the ones numbered 117 through 127. However, since the default configuration for ESX Server is set to enumerate the first 256 LUNs by default, it will move through each potential LUN even if the storage processor is preventing the LUN from being seen. In an effort to speed up the boot process, an ESX Server administrator can perform LUN masking at the server. In this example, if the administrator were to mask LUN 1 through LUN 116 and LUN 128 through LUN 256, then the server would only be enumerating the LUNs that it is allowed to see and, as a result, would boot quicker. To enable LUN masking on an ESX Server, you must edit the Disk.MaskLUN option (which you access by clicking the Advanced Settings link on the Configuration tab). The Disk.MaskLUN text box requires this format:

```
<adapter>:<target>:<LUN range lists separated by commas>;
```

For example, to mask the LUNs from the previous example (1 through 116 and 128 through 256) that are accessible through the first HBA and two different storage processors, you'd enter the following in the Disk.MaskLUN text box entry:

```
vmhba1:0:1-116,128-256;vmhba1:1:1-116,128-256;
```

The downside to configuring LUN masking on the ESX Server is the administrative overhead involved when a new LUN is presented to the server or servers. To continue with the previous example, if the VI3 administrator requests five new LUNs and the SAN administrator provisions LUNs with LUN IDs of 136 through 140, the VI3 administrator will have to edit all of the local masking configurations on each ESX Server host to read as follows:

Vmhba1:0:1-116,128-135,141-254;vmhba1:1:1-116,128-135,141-256;

In theory, LUN masking on each ESX Server host sounds like it could be a benefit. But in practice, masking LUNs at the ESX Server in an attempt to speed up the boot process is not worth the effort. An ESX Server host should not require frequent reboots, and therefore the effect of masking LUNs on each server would seldom be felt. Additional administrative effort would be needed since each host would have to be revisited every time new LUNs are presented to the server.

ESX LUN MAXIMUMS

Be sure that storage administrators do not carve LUNs for an ESX Server that have ID numbers greater than 255. ESX hosts have a maximum capability of 256 LUNs, beginning with ID 1 and on through ID 255. Clicking the Rescan link located in the Storage Adapters node of the Configuration tab on a host will force the host to identify new LUNs or new VMFS volumes, with the exception that any LUNs with IDs greater than 255 will not be discoverable by an ESX host.

Although adding a new HBA to an ESX Server host requires you to shut down the server, presenting and finding new LUNs only requires that you initiate a rescan from the ESX Server host.

To identify new storage devices and/or new VMFS volumes that have been added since the last scan, click the Rescan link located in the Storage node of the Configuration tab. The host will launch an enumeration process beginning with the lowest possible LUN ID to the highest (1 to 255), which can be a slow process (unless LUN masking has been configured on the host as well as the storage processor).

You have probably seen by now, and hopefully agree, that VMware has done a great job of creating a graphical user interface (GUI) that is friendly, intuitive, and easy to use. Administrators also have the ability to manage LUNs from a Service Console command line on an ESX Server host.

The ability to scan for new storage is available in the VI Client using the Rescan link in the Storage Adapters node of the Configuration page, but it is also possible to rescan from a command line.

ESTABLISHING CONSOLE ACCESS WITH ROOT PRIVILEGES

The root user account does not have secure shell (SSH) capability by default. You must set the Permit-RootLogin entry in the /etc/ssh/sshd_config file to Yes to allow access. Alternatively, you can log on to the console as a different user and use the #su - option to elevate the logon permissions. Opting to use the #su - option still requires that you know the root user's password but does not expose the system to allowing remote root logon via SSH.

Use the following syntax to rescan vmhba1 from a Service Console command line:

1. Log on to a console session as a nonroot user.

2. Type **su -** and then click Enter.

3. Type the root user password and then click Enter.

4. Type **esxcfg-rescan vmhba1** at the # prompt.

When multiple vmhba devices are available to the ESX Server, repeat the command, replacing **vmhba#** with each device.

You can identify LUNs using the physical address (i.e., vmhba#:target#:lun:partition), but the Service Console references the LUNs using the device filename (i.e., sda, sdb, etc.). You can see the device filenames when installing an ESX Server that is connected to a SAN with accessible LUNs. By using an SSH tool (putty.exe) to establish a connection and then issuing the esxcfg commands, you can perform command-line LUN management.

To display a list of available LUNs with their associated paths, device names, and UUIDs, perform the following steps:

1. Log on to a console session as a nonroot user.

2. Type **su -** and then click Enter.

3. Type the root user password and then click Enter.

4. Type **esxcfg-vmhbadevs -m** at the # prompt.

Figure 4.18 shows the resulting output for an ESX Server with an IP address of 172.30.0.106 and a nonroot user named *roottoo*.

FIGURE 4.18

The esxcfg commands offer parameters and switches for managing and identifying LUNs available to an ESX Server host.

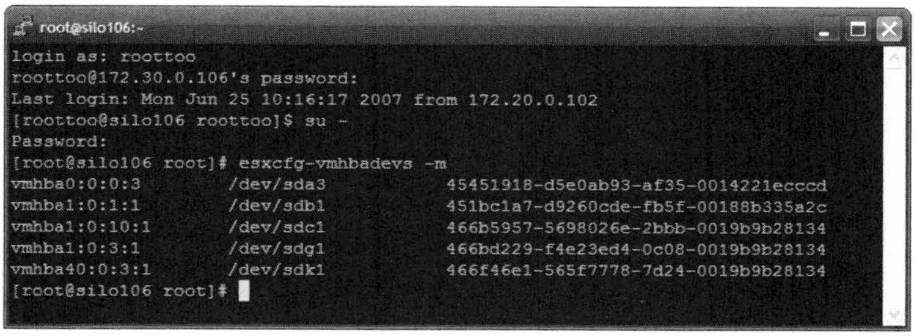

The UUIDs displayed in the output are unique identifiers used by the Service Console and VMkernel. These values are also reflected in the Virtual Infrastructure Client; however, we do not commonly refer to them because using the friendly names or even the physical paths is much easier.

Fibre channel storage has a strong performance history and will continue to progress in the areas of performance, manageability, reliability, and scalability. Unfortunately, the large financial investment required to implement a fibre channel solution has scared off many organizations looking to deploy a virtual infrastructure that offers all the VMotion, DRS, and HA bells that VI3 provides. Luckily for the IT community, VMware now offers lower-cost (and potentially lower-performance) options in iSCSI and NAS/NFS.

iSCSI Network Storage

As a response to the needs of not-so-deep-pocketed network administrators, Internet Small Computer Systems Interface (iSCSI) has become a strong alternative to fibre channel. The popularity of iSCSI storage, which offers both lower cost and increasing speeds, will continue to grow as it finds its place in virtualized networks.

UNDERSTANDING iSCSI STORAGE NETWORKS

iSCSI storage provides a block-level transfer of data using the SCSI communication protocol over a standard TCP/IP network. By using block-level transfer, as in a fibre channel solution, the storage device looks like a local device to the requesting host. With proper planning, an iSCSI SAN can perform nearly as well as a fibre channel SAN — or better. This depends on other factors, but we can dive into those in a moment. And before we make that dive into the configuration of iSCSI with ESX, let's first take a look at the components involved in an iSCSI SAN. Despite the fact that the goals and overall architecture of iSCSI are similar to fibre channel, when you dig into the configuration details, the communication architecture, and individual components of iSCSI, the differences are profound.

The components that make up an iSCSI SAN architecture, shown in Figure 4.19, include:

Hardware initiator   A hardware device referred to as an iSCSI host bus adapter (HBA) that resides in an ESX Server host and initiates storage communication to the storage processor (SP) of the iSCSI storage device.

Software initiator   A software-based storage driver initiator that does not require specific hardware and transmits over standard, supported Ethernet adapters.

Storage device   The physical device that houses the disk subsystem upon which LUNs are built.

Logical unit number (LUN)   A logical configuration of disk space created from one or more underlying physical disks. LUNs are most commonly created on multiple disks in a RAID configuration appropriate for the disk usage. LUN design considerations and methodologies will be covered later in this chapter.

Storage processor (SP)   A communication device in the storage device that receives storage requests from storage area network nodes.

Challenge Handshake Authentication Protocol (CHAP)   An authentication protocol used by the iSCSI initiator and target that involves validating a single set of credentials provided by any of the connecting ESX Server hosts.

Ethernet switches   Standard hardware devices used for managing the flow of traffic between ESX Server nodes and the storage device.

iSCSI qualified name (IQN)   The full name of an iSCSI node in the format of iqn.<*year*>-<*month*>.com.*domain*:*alias*. For example, iqn.1998-08.com.vmware:silo1-1 represents the registration of vmware.com on the Internet in August (08) of 1998. Nodes on an iSCSI deployment will have default IQNs that can be changed. However, changing an IQN requires a reboot of the ESX Server host.

iSCSI is thus a cheaper shared storage solution than fibre channel. Of course, the reduced cost does come at the expense of the better performance that fibre channel offers. Ultimately, the question comes down to that difference in performance. The performance difference can, in large part, reflect the storage design and the disk intensity of the virtual machines stored on the iSCSI LUNs. Although this is true for fibre channel storage as well, it is less of a concern given the greater bandwidth available via a 4GB fibre channel architecture. In either case, it is the duty of the ESX Server administrator and the SAN administrator to regularly monitor the saturation level of the storage network.

FIGURE 4.19
An iSCSI SAN includes an overall architecture similar to fibre channel, but the individual components differ in their communication mechanisms.

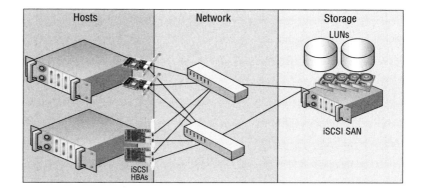

When deploying an iSCSI storage network, you'll find that adhering to the following rules can help mitigate performance degradation or security concerns:

◆ Always deploy iSCSI storage on a dedicated network.

◆ Configure all nodes on the storage network with static IP addresses.

◆ Configure the network adapters to use full-duplex, gigabit autonegotiated recommended communication.

◆ Avoid funneling storage requests from multiple servers into a single link between the network switch and the storage device.

Deploying a dedicated iSCSI storage network reduces network bandwidth contention between the storage traffic and other common network traffic types such as e-mail, Internet, and file transfer. A dedicated network also offers administrators the luxury of isolating the SCSI communication protocol from "prying eyes" that have no legitimate need to access the data on the storage device.

iSCSI storage deployments should always utilize dedicated storage networks to minimize contention and increase security. Achieving this goal is a matter of implementing a dedicated switch or switches to isolate the storage traffic from the rest of the network. Figure 4.20 shows the differences and one that is integrated with the other network segments.

If a dedicated physical network is not possible, using a virtual local area network (VLAN) will segregate the traffic to ensure storage traffic security. Figure 4.21 shows iSCSI implemented over a VLAN to achieve better security. However, this type of configuration still forces the iSCSI communication to compete with other types of network traffic.

Figure 4.21 iSCSI can be implemented across VLANs to enhance security.

FIGURE 4.20
iSCSI should have a dedicated and isolated network.

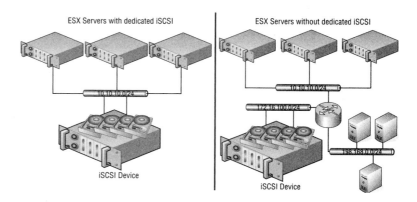

FIGURE 4.21
iSCSI communication traffic can be isoloated from other network traffic by using vLANs.

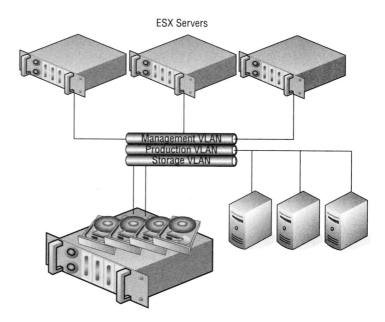

🌐 **Real World Scenario**

A COMMON ISCSI NETWORK INFRASTRUCTURE MISTAKE

A common deployment error with iSCSI storage networks is the failure to provide enough connectivity between the Ethernet switches and the storage device to adequately handle the traffic requests from the ESX Server hosts. In the sample architecture shown here, four ESX Server hosts are configured with redundant connections to two Ethernet switches, which each have a connection to the iSCSI storage device. At first glance, it looks as if the infrastructure has been designed to support a redundant storage communication strategy. And perhaps it has. But what it has not done is maximize the efficiency of the storage traffic.

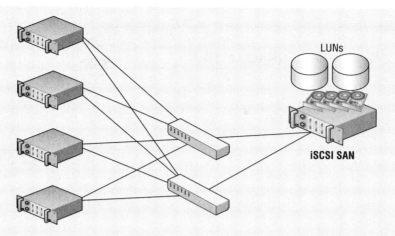

If each link between the ESX Server hosts and the Ethernet switches is a 1GB link, that means there is a total storage bandwidth of 8GB or 4GB per Ethernet switch. However, the connection between the Ethernet switches and the iSCSI storage device consists of a single 1GB link per switch. If each host maximizes the throughput from host to switch, the bandwidth needs will exceed the capabilities of the switch-to-storage link and will force packets to be dropped. Since TCP is a reliable transmission protocol, the dropped packets will be re-sent as needed until they have reached their destination. All of the new data processing, coupled with the persistent retries of dropped packets, consumes more and more resources and strains the communication, thus resulting in a degradation of server performance.

To protect against funneling too much data to the switch-to-storage link, the iSCSI storage network should be configured with multiple available links between the switches and the storage device. The image shown here represents an iSCSI storage network configuration that promotes redundancy and communication efficiency by increasing the available bandwidth between the switches and the storage device. This configuration will result in reduced resource usage as a result of less packet-dropping and less retrying.

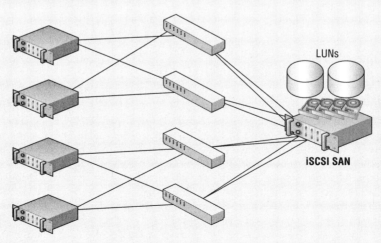

To learn more about iSCSI, visit the Storage Networking Industry Association website at `http://www.snia.org/tech_activities/ip_storage/iscsi`.

CONFIGURING ESX FOR ISCSI STORAGE

I can't go into the details of configuring the iSCSI storage side of things because each product has nuances that do not cross vendor boundaries, and companies don't typically carry an iSCSI SAN from each potential vendor. On the bright side, what I can and most certainly will cover in great detail is how to configure an ESX Server host to connect to an iSCSI storage device using both hardware and software iSCSI initiation.

As noted in the previous section, VMware is limited in its support for hardware device compatibility. As with fibre channel, you should always check VMware's website to review the latest SAN compatibility guide before purchasing any new storage devices. While software-initiated iSCSI has maintained full support since the release of ESX 3.0, hardware initiation with iSCSI devices did not garner full support until the ESX 3.0.1 release. The prior release, ESX 3.0, provided only experimental support for hardware-initiated iSCSI.

VMWARE ISCSI SAN COMPATIBILITY

Each of the manufacturers listed here provides an iSCSI storage solution that has been tested and approved for use by VMware:

- 3PAR: `http://www.3par.com`
- Compellent: `http://www.compellent.com`
- Dell: `http://www.dell.com`
- EMC: `http://www.emc.com`
- EqualLogic: `http://www.equallogic.com`
- Fujitsu Siemens: `http://www.fujitsu-siemens.com`
- HP: `http://www.hp.com`
- IBM: `http://www.ibm.com`
- LeftHand Networks: `http://www.lefthandnetworks.com`
- Network Appliance (NetApp): `http://www.netapp.com`
- Sun Microsystems: `http://www.sun.com`

An ESX Server host can initiate communication with an iSCSI storage device by using a hardware device with dedicated iSCSI technology built into the device, or by using a software-based initiator that utilizes standard Ethernet hardware and is managed like normal network communication. Using a dedicated iSCSI HBA that understands the TCP/IP stack and the iSCSI communication protocol provides an advantage over software initiation. Hardware initiation eliminates some processing overhead in the Service Console and VMkernel by offloading the TCP/IP stack to the hardware device. This technology is often referred to as the TCP/IP Offload Engine (TOE). When you use an iSCSI HBA for hardware initiation, the VMkernel needs only the drivers for the HBA and the rest is handled by the device.

For best performance, the iSCSI hardware-based initiation is the appropriate deployment. After you boot the server, the iSCSI HBA will display all its information in the Storage Adapters node of the Configuration tab, as shown in Figure 4.22. By default, as shown in Figure 4.23, iSCSI HBA devices will assign an IQN in the BIOS of the iSCSI HBA. Configuring the hardware iSCSI initiation with an HBA installed on the host is very similar to configuring a fibre channel HBA — the device will appear in the Storage Adapters node of the Configuration tab. The vmhba#'s for fibre channel and iSCSI HBAs will be enumerated numerically. For example, if an ESX Server host includes two fibre channel HBAs labeled vmhba1 and vmhba2, adding two iSCSI HBAs will result in labels of vmhba3 and vmhba4. The software iSCSI adapter in ESX Server 3.5 will always be labeled as vmhba32.. You can then configure the adapter(s) to support the storage infrastructure.

FIGURE 4.22
Supported iSCSI HBA devices will automatically be found and can be configured in the BIOS of the ESX host.

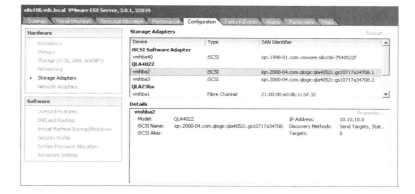

FIGURE 4.23
The BIOS of the QLogic card provides an opportunity to configure the iSCSI HBA. If it's not configured in the BIOS, the defaults pass into the configuration display in the VI Client.

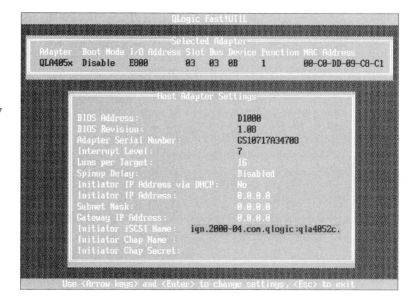

ISCSI HOST BUS ADAPTERS FOR ESX 3.0

At the time this book was written, the only supported iSCSI HBA was a specific set of QLogic cards in the 4050 series. Although a card may work, if it is not on the compatibility list, obtaining support from VMware will be challenging. As with other hardware situations in VI3, always check the VMware compatibility guide prior to purchasing or installing an iSCSI HBA.

To modify the setting of an iSCSI HBA, perform the following steps:

1. In the Storage Adapters node on the Configuration tab, select the appropriate iSCSI HBA (i.e., vmhba2 or vmhba3) from the list and click the Properties link.

2. Click the Configure button.

3. For a custom iSCSI qualified name, enter a new iSCSI name and iSCSI alias in the respective text boxes.

4. If desired, entire the static IP address, subnet mask, default gateway, and DNS server for the iSCSI HBA.

5. Click OK. Do not click Close.

Once you've configured the iSCSI HBA with the appropriate IP information, you must configure it to accurately find the target available via iSCSI storage devices. ESX provides for the two types of target identification:

◆ Static discovery

◆ Dynamic discovery

As the names suggest, one method involves manual configuration of target information (static) while the other involves a less cumbersome, administratively easier means of finding storage (dynamic). The dynamic discovery method is also referred to as the SendTargets method in light of the SendTarget request made by the ESX host. To dynamically discover the available storage targets, you must configure the host manually with the IP address of at least one node. Ironically, when configuring a host to perform a SendTarget request (dynamic discovery), you configure a target on the Dynamic Discovery tab of the iSCSI initiator Properties box, and all of the dynamically identified targets appear on the Static Discovery tab. You perform static assignment as well on the Dynamic Discovery tab so that dynamic targets appear on the Static Discovery tab. Figure 4.24 details the SendTargets method of iSCSI LUN discovery.

The hardware-initiated iSCSI allows for either dynamic or static discovery of targets. The iSCSI software initiator built into ESX 3.0 only allows for the SendTargets discovery method.

To configure the iSCSI HBA for target discovery using the SendTargets method, perform the following steps:

1. In the iSCSI Initiator Properties dialog box, select the Dynamic Discovery tab and click the Add button.

2. Enter the IP address of the iSCSI device and the port number (if it has been changed from the default port of 3260).

3. Click Close.

4. Click the Rescan link.

5. Review the Static Discovery tab of the iSCSI HBA properties.

FIGURE 4.24
The SendTargets iSCSI LUN discovery method requires that you manually configure at least one iSCSI target to issue a SendTargets request. The iSCSI device will then return information about all the targets available.

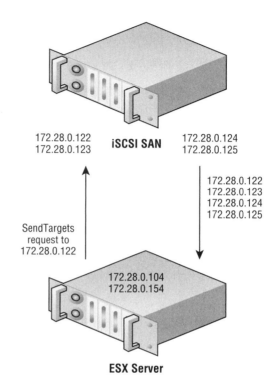

In this section I've hinted, or, better yet, blatantly stated, that iSCSI storage networks should be isolated from the other IP networks already configured in your infrastructure. However, this is not always a possibility due to such factors as budget constraints, IP addressing challenges, host limitations, and more. If you cannot isolate the iSCSI storage network, you can configure the storage device and the ESX nodes to use the Challenge Handshake Authentication Protocol (CHAP). CHAP provides a secure means of authenticating a user account without the need for exchanging the password over publicly accessible networks.

To configure an iSCSI HBA to authenticate using CHAP, follow these steps:

1. From the Storage Adapters node on the Configuration page, select the iSCSI HBA to be configured and click the Properties link.

2. Select the CHAP Authentication tab and click Configure.

3. Insert a custom name in the CHAP Name text box or select the Use Initiator Name checkbox.

4. Type a strong and secure string in the Chap Secret text box.

5. Click OK.

6. Click Close.

Software-initiated iSCSI is a cheaper solution than the iSCSI HBA hardware initiation because it does not require any special hardware. Software-based iSCSI initiation, as the name suggests, begins in the VMkernel and utilizes a normal Ethernet adapter installed on the ESX Server host. Unlike the iSCSI HBA solution, software initiation relies on a set of drivers and a TCP/IP stack that resides in the VMkernel. In addition, the iSCSI software initiator, of which there is only one, uses the name vmhba32 as opposed to being enumerated with the rest of the HBAs within a host. Figure 4.25 outlines the architectural differences between the hardware and software initiation mechanisms on ESX Server.

FIGURE 4.25
ESX Server supports using an iSCSI HBA hardware-based initiation, which reduces overhead on the VMkernel. For a cheaper solution, ESX Server also supports a software-based initiation that does not require specialized hardware.

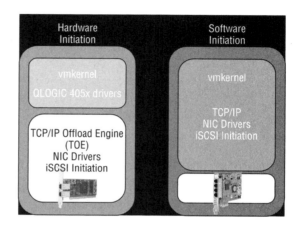

Using the iSCSI software initiation built into ESX Server provides an easy means of configuring the host to communicate with the iSCSI storage device. The iSCSI software initiator uses the Send-Targets method for obtaining information about target devices. The SendTargets request requires the manual entry of one of the IP addresses on the storage device. The software initiator will then query the provided IP address in search of all additional targets.

To enable iSCSI software initiation on an ESX Server, perform the following steps:

1. Enable the Software iSCSI client in the firewall of the ESX Server host as shown in Figure 4.26:

   ◆ On the Configuration tab of the ESX host, click the Security Profile link.

   ◆ Click the Properties link.

   ◆ Enable the Software iSCSI Client checkbox.

   or

   ◆ Open an SSH session with root privileges and type the following commands:

   ```
   esxcfg-firewall -r swISCSIClient
   ```

FIGURE 4.26
The iSCSI software must be enabled in the Service Console firewall.

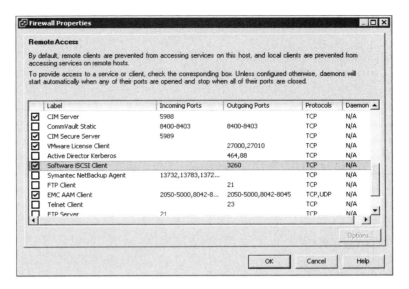

2. Create a virtual switch with a VMkernel port and a Service Console (vswif) port. Bind the virtual switch to a physical network adapter connected to the dedicated storage network. Figure 4.27 shows a correctly configured switch for use in connecting to an iSCSI storage device.

CREATING A VMKERNEL PORT FROM A COMMAND LINE

Log on to an ESX host using an SSH session and elevate the permissions using **#su** - if necessary. Follow these steps:

1. Add a new port group named **Storage** to the virtual switch on the dedicated storage network:

```
esxcfg-vswitch -A Storage vSwitch2
```

2. Configure the VMkernel NIC with an IP address of 172.28.0.106 and a subnet mask of 255.255.255.0:

```
esxcfg-vmknic -a -i 172.28.0.106 -n 255.255.255.0 Storage
```

3. Set the default gateway of the VMkernel to 172.28.0.1:

```
esxcfg-route 172.28.0.1
```

FIGURE 4.27
The VMkernel and Service Console must be able to communicate with the iSCSI storage device.

3. From the Storage Adapters node on the Configuration tab, shown in Figure 4.28, enable the iSCSI initiator. Alternatively, open an SSH session with root privileges and type the following command:

```
esxcfg-swiscsi -e
```

FIGURE 4.28
Enabling the iSCSI will automatically populate the iSCSI name and alias for the software initiator.

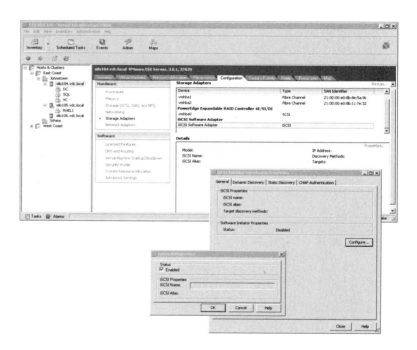

4. Select the vmhba40 option beneath the iSCSI Software Adapter and click the Properties link.

5. Select the Dynamic Discovery tab and click the Add button.

6. Enter the IP address of the iSCSI device and the port number (if it has been changed from the default port of 3260).

7. Click OK. Click Close.

8. Select the Rescan link from the Storage Adapters node on the Configuration tab.

9. Click OK to scan for both new storage devices and new VMFS volumes.

10. As shown in Figure 4.29, any available iSCSI LUNs will now be reflected in the Details section of the vmhba40 option.

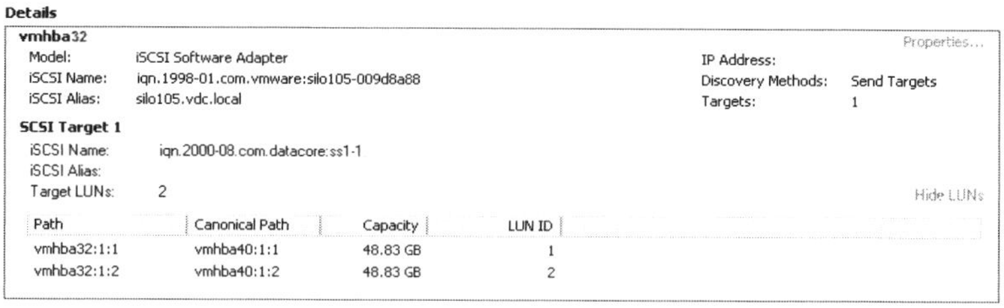

FIGURE 4.29

After configuring the iSCSI software adapter with the IP address of the iSCSI storage target, a rescan will identify the LUNs on the storage device that have been made available to the ESX host.

Details						
vmhba32						Properties...
Model:	iSCSI Software Adapter			IP Address:		
iSCSI Name:	iqn.1998-01.com.vmware:silo105-009d8a88			Discovery Methods:	Send Targets	
iSCSI Alias:	silo105.vdc.local			Targets:	1	
SCSI Target 1						
iSCSI Name:	iqn.2000-08.com.datacore:ss1-1					
iSCSI Alias:						
Target LUNs:	2					Hide LUNs
Path	Canonical Path	Capacity	LUN ID			
vmhba32:1:1	vmhba40:1:1	48.83 GB	1			
vmhba32:1:2	vmhba40:1:2	48.83 GB	2			

THE *VMKISCSI-TOOL* COMMAND

The `vmkiscsi-tool [options] vmhba##` command allows command-line management of the iSCSI software initiator. The options for this command-line tool include:

◆ `-I` is used with `-l` or `-a` to display or add the iSCSI name.

◆ `-k` is used with `-l` or `-a` to display or add the iSCSI alias.

◆ `-D` is used with `-a` to perform discovery of a specified target device.

◆ `-T` is used with `-l` to list found targets.

Review the following examples:

◆ To view the iSCSI name of the software initiator:

```
vmkiscsi-tool -I -l
```

◆ To view the iSCSI alias of the software initiator:

```
vmkiscsi-tool -k -l
```

◆ To discover additional iSCSI targets at 172.28.0.122:

```
vmkisci-tool -D -a 172.28.0.122 vmhba40
```

◆ To list found targets:

```
vmkiscsi-tool -T -l vmhba40
```

Network Attached Storage and Network File System

Although Network Attached Storage (NAS) devices do not hold up to the performance and efficiency of fibre channel and iSCSI networks, they most certainly have a place on some networks. Virtual machines stored on NAS devices are still capable of the advanced VirtualCenter features of VMotion, DRS, and HA. With a significantly lower cost and simplified implementation, NAS devices can prove valuable in providing network storage in a VI3 environment.

UNDERSTANDING NAS AND NFS

Unlike the block-level transfer of data performed by fibre channel and iSCSI networks, access to a NAS device happens at the file system level. You can access a NAS device by using Network File System (NFS) or Server Message Block (SMB), also referred to as Common Internet File System (CIFS). Windows administrators will be most familiar with SMB traffic, which occurs each time a user accesses a shared resource using a universal naming convention (UNC) like \\servername\sharename. Whereas Windows uses the SMB protocol for file transfer, Linux-based systems use NFS to accomplish the same thing.

Although you can configure the Service Console with a Samba client to allow communication with Windows-based computers, the VMkernel does not support using SMB and therefore lacks the ability to retrieve files from a computer running Windows. The VMkernel only supports NFS version 3 over TCP/IP.

Like the deployment of an iSCSI storage network, a NAS/NFS deployment can benefit greatly from being located on a dedicated IP network where traffic is isolated. Figure 4.30 shows a NAS/NFS deployment on a dedicated network.

FIGURE 4.30
An NAS Server deployed for shared storage among ESX Server hosts should be located on a dedicated network separated from the common intranet traffic.

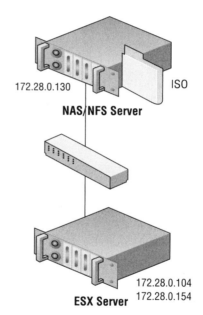

172.28.0.130

ISO

NAS/NFS Server

172.28.0.104
172.28.0.154
ESX Server

Without competition from other types of network traffic (e-mail, Internet, instant messaging, etc.), the transfer of virtual machine data will be much more efficient and provide better performance.

NFS SECURITY

NFS is unique because it does not force the user to enter a password when connecting to the shared directory. In the case of ESX, the connection to the NFS server happens under the context of root, thus making NFS a seamless process for the connecting client. However, you might be wondering about the inherent security. Security for NFS access is maintained by limiting access to only the specified or trusted hosts. In addition, the NFS server employs standard Linux file system permissions based on user and group IDs. The user IDs (UIDs) and group IDs (GIDs) of users on a client system are mapped from the server to the client. If a user or a client has the same UID and GID as a user on the server, they are both granted access to files in the NFS share owned by that same UID and GID. As you have seen, ESX Server accesses the NFS server under the context of the root user and therefore has all the permissions assigned to the root user on the NFS server.

When creating an NFS share on a Linux system, you must supply three pieces of information:

◆ The path to the share (i.e., `/nfs/ISOs`).

◆ The hosts that are allowed to connect to the share, which can include:

  ◆ A single host identified by name or IP address.

  ◆ Network Information Service (NIS) groups.

  ◆ Wildcard characters such as * and ? (i.e., `*.vdc.local`).

  ◆ An entire IP network (i.e., 172.30.0.0/24).

◆ Options for the share configuration, which can include:

  ◆ `root_squash`, which maps the root user to the nobody user and thus prevents root access to the NFS share.

  ◆ `no_root_squash`, which does not map the root user to the nobody user and thus provides the root user on the client system with full root privileges on the NFS server.

  ◆ `all_squash`, which maps all UIDs and GIDs to the nobody user for enabling a simple anonymous access NFS share.

  ◆ `ro`, for read-only access.

  ◆ `rw`, for read-write access.

  ◆ `sync`, which forces all data to be written to disk before servicing another request.

The configuration of the shared directories on an NFS server is managed through the `/etc/exports` file on the server. The following example shows a `/etc/exports` file configured to allow all hosts on the 172.30.0.0/24 network access to a shared directory named NFSShare:

```
root:~ # cat /etc/exports/mnt/NFSShare 172.30.0.0/24 (rw,no_root_squash,sync)
```

The next section explores the configuration requirements for connecting an ESX Server host to a shared directory on an NFS server.

CONFIGURING ESX TO USE NAS/NFS DATASTORES

Before an ESX Server host can be connected to an NFS share, the NFS server must be configured properly to allow the host. Creating an NFS share on a Linux system that allows an ESX Server host to connect requires that you configure the share with the following three parameters:

◆ `rw` (read-write)

◆ `no_root_squash`

◆ `sync`

To connect an ESX Server to an NAS/NFS datastore, you must create a virtual switch with a VMkernel port that has network access to the NFS server. As mentioned in the previous section, it would be ideal for the VMkernel port to be connected to the same physical network (the same IP subnet) as the NAS device. Unlike the iSCSI configuration, creating an NFS datastore does not require that the Service Console also have access to the NFS server. Figure 4.31 details the configuration of an ESX Server host connecting to a NAS device on a dedicated storage network.

FIGURE 4.31
Connecting an ESX
Server to a NAS device
with an NFS share
requires the creation
and configuration of a
virtual switch with a
VMkernel port.

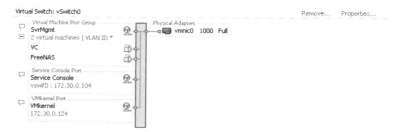

To create a VMkernel port for connecting an ESX Server to a NAS device, perform these steps:

1. Use the VI Client to connect to VirtualCenter or an ESX Server host.

2. Select the hostname in the inventory panel and then click the Configuration tab.

3. Select Networking from the Hardware menu.

4. Select the virtual switch that is bound to a network adapter that connects to a physical network with access to the NAS device. (Create a new virtual switch if necessary.)

5. Click the Properties link of the virtual switch.

6. In the vSwitch# Properties box, click the Add button.

7. Select the radio button labeled VMkernel, as shown in Figure 4.32, and then click Next.

FIGURE 4.32
A VMkernel port is
used for performing
VMotion or communi-
cating with an iSCSI or
NFS storage device.

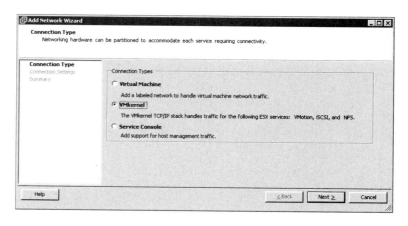

8. As shown in Figure 4.33, type a name for the port in the Network Label text box. Then provide an IP address and subnet mask appropriate for the physical network the virtual switch is bound to.

FIGURE 4.33
Connecting an ESX Host to an NFS server requires a VMkernel port with a valid IP address and subnet mask for the network on which the virtual switch is configured to communicate.

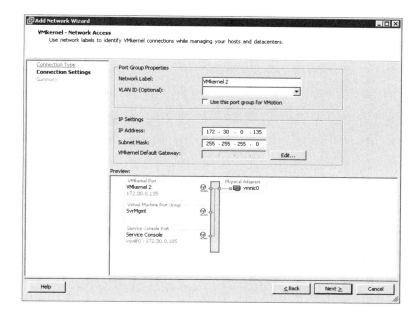

9. Click Next, review the configuration, and then click Finish.

VMKERNEL DEFAULT GATEWAY

If you are prompted to enter a default gateway, choose No if one has already been assigned to a Service Console port on the same switch or if the VMkernel port is configured with an IP address on the same subnet as the NAS device. Select the Yes option if the VMkernel port is not on the same subnet as the NAS device.

Unlike fibre channel and iSCSI storage, an NFS datastore cannot be formatted as VMFS. For this reason it is recommended that NFS datastores not be used for the storage of virtual machines in large enterprise environments. In non-business-critical situations such as test environments and small branch offices, or for storing ISO files and templates, NFS datastores are an excellent solution.

Once you've configured the VMkernel port, the next step is to create a new NFS datastore. To create an NFS datastore on an ESX Server host, perform the following steps:

1. Use the VI Client to connect to a VirtualCenter or an ESX Server host.

2. Select the hostname in the inventory panel and then select the Configuration tab.

3. Select Storage (SCSI, SAN, and NFS) from the Hardware menu.

4. Click the Add Storage link.

5. Select the radio button labeled Network File System, as shown in Figure 4.34.

FIGURE 4.34
The option to create an NFS datastore is separated from the disk or LUN option that can be formatted as VMFS.

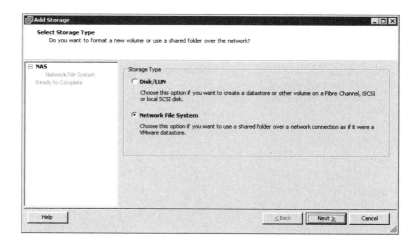

6. Type the name or IP address of the NFS server in the Server text box.

7. Type the name of the shared directory on the NFS server in the Folder text box. Ensure that the folder listed here matches the entry of the `/etc/hosts` file on the NFS server. If the folder in `/etc/hosts` is listed as /ISOShare, then enter **/ISOShare** in this text box. If the folder is listed as /mnt/NFSShare then enter /mnt/NFSShare in the Folder text box of the Add Storage wizard.

8. Type a unique datastore name in the Datastore Name text box and click Next, as shown in Figure 4.35.

FIGURE 4.35
To create an NFS datastore, you must enter the name or IP address of the NFS server, the name of the directory that has been shared, and a unique datastore name.

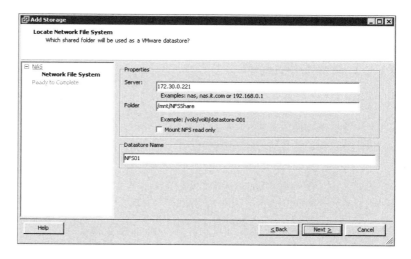

9. Click Finish to view the NFS datastore in the list of Storage locations for the ESX Server host.

Creating and Managing VMFS Datastores

Microsoft has NTFS, Linux has EXT3, and so it is only fair that VMware have its own proprietary file system: VMFS. The VMware File System (VMFS) is a high-performance, distributed journaling file system used to house virtual machine files, ISO files, and templates in a VI3 environment. Any fibre channel, iSCSI, or local storage pool can be formatted as VMFS and used by an ESX Server host. Network storage located on NAS devices cannot be formatted as VMFS datastores but still offer some of the same advantages. The VMFS found in the latest version of ESX Server is VMFS-3, which presents a significant upgrade from its predecessor VMFS-2.

VMFS protects against data integrity problems by writing all updates to a serial log on the disk before updating the original log. Postfailure, the server will restore the data to the prefailure state and recover any unsaved data by writing it to the intended prefailure location. Perhaps the most significant enhancement to VMFS-3 is its ability to have subdirectories, thus allowing virtual machine disk files to be located in respective folders under the VMFS volume parent label.

A VMFS volume stores all of the files needed by virtual machines, including:

◆ .vmx, the virtual machine configuration file.

◆ .vmx.lck, the virtual machine lock file created when a virtual machine is in a powered-on state.

◆ .nvram, the virtual machine BIOS.

◆ .vmdk, the virtual machine hard disk.

◆ .vmsd, the dictionary file for snapshots and the associated vmdk.

◆ .vmem, the virtual machine memory mapped to a file when the virtual machine is in a powered-on state.

◆ .vmss, the virtual machine suspend file created when a virtual machine is in a suspended state.

◆ -Snapshot#.vmsn, the virtual machine snapshot configuration.

◆ .vmtm, the configuration file for virtual machines in a team.

◆ -flat.vmdk, a pre-allocated disk file that holds virtual machine data.

◆ f001.vmdk, the first extent of pre-allocated disk files that hold virtual machine data split into 2GB files; additional files increment the numerical value.

◆ s001.vmdk, the first extent of expandable disk files that are split into 2GB files; additional files increment the numerical value.

◆ -delta.vmdk, the snapshot differences file.

VMFS is a clustered file system that allows multiple physical ESX Server hosts to simultaneously read and write to the same shared storage location. The block size of a VMFS volume can be configured as 1 MB, 2 MB, 4 MB, or 8 MB. Each of the block sizes corresponds to a maximum file size of 256GB, 512GB, 1024GB, and 2048GB, respectively.

> ### 2TB LIMIT?
>
> Although the VMFS file system does not allow for files larger than 2048GB or 2TB, don't think of this as a limitation that prevents you from virtualizing specific servers. There might be scenarios in which large enterprise databases consume more than 2TB of space, but keep in mind that good file management practices should not have all of the data confined in a single database file. With the capabilities of Raw Device Mappings (RDMs), it is possible to virtualize even in situations where storage requirements exceed the 2TB limit that exists for a file on a VMFS volume.

To create a VMFS datastore on a fibre channel or iSCSI LUN using the VI Client, follow these steps:

1. Use the VI Client to connect to a VirtualCenter or an ESX Server host.

2. Select the hostname in the inventory panel and then click the Configuration tab.

3. Select Storage (SCSI, SAN, and NFS) from the Hardware menu.

4. Click the Add Storage link.

5. As shown in Figure 4.36, select the radio button labeled Disk/LUN and then click Next.

FIGURE 4.36
The Disk/LUN option in the Add Storage wizard formats allows you to configure a fibre channel or iSCSI SAN LUN as a VMFS volume.

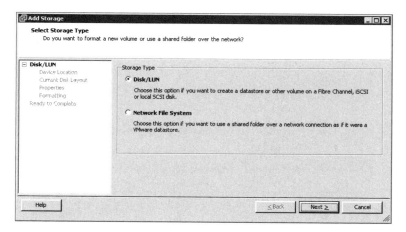

6. As shown in Figure 4.37, select the appropriate SAN device for the VMFS datastore (i.e., vmhba1:0:21) and click Next.

FIGURE 4.37
The list of SAN LUNs will include only the non-VMFS LUNs as available candidates for the new VMFS volume.

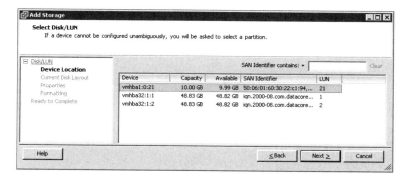

7. Click Next on the Current Disk Layout page.

8. Type a name for the new datastore in the Datastore Name text box and then click Next.

9. As shown in Figure 4.38, select a maximum file size and block size from the Maximum File Size drop-down list.

FIGURE 4.38
VMFS volumes can be configured to support a greater block size, which translates into greater file size capacity.

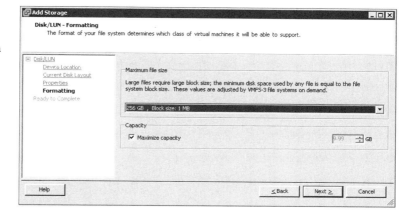

10. (*Optional*) If desired, though it's not recommended, the new VMFS datastore can be a portion of the full SAN LUN. Deselect the Maximize Capacity checkbox and specify a new size.

11. Review the VMFS volume configuration and then click Finish.

DON'T PARTITION LUNS

When creating datastores, avoid partitioning LUNs. Use the maximum capacity of the LUN for each datastore created.

Although using the VI Client to create VMFS volumes through VirtualCenter is a GUI-oriented and simplified approach, it is also possible to create VMFS volumes from a command line using the fdisk and vmkfstools utilities. Perform these steps to create a VMFS volume from a command line:

1. Log in to a console session or use an application like Putty.exe to establish an SSH session to an ESX Server host.

2. Type the following command at the # prompt:

   esxcfg-vmhbadevs

3. Determine if a valid partition table exists for the respective LUN by typing the following command at the # prompt:

   fdisk -l /dev/sd?

   where ? is the letter for the respective LUN. For example, /dev/sdf is shown in Figure 4.39.

FIGURE 4.39
The `esxcfg-vmhbadevs` command identifies all the available LUNs for an ESX Server host; the `fdisk -l /dev/sd?` command will identify a valid partition table on a LUN.

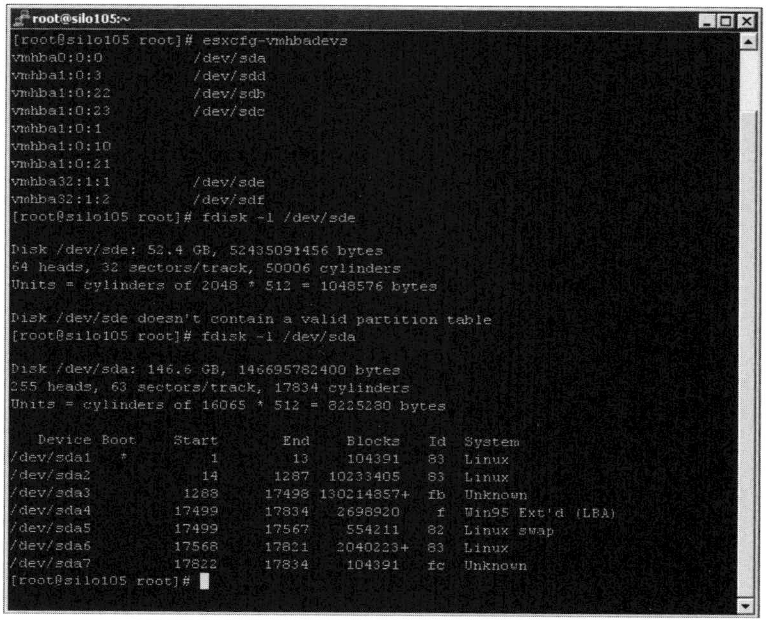

```
root@silo105:~
[root@silo105 root]# esxcfg-vmhbadevs
vmhba0:0:0          /dev/sda
vmhba1:0:3          /dev/sdd
vmhba1:0:22         /dev/sdb
vmhba1:0:23         /dev/sdc
vmhba1:0:1
vmhba1:0:10
vmhba1:0:21
vmhba32:1:1         /dev/sde
vmhba32:1:2         /dev/sdf
[root@silo105 root]# fdisk -l /dev/sde

Disk /dev/sde: 52.4 GB, 52435091456 bytes
64 heads, 32 sectors/track, 50006 cylinders
Units = cylinders of 2048 * 512 = 1048576 bytes

Disk /dev/sde doesn't contain a valid partition table
[root@silo105 root]# fdisk -l /dev/sda

Disk /dev/sda: 146.6 GB, 146695782400 bytes
255 heads, 63 sectors/track, 17834 cylinders
Units = cylinders of 16065 * 512 = 8225280 bytes

   Device Boot    Start       End    Blocks   Id  System
/dev/sda1   *         1        13    104391   83  Linux
/dev/sda2            14      1287  10233405   83  Linux
/dev/sda3          1288     17498 130214857+  fb  Unknown
/dev/sda4         17499     17834   2698920    f  Win95 Ext'd (LBA)
/dev/sda5         17499     17567    554211   82  Linux swap
/dev/sda6         17568     17821   2040223+  83  Linux
/dev/sda7         17822     17834    104391   fc  Unknown
[root@silo105 root]#
```

4. To create a new partition on a LUN, type the following at a # prompt:

   `fdisk /dev/sd?`

   where *?* is the letter for the respective LUN.

5. Type **n** to add a new partition.
6. Type **p** to create the partition as a primary partition.
7. Type **1** for a partition number of 1.
8. Press the Enter key twice to accept the default values for the first and last cylinders.
9. Type **p** to view the partition configuration. Steps 5 through 9 are displayed in Figure 4.40.

FIGURE 4.40
To create a VMFS volume from the command line, you must create a partition on the target LUN.

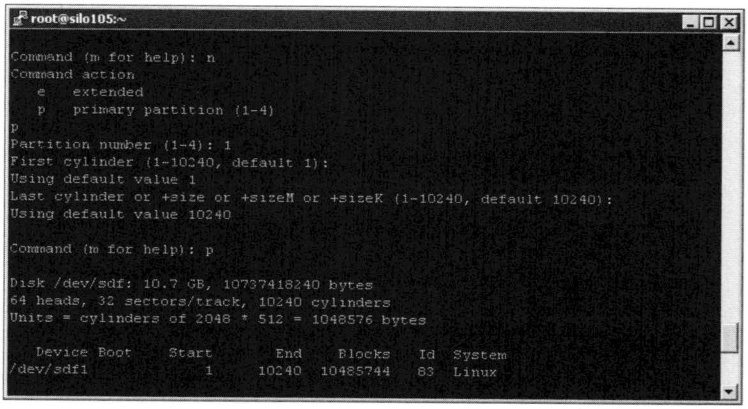

```
root@silo105:~

Command (m for help): n
Command action
   e   extended
   p   primary partition (1-4)
p
Partition number (1-4): 1
First cylinder (1-10240, default 1):
Using default value 1
Last cylinder or +size or +sizeM or +sizeK (1-10240, default 10240):
Using default value 10240

Command (m for help): p

Disk /dev/sdf: 10.7 GB, 10737418240 bytes
64 heads, 32 sectors/track, 10240 cylinders
Units = cylinders of 2048 * 512 = 1048576 bytes

   Device Boot    Start       End    Blocks   Id  System
/dev/sdf1             1     10240  10485744   83  Linux
```

10. Once you've created the partition, define the partition type. At the Command (**m** for help) prompt, press the T key to enter the partition type.

11. At the Hex code prompt (type **L** to list codes), type **fb** to select the unknown code that corresponds to VMFS.

12. Type **w** to save the configuration changes. Figure 4.41 shows steps 10 through 12.

FIGURE 4.41
Once the partition is created, adjust the partition type to reflect the VMFS volume that will be created.

13. As shown in Figure 4.42, type the following command at the # prompt:

```
vmkfstools -C vmfs3 -S <VMFS_NAME> vmhbaw:x:y:z
```

where *<VMFS_NAME>* is the label to provide the VMFS volume, w is the HBA to use, x is the target ID for the storage processor, *y* is the LUN ID, and *z* is the partition.

FIGURE 4.42
After the LUN is configured, use vmkfstools to create the VMFS volume.

ALIGNING VMFS VOLUMES

Using the VI Client to create VMFS volumes will properly align the volume to achieve optimal performance in virtual environments with significant I/O. However, if you opt to create VMFS volumes using the command line, I recommend that you perform a few extra steps in the `fdisk` process to align the partition properly.

In the previous exercise insert the following steps between steps 11 and 12.

1. Type **x** to enter expert mode.

2. Type **b** to set the starting block number.

3. Type **1** to choose partition 1.

4. Type **128**.

Note that the tests to identify the performance boosts were conducted against an EMC CX series storage area network device. The recommendations from VMware on alignment are consistent across fibre solutions and are not relevant for IP-based storage technologies. The tests concluded that proper alignment of the VMFS volume and the virtual machine disks produces increased throughput and reduced latency. Chapter 6 will list the recommended steps for aligning virtual machine file systems.

Once the VMFS volume is created, the VI Client provides an easy means of managing the various properties of the VMFS volume. The LUN properties offer the ability to add extents as well as to change the datastore name, the active path, and the path selection policy.

Adding extents to a datastore lets you increase the size of an extent greater than the 2TB limit. This does not allow file sizes to exceed the 2TB limit but only the size of the VMFS volume. Be careful when working with adding extents because the LUN that is added as an extent is wiped of all its data during the process. This can result in unintentional data loss. LUNs that are available as extent candidates are those that are not already formatted with VMFS, leaving empty or NTFS-formatted LUNS as viable candidates. (In other words, ESX will not eat its own!)

ADDING VMFS EXTENTS

When adding an extent to a VMFS volume, be sure to check for any existing data on the extent candidate. A simple method to do this is to compare the maximum size of the LUN with the available space to identify whether there is any existing data on the LUN. If the two sizes are almost identical, it is safe to say there is no data. For example, a 10GB LUN might reflect 9.99GB of free space. Check and double-check the LUNs. Since adding the extent will wipe all data from the extent candidate, you cannot be too sure.

While adding an extent through the VI Client or command line is an easy way to provide more space, it is a better practice to manage VMFS volume size from the storage device. To add an extent to an existing datastore, perform these steps:

1. Use the VI Client to connect to a VirtualCenter or an ESX Server host.

2. Select the hostname from the inventory pane and then click the Configuration tab.

3. Select Storage (SCSI, SAN, and NFS) from the Hardware menu.

4. Select the datastore to which the extent will be added.

5. Click the Properties link.

6. Click the Add Extent button, shown in Figure 4.43, on the datastore properties.

FIGURE 4.43
The properties page of a datastore lets you add an extent to increase the available storage space a datastore offers.

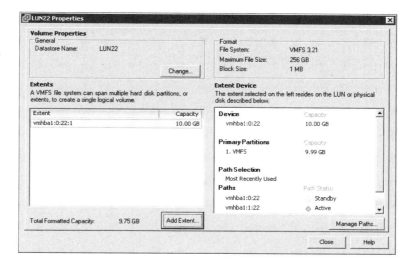

7. Choose an extent candidate on the Extent Device page of the Add Extent wizard, shown in Figure 4.44, and then click Next.

FIGURE 4.44
When adding an extent, be sure the selected extent candidate does not currently hold any critical data. All data is removed from an extent candidate when added to a datastore.

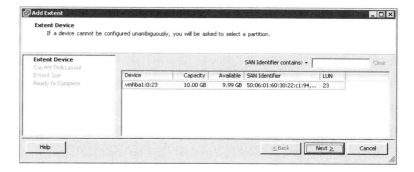

8. Click Next on the Current Disk Layout page.

9. (*Optional*) Although it is not recommended, the Maximum Capacity checkbox can be deselected and a custom value can be provided for the amount of space to use from the LUN.

10. Click Next on the Extent Size page.

11. Review the settings for the new extent and then click Finish.

12. Identify the new extent displayed in the Extents list and the new Total Formatted Capacity of the datastore, and then click Close.

13. As shown in Figure 4.45, identify the additional extent in the details pane for the datastore.

FIGURE 4.45

All extents for a datastore are reflected in the Total Formatted Capacity for the datastore and can be seen in the Extents section of the datastore details.

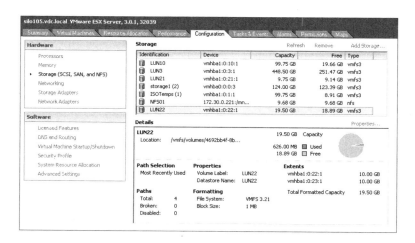

Once an extent is complete, the datastore will maintain the relationship until the datastore is removed from the host computer. An individual extent cannot be removed from a datastore.

 Real World Scenario

RESIZING A VIRTUAL MACHINE'S SYSTEM VOLUME

The time will come when a critical virtual machine in your Windows environment will run out of space on the system volume. If you've been around Windows long enough, you know that it is not a fun issue to have to deal with. Though adding an extent can make a VMFS volume bigger, it does nothing to help this situation. There are third-party solutions to this problem; for example, use Symantec Ghost to create an image of the virtual machine and then deploy the image back to a new virtual machine with a larger hard drive. The solution described here comes completely at the hand of tools that are already available to you within ESX and Windows and will incur no financial charge.

As a first step to solving this problem, you must increase the size of the VMDK file that corresponds to the C drive. Using the `vmkfstools` command, you can expand the VMDK file to a new size. For example, to increase the size of a VMDK file named `server1.vmdk` from 20GB to 60GB:

1. Use the virtual machines properties to resize the virtual machine disk file size.

2. Mount the `server1.vmdk` file as a secondary drive in a different virtual machine.

3. Open a command window in the second virtual machine.

4. At the command prompt, type **`diskpart.exe`**.

5. To display the existing volumes, type **`list volume`**.

6. Type **`select volume`** *`<volume number>`*, where *`<volume number>`* is the number of the volume to extend.

7. To add the additional 40GB of space to the drive, type **extend size=40000**.

8. To quit di skpart.exe, type **exit**.

9. Shut down the second virtual machine to remove server1.vmdk.

10. Turn on the original virtual machine to reveal a new, larger C drive.

Free third-party utilities like QtParted and GParted can resize most types of file systems, including those from Windows and Linux. No matter which tool or procedure you use, be sure to always back up your VMDK before resizing.

If budget is not a concern, you can replace the mounting of the VMDK and use of the diskpart.exe utility with a third-party product like Acronis Disk Director. Disk Director is a graphical utility that simplifies managing volumes, even system volumes, on a Windows computer.

With the release of Windows Server 2008, Microsoft has now added the native ability to grow and shrink the system volume making it even easier to make these same types of adjustments without third part tools or fancy tricks.

All the financial, human, and time investment put into building a solid virtual infrastructure would be for nothing if ESX Server did not offer a way of ensuring accessing to VMFS volumes in the face of hardware failure. ESX Server has a native multipathing feature that allows for redundant access to VMFS volumes across an available path.

ESX SERVER MULTIPATHING

ESX Server does *not* require third-party software, like EMC PowerPath, to gain the benefits of understanding and/or identifying redundant paths to network storage devices.

It doesn't seem likely that critical production systems with large financial investments in network storage would be left susceptible to single points of failure — which is why, in most cases, a storage infrastructure built to host critical data is done with redundancy at each level of the deployment. For example, a solid fibre channel infrastructure would include multiple HBAs per ESX host, connected to multiple fibre channel switches, connected to multiple storage processors on the storage device. In a situation where an ESX host has two HBAs and a storage device has two storage processors, there are four (2×2) different paths that can be assembled to provide access to LUNs. This concept, called multipathing, involves the use of redundant storage components to ensure consistent and reliable transfer of data. Figure 4.46 depicts a fibre channel infrastructure with redundant components at each level, which provides for exactly four distinct paths for accessing the available LUNs.

The multipathing capability built into ESX Server offers two different methods for ensuring consistent access: the most recently used (MRU) and the fixed path. As shown in Figure 4.47, the details section of an ESX datastore will identify the current path selection policy as well as the total number of available paths. The default policy, MRU, provides failover when a device is not functional but does not failback to the original device when the device is repaired. As the name suggests, an ESX host configured with an MRU policy will continue to transfer data across the most recently used path until that path is no longer available or is manually adjusted.

FIGURE 4.46
ESX Server has a native multipathing capability that allows for continued access to storage data in the event of hardware failure. With two HBAs and two storage processors, there exist exactly four paths that can be used to reach LUNs on a fibre channel storage device.

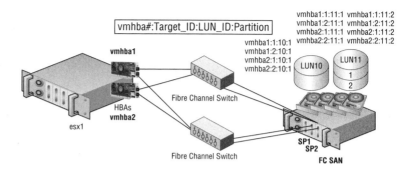

FIGURE 4.47
The Details of a datastore configured on a fibre channel LUN identifies the current path selection policy.

Storage   Refresh   Remove   Add Storage...

Identification	Device	Capacity	Free	Type
LUN10	vmhba1:0:10:1	99.75 GB	19.66 GB	vmfs3
LUN3	vmhba1:0:3:1	448.50 GB	251.47 GB	vmfs3
storage1 (2)	vmhba0:0:0:3	124.00 GB	123.39 GB	vmfs3
ISOTemps (1)	vmhba1:0:1:1	99.75 GB	8.91 GB	vmfs3
NFS01	172.30.0.221:/mn...	9.68 GB	9.68 GB	nfs
LUN22	vmhba1:0:22:1	19.50 GB	18.89 GB	vmfs3

Details   Properties...

LUN22   19.50 GB   Capacity
Location: /vmfs/volumes/4692bb4f-8b...
                                                   626.00 MB ☐ Used
                                                   18.89 GB   ☐ Free

Path Selection	**Properties**		**Extents**	
Most Recently Used	Volume Label:	LUN22	vmhba1:0:22:1	10.00 GB
	Datastore Name:	LUN22	vmhba1:0:23:1	10.00 GB
Paths	**Formatting**		Total Formatted Capacity	19.50 GB
Total: 4	File System:	VMFS 3.21		
Broken: 0	Block Size:	1 MB		
Disabled: 0				

The second policy, fixed path, requires administrators to define the order of preference for the available paths. The fixed path policy, like the MRU, provides failover in the event that hardware fails, but it also provides failback upon availability of any preferred path as defined.

MRU vs. Fixed Path

Virtual infrastructure administrators should strive to spread the I/O loads over all available paths. An optimal configuration would utilize all HBAs and storage processors in an attempt to maximize data transfer efficiency. Once the path selections have been optimized, the decision will have to be made regarding the path selection policy. When comparing the MRU with fixed policies, you will find that each provides a set of advantages and disadvantages.

The MRU policy requires very little, if any, effort on the front end but requires an administrative reaction once failure (failover) has occurred. Once the failed hardware is fixed, the administrator must regain the I/O balance achieved prior to the failure.

The fixed path policy requires significant administrative overhead on the front end by requiring the administrator to define the order of preference. The manual path definition that must occur is a proactive effort for each LUN on each ESX Server host. However, after failover there will be an automatic failback, thereby eliminating any type of reactive steps on the part of the administrator.

Ultimately, it boils down to a "pay me now or pay me later" type configuration. Since hardware failure is not something we count on and is certainly something we hope happens on an infrequent basis, it seems that the MRU policy would require the least amount of administrative effort over the long haul.

Perform the following steps to edit the path selection policy for a datastore:

1. Use the VI Client to connect to a VirtualCenter or an ESX Server host.

2. Select the hostname in the inventory panel and then click the Configuration tab.

3. Select Storage (SCSI, SAN, and NFS) from the Hardware menu.

4. Select a datastore and review the details section.

5. Click the Properties link for the selected datastore.

6. Click the Manage Paths button in the Datastore properties box.

7. Click the Change button in the Policy section of the properties box.

8. As shown in Figure 4.48, select the Fixed radio button.

FIGURE 4.48
You can edit the path selection policy on a per-LUN basis.

9. Click OK.

10. Click OK.

11. Click Close.

Perform the following steps to change the active path for a LUN:

1. Use the VI Client to connect to a VirtualCenter or an ESX Server host.

2. Select the hostname in the inventory panel and then click the Configuration tab.

3. Select Storage (SCSI, SAN, and NFS) from the Hardware menu.

4. Select a datastore and review the details section.

5. Click the Properties link for the selected datastore.

6. Click the Manage Paths button in the Datastore properties box, shown in Figure 4.49.

FIGURE 4.49
The Manage Paths detail box identifies the active and standby paths for a LUN and can be used to manually select a new active path.

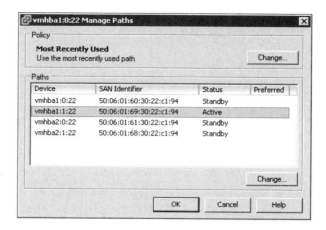

7. Select the existing Active path and then click the Change button beneath the list of available paths.

8. Click the Disabled radio button to force the path to change to a different available path, shown in Figure 4.50.

FIGURE 4.50
Disabling the active path of a LUN forces a new active path.

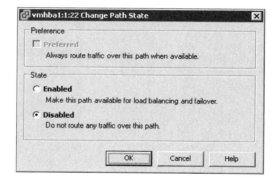

9. Repeat the process until the desired path is shown as the Active path.

Regardless of the LUN design strategy or multipathing policy put in place, virtual infrastructure administrators should take a very active approach to monitoring virtual machines to ensure that their strategies continue to maintain adequate performance levels.

The Bottom Line

Differentiate among the various storage options available to VI3.   The storage technologies available for VMware Infrastructure 3 offer a wide range of performance and cost options. From the high-speed, high-cost fibre channel solution to the efficient, cost-effective iSCSI solution, to the slower, yet cheaper NAS/NFS, each solution has a place in any organization on a mission to virtualize.

Master It   Identify the characteristics of each storage technology and which VI3 features each supports.

Design a storage area network for VI3.   Once you've selected a storage technology, begin with the implementation of a dedicated storage network to optimize the transfer of storage traffic. A dedicated network for an iSCSI or NAS/NFS deployment will isolate the storage traffic from the e-mail, Internet, and file transfer traffic of the standard corporate LAN. From there, the LUN design for a fibre channel or iSCSI storage solution will work itself out in the form of the adaptive approach, predictive approach, or a hybrid of the two.

Master It   Identify use cases for the adaptive and predictive LUN design schemes.

Configure and manage Fibre Channel and iSCSI storage networks.   Deploying a fibre channel SAN involves the development of zoning and LUN masking strategies that ensure data security across ESX Server hosts while still providing for the needs of VMotion, HA, and DRS. The nodes in the fibre channel infrastructure are identified by 64-bit unique addresses called World Wide Names (WWNs). The iSCSI storage solution continues to use IP and MAC addresses for node identification and communication. ESX Server hosts use a four-part naming structure for accessing pools of storage on a SAN. Communication to an iSCSI storage device requires that both the Service Console and the VMkernel be able to communicate with the device.

Master It   Identify the SAN LUNs that have been available to an ESX Server host.

Configure and manage NAS storage.   NAS storage offers a cheap solution for providing a shared storage pool for ESX Server hosts. Since the ESX Server host connects under the context of root, the NFS server must be configured with the no_root_squash parameter. A VMkernel port with access to the NAS server is required for an ESX Server host to function.

Master It   Identify the ESX Server and NFS server requirements for using a NAS/NFS device.

Create and manage VMFS volumes.   VMFS is the proprietary, highly efficient file system used by ESX Server hosts for storing virtual machine files, ISO files, and templates. VMFS volumes can be extended to overcome the 2TB limitation, but the file sizes within the VMFS volume still keep a maximum of 2TB. VMFS is managed through the VI Client or from a series of command-line tools, including vmkfstools and esxcfg-vmhbadevs.

Master It   Increase the size of a VMFS volume.

Master It   Balance the I/O of an ESX Server to use all existing hardware.

Chapter 5

Installing and Configuring VirtualCenter 2.0

In the majority of today's information systems, the client-server domain environment is king. This is because the client-server domain has the ability to centralize management of resources and to provide end users and client systems with access to those resources in a simplified manner. Imagine, or recall if you can, the days when information systems existed in a flat, peer-to-peer model. . . when user accounts were required on every system where resource access was needed, and significant administrative overhead was needed simply to make things work. The advent of the domain model brought about tremendous changes in the way we design and manage all the components of our infrastructure. Today we would not think twice about deploying a client-server network infrastructure.

In this chapter you will learn to:

◆ Understand the features and role of VirtualCenter

◆ Install and configure a VirtualCenter database

◆ Install and configure a VirtualCenter Server

◆ Use VirtualCenter topology maps

◆ Plan a VirtualCenter deployment

Introducing VirtualCenter 2.5

As the size of a virtual infrastructure grows, the ability to manage the infrastructure from a central location becomes significantly more important. VirtualCenter 2.5 is a Windows-based application that serves as a centralized ESX Server and virtual machine management tool. VirtualCenter acts as a proxy that performs tasks on the individual ESX Server hosts that have been added as members of a VirtualCenter installation. VirtualCenter is licensed and sold as an optional component in the VI3 product suite. VirtualCenter offers terrific enhancements in the areas of:

◆ Resource management for ESX Server and virtual machines

◆ Template management and virtual machine deployment

◆ ESX Server and virtual machine management

◆ Scheduled tasks

◆ Statistics and logging

◆ Alarms and event management

Figure 5.1 outlines the cores services available through a VirtualCenter installation.

FIGURE 5.1
VirtualCenter 2.0 is a
Windows-based applica-
tion that allows virtual
infrastructure admin-
istrators to centrally
manage ESX Server
hosts and their respec-
tive virtual machines.

In a virtual infrastructure with only one or two servers, administrative effort is not a major concern. Administration of one or two servers would not incur incredible effort on the part of the administrator, and the creation of user accounts for virtual infrastructure administrators would not be too much of a burden. In situations like this, VirtualCenter may not be missed from a management perspective, but it will certainly be missed from a feature set viewpoint. In addition to its management capabilities, VirtualCenter offers the ability to perform VMware VMotion, configure VMware Distributed Resource Scheduler (DRS), and establish VMware High Availability (HA). These features are not accessible when ESX Servers act as individual servers running under a host-based license. VirtualCenter should be considered a requirement for any enterprise-level virtualization projects.

VIRTUALCENTER REQUIREMENT

VirtualCenter is not a requirement for a virtualized server environment. However, to utilize the advanced features of ESX Server (such as Update Manager, VMotion, DRS, and HA), VirtualCenter must be licensed, installed, and configured accordingly.

As a byproduct of an ever-growing virtual infrastructure, new users will consistently be brought into the environment. These users will likely need various levels of permissions to perform their job. VirtualCenter includes a scalable framework for providing Windows users and groups with varying levels of access to objects throughout the inventory.

VirtualCenter, acting as proxy for host and virtual machine management, does not store the virtual infrastructure data locally on the VirtualCenter server. Instead, all data is stored on a back-end database server that runs either Microsoft SQL Server or Oracle. In the section "Installing the VirtualCenter Back-end Database" later in this chapter, we will dig deeper into VirtualCenter planning. We will discuss the importance of data availability from the database server perspective.

In Chapter 2, we discussed a user's authentication to an ESX Server under the context of a user account created and stored in the Service Console. Without VirtualCenter, a user account on each ESX Server would be required for each administrator who needed access to the server.

VirtualCenter installs on a Windows Server operating system, and uses Windows' user accounts and groups to authenticate to VirtualCenter. These users and groups can reside in the local security accounts manager (SAM) of VirtualCenter, or they can belong to the Windows Active Directory domain to which VirtualCenter server belongs. For example, if a user account named Shane is created in the Service Console of an ESX Server host named silo3504.vdc.local and the user account is granted the permissions necessary to manage the host, Shane will not be able to utilize the Virtual Infrastructure Client connected to VirtualCenter to perform his management capabilities. The inverse is also true. If a Windows user account named Elaine is granted permissions through VirtualCenter to manage an ESX Server host named silo3505.vdc.local, then Elaine will not be able to manage the host by using the Virtual Infrastructure Client to connect directly to the ESX Server. Figure 5.2 exemplifies the authentication agents when using the Virtual Infrastructure client to connect to an ESX Server host or a VirtualCenter Server.

FIGURE 5.2
The Virtual Infrastructure client can be used to connect directly to an ESX Server under the context of a Service Console (Linux) user, or it can be used to connect to a VirtualCenter under the context of a Windows user.

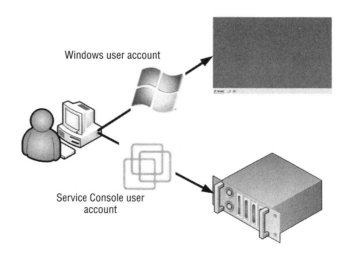

Windows user account

Service Console user account

VIRTUAL INFRASTRUCTURE CLIENT

Logging on to an ESX Server host using the Virtual Infrastructure (VI) Client requires the use of an account created and stored in the Service Console. Using the same VI Client to connect to a Virtual-Center requires the use of a Windows user account. Keep in mind that VirtualCenter and an ESX Server host do not make any attempt to reconcile the user account for each respective accounts database.

Using the Virtual Infrastructure Client to connect directly to an ESX Server that is currently being managed by a VirtualCenter server can cause negative effects in VirtualCenter. Successful logon to a managed host will result in a pop-up box warning you of this potential problem.

The VirtualCenter component of VI3 is the most extensible in regard to allowing third-party support. Some of these applications will be covered in Appendix A. Figure 5.3 shows the many components that revolve around the core services of VirtualCenter 2.5.

FIGURE 5.3
Although the foundation of virtual infrastructure is the ESX Server product, it is VirtualCenter that provides enhanced functionality and added features like HA, DRS, and VMotion as well as centralized management.

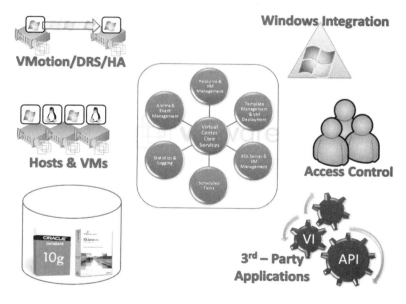

A key aspect for the success of virtualization is the ability to allow third-party companies to provide additional products that add value, ease, and functionality to existing products. VMware has shown its interest in allowing third-party software development houses to play an integral part in virtualization by providing an application programming interface (API) to VirtualCenter. This API allows companies to develop custom applications that can take advantage of the virtual infrastructure created in VirtualCenter. For example, Vizioncore's vRanger Pro, a product we will look at in our appendix of tools, is a simplified backup utility that works off the exact inventory created inside VirtualCenter to allow for advanced backup options of virtual machines.

This chapter will cover the installation, configuration, and management of VirtualCenter. In addition, you will find helpful information about best practices for VirtualCenter maintenance, availability, and disaster recovery. A detailed look at templates will be provided in Chapter 6, and Chapter 11 will offer an in-depth look at ESX Server and virtual machine monitoring.

Installing the VirtualCenter Back-end Database

By now, you have a good understanding of the importance of VirtualCenter in a large enterprise environment. As noted in the introduction to this chapter, all things VirtualCenter are stored in a back-end database. So the truth is that the back-end database, not so much the front-end VirtualCenter, is the key component. Without the back-end database, you will find yourself rebuilding an entire infrastructure. Figure 5.4 illustrates the components of a typical Virtual Server infrastructure.

FIGURE 5.4
VirtualCenter acts as a proxy for managing ESX Server 3.0 hosts. All of the data for Virtual-Center is stored in an external database.

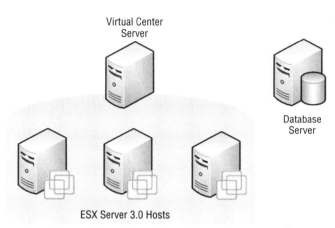

Virtual Center Server

Database Server

ESX Server 3.0 Hosts

VIRTUALCENTER BUSINESS CONTINUITY

Losing the server that runs VirtualCenter might result in a small period of downtime; however, losing the back-end database to VirtualCenter could result in days of downtime and extended periods of rebuilding.

As with most enterprise-level databases that store critical company data, you will want to take especially good care of and take precautions with the VirtualCenter database. Whether this means building the database on a server cluster that provides high availability, or developing a rock-solid backup strategy to ensure smooth and timely restore in the event of loss, measures must be taken to guarantee access and availability of VirtualCenter data.

In light of the sensitive and critical nature of the data in the VirtualCenter database, VMware will only support VirtualCenter issues with back-end databases on enterprise-level database applications. VirtualCenter 2.0.1 supports the following database applications:

◆ Oracle 9*i*

◆ Oracle 10*g*

◆ Microsoft SQL Server 2000 with Service Pack 4

◆ Microsoft SQL Server 2005 with Service Pack 1

◆ Microsoft SQL Server Desktop Engine (MSDE)

VIRTUALCENTER DATABASE SUPPORT

SQL Server 2005 Service Pack 1 is not supported on VirtualCenter 2.0.0. To use SQL Server 2005 Service Pack 1 as the back-end database for VirtualCenter, you must be running VirtualCenter 2.0.1 or higher.

For administrative purposes, you might find it easy to install the database application and the VirtualCenter application on the same computer. This configuration, however, is not considered best practice as you would then have a single point of failure for two core components of the virtual infrastructure. The more common, and recommended, infrastructure design includes deploying VirtualCenter and its back-end database on two different computers. Later in this chapter we will explore some options for building a highly available VirtualCenter installation.

Connecting VirtualCenter to its back-end database requires that an Open Database Connectivity (ODBC) connection be created on VirtualCenter. The ODBC connection should be created under the context of a database user who has full rights and permissions to a database that has been created specifically for storing VirtualCenter data.

Working with Oracle Databases

Working with Oracle as the back-end database naturally involves more effort than using a SQL Server back-end. I stress the naturally part only because VirtualCenter is a Windows-based application and therefore seems to have a tighter integration with SQL Server that facilitates the configuration. To use Oracle 9*i* or 10*g*, you will need to install Oracle and create a database for VirtualCenter to use. If your Oracle database resides on the same computer as VirtualCenter, perform the following steps to prepare Oracle for VirtualCenter:

1. Install the Oracle database driver to the VirtualCenter server.

2. Increase the number of open available cursors for the database by adding the following line:

    ```
    open_cursors - 300 to the C:\Oracle\Admin\VPX\pfile\init.ora
    ```

3. Create a new tablespace dedicated to the VirtualCenter:

    ```
    CREATE TABLESPACE vc DATAFILE 'C:\Oracle\ORADATA\VPX\vpx.dat' SIZE 250M;
    ```

4. Create a new Oracle user account (i.e., vdcdbuser) to use in the ODBC connection string:

    ```
    CREATE USER vdcdbuser IDENTIFIED BY vdcdbuser DEFAULT TABLESPACE vc;
    ```

5. Ensure the database user has been given the CONNECT and DBA privileges.

6. Finally, create an ODBC connection string in the VirtualCenter server using Administrative Tools. Give the ODBC connection a meaningful name and utilize the account created for VirtualCenter access.

For larger enterprise networks where the Oracle 9*i* or 10*g* database server is a separate computer, you will need to perform the following tasks on the computer running VirtualCenter:

1. If necessary, download and install the Oracle client on the VirtualCenter server.

2. Download and install the Oracle ODBC driver on the VirtualCenter database.

3. Open the `tnsnames.ora` file in the `C:\Oracle\Oraxx\network\admin` directory, where *xx* is the version number of your ESX server.

4. Add the following text to the `tnsnames.ora` file:

```
VPX =
(Description =
(Description=
(Address_List=
Address=(Protocol=TCP)(Host=vpxd-Oracle)(Port1521)))
Host =
```

VIRTUALCENTER AND ORACLE

All of the downloadable files required to make VirtualCenter work with Oracle can be found on Oracle's website at `http://www.oracle.com/technology/software/index.html`.

Working with Microsoft SQL Server Databases

In light of the existing widespread deployment of Microsoft SQL Server 2000 and Microsoft SQL Server 2005, it is most common to find SQL Server as the back-end database for VirtualCenter. This is not to say that Oracle does not perform as well or that there is any downside to using Oracle. Microsoft SQL Server just happens to be implemented more commonly than Oracle and therefore is a more common back-end for VirtualCenter.

USING SQL SERVER 2005 EXPRESS EDITION

With the introduction of VirtualCenter 2.5, SQL Server 2005 Express Edition is now the minimum database available as a back-end to VirtualCenter. In fact, SQL Server 2005 Express Edition has replaced the MSDE option for demo or trial installations.

Microsoft SQL Server 2005 Express Edition, like MSDE, has physical limitations that include:

◆ 1 CPU maximum

◆ 1GB of maximum of addressable RAM

◆ 4GB database maximum

Large virtual enterprises will quickly outgrow these SQL Server 2005 Express edition limitations. Therefore, you might assume that any virtual infrastructures using SQL Server 2005 Express Edition are smaller deployments with little projections, if any, for growth. VMware suggests the use of SQL Server 2005 Express Edition only for VI3 deployments with 5 or fewer hosts and 50 or fewer virtual machines.

Connecting VirtualCenter to a Microsoft SQL Server database, like the Oracle implementation, requires some specific configuration steps. The SQL Server computer must be configured in Mixed Mode authentication, as shown in Figure 5.5. This setting allows authentication to be performed by either Windows or SQL Server (see the sidebar "Windows Authentication vs. SQL Server Authentication"). Once you configure the SQL Server to allow the appropriate authentication, you must create a new database for VirtualCenter. Finally, you must create a SQL Server user account that has full access to the database you created for VirtualCenter. You can easily set the appropriate permissions for the account by making the account a member of the db_owner database role, as shown in Figure 5.6.

FIGURE 5.5
Using SQL Server 2000 or SQL Server 2005 requires that the database server allow Windows and SQL Server Authentication.

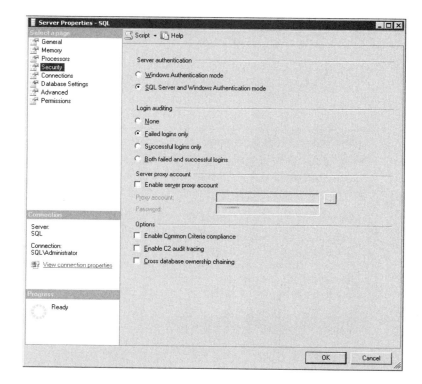

Take these steps prior to creating the ODBC connection to the SQL Server database. Using SQL Server 2005 requires not only that the account have dbo (db_owner) privileges, but that the account created actually own the database. In addition, the account used by VirtualCenter to access the SQL Server 2005 database must have membership in the db_owner database role in the msdb for the duration of the installation process. Figure 5.7 shows the creation of a new SQL Server 2005 database with the default owner changed to a custom SQL Server user account.

FIGURE 5.6
The user account VirtualCenter uses to access the back-end SQL 2000 Server database requires database owner privileges to build the table structure and populate the tables with data.

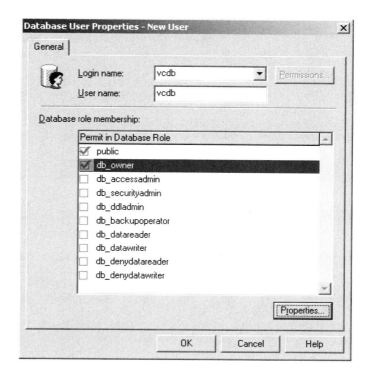

FIGURE 5.7
SQL Server 2005 databases used by VirtualCenter must be owned by the account VirtualCenter uses to connect to the database.

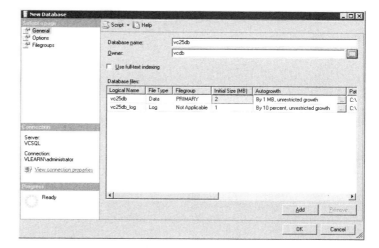

SQL SERVER 2005 PERMISSIONS

Not only will most database administrators cringe at the thought of over extending privileges to a SQL Server computer, it is not good practice to do so. As a best and strong security practice, it is best to minimize the permissions of each account that access the SQL Server computer. Therefore, in the case of the VirtualCenter 2.5 installation procedure, you will need to grant a SQL Server user account the db_owner membership on the MSDB database. However, once the installation is complete this role membership can be removed, and should be removed. Normal day-to-day operation of and access to the VirtualCenter database does not require this permission. It is a temporary requirement needed for the installation of VirtualCenter 2.5.

If you have an existing SQL Server 2005 database that needs to be used as the back-end for VirtualCenter, you can use the sp_changedbowner stored procedure command to change the database ownership accordingly. For example, EXEC sp_changedbowner @loginame='vcdbuser', @map='true' would change the database owner to a user account named vcdbuser.

WINDOWS AUTHENTICATION VS. SQL SERVER AUTHENTICATION

Microsoft SQL Server, both the 2000 and 2005 versions, supports two methods of authentication: Windows and SQL Server. While a default installation of SQL Server will allow only the Windows authentication method, this setting can be changed and in some cases, as with VirtualCenter, must be changed. Figure 5.8 shows a SQL Server 2005 server configured to allow Windows and SQL Server authentication, or what is often called Mixed Mode authentication.

Windows Authentication, as the name implies, involves authentication at the operating system level. The Windows operating system checks the username and password for a user attempting to use SQL Server. The SQL Server then only looks at the user's identity, including group memberships, to determine the level of access allowed to the SQL Server.

SQL Server authentication removes the Windows aspect of the authentication leaving the SQL Server to check the requesting user's username and password. SQL Server authentication is most commonly used when connecting non-Windows clients to a SQL Server database.

SQL Server 2000 and SQL Server 2005 can be configured to allow Windows-only authentication or to allow Windows and SQL Authentication (Mixed Mode), but there is no way to enforce a SQL Server authentication–only mode.

The configuration necessary to allow VirtualCenter to communicate with SQL Server is not an uncommon one and should result in little resistance from seasoned database administrators. In some cases, however, company policy may prevent the use of SQL Server authentication on specific SQL Servers or perhaps entirely. In this case, administrators might have to install and configure a new SQL Server computer or SQL instance to host the VirtualCenter database. If your company policy does not allow SQL Authentication to be used anywhere on the network, you will have to install SQL Server on the same computer as VirtualCenter. Figure 5.8 illustrates the scenarios in which VirtualCenter and SQL Server can communicate.

FIGURE 5.8
Authentication from VirtualCenter to SQL Server must use SQL Authentication for a SQL Server user account; however, if VirtualCenter and SQL Server are on the same computer, a Windows user account can be used for authentication.

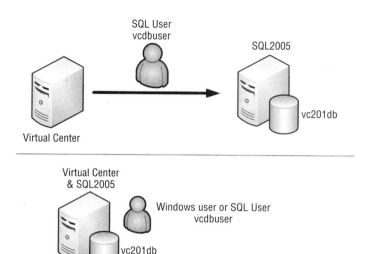

VIRTUALCENTER AUTHENTICATION TO SQL SERVER

VirtualCenter will only support the Windows Authentication method to a SQL Server if VirtualCenter and SQL Server are installed on the same computer.

Once your database is setup you can create the ODBC connection to be used during the VirtualCenter Server installation wizard. If using SQL Server 2000, the ODBC connection can be created with the SQL Server driver. However, using SQL Server 2005 requires use of the SQL Native Client. Figure 5.9 shows both options available in the Create New Data Source wizard.

FIGURE 5.9
ODBC connections to SQL Server 2005 require the SQL Native Client driver.

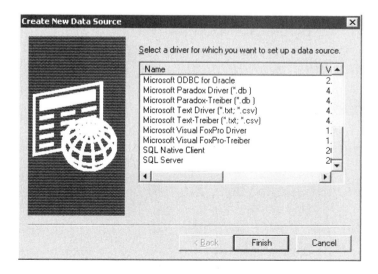

If you do not find the SQL Native Client option during the creation of the ODBC Connection string you can download it from Microsoft's Web site or install it off of a SQL Server 2005 installation CD-Rom.

On the server where VirtualCenter will be installed perform the following steps to create an ODBC connection to a SQL Server 2005 database:

1. Open the Data Sources (ODBC) applet from the Administrative Tools menu.

2. Select the System DSN tab.

3. Click the Add button.

4. Select the SQL Native Client from the list of available drivers and click the Finish button. If the SQL Native Client is not in the list it can be downloaded from Microsoft's Web site.

5. The Create New Data Source to SQL Server dialog box will open. In the Name text box, type the name you want to use to reference the ODBC connection. This is the name you will give to VirtualCenter to establish the database connection.

6. In the Server drop down list, select the SQL Server 2005 computer where the database has been created.

7. Click the Next button.

8. Select the With SQL Server authentication using a login ID and password entered by the user radio button.

9. Enter the username and password for the SQL Server authenticated user account that has the appropriate permissions to the VirtualCenter database and the MSDB database.

10. Click the Next button.

11. If the default database is listed as Master select the Change the default database to: checkbox and then select the name of the VirtualCenter database as the default. The appropriate database might be selected if the SQL Server user account was configured with the VirtualCenter database as the default.

12. Click the Next button.

13. Click the Finish button.

14. Click the Test Data Source button to test the ODBC connection.

15. Click the OK button twice.

Migrating from MSDE Databases

VIRTUALCENTER AND MSDE

VMware does not support MSDE or SQL Server 2005 Express Edition databases as the back-end database for production VirtualCenter installations.

Older versions of VirtualCenter (pre VC 2.5) were able to use the free Microsoft SQL Server Desktop Engine (MSDE) as the back-end database for a VirtualCenter installation, however doing so would not earn support from VMware. The use of MSDE as a VirtualCenter database should be restricted to demonstration or development implementations where loss of data or excess downtime is not a major concern.

If the threat of nonsupport isn't enough to scare you away from relying on MSDE for production environments, perhaps knowing the limitations of MSDE will. The MSDE database, though robust enough to support development, test, and training environments for previous VirtualCenter versions, is hard-coded with a database size limit of 2GB and maximum RAM use of 2GB.

If you use an MSDE database simply to get your virtual infrastructure up and running without incurring the administrative or financial overhead of a full-blown SQL Server 2005 computer, it's possible to make the transition later. Use the following procedure to move an MSDE or SQL Server 2000 database to SQL Server 2005e:

1. Stop the SQL Server service on the existing VirtualCenter that runs the MSDE database.

2. Copy the `*.mdf` and `*.ldf` for the respective VirtualCenter database to a directory on the SQL Server 2005 computer.

3. Open the SQL Server 2005 Management Studio on the SQL Server computer. Authenticate to the local SQL Server installation and navigate through the tree structure to find the imported database.

4. Right-click the databases node and select the Attach option.

5. In the Attach Databases window, select the MDF file for the database you wish to attach.

6. Modify the database owner to match the name of the user account that VirtualCenter uses in its ODBC connection, as shown in Figure 5.10.

7. Perform a simple query against the VPX_HOST table, as shown in Figure 5.11.

FIGURE 5.10
Attaching an MSDE database requires selecting the appropriate database files and assigning a new database owner to match the name on the user account used by VirtualCenter.

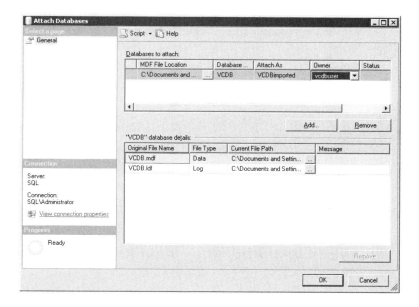

FIGURE 5.11
A simple query against
the VPX_HOST table
is a good way to test
that your data migration
process is complete.

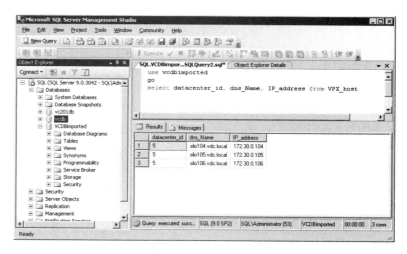

MICROSOFT ACCESS

Microsoft Access is no longer supported as the back-end database for any installation of VirtualCenter.

ESX 3.5 and VirtualCenter 2.5 Licensing Strategies

The latest release of the VirtualCenter application, VirtualCenter 2.5, includes significant enhancements that make it much more powerful than any of the previous versions. The new features include VMware Update Manager, a built-in Vmware Converter tool, expanded licensing options, and more. The installation of VirtualCenter 2.5 requires a system with the following minimum hardware specifications:

◆ 2.0 GHz processor or faster

◆ 2 GB of RAM or more

◆ 560 MB of free disk space or more

◆ A network adapter (preferably gigabit)

◆ Windows 2000 Server with Service Pack 4 or Windows Server 2003 with Service Pack 1 or Windows Server 2003 R2

◆ Internet Explorer 5.5 or higher

VIRTUALCENTER 2.5 PRE-INSTALLATION TASKS

Before installing VirtualCenter 2.5, you should ensure that the computer has been updated with the latest updates from the Microsoft Windows Update site. This will ensure updates like Windows Installer 3.1 and all required .NET components are installed.

TABLE 5.1:   Features of ESX Server Editions

FEATURE	VI ENTERPRISE	VI STANDARD	VI FOUNDATION
License type	Flex	Flex	Flex
VMFS	Yes	Yes	Yes
Virtual SMP	Yes	Yes	Yes
VCB	Yes	Yes	Yes
Vmware Update Manager	Yes	Yes	Yes
Guided Consolidation	Yes	Yes	Yes
Remote CLI Access	Yes	Yes	Yes
Evaluation mode support	Yes	Yes	Yes
Virtual Center Management Agent	Yes	Yes	Yes
HA	Yes	Yes	Purchased Option
VMotion	Yes	Purchased Option	Purchased Option
Storage VMotion	Yes	Purchased Option	Purchased Option
DRS	Yes	Purchased Option	Purchased Option
DPM	Yes	Purchased Option	Purchased Option
2 Processor license with 3 year platinum support	$9,416	$4,905	$2,640

Large enterprise environment with many ESX Server hosts and virtual machines should scale the VirtualCenter server accordingly. In addition, if your VirtualCenter computer will also function as the database server, the hardware specifications should be adjusted to support the additional overhead.

In Chapter 2 on installation we did not spend much time on licensing because the reality of the virtual environment is that server based licensing will be the dominate scenario. VirtualCenter 2.5 combined with ESX Server 3.5 introduces a new line of licensing options for VMware Infrastructure 3. This new strategy makes virtualization readily available to the small and medium businesses by making the licensing more affordable for those types of environments. Table 5.1 outlines the features available with each of the new ESX 3.5 editions.

The host-based licensing configuration for ESX sets limitation that result in the inability to have floating licenses and, more importantly, the inability to use the advanced VMotion, DRS, and HA features of ESX and VirtualCenter. As previously mentioned, managing ESX servers individually becomes an administrative hassle as the number of servers is increased. Once the decision is made to move away from the individual host management, the first step in moving to a more centralized model is to install VirtualCenter Server's back-end database. (See the previous section for more about this.) Once the database is ready to go, the next step is to install the VMware License Server. The license server is most commonly installed on the same computer that will run VirtualCenter, though that approach is not mandatory. The VMware License Server will allow the migration from host-based licensing to a centralized license repository, where licenses can float between ESX hosts. Figure 5.12 illustrates the difference between a host-based licensing strategy and a server-based licensing strategy.

FIGURE 5.12
VMware ESX Server computers can be licensed individually with host-based licensing or can share a license repository using the VMware License Server.

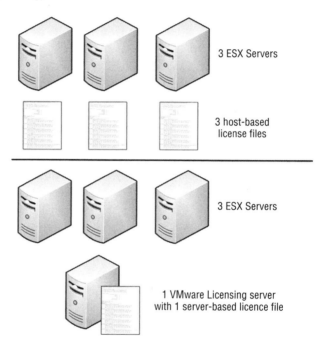

3 ESX Servers

3 host-based license files

3 ESX Servers

1 VMware Licensing server with 1 server-based licence file

VirtualCenter 2.5 can be deployed with either of the following license types:

◆ VirtualCenter Foundation edition

◆ VirtualCenter edition

VirtualCenter Foundation

Earlier I mentioned some changes to the VI3 licensing strategy that made virtualization on VMware products more readily available to smaller network environments. The VirtualCenter Foundation edition is the licensing option for the small and medium business. This edition allows for managing a maximum of three ESX server hosts. Although they can be purchased separately, VMotion, DRS, and HA are not available with the Foundation Edition of VirtualCenter 2.5. VC Foundation with three years of platinum support retails for $3,140.

VirtualCenter

The VirtualCenter edition of VirtualCenter 2.5 (I know it sounds weird) is the larger enterprise version that is not limited to only three hosts. All of the enterprise features of VMotion, DRS, and HA are supported. VirtualCenter Server Virtual Center edition (still weird) with three years of platinum support retails for $8,180.

Starting out your virtual infrastructure with the Foundation edition of VirtualCenter or ESX Server does not lock you into those editions. As your virtual infrastructure grows, and potentially outgrows the Foundation Edition, you can purchase upgrades for the VirtualCenter Server and ESX Server products. Naturally these upgrades will include the additional features and function-ality as outlined in Table 5.1.

The options and features available to you are dependent on the license file that is configured for use by the licensing server. License keys are able to open up or prevent features. With the exception of the VirtualCenter 2.5 product, all other products and features of the VI3 suite are licensed on a per-processor basis. This includes ESX Server, VMotion, Storage VMotion, HA, DRS, and VCB.

You can obtain a VMWare your server licenses by visiting the website (`http://www.vmware.com`) and entering the activation codes provided. The FLEXnet licensing, as it is called, lets you combine and download licenses to ensure the target ESX Server infrastructure works correctly. Figure 5.13 shows the license management website, and Figure 5.14 shows a sample license file obtained from the site.

FIGURE 5.13
Licenses can be com-bined on VMware's website and then down-loaded and installed to a license server.

FIGURE 5.14
This sample
server.lic file is
human readable, is
shared by all virtual
machines, and has more
items appended to it.

```
#######################################################################
# Produced by lic_check, ver. 1.2, Wed May 23 12:35:53 PDT 2007
#----------------------------------------------------------------------
# Licensing Quickstart Guide:
#      http://www.vmware.com/pdf/vi3_license_redemption.pdf
# Licensing Chapter of the Installation & Upgrade Guide:
#      http://www.vmware.com/pdf/vi3_installation_guide.pdf
#----------------------------------------------------------------------
# License Counts
#                 VC Management Server      1
#                            vMotion       16
#                        VC_ESXHOST        16
#                           VC_DAS         16
#                              DRS         16
#                      PROD_ESX_FULL       16
#                      ESX_FULL_BACKUP     16
#----------------------------------------------------------------------
SERVER this_host ANY 27000
VENDOR VMWARELM port=27010
USE_SERVER
INCREMENT PROD_VC VMWARELM 2005.05 21-jun-2007 1 \
        VENDOR_STRING=licenseType=Server \
        ISSUED=23-May-2007 NOTICE=FulfillmentId=488873 SIGN="1370 E44E \
        98C4 4F25 46FD F446 1843 4BB2 7ABB 5F1D 7F4A 3B7A B8ED E211 \
        7EDF 140C E580 A276 B50A 0A7B DBE1 B973 1FBB 7681 52E2 09C4 \
        3704 CECF 021E 33F4"
INCREMENT VC_VMOTION VMWARELM 2005.05 21-jun-2007 16 \
        VENDOR_STRING=licenseType=Server;capacityType=cpuPackage \
        ISSUED=23-May-2007 NOTICE=FulfillmentId=488872 SIGN="0F59 EAA7 \
        8724 B44E 5C04 184F 06FB 2407 D125 5A9F 258F 72AE E3E4 F248 \
        04B9 14A2 4403 588D 7E25 E7EA 3594 C90D B1C1 51EC B836 0974 \
        B61D 5813 FD6E C19F"
INCREMENT VC_ESXHOST VMWARELM 2005.05 21-jun-2007 16 \
        VENDOR_STRING=licenseType=Server;capacityType=cpuPackage \
        ISSUED=23-May-2007 NOTICE=FulfillmentId=488872 SIGN="0AF6 4803 \
        B76A 1E9E 7AE6 FE65 B75C 2EBA 3BD9 946F 097D 4C57 A82C 5F52 \
        635E 0014 AB6D B60D 2EB5 E9BC E1F1 D66A FFDC F043 6EA1 7EA0 \
        77DD 8BB4 B52D F741"
INCREMENT VC_DAS VMWARELM 2005.05 21-jun-2007 16 \
        VENDOR_STRING=licenseType=Server;capacityType=cpuPackage \
        ISSUED=23-May-2007 NOTICE=FulfillmentId=488872 SIGN="0B11 01A1 \
        54B8 6FB7 BBCA 32D8 F793 A12A AD66 4351 A2AA 04FE 0E7D A08A \
        34FC 17CC 0C48 A1E3 AC8C 52AE B6A7 BA81 07AA 5D7C 92D9 5BB2 \
        185B A0E2 363E CBC8"
INCREMENT VC_DRS VMWARELM 2005.05 21-jun-2007 16 \
        VENDOR_STRING=licenseType=Server;capacityType=cpuPackage \
        ISSUED=23-May-2007 NOTICE=FulfillmentId=488872 SIGN="19C1 C17D \
        D3F3 3960 AAAE E8E0 93E7 9144 13E5 D3DE C854 2048 C2BC FFA0 \
        79FB 0B96 8B8A 8FB3 FE32 17F8 DF4C 0533 0044 8B3B 0B48 F84B \
        B6CF BB58 709E B44F"
INCREMENT PROD_ESX_FULL VMWARELM 2005.05 21-jun-2007 16 \
        VENDOR_STRING=licenseType=Server;capacityType=cpuPackage;gp=14;exclude=BACKUP \
        ISSUED=23-May-2007 NOTICE=FulfillmentId=488872 SIGN="0FE4 709D \
        2529 609B 1069 11C9 4C7E 0DDD 067C 0250 7003 547D DB58 1FD5 \
        DC82 139C 7EA0 20CC DF0B 7334 E744 5E83 25FE CD66 454C C6F5 \
        7197 F6A2 41F2 9378"
INCREMENT ESX_FULL_BACKUP VMWARELM 2005.05 21-jun-2007 16 \
        VENDOR_STRING=licenseType=Server;capacityType=cpuPackage \
        ISSUED=23-May-2007 NOTICE=FulfillmentId=488872 SIGN="079A 515B \
        EF06 B4B6 3CB8 A1D6 7EF4 C566 E929 9E69 50CF D4F0 4915 864F \
        1E6C 0AD0 31E3 6EDD 6B62 AFB1 C56E 2082 9ECC CF1C F042 9E00 \
        9B6A 8172 0D85 BA73"
# Add any additional licenses BELOW this comment.
#######################################################################
```

Even after the license server is installed, there may come a time when a company outgrows an existing license and must download and install a new license. Figure 5.15 shows one of the tabs available in the LMTOOLS licensing tool (a Macrovision product installed with VMware) used to start, stop, and read license files.

Growing a VI3 deployment is quite easy because VMware has constructed the product to use a license directory as opposed to a single file. Certainly, as you will soon see, you can specify a single license file during the installation of VirtualCenter, however, adding new licenses to support more ESX Server hosts requires downloading a new license and saving it to the C:\Program Files\VMware\VMware License Server\Licenses directory on the licensing server. After a restart of the VMware License Server service the new licenses will be effective.

Many IT professionals have the misconception that using a centralized license server introduces a single point of failure for which we so diligently try to maintain high availability. In the event that an ESX host is unable to communicate with a license server, there will be a 14-day grace period during which all network management practices and virtual machines will continue to run. At the end of the 14 days, additional restrictions are imposed. Tasks that are not permitted after the 14-day grace period has expired include:

◆ Turning on a virtual machine

◆ Restarting virtual machines that failed because of a failed host that belongs to a DRS cluster

Tasks that are not permitted once the licensing server becomes unavailable include:

◆ Adding an ESX host to inventory

◆ Moving an ESX host into a VMotion/HA/DRS cluster

◆ Adding/removing licenses

Some of the more common tasks that are still permitted once the license server becomes unavailable include:

◆ Creating and deleting virtual machines

◆ Suspending and resuming virtual machines

◆ Turning an ESX host on or off

◆ Configuring an VirtualCenter or ESX host using the VI Client

◆ Removing an ESX host from inventory

◆ Maintaining DRS automated efficiency

FIGURE 5.15
The LMTOOLS program allows you to update server-based licenses when you want to add more licenses to your virtual infrastructure.

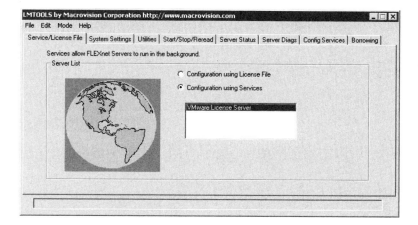

DON'T WAIT. FIX IT.

When a license server becomes unavailable, it is best to fix the server immediately despite having the 14-day grace period.

While a licensing server can be installed on its own, it is more convenient to install it as part of the VirtualCenter installation procedure. If you wish to install the licensing server separately, use VMware-licenseserver.exe in the \vpx directory of the VirtualCenter installation folder (VMware-VIMSetup-2.5.0-xxxxxx).

Installing VirtualCenter 2.5

With the database in place and a solid understanding of the licensing options, you can now install and properly configure VirtualCenter. Once you've done that, you can add servers and continue the configuration of your virtual infrastructure.

VIRTUALCENTER 2.5

Remember that the latest version of VirtualCenter is available for download from the http://www.vmware.com/download website. It is often best to install the latest version of the software to ensure the highest levels of compatibility, security, and simplicity. VirtualCenter 2.5 was the latest update available at the time of this writing and was used as the source of the images for this section.

The VirtualCenter 2.5 installation takes only a few minutes and is not administratively intensive, assuming all of the pre-installation tasks have been completed. The VirtualCenter 2.5 installation can be started by double-clicking autorun.exe inside the VirtualCenter installation directory.

After a brief overview of the benefits of VirtualCenter the installation will continue through the acceptance of a license agreement and the provision of the organization information. At this point, you must select the role to be played by the server. As shown in Figure 5.16, the installation procedure offers the following installation types:

◆   VMware Infrastructure Client

◆   VMware VirtualCenter Server (default)

◆   Custom

FIGURE 5.16
VirtualCenter Server installation types provided during the installation wizard.

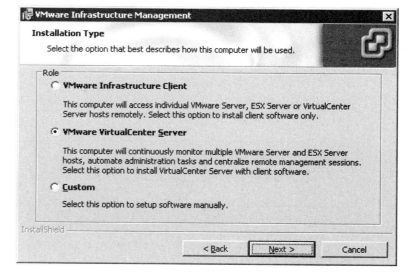

Selecting the Custom option leads to a components selection screen shown in Figure 5.17. This page of the installation wizard offers the following component selections which are all selected by default:

◆   VMware Infrastructure Client

◆   VMware VirtualCenter Server

◆   VMware Update Manager

◆   VMware Converter Enterprise for VirtualCenter

FIGURE 5.17
Custom options are available during the VirtualCenter installation wizard to allow for selection of individual components.

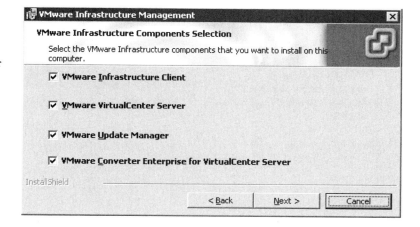

The latter two options in the list are new features of VirtualCenter 2.5. Chapter 12, "Securing and Managing a VMware Virtual Infrastructure" and Chapter 7, "Migrating and Importing Virtual Machines" will provide more detail on the VMware Update Manager and VMware Converter Enterprise features respectively.

The next step in the installation process is to identify the location of the back-end database. Figure 5.18 shows the two options of installing a local database on SQL Server 2005 Express Edition or using an existing (separate or local) database server. The Use existing database server option should be selected for remote back-end SQL Server 2000/2005 or Oracle databases.

ODBC TO DB

An ODBC connection must be defined and the name must match in order to move past the database configuration page of the installation wizard. Remember to set the appropriate authentication strategy and user permissions for an existing database server. If you receive an error at this point in the installation revisit the database configuration steps. Remember to set the appropriate database ownership and database roles.

After successfully connecting to a pre-configured VirtualCenter database running on SQL Server 2005, you will receive a warning message regarding the database being set to the Full recovery model. The warning message continues on identifying that this model runs the risk of growing large transaction logs for the VirtualCenter database. The knowledge base article identified in the warning message suggests reconfiguring the VirtualCenter database into the

Simple recovery model. What the warning does not tell you is that doing this means that you will lose the ability to backup transaction logs for the VirtualCenter database. If you leave the database set to Full recovery, be sure to work with the database administrator to routinely backup and truncate the transaction logs. By having transaction log backups from a database in Full recovery you will have the option to restore to an exact point in time should any type of data corruption occur. If you alter the recovery model as suggested be sure you are taking consistent full backups of the database, but understand that you will only be able to recover to the point of the last full backup as transaction logs will be unavailable.

FIGURE 5.18
The VirtualCenter installation wizard provides options for installing a local SQL Server 2005 Express Edition instance or using an existing database server running SQL Server 2000/2005 or Oracle.

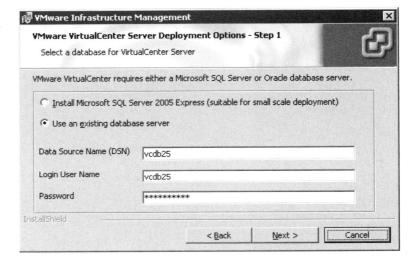

The next step in the VirtualCenter installation wizard is to select the VirtualCenter License Server configuration. The default setting on this page is a new option that allows a 60-day evaluation mode, shown in Figure 5.19. This new option allows administrators that are interested in virtualization to deploy test or proof-of-concept environments that support all of the features of VI3. The Virtual Infrastructure client will reflect the number of days remaining in the evaluation period. Once the evaluation period has expired, you can purchase license to install, thereby allowing you to maintain all of the work performed to assemble the evaluation environment.

Opting out of the evaluation mode by deselecting the option opens up the ability to choose between using and existing licensing server, shown in Figure 5.20, or to install a new licensing server as shown in Figure 5.21. An existing licensing server is references by 27000@<servername> to indicate the licensing port of 27000 and the host functioning as the licensing server. If the local system is also the licensing server then the name localhost can be used in place of the actual host name. By not selecting the **Use an Existing License Server** option, you will need to browse to find a license file that has been obtained from the VMware Web site. In either case you must also select the appropriate edition of VirtualCenter from the Management Server and Foundation Management Server options.

By default VirtualCenter is setup to use a set of default ports for the various types of communication it engages in, as shown in Figure 5.22. These default ports include:

◆ Port 80 for the HTTP Web Service

◆ Port 443 for the HTTPS Web Service

FIGURE 5.19
A new 60-day evaluation mode is available for VirtualCenter.

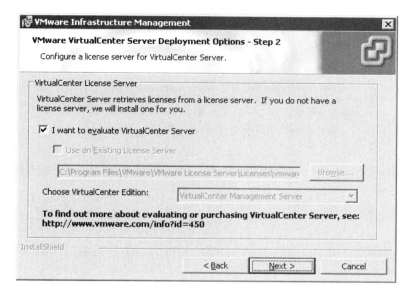

FIGURE 5.20
An existing license server is referenced by using <licensing_port>@hostname syntax.

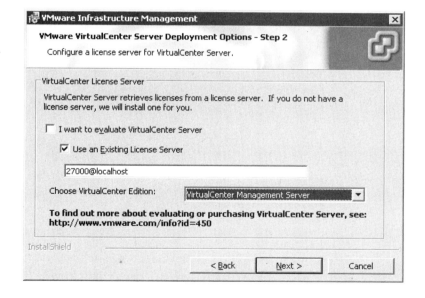

◆ Port 902 (UDP) for the Heartbeat

◆ Port 8086 for the Web Server management (running on Apache Tomcat)

Although these ports can be altered but it is not recommended to do as it would incur additional administrative overhead in ensuring that all other application accessing VirtualCenter were aware of the port alterations.

FIGURE 5.21
The system where Vir-
tualCenter is being
installed can be con-
figured as the licensing
server by browsing for
the appropriate down-
loaded .LIC file.

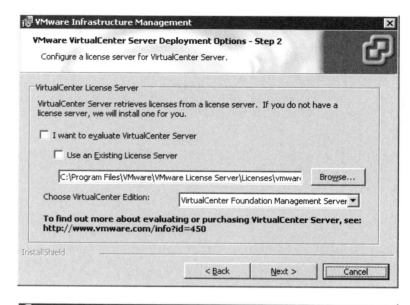

FIGURE 5.22
VirtualCenter ports are
defined for the various
types of management
communication.

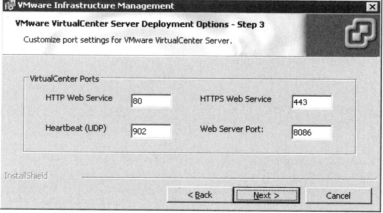

VirtualCenter extensions add new functionality in the areas of ESX Server updates management and consolidation assistance. Figure 5.x shows the configuration of administrative credentials in support of the installation of the VMware Converter Enterprise for VirtualCenter Server
and VMware Update Manager extensions. Later in this chapter we will discuss enabling and
configuring these new extensions.

The VMware Update Manager maintains data in its own back-end database. The next page of
the installation wizard identifies a local or remote database to be used by the VMware Update
Manager. Similar to the VirtualCenter database, there is an option for installing SQL Server 2005
Express Edition or for using an existing remote database. If you wish, you can even use the same
database used for VirtualCenter.

FIGURE 5.23
New extensions available in VirtualCenter 2.5 allow for VMware Update Manager and VMware Converter Enterprise to be integrated into VirtualCenter.

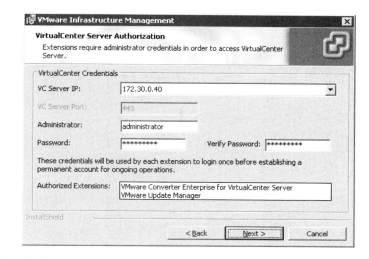

VMWARE UPDATE MANAGER DATABASE

If you choose to use a different database for VMware Update Manager data, you must create a second ODBC connection to the new database. The user account used in the ODBC connection must be a member of the db_owner database role for the database.

The VMware Update Manager installation includes some additional configuration for the SOAP and Web ports to be used for the downloading of updates. As shown in Figure 5.24, you can also enable and configure a proxy server for use by the VMware Update Manager.

FIGURE 5.24
VMware Update Manager ports are used to download ESX Server updates directly from the VMware Web site.

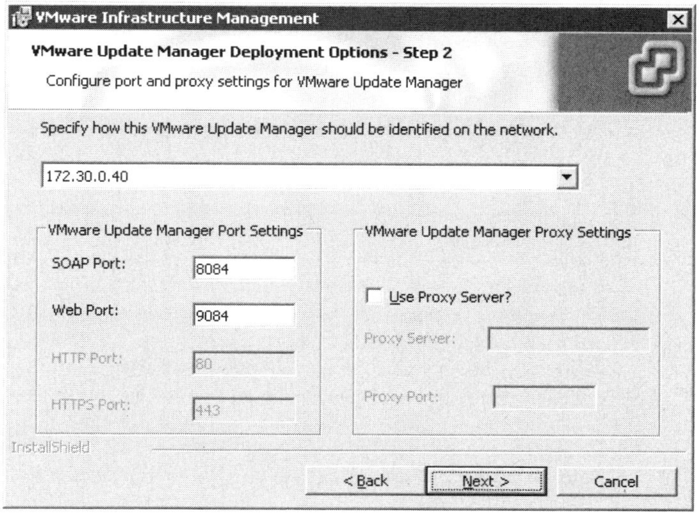

After the configuration of the VMware Update Manager the next page in the wizard, shown in Figure 5.25, allows for the ports configuration for the VMware Converter Enterprise that is now built into VirtualCenter.

FIGURE 5.25
VMware Converter Enterprise is now built into VirtualCenter for facilitating consolidation of physical serves into virtual machines.

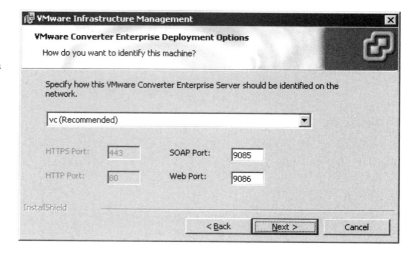

MISSING PIECES

If the VirtualCenter installation procedure identifies any missing Windows components, for example .NET updates, you will be prompted to allow VirtualCenter to install the necessary pieces. If you select the option to use SQL Server 2005 Express Edition you will also witness its installation as part of the VirtualCenter installation process.

Upon completion of the VirtualCenter installation, browsing to VirtualCenter's URL (`http://<server name>` or `http://<server ip address>`) will turn up a page that allows for the installation of the VI Client, or the use of a web-based tool for managing the individual virtual machines hosted by the ESX Server 3.0 hosts within the VirtualCenter inventory. Figure 5.26 shows a sample home page for VirtualCenter.

VIRTUALCENTER AND IIS

Despite the fact that VirtualCenter is accessible via a Web browser, it is not necessary to install Internet Information Services on the VirtualCenter server. VirtualCenter access via a browser relies on the Apache Tomcat Web Service which is installed as part of the VirtualCenter installation. IIS should be uninstalled as it can cause conflicts with Apache Tomcat.

The VI Client connected to VirtualCenter should be the primary management tool for managing ESX Server 3.5 hosts and their respective virtual machines. The VI Client can connect directly to ESX Server 3.5 hosts under the context of a user account defined in the Service Console, or it can connect to a VirtualCenter server under the context of a Windows user account defined in Active Directory or the local security accounts manager (SAM) of the VirtualCenter computer.

FIGURE 5.26
The home page of an ESX Server host or a VirtualCenter both offer a download of the VI Client and a web access login.

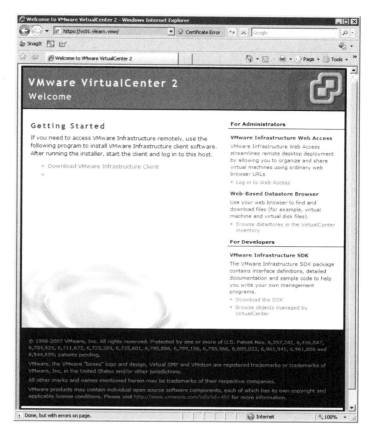

VirtualCenter is a critical application for the management of your virtual infrastructure. Its implementation should be carefully designed and executed to ensure availability and data protection.

MANAGING VIRTUALCENTER SERVICES

After the installation of VirtualCenter, having included licensing and the extensions, there will be ten new services installed to facilitate the operation of VirtualCenter and all its features. These services include:

◆ **VMware Capacity Planner Service**-used by the Guided Consolidation feature to gather performance data about target systems.

◆ **VMware Converter Enterprise Service**-used by the built in VMware Converter Enterprise tool for migrating physical and virtual machines into VirtualCenter.

◆ **VMware Descheduled Time Accounting Service**-used to facilitate the management of time within a virtual machine.

◆ **VMware Infrastructure Web Access**-used to allow browser-based access to the VirtualCenter Server application.

◆ VMware License Server-used to manage VI3 server based product licensing.

◆ VMware Mount Service for Virtual Center-used to support VirtualCenter integration with VMware Consolidated Backup (VCB).

◆ VMware Physical Disk Helper Service-used to support running a virtual machine from a physical disk partition.

◆ VMware Tools Service-used to support the synchronization of objects between the virtualization host and the guest operating systems running in virtual machines.

◆ VMware Update Manager Service-used to provide update or patch management capability.

◆ VMware VirtualCenter Server-used to provide centralized management of ESX Server hosts and virtual machines.

The following graphic displays the default status and configuration of all the VirtualCenter Server services.

As a virtual infrastructure administrator, you should be familiar with the default states of these services. In times of troubleshooting, check the status of the services to see if they have changed. Keep in mind the dependencies that exist between VirtualCenter and other services on the network. For example, if the VirtualCenter Server service is failing to start, be sure to check that the system has access to the SQL Server (or Oracle) database. If VirtualCenter cannot access the database due to lack of connectivity or the database service not running, then it will not start.Perform the following steps to install VirtualCenter 2.5 and all of the additional licensing and extension components:

1. Ensure that the appropriate ODBC connections have been created for connectivity to the VirtualCenter database and the VMware Update Manager Database.

2. Initiate the VirtualCenter 2.5 installation from a CD-ROM or a downloaded set of files. If the files have been downloaded from the `http://www.vmware.com/download` site the installation can be initiated by double-clicking the autorun.exe file in the Vmware-VIMSetup-2.5.0-xxxxx folder.

3. Once the VMware Infrastructure Management installation wizard appears click the Next button.

4. Click the Next button after reviewing the introduction page that highlights the features of VirtualCenter.

5. Select the I accept the terms in the license agreement radio button and then click the Next button.

6. Provide a User Name and Organization in the appropriate text boxes and then click the Next button.

7. Select the VMware Infrastructure Client radio button to install only the management client, select the VMware VirtualCenter Server radio to accept the defaults of all options, or select the Custom radio button to choose which options to be installed. Choosing the custom option allows for choosing between the following:

   ◆ VMware Infrastructure Client

   ◆ VMware VirtualCenter Server

   ◆ VMware Update Manager

   ◆ VMware Converter Enterprise for VirtualCenter Server

8. On the VMware VirtualCenter Server Deployment Options-Step 1 page select the appropriate database option. Choose SQL Server 2005 Express for small deployments or demo installation. Choose use an existing database server for enterprise deployments that will use SQL Server 2005 or Oracle.

9. If using SQL Server 2005 or Oracle provide the ODBC data source name and the appropriate user account information. For SQL Server 2005 this is the SQL user account that has been granted ownership of the VirtualCenter database and db_owner database role for the MSDB database. It is also the use account used for the creation of the ODBC connection to the SQL Server 2005 computer.

DATABASE PERMISSIONS ERROR

At this stage in the installation you might receive the following error:

The DB user entered does not have the required permissions needed to install and configure VMware VirtualCenter Server with the selected DB. Please see the installation documentation for detailed DB permission requirements.

This is most commonly due to not providing the SQL user account with ownership of the VirtualCenter database or not providing db_owner database role membership for the MSDB database. It might be a bit of a struggle to convince database administrators to allow the db_owner membership for MSDB, but remember that the permission assignment can be removed once the installation is complete.

If you have the luxury of making the SQL user account a sysadmin the installation will also run fine, however, if this is done it should be immediately undone after the installation. If you are using an existing SQL server managed by other database administrators chances are that they are not going to allow even temporary sysadmin membership.

---

10. Click the OK button if your receive the following warning message:

11. Please make sure SQL Server Agent service is running on the database server.

12. If the SQL Server 2005 database has been left with the default configuration it will be set to Full Recovery model and a warning message will appear, click the OK button. The warning will suggest a VMware knowledge base article that will direct you to change

the recovery model to Simple. If you are unsure of the ramifications of doing this please revisit an earlier section of this chapter where we discussed the Full versus Simple recovery model. Or ask your friendly neighborhood database administrator.

13. On the VMware VirtualCenter Server Deployment Options-Step 2 page select the appropriate licensing strategy. The default selection will allow a 60 day evaluation. It is also possible to select the use of an existing licensing server or to configure the local server as a licensing server by using the Browse button to find a valid server-based licensing license file. If you choose to use and existing license server or configure the local server as a licensing server select the VirtualCenter edition from the drop down list. It is important to select the version that matches the license you have purchased else you will have to reconfigure VirtualCenter after installation. You can revisit the earlier section of this chapter that discussed the differences in licensing.

14. If the installation is being installed to use the 60 day trial you will receive an information box regarding the trial period. Click the OK button to continue.

15. On the VMware VirtualCenter Server Deployment Options-Step 3 page click the OK button to accept the default VirtualCenter port configuration. The ports can be edited if conflicts might occur with existing applications using similar ports. You should avoid altering the default port settings.

16. On the VirtualCenter Server Authorization page provide the administrative credentials necessary for VirtualCenter to install the VirtualCenter extensions. Click the Next button to continue.

17. On the VMware Update Manager Deployment Options-Step1 page, select the appropriate back-end database option for use by the VMware Update Manager. Provide the appropriate ODBC connection name and corresponding username and password. Once again a warning regarding the database recovery model might be presented. Click the OK button to proceed past the warning, then click the Next button to continue.

18. On the VMware Update Manager Deployment Options-Step 2 page configure the appropriate name and port setting for the VMware Update Manager to use. You should avoid altering the default port settings. Click the Next button to continue.

19. On the VMware Converter Enterprise Deployment Options page configure the appropriate name and port setting for use by the VMware Converter built into VirtualCenter. You should avoid altering the default port settings. Click the Next button to continue.

20. On the Destination Folder selection page configure the installation directory for Virtual-Center and its components and the directory for storing updates downloaded by VMware Update Manager. Click the Next button to continue.

21. Click the Install button to initiate the installation.

22. After the installation is complete use the VMware Virtual Infrastructure Client to connection to the VirtualCenter Server installation.

Creating and Managing a VirtualCenter Inventory

Upon first connecting to VirtualCenter you will notice a getting started tab that facilitates the construction of a new datacenter. The starting point for the VirtualCenter inventory is called the root, while the building block of the VirtualCenter inventory is called a datacenter object. Along with the link for creating new data is a set of links to help you quickly find more information about getting the VirtualCenter up and running. The links in the Explore Further menu include:

◆ Learn more about inventory views

◆ Learn more about virtualization

◆ Learn more about datacenter

From the Hosts & Clusters node in the inventory tree, there are several tabs across (see Figure 5.27) for reviewing data about all objects beneath the Hosts & Clusters view root. Within each tab you can right click the column headers and select additional data to be reviewed or existing data to be removed. In addition to the Getting Started tab, the tabs available from the Hosts & Clusters root include:

◆ Datacenters-viewing all datacenter objects as well as the number of hosts and virtual machines within

◆ Virtual Machines-provides a list of virtual machines within the root as well as performance data, state, and host.

◆ Hosts-provides a list of each host within the root as well as performance data and state of each host.

◆ Tasks & Events-provides a listing of the most recent tasks and events that have taken place

◆ Alarms-displays a list of alarms that have been defined to fire for each host or VM within the root

◆ Permissions-provides information and configuration capability for delegating authority at the root level

◆ Map-provides a tool for reviewing the virtualization architecture and the relationships between the various components.

FIGURE 5.27
Hosts & Clusters is the root of the VirtualCenter management utility.

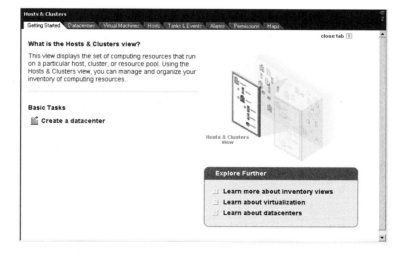

VirtualCenter is a dynamic application in that when a different object in the inventory is selected, the available tabs become customized for the selected object. For example, when an ESX Server host is selected in the inventory the available tabs change to reflect the administrative tasks and data for the host, shown in Figure 5.28. The tabs available when a host is selected include:

◆ Summary

◆ Virtual Machines

◆ Resource Allocation

◆ Performance

◆ Configuration

◆ Tasks & Events

◆ Alarms

◆ Permissions

◆ Topology Maps

FIGURE 5.28
VirtualCenter management tools are dynamic. The tools change based on the object selected from the inventory.

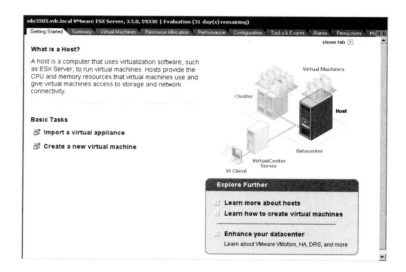

VIRTUALCENTER INVENTORY DESIGN

If you are familiar with objects used in a Microsoft Windows Active Directory (AD), you may recognize a strong similarity in the best practices of AD design and the design of a VirtualCenter inventory. A close parallel can even be drawn between a Datacenter object and an organizational unit, as both are the building blocks of their respective infrastructures.

Prior to adding a host to a VirtualCenter inventory, you must create a datacenter object. Keep in mind that the naming strategy you provide for the objects in VirtualCenter should mirror the way that network management is performed. For example, if you have qualified IT staff at each of your three datacenters across the country, then you would most likely create a hierarchical inventory that mirrors that management style. On the other hand, if your IT management was most profoundly set by the various departments in your company, then the datacenter objects might be named after each respective department. In most enterprise environments, the VirtualCenter inventory will be a hybrid that involves management by geography, department, server type, and even project title.

The VirtualCenter inventory can be structured as needed to support a company's IT management needs. Folders can be created above and below the datacenter object to provide higher or more granular levels of control that can propagate to lower-level child objects. Figure 5.29 shows a Hosts & Clusters view of a VirtualCenter inventory that is based on a geographical management style.

FIGURE 5.29
The VirtualCenter inventory should reflect a company's IT management needs. Folders can be created above the datacenter object to grant permission at a level that can propagate to multiple datacenter objects, or folders can be created beneath a datacenter to manage the objects within the datacenter.

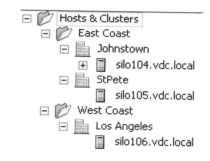

Should a company use more of a departmental approach to IT resource management, then the VirtualCenter inventory can be shifted to match the new management style. Figure 5.30 reflects a VirtualCenter inventory based on a departmental management style.

FIGURE 5.30
A departmental Virtual-Center inventory allows the IT administrator to implement controls within each organizational department.

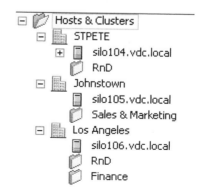

In most enterprise environments, the VirtualCenter inventory will be a hybrid of the different topologies. Perhaps one topology might be a geographical top level, followed by departmental management, followed by project-based resource configuration.

Along the top of the VirtualCenter user interface there are six menu buttons for changing the scope of management in VirtualCenter. The buttons include:

◆ Inventory-menu selection for changing the list of inventory objects

◆ Scheduled Tasks-menu selection for creating a job to be executed

◆ Events-a look at recent events that have occurred in the VirtualCenter deployment

◆ Administration-menu selection for accessing VirtualCenter data about roles, sessions, licenses, and VirtualCenter logs

◆ Maps-menu selection for reviewing topology maps for selected inventory objects

◆ Consolidation-menu selection for managing the guided consolidation feature in Virtual-Center

The VirtualCenter application has four views, accessible from the Inventory drop down list, that can be used to shift the focus between the various components in the virtual infrastructure:

◆ Hosts & Clusters

◆ Virtual Machines & Templates

◆ Networks

◆ Datastores

Each of the views has a distinct advantage because they can filter out unnecessary objects to allow administrators to concentrate on one particular aspect of the virtual infrastructure. Figure 5.31 compares three of the VirtualCenter views.

FIGURE 5.31
Each of the views available through VirtualCenter provide an insight into some aspect of the virtual environment.

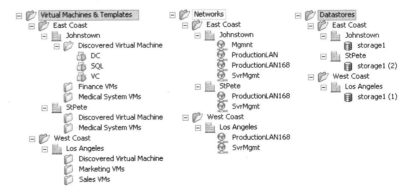

The VirtualCenter inventory is the framework built to deliver a management infrastructure for hosts, virtual machines, and templates. Hosts are added to VirtualCenter under the context of the root user account, as shown in Figure 5.32. At this point, a new VirtualCenter agent

service is installed on the ESX Server host. This new service is installed with the name vpxa and is responsible for VirtualCenter to ESX Server communication. All subsequent connections from a VirtualCenter server to an ESX Server 3.0 host happen under the context of a vpxuser account created by root when the new host is added to the inventory.

FIGURE 5.32
Adding an ESX Server 3.5 host into a VirtualCenter under the context of root allows root to create a new user account named vpxuser that will be used for all subsequent logins and actions.

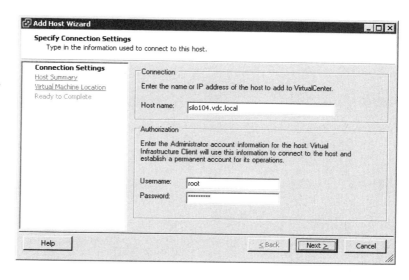

Chapter 8 will describe the security model of VirtualCenter that will work hand-in-hand with the management-driven inventory design.

From the Scheduled Tasks menu you can create jobs to run based on a defined logic. The list of tasks that can be scheduled include:

◆ Change the power state of a virtual machine

◆ Clone a virtual machine

◆ Deploy a virtual machine

◆ Move a virtual machine with VMotion

◆ Relocate a virtual machine

◆ Create a virtual machine

◆ Make a snapshot of a virtual machine

◆ Add a host

◆ Export a virtual machine

◆ Import a virtual machine

The data to be provided for each task varies and therefore each of the wizards that results from the task selection is unique in its own way.

Using VirtualCenter Topology Maps

The new Maps feature of VirtualCenter is a great tool for quickly infrastructure. Topology maps graphically represent the relationship that exists between different types of objects in the virtual infrastructure. The maps can display any of the following relationships:

◆ Host to Virtual Machine

◆ Host to Network

◆ Host to Datastore

◆ Virtual Machine to Network

◆ Virtual Machine to Datastore

In addition to defining the relationships to display, you can include or exclude specific objects from the inventory. Perhaps you are only interested in the relationship that exists between the virtual machines and the networks that are on a single host. In this case, you can exclude all other hosts from the list of relationships by deselecting their icons in the VirtualCenter inventory. Figure 5.33 shows a series of topology maps that defines the relationships for a set of objects in the VirtualCenter inventory. For historical purposes or further analysis, topology maps can be saved as JPG, BMP, or EMF file formats.

FIGURE 5.33
VirtualCenter's Maps feature is a flexible, graphical utility that helps identify the relationships that exist between the various objects in the virtual infrastructure.

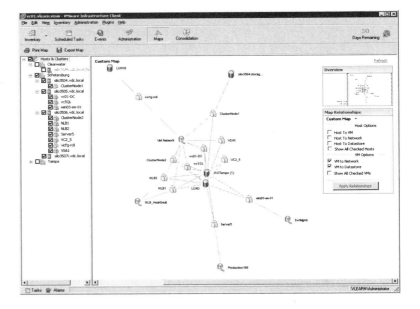

Topology maps are available by clicking the Maps button on the VirtualCenter menu or by selecting an inventory object and then selecting the Maps tab. Figure 5.33 showed the Maps feature from the VirtualCenter menu while Figure 5.34 shows the Maps tab available for each inventory object. In either case the depth of the relationship can be identified by enabling or disabling options in the list of relationships.

FIGURE 5.34
The Maps tab for inventory objects limits the scope of the map to the selected object.

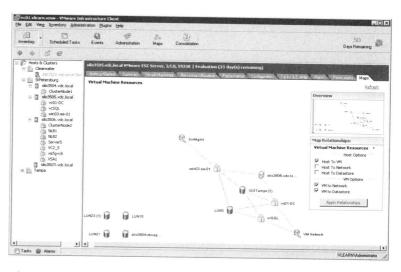

The Maps button on the menu allows for the scope of the relationship to be edited by enabling and disabling objects in the VirtualCenter inventory. By selecting an inventory object and then viewing the topology map the focus is limited to just that object.

Planning a VirtualCenter Deployment

When discussing the deployment of VirtualCenter, some of the most common topics include:

◆ How much hardware do I need to power VirtualCenter?

◆ How do I prepare VirtualCenter for disaster recovery?

◆ Should I run VirtualCenter in a virtual machine?

The amount of hardware required by VirtualCenter is directly related to the number of hosts and virtual machines it will be managing.

LOCAL DISKS ON VIRTUALCENTER SERVER

Disk storage allocation is of minimal concern when planning a VirtualCenter installation because the data will be stored in a SQL Server or Oracle database on a remote server.

The operating system running VirtualCenter has a maximum memory limit of 4GB: 2GB for use by the operating system and the other 2GB allocated for the application. In addition, VirtualCenter with multiple processors can support large enterprise environments.

VMware suggests that VirtualCenter be configured with two processors and 3GB of RAM to support up to 100 ESX Server hosts and 2,000 virtual machines. An environment of that size is much larger than a typical environment might be, so it's feasible to simply scale the specifications back to meet your needs. For example, a single processor and 1.5GB of RAM should suffice for up to 50 ESX Server hosts and 1,000 virtual machines. Though it helps to have a good starting point for the deployment of VirtualCenter, you can always alter the specifications to achieve adequate performance levels.

More important than detailing the CPU and memory allocations for VirtualCenter is the plan devised for recovery in the event of disaster. Remember, the heart of the VirtualCenter content is stored in a back-end SQL Server or Oracle database. Any good disaster recovery or business continuity plan should include instructions on how to handle data loss or corruption on the back-end.

If the VirtualCenter server is a physical box, the best approach to providing availability is to create a stand-by VirtualCenter server that can be turned on in the event of a failure of the online VirtualCenter server. After failure, the stand-by server can be brought online and attached to the existing SQL Server database, and then the hosts can be added to the new VirtualCenter server.

For high availability of the data component of VirtualCenter, you can configure the back-end database on a SQL Server cluster. Figure 5.35 illustrates using a SQL Server cluster for the back-end database and a stand-by VirtualCenter computer. If a SQL Server cluster is not available or not within fiscal reach, you should strengthen your database backup strategy to support easy recovery in the event of data loss or corruption. Using the native SQL Server tools, you can create a backup strategy that combines full, differential, and transaction log backups. This strategy will allow you to restore data up to the minute when loss or corruption occurred.

FIGURE 5.35
A good disaster recovery plan for VirtualCenter should include a quick means of regaining the user interface as well as ensuring the data is highly available and protected against damage.

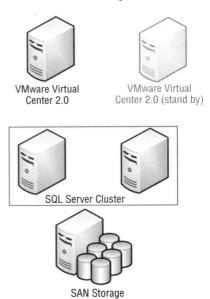

VMware Virtual Center 2.0

VMware Virtual Center 2.0 (stand by)

SQL Server Cluster

SAN Storage

VIRTUALIZING VIRTUALCENTER

Another option for VirtualCenter is to install it into a virtual machine. Though you might hesitate to do so, there are really some great advantages to doing this. The most common concern is the misconception that losing the VirtualCenter server causes a domino effect that results in losing the functionality of VMware High Availability (HA). The truth, however, is that HA is an advantage to virtualizing the VirtualCenter server. In addition to taking advantage of the HA feature, a VirtualCenter server installed as a virtual machine offers increased portability, snapshot functionality, and cloning functionality (though not in the traditional sense).

Although there are advantages to installing VirtualCenter in a virtual machine, you should also understand the disadvantages. Features like cold migration, cloning, and editing hardware will not be available for the virtual machine running VirtualCenter.

Snapshot functionality will give you the ability to return to a point in time for your VirtualCenter. VMotion will give you the portability required to move the server from host to host without experiencing server downtime. But what happens when a snapshot is corrupted or the virtual machine is corrupt altogether? With VirtualCenter as your virtual machine, you can make regular copies of the .vmdk file and keep a "clone" of the server ready to go in the event of server failure. The clone will have the same system configuration used in the last .vmdk copy process, which should not be extremely different, given that the bulk of the data processing by VirtualCenter ends up in a back-end database running on a different server. Figure 5.36 illustrates the setup of a manual cloning of the VirtualCenter server.

FIGURE 5.36
If VirtualCenter is installed and configured as a virtual machine, its .vmdk file can be copied regularly and used as the hard drive for a new virtual machine, effectively providing a point in time restore in the event of complete server failure or loss.

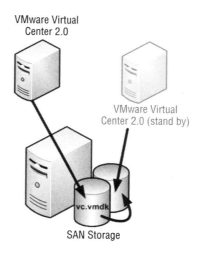

As a last resort for recovering VirtualCenter, it's possible to just reinstall the software, point to the existing database, and connect the host systems. The installation of VirtualCenter is not a time-consuming process. Ultimately the most important part of the VirtualCenter recovery plan is to ensure that the database server is redundant and protected.

Managing VirtualCenter Settings

The Administration menu in VirtualCenter allows for post-installation configuration of the VirtualCenter. In fact, it even contains configuration options that are not provided during installation. The Administration menu contains the following items:

- Custom Attributes
- VirtualCenter Management Server Configuration

◆ Roles

◆ Session

◆ Edit Message of the Day

◆ Export Diagnostic Data

◆ Consolidation Settings

CUSTOM ATTRIBUTES

The custom attributes option let you define custom identification or information options for virtual machines, hosts, or both (global). Let's look at a good example of how the Custom Attributes can be used. Say that you want to add metadata to each virtual machine to identify if it is an application server, infrastructure server (I.E. DHCP Server, DNS Server), or a domain controller.

Adding a custom virtual machine attribute named VM role as shown in Figure 5.37 will allow you to add the required information.

FIGURE 5.37
Custom attributes allow you to store metadata about virtual machines and hosts.

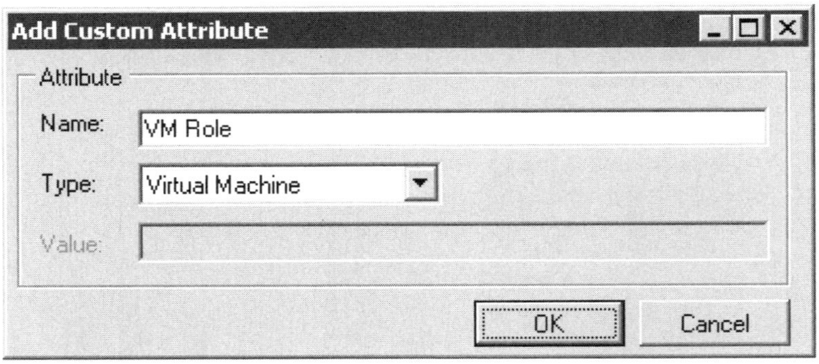

Once a custom attribute is created, the attribute data can be edited from the Summary tab of the object. . Once the custom attribute is added to the Annotations section of the object, as shown in Figure 5.38, you can use the Edit button to pull up the Custom Attributes window and add the required metadata, as shown in Figure 5.39.

With the metadata clearly defined for various object you can then search based on that data. Figure 5.40 shows a custom search for all virtual machines with a VM role equal to domain controller.

VIRTUALCENTER MANAGEMENT SERVER CONFIGURATION

The VirtualCenter Management Server Configuration dialog box contains 12 VirtualCenter settings:

◆ License Server

◆ Statistics

◆ Runtime Settings

◆ Active Directory

◆ Mail

FIGURE 5.38
Custom attributes will show in the Annotatons section of the Summary tab for an object.

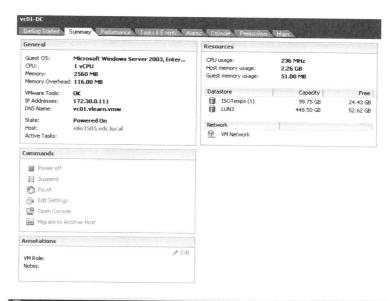

FIGURE 5.39
Metadata can be added to objects by editing the values of the custom attributes.

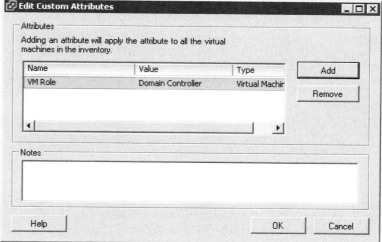

FIGURE 5.40
Once the data for a custom attribute is defined it can be used as search criteria for quickly finding objects with similar metadata.

- ◆ SNMP

- ◆ Web Service

- ◆ Timeout Settings

- ◆ Logging Options

- ◆ Database

- ◆ SSL Settings

- ◆ Advanced Settings

License Server

The License Server configuration page, shown in Figure 5.41, of the VirtualCenter Management Server Configuration dialog box provides the parameters for establishing the location of the license server. The options include using an evaluation mode, a local license server, or pointing to a specific license server hosted on another server. Clicking the Use the Following License Server radio button lets you configure different license servers in the format of port@server. For example, using port 27000 on a server named License1 would be identified as 27000@License1.

FIGURE 5.41
The licensing mode of VirtualCenter is managed through the VirtualCenter Management Server Configuration.

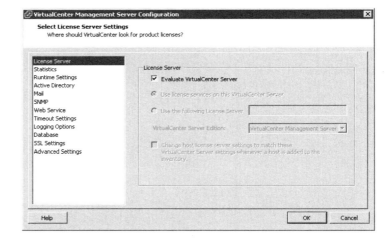

When an evaluation of VI3 is no longer required and the appropriate licenses have been purchased you must deselect the evaluation option and configure the appropriate licensing strategy. When the evaluation option is unchecked a warning message is presented as shown in Figure 5.42.

A checkbox labeled Change Host License Server Settings to Match These VirtualCenter Settings Whenever a Host Is Added to the Inventory is available for facilitating the configuration of new hosts that are added to the VirtualCenter inventory. With this box selected, any host added to VirtualCenter will automatically be reconfigured to use the license server as configured here.

Statistics

The Statistics page, shown in Figure 5.43, offers the ability to configure the collection intervals and the system resources for accumulating statistical performance data in VirtualCenter.

FIGURE 5.42
Upgrading from an evaluation of VI3 requires purchase of a license and configuration of a licensing server.

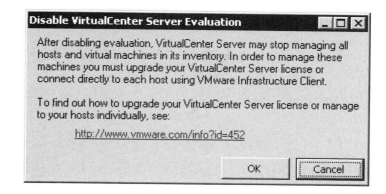

In addition it also provides a database sizing calculator that can estimate the size of a VirtualCenter database based upon the configuration of statistics intervals. By default, four collection intervals are available:

◆ Past day: 5 minutes per sample at statistics level 1

◆ Past week: 30 minutes per sample at statistics level 1

◆ Past month: 2 hour per sample at statistics level 1

◆ Past year: 1 day per sample at statistics level 1

FIGURE 5.43
Statistics collection intervals can be customized to support broad or detailed logging.

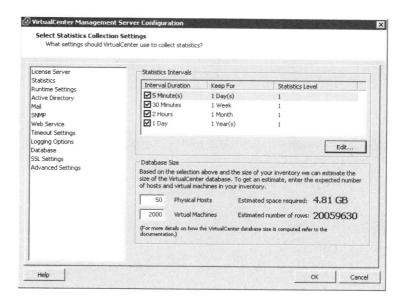

By selecting an interval from the list and clicking the Edit button you can customize the interval configuration. Figure 5.44 shows the Edit Statistics Interval page where the interval, how long to keep the sample, and the statistics level can be set.

FIGURE 5.44
Statistics collection can be customized to keep as much or as little information as needed.

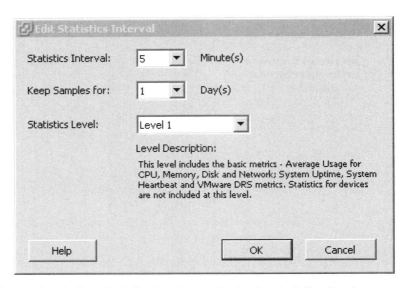

The Statistics Collection level offers the following four collection levels defined in the user interface:

Level 1 Basic metrics for average usage of CPU, Memory, Disk, and Network. Also includes data about system uptime, system heartbeat, and DRS metrics. Statistics for devices are not included.

Level 2 Includes all the average, summation, and rollup metrics for CPU, Memory, Disk, and Network. Also includes system uptime, system heartbeat, and DRS metrics. Maximum and minimum rollup types as well as statistics for devices are not included.

Level 3 Includes all metrics for all counter groups, including devices, except for minimum and maximum rollups. Maximum and minimum rollup types are not included.

Level 4 Includes all metrics supported by VirtualCenter.

DATABASE ESTIMATES

By editing the statistics collection configuration, you can see watch the estimated database size change accordingly. For example, by reducing the one day collection interval to 1 minute as opposed to 5 minutes the database size jumps from an estimated 4.81 GB to an estimated 8.93 GB. Similarly if the collection samples taken once per day are kept for 5 years instead of 1 year the database size jumps from an estimated 4.81 GB to an estimated 10.02 GB. The collection intervals and retention durations should be set to a level required by your company's audit policy.

Runtime Settings

The Runtime Settings, shown in Figure 5.45, let you configure the VirtualCenter Unique ID, the port over which VirtualCenter communicates, and the IP address used to manage VirtualCenter. The unique ID and port will be populated by default and each requires a restart of the VirtualCenter Server service. By default VirtualCenter uses port 902. These settings would normally require changing only when multiple virtual center instances exist in the same environment and conflicts might exist if not altered.

FIGURE 5.45

VirtualCenter ID, port settings, and Managed IP address can be altered from the RunTime Settings page of the VirtualCenter Management Server Configuration dialog box.

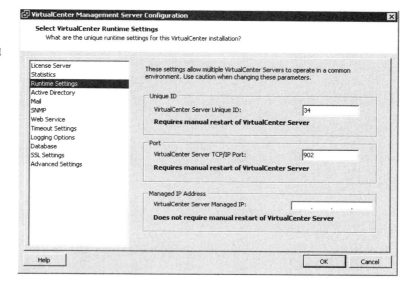

Active Directory

Figure 5.46 shows the Active Directory settings for VirtualCenter. This page includes the ability to set the Active Directory timeout value, a limit for the number of users and groups returned in a query against the Active Directory database, and the validation period (in minutes) for synchronizing users and groups used by VirtualCenter.

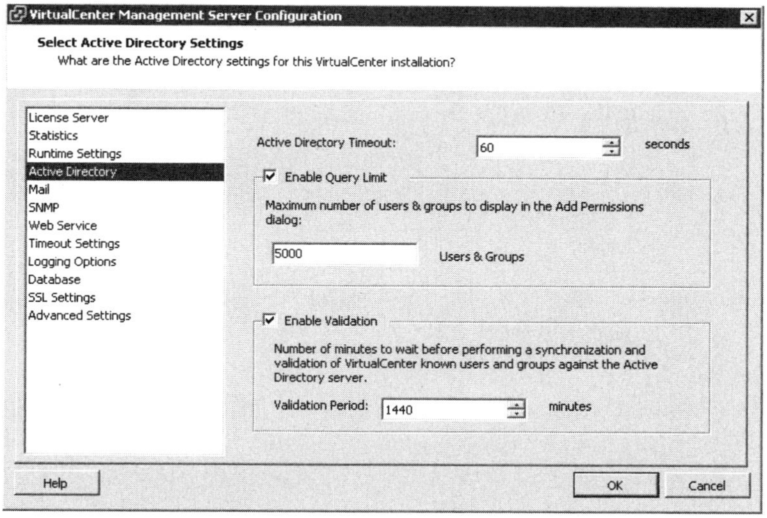

FIGURE 5.46

You can customize the communication and relationship between VirtualCenter and Active Directory for each VirtualCenter deployment.

Mail

The Mail page, shown in Figure 5.47, might be the most commonly customized page as its configuration is crucial to the sending of alarm results. The mail SMTP server name or IP address and the sender account will determine the server and the account from which alarm results will be sent.

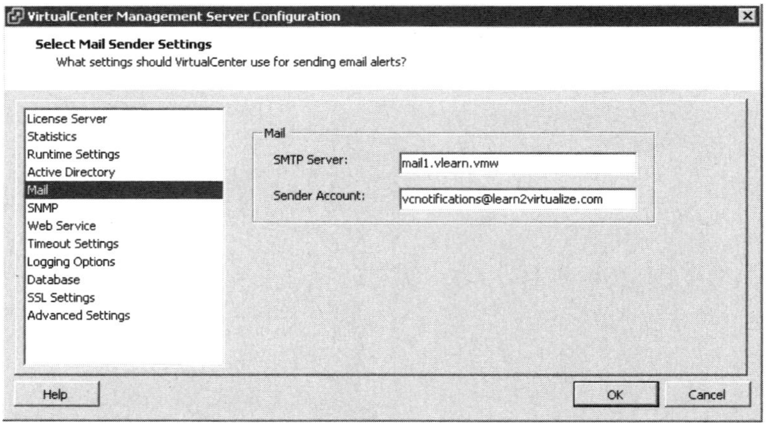

FIGURE 5.47
Mail settings in Virtual-Center are important for sending VirtualCenter alarm results.

SNMP

Figure 5.48 shows the SNMP configuration page. The receiver URL should be the name or IP address of the server with the appropriate SNMP trap receiver. The SNMP port, if not configured away from the default, should be set at 162, and the community string should be configured appropriately (public is the default).

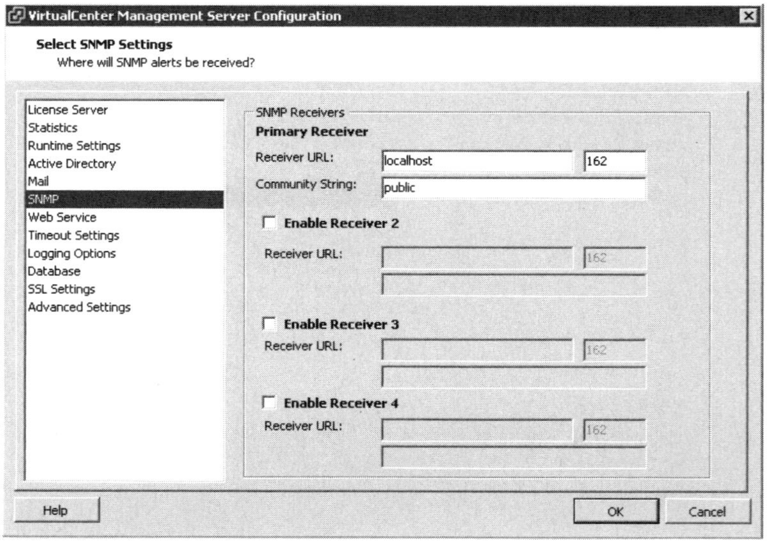

FIGURE 5.48
VirtualCenter can be configured to send SNMP traps as a result of VirtualCenter alarms.

Web Service

The Web Service page, shown in Figure 5.49, is used to configure the HTTP and HTTPS ports used by the VirtualCenter Web Access feature.

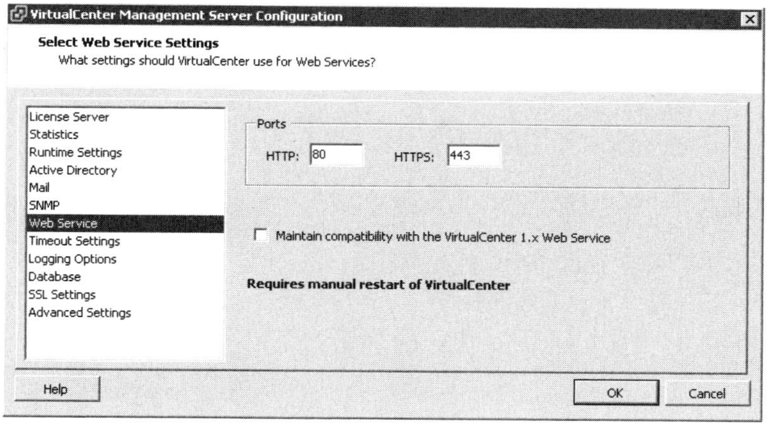

FIGURE 5.49
VirtualCenter Web Access uses default HTTP and HTTPS ports by default but you can change that.

Timeout Settings

Figure 5.50 highlights the Timeout Settings where client connection timeouts are configured. The settings by default allow for a 30-second timeout for normal operations or 120 minutes for long operations.

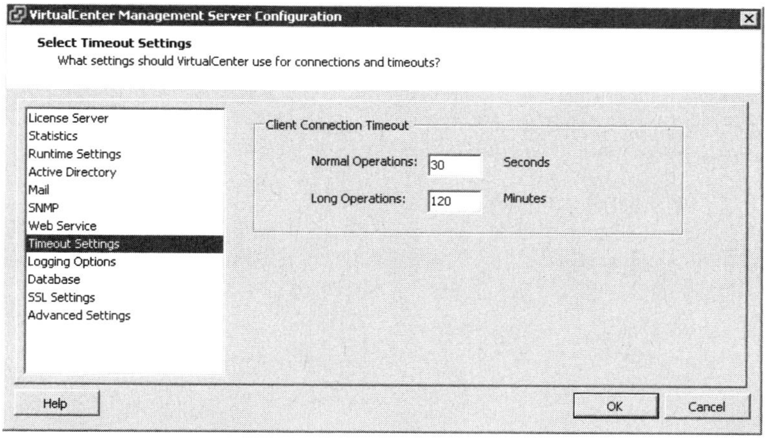

FIGURE 5.50
You can adjust Virtual-Center timeout settings in the VirtualCenter Management Server Configuration dialog box.

Logging Options

The Logging Options page, shown in Figure 5.51, customizes the level of detail accumulated in VirtualCenter logs. The logging options include:

◆ None (Disable Logging)

◆ Errors (Errors Only)

◆ Warning (Errors and Warnings)

◆ Info (Normal Logging)

◆ Verbose (Verbose)

◆ Trivia (Extended Verbose)

FIGURE 5.51
VirtualCenter offers
several options for con-
figuring the amount of
data to be stored in Vir-
tualCenter logs.

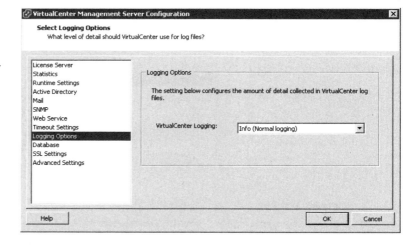

Database

The Database page, shown in Figure 5.52, lets you configure the database password and the maximum number of connections.

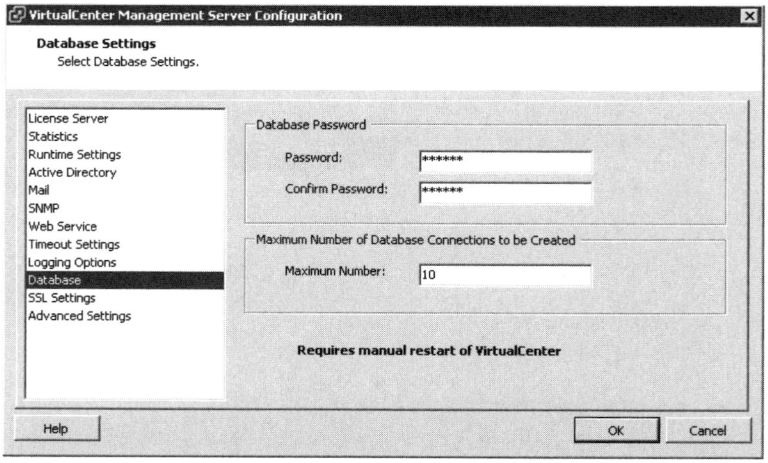

FIGURE 5.52
Database settings can
be configured through
the Database page
of the VirtualCenter
Management Server
Configuration dialog
box.

SSL Settings

Figure 5.53 shows the SSL settings configuration for VirtualCenter. This page includes the ability to configure a certificate validity check between VirtualCenter Server and the VI Client. If enabled, both systems will check the trust of the SSL certificate presented by the remote host when performing tasks like adding a host to inventory or establishing a remote console to a virtual machine.

FIGURE 5.53

VirtualCenter and the VI Client can be forced into checking the trust of an SSL certificate presented by a remote host.

Advanced Settings

The Advanced Settings page provides for an extensible configuration interface.

ROLES

The Roles option from the Administration menu is only available when the view is set to Administration and the Roles tab is selected. This menu works like a right-click context menu that offers the ability add, edit, rename, or remove roles based on what object is selected.

SESSIONS

The Sessions menu option is only available when the view is set to Administration and the Sessions tab is selected. As shown in Figure 5.54 the session tab allows for terminating all sessions and editing the text that makes up the Message of the Day (MOTD). The currently used session identified by the status "This Session" cannot be terminated.

EDIT MESSAGE OF THE DAY

As the name suggests this menu item allows for editing the Message of the Day (MOTD). The MOTD is displayed to users each time they log in to VirtualCenter. This provides an excellent means of distributing information regarding maintenance schedules or other important information.

FIGURE 5.54
The sessions tab (and menu) control the termination of sessions and the message of the day.

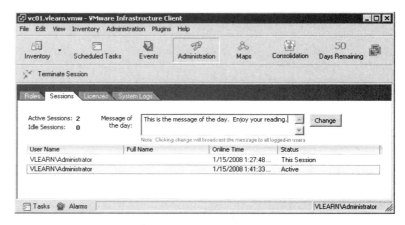

CONSOLIDATION SETTINGS

The Consolidation Settings menu item provides an interface for establishing the credentials used when using the Guided Consolidation feature of VirtualCenter. We will discuss the Guided Consolidation feature in much more detail in Chapter 7, however, as shown in Figure 5.55, the Service Credentials and Default Credential for the Guided Consolidation feature can be established here.

FIGURE 5.55
The service and default credentials for Guided Consolidation can be established using the Consolidation Settings menu item.

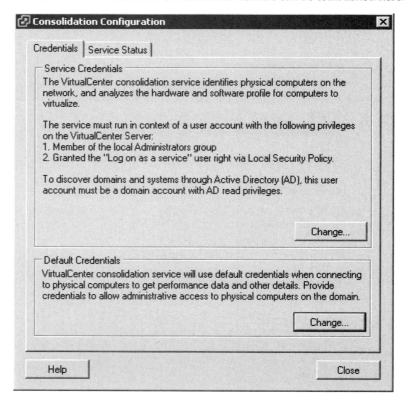

The Bottom Line

Understand the features and role of VirtualCenter.   If ESX Server 3.0 is the heart and soul of the virtual infrastructure, then VirtualCenter is the equivalent of the brain that keeps it all moving. VirtualCenter keeps the management capabilities within a defined framework and allows for controlled, detailed delegation of permissions assignment to meet a company's management needs. Access control strategies maintain the principle of least privilege, while VMotion and DRS maintain performance levels and resource fairness.

The VirtualCenter inventory will be a living entity in your virtual world; it will change regularly in response to the changing demands of the network and the consistently changing management practices of today's IT environments. There is no single way to design or implement a VirtualCenter inventory, just as there is no single design implementation that will stand the test of time. Be open to change and to utilizing the dynamic nature of VirtualCenter to allow your infrastructure to be flexible, scalable, and secure.

Install and configure a VirtualCenter database.   VirtualCenter can use Oracle, SQL Server, or MSDE as its back-end database platform. Production environments will not be supported unless running on Oracle or SQL Server, reserving MSDE for nonproduction, demonstration, or evaluation purposes.

Master It   Configure a SQL Server 2000 database to support VirtualCenter.

Master It   Configure a SQL 2005 database to support VirtualCenter.

Install and configure a VirtualCenter Server.   VirtualCenter and the VirtualCenter License Server should be installed on the same server. For web access to VirtualCenter, the Apache Tomcat service can be installed and enabled.

Use VirtualCenter topology maps.   VirtualCenter topology maps offer a graphical display of the relationships that exist between hosts, virtual machines, datastores, and networks.

Plan a VirtualCenter deployment.   The VirtualCenter application is a proxy that acts on the ESX Server hosts that are in the inventory. Ensuring availability of the VirtualCenter application requires planning the redundancy and availability of the back-end database and the application itself.

Chapter 6

Creating and Managing Virtual Machines

The ESX Servers are installed, VirtualCenter is running, the networks are blinking, the SAN is carved, and the VMFS volumes are formatted... and so the virtualization begins. With the virtual infrastructure in place, the attention and focus of the administrator shifts to the deployment of virtual machines.

In this chapter you will learn to:

- ◆ Create a virtual machine

- ◆ Install a guest operating system

- ◆ Install the VMware Tools

- ◆ Manage and modify a virtual machine

- ◆ Create templates and deploy virtual machines

Creating a Virtual Machine

Before we get too deep into the virtual machine creation and management process, we must first establish a few distinctions with regard to the terminology we will use. It is common for IT folk to commonly refer to a Windows or Linux system running on an ESX Server host as a *virtual machine*. Technically, the statement is not 100 percent accurate. I am not here to change the world, so I won't try to force a change; however, a virtual machine actually deserves a separate distinction from the guest operating system. The assembly of a set of virtual hardware that makes up the virtual machine is still a virtual machine prior to the installation of the guest operating system, just as a physical server without an operating system is still a physical machine. So, from a technical perspective, a virtual machine is a set of virtual hardware selected for the purpose of running a guest operating system. However, from a practical perspective you can go on calling the Windows or Linux system a virtual machine.

A virtual machine can consist of different virtual hardware components that utilize drivers written by VMware. These drivers are not as complex as using manufacturer-released drivers for specific hardware components. For example, the drivers for the VMware SVGA II are not as heavy or invasive as the drivers for an ATI Radeon video adapter. Figure 6.1 shows virtual hardware identified in the Device Manager of a virtual machine. Noticeably, much of the third-party device driver installation is replaced with the virtualized hardware that the ESX Server is providing.

FIGURE 6.1
The drivers for hardware in a virtual machine are much lighter than the third-party drivers found on physical computers.

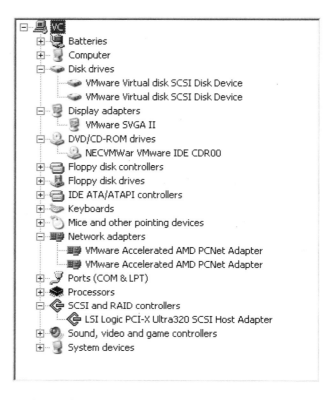

The lighter and less intrusive drivers found in a virtual machine result in an easier hardware maintenance schedule and reduced opportunity for server failures due to driver incompatibilities.

A virtual machine consists of several types of files; the two most common are the configuration file and the virtual hard disk file. The configuration file is identified by a .vmx extension and functions as the structural definition of the virtual machine. The VMX file defines the virtual hardware that resides in a virtual machine. The number of processors, the amount of RAM, the number of network adapters, associated MAC addresses, and the number, names, and locations of all virtual hard drives are stored in the configuration file.

The virtual hard disk file (identified by a .vmdk extension) holds the data stored by a virtual machine. Typically the first VMDK file is the storage location for the C drive of the virtual machine that holds the operating system. Additional virtual hard disks (VMDK files) can be added to provide additional storage locations for the virtual machine.

A virtual machine, as shown in Figure 6.2, can consist of the following virtual hardware devices:

◆ Processors — one, two, or four processors with VMware Virtual SMP

◆ Memory — Maximum of 16GB of RAM

◆ SCSI adapter — Maximum of four SCSI adapters with 15 devices per adapter

◆ Network adapter — Maximum of four network adapters

◆ Parallel port — Maximum of three parallel ports

◆ Serial port — Maximum of four serial ports

◆ CD/DVD ROM — Maximum of two CD/DVD ROM drives

◆ Floppy drive — Maximum of two floppy disk drives

◆ Keyboard, video card, and mouse

FIGURE 6.2
A virtual machine consists of virtual processors, SCSI adapters, network adapter, CD/DVD drives, memory, and more.

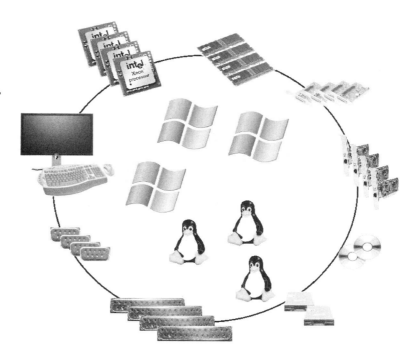

Hard drives are not listed in the virtual hardware because virtual machine hard drives are added as SCSI devices. With up to four SCSI adapters and 15 SCSI devices per adapter, it is possible to attach 60 hard drivers to a virtual machine. Keep in mind, however, that the size limit for a virtual hard drive is 2TB.

Perform the following steps to create a virtual machine:

1. Use the VI Client to connect to a VirtualCenter server or an individual ESX Server host.

2. In the inventory tree, right-click on the name of a cluster or an individual ESX Server host and select the New Virtual Machine option, as shown in Figure 6.3. Alternatively, use the File menu or the Ctrl+N keyboard shortcut to launch the wizard.

3. When the New Virtual Machine Wizard opens, select the Custom radio button, shown in Figure 6.4, and then click Next. The Custom selection lets you configure input/output (I/O) adapters during the virtual machine creation process.

4. As shown in Figure 6.5, type a name for the virtual machine in the Virtual Machine Name text box, select a location in the inventory where the virtual machine should reside, and click Next.

Real World Scenario

VIRTUAL MACHINE NAMING

The display name given to a virtual machine might seem like a trivial assignment, but you must ensure an appropriate naming strategy is in place. As a rule, the display names of virtual machines should, but don't have to, match the hostnames configured in the guest operating system being installed. For example, if the intention is to name the guest operating system host Server1, then the virtual machine display name should match with Server1. If spaces are used in the virtual display name, which is allowed, then using command-line tools to manage virtual machines becomes a bit tricky because the spaces will have to be quoted out in the command-line use. In addition, since DNS hostnames cannot include spaces, using spaces in the virtual machine name would create a disparity between the virtual machine name and the guest operating system hostname. Ultimately, this means you should avoid using spaces and special characters that are not allowed in standard DNS naming strategies to ensure similar names both inside and outside the virtual machine.

The display name assigned to a virtual machine also becomes the name of the folder in the VMFS volume where the virtual machine files will live. At the file level, the associated configuration (VMX) and virtual hard drive (VMDK) files will assume the name supplied in the display named text box during virtual machine creation.

FIGURE 6.3
You can launch the New Virtual Machine Wizard from the context menu of an ESX Server cluster or an individual ESX Server host.

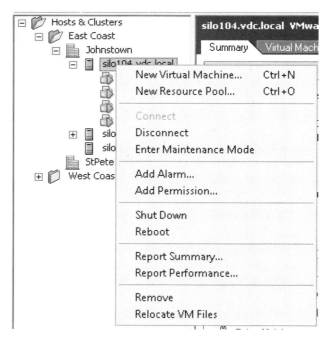

5. Select a datastore where the virtual machine files should be located, as shown in Figure 6.6, and then click Next.

FIGURE 6.4
The Custom option lets you adjust the type of I/O adapter in the virtual machine.

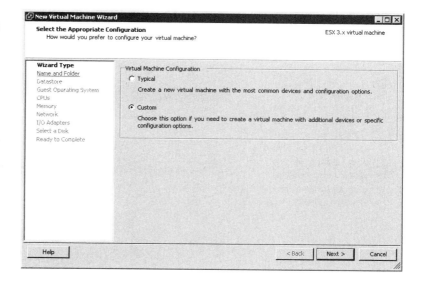

FIGURE 6.5
The name provided for the display name of the virtual machine becomes the name of the folder it resides in and the prefix for all of the corresponding virtual machine files (i.e., VMX and VMDK).

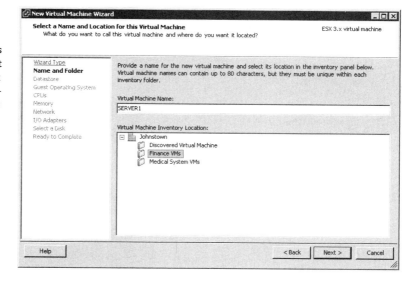

6. As shown in Figure 6.7, select the radio button that corresponds to the operating system vendor, select the correct operating system version, and then click Next.

7. As shown in Figure 6.8, select the number of virtual processors to include in the virtual machine, and then click Next.

8. Configure the virtual machine with the determined amount of RAM by adjusting the slider bar or typing the value, as shown in Figure 6.9, and then click Next.

The amount of RAM configured on this page is the amount of RAM the guest operating system reflects in its system properties. The setting on this page is not a guarantee that physical memory will be used to achieve the configured value. As discussed in later chapters, memory for a virtual machine can be physical RAM, VMkernel swap file space, or a combination of both.

FIGURE 6.6
Virtual machines can be stored in any of the datastores available to an ESX Server host as long as the space requirements meet the needs of the virtual machine.

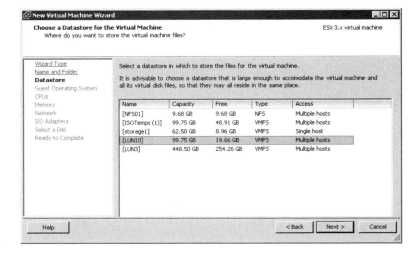

FIGURE 6.7
Selecting the appropriate operating system vendor and version ensures that the correct I/O adapter is automatically chosen for the virtual machine.

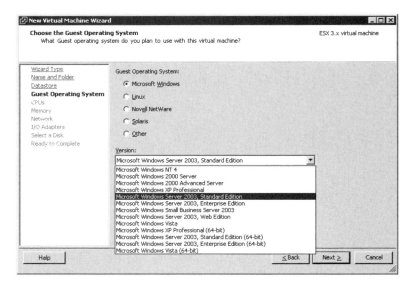

9. As shown in Figure 6.10, select the number of network adapters to include in the virtual machine, configure each NIC for the appropriate network, and then click Next.

10. Select the radio button that corresponds to the appropriate SCSI adapter for the operating system selected on the Guest Operating System page of the New Virtual Machine Wizard. The correct default driver should already be selected based on the previously selected operating system.

VIRTUAL MACHINE SCSI CONTROLLERS

Typically, Windows 2000 and Windows XP have built-in support for the BusLogic SCSI controller, while Windows Server 2003 and later operating systems have built-in support for the LSI Logic controller. Choosing the wrong controller will result in an error during the operating system installation. The error states that hard drives cannot be found. Choosing the wrong SCSI controller during a physical to virtual (P2V) operation will result in an "inaccessible boot device blue screen error" inside the virtual machine.

FIGURE 6.8
You can configure virtual machines with one, two, or four processors with VMware Virtual SMP (which is included in the VMware Standard and Enterprise editions).

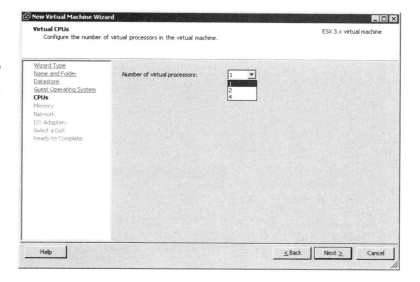

FIGURE 6.9
The RAM configured on the Memory page of the New Virtual Machine Wizard equates to the amount of RAM the guest operating system reflects when viewing the system properties.

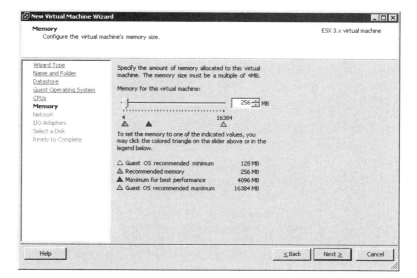

FIGURE 6.10
A virtual machine can
be configured with
up to four network
adapters that reside on
the same or different
networks as needed.

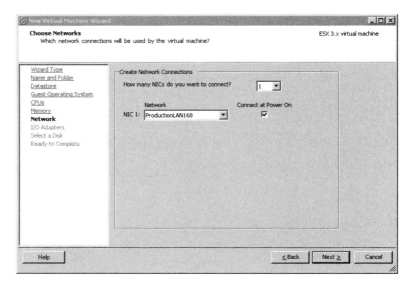

11. Select the appropriate radio button for the virtual disk to be used, as shown in Figure 6.11, and then click Next.

FIGURE 6.11
A virtual disk can be
created as new, from an
existing virtual disk,
or with access to a
raw SAN LUN.

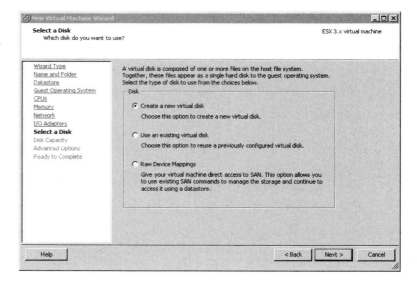

The option Use an Existing Virtual Disk allows a virtual machine to be created from a virtual disk that is already configured with an operating system and residing in an available datastore.

The option Raw Device Mappings allows a virtual machine to have raw SAN LUN access. We will discuss this in more detail later in the book.

ADDING EXISTING DISKS

The existing virtual disk doesn't have to contain an OS; it can contain data that perhaps will serve as a secondary drive inside the virtual machine. The ability to add existing disks with data makes virtual hard drives extremely portable as they can be moved from virtual machine to virtual machine without repercussions.

---

12. As shown in Figure 6.12, configure the desired disk size for the virtual machine hard drive and specify the location where the file should be stored; then click Next. The disk size configuration cannot exceed the maximum file size as defined by the format of the VMFS volume on which the file is being stored.

FIGURE 6.12
A virtual machine disk will consume the full amount of disk space by default. The size of the virtual machine's hard drive should be carefully considered.

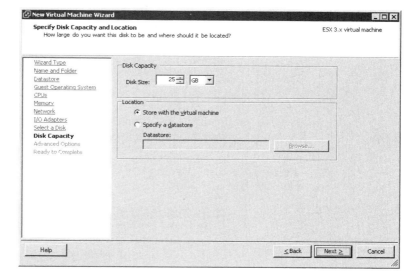

The option Store with the Virtual Machine will place the file in the same subdirectory as the configuration file and the rest of the virtual machine files. This is the most commonly selected option and makes managing the virtual machine files administratively easier.

The option Specify a Datastore allows you to store the virtual machine file separately from the rest of the files. You'd typically select this option when adding new virtual hard disks to a virtual machine and when you need to separate the operating system virtual disk from a data virtual disk.

13. As shown in Figure 6.13, the Advanced Options page lets you specify the SCSI node the virtual disk is connected to and also allows you to configure a virtual disk in Independent mode. As noted in the wizard, this page is normally not altered and can be accepted by clicking Next.

The Node drop-down list reflects the 15 different SCSI nodes available on each of the four SCSI adapters a virtual machine supports.

FIGURE 6.13
The virtual device node defines where in the virtual SCSI adapter the virtual hard disk is connected, while the virtual disk node defines the characteristics of the data storage. The Snapshots (Allowed) disk mode is the default configuration, which permanently writes to the disk and permits snapshots.

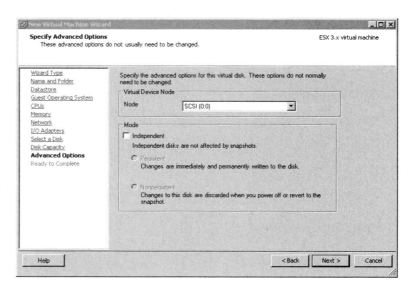

By not selecting the Independent mode option, you ensure that the virtual disk remains in the default state that allows virtual machine snapshots to be created. If you select the Independent checkbox, you can configure the virtual disk as a Persistent disk, in which changes are written immediately and permanently to the disk, or as a Nonpersistent disk, which discards all changes when the virtual machine is turned off.

14. As shown in Figure 6.14, complete a final review of the virtual machine configuration and then click Finish.

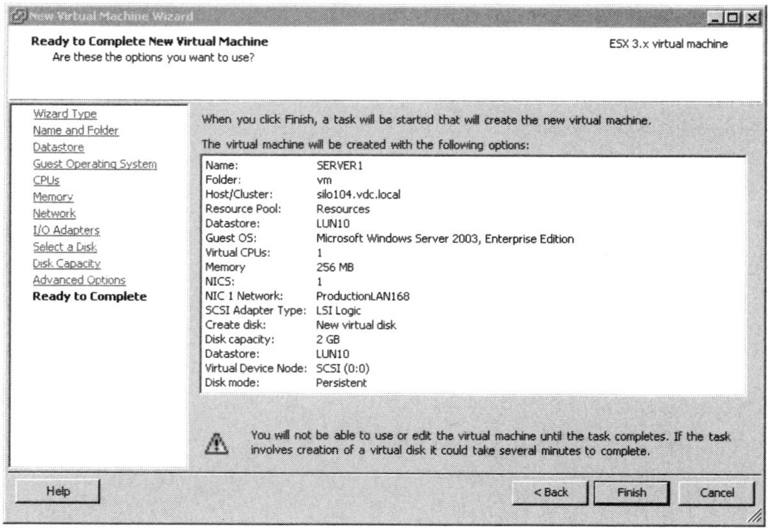

FIGURE 6.14
Reviewing the configuration of the New Virtual Machine Wizard ensures the correct settings for the virtual machine and prevents mistakes that require deleting and re-creating the virtual machine.

BUILDING SCALABLE VIRTUAL MACHINES

Although many configuration options are available for creating virtual machines, there are some best practices that facilitate the management, scalability, and backup of virtual machines. First and foremost, virtual machines should be created with multiple virtual disk files as a means of separating the operating system from the custom user data. Separating the system files and the user data will make it easier to increase the number of data drives in the future and will allow for a more practical backup strategy. A system drive of 25GB to 30GB, for example, will provide ample room for the initial installation and continued growth of the operating system. The data drives across different virtual machines will vary in size due to the installed applications, the function of the system, and the number of users who connect to the computer. However, due to the fact that the extra hard drives are not operating system data, it will be easier to make adjustments to those drives when needed.

Additional virtual hard drives will pick up on the same naming scheme as the original virtual hard drive. For example, a virtual machine named SERVER1 that has an original virtual hard disk file named SERVER1.vmdk will name the new virtual hard disk file SERVER1_1.vmdk. Each additional file will increment the last number, making it administratively easy to identify all virtual disk files related to a particular virtual machine. This image shows a virtual machine configuration with operating system hard drives and an extra hard drive added for storing user nonsystem data:

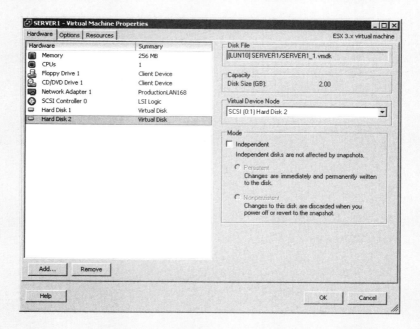

Later in this chapter, we will revisit this concept to see how templates can be used to implement and maintain an optimal virtual machine configuration that separates the system data from the user data.

Installing a Guest Operating System

A new virtual machine is analogous to a physical computer with an empty hard drive. All the components are installed but there is no operating system. Once the virtual machine has been created, a supported guest operating system can be installed. Some of the more commonly installed guest operating systems supported by ESX 3.0 include:

◆ Windows Vista

◆ Windows Server 2003 Web/Standard/Enterprise/Datacenter

◆ Windows Small Business Server 2003

◆ Windows XP

◆ Windows 2000

◆ Windows NT 4

◆ Red Hat Enterprise Linux 2.1/3.0/4.0

◆ SUSE Linux Enterprise Server 8/9/10

◆ NetWare 5.1/6.0/6.5

◆ Solaris 10 operating system for x86 platforms

Installing any of these supported guest operating systems follows the same common order of steps for installation on the physical server, but the nuances and information provided during the install of each guest operating might vary greatly.

Perform the following steps to install a guest operating system using an ISO file on a shared datastore:

1. Use the VI Client to connect to a VirtualCenter server or an individual ESX Server host where a virtual machine has been created.

2. In the inventory tree, right-click the new virtual machine and select the Edit Settings menu option. The virtual machine properties window will open.

3. Select the CD/DVD Drive 1 hardware option.

4. Select the Datastore ISO File radio button and enable the checkbox Connect At Power On.

5. Click the Browse button to browse a datastore for the ISO file of the guest operating system.

6. Navigate through the available datastore options to find the ISO file of the guest operating system to be installed. Once the ISO file is selected, the properties page will be configured similar to Figure 6.15.

7. Right-click the virtual machine and select the Open Console option. Alternatively, you can use the Console in the details pane of the VI Client application.

8. Click the green Power On button from the toolbar of the console session. Alternatively, you can click the VM menu and select the Power On option. The virtual machine will boot from the mounted CD-ROM ISO file and begin the installation of the guest operating system, as shown in Figure 6.16.

FIGURE 6.15
A CD-ROM or an ISO file must be configured for the virtual machine to install a guest operating system.

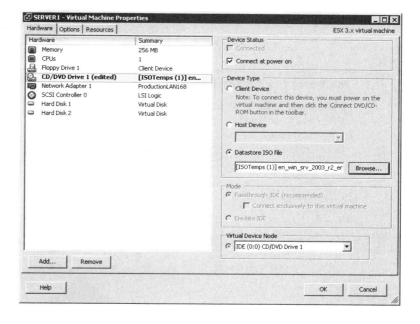

FIGURE 6.16
When the new virtual machine is turned on for the first time, it will boot from the CD-ROM to begin the installation of the guest operating system.

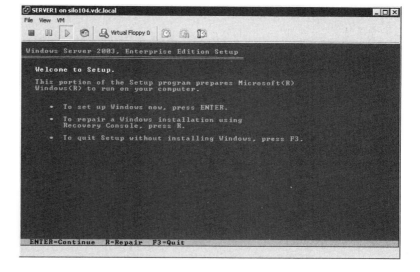

9. Follow the onscreen instructions to complete the guest operating system installation.

After installing the guest operating system, you should then install the VMware Tools. We will discuss the VMware Tools installation and configuration in the next section.

MICROSOFT LICENSING AND WINDOWS ACTIVATION FOR VIRTUAL MACHINES

In the fourth quarter of 2005 Microsoft announced a radical change in the licensing of Windows Server 2003 operating system within a virtual infrastructure. To date, there is still confusion about the virtualization licensing available for the Windows Server 2003 operating system. The following list of licensing data is a culmination of information from both Microsoft and VMware:

◆ A single licensed copy of Windows Server 2003 R2 Datacenter Edition can be use to install and run an unlimited number of virtual machines on a single physical server. The following image shows the Windows Server 2003 R2 Enterprise and Datacenter Edition licensing schemes:

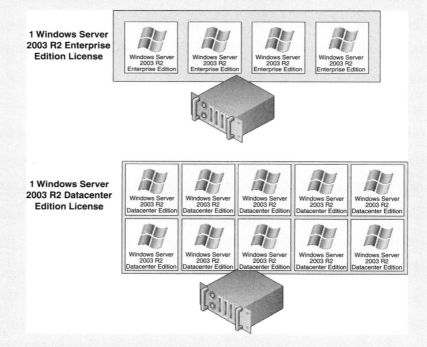

◆ Windows Server 2003 Web Edition and Windows Server 2003 Standard Edition are not affected by the new licensing terms and must be licensed on a per-virtual machine basis to maintain compliance with the Microsoft Licensing agreement.

◆ VMotion, moving a running virtual machine to a new host, does not violate a Microsoft Licensing agreement as long as the target ESX Server host is licensed for the post-VMotion number of virtual machines. For example, if an ESX Server host named SILO101 has four running virtual machines and a second ESX host named SILO102 has three running virtual machines, it is within the licensing agreement to perform a VMotion of one virtual machine from SILO101 to

SILO102. However, a VMotion from SILO102 to SILO101 would violate the licensing agreement. The next image exemplifies this scenario:

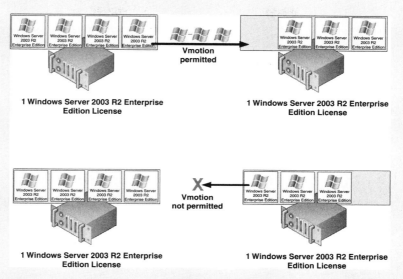

- ◆ Microsoft applications licensed on a per-processor basis must be licensed per virtual processor. For example, installing SQL Server 2005 in two virtual machines with two virtual processors requires four licenses for SQL Server 2005.

With the new licensing structure in place, using ESX Server with multicore processors and a hefty helping of RAM provides a substantial return on investment.

If your licensing structure for a Windows Server guest operating system does not fall under the umbrella of a volume licensing agreement, you will be required to activate the operating system with Microsoft within 60 days of installation. Activation can be done automatically over the Internet or by calling the provided regional phone number. With Windows Server operating systems specifically, the activation algorithm takes into account the hardware specifications of the server. In light of this, Windows must be reactivated when enough hardware changes have been made to significantly change the operating systems. To facilitate the activation process and especially to reduce the possibility of reactivation, the VMware Tools installation, memory adjustments, and processor adjustments should be made prior to performing the activation.

In addition to installing the VMware Tools, you should perform any necessary tweaks or adjustments to enhance the performance of the virtual machine. For example, in a Windows guest operating system, configuring the hardware acceleration to its maximum setting provides a much smoother console session performance.

Perform the following steps to adjust the hardware acceleration in a Windows guest operating system:

1. Right-click an empty area of the Windows desktop and select the Properties option.

2. Select the Settings tab and click the Advanced button.

3. Select the Troubleshooting tab.

4. As shown in Figure 6.17, move the Hardware Acceleration slider bar to the Full setting on the right.

FIGURE 6.17
Adjusting the hardware acceleration feature of a Windows guest operating system is a common and helpful adjustment for improving mouse performance.

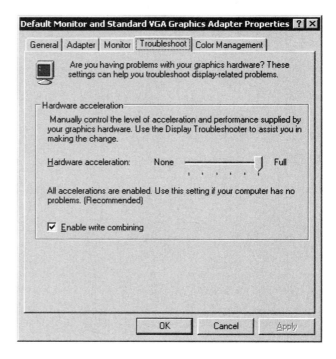

VIRTUAL MACHINE GUEST OPERATING SYSTEMS

For a complete list of guest operating systems and all respective information regarding installation notes and known issues, please refer to the PDF available from the VMware.com website at `http://www.vmware.com/pdf/GuestOS_guide.pdf`.

Installing the VMware Tools

Although the VMware Tools are not installed by default, they are an important part of a virtual machine. The VMware Tools offer several great benefits without any detriments. In other words, installing the VMware Tools should be a standard practice and not a debatable step in the deployment of a virtual machine. The VMware Tools provide for:

◆ Optimized SCSI driver

◆ Enhanced video and mouse performance

♦ Virtual machine heartbeat

♦ Virtual machine quiescing for snapshots and backups

♦ Enhanced memory management

The VMware Tools are available for both Windows and Linux guest operating systems; however, the installation methods vary due to the differences in the operating systems. In either case, after you select the option to install the VMware Tools, the guest operating system will reflect a mounted CD-ROM that has the VMware Tools install bits. The VMware Tools ISO images are located in the /vmimages directory in the root file system on the ESX. They do not have to be downloaded or obtained from the installation CD-ROM.

Follow these steps to install the VMware Tools in virtual machines with a Windows guest operating system:

1. Use the VI Client to connect to a VirtualCenter server or an individual ESX Server host.

2. Right-click the virtual machine in the inventory tree and select the Install VMware Tools option.

3. If a warning message is displayed, click OK.

4. If the VMware Tools installation process does not begin automatically, open Windows Explorer, navigate to the CD/DVD drive, and double-click the file named setup.exe.

5. Click Next on the VMware Tools installation wizard welcome page.

6. Select the appropriate setup type for the VMware Tools installation and click Next. The Typical radio button will suffice for most situations. The Complete installation option installs more features than are used by the current product, while the Custom installation option allows for the greatest level of feature customization.

7. Click Install.

8. Once the installation is complete, click Finish.

9. Click Yes to restart the virtual machine immediately or click No to manually restart the virtual machine at a later time.

Once the VMware Tools installation is complete and the virtual machine is rebooted, the system tray will display an icon of the VMware logo. The logo in the system tray, shown in Figure 6.18, indicates a successful VMware Tools installation.

By double-clicking on the VMware logo in the system tray, you open the VMware Tools Properties, shown in Figure 6.19. Here you can configure time synchronization, hide the VMware Tools from the taskbar, and create scripts to suspend, resume, shut down or turn on a virtual machine.

Use caution when enabling time synchronization between the guest operating system and the console operating system host since Windows domain members rely on Kerberos for authentication and Kerberos is very sensitive to time differences between computers. A Windows-based guest operating system that belongs to an Active Directory domain is already configured with a native time synchronization process against the domain controller of its domain that functions as the PDC Emulator operations master. If the Service Console time is different from the PDC Emulator operations master domain controller, the guest operating system could end up moving outside the five-minute window that Kerberos will allow. Once the five-minute window is exceeded, Kerberos begins to experience errors with authentication and replication.

FIGURE 6.18
Once the VMware Tools are installed on a Windows-based virtual machine, an icon of the VMware logo will be displayed in the system tray.

FIGURE 6.19
Use the VMware Tools to configure time synchronization with the Service Console.

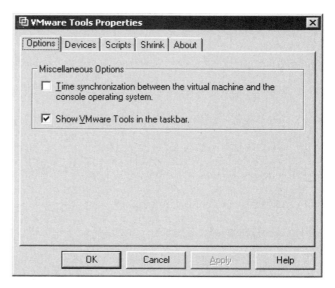

There are a few different approaches you can take to manage time synchronizations in a virtual environment. The first approach involves not using the VMware Tools time synchronization and relying instead on the W32Time service and a PDC Emulator with a registry edit that configures a synchronization with an external time server. Another approach involves disabling the native time synchronization across the Windows domain and then relying on the VMware Tools feature.

A third approach might be to synchronize the ESX Server hosts and the PDC Emulator operations master with the same external time server and then to enable the VMware Tools option for synchronization. In this case both the native W32Time service and the VMware Tools should be adjusting the time to the same value.

CONFIGURING NTP ON ESX SERVER

By tweaking the Service Console firewall and editing a few files, you can configure an ESX Server to consistently synchronize with an external time server. Perform the following steps to synchronize an ESX host with a set of external time servers:

1. From a console with root permission, enter the following command to open the required ports for allowing the NTP daemon to communicate with an external time server:

   ```
   # esxcfg-firewall --enableService ntpClient
   ```

   or

   ```
   # esxcfg-firewall -e ntpClient
   ```

   where **-e** is shorthand for –enableService).

2. Once the firewall port has been opened, you must edit the /etc/ntp.conf file to include the address or addresses of the external time server(s). Edit ntp.conf to include the following uncommented lines:

   ```
   Restrict 127.0.0.1
   Restrict default kod nomodify notrap
   server name.of.time.server.1
   server name.of.time.server.2
   driftfile /var/lib/ntp/drift
   ```

3. Edit the /etc/ntp/step-kickers file to include all of the names of the time servers that were configured in the ntp.conf file.

4. Edit the /etc/hosts file to define name to IP addresses for the time servers. If an existing DNS server is capable of providing the name resolution, the last step does not have to be performed.

INSTALL THE RPM, NOT THE ZIP, THEN, RUN the perl script

Use the following steps to install the VMware Tools on a Linux host:

1. Use the VI Client to connect to a VirtualCenter or an individual ESX Server host.

2. Right-click the virtual machine in the inventory tree and select the Install VMware Tools option.

3. If a warning message is displayed, click OK.

4. Open a terminal window and change directories to the location of the VMware Tools mount point using the following commands:

   ```
   [root@rhel5-1 /]# cd /media/"VMware Tools"
   ```

5. Copy the `gzip` tar file to a temporary directory and then change to the temporary directory using the following commands:

```
[root@rhel5-1 VMware Tools]# cp VMwareTools-3.0.x- nnnn.tar.gz /tmp
[root@silo104 VMware Tools]# cd /tmp
```

6. Extract the contents of the tar file. By default, the file will extract to a directory named `vmware-tools-distrib`. *tar -xzf VMwareTools* *

7. Change to the `vmware-tools-distrib` directory and run the `vmware-install.pl` Perl script using the following commands:

```
[root@rhel5-1 tmp]#cd vmware-tools-distrib
[root@rhel5-1 vmware-tools-distrib]# ./vmware-install.pl
```

Figure 6.20 shows the commands for steps 4 through 7.

FIGURE 6.20
Installing the VMware Tools for Linux from the command line involves extracting the tools and running the install file.

```
[root@rhel5-1 /]# cd /media/"VMware Tools"
[root@rhel5-1 VMware Tools]# ls
VMwareTools-3.0.1-32039.i386.rpm  VMwareTools-3.0.1-32039.tar.gz
[root@rhel5-1 VMware Tools]# cp VMwareTools-3.0.1-32039.tar.gz /tmp
cp: overwrite `/tmp/VMwareTools-3.0.1-32039.tar.gz'? y
[root@rhel5-1 VMware Tools]# cd /tmp
[root@rhel5-1 tmp]# cd vmware-tools-distrib/
[root@rhel5-1 vmware-tools-distrib]# ./vmware-install.pl
```

/usr/bin/vmware-config-tools.pl
This is your
-networking
-BUI interface
-VI interaction
(copy/pasting etc)

8. After the Perl script completes, restart the X session using `startx`.

9. Start the VMware Tools running in the background of an X server session using the following command:

```
[root@silo104~]# /usr/bin/vmware-toolbox &
```

10. Remove the tar file copy and the extracted directory using these commands:

```
[root@silo104~]# rm /tmp/VMwareTools-3.0.x-nnnn.tar.gz
[root@silo104~]# rm -rf /tmp/vmware-tools-distrib
```

VMWARE TOOLS FOR LINUX

When installing the VMware Tools to a Linux guest operating system, the path to the tar file and the numbers in the tar filename will vary.

You can determine the existence of VMware Tools by checking for the icon displayed on the notification bar inside the guest operating system or by using the VI client. As shown in Figure 6.21, the Summary tab of a virtual machine object identifies the status of the VMware Tools as well as other information such as operating system, CPU, memory, DNS (host) name, IP address, and current host.

FIGURE 6.21
You can view details about VMware Tools, DNS name, IP address, and so forth from the Summary tab of a virtual machine object.

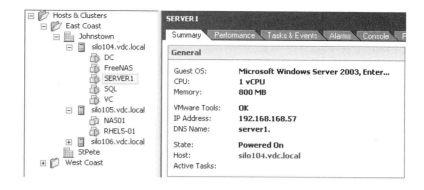

Managing and Modifying Virtual Machines

Just as physical machines require upgrading of hardware, a virtual machine may require scaling up on hardware due to performance demands. Perhaps a new memory-intensive client-server application requires an increase in memory, or a new data-mining application requires a second processor or additional network adapters for a bandwidth-heavy FTP site. In each of these cases, the virtual machine requires a modification of the virtual hardware configured for the guest operating system to use.

Modifying a virtual machine requires that the virtual machine exist in a powered-off state for all hardware — except when adding a new hard drive. You can add a new hard drive to a virtual machine with the machine turned off or on. This is a "hot add" process only because a hard disk cannot be removed while the virtual machine continues to run. CD and DVD-ROMs can be mounted and unmounted while a virtual machine is turned on, but new CD/DVD-ROM devices cannot be added. Floppy disk images can be mounted or unmounted while a virtual machine is turned on, but new floppy devices cannot be added. You can assign and reassign adapters to virtual networks while a virtual machine is running, but new adapters cannot be added. Figure 6.22 shows the CD/DVD mapping and the Add Hardware Wizard for a virtual machine. Note how the CD/DVD-ROM can be associated with a new ISO on a datastore; however, adding hardware to a running virtual machine is limited to adding virtual hard drives.

As administrators, we are consistently working with virtual machines, but on occasion we have to work directly with the files that make up the virtual machine. By browsing a datastore, as shown in Figure 6.23, or using an SSH session, you'll find there are many files that relate to a working virtual machine.

Most often, when dealing directly with virtual machine files, we deal with either the VMX configuration file or the VMDK virtual hard disk file. The VMX file identifies the configuration of the virtual machine with respect to the virtual hardware allocated to the virtual machine. Figure 6.24 shows a sample VMX file for a virtual machine named vdcSQL. Reading through the vdcSQL.vmx file, you will notice that the virtual machine uses the following configuration:

◆ A virtual machine named vdcSQL that runs Windows Server 2003 Standard Edition

◆ RAM: 1564 MB

◆ A single hard drive located at vdcSQL-000001.vmdk

◆ A single CD-ROM that starts connected but not mounted to an image

◆ A floppy drive that does not start connected

◆ A single network adapter configured on the ProductionLAN168 virtual switch and a MAC address of 00:0 C:29:9b:1e:b2

FIGURE 6.22
A new hard disk is the only hardware that can be added to a running virtual machine. CD/DVD-ROMs, floppy drives, and network adapters can be edited but not added.

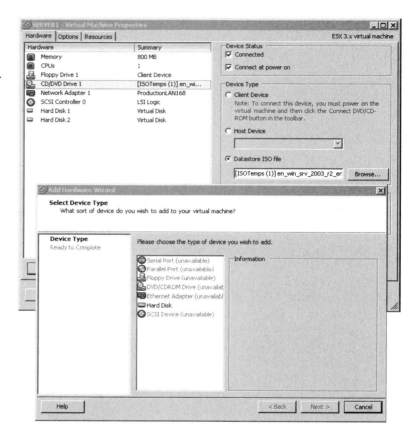

FIGURE 6.23
A virtual machine consists of many files that can be viewed by browsing a datastore using the VI Client.

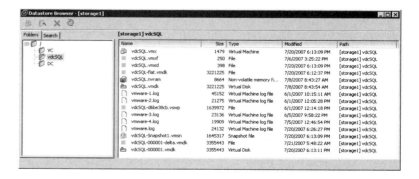

While the VMDK file is not human readable, it is arguably the most important file for a virtual machine. You can rebuild a VMX configuration file quite easily, but a VMDK is the data behind the virtual hard drive and is not as easy to rebuild. If you revisit Figure 6.23 and review the files that reside in the folder of a virtual machine's associated files, you will notice the existence of a file that ends with -flat.vmdk. The -flat.vmdk file for a virtual machine is where the actual virtual machine data is stored.

FIGURE 6.24
A virtual machine's configuration file (VMX) details the virtual hardware available for use by the guest operating system.

Although the -flat.vmdk and the VMDK are the same size, they do not actually both consume the full amount of disk space that is listed. Take, for example, the virtual machine vdcSQL. The virtual machine is configured with a 30GB hard drive. If both the VMDK and the `-flat.vmdk` files were holding 30GB of data, the total between the two would be 60GB. However, in looking at the total storage capacity and the free space of the datastore where vdcSQL resides, as shown in Figure 6.25, you will notice that the total capacity for the datastore is 62GB and that 7.83GB still remains. Figure 6.26 shows the contents of the storage1 datastore, which identifies the existence of two other virtual machines and a handful of ISO files on the datastore. The file size calculation of the vdcSQL virtual machine, coupled with a look at all of the other data in the datastore, clearly shows that both the VMDK and the `-flat.vmdk` do not store the full capacity of the space allocated to the virtual machine.

FIGURE 6.25

The total size of the datastore is 62.5GB with 7.38GB of free space remaining.

FIGURE 6.26

The storage1 datastore houses three virtual machines and several ISO images. The existence of free space on the storage1 datastore indicates that the `-flat.vmdk` and VMDK files are not each consuming the total space of the virtual hard drive.

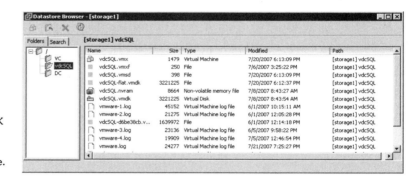

ESX 3.0 introduces a new snapshot feature that's found in the VMware Workstation product. Snapshots provide administrators with the ability to create point-in-time snapshots of a virtual machine. In addition, snapshots are used heavily by the VMware Consolidated Backup product. A snapshot is not a full copy of a virtual machine. VMware's snapshot technology allows for minimal space consumption while still reverting to a previous snapshot.

VMDK FILE SIZE IDENTIFICATION

The VMDK file size is misleading if viewed from the VI Client. Consider the virtual machine with a 30GB hard drive. Using the VI Client, it looks as if the virtual machine hard disk file consumes the exact amount that it was configured as. As noted, this is not the case. If you look at the VMDK file using an SSH client connection to the Service Console, the VMDK file is a few bytes in size, which is a more accurate reflection. However, the `-flat.vmdk` file is 30GB.

ALIGNING VIRTUAL MACHINE FILE SYSTEMS

In Chapter 4 I introduced the concept of aligning the VMFS file system, and I also suggested the virtual machine's file system should be aligned as well. If you construct virtual machines with separate virtual hard drives for operating system and data, then you are most concerned with the alignment of the file system for the data drive because the greatest amount of I/O will occur on that drive. For example, a virtual machine with Disk 0 (that holds the operating system) and a blank disk, Disk 1 (that holds data that will incur significant I/O), should have Disk 1 aligned.

Perform the following steps to align Disk 1 of the virtual machine:

1. Log in to the virtual machine using an account with administrative credentials.

2. Open a command prompt and type **Diskpart**.

3. Type **list disk** and press Enter.

4. Type **select disk 1** and press Enter.

5. Type **create partition primary align = 64** and press Enter.

6. Type **assign letter = X**, where *X* is an open letter that can be assigned.

7. Type **list part** to verify the 64 KB offset for the new partition.

8. Format the partition.

Perhaps you are thinking that this seems like a tedious task to perform for all your virtual machines. It *is* a tedious task; however, the benefit of doing this is realized most when there is a significant I/O requirement. Also keep in mind that you could also perform this task in the template that is used to provision new virtual machines.

Figure 6.27 shows the details of a folder named SERVER1 that holds virtual machine files and resides on a datastore named LUN10. LUN10, at this point shows a 99.75GB capacity with 14.88GB of free space.

FIGURE 6.27
A datastore with all the virtual machine files that exist as a default.

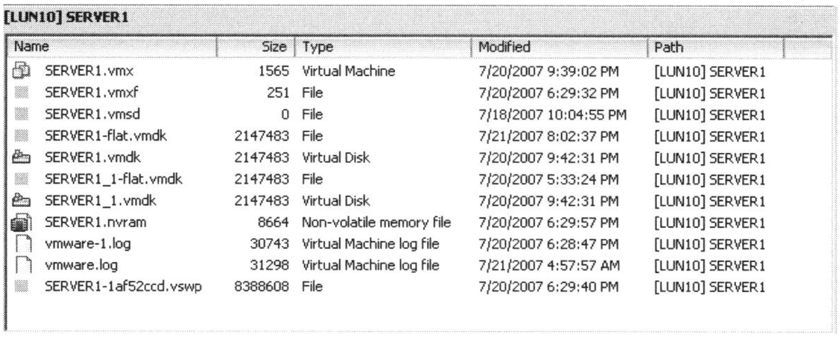

[LUN10] SERVER1				
Name	Size	Type	Modified	Path
SERVER1.vmx	1565	Virtual Machine	7/20/2007 9:39:02 PM	[LUN10] SERVER1
SERVER1.vmxf	251	File	7/20/2007 6:29:32 PM	[LUN10] SERVER1
SERVER1.vmsd	0	File	7/18/2007 10:04:55 PM	[LUN10] SERVER1
SERVER1-flat.vmdk	2147483	File	7/21/2007 8:02:37 PM	[LUN10] SERVER1
SERVER1.vmdk	2147483	Virtual Disk	7/20/2007 9:42:31 PM	[LUN10] SERVER1
SERVER1_1-flat.vmdk	2147483	File	7/20/2007 5:33:24 PM	[LUN10] SERVER1
SERVER1_1.vmdk	2147483	Virtual Disk	7/20/2007 9:42:31 PM	[LUN10] SERVER1
SERVER1.nvram	8664	Non-volatile memory file	7/20/2007 6:29:57 PM	[LUN10] SERVER1
vmware-1.log	30743	Virtual Machine log file	7/20/2007 6:28:47 PM	[LUN10] SERVER1
vmware.log	31298	Virtual Machine log file	7/21/2007 4:57:57 AM	[LUN10] SERVER1
SERVER1-1af52ccd.vswp	8388608	File	7/20/2007 6:29:40 PM	[LUN10] SERVER1

Perform the following steps to create a snapshot of a virtual machine:

1. Use the VI Client to connect to a VirtualCenter or an individual ESX Server host.

2. Right-click on the virtual machine name in the inventory tree, select Snapshot, and then select Take Snapshot.

3. As shown in Figure 6.28 provide a name and description for the snapshot and then click OK.

FIGURE 6.28
Providing names and descriptions for snapshots is an easy way to manage multiple historical snapshots.

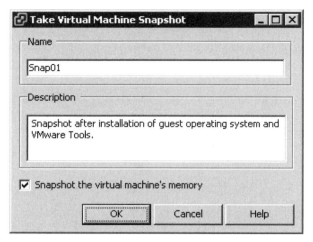

It is a common misconception for administrators to think of snapshots as full copies of virtual machine files. SERVER1 is a new virtual machine that runs Windows Server 2003 Enterprise Edition with the VMware Tools installed. The virtual hard drives have been created as a rather small 2GB hard drive for the operating system and a 2GB hard drive for data. For the purposes of explaining the snapshot technology, these smaller drives will suffice. SERVER1 is configured as follows:

◆ The C: drive maps to the SERVER1.vmdk file with a corresponding SERVER1-flat.vmdk file.

◆ The E: drive maps to the SERVER1_1.vmdk file with a corresponding SERVER1_1-flat.vmdk file.

To demonstrate snapshot technology, I took the following steps:

1. I created the virtual machine with a default installation of Windows Server 2003 with two hard drives (C and E) as outlined earlier.

2. I took a snapshot named SNAP1.

3. I added approximately 500 MB of data to drive E (SERVER1_1.vmdk).

4. I took a second snapshot named SNAP2.

5. I once again added approximately 500 MB of data to drive E (SERVER1_1.vmdk).

Review Table 6.1 for the results I recorded after each step.

Despite the storage efficiency that snapshots attempt to maintain, they can over time eat up a considerable amount of disk space. Therefore, you should use them as needed but also remove older snapshots on a regular basis. There are performance ramifications to using snapshots. Virtual machines will perform more slowly and LUNs will become locked each time the snapshot grows. Snapshot files grow in 16 MB increments to minimize the LUN locking that the ESX Server host performs to update the metadata files (.sf files) in order to prevent corruption by other ESX Server hosts (which see a change to the LUN and could want to update the metadata files at the same time).

TABLE 6.1: Snapshot Demonstration Results

POST STEP1	VMFS SIZE	NTFS SIZE	NTFS FREE SPACE
SERVER1.vmdk	2GB	1.99GB	855 MB
SERVER1-flat.vmdk	2GB	–	–
SERVER1_1.vmdk	2GB	1.99GB	1.97GB
SERVER1_1-flat.vmdk	2GB	–	–
Post Step 2 (SNAP1)			
SERVER1.vmdk	2GB	1.99GB	855 MB
SERVER1-flat.vmdk	2GB	–	–
SERVER1_1.vmdk	2GB	1.99GB	1.97GB
SERVER1_1-flat.vmdk	2GB	–	–
Created by SNAP1 — SERVER1-Snapshot1.vmsn	805 MB	–	–
SERVER1-000001.vmdk	16 MB	–	–
SERVER1-000001-delta.vmdk	16 MB	–	–
SERVER1_1-000001.vmdk	16 MB	–	–
SERVER1_1-000001-delta.vmdk	16 MB	–	–
Post Step 3 (Add 500 MB to Drive E)			
SERVER1.vmdk	2GB	1.99GB	855
SERVER1-flat.vmdk	2GB	–	–
SERVER1_1.vmdk	2GB	1.99GB	**1.5GB***
SERVER1_1-flat.vmdk	2GB	–	–
SERVER1-Snapshot1.vmsn	800 MB	–	–
SERVER1-000001.vmdk	16 MB	–	–
SERVER1-000001-delta.vmdk	16 MB	–	–
SERVER1_1-000001.vmdk	**512 MB***	–	–
SERVER1_1-000001-delta.vmdk	**512 MB***	–	–

(CONTINUED)

TABLE 6.1: Snapshot Demonstration Results *(CONTINUED)*

POST STEP1	VMFS SIZE	NTFS SIZE	NTFS FREE SPACE
Post Step 4 (Snap 2)			
SERVER1.vmdk	2GB	1.99GB	855 MB
SERVER1-flat.vmdk	2GB	–	–
SERVER1_1.vmdk	2GB	1.99GB	1.5GB
SERVER1_1-flat.vmdk	2GB	–	–
SERVER1-Snapshot1.vmsn	800 MB	–	–
SERVER1-000001.vmdk	16 MB	–	–
SERVER1-000001-delta.vmdk	16 MB	–	–
SERVER1_1-000001.vmdk	512 MB	–	–
SERVER1_1-000001-delta.vmdk	512 MB	–	–
Created by SNAP2 SERVER1-Snapshot2.vmsn	800 MB	–	–
SERVER1-000002.vmdk	16 MB	–	–
SERVER1-000002-delta.vmdk	16 MB	–	–
SERVER1_1-000002.vmdk	16 MB	–	–
SERVER1_1-000002-delta.vmdk	16 MB	–	–
Post Step 5 (Add Another 500 MB to Drive E)			
SERVER1.vmdk	2GB	1.99GB	855 MB
SERVER1-flat.vmdk	2GB	–	–
SERVER1_1.vmdk	2GB	1.99GB	**1.02***
SERVER1_1-flat.vmdk	2GB	–	–
SERVER1-Snapshot1.vmsn	800 MB	–	–
SERVER1-000001.vmdk	16 MB	–	–
SERVER1-000001-delta.vmdk	16 MB	–	–

TABLE 6.1:   Snapshot Demonstration Results *(CONTINUED)*

POST STEP1	VMFS SIZE	NTFS SIZE	NTFS FREE SPACE
SERVER1_1-000001.vmdk	512 MB	–	–
SERVER1_1-000001-delta.vmdk	512 MB	–	–
SERVER1-Snapshot2.vmsn	800 MB	–	–
SERVER1-000002.vmdk	16 MB	–	–
SERVER1-000002-delta.vmdk	16 MB	–	–
SERVER1_1-000002.vmdk	**496 MB***	–	–
SERVER1_1-000002-delta.vmdk	**496 MB***	–	–

Snapshots are an excellent addition to the feature set of ESX 3.0. You'll find snapshots helpful when making risky changes to production servers (such as renaming the domain or installing service packs). You use the Snapshot Manager to view and delete snapshots or revert to an earlier snapshot.

Perform the following steps to access the Snapshot Manager:

1. Use the VI Client to connect to a VirtualCenter or an individual ESX Server host.

2. In the inventory tree, right-click on the name of the virtual machine to restore a snapshot.

3. Select Snapshot and then click Snapshot Manager.

4. Select the appropriate snapshot to fall back to and then click the Go To button, as shown in Figure 6.29.

REVERTING TO A SNAPSHOT

Reverting back to a snapshot incurs a loss of data. Any data that was written since the snapshot has occurred will no longer be available, along with any applications that were installed since the snapshot was taken. Therefore, revert to snapshots only if you have determined that the loss of data is acceptable.

Creating Templates and Deploying Virtual Machines

If you've ever wished there were a faster way to provision a new server into your environment, then VMware fulfills that wish in a big way. In a VI3 environment, what would traditionally take several hours to do is now reduced to a matter of minutes. With the templates feature of VirtualCenter, you can roll out new virtual machines quickly and easily with limited administrative effort.

FIGURE 6.29
The Snapshot Manager can revert to original virtual machines, but all data written between now and the last backup will be lost.

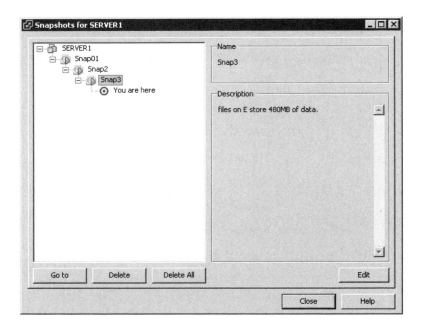

VirtualCenter offers two different options for creating templates: Clone to Template and Convert to Template. As the name suggests, the Clone to Template feature copies a virtual machine to a template format, leaving the original virtual machine intact. Similarly, the Convert to Template feature involves a virtual machine that is changed to a template format, thereby removing the ability to turn on the virtual machine without converting back to a virtual machine format.

Virtual machines that become templates should not be critical servers for production environments. The idea behind a template is to have a pristine system configuration that can be customized as needed for deployment to the target environment. Any information stored on a virtual machine that becomes a template will become part of the new system that is deployed from that template. Thus, if a template is updated, all of the virtual machines previously deployed from that template do not experience the same update.

You can convert a virtual machine to a template using the right-click menu of the virtual machine or the Convert to Template link in the Commands list. Figure 6.30 shows two ways an existing virtual machine can be converted into a template format. To make updates to a template, you must first convert the template back to a virtual machine, then update it, and finally convert it back to a template.

The Clone to Template feature provides the same end result as the conversion method in creating a template that can be deployed as a new virtual machine, but it differs from the conversion method in that the virtual machine remains intact. By leaving the virtual machine in a format that can be turned on, the Clone to Template feature facilitates making updates to the template. This means you don't have to store the template object definition in the same datastore from which the virtual machine was built.

Follow these steps to clone a virtual machine into a template format:

1. Use the VI Client to connect to a VirtualCenter server or an individual ESX Server host.

2. Right-click the virtual machine to be used as a template and select the Clone to Template option.

3. Type a name for the new template in the Template Name text box, select a location in the inventory to store the template, and then click Next, as shown in Figure 6.31.

4. Select the host or cluster where the template should be hosted and click Next.

5. Select the datastore where the template should be stored and click Next.

6. Select the disk format for the template, shown in Figure 6.32, and click Next.
   The Normal template disk format allows for quicker conversion back into a running virtual machine.
   The Compact template disk format creates a more compact template, which is a benefit when portability is a key requirement.

7. Review the template configuration information and click Finish.

FIGURE 6.30
A virtual machine can be converted to a template.

A completed template is signified by a different icon than the one used to identify a virtual machine in the VirtualCenter inventory. The template objects are available by clicking on a datacenter object and then selecting the Virtual Machines tab, or by adjusting the inventory view to the Virtual Machines & Templates view.

Once you've created a library of templates, provisioning a new virtual machine is as simple as right-clicking on the template required as the system image baseline. For virtual machines running Windows as the guest operating system, VMware has included a component within the template processes that eliminates the need for administrators to perform tasks that force uniqueness on the virtual machine upon which the template is created. The catch is that the component must extract sysprep and its associated files to a directory on the VirtualCenter server that was created during the installation. If these files are not extracted before you deploy a virtual machine, the guest customization page of the Deploy Template Wizard will be unavailable. Figure 6.33 shows the Guest Customization page of the Deploy Template Wizard on a VirtualCenter that has not had the sysprep files extracted.

FIGURE 6.31
Templates should have meaningful names that describe the pristine environment provided by the template.

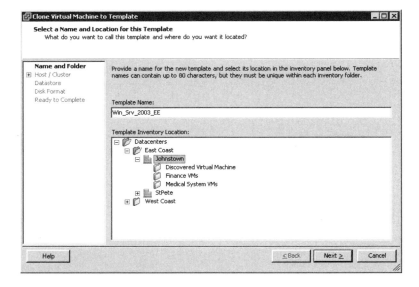

FIGURE 6.32
Templates can be stored in a format that supports quicker provisioning or that provides greater portability.

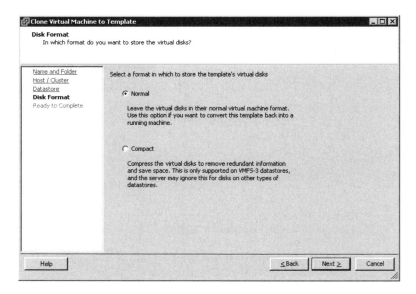

Perform these steps to allow guest operating system customization of Windows guest operating system templates:

1. Insert the Windows Server 2003 CD into the disk drive of the VirtualCenter server.

2. Navigate to the ../support/tools/deploy.cab directory on the Windows Server 2003 CD.

FIGURE 6.33
If the `sysprep` files are not extracted and stored on the VirtualCenter server, you won't be able to customize the guest operating system when you deploy from a template.

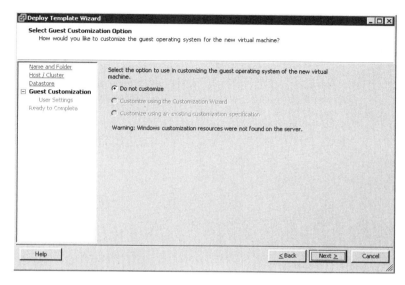

3. Copy the `sysprep.exe` and `setupcl.exe` files to this directory:

```
C:\Documents and Settings\All Users\Application
    Data\VMware\VMware Virtual Center\svr2003
```

As shown in Figure 6.34.

FIGURE 6.34
Customizing the Windows guest operating system requires the extraction of the `sysprep.exe` and `setupcl.exe` files to an existing directory on the VirtualCenter server.

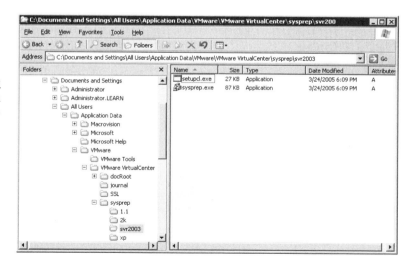

Follow these steps to deploy a virtual machine from a template:

1. Use the VI Client to connect to a VirtualCenter server.

2. Locate the template object to be used as the virtual machine baseline.

3. Right-click the template object and select Deploy Virtual Machine from This Template.

4. As shown in Figure 6.35, type a name for the new virtual machine in the Virtual Machine Name text box, select a location in the inventory to store the virtual machine, and then click Next. Click the Advanced button if you want to specify an alternate storage location for virtual machine disk files.

FIGURE 6.35
The virtual machine's display name is the friendly name reflected in the VirtualCenter inventory and should match the guest operating system's hostname.

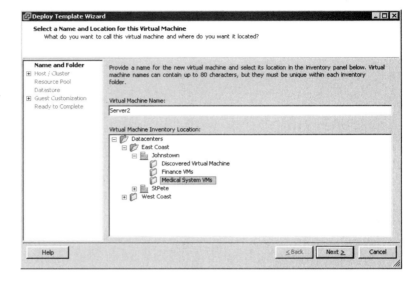

5. Select a host on which the virtual machine should run and then click Next.

6. Select a datastore location for the virtual machine files, as shown in Figure 6.36.

FIGURE 6.36
Select a datastore for a new virtual machine based on the VMotion, DRS, and HA constraints of your organization.

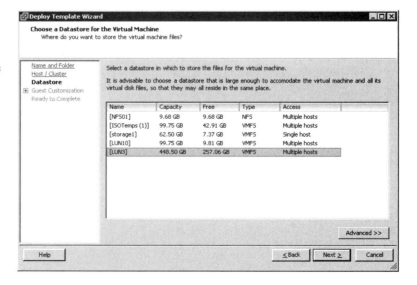

7. For first-time template deployments, as shown in Figure 6.37, select the Customize Using the Customization Wizard option to create a new XML-based answer file, and then click Next.

FIGURE 6.37
The Guest Customization Wizard allows you to create an answer file that provides zero-touch installs of a guest operating system. The answer file data is stored in the Virtual-Center database.

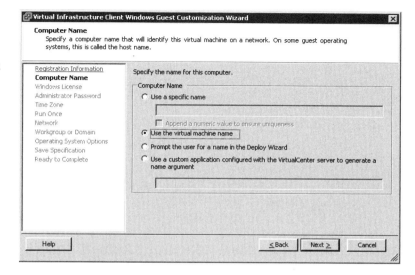

8. Provide a name and organization to be used for virtual machines built from the customization file.

9. For simplicity and consistency, as shown in Figure 6.37, select the Use the Virtual Machine Name option to specify that the guest operating system hostname be the same as the display name, and then click Next.

10. Enter a valid Windows product key, configure the licensing mode, and click Next.

11. Enter an administrator password and click Next.

12. Enter the appropriate time zone for the new virtual machine and click Next.

13. Enter any commands that should run one time at the end of setup and click Next.

14. Configure the Network Interface Settings for DHCP obtained addressing (Typical) or static addressing (Custom) and then click Next.

15. Specify the workgroup or domain membership of the new guest operating system and click Next.

16. For mass virtual machine deployments, ensure that the Generate New Security ID (SID) checkbox is selected. Select the Delete All User Accounts checkbox as needed to clear the local security accounts manager (SAM) of the new guest operating system to allow for a change to the administrator password. Click Next.

17. As shown in Figure 6.38, ensure the Save This Customization Specification for Later Use checkbox is selected, provide a name for the customization file, enter a description as needed, and then click Next.

FIGURE 6.38
Customizations can be saved for zero-touch deployments of new guest operating systems.

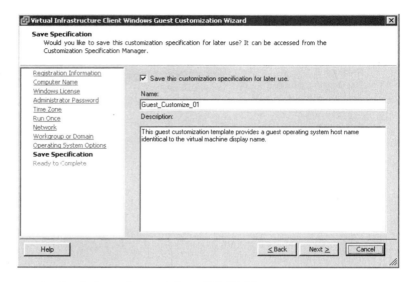

18. Review the customization information and then click Finish.

19. Review the template deployment information, select the Power On the New Virtual Machine After Creation option as needed, and then click Finish.

VIRTUAL MACHINE CLONING

While templates might be the most common means of deploying a new virtual machine, it is possible to clone any virtual machine in a powered-off state. The right-click menu of a powered-off virtual machine provides a Clone option that allows you to make a copy without first converting to a template. The Clone to New Virtual Machine option from the Commands list on a virtual machine summary page accomplishes the same task. The wizard that initiates this will provide similar options to the wizard you use when cloning from a template. Keep in mind that unless you customize the guest operating system, an exact copy of the original virtual machine will be made. This could be especially useful when you're looking to create a test environment that mirrors a live production environment.

The Bottom Line

While company policy should ultimately drive virtual machine creation, there are best practices that can be followed to ensure performance and ease management. Virtual machines should always start as single virtual CPU systems with a minimum of two hard drives for separating the operating system from the user data.

Install a guest operating system. Installing a guest operating system on a set of virtual machine hardware is similar to an installation on physical hardware and requires the same licensing considerations.

Install the VMware Tools. The VMware Tools provide valuable additions to virtual machines and, although they are not installed by default, they should not be treated as an optional component. The VMware Tools install drivers and features for better memory management, optimized SCSI drivers, and enhanced video and mouse, among other benefits.

Master It Install the VMware Tools into a guest operating system.

Manage and modify a virtual machine. A running virtual machine is limited in its modifications. Only a hard disk can be added to a running virtual machine, but CD/DVD-ROM drives, floppy drives, and network adapters can all be configured while the virtual machine is in a powered-on state.

Master It Add a new network adapter to a virtual machine.

Master It Add a new hard drive to a virtual machine.

Create templates and deploy virtual machines. Templates save administrators a great deal of time when deploying new virtual machines. Not only will templates reduce deployment times, but they also help reduce mistakes for new machines.

Master It Prepare VirtualCenter for guest operating system customizations.

Chapter 7

Migrating and Importing Virtual Machines

The process of building a virtual infrastructure is at its peak with the conversion of existing systems into virtual machines. Consolidating physical systems provides significant intrinsic savings in the areas of physical space, power consumption, and hardware costs. In this chapter, we'll look at the native tools available for performing a server consolidation by migrating physical computers into virtual machines.

In this chapter you will learn to:

◆ Use the VirtualCenter 2.5 Consolidation feature.

◆ Perform physical-to-virtual migrations of running computers

◆ Perform physical-to-virtual migrations of computers that are powered off

◆ Import virtual appliances

Guided Consolidation

VMware VirtualCenter 2.5 includes a new feature called Consolidation that provides a simple-to-use capacity-planning utility. This utility allows administrators to monitor physical computers as potential virtualization candidates. As the monitoring period goes on, the guided Consolidation capacity planner becomes increasingly confident about its recommendations for virtualization.

Before consolidation can begin, there must be a datacenter object and a host added to the VirtualCenter inventory. The Consolidation feature is accessible from the Consolidation button on the top menu of VirtualCenter 2.5. The feature is installed as part of VirtualCenter 2.5 and has its own corresponding Windows service called the VMware Capacity Planner Service. The service must run under the context of a user account with the following settings on the VirtualCenter Server:

◆ Membership in the local administrators group

◆ The Log On as a Service right

LOG ON AS A SERVICE

The Log On as a Service right can be configured through the Local Security Policy on the VirtualCenter Server computer or via a Group Policy Object (GPO) in Windows Active Directory. You can find the Log On as a Service right in the following location in the Group Policy Object Editor (gpedit.msc): Computer Configuration | Windows Settings | Security Settings | Local Policies | User Rights Assignment.

While VMware has a more robust product in the VMware Capacity Planner, this light version is a perfect fit for the small- and medium-sized businesses. The Consolidation feature can scan systems that exist as members of a workgroup or part of a domain. A set of default credentials can be configured when scanning systems with similar administrator account settings, while at the same time custom credentials can be set for the nondomain systems or those with nonstandard administrator account settings.

Perform the following steps to configure the Service and Default.credentials for the VirtualCenter Consolidation feature:

1. Use the Virtual Infrastructure (VI) Client to connect to the VirtualCenter 2.5 Server.

2. Click the Administration menu button and then select the Consolidation Settings option.

3. In the Consolidation Configuration dialog box, shown in Figure 7.1, click the Change button in the Service Credentials section.

FIGURE 7.1
The Consolidation feature defaults must be configured with accounts that include the appropriate administrative rights.

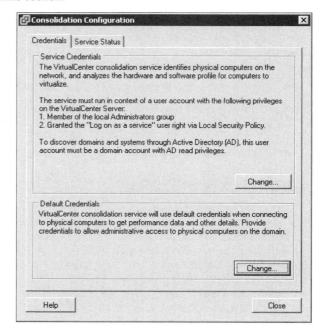

4. In the Enter Credentials dialog box, shown in Figure 7.2, enter the username and password for a user account with membership in the local administrators group and the Log On as a Service user right. Preface the user account with the appropriate domain name for a domain account or the server name for a nondomain account.

5. Click the OK button.

6. Click the Change button in the Default Credentials section of the Consolidation Configuration dialog box.

7. Enter the username and password with administrative rights on the target systems to be monitored.

8. Click OK.

FIGURE 7.2
The service account credentials should be prefaced with the domain or server name where the account is stored.

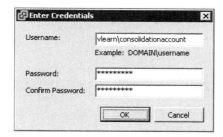

The various services involved in the Consolidation feature can be monitored from the Service Status tab of the Consolidation Configuration dialog box, as shown in Figure 7.3.

FIGURE 7.3
The Consolidation feature includes several child services that facilitate the data-gathering and recommendation processes.

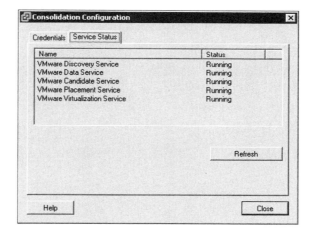

Once you've set the defaults, you can initiate an analysis of systems from the Analysis tab. As noted earlier, the analysis of target systems becomes more confident as time passes and the amount of data collected increases. Typically, it takes about 24 hours for the analysis algorithms to become confident in the consolidation plan. As the confidence builds, it will be reflected in the Confidence column on the Analysis tab, as shown in Figure 7.4.

FIGURE 7.4
The Consolidation feature generally takes about 24 hours to gain confidence in its recommendations.

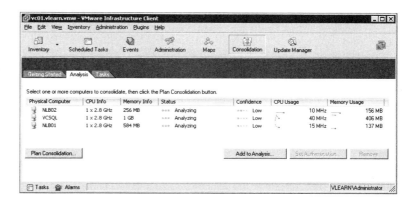

Perform the following steps to begin an analysis with the Consolidation feature of VirtualCenter 2.5:

1. Use the VI Client to connect to the VirtualCenter 2.5 Server.

2. Click the Consolidation menu button and then click the Analysis tab.

3. Click the Add to Analysis button.

4. In the Add to Analysis dialog box, shown in Figure 7.5, click the Show domain drop-down list to view the list of domains and workgroups discovered by the VirtualCenter Consolidation feature.

FIGURE 7.5
The Consolidation feature discovers domains and workgroups of potential target computers.

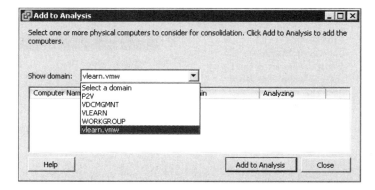

5. Select the appropriate domain or workgroup to which the target computers belong.

6. Once the list of computers is displayed, select the computer or computers to be monitored. You can select multiple computer names by holding the Ctrl key while clicking each name.

7. Once you've selected all the desired targets, click the Add to Analysis button.

8. As shown in Figure 7.6, select the custom Username and Password option or the Use the configured default credentials option. If the credentials defined in the default are not appropriate for the system to be monitored, enter the appropriate username and password in the Set Authentication dialog box. If three systems require three different sets of credentials, then you must select each system individually from the list of computer names.

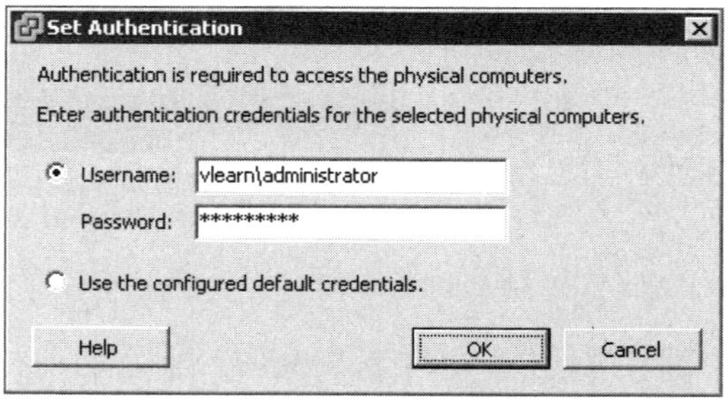

FIGURE 7.6
Authentication credentials can be customized for nondomain systems, or the default credentials can be passed through to the target systems.

9. Click OK.

Once these steps have been completed, the analysis will begin and will run until the confidence level is sufficient for making a recommendation about virtualizing the physical target system.

ANALYZING PHYSICAL COMPUTERS

Analyzing a physical computer requires the appropriate administrative rights and IP connectivity to the computer. Be sure to disable any software firewalls that might be preventing communication with the physical computer.

After a period of time, the VirtualCenter Consolidation feature gains confidence with the consolidation plan and the status value of the analyzed systems changes, as shown in Figure 7.7.

FIGURE 7.7
Once the confidence of the Consolidation feature reaches a high level, the analyzed systems will be noted as ready for consolidation.

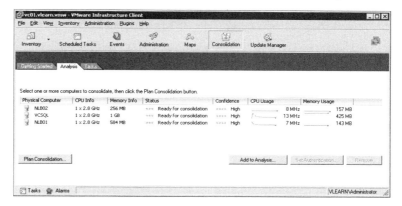

You can observe a consolidation plan for one or more of the analyzed systems by selecting the system or systems and then clicking the Plan Consolidation button. As shown in Figure 7.8, the Consolidation Plan dialog box will detail the computer name, the recommended destination, and a star rating to identify how likely a candidate the system is for virtualization. The rating system ranges from one to five; with five stars indicating that the system is an excellent virtualization candidate for the given host.

FIGURE 7.8
A consolidation plan is generated for each of the analyzed systems. The plan includes a recommended destination host and rating.

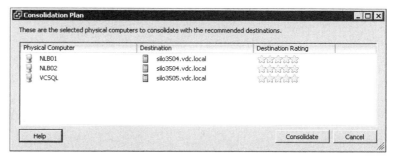

From the Consolidation Plan dialog box, you can select one or more of the analyzed systems and then click the Consolidate button. Clicking the Consolidate button will cause the VMware Converter to import the system as a virtual machine into the existing VirtualCenter inventory, as shown in Figure 7.9.

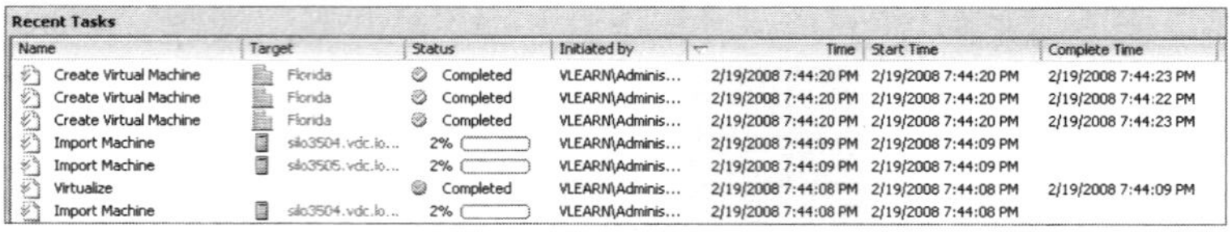

FIGURE 7.9
Multiple systems can be converted to virtual machines with a single click as part of the consolidation plan generated by VirtualCenter.

The Consolidation feature of VirtualCenter will provide many small and medium businesses with a simplified physical-to-virtual migration strategy through its simple and intuitive interface. While it may not be as robust as the full VMware Capacity Planner utility, it is free and does not require any outside experience or assistance. In truth, the best migration plans will come from the intimate knowledge an administrator has about the physical systems that have been deployed over his/her tenure. The Consolidation tools and Capacity Planner tools are an excellent way to provide validated and documented proof of the benefits and capabilities of constructing a virtual infrastructure on VI3.

Performing Physical-to-Virtual Migrations

You can migrate physical machines into virtual machines by performing one of the following:

◆ A hot (or live) migration — the conversion of a running physical computer.

◆ A cold migration — the conversion of a physical computer that is powered off.

Both types of migrations can be performed with the VMware Converter. The VMware Converter has traditionally been a stand-alone product that can be downloaded and installed for free. However, with the release of VirtualCenter 2.5, VMware has made the VMware Converter even more convenient by adding it into VirtualCenter as a plug-in accessible directly from the VirtualCenter 2.5 interface.

Perform the following steps on each VI Client that will manage physical-to-vertical (P2V) migration to enable the VMware Converter Enterprise feature of VirtualCenter 2.5:

1. Use the VI Client to connect to the VirtualCenter 2.5 Server.

2. Click the Plugins menu and select the Manage Plugins option.

3. In the Plugin Manager dialog box, shown in Figure 7.10, click the Download and Install button under VMware Converter Enterprise.

4. Click the Next button on the VMware Converter Enterprise Client installation wizard.

5. Click the Install button to begin the installation.

6. Click OK once the installation is complete.

7. As shown in Figure 7.11, click the Installed tab and enable the VMware Converter Enterprise Client plug-in by selecting the Enabled check box. You may need to exit the VI Client and log back in before the Installed tab displays the VMware Converter Enterprise Client plug-in.

FIGURE 7.10
The VMware Converter
Enterprise feature must
be installed on each VI
Client that will
manage conversions.

FIGURE 7.11
Once installed, the
VMware Converter
Enterprise Client plug-in
must be enabled.

VMWARE CONVERTER STAND-ALONE ENTERPRISE AND STARTER EDITIONS

The VMware Converter is also available in a stand-alone product that can be installed and used outside the scope of VirtualCenter 2.5. The VMware website at http://www.vmware.com offers the VMware Converter Standalone Enterprise Edition and the VMware Converter Starter Edition.

The VMware Converter Enterprise edition found in VirtualCenter is equal in functionality to the Standalone Enterprise Edition, while the Starter Edition is less functional than both. The VMware Converter Starter Edition provides single-machine conversions by requiring an installation on each virtualization candidate. The end result of all the VMware Converter products is the ability to convert physical systems into virtual machines; the Enterprise Edition just makes it easier to accomplish this by providing a centralized management and operations interface.

The new and improved VMware Converter is a marriage of two older tools: P2V Assistant and VMware Importer. Functionality is enhanced and the interface is simplified, but the result is an easier to use and easier to manage conversion process. All of the following virtual machine types can be imported with the VMware Converter tool:

- VMware Workstation 4.x, 5.x, and 6.x
- VMware Ace 2.x
- VMware Fusion 1.x
- VMware Player 1.x and 2.x
- ESX Server 3.x
- ESX Server 2.5 if managed by VirtualCenter 2.x
- GSX Server 3.x
- VMware Server 1.x
- VirtualCenter 2.x
- Microsoft Virtual PC 7 and later
- Microsoft Virtual Server

In addition to these virtual machine formats, VMware Converter can import third-party system images created with the following products:

- Symantec Backup Exec System Recovery 7 (formerly LiveState Recovery)
- Norton Ghost
- Acronis True Image 9

VMware Converter and the VMware Converter agent can be run on any of the following operating systems:

- Windows Vista 32-bit (experimental on 64-bit)
- Windows Server 2003 32-bit and 64-bit
- Windows XP Professional 32-bit and 64-bit

◆ Windows 2000

◆ Windows NT with Service Pack 6 and Internet Explorer 5 and later

---

GREATER THAN OR EQUAL TO

The operating system on which VMware Converter is running must be equal to or greater than the operating system being converted to a virtual machine. For example, if the system running the VMware Converter is Windows NT with Service Pack 6, then it can only handle migrations of source computers running Windows NT with Service Pack 6. If VMware Converter is installed on Windows Server 2003 or Windows Vista, then the source computer can be any of the listed operating systems.

WINDOWS ACTIVATION

Servers that run Windows Server 2003 that are installed using retail media and keys that require activation will require a reactivation after the physical-to-virtual migration. The Windows Activation algorithm tracks changes to hardware specifications in a system, and when the amount of hardware change is deemed significant, the Windows Activation is once again required.

The migration of a physical system to a virtual machine incurs drastic changes to the hardware specifications of the system. Everything from the CPU to network card to video adapter to disk controllers is altered as part of the migration process. It is these changes that force the Windows Activation algorithm to require a reactivation. In addition, do not be surprised if the Internet-based activation procedure is not successful. You may find that you are forced into calling the toll-free Windows Activation phone line to explain that the old system is being decommissioned in favor of the new virtual machine and that you are not in breach of your licensing agreement with Microsoft.

Performing Hot Migrations

Hot migration, or migration of a running physical computer, is ideal for those systems that cannot afford to be taken offline and do not perform consistent changes to local data. Systems like domain controllers, web servers, and print servers are excellent candidates for hot migrations because they generally have a static set of data. Hot migration allows administrators to convert the physical system to a virtual machine and then to cut over to the virtual machine and decommission the physical machine without losing data.

Perform the following steps to conduct a hot migration of a running computer:

1. Use the VI Client to connect to a VirtualCenter 2.5 server.

2. Right-click on a cluster or ESX Server host object in the VirtualCenter inventory and select the Import Machine option.

3. Click the Next button on the Source page of the Import Wizard.

4. As shown in Figure 7.12, select the radio button labeled Physical Computer and click the Next button.

5. Enter the target computer information, including name or IP address and the appropriate user account information, as shown in Figure 7.13, then click the Next button. The user account must have administrative privileges on the target computer being converted to a virtual machine.

FIGURE 7.12
The VMware Converter Enterprise converts physical computers into virtual machines.

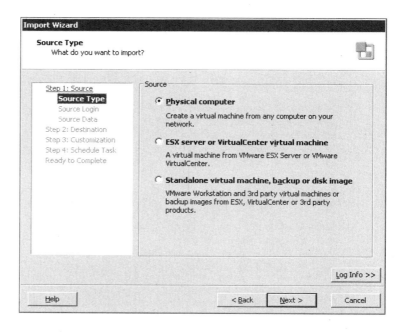

FIGURE 7.13
In addition to identifying the target computer by name or IP address, you must supply administrative credentials to perform a hot migration.

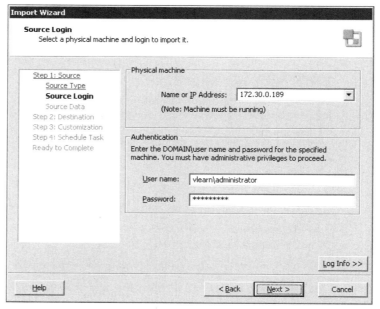

6. Select to uninstall the VMware Converter Agent automatically or manually in the Remote Installation Required warning dialog box shown in Figure 7.14, then click the Yes button to continue.

FIGURE 7.14
The VMware Converter
Agent can be unin-
stalled automatically
or manually once the
conversion is complete.

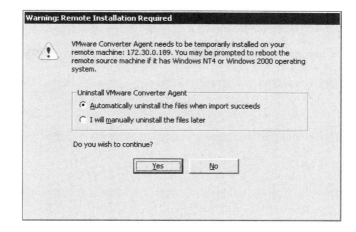

7. On the Source Data page, shown in Figure 7.15, select the volumes that should be converted
as part of the physical-to-virtual migration process. Volumes can be ignored by deselecting
the respective check box.

FIGURE 7.15
The VMware Converter
can migrate all, some,
or only one of the
volumes that exist on
the physical server.

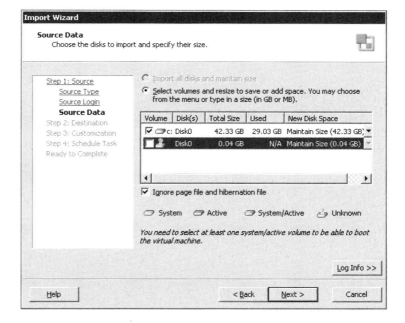

As part of the migration process, volumes can be resized. Notice in Figure 7.15 that the total
size of volume C: on Disk0 is 42.33GB with 29.03GB used. The default value in the New Disk
Space column is equal to the existing total size. Figure 7.16 shows the New Disk Space value
has been increased by 10GB to give more space to the volume.

8. Click Next once the Source Data page is configured appropriately for the migration.

FIGURE 7.16
The VMware Converter allows volumes to be resized (increased or decreased) as part of the migration process.

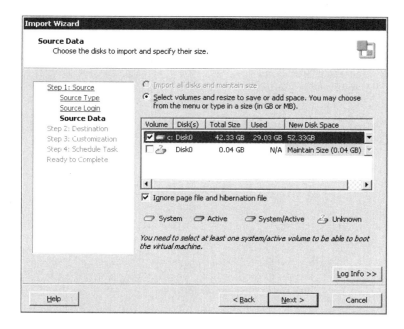

9. Click Next to begin configuration of the destination details of the migration process.

10. As shown in Figure 7.17, provide a virtual machine name and the location in the inventory where the virtual machine will reside, and then click Next.

FIGURE 7.17
The new virtual machine can be placed any-where throughout the Virtual Machines & Templates inventory.

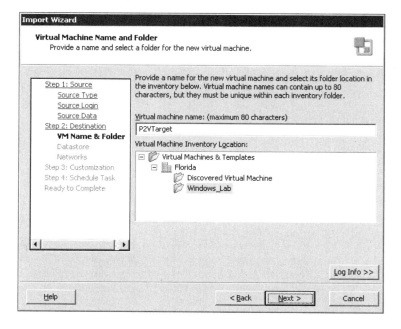

11. As shown in Figure 7.18, select a datastore with ample storage for the new virtual machine disk files, and then click Next.

FIGURE 7.18

The conversion process details the storage location for the new virtual machine disk files.

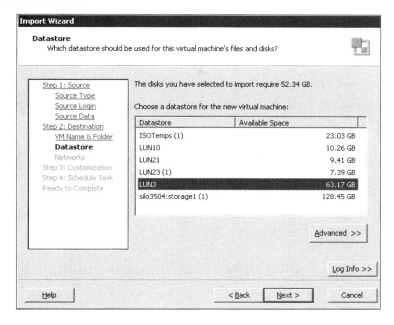

Clicking the Advanced button lets you place each new virtual machine disk file in different datastores, as shown in Figure 7.19.

FIGURE 7.19

The Advanced configuration allows virtual machine files to be spread across different datastores.

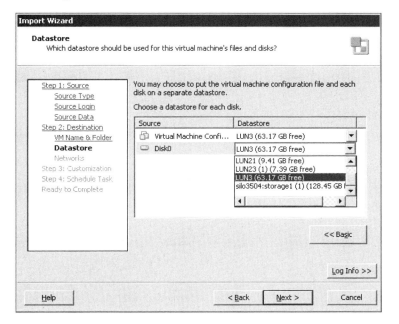

12. On the Networks page, shown in Figure 7.20, select the number of network adapters for the new virtual machine and then select the network that each network adapter should be connected to. Then click Next.

FIGURE 7.20
The new virtual machine can be configured with up to four network adapters on any of the available virtual machine networks.

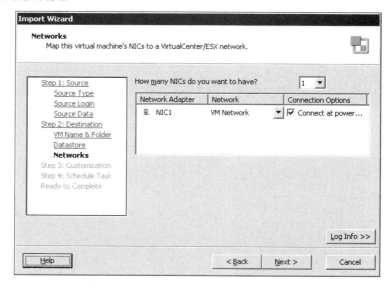

13. On the Customization page, shown in Figure 7.21, select the check box labeled Install VMware tools, and then click Next.

FIGURE 7.21
The new virtual machine can be customized by installing VMware tools or by changing the entire identity of the virtual machine.

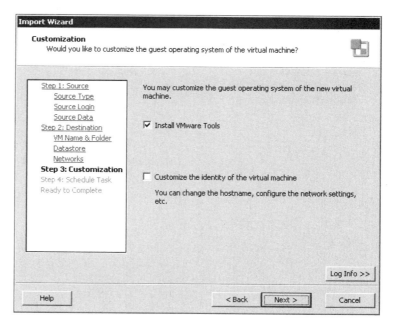

In the option labeled Customize, the identity of the virtual machine should only be selected if the physical machine and virtual machine will both remain part of the production network. Leave the box unchecked to maintain all existing settings of the physical computer. Selecting the option to customize the wizard includes the following additional pages:

◆ Computer Info

◆ Windows License

◆ Time Zone

◆ Network Settings

◆ Workgroup/Domain

14. On the Schedule Task page, select to perform the migration immediately or schedule it to take place at a later time, and then click Next.

15. To power on the virtual machine after the migration is complete, select the Power check box on the new virtual machine after creation. If you want to wait until the physical box is powered off before using the virtual machine, then leave this check box unselected. Click the Finish button to begin the conversion.

16. The Recent Tasks pane of VirtualCenter will detail the progress of the conversion process, as shown in Figure 7.22.

FIGURE 7.22
VirtualCenter's Recent Tasks pane will monitor the progress of the physical-to-virtual migration.

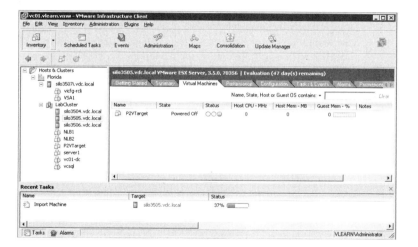

ELIMINATING EXCESS IN A P2V

Often times physical servers are purchased with more hardware than is required simply because the budget is there to support it. For example, it is not uncommon to find simple domain controllers or print servers with hundreds of gigabytes of empty space. While this is not a huge administrative concern in a physical server environment, it is a red flag in the physical-to-virtual migration process. The process of converting a physical machine to a virtual machine should involve an inspection of the resources assigned to the physical server as it is migrated. In this case, when converting a domain controller or print server with hundreds of gigabytes of free storage, it is best to adjust the disk size as part of the conversion process. This ensures that expensive SAN storage is not aimlessly consumed by virtual machines that will never utilize the resource to its full capacity.

The same can be said for memory and CPU resource allocation. As part of the migration, RAM and CPU allocations should be revisited and adjusted to better suit the demands of the virtual machine. For example, a domain controller with two dual-core processors and 4GB of RAM is severely overallocated. While the conversion process does not directly allow these two resources to be adjusted as part of the conversion wizard, they can easily be adjusted after the virtual machine has been created, prior to the first power-on.

Performing Cold Migrations

The process referred to as a *cold migration* involves the conversion of a physical machine to a virtual machine while the physical machine is not in a running state. This type of conversion is best for servers that have constantly changing data sets. For example, computers that run SQL Server or Exchange Server are good candidates for cold migrations. The downside is that the server must be taken offline as part of a planned outage. Cold migrations are preferable for database and mail servers because the hot migration does not continuously update as the conversion is in progress. Therefore, if a hot migration begins at 9:00 ~PM, the virtual machine would be consistent as of that time. Any updates since the 9:00 ~PM start time would not be captured in the virtual machine.

Naturally, a computer cannot be migrated while powered off completely, so the cold migration is not about migrating a physical computer that is powered off. Rather, it is the migration of a physical computer not booted into the standard default operating system. The cold clone process begins by booting the computer from the CD/DVD-ROM drive with the VMware Converter boot CD installed. You can download the VMware Converter boot CD from VMware's website and then burn it to CD or DVD media.

The target physical computer must be configured with more than 264 MB of RAM to perform a cold migration or an error will be thrown, as shown in Figure 7.23.

FIGURE 7.23
Target machines to be converted to virtual machines must be configured with more than 264 MB of RAM.

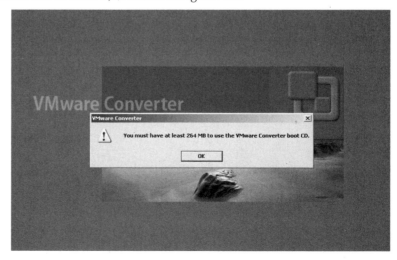

Perform the following steps to cold-migrate a physical computer into a virtual machine:

1. Boot the target computer from the VMware Converter boot CD.

2. Click the I Accept the Terms in the License Agreement radio button and then click OK.

3. If the target computer has less than 364 MB of RAM, a warning message, shown in Figure 7.24, will be thrown. If the target computer has more than 364 MB of RAM, skip to step 4.

FIGURE 7.24
The VMware Converter will suggest using a temporary directory for target machines with less than 364 MB of RAM.

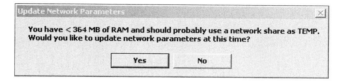

Click the Yes button to edit the network configuration, as shown in Figure 7.25. This is just a suggestion by the VMware Converter and does not have to be done.

FIGURE 7.25
A mapped network drive can serve as the temporary directory used by the VMware Converter.

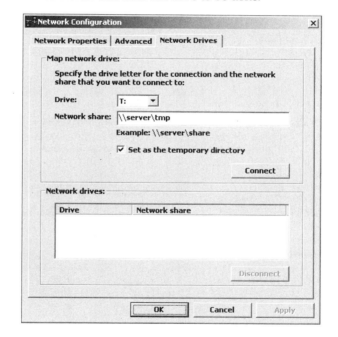

4. After accepting the license agreement, you will be prompted to update the network parameters. Click the Yes button to adjust the network properties shown in Figure 7.26.

5. Click OK once the network properties are adjusted as needed.

6. The VMware Converter window will open. Click the Import Machine button to launch the VMware Converter Import Wizard.

7. Click Next.

FIGURE 7.26

The network properties of the target system can be adjusted as part of the cold clone process.

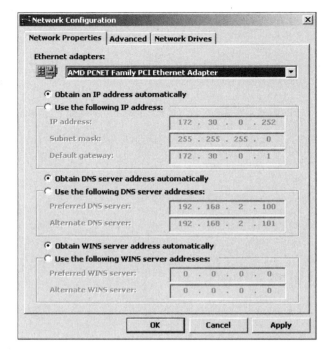

8. On the Source Data page of the wizard, select either the Import all disks and maintain size option or the Select volumes and resize to save or add space option, as shown in Figure 7.27. Use the latter option to increase or decrease the amount of space on the volume. Figure 7.27 shows an increase in size on volume C: from 1.99GB to 10GB.

FIGURE 7.27

The cold clone process allows for increasing or decreasing the space allocated to converted volumes.

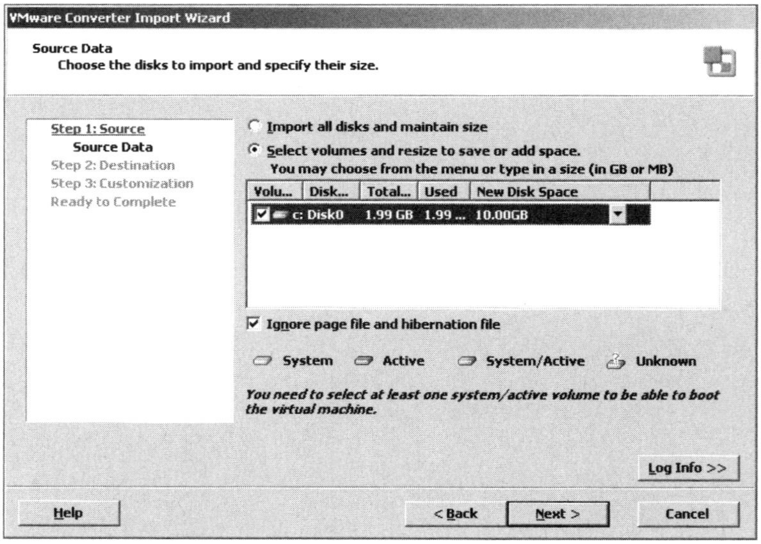

9. Once the volumes have been resized as needed, click Next to continue.

10. On the Destination Type page, select the destination for the import. For enterprise physical-to-virtual migrations, the VMware ESX Server or VirtualCenter virtual machine option, shown in Figure 7.28, will be the most appropriate. Click Next.

FIGURE 7.28
The VMware Converter Import Wizard offers destinations of ESX Server, VirtualCenter, Workstation, Fusion, and Server.

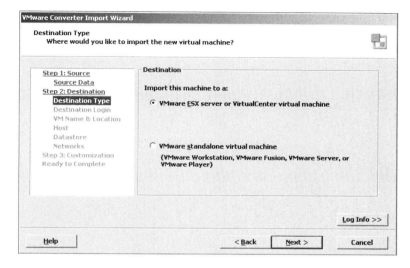

11. On the Destination Login page, provide the name or IP address of the ESX Server or Virtual-Center Server and the appropriate credentials to authenticate, as shown in Figure 7.29. Click Next.

FIGURE 7.29
Identification and authentication of the destination server require name resolution or the use of an IP address.

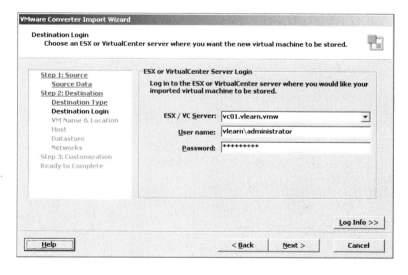

12. On the Virtual Machine Name and Folder page, type a display name for the virtual machine and select the desired location in the VirtualCenter inventory. Click Next.

13. On the Host or Cluster page, select the host, cluster, or resource pool under which the virtual machine will run, as shown in Figure 7.30. Click Next.

FIGURE 7.30
Migrated virtual machines can be placed under a host, cluster, or resource pool.

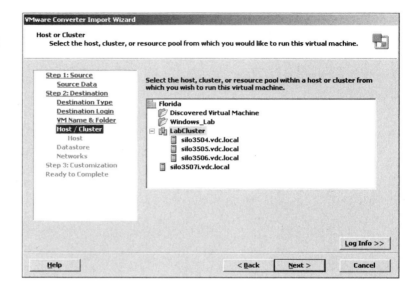

If a cluster is selected from the inventory list, the next page in the wizard will require the selection of a specific host. If a host is selected, the wizard will move on to the Datastore page.

14. On the Datastore page, select the datastore where the virtual machine disk files will be stored. Use the Advanced button to supply unique datastores for the different virtual machine disk files. Click Next.

15. On the Networks page, select the number of network adapters to include in the new virtual machine, and then select the virtual machine network that each network adapter should be connected to. Click Next.

16. On the Customization page, select the check box Install VMware Tools. If you want to change the identity of the virtual machine to be different from the target system, select the check box Customize the Identity of the Virtual Machine. Selecting this option adds the following pages to the VMware Converter Import Wizard:

- ◆ Computer Info
- ◆ Windows License
- ◆ Time Zone
- ◆ Network Settings
- ◆ Workgroup/Domain

17. Click Next to continue.

18. On the Ready to Complete page, select the check box Power On the Virtual Machine after Creation and then click the Finish button. The cold clone process will be detailed in the VMware Converter utility, as shown in Figure 7.31.

FIGURE 7.31
The VMware Converter provides detailed information about the progress of the cold migration process.

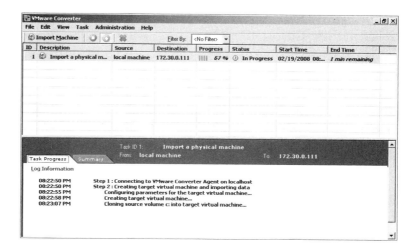

P2V OR V2V ONE AND THE SAME

While all of the samples here discuss the use of the VMware Converter to perform physical-to-virtual migrations, the tool can also be used to perform virtual-to-virtual migrations.

This can be a powerful utility for solving problems regarding the over- or under-allocation of disk space for a virtual machine. By using the VMware Converter, as you have seen in this chapter, the amount of space allocated to a volume can be decreased or increased as needed. This allows administrators to use a nondestructive process to easily manage volume sizes in Windows virtual machines. Typically, doing this requires costly third-party tools and can incur damage to the system if not done properly.

Importing Virtual Appliances

An interesting new feature of VirtualCenter 2.5 is the ability to import virtual appliances directly from the VMware Virtual Appliance marketplace. A virtual appliance is a specialized virtual machine with a dedicated purpose. If you browse the Virtual Appliance Marketplace at `http://www.vmware.com/appliances`, you will find that appliances exist across a multitude of categories, including:

◆ Administration

◆ App/Web Server

◆ Communications

◆ Database

◆ Networking

◆ Security

To import a virtual appliance in VirtualCenter 2.5, select File ≻ Virtual Appliance ≻ Import. As shown in Figure 7.32, virtual appliances can be imported from the VMware website, a local file, or a designated URL.

FIGURE 7.32
Virtual appliances are prebuilt virtual machines with specific purposes and can be imported directly into VirtualCenter 2.5.

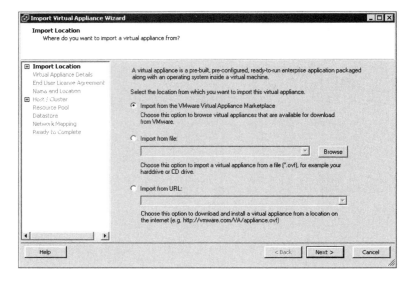

The virtual appliances available for import directly from the VMware website are extremely limited, as this feature is so new. At the time of this writing, only three appliances were viable import options from the site.

The ability to import from a file or URL supports the open virtual machine format (OVF). OVF is an attempt to standardize virtual machine formats across various platforms.

The process of importing a virtual appliance continues with the configuration of the following:

◆ Virtual machine name and location.

◆ Host or cluster under which the virtual machine will run.

◆ Resource pool under which the virtual machine will run.

◆ The datastore that will host the virtual machine files.

◆ The network configuration for the virtual machine.

The virtual appliances imported into VirtualCenter 2.5 by whichever means are treated as any other virtual machine in the inventory. While some of the available appliances are production ready and free for use, others are operated under trial conditions and must be purchased for extended production utilization.

The Bottom Line

Use the VirtualCenter 2.5 Consolidation feature.   The Consolidation feature of VirtualCenter 2.5 offers a simplified utility for creating a consolidation plan for small- and medium-sized businesses.

> **Master It**   Your company has 27 physical servers that it has identified as virtualization candidates. You need to provide a documented effort for determining which systems are ideal candidates and where on the four-node cluster the virtual machine should run.

Perform physical-to-virtual migrations of running computers.   A hot migration, or hot clone, is the conversion of a running computer into a virtual machine. The hot cloning process is ideal for systems with relatively static data sets to ensure time-consistent conversions of the target computer.

> **Master It**   Your company's business hours are 8:00 ~AM to 6:00 ~PM. There are four physical servers that function as domain controllers. You want to convert three of them to virtual machines running in your new three-node ESX Server cluster.

> **Master It**   You have an existing virtual machine that has a 10GB C drive with only 1 MB of space remaining. You need to provide an additional 20GB of space to the C drive.

Perform physical-to-virtual migrations of computers that are powered off.   A cold migration, or cold clone, is the conversion of a computer into a virtual machine while booted from the VMware Converter boot CD. The cold cloning process is ideal for systems that rely on frequently changing data sets since the data cannot be modified during the conversion process.

> **Master It**   Your company has a computer that runs Microsoft SQL Server 2005. The IT staff has identified the system as a good target for becoming a virtual machine. You need to plan the conversion of the SQL Server 2005 computer into a virtual machine.

Import virtual appliances.   The ability to import virtual appliances is a new feature of VirtualCenter 2.5. Appliances can be pulled directly from VMware or can be imported from a local file or URL.

> **Master It**   You need to deploy the remote command-line management tool as a virtual appliance in your VirtualCenter 2.5 inventory.

Chapter 8

Configuring and Managing Virtual Infrastructure Access Controls

As indicated in the introduction to Chapter 5, centralizing management of the sheer number of virtual machines and their ESX hosts has become an issue in most growing datacenters. Delegating control to the appropriate users so they can assist in managing the virtual infrastructure is also a large part of the centralized management model. For instance, how do you assign permissions to a group of users responsible for setting up virtual machines to test a new application? They might need to create the virtual machine and manage its access to resources, but they may need to be restricted in what they can do in other areas of the virtual infrastructure.

Permissions to a virtual infrastructure can be managed through a VirtualCenter server or directly through an ESX Server host.

In this chapter you will learn to:

Manage and maintain ESX Server permissions

Manage and maintain VirtualCenter permissions

Manage virtual machines using the web console

Managing and Maintaining ESX Server Permissions

Both the VirtualCenter Server and the ESX Server use the same structured security model to grant users the ability to manage portions of the virtual infrastructure. As shown in Figure 8.1, this model consists of users (groups), roles, privileges, and permissions.

The items that differ between the non-VirtualCenter environment and the VirtualCenter environment are predominantly in two areas:

◆ The location of the user and group objects created

◆ The level of granularity of the roles and privileges available in each environment

For environments that don't have VirtualCenter, or where the administrator chooses to have users authenticate directly to the ESX Server to perform management tasks, it is important to start with a discussion of the security model.

Permissions to an ESX Server host are assigned to Linux-based users and groups that exist in the Service Console. Perform the following steps to view the ESX Server users and groups:

1. Use the VI Client to connect to an ESX Server host.

2. Select the host in the inventory panel and then click the Users & Groups tab, as shown in Figure 8.2.

FIGURE 8.1
VI3 security model for
assigning access control

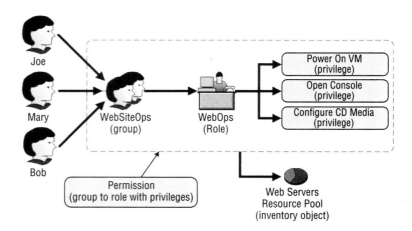

FIGURE 8.2
ESX users and groups
are stored in the Ser-
vice Console.

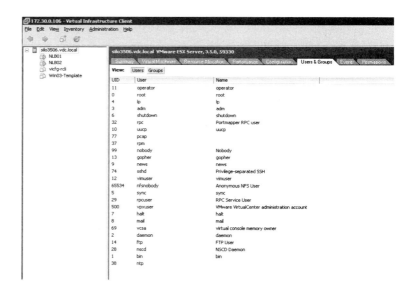

When constructing a virtual infrastructure, it is important from a security standpoint to identify who in your organization needs access to your ESX host to perform any level of management, using either an SSH connection (like Putty, WinSCP, FastSCP, etc.), the VI Client, and/or the web interface that we will discuss later in this chapter. The root username and password should be distributed with caution. If you determine that multiple users should be allowed direct access to an ESX Server host, provide each user with their own user account.

As mentioned in the introduction, the VI3 and ESX Server security model are composed of users (or groups), roles, privileges, and permissions. In its most basic format, **users or groups are** assigned to a role that has privileges. The user-role-privilege combination is **then associated with** an object in the inventory as a permission.

There are two buttons on the Users & Groups tab, the Users button and the Groups button, as shown in Figure 8.2. Users and groups — or at least the groups — are created in order to assign the group to the appropriate role. So what exactly is a role?

ESX Server permissions are set up to help simplify assignment. Rather than choose the individual privilege to be assigned each time you need to delegate, you assign a user or group to a role. Then, the role is granted role a privilege or group of privileges. As shown in Figure 8.3, the Service Console houses three default roles: No Access, Read-only, and Administrator.

FIGURE 8.3
The Service Console includes default roles for assigning capabilities on an ESX Server host.

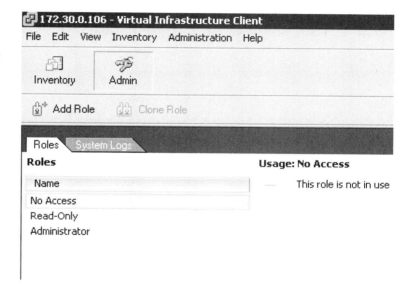

The No Access role works as the name suggests. This role prevents access to an object or objects in the inventory. The No Access role can be used if a user was granted access higher up in the inventory. The No Access role can also be used at lower-level objects to prevent object access. For example, if a user is granted permissions at the ESX Server host but should be prevented access to a specific virtual machine, use the No Access role.

Read-Only allows a user to see the objects within the VI Client inventory. It does not allow the user to interact with any of the visible objects in any way. For example, a user with the Read-Only permission would be able to see a list of virtual machines in the inventory but could not act on any of them.

The Administrator role by nature has the utmost authority, but it is only a role, and it needs to be assigned using a combination of a user or group object and an inventory object like a virtual machine.

With only three built-in roles in the Service Console, the defaults don't leave room for much flexibility. However, don't let that slow you down. The limits of the default roles are easily overcome by creating custom roles. You can create custom roles that will better suit your needs, or you can clone existing roles to make additional roles to modify for your own purposes.

The default roles should not be modified. If a role does not suit the management needs, create a custom role. If you alter a default role, it may present a scenario where other administrators unknowingly grant too much or too little permission by assigning membership in a default role.

DEFAULT ESX SERVER PERMISSION ASSIGNMENTS

By default, when ESX is installed the only user that exists is the root user, and root has full administrative permissions to the entire server, as shown in this image:

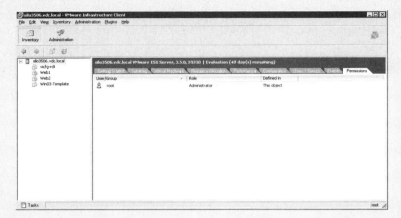

This default set of permissions changes when an ESX Server is managed by VirtualCenter. The process of adding a host to VirtualCenter adds an agent (the VirtualCenter Agent) and an additional Service Console account called vpxuser. The vpxuser account has a 32-character, complex, and randomly generated password that is also granted membership in the Administrator role on an ESX Server host. This assignment enables the VirtualCenter service to carry out tasks on the ESX hosts in the inventory.

For example, assume that a set of users needs to interact with the console of a virtual machine, and also needs to change the CD and floppy media of those virtual machines. In the following steps, you'll create a custom role named VMusers:

1. Use the VI Client to connect to an ESX Server host.

2. Click the Admin button from the menu bar.

3. Ensure the Roles tab is selected and click the Add Role button.

4. Type the name of the new role in the Enter Name text box (in this example, **VMUsers**) and then select the privileges that will be required by members of the role, as shown in Figure 8.4.

5. Click OK to complete the custom role creation.

PERMISSIONS FOR CHANGING VIRTUAL MEDIA

To change floppy and CD media using FLP and ISO images that are stored on a SAN volume, you will also need to grant that group browse datastore privileges at the root of the hierarchy — in this case, at the ESX host itself.

FIGURE 8.4
Custom roles strengthen management capabilities and add flexibility to permission delegations.

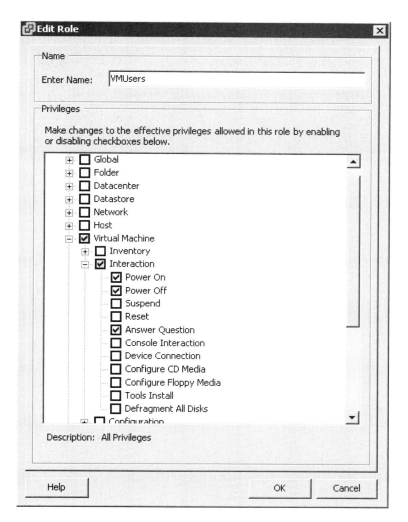

As simple and useful as roles are, they are not functional until a user or group is assigned to the role, and then the role is assigned to an inventory object. Assume that a group of users exists that needs to interact with all virtual machines that are web servers. If access control is managed through the ESX Server, then you have to create a user account in the Service Console along with a new group — for example, SiteOperators. Once you've created these Linux-based users and groups, you can execute the security model. Follow these steps to grant virtual machine access control to a Service Console user or group:

1. Use the VI Client to connect to an ESX Server host.

2. Right-click the object in the inventory to which permission should be assigned and click the Add Permission option, as shown in Figure 8.5.

FIGURE 8.5
Granting access control
begins with selecting
the inventory object
to which access must
be granted.

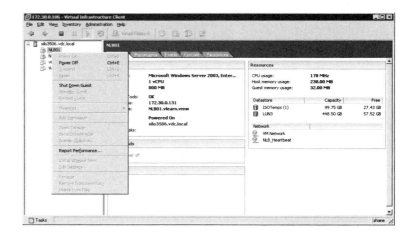

3. Click the Add button in the Assign Permissions dialog box, as shown in Figure 8.6.

FIGURE 8.6
The Assign Permissions
dialog box allows you to
select a user or group
and associate it with
an ESX Server role.

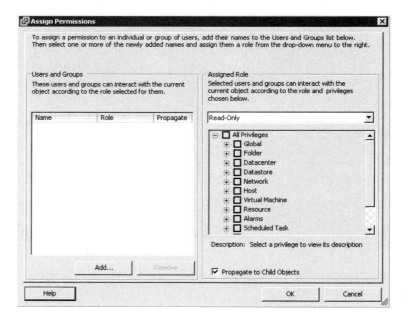

4. Select the appropriate user or group (in this case, SiteOperators) and then click the Add button, as shown in Figure 8.7.

5. Select the role that the Service Console users or groups should belong to, as shown in Figure 8.8.

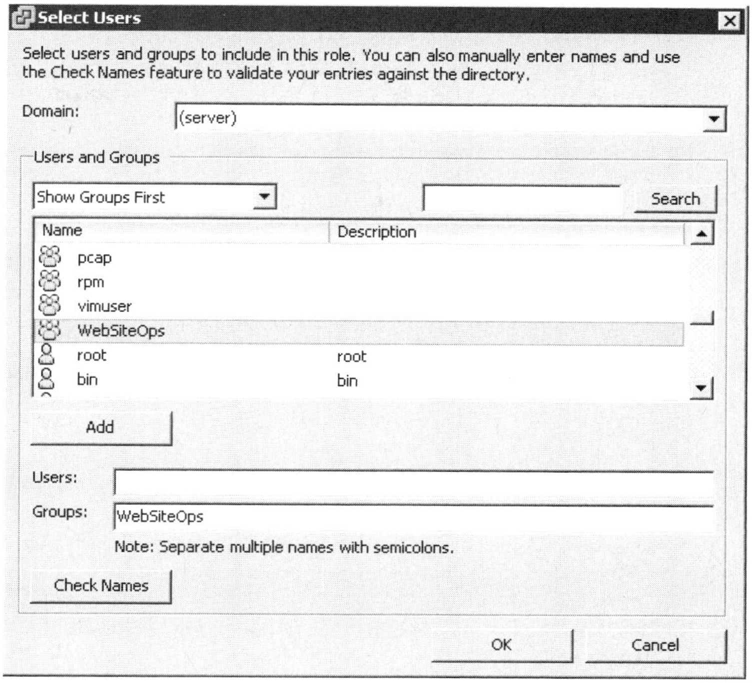

FIGURE 8.7
Service console users
and groups can be
granted access to inven-
tory objects.

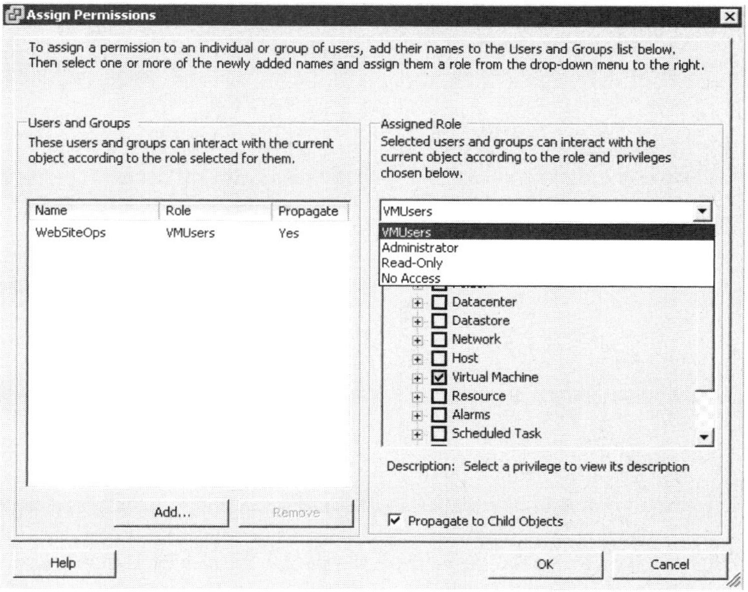

FIGURE 8.8
The selection of a role
ultimately dictates the
privilege level a user or
group has on an object.

What if you have an ESX Server that will host 30 virtual machines and 10 of those are the web server virtual machines? As previously demonstrated, this approach then requires that you assign permissions on each of the ten web server virtual machines. This is not an efficient process. Further growth resulting in more web server virtual machines would require additional administrative effort to ensure access control. When creating a role, you'll notice an option, Propagate to Child Objects, that you can use to facilitate access control implementation. This option works like the inheritance settings in a Windows file system. It allows the privileges assigned in this role to be applied to objects beneath the selected object. For example, if the VMUsers role is applied as a permission on the ESX Server host in the inventory panel, and the Propagate to Child Objects option is enabled, all members of the VMusers role could interact with all the virtual machines hosted on the ESX Server. While this certainly simplifies access control implementation, it adds another problem: the permissions of the VMUsers role has been overextended and now applies to all virtual machines and not just the web server. With access control granted at the host level, VMUsers will be able to change floppy and CD media and use the console of the web server virtual machines, but they will also be able to do that on any other virtual machine in the inventory.

This issue presents one of the drawbacks of managing access control on an individual ESX Server host. Keep in mind as well that all of the steps we have discussed so far would have to be performed on each ESX Server in the virtual infrastructure. What if there was a way to organize the inventory of virtual machines? In other words, what if we could create an object for the web server virtual machines and put all of the web server virtual machines within that object? Then we could assign the group to the role at the parent object level and let inheritance take over. As shown in Figure 8.9, the problem is that folder objects are not possible on a single ESX Server host.

FIGURE 8.9

Folder objects cannot be added to an individual ESX Server, leaving resource pools as the only viable solution for organizing virtual machines.

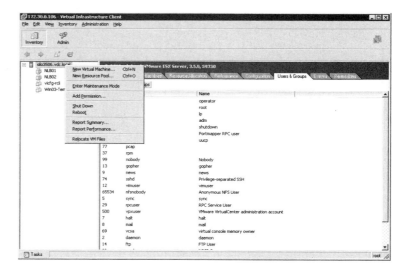

A resource pool is actually a special object, a folder of sorts, that we will discuss in the next chapter in great detail, but the good news is that it will also help to organize our virtual machines. One byproduct of the resource pool is the ability to manipulate and manage many virtual machines as objects within the logical resource pool object.

Perform the following steps to create a resource pool:

1. Use the VI Client to connect to an ESX Server host.

2. Right-click the hostname and select New Resource Pool, as shown in Figure 8.10.

3. Type a resource pool name in the Name text box, in this case **WebServers**, as shown in Figure 8.10.

FIGURE 8.10
Resource pools provide a means of allocating resources as well as organizing virtual machines.

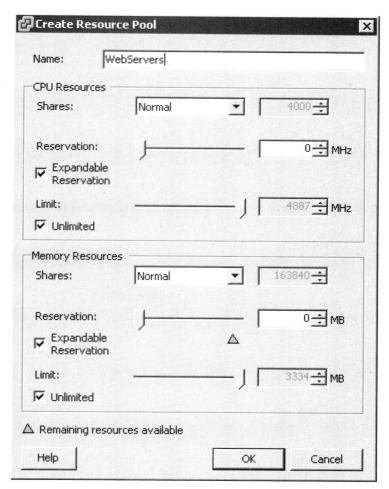

4. Configure the resource allocations if desired to establish limits and reservations for the resource pool. The limit will establish a hard cap on the resource usage while the reservations establish a resource guarantee.

5. Click OK.

So now that we've created a WebServers resource pool, virtual machines can be placed under the resource pool, as shown in Figure 8.11.

FIGURE 8.11
Virtual machines can
be placed into resource
pools for resource man-
agement purposes.

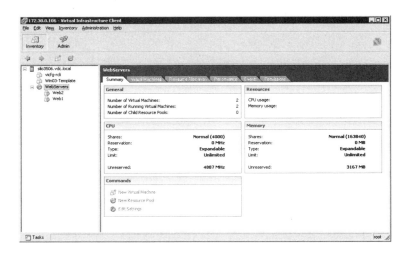

Resource pools become inventory objects to which permissions can be assigned, as shown in
Figure 8.12.

FIGURE 8.12
As an object in the
inventory, resource
pools are potential levels
of infrastructure man-
agement.

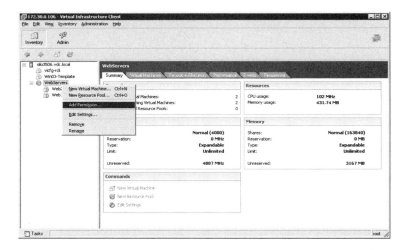

Permissions can be removed from inventory objects when management needs change or when
improper assignments have been made. In the previous example, the inappropriate permission
previously applied to the host itself should be removed now that more appropriate permissions
have been configured at the resource pool object.

Use the following steps to remove permissions on an object in the inventory:

1. Use the VI Client to connect to an ESX Server host.

2. Select the object in the inventory and then select the Permissions tab.

3. Right-click the permissions entry to be deleted from the list of existing permissions and
   then click the Delete option, as shown in Figure 8.13.

FIGURE 8.13

Permissions are removed from inventory objects as easily as they are added.

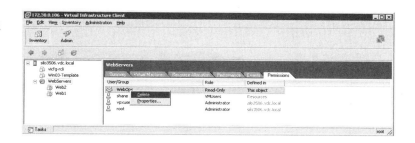

You should see a warning indicating that users may retain their permissions because of an assignment higher in the hierarchy; however, in this case, that is what we are trying to accomplish. We want the users to have access to the virtual machines as a result of permissions applied at the resource pool, not the ESX Server.

Once permissions have been assigned throughout the inventory, it is easy to lose track of what has been previously been done. Of course, if your company mandates documentation, there might already be a solid audit trail. However, it is easy to see existing role usage from within the VI Client.

To identify where a role has been assigned as a permission:

1. Use the VI Client to connect to an ESX Server host.

2. Click the Admin button from the toolbar.

3. Click on the role whose usage you wish to identify.

As shown in Figure 8.14, the details pane will identify where in the inventory the role has been used.

FIGURE 8.14

The VI Client makes it easy to identify where a role has been assigned as a permission.

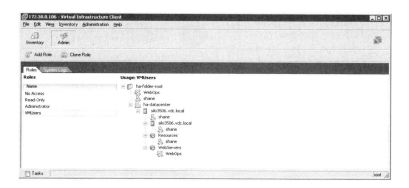

Over time, it is almost inevitable that management needs will change. At times, you may have to create new roles, edit an existing role, or even delete a role. If a role is not used, it should be removed simply to minimize the number of objects to be viewed and managed.

To delete a role:

1. Use the VI Client to connect to an ESX Server host.

2. Click the Admin button from the toolbar.

3. From the Roles tab, right-click the role to be deleted and select the Remove option, as shown in Figure 8.15.

FIGURE 8.15
Unused roles should be removed to minimize the objects viewed and managed on an ESX Server.

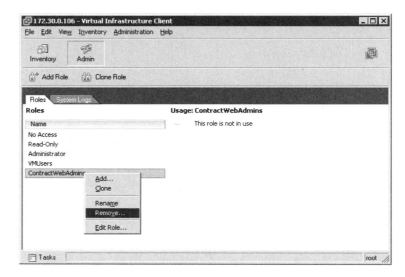

When a role is in use and is selected for removal, the ESX Server will offer the opportunity to transfer the existing role members to a new role or simply to drop all members from the role, as shown in Figure 8.16. This eliminates the opportunity for accidentally deleting roles that are being used in the inventory.

FIGURE 8.16
When you attempt to delete a role that is in use, you'll see a prompt that asks if you want to drop or reassign the role members.

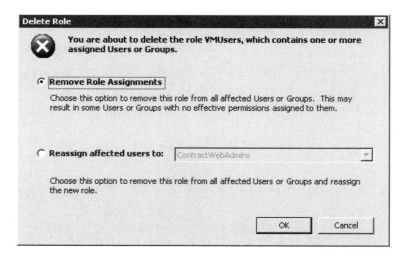

Now that you understand how to work with Linux-based users, groups, roles, and permissions on an ESX Server host, be aware that you more than likely will not be doing much of this. Managing the Linux-based user accounts is administratively more cumbersome because of the lack of centralized management and authentication. This is, of course, because the bulk, if not all, of your access control strategies should revolve around Windows-based user accounts accessing the VirtualCenter environment. This offers the advantage of having a centralized user database with a single password management process.

Managing and Maintaining VirtualCenter Permissions

The security model for VirtualCenter is identical to that explained in the previous section for an ESX Server: take a user or group and assign them to a role for a specific inventory object. The difference in the VirtualCenter security model is the origin of the user or group objects. In the VirtualCenter environment, the users and groups are actually Windows users and groups, but exactly which users will depend on whether your VirtualCenter server is a part of a domain or not. If the VirtualCenter server belongs to a workgroup, then the users and groups are stored in the local Security Accounts Manager (SAM) on that server and are managed through the Local Users and Groups node of the Computer Management snap-in. If the VirtualCenter server belongs to an Active Directory domain, then the users and groups available for assignment to roles are pulled from the Active Directory database and are managed through the Active Directory Users and Groups snap-in. This is fairly typical for a Windows server-based application, and also helps us to continue to manage all of the users in our network in one place: Active Directory. If you don't have the ability to create users and/or groups in Active Directory, you will need to make arrangements with your Active Directory administration team to assist you in that area. Once the users and/or groups are created, they will be available for you to assign roles to them through VirtualCenter.

We will assume that the VirtualCenter environment is based on a server that is a part of an Active Directory domain for the purposes of this discussion, although the procedures for assigning permissions remains essentially the same if you have a workgroup-based installation. The key is to remember where to create the users and groups you need to use.

 **Real World Scenario**

VIRTUALCENTER IN A WORKGROUP VS. VIRTUALCENTER IN A DOMAIN

You can install VirtualCenter on a Windows Server 2003 system that belongs to a workgroup or a domain. Although the security model and configuration steps are identical in both cases, there are significant concerns that arise in both cases.

In most cases, you'll install VirtualCenter on a computer that belongs to a Windows Active Directory domain. Doing this means users and groups that are granted access will likely reside in the Active Directory database. It also means signing into a VirtualCenter will take place under the context of a domain account, which in turn means passwords for accessing VirtualCenter will be susceptible to the domain password policies in effect. Even though the account information is the same, VirtualCenter does not currently support any type of single sign-on method in which your existing credentials are passed to the application. You will still have to type your username and password for VirtualCenter access. From a management perspective, installing VirtualCenter on a domain member eliminates the need to manage multiple user accounts, but it does pose a security risk that must be addressed.

The default permissions in a VirtualCenter installation provide the local Administrators group of the VirtualCenter server with membership in the Administrator role at the root of the inventory. As you learned in the previous section, this role has all privileges for virtual infrastructure management. The problem with this is that the Domain Admins group is, by default, a member of the local Administrators group, thereby granting all Domain Admins complete rights in the VirtualCenter infrastructure. In most cases, this will violate the principle of least privilege as all Domain Admins are not necessarily qualified or hired to be virtual infrastructure administrators. To mitigate the risk involved with the default configuration, create a new Active Directory organizational unit (OU) that includes the user accounts and groups for the virtual infrastructure administrators. Then, change the Active Directory permissions to prevent the Domain Admins from managing the new OU.

As shown in this image, you can create and configure an Active Directory group to prevent Domain Admins from managing the group membership. This group can then replace the local Administrators group in the VirtualCenter root permissions list.

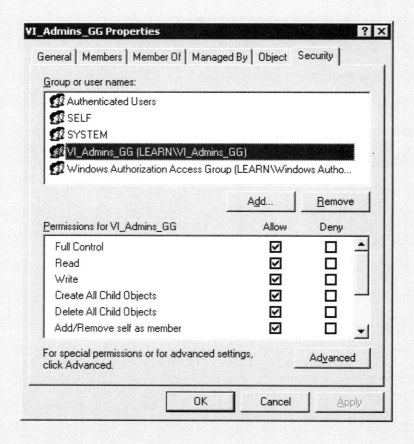

Once you've created the new group and granted it rights in VirtualCenter, you can remove the local Administrators permissions entry from the root of the VirtualCenter inventory, which will remove the original security concern. The following image shows how replacing local Administrators with a custom group eliminates a Domain Admin's ability to manage the virtual infrastructure:

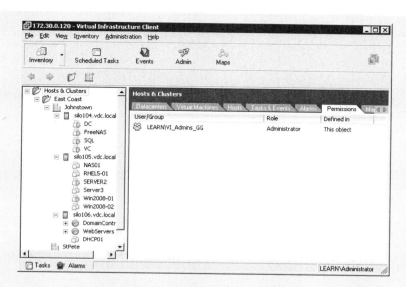

Alternatively, you can install VirtualCenter on a Windows Server 2003 system that belongs to a workgroup. As part of a workgroup, the Domain Admins will not have a default membership in the local Administrators group. The downside to the workgroup configuration is the multiuser account management now in place. Users accessing VirtualCenter will now use a completely different user account that is not susceptible to the domain password policies.

VirtualCenter has a more structured hierarchy with greater depth than an ESX Server host. As outlined in the previous section, the only way to organize virtual machines on an individual ESX host is to build a resource pool, and then move the appropriate virtual machines into that resource pool. The VirtualCenter hierarchy opens opportunities to create folder structures for organizing objects like datacenters and virtual machines.

In the VirtualCenter environment, start by creating, as a minimum, a datacenter. The datacenter object is the building block of a VirtualCenter hierarchy.

Perform the following steps to create a datacenter object:

1. Use the VI Client to connect to a VirtualCenter server.

2. Right-click the Hosts & Clusters root node in the inventory and select the New Datacenter option, as shown in Figure 8.17.

3. Type a name for the new datacenter object.

So what exactly is a datacenter object used for? A datacenter is used to organize ESX Server hosts, resource pools, virtual machines, and templates based on a company's management style. It is the building block of the VirtualCenter inventory, much like organizational units are the foundation of an Active Directory structure. An ESX host cannot be added directly to the VirtualCenter. A datacenter must exist in order to add an ESX Server. VirtualCenter is designed as an enterprise management application for all of the ESX servers in your worldwide organization. So the question remains: How do you manage resources? Is your management strategy based on geography, departments, or projects? Or do you prefer an arbitrary management style? In any case, Virtual-Center supports your style. Datacenters can be named by location, department, project, or can be given generic names like Datacenter1, Datacenter2, and so forth.

FIGURE 8.17

The Datacenter object is the building block of the VirtualCenter inventory.

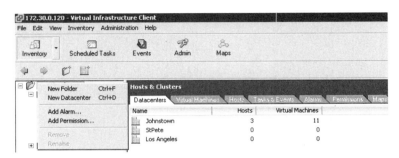

Think about what would happen if you were to place every document in your computer at the root of your hard drive. Finding documents would be difficult to say the very least, and assigning permissions to objects would be similarly difficult. Thus would be the case if our virtual infrastructure objects (hosts, resource pools, virtual machines, templates) were all located in a flat structure under the root.

Take, for example, an organization with offices in St. Petersburg, Florida, and Los Angeles, California, where each office will have several ESX hosts and dozens of virtual machines and template objects. The infrastructure might be constructed so that the hosts in Los Angeles are attached to a shared storage device in Los Angeles, and the St. Petersburg ESX Server hosts are attached to a second shared storage device local to their site. Keep in mind that these servers will be able to talk to each other via a WAN connection, but they can only access storage in their specific region. In addition, if the company has an IT staff in each location, then the administrators will create logical datacenter objects based on physical location.

This example could just as easily have been detailed as a departmental-specific configuration in which the finance, marketing, and sales departments have their own respective ESX Server hosts. In this case, the logical datacenter objects would be labeled by department rather than physical location.

This organization also does one more thing: a datacenter is a boundary for the configuration of VMotion, HA, and DRS. In other words, you can only migrate a virtual machine with VMotion to another host in the same datacenter where it is currently running, in the same way that HA can only fail over to another host in the same datacenter. The VMotion, HA, and DRS topics will be covered in more detail in Chapters 9 and 10.

But what happens if there are 30 datacenters in your organization, some located in Europe, some in North America, some in South America — and all with different teams of administrators managing them? The simple answer is to create folders under the root object in VirtualCenter and then create (or move) your datacenter objects under those folders. Creating folders under the root and placing datacenter objects beneath them allows for broader access control management. Think about why you create folders on network drives: to organize files and other folders and to simplify the assignment of permissions to many objects. Designing a VirtualCenter inventory employs the same logic. Figure 8.18 details a VirtualCenter inventory where multiple datacenter objects exist beneath a folder structure that provides an additional layer of management and access control. In this case, the datacenters are managed by geography: East Coast or West Coast.

FIGURE 8.18
Folders created above the datacenter object offer flexibility in providing broader access control.

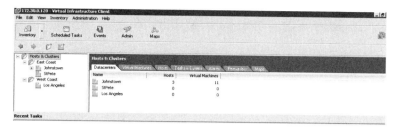

In the same way you can use folders to organize datacenters, you can also create folders within the datacenter to organize virtual machines according to your needs. For more detailed micromanaging scenarios, folders within folders can be created. Figure 8.19 details an inventory structure where datacenters are organized by geography and servers are managed by the rack in which they exist.

FIGURE 8.19
Creating folders beneath a datacenter provides more granular access control and management strategies.

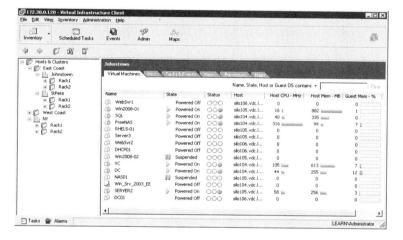

As explained in the previous section, a special type of folder called a resource pool is used to organize virtual machines. The key difference between a regular folder and a resource pool is that a resource pool allows for the carving of CPU and memory resources to provide resource limitation to virtual machines within the pool. Resource pool functionality will be discussed with more detail in Chapter 9; for now, our focus is on the access control capabilities of the resource pool as an object in the inventory.

VirtualCenter offers two main views of the objects within the inventory: Hosts & Clusters and Virtual Machines & Templates. Until now we have remained in the default view of Hosts & Clusters, but the Virtual Machines & Templates view is extremely valuable for organizing virtual machines with respect to the management and access control needs of the traditional Windows administrators. The alternate views available in VirtualCenter maintain their own respective structures to support management of the various objects. For example, changes to objects in the Hosts & Clusters view does not necessarily result in changes to the objects in the Virtual Machines & Templates view. Figure 8.20 shows details of a Virtual Machines & Templates view constructed to support access control implementation based on the types of virtual machines in the infrastructure. The inventory is made up of several custom folders called Finance VMs, Medical System VMs, Infrastructure VMs, and the default Discovered Virtual Machine, which catches any unassigned virtual machines. These folders, like those in the Hosts & Clusters view, provide a boundary for assigning permissions.

FIGURE 8.20

The Virtual Machines & Templates view maintains its own hierarchical structure to enhance access control possibilities.

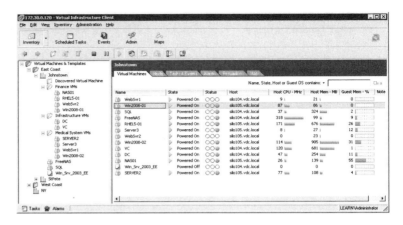

The remaining views in VirtualCenter, Networks and Datastores, though not more common utilities, provide consolidated looks at all the networks and datastores configured within the available datacenter objects. Figures 8.21 and 8.22 show examples of these views.

FIGURE 8.21

The Networks view provides a consolidated look at all the available networks and the virtual machines connected to each respective network.

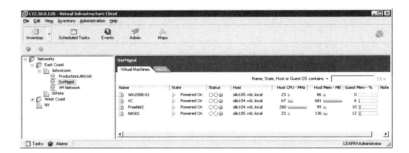

FIGURE 8.22

The Datastores view provides a consolidated look at all datastores available in a datacenter as well as a summary of the datastore, the virtual machines it contains, and the hosts that have access.

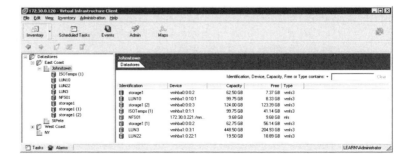

Where the ESX Server host was quite limited in its default roles, VirtualCenter provides more default roles, thereby offering a much greater degree of flexibility in constructing access control. Although both security models offer the flexibility of creating custom roles, ESX Server included three default roles while VirtualCenter provides eight default roles, including the same three offered in ESX Server. Figure 8.23 details the default VirtualCenter roles.

FIGURE 8.23
The VirtualCenter default roles offer much more flexibility than an individual ESX Server.

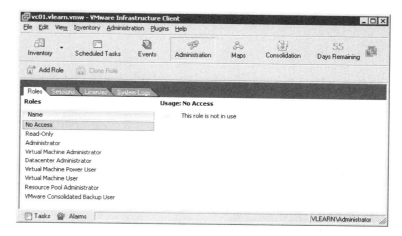

As you can see, there are a large number of roles provided by VMware in a default Virtual-Center installation. Remember, just like the default ESX roles, it is considered a best practice to *not* modify the default roles provided by VMware. Editing the defaults could result in over- or under-assigning permissions. If the default roles are edited and other administrators are unaware of the alteration, the use of the default role results in unexpected privileges or a lack of any privileges. If you need a similar role to one that is a default, then clone that role and change the permissions assignment for the cloned role. The key to using these roles effectively is to understand the functions of each of the roles provided by VMware:

No Access   This role is just what it sounds like — it permits a user or group no access. But why do we need it? The idea behind this role is to prevent a user or group that has permissions at some point higher in the hierarchy from having permissions on the object to which this role is assigned. For instance, you may have granted Bob the Virtual Machine Administrator a role at the datacenter level, which would permit him to administer all of the virtual machines in the datacenter, but there is a security concern about him having access to one of the accounting virtual machines in that datacenter. You could assign Bob to the No Access role on the Accounting virtual machine, which would effectively supersede his Virtual Machine Administrator privileges.

Read-Only   Read-Only allows users to see the VirtualCenter inventory. It does not allow them to interact with any of the virtual machines in any way through the VI Client or the web client except to see what the power status of each virtual machine is in the inventory where they have the Read-Only role applied.

Administrator   A user assigned to an object with the Administrator role will have full administrative capabilities over that object in VirtualCenter. Note that this does *not* grant *any* Windows privileges. For instance, a user assigned the Administrator role for a virtual machine may be able to change the RAM assigned to the virtual machine and alter its performance parameters (Shares, Reservations, and Limits), but may not even have the permissions to log into that Windows virtual machine unless his or her Windows account has those permissions.

The Administrator role can be granted at any object level in the hierarchy and the user or group that is assigned the role at that level will have VirtualCenter administrative privileges over that object and (if the inheritance box is checked) any child objects in the hierarchy. This is in contrast to the Virtual Machine Administrator, who has limited privileges on certain inventory objects but full administrative capabilities over virtual machines.

Virtual Machine Administrator   The VM Administrator role is used to assign full administrative privileges to a user or group, but only to virtual machines. The idea here is, as an example, if a user is granted the VM Administrator role at a datacenter level, he or she would only be able to fully administer virtual machines in that datacenter, but that user would not be able to change settings on objects such as resource pools in that datacenter.

Datacenter Administrator   The Datacenter Administrator role is targeted at users whose primary function is to set up the infrastructure of the hosts, clusters, and networks within the Datacenter object. Interestingly enough, the Datacenter Administrator Role does not include the ability to create virtual machines, although the administrator can set up folders and resource pools for the virtual machines to be placed into.

Resource Pool Administrator   The Resource Pool administrator is able to manage and configure resources with a resource pool including virtual machines, child pools, scheduled tasks, and alarms.

VMware Consolidated Backup User   As the role name suggests, the VMware Consolidated Backup user has the privileges required for performing a backup of a virtual machine using VCB.

Virtual Machine Power User   The VM Power User role grants a user the ability to interact with and change the configuration of an existing virtual machine. The VM Power User role is essentially a VM Administrator without the ability to create or delete a virtual machine. In addition, a user cannot move a virtual machine within the VirtualCenter hierarchy.

Virtual Machine User   The Virtual Machine User role grants the user the ability to interact with a virtual machine, but not the ability to change its configuration. Users can operate the virtual machine's power controls and change the media in the virtual CD-ROM drive or floppy drive as long as they also have access to the media they wish to change. For instance, a user who is assigned this role for a virtual machine will be able to change the CD media from an ISO image on a shared storage volume to their own client system's physical CD-ROM drive. If you want them to have the ability to change from one ISO file to another (both stored on a Virtual Machine File System [VMFS] volume or Network File [NFS] volume), they will also need to be granted the Browse Datastore permission at the parent of the Datastore object in the VirtualCenter hierarchy — usually the datacenter that the ESX host is located in.

What if the roles listed here don't provide you with the necessary functionality for a particular grouping of users? Well, it depends on what the problem is. Let's take the most basic problem. You've chosen a best fit role to assign a user privileges, but you just want them to do one more thing — or perhaps it's that the role assigns too many privileges. For such cases, it is best to clone the existing role and make the minor adjustments.

Perform the following steps to clone a role in VirtualCenter:

1. Use the VI Client to connect to a VirtualCenter server.

2. Click the Admin button on the toolbar and then select the Roles tab.

3. Right-click on the role that is to be cloned and then click the Clone option, as shown in Figure 8.24.

FIGURE 8.24
Cloning an existing role provides a starting point for role customization.

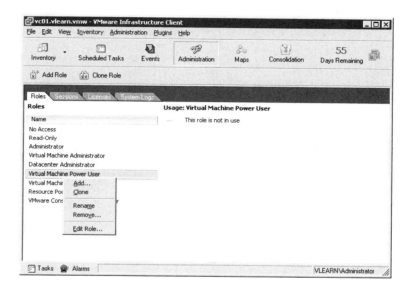

Once you've cloned the role, you can add or remove privileges as needed.

That takes care of just tweaking a role for your own purposes, but what if a user needs permissions on two different objects in the inventory? The example we discussed previously is when the user needs to change the ISO image that's mounted in the CD-ROM drive of the virtual machine to a different ISO. A Virtual Machine User has access to the CD-ROM properties of a virtual machine, but they don't have access (by default) to browse the datastores where the ISO images are stored. In this case, you would perform two separate permissions assignments. First, you would assign the user to the VM User role directly on the virtual machine or on the folder in which the virtual machines are stored. Next, you would create a custom role, grant the Browse Datastore privilege to the role, and assign the user to the role. Last, you would assign the permission in the inventory.

 **Real World Scenario**

REAL WORLD SCENARIO: VIRTUALCENTER PERMISSIONS INTERACTION

In organizations, both large and small users will often belong to multiple groups, and those groups will be assigned different levels of permissions on different objects. Let's observe the effects of multiple group memberships and multiple permission assignments in the virtual infrastructure.

In the first scenario, we look at the effective permissions when a user belongs to multiple groups that have different permissions on objects at different levels in the inventory. In the example, a user named Rick Avsom is a member of the Res_Pool_Admins and VM_Auditors Windows groups. As shown in the next images, the Res_Pool_Admins group is assigned membership in the Resource Pool Admins VirtualCenter role and the permission is set at the Production Resource Pool while the VM_Auditors group is assigned membership in the Read-Only VirtualCenter role and the permission is set at the Win2008-02 virtual machine.

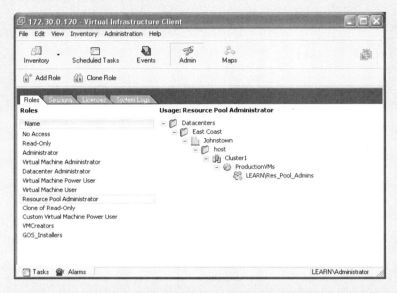

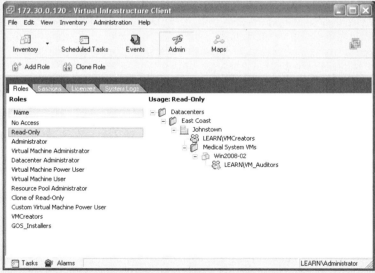

When logged on to the VirtualCenter server as Rick Avsom, the inventory will reflect only the objects available to him through his permissions application. Based on the permission assignment shown in the images above, Rick Avsom will be able to manage the Production resource pool and will have full privileges over the Win2008-01 virtual machine to which the Resource Pool Admin privileges are propagating. However, Rick Avsom will not be able to manage the Win2008-02 virtual machine to which he is limited to Read-Only privileges. The conclusion to this scenario is that users in multiple groups with conflicting permissions on objects lower in the inventory will be granted only the permissions configured directly on the object.

Another common scenario to understand is the effective permissions when a user belongs to multiple groups that have different permissions on the same objects. In this example, a user named Sue Rindlee is a member of the VM_Admins and VM_Auditors Windows groups. The VM_Admins group has been assigned membership in the Virtual Machine Administrator VirtualCenter role while the VM_Auditors group has been assigned membership in the Read-Only VirtualCenter role. As shown in the image here, both of these roles have been assigned permissions on the Production resource pool.

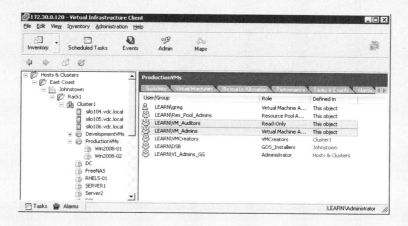

When logged on to the VirtualCenter Server as Sue Rindlee, the inventory will reflect only the objects available to her through her permissions application. Based on the permission assignment shown in the image, Sue Rindlee will be able to fully manage all of the virtual machines in the production resource pool. The image shown here validates that Sue's Virtual Machine Administrator status through membership in the VM_Admin group prevails over the Read-Only status obtained through her membership in the VM_Auditors group.

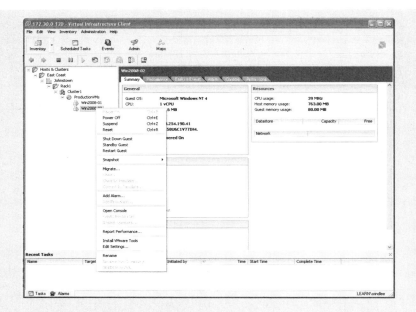

The conclusion to this scenario is that the effective permission is a cumulative permission when a user belongs to multiple groups with different permissions on the same object. Even if Sue Rindlee belonged to a group that had been assigned to the No Access VirtualCenter role, her Virtual Machine Administrator role would prevail. However, if Sue Rindlee's user account was added directly to a VirtualCenter object and assigned the No Access role, as shown in this image, then she would not have access to any of the objects to which that permission has propagated, as shown in the next image.

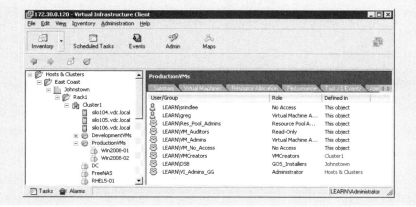

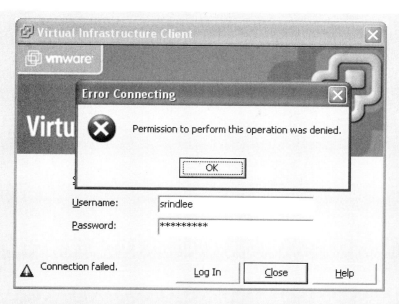

Even with a good understanding of permission propagation, you should always proceed with caution and always maintain the principle of least privilege to ensure that no user has been extended privileges beyond those that are needed as part of a job role.

Roles are very useful, but now that we've started to peek into the properties of the roles, we should take a look at what each of the privileges are and what they do for you in terms of customizing roles. Remember that privileges are individual tasks that are assigned to roles. This is a rather long list of privileges, but it's broken down into some general categories, so we'll begin by looking at what each of the categories means in general terms:

Global   Includes the ability to manage VirtualCenter license settings and server settings like SNMP and SMTP.

Folder   Controls the creation, deletion, and general manipulation of folders in the Virtual-Center hierarchy.

Datacenter   Controls the ability to create, delete, move, and rename datacenters inside VirtualCenter.

Datastore   Controls who can access files stored on an ESX attached volume. This permission needs to be assigned at the parent object of the ESX host itself — for instance, a datacenter, an ESX cluster, or a folder that contains ESX hosts.

Network   Controls the removal of networks from the VirtualCenter inventory.

Host   Controls what users can do with the ESX host itself in inventory. This includes tasks like adding and removing ESX hosts from the inventory, changing the host's memory configuration, or changing the Service Console firewall setting's network configuration.

Virtual Machine   Controls the manipulation of Virtual machines in the VirtualCenter inventory, including the ability to create, delete, or connect to the remote console of a virtual machine, to control the power state of a virtual machine, to change floppy and CD media, and to manipulate templates among other privileges.

Resource   Controls resource pool manipulation, including creating, deleting, or renaming the pool itself, and controls migration by using VMotion and applying DRS recommendations.

Alarms   Controls the configuration of alarms in the VirtualCenter hierarchy.

Scheduled Task   Controls the configuration of tasks and the ability to run a task that is scheduled inside VirtualCenter.

Sessions   Controls the ability to view and disconnect VI Client sessions connected to VirtualCenter and to send a global message to connected VI client users. As shown in Figure 8.25, a user without Sessions privileges cannot terminate VI Client sessions.

FIGURE 8.25
Session Control in VirtualCenter allows a user to disconnect VI Client sessions.

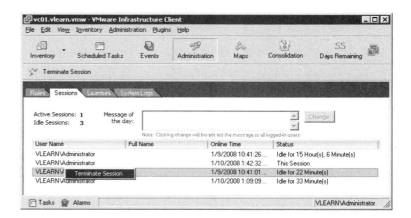

Performance   Controls the ability of users to modify the intervals at which the performance chart information is displayed on the performance tab of an object.

Permissions   Controls who has the ability to modify the permissions assigned to a role and who can manipulate a role/user combination for a particular object.

Extensions   Controls the ability to register, update, or unregister extension in VirtualCenter. The two existing extensions include VMware Update Manager and VMware Converter.

VMware Update Manager   Controls who has the ability to manage system baselines and updates as well as configure the VMware Update Manager service.

Table 8.1 details the default privileges assigned to each of the VirtualCenter roles.

TABLE 8.1:   Table of Privileges for Default Roles

	ADMINISTRATOR	DATACENTER ADMINISTRA- TOR	VIRTUAL MACHINE ADMINIS- TRATOR	VIRTUAL MACHINE POWER USER	VIRTUAL MACHINE USER	RESOURCE POOL ADMIN- ISTRATOR
All Privileges	✓		✓		✓	✓
Global	✓	✓	✓	✓	✓	
Manage Custom Attributes	✓		✓	✓		
Set Custom Attribute	✓	✓	✓			
Log Event	✓	✓	✓			
Cancel Task	✓	✓	✓	✓	✓	
Licenses	✓	✓	✓			
Diagnostics	✓	✓	✓			
Settings	✓	✓	✓			
VC Server	✓	✓	✓			
Folder	✓	✓	✓			
Create Folder	✓	✓	✓			✓
Delete Folder	✓	✓	✓			✓
Rename Folder	✓	✓	✓			✓
Move Folder	✓	✓	✓			✓
Datacenter	✓	✓	✓			
Create Datacenter	✓	✓	✓			
Remove Datacenter	✓	✓	✓			
Rename Datacenter	✓	✓	✓			
Move Datacenter	✓	✓	✓			

TABLE 8.1:   Table of Privileges for Default Roles *(CONTINUED)*

	ADMINISTRATOR	DATACENTER ADMINISTRA-TOR	VIRTUAL MACHINE ADMINIS-TRATOR	VIRTUAL MACHINE POWER USER	VIRTUAL MACHINE USER	RESOURCE POOL ADMIN-ISTRATOR
Datastore	✓	✓	✓	✓		✓
Rename File	✓	✓	✓			
Remove Datastore	✓	✓	✓			
Browse Datastore	✓	✓	✓	✓		✓
Remove File	✓	✓	✓			
Network	✓	✓	✓			
Remove	✓	✓	✓			
Host	✓	✓	✓			
Inventory	✓	✓	✓			
Add Standalone Host	✓	✓	✓			
Create Cluster	✓	✓	✓			
Add Host To Cluster	✓	✓	✓			
Remove Host	✓	✓	✓			
Move Cluster/Standalone Host	✓	✓	✓			
Rename Cluster	✓	✓	✓			
Remove Cluster	✓	✓	✓			
Modify Cluster	✓	✓	✓			
Move Host	✓	✓	✓			

TABLE 8.1:   Table of Privileges for Default Roles *(CONTINUED)*

	ADMINISTRATOR	DATACENTER ADMINISTRATOR	VIRTUAL MACHINE ADMINISTRATOR	VIRTUAL MACHINE POWER USER	VIRTUAL MACHINE USER	RESOURCE POOL ADMINISTRATOR
Configuration	✓	✓	✓			
Connection	✓	✓	✓			
Maintenance	✓	✓	✓			
Virtual Machine Auto-Start Configuration	✓		✓			
HyperThreading	✓	✓	✓			
Storage Partition Configuration	✓		✓			
Security Profile and Firewall	✓	✓	✓			
Memory Configuration	✓	✓	✓			
Network Configuration	✓		✓			
Advanced Settings	✓	✓	✓			
System Resource Allocation	✓	✓	✓			
Change SNMP settings	✓	✓	✓			
Local Operations	✓		✓			
Add Host to VirtualCenter	✓		✓			
Manage User Groups	✓		✓			
Create Virtual Machine	✓		✓			
Delete Virtual Machine	✓		✓			

TABLE 8.1:   Table of Privileges for Default Roles *(CONTINUED)*

	ADMINISTRATOR	DATACENTER ADMINISTRATOR	VIRTUAL MACHINE ADMINISTRATOR	VIRTUAL MACHINE POWER USER	VIRTUAL MACHINE USER	RESOURCE POOL ADMINISTRATOR
Virtual Machine	✓	✓	✓	✓	✓	✓
Inventory	✓		✓			✓
Create	✓		✓			✓
Remove	✓		✓			✓
Move	✓		✓			✓
Interaction	✓		✓	✓	✓	✓
Power On	✓		✓	✓	✓	✓
Power Off	✓		✓	✓	✓	✓
Suspend	✓		✓	✓	✓	✓
Reset	✓		✓	✓	✓	✓
Answer Question	✓		✓	✓	✓	✓
Console Interaction	✓		✓	✓	✓	✓
Device Connection	✓		✓	✓	✓	✓
Configure CD Media	✓		✓	✓	✓	✓
Configure Floppy Media	✓		✓	✓	✓	✓
Tools Install	✓		✓	✓	✓	✓
Configuration	✓		✓	✓		✓
Rename	✓		✓	✓		✓
Add Existing Disk	✓		✓	✓		✓
Add New Disk	✓		✓	✓		✓
Remove Disk	✓		✓	✓		✓

TABLE 8.1:   Table of Privileges for Default Roles *(CONTINUED)*

	ADMINISTRATOR	DATACENTER ADMINISTRATOR	VIRTUAL MACHINE ADMINISTRATOR	VIRTUAL MACHINE POWER USER	VIRTUAL MACHINE USER	RESOURCE POOL ADMINISTRATOR
Raw Device	✓		✓	✓		✓
Change CPU Count	✓		✓	✓		✓
Memory	✓		✓	✓		✓
Add or Remove Device	✓		✓	✓		✓
Modify Device Settings	✓		✓	✓		✓
Settings	✓		✓	✓		✓
Change Resource	✓		✓	✓		✓
Upgrade Guest Information	✓		✓	✓		✓
Advanced	✓		✓	✓		✓
Disk Lease	✓		✓	✓		✓
State	✓		✓	✓		✓
Create Snapshot	✓		✓	✓		✓
Revert To Snapshot	✓		✓	✓		✓
Remove Snapshot	✓		✓	✓		✓
Rename Snapshot	✓		✓	✓		✓
Provisioning	✓	✓	✓			✓
Customize	✓		✓			✓
Clone	✓		✓			✓
Create Template From Virtual Machine	✓		✓			✓

TABLE 8.1: Table of Privileges for Default Roles *(CONTINUED)*

	ADMINISTRATOR	DATACENTER ADMINISTRATOR	VIRTUAL MACHINE ADMINISTRATOR	VIRTUAL MACHINE POWER USER	VIRTUAL MACHINE USER	RESOURCE POOL ADMINISTRATOR
Deploy Template	✓		✓			✓
Clone Template	✓		✓			✓
Mark As Template	✓		✓			✓
Mark As Virtual Machine	✓		✓			✓
Read Customization Specifications	✓	✓	✓			✓
Modify Customization Specifications	✓	✓	✓			✓
Allow Disk Access	✓		✓			✓
Allow Read-Only Disk Access	✓		✓			✓
Allow Virtual Machine Download	✓		✓			✓
Allow Virtual Machine Files Upload	✓		✓			✓
Resource	✓	✓	✓			✓
Assign Virtual Machine to Resource Pool	✓	✓	✓			✓
Apply Recommendation	✓	✓	✓			
Create Pool	✓	✓	✓			✓
Rename Pool	✓	✓	✓			✓
Modify Pool	✓	✓	✓			✓

TABLE 8.1:   Table of Privileges for Default Roles *(CONTINUED)*

	ADMINISTRATOR	DATACENTER ADMINISTRA-TOR	VIRTUAL MACHINE ADMINIS-TRATOR	VIRTUAL MACHINE POWER USER	VIRTUAL MACHINE USER	RESOURCE POOL ADMIN-ISTRATOR
Move Pool	✓	✓	✓			✓
Remove Pool	✓	✓	✓			✓
Migrate	✓	✓	✓			✓
Relocate	✓	✓	✓			✓
Query VMotion	✓	✓	✓			✓
Alarms	✓	✓	✓			✓
Create Alarm	✓	✓	✓			✓
Remove Alarm	✓	✓	✓			✓
Modify Alarm	✓	✓	✓			✓
Scheduled Task	✓	✓	✓	✓	✓	✓
Create Tasks	✓	✓	✓	✓	✓	✓
Remove Task	✓	✓	✓	✓	✓	✓
Run Task	✓	✓	✓	✓	✓	✓
Modify Task	✓	✓	✓	✓	✓	✓
Sessions	✓		✓			
View and Terminate Sessions	✓		✓			
Global Message	✓		✓			
Performance	✓		✓			
Modify Intervals	✓		✓			
Permissions	✓					✓
Modify Role	✓					
Reassign Role Permissions	✓					
Modify Permission	✓					✓

 **Real World Scenario**

DELEGATING THE ABILITY TO CREATE VIRTUAL MACHINES AND INSTALL A GUEST OPERATING SYSTEM

One common access control delegation in a virtual infrastructure is to give a group of users the rights to create virtual machines. After just browsing through the list of available privileges, it might seem simple to accomplish this. It is, however, more complex than meets the eye. Providing a user with the ability to create a virtual machine involves assigning a combination of privileges at multiple levels throughout the VirtualCenter inventory.

Follow these steps to allow a Windows-based user or group to create virtual machines:

1. Use the VI Client to connect to a virtual server. Log in with a user account that has been assigned the Administrator role.

2. Create a new role called **VMCreators**.

3. Select the following privileges:

```
Virtual Machine | Inventory | Create
Virtual Machine | Inventory | Add new disk
Virtual Machine | Inventory | Add existing disk
Virtual Machine | Configuration | Raw Device
```

4. Create a new role called **VMAssigners**:

```
Resource | Assign virtual machine to Resource Pool
```

5. Assign a Windows-based user or group the VMCreators role on a folder or datacenter object.

6. Assign the same Windows-based user or group the VMAssigners role on a resource pool, host, or cluster.

7. Assign the same Windows-based user or group the Read-Only role on a datacenter object or a folder containing a datacenter object. Disable the propagation if the role is assigned directly to the datacenter. Leave the propagation enabled if the role is assigned to a folder that contains the datacenter object.

At this point, the privileges for creating a virtual machine are complete; however, the user or group from steps 5 through 7 does not have the rights to mount an ISO image and therefore could not install a guest operating system.

Perform these steps to allow a Windows-based user or group to install a guest operating system from an ISO file:

1. Use the VI Client to connect to a virtual server. Log in with a user account that has been assigned the Administrator role.

2. Create a new role named **GOS_Installers**.

3. Select the following privileges:

```
Datastore | Browse Datastore
Virtual Machine | Configuration
Virtual Machine | Interaction
```

4. Assign a Windows-based user or group the GOS_Installers role on the datacenter object.

Manage your permissions carefully. Do not provide more permissions than are necessary for the job role at hand. It is always better to err on the side of caution when it comes to delegating authority. Just as in any other information systems environment, your access control implementation will be a living object that will consistently require consideration and revision. Be flexible, and expect that users and administrators alike are going to be curious and will push their access levels to the limits. Stay a step ahead and always remember the principle of least privilege.

Virtual Machine Management Using the Web Console

Imagine a situation where you are away from your desk at the office and you get a call or a page indicating that there is a problem with a virtual machine in one of your datacenters. These types of situations have been known to happen. Your desk isn't close at hand and you don't have your laptop with you. How can you quickly take a look at the virtual machine in order to diagnose the issue?

Fortunately, VMware has included an optional web service that can be installed on your VirtualCenter server and is installed by default on all of your ESX hosts. All it requires is a web browser and IP connectivity.

VIRTUALCENTER WEB ACCESS BROWSER REQUIREMENTS

Connecting to the VirtualCenter web access utility from a Windows or Linux client requires any of the following browsers:

◆ Internet Explorer 6.0 or later (Windows only)

◆ Netscape Navigator 7.0

◆ Mozilla 1.x

◆ Firefox 1.0.7 or later

This service can give you access to the virtual machines running in your infrastructure, and it is based on the Apache Tomcat web service. The Apache Tomcat web service is part of the VirtualCenter installation, as you learned in Chapter 5. Tomcat is most commonly known for its use as a web server running on Linux operating systems. However, the Windows version of Tomcat is used for the web access component of VirtualCenter instead of building on top of the Internet Information Services (IIS) web server available natively in Windows. This web access component, like the VI Client, maintains the level of security as defined by the permissions established in VirtualCenter.

To use the web console to access and manage virtual machines on a VirtualCenter server:

1. Open a web browser and type in the IP address or fully qualified domain name of the VirtualCenter server.

2. At the default VirtualCenter web page, shown in Figure 8.26, click the Log In to Web Access link.

FIGURE 8.26
VirtualCenter default web page

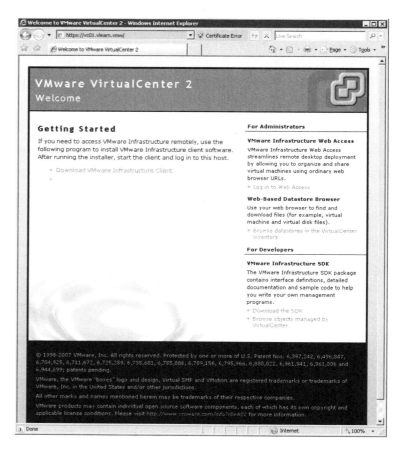

3. Type a valid username and password at the VMware Virtual Infrastructure Web Access login page, shown in Figure 8.27.

Once you have entered a valid Windows username and password for a user that has permissions in VirtualCenter, you'll see an inventory of the virtual machines, as shown in Figure 8.28.

FIGURE 8.27
By logging in to Virtual-Center via the web page, you maintain the same security as the VI Client.

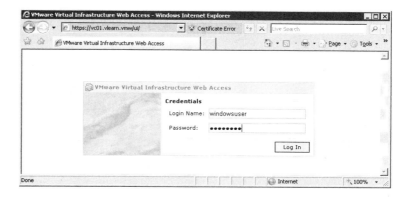

FIGURE 8.28
The web console lets you access and manage the virtual machines that are available to you.

WEB-BASED VIRTUAL MACHINE MANAGEMENT

The VirtualCenter web console is used solely for the purpose of accessing and managing virtual machines. There will not be any ESX Server hosts listed in the inventory; you must perform all host management tasks through the VI Client or from a command line.

Selecting an individual virtual machine alters the layout of the web console by offering additional tabs and links for managing the virtual machine. Figure 8.29 shows the default view once a virtual machine has been selected in the inventory. In addition to the five management tabs, the toolbar at the top of the page contains buttons for managing virtual machine power states as well as CD-ROM, floppy, and network devices.

FIGURE 8.29

You can view details on console access, hardware management, and power management.

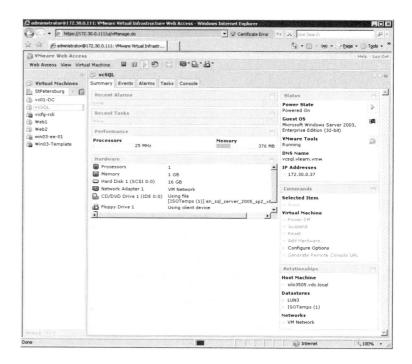

The Events tab, shown in Figure 8.30, details the most recent events that have occurred for the selected virtual machine. Events in this view include information on changes in power state as well as resource utilization.

The Alarms tab will allow you to examine the recent alerts that this virtual machine has triggered according to the Alarms that are configured for the virtual machine. Alarm creation and management will be discussed in great detail in Chapter 11.

The Tasks tab lists any recent tasks that have recently taken place upon the virtual machine along with any tasks that might still be in progress.

As shown in Figure 8.31, the Console tab provides access to a console session for the virtual machine that grants access similar to using a keyboard and mouse connected directly to a physical server.

FIGURE 8.30
Events tab in the web console

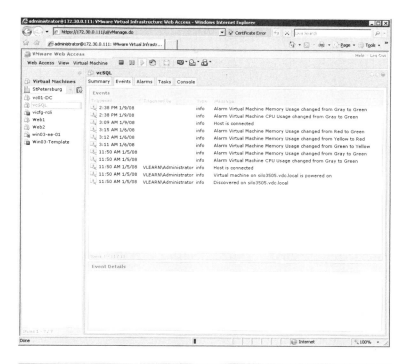

FIGURE 8.31
The Console tab provides desktop access to a virtual machine when traditional in-band management tools are inoperable.

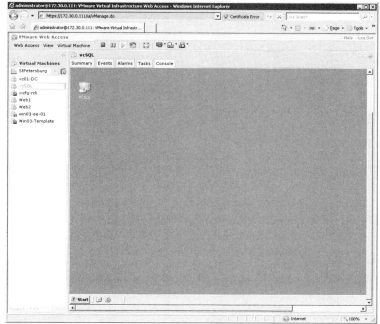

WEB SERVICE CONNECTIONS

The web console is not meant to be a replacement for Terminal Services, Remote Desktop, VNC, Citrix, or any other remote management tool. The greatest value to the web console is during the situation where the aforementioned in-band management tools are unable to connect to a server. The web console will provide access for the purposes of troubleshooting and restoring common remote management tools. However, the web console also poses problems when multiple users establish connections. Since the connection is considered a console session, multiple users would be forced to share mouse and keyboard control unlike a typical Remote Desktop or Terminal Services connection, where users would be unaware of each other's presence without some investigation.

You can log in to a virtual machine desktop through the web console by pressing Ctrl+Alt+ Insert or by clicking the Virtual Machine menu in the toolbar and then selecting the Send Ctrl+Alt+ Delete option.

Quickly revisit Figure 8.32, noting the Commands section on the right side of the page. This section contains a Generate Remote Console URL link, which generates a URL that provides direct access to a virtual machine. Figure 8.32 shows the details of the remote URL generation page. By default, the Limit View to the Remote Console and Limit View to a Single Virtual Machine options are selected, thereby confining the remote console URL to only the target virtual machine. The URL begins with the IP address or fully qualified domain name of the VirtualCenter depending on how the connection has been established in the web browser.

FIGURE 8.32
A URL generated for a virtual machine provides direct access to a console session; however, successful access still requires authentication and privileges.

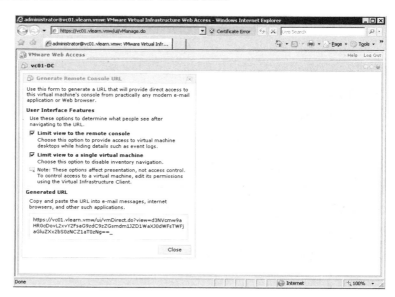

The URL is rather long and therefore not one to be committed to memory. For the user who needs occasional access to a virtual machine, the remote console URL can be pasted into an e-mail message or instant messaging session. Once the user clicks on the link, an authentication page much like the one seen earlier in this section will open. The ID that the user authenticates with must have at least the Virtual Machine User role assigned to it for the link to function as expected.

REMOTE CONSOLE URLS

The web access component of an individual ESX Server host is identical in nature to the one shown here for VirtualCenter. However, you can view only the virtual machines on that specific host. In addition, if a remote console URL is created by connecting to an individual host, the URL will begin with the IP address or fully qualified domain name of that host instead of the VirtualCenter server's information. The problem with this arises when the virtual machine is relocated to new host as a result of VMotion or HA. The relocation of the virtual machine in this case invalidates the URL. Because of these limitations, you should always create remote console URLs by connecting to a VirtualCenter server and not an ESX Server host.

The Bottom Line

Manage and maintain ESX Server permissions. Grant permissions to an ESX Server host with caution. Ideally, the number of individuals who have the ability to connect directly to an ESX Server host should be minimized.

> **Master It** A group of administrators need the ability to connect directly to an ESX Server host to perform management tasks.

Manage and maintain VirtualCenter permissions. The VirtualCenter permissions model builds off Windows-based user accounts and provides a great degree of flexibility, thus allowing virtual infrastructure administrators to maintain the principle of least privilege.

> **Master It** Domain administrators from a Windows Active Directory domain should not be able to manage the virtual infrastructure.

> **Master It** Users with Windows-based groups need varying levels of access to the VirtualCenter inventory.

> **Master It** A default VirtualCenter role provides too much permission for a new user who needs access to VirtualCenter objects.

Manage virtual machines using the web console. The web console utility is solely for the management of virtual machines. It is a great tool for allowing virtual machine administrators management capabilities without using the full VI Client. Like the VI Client, however, the web console is an excellent means for connecting to a virtual machine when traditional in-band management tools are not available.

> **Master It** You need to access a virtual machine but the corporate firewall does not permit traffic on nonstandard ports.

> **Master It** You need to send a Windows administrator a link that will provide access to a virtual machine console. The administrator wants to establish this link as an Internet Explorer favorite.

Chapter 9

Managing and Monitoring Resource Access

The idea that we can take a single physical server and host many virtual machines has a great deal of value in today's dynamic datacenter environments, but let's face it — there are limits to how many virtual machines can be hosted on an ESX Server platform. The key to making the most of your virtualization platform is understanding how resources are consumed by the virtual machines running on the host and how the host itself consumes resources. Then, there's the issue of how we, the administrators, can exercise control over the way a virtual machine or group of virtual machines uses resources.

The key resources are memory, processors, disks, and networks. When a number of virtual machines are hosted on an ESX host, each virtual machine consumes some of these resources; however, the method the ESX Server uses to arbitrate access to each resource is a bit different. This chapter will discuss how the ESX Server allocates these resources, how you can change the way these resources are allocated, and how you can monitor the consumption of these resources over time.

In this chapter you will learn to:

◆ Manage virtual machine memory

◆ Manage virtual machine CPU allocation

◆ Create and manage resource pools

◆ Configure and execute VMotion

◆ Create and manage clusters

◆ Configure and manage Distributed Resource Scheduling (DRS)

Allocating Virtual Machine Memory

One of the most significant advantages of server virtualization is the ability to allocate resources to a virtual machine based on the machine's actual performance needs. In the traditional physical server environment, a server is often provided with more resources than it really needs because it was purchased with a specific budget in mind and the server specifications were maximized for the budget provided. For example, does a DHCP server really need dual processors, 4GB of RAM, and 146GB mirrored hard drives? In most situations, the DHCP server will most certainly under-utilize those resources. In the virtual world, we can create a virtual machine better suited for the DHCP services provided by the virtual machine. For this DHCP server, then, we would assemble a virtual machine with a more suitable 1GB of RAM, access to a single CPU, and 20GB of disk space, all of which are provided by the ESX host that the virtual machine is running on. Then, we can create additional virtual machines with the resources they need to operate effectively without wasting valuable memory, CPU cycles, and disk storage. As we add more virtual machines, each machine places additional demand on the ESX Server, and the host's resources are consumed to support the virtual machines. At a certain point, either the host will run out of resources or we will need to find an alternate way to share access to a limited resource.

THE GAME PLAN FOR GROWTH

One of the most challenging aspects of managing a virtual infrastructure is managing growth without jeopardizing performance and without overestimating. From small business to large enterprise, it is critical to establish a plan for managing virtual machine and ESX Server growth.

The easiest approach is to construct a resource consumption document that details the following:

◆ What is the standard configuration for a new virtual machine to be added to the inventory? What is the size of the operating system drive? What is the size of the data drive? How much RAM will it be allocated?

◆ What are the decision points for creating a virtual machine with specifications beyond the standard configuration?

◆ How much of a server's resources can be consumed before availability and performance levels are jeopardized?

◆ At the point where the resources for an ESX Server (or an entire cluster) are consumed, do we add a single host or multiple hosts at one time?

◆ What is the maximum size of a cluster for our environment? When does adding another host (or set of hosts) constitute building a new cluster?

Let's start with how memory is allocated to a virtual machine. Then, we'll discuss the mechanisms ESX will use to arbitrate access to the memory under contention and what you as administrator can do to change how virtual machines access memory.

When you create a new virtual machine through the VI Client, the wizard will ask you how much memory the virtual machine should have, as shown in Figure 9.1.

The amount of memory you allocate on this screen is the amount the guest operating system will see — in this example, it is 1024MB. This is the same as when you build a system and put two 512MB memory sticks into the system board. If we install Windows 2003 in this virtual machine, Windows will report 1024MB of RAM installed. Ultimately this is the amount of memory the virtual machine "thinks" that it has.

Let's assume we have an ESX Server with 4GB of physical RAM available to run virtual machines (in other words, the Service Console and VMkernel are using some RAM and there's 4GB left over for the virtual machines). In the case of our new virtual machine, it will comfortably run, leaving approximately 3GB for other virtual machines (there is some additional overhead that we will discuss later, but for now let's assume that the 3GB is available to other virtual machines).

What happens when we run three more virtual machines each configured with 1GB of RAM? Each of the additional virtual machines will request 1GB of RAM from the ESX host. At this point, four virtual machines will be accessing the physical memory.

What happens when you launch a fifth virtual machine? Will it run? The short answer is yes, but the key to understanding why this is so is the mechanism that ESX Server employs — and it is based on some default settings in the virtual machines' configuration that administrators have control over.

FIGURE 9.1
Initial Memory settings for a virtual machine indicate the amount of RAM the virtual machine "thinks" that it has.

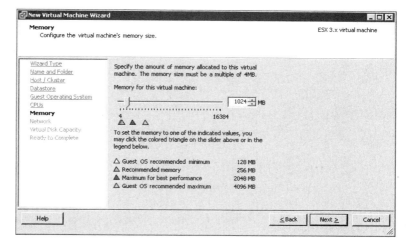

In the advanced settings for a virtual machine, as shown in Figure 9.2, we can see there is a setting for a reservation, a limit, and shares. In this discussion, we will examine the limit and reservation settings and then come back later to deal with the shares.

FIGURE 9.2
Each virtual machine can be configured with a shares value, a reservation, and a limit.

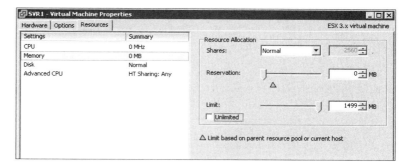

To edit the reservation, limit, or shares of a virtual machine:

1. Use the VI Client to connect to a VirtualCenter Server or directly to an ESX Server host.

2. Drill down through the inventory to find the virtual machine to be edited.

3. Right-click the virtual machine and select the Edit Settings option.

4. Click the Resources tab.

5. On the Resources tab, select the CPU or Memory options from the Settings list on the left.

6. Adjust the Shares, Reservation, and Limit values as desired.

The following sections will detail the ramifications of setting custom Reservation, Limit, and Shares values.

Memory Reservation

The Reservation value is an optional setting you can set for each virtual machine — but note that the default value is 0MB, as this has a potential impact on virtual machine performance. The Reservation amount specified on the Resource tab of the virtual machine settings is the amount of actual, real physical memory that the ESX Server *must* provide to this virtual machine for the virtual machine to power on. A virtual machine with a reservation is guaranteed the amount of RAM configured in its Reservation setting. In our previous example, the virtual machine config-ured with 1GB of RAM and the default reservation of 0MB means the ESX Server does not have to provide the virtual machine with any physical memory. If the ESX Server is not required to provide actual RAM to the virtual machine, then where will the virtual machine get its memory? The answer is that it provides swap, or more specifically something called VMkernel swap.

VMkernel swap is a file created when a virtual machine is powered on with a .vswp extension. The per-virtual machine swap files created by the VMkernel reside by default in the same datastore location as the virtual machine's configuration file and virtual disk files. By default, this file will be equal to the size of the RAM that you configured the virtual machine with, and you will find it in the same folder where the rest of the virtual machines files are stored, as shown in Figure 9.3.

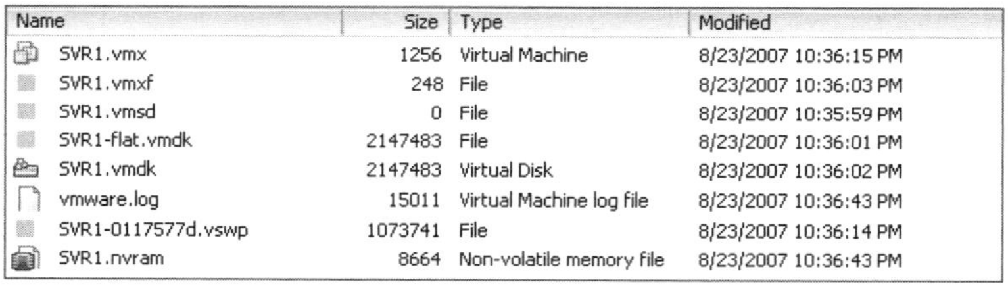

FIGURE 9.3
The VMkernel creates a per-virtual machine swap file stored in the same datastore as the other virtual machine files. The swap file has a .vswp extension.

Name	Size	Type	Modified
SVR1.vmx	1256	Virtual Machine	8/23/2007 10:36:15 PM
SVR1.vmxf	248	File	8/23/2007 10:36:03 PM
SVR1.vmsd	0	File	8/23/2007 10:35:59 PM
SVR1-flat.vmdk	2147483	File	8/23/2007 10:36:01 PM
SVR1.vmdk	2147483	Virtual Disk	8/23/2007 10:36:02 PM
vmware.log	15011	Virtual Machine log file	8/23/2007 10:36:43 PM
SVR1-0117577d.vswp	1073741	File	8/23/2007 10:36:14 PM
SVR1.nvram	8664	Non-volatile memory file	8/23/2007 10:36:43 PM

In theory, this means a virtual machine can get its memory allocation entirely from VMkernel swap — or disk — resulting in virtual machine performance degradation. If the virtual machine is configured with a reservation or a limit, the VMkernel swap file could differ.

THE SPEED OF RAM

How slow is VMkernel swap when compared to RAM? If we make some basic assumptions regarding RAM access times and disk seek times, we can see that both appear fairly fast in terms of a human but that in relation to each other RAM is faster:

RAM access time = 10 nanoseconds (for example)

Disk seek time = 8 milliseconds (for example)

The difference between these is calculated as follows:

$0.008 \div 0.000000010 = 800,000$

RAM is accessed 800,000 times faster than disk. Or to put it another way, if RAM takes 1 second to access, then disk would take 800,000 seconds to access — or nine and a quarter days — ((800,000 ÷ 60 seconds) ÷ 60 minutes) ÷ 24 hours).

As you can see, if virtual machine performance is your goal, it is prudent to spend your money on enough RAM to support the virtual machines you plan to run. There are other factors, but this is a very significant one.

Does this mean that a virtual machine will get all of its memory from swap when ESX Server RAM is available? No. What this means is that if an ESX host doesn't have enough RAM available to provide all of the virtual machines currently running on the host with their memory allocation, the VMkernel will page some of each virtual machine's memory out to the individual virtual machine's VMkernel swap file (VSWP), as shown in Figure 9.4.

FIGURE 9.4

Memory allocation for a virtual machine with 1024MB of memory configured and no reservation

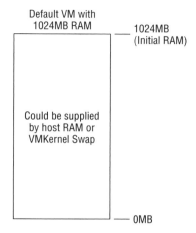

How do we control how much of an individual virtual machine's memory allocation can be provided by swap and how much must be provided by real physical RAM? This is where a memory reservation comes into play.

Let's look at what happens if we decide to set a memory reservation of 512MB for this virtual machine, shown in Figure 9.5. How does this change the way this virtual machine gets memory?

FIGURE 9.5

A virtual machine configured with a memory reservation of 512MB

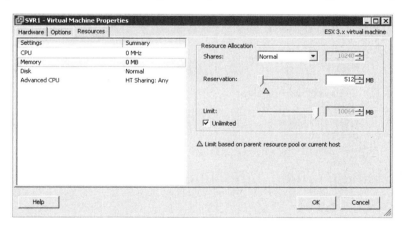

In this example, when this virtual machine is started, the host must provide at least 512MB of real RAM to support this virtual machine's memory allocation, and the host could provide the remaining 512MB of RAM from VMkernel swap. See Figure 9.6.

This ensures that a virtual machine has at least some high-speed memory available to it if the ESX host is running more virtual machines than it has actual RAM to support, but there's also a downside. If we assume that each of the virtual machines we start on this host have a 512MB reservation and we have 4GB of available RAM in the host to run virtual machines, then we will only be able to launch eight virtual machines concurrently (8 × 512MB = 4096MB). On a more positive note, if each virtual machine is configured with an initial RAM allocation of 1024MB, then we're now running virtual machines that would need 8GB of RAM on a host with only 4GB.

FIGURE 9.6
Memory allocation for a virtual machine with 1024MB of memory configured and a 512MB reservation

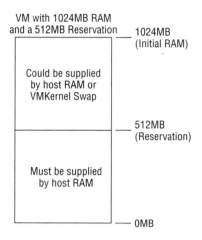

Memory Limit

If we look back at Figure 9.5, you will also see a setting for a memory limit. By default, all new virtual machines are created without a limit, which means that the initial RAM you assigned to it in the wizard is its effective limit. So, what exactly is the purpose of the limit setting? The limit sets the actual limit. A virtual machine cannot be allocated more physical memory than is configured in the limit setting.

Let's now change the limit on this virtual machine from the unlimited default setting to 768MB, as shown in Figure 9.7.

FIGURE 9.7
A virtual machine configured with 1024MB of memory, a 512MB reservation, and a 768MB limit

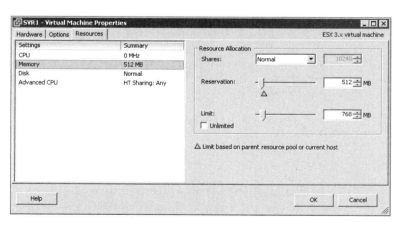

This means that the top 256MB of RAM will *always* be provided by swap, as shown in Figure 9.8.

FIGURE 9.8
Memory allocation for
a virtual machine with
1024MB of memory
configured, a 512MB
reservation, and a
768MB limit

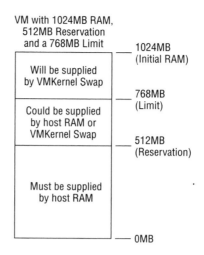

VM with 1024MB RAM,
512MB Reservation
and a 768MB Limit

1024MB
(Initial RAM)

Will be supplied
by VMKernel Swap

768MB
(Limit)

Could be supplied
by host RAM or
VMKernel Swap

512MB
(Reservation)

Must be supplied
by host RAM

0MB

Think about the server administrator who wants a new virtual machine with 16GB of RAM.
You know his application doesn't need it, but you can't talk him out of his request — and worse
than that, your supervisor has decided you need to build a virtual machine that actually has
16GB of RAM. Consider creating the virtual machine with an initial allocation of 16GB, and set a
reservation of 1GB and a limit of 2GB. The operating system installed in the virtual machine will
report 16GB of RAM (making that person happy and keeping your supervisor happy, too). The
virtual machine will always consume 1GB of host memory. If your host has available RAM, then
the virtual machine might consume up to 2GB of real physical memory with the top 14GB always
being provided by VMkernel swap. Of course, the virtual machine performance should not be
expected to perform as if it had all 16GB of memory from physical RAM.

Working together, an initial allocation of memory, a memory reservation, and a memory limit
can be powerful tools in efficiently managing the memory available on an ESX Server host.

Memory Shares

In Figure 9.5, there was a third setting called Shares that we have not discussed. The share system
in VMware is a proportional share system that provides administrators with a means of assigning
resource priority to virtual machines. For example, with memory settings, shares are a way of
establishing a priority setting for a virtual machine requesting memory that is above the virtual
machine's reservation but below its limit. In other words, if two virtual machines want more
memory than their reservation limit, and the ESX host can't satisfy both of them using RAM, we
can set share values on each virtual machine so that one gets higher-priority access to the RAM
in the ESX host than the other. Some would say that you should just increase the reservation for
that virtual machine. While that may be a valid technique, it may limit the total number of virtual
machines that a host can run, as indicated earlier in this chapter. Increasing the limit also requires
a reboot of the virtual machine to become effective, but shares can be dynamically adjusted while
the virtual machine remains powered on.

For the sake of this discussion, let's assume we have two virtual machines (VM1 and VM2)
each with a 512MB Reservation and a 1024MB Limit, and both running on an ESX host with less
than 2GB of RAM available to the virtual machines. If the two virtual machines in question have
an equal number of shares (let's assume it's 1000 each), then as each virtual machine requests
memory above its reservation value, each virtual machine will receive an equal quantity of RAM

from the ESX host and, because the host cannot supply all of the RAM to both virtual machines, each virtual machine will swap equally to disk (VMkernel pagefile VSWP).

If we change VM1's Shares setting to 2000, then VM1 now has twice the shares VM2 has assigned to it. This also means that when VM1 and VM2 are requesting the RAM above their respective reservation values, VM1 will swap one page to VMkernel pagefile for every two pages that VM2 swaps. Stated another way, VM1 gets two RAM pages for every one RAM page that VM2 gets. If VM1 has more shares, VM1 has a higher-priority access to available memory in the host.

It gets more difficult to predict the actual memory utilization and the amount of access each virtual machine gets as more virtual machines run on the same host. Later in this chapter we will discuss more sophisticated methods of assigning memory limits, reservations, and shares to a group of virtual machines using resource pools.

Allocating Virtual Machine CPU

When creating a new virtual machine using the VI Client, the only question you are asked related to CPU is, "Number of virtual processors?", as shown in Figure 9.9.

FIGURE 9.9
When a virtual machine is created, the wizard provides the opportunity to configure the virtual machine with one, two, or four virtual CPUs.

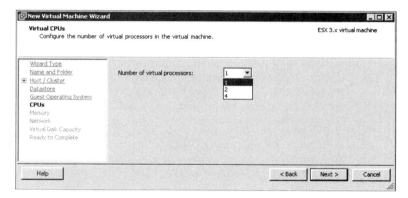

The CPU setting effectively lets the guest operating system utilize one, two, or four virtual CPUs on the host system. When the VMware engineers designed the virtualization platform, they started with a real system board and modeled the virtual machine after it — in this case, it was based on the Intel 440BX chipset. The PCI bus was something the virtual machine could emulate, and could be mapped to input/output devices through a standard interface, but how could a virtual machine emulate a CPU? The answer was "no emulation." Think about a virtual system board that has a "hole" where the CPU socket goes — and the guest operating system simply looks through the hole and sees one of the cores in the host server. This allowed the VMware engineers to avoid writing CPU emulation software that would need to change each time the CPU vendors introduced new instruction sets. If there was an emulation layer, it would also add a significant quantity of overhead, which would limit the performance of the virtualization platform by adding more computational overhead.

So how many CPUs should a virtual machine have? Creating a virtual machine to replace a physical DHCP server that runs at less than 10 percent CPU utilization at its busiest point in the day surely does not need more than one virtual CPU. As a matter of fact, if we give this virtual machine two virtual CPUs (vCPUs), then we would effectively limit the scalability of the entire host.

The VMkernel simultaneously schedules CPU cycles for multi-CPU virtual machines. This means that when a dual-CPU virtual machine places a request for CPU cycles, the request goes into a queue for the host to process, and the host has to wait until there are at least two cores with concurrent idle cycles to schedule that virtual machine. This occurs even if the virtual machine only needs a few clock cycles to do some menial task that could be done with a single processor. Think about it this way: You need to cash a check at the bank, but because of the type of account you have, you need to wait in line until two bank tellers are available *at the same time*. Normally, one teller could handle your request and you would be on your way — but now you have to wait. What about the folks behind you in the queue as you wait for two tellers? They are also waiting longer because of you.

On the other hand, if a virtual machine needs two CPUs because of the load it will be processing on a constant basis, then it makes sense to assign two CPUs to that virtual machine — but only if the host has four or more CPU cores total. If your ESX host is an older generation dual-processor single-core system, then assigning a virtual machine two vCPUs will mean that the virtual machine owns all of the CPU processing power on that host every time it gets CPU cycles. You will find that the overall performance of the host and any other virtual machines will be less than stellar.

ONE (CPU) FOR ALL. . .AT LEAST TO BEGIN WITH

Every virtual machine should be created with only a single virtual CPU so as not to create unnecessary contention for physical processor time. Only when a virtual machine's performance level dictates the need for an additional CPU should one be allocated. Remember that multi-CPU virtual machines should only be created on ESX Server hosts that have more cores than the number of virtual CPUs being assigned to the virtual machine. A dual-CPU virtual machine should only be created on a host with two or more cores, and a quad-CPU virtual machine should only be created on a host with four or more cores.

Default CPU Allocation

Like the memory settings discussed, the settings Shares, Reservation, and Limit can be configured for CPU. Figure 9.10 shows the default values for CPU Resource settings.

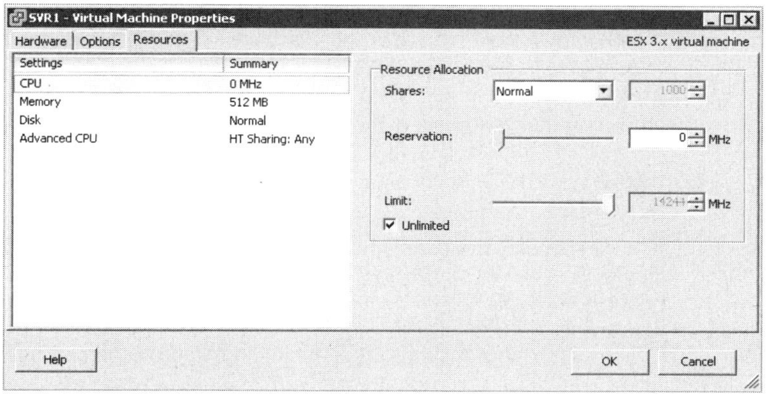

FIGURE 9.10
A virtual machine's CPU can be configured with Shares, Reservation, and Limit values.

When a new virtual machine is created with a single vCPU, the total maximum CPU cycles for that virtual machine equals the clock speed of the host system's core. In other words, if you create a new virtual machine, it can see through the "hole in the system board" and it sees whatever the core is in terms of clock cycles per second — an ESX host with 3GHz CPUs in it will allow the virtual machine to see one 3GHz core.

CPU Reservation

As shown in Figure 9.10, the default CPU reservation for a new virtual machine starts at 0MHz. Therefore, by default a virtual machine is not guaranteed any CPU activity by the VMkernel. This means that when the virtual machine has work to be done, it places its CPU request into the CPU queue so that the VMkernel can handle the request in sequence along with all of the other virtual machines' requests. On a lightly loaded ESX host, it's unlikely the virtual machine will wait long for CPU time; however, on a heavily loaded host, the time this virtual machine may have to wait could be significant.

If we were to set a 300MHz reservation, as shown in Figure 9.11, this would effectively make that amount of CPU available instantly to this virtual machine if there is a need for CPU cycles.

FIGURE 9.11
A virtual machine configured with a 300 MHz reservation for CPU activity

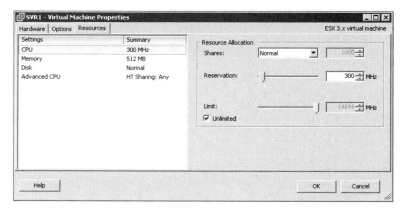

This option also has another effect similar to that of setting a memory reservation. If each virtual machine you create has a 300MHz reservation and your host has 6000MHz of CPU capabilities, you can deploy no more than 20 virtual machines even if all of them are idle. The host system must be able to satisfy all of the reservation values concurrently. Now, does that mean each virtual machine is limited to its 300MHz? Absolutely not — that's the good news. If VM1 is idle and VM2 needs more than its CPU reservation, the ESX host will schedule more clock cycles to VM2. If VM1 suddenly needs cycles, VM2 doesn't get them any more and they are assigned to VM1.

CPU Limit

Every virtual machine has an option that you can set to place a limit on the amount of CPU allocated. This will effectively limit the virtual machine's ability to see a maximum number of clock cycles per second, regardless of what the host has available. Keep in mind that a single virtual CPU virtual machine hosted on a 3GHz, quad-processor ESX Server will only see a single 3GHz core as its maximum, but as administrator you could alter the limit to hide the actual maximum core speed from the virtual machine. For instance, you could set a 500MHz limit on that DHCP server so that when it reindexes the DHCP database, it won't try to take all of the 3GHz on the processor that it can see. The CPU limit provides you with the ability to show the virtual machine less processing power than is available on a core on the physical host. Not every virtual machine needs to have access to the entire processing capability of the physical processor core.

🌐 **Real World Scenario**

INCREASING CONTENTION IN THE FACE OF GROWTH

One of the most common problems administrators can encounter occurs when several virtual machines without limits are deployed on a new virtualized environment. The users get accustomed to stellar performance levels early in the environment lifecycle, but as more virtual machines are deployed and start to compete for CPU cycles, the relative performance of the first virtual machines deployed will degrade. One approach to this issue is to set a reservation of approximately 10 to 20 percent of a single core's clock rate as a reservation and add approximately 20 percent to that value for a limit on the virtual machine. For example, with 3GHz CPUs in the host, each virtual machine would start with a 300 MHz reservation and a 350 MHz limit. This would ensure that the virtual machine would perform similarly on a lightly loaded ESX host, as it will when that host becomes more heavily loaded. Consider setting these values on the virtual machine that you use to create a template since these values will pass to any new virtual machines that were deployed from that template. Please note that this is only a starting point. It is possible to limit a virtual machine that really does need more CPU capabilities, and you should always actively monitor the virtual machines to determine if they are using all of the CPU you are providing them with.

If the numbers seem low, feel free to increase them as needed. More important is the concept of setting expectations for virtual machine performance.

CPU Shares

In a manner similar to memory allocation, you can assign CPU share values to a virtual machine. The shares for CPU will determine how much CPU is provided to a virtual machine in the face of contention with other virtual machines needing CPU activity. All virtual machines, by default, start with an equal number of shares, which means that if there is competition for CPU cycles on an ESX host, each virtual machine gets serviced with equal priority. Keep in mind that this share value only affects CPU cycles that are above the reservation set for the virtual machine. In other words, the virtual machine is granted access to its reservation cycles regardless of what else is happening on the host, but if the virtual machine needs more — and there's competition — then the share values come into play.

Several conditions have to be met for shares to even be considered for allocating CPU cycles. The best way to determine this is to consider several examples. For the examples to be covered, we will assume the following details about the environment:

- The ESX Server host includes dual single-core, 3GHz CPUs.

- The ESX Server host has one or more virtual machines.

Scenario 1   The ESX host has a single virtual machine running. The shares are set at default for the running virtual machines. Will the shares value have any effect in this scenario? No — there's no competition between virtual machines for CPU time.

Scenario 2   The ESX host has two idle virtual machines running. The shares are set at default for the running virtual machines. Will the shares values have any effect in this scenario? No — there's no competition between virtual machines for CPU time as both are idle.

Scenario 3   The ESX host has two equally busy virtual machines running (both requesting maximum CPU capabilities). The shares are set at default for the running virtual machines.

Will the shares values have any effect in this scenario? No. Again, there's no competition between virtual machines for CPU time, this time because each virtual machine is serviced by a different core in the host.

Scenario 4 To force contention, both virtual machines are configured to use the same CPU by setting the CPU affinity, shown in Figure 9.12. The ESX host has two equally busy virtual machines running (both requesting maximum CPU capabilities). This ensures contention between the virtual machines.

FIGURE 9.12
CPU affinity can tie a virtual machine to physical CPU at the expense of eliminating VMotion capability.

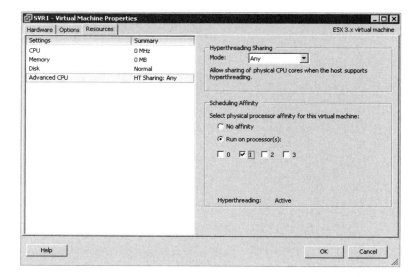

The shares are set at default for the running virtual machines. Will the shares values have any effect in this scenario? Yes! But in this case, since all virtual machines have equal share values, this ensures that each virtual machine has equal access to the host's CPU queue, so we don't see any effects from the share values.

Scenario 5 The ESX host has two equally busy virtual machines running (both requesting maximum CPU capabilities with CPU affinity set to the same core). The shares are set as follows: VM1 = 2000 CPU shares and VM2 is set to the default 1000 CPU shares. Will the shares values have any effect in this scenario? Yes. In this case, VM1 has double the number of shares that VM2 has. This means that for every clock cycle that VM2 is assigned by the host, VM1 is assigned two clock cycles. Stated another way, out of every three clock cycles assigned to virtual machines by the ESX host: two are assigned to VM1 and one is assigned to VM2.

CPU AFFINITY SETTINGS

If the option for CPU affinity is not present on a virtual machine, then check if this virtual machine is being hosted by a DRS cluster. CPU affinity is one of the items that must not be set for VMotion to function, and DRS uses VMotion to perform load balancing across the cluster. If CPU affinity is required on a virtual machine, it cannot be hosted by a DRS cluster. In addition, if you have CPU affinity set on a virtual machine and you then enable DRS, it will remove those CPU affinity settings.

The CPU affinity setting should be avoided at all costs. Even if a virtual machine is configured to use a single CPU (for example, CPU1), it does not guarantee that it will be the only virtual machine accessing that CPU unless every other virtual machine is configured not to use that CPU. At this point, VMotion capability will be unavailable for every virtual machine. In short, don't do it. It's not worth losing VMotion. Use shares, limits, and reservations as an alternative.

Scenario 6 The ESX host has three equally busy virtual machines running (each requesting maximum CPU capabilities with CPU affinity set to the same core). The shares are set as follows: VM1 = 2000 CPU shares and VM2 and VM3 are set to the default 1000 CPU shares. Will the shares values have any effect in this scenario? Yes. In this case, VM1 has double the number of shares that VM2and VM3 have assigned. This means that for every two clock cycles that VM1 is assigned by the host, VM2 and VM3 are each assigned a single clock cycle. Stated another way, out of every four clock cycles assigned to virtual machines by the ESX host: two cycles are assigned to VM1, one is assigned to VM2, and one is assigned to VM3. You can see that this has effectively watered down VM1's CPU capabilities.

Scenario 7 The ESX host has three virtual machines running. VM1 is idle while VM2 and VM3 are equally busy (each requesting maximum CPU capabilities, and all three virtual machines are set with the same CPU affinity). The shares are set as follows: VM1 = 2000 CPU shares and VM2 and VM3 are set to the default 1000 CPU shares. Will the shares values have any effect in this scenario? Yes. But in this case VM1 is idle, which means it isn't requesting any CPU cycles. This means that VM1's shares value is not considered when apportioning host CPU to the active virtual machines. In this case, VM2 and VM3 would equally share the host CPU cycles as their shares are set to an equal value.

Given these scenarios, if we were to extrapolate to an eight-core host with 30 or so virtual machines it would be difficult to set share values on a virtual machine–by–virtual machine basis and to predict how the system will respond. Additionally, if the scenario were played out on a DRS cluster, where virtual machines can dynamically move from host to host based on available host resources, it would be even more difficult to predict how an individual virtual machine would get CPU resources based strictly on the share mechanisms. The question then becomes, "Are shares a useful tool?" The answer is yes, but in large enterprise environments, we need to examine resource pools and the ability to set share parameters along with reservations and limits on collections of virtual machines. And with that, let's introduce resource pools.

Resource Pools

The previously discussed settings for virtual machine resource allocation (memory and CPU reservations, limits, and shares) are methods used to designate the priority of an individual virtual machine compared to other virtual machines also seeking access to resources. In much the same way as we assign users to groups and then assign permissions to the groups, we can leverage resource pools to make the allocation of resources to collections of virtual machines a less tedious and more effective process.

A resource pool is a special type of container object, much like a folder, in the Hosts & Clusters view of inventory. We can create a resource pool on a stand-alone host or as a management object in a DRS cluster (discussed later in this chapter). Figure 9.13 shows the creation of a resource pool.

If you examine the properties of the resource pool, as shown in Figure 9.14, you'll see there are two sections: one for CPU settings (reservation, limit, and shares) and another section with similar settings for memory.

FIGURE 9.13
Resource pools can be created on individual hosts and within clusters. A resource pool provides a management and performance configuration layer in VirtualCenter inventory.

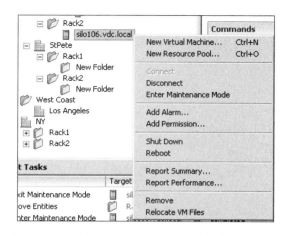

FIGURE 9.14
A resource pool is used for managing CPU and memory resources for multiple virtual machines contained within the resource pool.

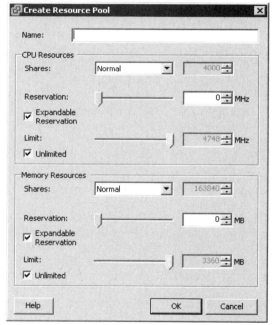

To describe the function of resource pools, consider the following example. A company has two main classifications of servers: production and development. The goal of resource allocation in this scenario is to ensure that if there's competition for a particular resource, the virtual machines in production should be assigned higher-priority access to that resource. In addition to that goal, we need to ensure that the virtual machines in development cannot consume more than 4GB of physical memory with their running virtual machines. We don't care how many virtual machines run concurrently as part of the development group as long as they don't collectively consume more than 4GB of RAM.

The first step in creating the infrastructure to support the outlined goal is to create two resource pools: one called ProductionVMs and one called DevelopmentVMs, shown in Figure 9.15.

FIGURE 9.15
Two resource pools created on an ESX Server host

We will then modify the resource pool settings for each resource pool to reflect the goals of the organization, as shown in Figures 9.16 and 9.17.

FIGURE 9.16
The ProductionVMs resource pool is configured to be able to consume more resources in the face of contention.

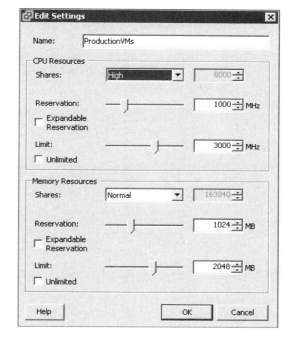

As a final step in configuring the environment, the virtual machines must be moved into the appropriate resource pool by clicking on the virtual machine in the inventory panel and dragging it onto the appropriate resource pool. The result will be similar to that shown in Figure 9.18.

Now that we've got an example to work with, let's examine what the settings on each of these resource pools will do for the virtual machines contained in each of the resource pools.

In Figure 9.16, we set the ProductionVMs CPU shares to High (8000). In Figure 9.17, we set the DevelopmentVMs CPU shares to Low (2000). The effect of these two settings is similar to that of comparing two virtual machines' CPU share values — except in this case, if there is any competition for CPU resources between virtual machines in the ProductionVMs and the DevelopmentVMs resource pool, the ProductionVMs would have higher priority. To make this clearer, let's examine Figure 9.19 with the assumption that all the available virtual machines are competing for CPU cycles on the same physical CPU. Remember that share allocations only come into play when virtual machines are fighting one another for a resource. If an ESX Server host is only running four virtual machines on top of two dual-core processors, there won't be much contention to manage.

If there are two or more virtual machines in a resource pool that require different priority access to resources, we can still set individual Shares values on the virtual machines, or if we have groupings of virtual machines within a resource pool, we can also build a resource pool in a resource pool. A resource pool within a resource pool is called a child resource pool, and it contains its own shares, limits, and reservations separate from the parent resource pool.

FIGURE 9.17
The DevelopmentVMs resource pool is configured not to be able to consume more resources in the face of contention.

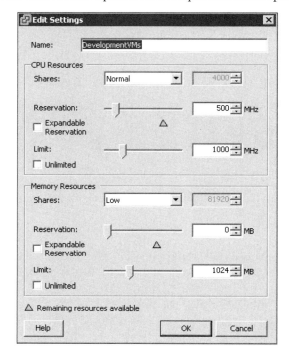

FIGURE 9.18
Virtual machines assigned to a resource pool consume resources allocated to the resource pool.

The next setting in the Resource Pool properties to evaluate is CPU Reservation (Figure 9.14). In the example, a CPU Reservation value of 1000MHz has been set on the ProductionVMs resource pool. This will ensure that at least 1000MHz of CPU time is available for all of the virtual machines located in that resource pool. This setting will have an additional effect: assuming that the ESX Server host has a total of 6000MHz of total CPU, this means 5000MHz of CPU time is available to other resource pools. If two more resource pools are created with a reservation value of 2500MHz each, then the cumulative reservations on the system have reserved all available host CPU (1000 + 2500 + 2500). This essentially means the administrator will not be able to create additional resource pools with reservation values set.

The third setting on the Resource Pool is the CPU Limit field. This is similar to the individual virtual machines CPU Limit field, except in this case all virtual machines in the resource pool combined can consume up to this value. The limit applies to the collective sum of the virtual machines within the resource pool. In the example, the ProductionVMs resource pool has been configured with a CPU limit of 3000MHz. In this case, no matter how many virtual machines are running in this resource pool, they can only consume a maximum of 3000MHz of host CPU cycles.

FIGURE 9.19

Two resource pools with different Shares values will be allocated resources proportional to their percentage of share ownership.

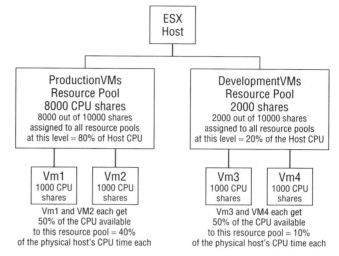

Each resource pool also includes a setting to determine if the pool has an Expandable Reservation. The Expandable Reservation dictates whether a resource pool is allowed to ask the parent pool for more resources once it has consumed all its allocated resources. Consider a child who is given a weekly allowance of $10 by their parent. Suppose the child wants to make a purchase that costs $20. If the child's allowance is set to allow Expandable Reservations, then the child could ask the parent for the additional resource, and if the parent has the resource, it will be given. If the child's allowance is not set to allow Expandable Reservations, then they cannot ask the parent for additional resources.

Therefore, if the intent is to limit the total amount of CPU available to virtual machines in a resource pool, then the Expandable Reservation check box should be left empty. If left selected, a new virtual machine with a reservation configured that exceeds the capacity of the resource pool will be powered on if the parent is able to provide the necessary resource. In this case, the pool has not provided a hard cap on the amount of reserved resources.

Moving on to the Memory portion of the Resource Pool settings, the first setting is the Shares value. This setting works in much the same way as Memory Shares worked on individual virtual machines. It determines which pool of virtual machines will be the first to page in the face of contention. However, this setting is used to set a priority value for any virtual machine in the resource pool when competing for resources with virtual machines in other resource pools. Looking at the Memory Share settings in our example (ProductionVMs = Normal and DevelopmentVMs = Low), this would generally mean that if host memory was limited, virtual machines in the DevelopmentVMs area that need more memory than their reservation would use more pages in VMkernel swap than an equivalent virtual machine in the ProductionVMs resource pool.

The Memory Reservation value will reserve this amount of host RAM for virtual machines in this resource pool to run, which effectively ensures that there is some actual RAM that the virtual machines in this resource pool are guaranteed.

The Memory Limit value is an excellent way of setting a limit on how much host RAM a particular set of virtual machines can consume. If administrators have been given the "Create Virtual machines" permission in the DevelopmentVMs resource pool, then the Memory Limit value would prevent those administrators from running virtual machines that will consume more than that amount of actual host RAM. In our example, the Memory Limit value on the Development VMs resource pool is set to be 1024MB. How many virtual machines can administrators in Development create? They can create as many as they wish. But the number of virtual machines they will be able to run will be less. Unfortunately, this setting has nothing to do with the creation of virtual machines, but it will prevent administrators from running too many virtual machines at once. So how many can they run? The cap placed on memory use is not a per virtual machine setting but a cumulative setting. They might be able to run only one virtual machine with all the memory, or multiple virtual machines with lower memory configurations. Assuming that each virtual machine is created without an individual Memory Reservation value, the administrator can run as many virtual machines concurrently as she wants! The problem will be that once the virtual machines consume 1024MB of host RAM, anything above that amount will need to be provided by VMkernel swap. If she builds four virtual machines with 256MB as the initial memory amount, then all four virtual machines will consume 1024MB (assuming no overhead) and will run in real RAM. If she tries to run 20 of the same type of virtual machine, then all 20 virtual machines will share the 1024MB of RAM, even though their requirement is for 5120MB (20 × 256MB) — the remaining 4096MB would be provided by VMkernel swap. At this point performance might be noticeably slow.

The Unlimited check box should be cleared to set a limit value. The Expandable Reservation check box functions in the same way as the equivalent CPU setting. If you truly want to limit the resource pool's memory, then clear this check box.

GO BIG IF JUST FOR A MOMENT

An Expandable Reservation may not seem that useful given the comments in the text. However, think about temporarily allowing a resource pool to exceed its limit by using an expandable reservation. Consider a scenario where the Infrastructure resource pool needs more memory to deploy a new Windows 2003 virtual machine. They will use this new virtual machine to retire a Windows 2000 virtual machine and they will be doing this over the weekend. Simply select the Expandable Reservation option on Friday to effectively give them room to run both virtual machines at the same time to allow the data migration from the old virtual machine to the new one. After the weekend, verify that they have shut off the old virtual machine, clear the Expandable Reservation checkbox, and then everything is back to normal.

Memory Overhead

As they say, nothing in this world is free. There are several basic processes on an ESX host that will consume host memory. The VMkernel itself, the Service Console (272MB by default, 800MB maximum), and each virtual machine that is running will cause the VMkernel to allocate some memory to host the virtual machine above the initial amount that we assigned to it. The amount of RAM allocated to host each virtual machine depends on the configuration of each virtual machine, as shown in Table 9.1.

Exploring VMotion

We've defined the VMware VMotion feature as the ability to perform a hot migration of a virtual machine from one ESX Server host to another without service interruption. This is an extremely effective tool for load-balancing virtual machines across ESX Server hosts. Additionally, if an ESX Server host needs to be powered off for hardware maintenance or some other function that would take it out of production, VMotion can be used to migrate all active virtual machines from the host going offline to another host without waiting for a hardware maintenance window since the virtual machines will remain available to the users that need them.

TABLE 9.1:   Virtual Machine Memory Overhead

VIRTUAL CPUs	MEMORY ASSIGNED (MB)	OVERHEAD FOR 32-BIT	OVERHEAD FOR 64-BIT
		Virtual machine (MB)	Virtual machine (MB)
1	256	79	174
1	512	79	176
1	1024	84	180
1	2048	91	188
1	4096	107	204
1	8192	139	236
1	16384	203	300
2	256	97	288
2	512	101	292
2	1024	101	300
2	2048	125	316
2	4096	157	349
2	8192	221	413
2	16384	349	541
4	256	129	511
4	512	133	515
4	1024	141	523
4	2048	157	540
4	4096	189	572
4	8192	222	605
4	16384	350	734

VMotion works by copying the contents of virtual machine memory from one ESX host to another and then transferring control of the virtual machines' disk files to the target host.

VMotion operates in the following sequence of steps:

1. An administrator initiates a migration of a running virtual machine (VM1) from one ESX Server (Silo104) to another (Silo105), shown in Figure 9.20.

FIGURE 9.20
Step 1 in a VMotion migration: invoking a migration while the virtual machine is powered on.

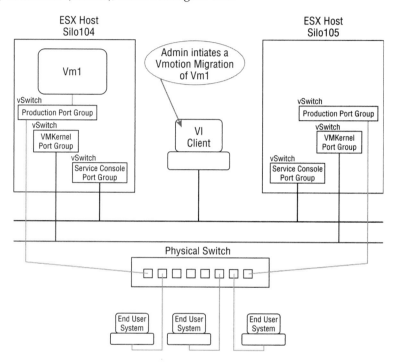

2. The source hosts (Silo104) begins copying the active memory pages VM1 has in host memory to the destination host (Silo105). During this time, the virtual machine still services clients on the source (Silo104). As the memory is copied from the source host to the target, pages in memory could be changed. ESX Server handles this by keeping a log of changes that occur in the memory of the virtual machine on the source host after that memory address has been copied to the target host. This log is called a memory bitmap as shown in Figure 9.21.

THE MEMORY BITMAP

The memory bitmap does not include the contents of the memory address that has changed; it simply includes the addresses of the memory that has changed — often referred to the "dirty memory."

---

3. Once the entire contents of RAM for the virtual machine being migrated have been transferred to the target host (SILO105), then VM1 on the source ESX Server (SILO104) is *quiesced*. This means that it is still in memory but is no longer servicing client requests for data. The memory bitmap file is then transferred to the target (Silo105). See Figure 9.22.

4. The target host (SILO105) reads the addresses in the memory bitmap file and requests the contents of those addresses from the source (SILO104). See Figure 9.23.

FIGURE 9.21
Step 2 in a VMotion migration: starting the memory copy and adding a memory bitmap

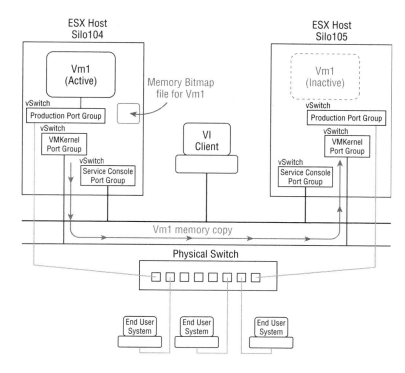

FIGURE 9.22
Step 3 in a VMotion migration: quiescing VM1 and transferring the memory bitmap file from the source ESX host to the destination ESX host

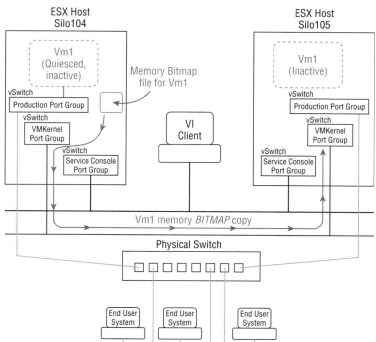

FIGURE 9.23
Step 4 in a VMotion migration: fetching the actual memory listed in the bitmap file from the source to the destination (dirty memory)

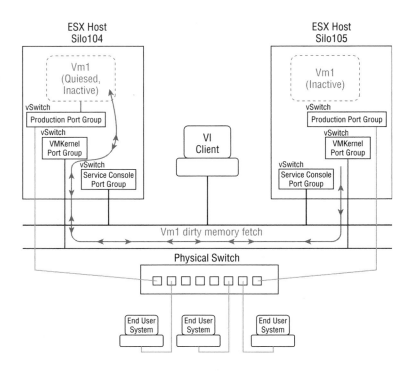

5. Once the contents of the memory referred to in the memory bitmap file have been transferred to the target host, the virtual machine starts on that host. Note that this is not a reboot — the virtual machine's state is in RAM, so the host simply enables it. This will cause a Reverse Address Resolution Protocol (RARP) from the host to register its MAC address against the physical switch port the target ESX server is plugged into. This process enables the switch infrastructure to send network packets to the appropriate ESX host from the clients who are attached to the virtual machine that just moved. See Figure 9.24.

6. Once the virtual machine is successfully operating on the target host, the memory the virtual machine was using on the source host is deleted. This memory becomes available to the VMkernel to use as appropriate. See Figure 9.25.

TRY IT WITH PING -T

Following the previous procedure carefully, you'll note there will be a time when the virtual machine being moved is not running on either the source host *or* the target host. This is typically a very short period of time. Testing has shown a continuous ping (ping -t) of the virtual machine being moved might, on a bad day, result in the loss of one ping packet. Most client-server applications are built to withstand the loss of more than a packet or two before the client is notified of a problem.

FIGURE 9.24
Step 5 in a VMotion migration: enabling the virtual machine on the target host and registering with the network infrastructure

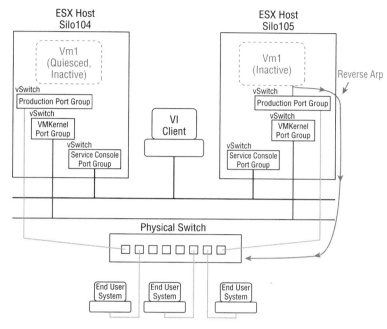

FIGURE 9.25
Step 6 in a VMotion migration: deleting the virtual machine from the source ESX host

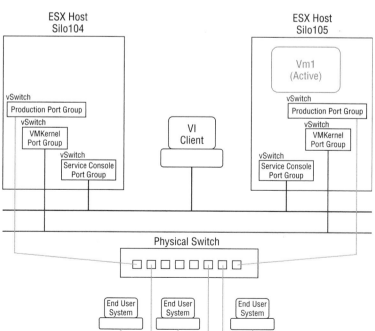

VMotion Requirements

The VMotion migration is pretty amazing, and when they see it work for the first time in a live environment, most people are extremely impressed. However, detailed planning is necessary for this procedure to function properly. The hosts involved in the VMotion process have to meet certain requirements, along with the virtual machines being migrated.

Each of the ESX Server hosts that are involved in VMotion must meet the following requirements:

◆ Shared VMFS storage for the virtual machines files

◆ A gigabit network card with a VMkernel port defined and enabled for VMotion on each host (see Figure 9.26 through Figure 9.32)

Perform these steps to create a virtual switch with a VMotion-capable VMkernel port:

1. Add a new switch that includes a VMkernel port, as shown in Figure 9.26.

FIGURE 9.26
A VMotion enabled VMkernel port is required to perform a hot migration of a virtual machine.

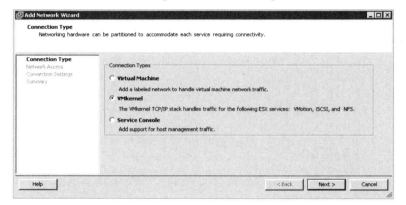

2. Choose the network adapter that is connected to the VMotion network, as shown in Figure 9.27.

FIGURE 9.27
VMotion requires a virtual switch associated to a physical network adapter, preferably on a dedicated physical network.

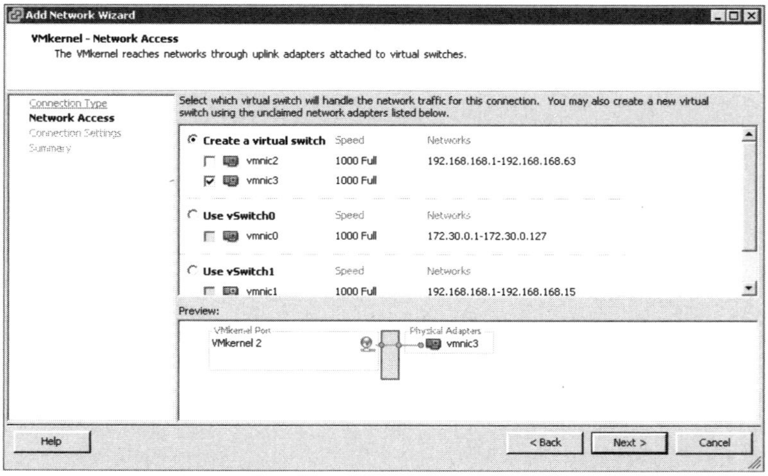

3. Enable the Use This Port Group for VMotion option and assign an IP address appropriate for the VMotion network, as shown in Figure 9.28.

FIGURE 9.28
The vSwitch with the VMkernel port group for VMotion must be VMotion capable.

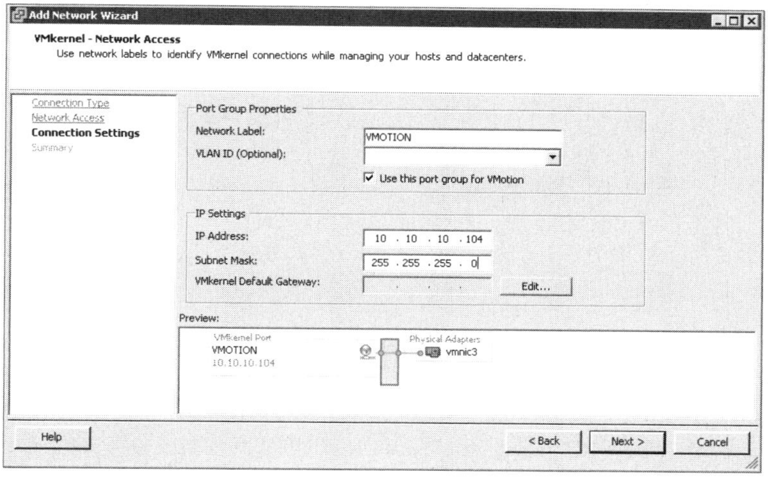

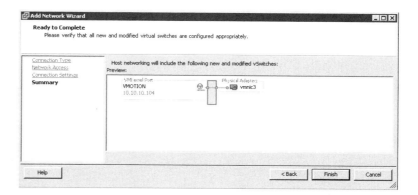

4. Click Finish. Add a default gateway if needed, as shown in Figures 9.29 and 9.30.

FIGURE 9.29
Finish the VMkernel port configuration to allow VMotion migrations.

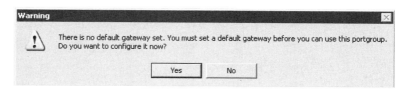

FIGURE 9.30
A default gateway can be created for the VMkernel port if one is required. VMkernel ports with VMotion enabled should not require a default getaway.

If the VMotion network is nonroutable, leave the default gateway blank or simply use the default gateway assigned for the Service Console, as shown in Figure 9.31.

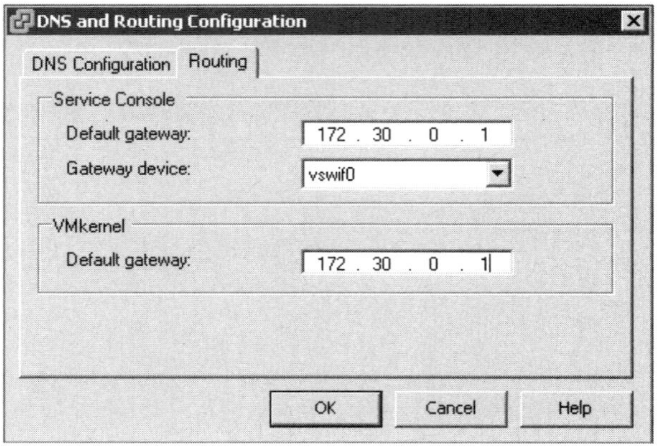

FIGURE 9.31
VMotion networks without a router do not need a default or the same default gateway as the Service Console can be entered.

DNS and Routing Configuration ☒

DNS Configuration | Routing

┌─ Service Console ─────────────────────────┐
│ Default gateway: 172 . 30 . 0 . 1   │
│ Gateway device: vswif0   ▼ │
└──┘

┌─ VMkernel ────────────────────────────────┐
│ Default gateway: 172 . 30 . 0 . 1│ │
└──┘

[OK]   [Cancel]   [Help]

A successful VMotion migration between two hosts relies on all of the following conditions being met:

◆ Both the source and destination hosts must be configured with identical virtual switches that have VMkernel port groups. The names of the switches must be the same as shown in Figure 9.32.

FIGURE 9.32
The two hosts involved in the VMotion migration must have similarly configured VMotion enabled virtual switches.

◆ All port groups to which the virtual machine being migrated is attached must exist on both ESX hosts. Port group naming is case sensitive, so create identical port groups on each host and make sure they plug into the same physical subnets or VLANs. A virtual switch named Production is not the same as a virtual switch named PRODUCTION. Remember that to prevent downtime the virtual machine is not going to change its network address as it is moved. The virtual machine will retain its MAC address and IP address so clients connected to it don't have to resolve any new information to reconnect.

◆ Processors in both hosts must be compatible. When a virtual machine is transferred between hosts, the virtual machine has already detected the type of processor it is running on when it booted. Since the virtual machine is not rebooted during a VMotion, the guest assumes the CPU instruction set on the target host is the same as on the source host. We can get away with slightly dissimilar processors, but in general the processors in two hosts that perform VMotion must meet the following requirements:

◆ CPUs must be from the same vendor (Intel or AMD).

◆ CPUs must be from the same CPU family (PIII, P4, Opteron).

- ◆ CPUs must support the same features, such as the presence of SSE2, SSE3, and SSE4, and NX or XD (see the sidebar, "Processor Instruction").

- ◆ For 64-bit virtual machines, CPUs must have virtualization technology enabled (Intel VT or AMD-v).

PROCESSOR INSTRUCTION

SSE2 (Streaming SIMD Extensions 2) was an enhancement to the original MMX instruction set found in the PIII processor. The enhancement was targeted at the floating-point calculation capabilities of the processor by providing 144 new instructions. SSE3 instruction sets are an enhancement to the SSE2 standard targeted at multimedia and graphics applications. The new SSE4 extensions target both the graphics and application server.

AMD's XD (eXecute Disable) and Intel's NX (NoExecute) are features of processors that mark memory pages as data only, which prevents a virus from running executable code at that address. The operating system needs to be written to take advantage of this feature, and in general, versions of Windows starting with Windows 2003 SP1 and Windows XP SP2 support this CPU feature.

The latest processors from Intel and AMD have specialized support for virtualization. The AMD-V and Intel Virtualization Technology (VT) must be enabled in the BIOS in order to create 64-bit virtual machines.

VMware includes a utility named `cupid.iso.gz` in the `images` subdirectory of the ESX Server installation CD. This tool can test a server to see what CPU features the host processors have. To perform the test, unzip it and make a bootable CD, then boot each ESX host from the `cupid` CD and compare the output. If they match, then VMotion is CPU compatible. If they don't match, then you need to determine what doesn't match.

On a per-virtual machine basis, you'll find a setting that tells the virtual machine to show or mask the NX/XD bit in the host CPU. Masking the NX/XD bit from the virtual machine tells the virtual machine that there's no NX/XD bit present. This is useful if you have two otherwise compatible hosts with an NX/XD bit mismatch. If the virtual machine doesn't know there's an NX or XD bit on one of the hosts, it won't care if the target host has or doesn't have that bit if you migrate that virtual machine using VMotion. The greatest VMotion compatibility is achieved by masking the NX/XD bit. If the NX/XD bit is exposed to the virtual machine, as shown in Figure 9.33, the BIOS setting for NX/XD must match on both the source and destination ESX Server host.

What happens if you have SSE3 features on one host and not on the other? For mismatched SSE3 and SSE4 processors, you can change the masking by clicking the Advanced button, shown in Figure 9.33, and entering the CPU parameters you wish to mask, as shown in Figure 9.34.

Some administrators might recognize that this is a tedious task if you already have dozens of virtual machines built. The setting is changed on *each* virtual machine. However, if you know you have mismatched NX/XD bits or SSE3/SSE4 masks, you can change your template virtual machine and any virtual machine deployed from that template will also have the same setting.

FIGURE 9.33
Masking the NX/XD bit
on a virtual machine

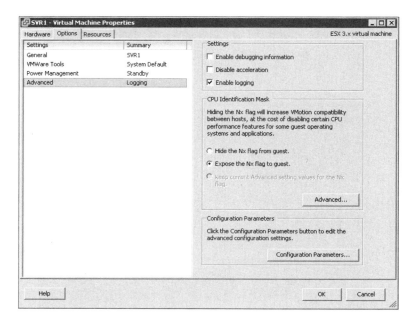

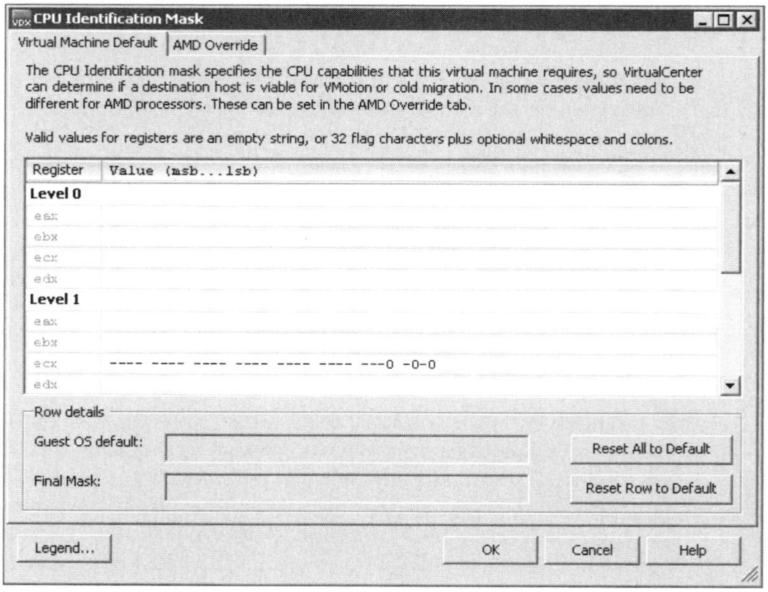

FIGURE 9.34
Masking SSE3
extensions for an Intel
CPU

In addition to the VMotion requirements for the hosts involved, there are requirements that must be met by the virtual machine to be migrated:

◆ The virtual machine must not be connected to any device physically available to only one ESX host. This includes disk storage, CD-ROMs, floppy drives, serial ports, or parallel ports. If the virtual machine to be migrated has one of these mappings, simply clear the Connected check box beside the offending device, as shown in Figure 9.35.

FIGURE 9.35
Clear the Connected box for any locally mapped device prior to migrating with VMotion.

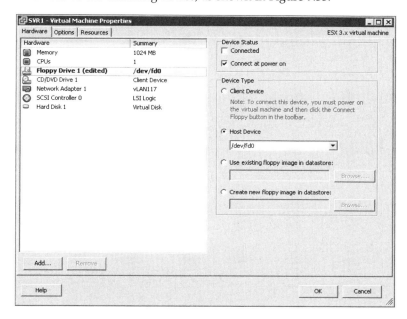

◆ The virtual machine must not be connected to an internal-only switch.

◆ The virtual machine must not have its CPU affinity set to a specific CPU.

◆ The virtual machine must not have a RAW disk mapping as part of a Microsoft Cluster Services (MSCS) configuration.

◆ The virtual machine must have all disk, configuration, log, and nonvolatile random access memory (NVRAM) files stored on a volume visible to both the source and the destination ESX Server host.

If you start a VMotion migration and VirtualCenter finds an issue that is considered a violation of the VMotion compatibility rules, you will see an error message. In some cases, a warning, not an error, will be issued. In the case of a warning, the VMotion migration will still succeed. For instance, if you have cleared the check box on the host-attached floppy drive, VirtualCenter will tell you there is a mapping to a host-only device that is not active. You'll see a prompt asking if the migration should take place anyway.

VMware states that you need a gigabit network card for VMotion; however, it does not have to be dedicated to VMotion. When you're designing the ESX Server host, dedicate a network adapter to VMotion if possible. You thus reduce the contention on the VMotion network, and the VMotion process can happen in a fast and efficient manner.

To perform a VMotion migration of a virtual machine:

1. Select a powered-on virtual machine in your inventory, right-click the virtual machine, and select Migrate, as shown in Figure 9.36.

FIGURE 9.36
Starting the
VMotion process

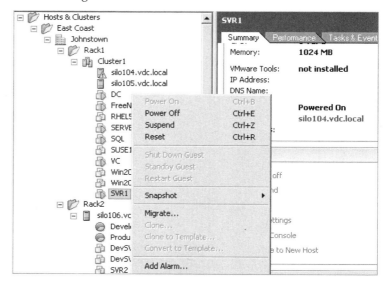

2. Choose the target host, as shown in Figure 9.37.

FIGURE 9.37
Choose the target host.

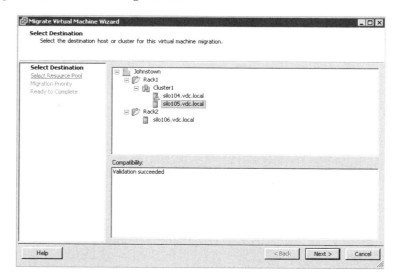

3. Choose the target resource pool (or cluster). Most of the time the same resource pool (or cluster) that the virtual machine currently resides in will suffice. Choosing a different resource pool might change that virtual machine's priority access to resources, as shown in Figure 9.38.

FIGURE 9.38
Choose a target resource pool for the virtual machine being migrated.

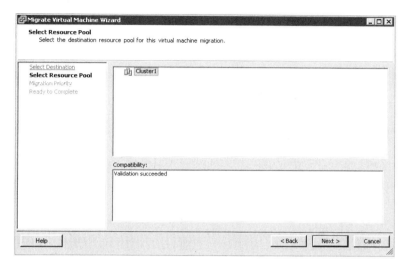

4. Select the priority that the VMotion migration needs to proceed with. Be aware that choosing high priority will cause CPU stress on the hosts involved in the migration, as described in the option shown in Figure 9.39.

FIGURE 9.39
Choosing a priority level for the migration

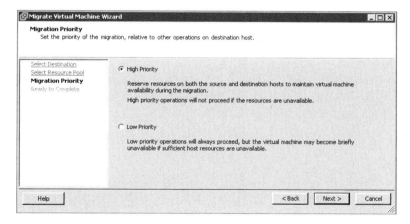

5. Click Finish once the validation has concluded and you have reviewed the information on the summary screen, as shown in Figure 9.40.

6. The virtual machine should start to migrate. Often, the process will pause at about 10% in the progress dialog box, and then again at 90%. The 10% pause occurs while the hosts

in question establish communications and gather the information for the pages in memory to be migrated; the 90% pause occurs when the source virtual machine is quiesced and the dirty memory pages are fetched from the source host, as shown in Figure 9.41.

FIGURE 9.40
Click Finish to start the
actual migration.

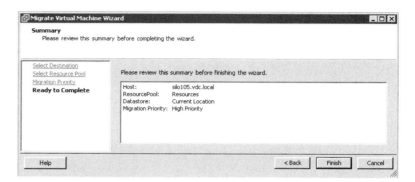

VMotion is an invaluable tool for virtual administrators, and certainly the feature that put ESX Server on the map. But VMotion, in this latest version of ESX Server, has evolved into more than just a simple tool for moving virtual machines. VMotion is the backbone for the new Distributed Resource Scheduler (DRS) feature that can be enabled on ESX Server clusters. Before we get to the details of DRS, you need to understand clusters.

FIGURE 9.41
Progress of a
VMotion migration

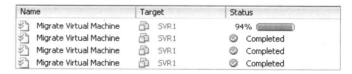

Clusters

As virtual environments grow, organizations can and will add multiple ESX Server hosts to handle the workload of the ever-increasing, sometimes exponentially increasing, number of virtual machines. Some of the concerns with adding a number of stand-alone ESX hosts, even those managed by VirtualCenter, include issues such as "What happens when a host fails" and "How can I effectively balance the load across more than one ESX host?" VMware Infrastructure 3 (VI3) handles both of these issues by creating a cluster of ESX Servers.

What is a cluster? A cluster is 2 to 32 ESX Servers that work cooperatively to provide for features such as High Availability and Distributed Resource Scheduler (DRS). Clusters themselves are implicitly resource pools; however, resource pools can be built under a cluster. This gives the administrator a larger collection of resources to carve up, and the virtual machine can run on any node in the cluster and still be affected by its membership in the resource pool.

Cluster setup is fairly straightforward. There are no special hardware requirements above what an ESX host should already have. Each of the hosts has to be able to talk to the other host on the Service Console network, and all nodes of the cluster must be managed by the same VirtualCenter. Additionally, all hosts in the cluster must belong to the same datacenter in VirtualCenter because the cluster is a child of a Datacenter object.

To create a cluster, right-click a Datacenter object in the VirtualCenter inventory and select the New Cluster option as shown in Figure 9.42.

FIGURE 9.42
Cluster creation

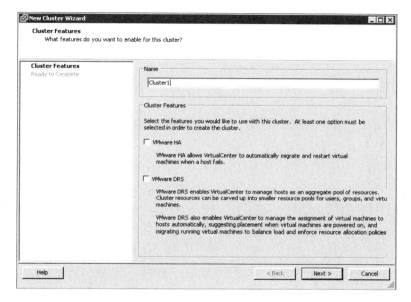

Once the cluster has been created, ESX hosts can be moved into the cluster by dragging and dropping them onto the cluster object.

CLUSTER LIMITS

There is a functional limit to the number of hosts in an ESX cluster, but it depends on which features are enabled on the cluster itself. For ESX 3.5 with VirtualCenter 2.5, the absolute limit is 32 ESX hosts per cluster. However, VMware's *recommended* maximum number of hosts is 16 in each circumstance. If you have more hosts in the datacenter than will (or can) be used in one cluster, consider building multiple clusters, which can be a benefit based on processor matching for VMotion and different cluster settings.

If an ESX Server host contains resource pools and is added to a non-DRS cluster, a warning message stating that existing resource pools will be removed appears, as shown in Figure 9.43.

FIGURE 9.43
Adding a host with an existing resource pool to a non-DRS-enabled cluster

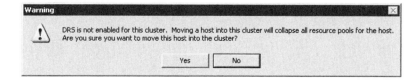

To preserve resource pools and the settings on the host added to the cluster, select the No option on the warning message shown in Figure 9.43.

Once a cluster is created, DRS can be enabled. To enable DRS, right-click the cluster to edit the settings. Then enable DRS on the cluster, as shown in Figure 9.44.

FIGURE 9.44
Enabling DRS on a cluster

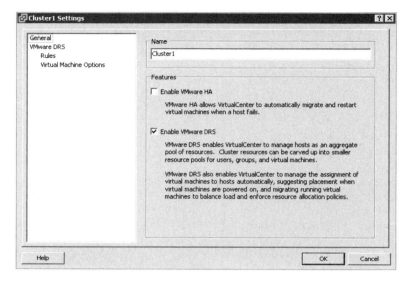

If an ESX Server host contains resource pools and is added to a DRS-enabled cluster, a wizard will be initiated that allows existing resource pools to be deleted or maintained, as shown in Figure 9.45.

FIGURE 9.45
Adding an ESX Server host that contains resource pools to a DRS-enabled cluster offers the option to keep the existing resource pools or delete them.

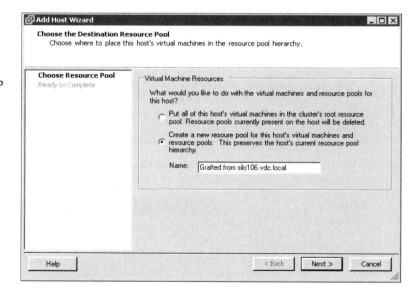

The options provided, as shown in Figure 9.45, are just as they sound. The first option will delete any existing resource pools on the host, and the virtual machines in them will be a part of the cluster but not part of a resource pool. The second option will add the existing resource pools on the host as child objects of a new resource pool created in the cluster, as shown in Figures 9.46 and 9.47.

FIGURE 9.46
Confirm the addition of a host to the cluster.

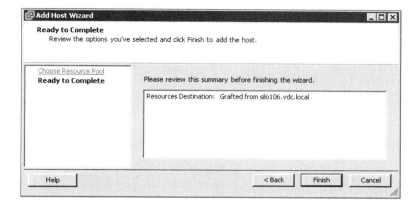

FIGURE 9.47
Resource pools kept when a host is added to a cluster will, by default, fall under a parent pool that begins with the name "Grafted from" followed by the hostname.

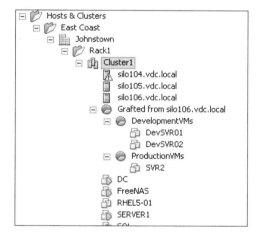

Once the resource pools have been migrated, eliminate the additional resource pool (Grafted from. . .) created using one of two methods:

◆ Drag the child resource pools from the newly created resource pool and drop them onto the cluster itself.

◆ Move the virtual machines from the imported resource pools into other existing resource pools in the cluster (after adjusting the resource pools to reflect the new reservations and/or limits required to support the newly added virtual machines).

Since Chapter 10 will extensively deal with HA, we'll focus on DRS and how it affects resource management.

Exploring Distributed Resource Scheduler (DRS)

DRS is a feature of VirtualCenter on the properties of a cluster that balances load across multiple ESX hosts. It has two main functions: the first is to decide which node of a cluster should run a virtual machine when it's powered on, and the second is to evaluate the load on the cluster over time and either make recommendations for migrations or automatically move virtual machines to create a more balanced cluster workload using VMotion. Fortunately for those of us who like to retain control, there are parameters that set how aggressively DRS will automatically move virtual machines around the cluster.

If we start by looking at the DRS properties, as shown in Figure 9.48, there are three selections regarding the automation level of the DRS cluster: Manual, Partially Automated, and Fully Automated. The slider bar only affects the actions of the fully automated setting on the cluster. These settings control the initial placement of a virtual machine and the automatic movement of virtual machines between hosts.

FIGURE 9.48
A DRS cluster can be set to automate as much or as little as desired.

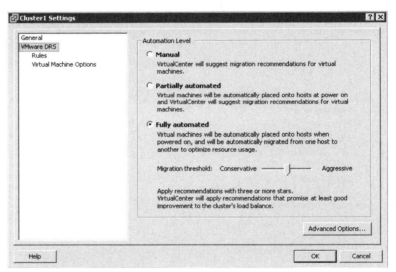

Manual

The Manual setting of the DRS cluster will prompt you every time you power on a virtual machine for the node that you want to launch that virtual machine on. The dialog box rates the available hosts according to suitability at that moment in time: the more stars, the better the choice, as shown in Figure 9.49.

The Manual setting will also suggest Migrations when DRS detects an imbalance between ESX hosts in the cluster. This is an averaging process that works over longer periods of time than many of us are used to in the information technology field. It is unusual to see DRS make any recommendations unless an imbalance has existed for longer than 5 minutes. The recommended list of migrations is available by selecting the cluster in Inventory and then selecting the Migrations tab, as shown in Figure 9.50.

Figure 9.50 shows that DRS rates both the SERVER1 virtual machine and the Win2008-02 virtual machine as very strong candidates to move from host Silo106 to Silo105 and Silo104, respectively. The number of stars a migration can have ranges from one to five: a one-star migration suggestion is a gentle recommendation and a four-star migration is a much stronger suggestion.

FIGURE 9.49
A DRS cluster set to Manual will let you specify where the virtual machine should be powered on.

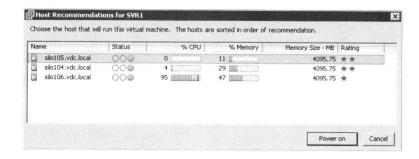

FIGURE 9.50
Recommended migrations for a DRS cluster

To agree with DRS and start the migration, select the virtual machine you want to migrate on the Migrations tab and click the Apply Migration Recommendation button. VMotion will handle the migration automatically.

Partially Automated

If you select the Partially Automated setting on the DRS properties, as shown in Figure 9.48, DRS will make an automatic decision about which host a virtual machine should run on when it is initially powered on (without prompting the admin who is performing the power on task), but it will still prompt for all migrations on the Migration tab.

Fully Automated

The third setting for DRS is Fully Automated. This setting will make decisions for initial placement without prompting and will also make automatic VMotion decisions based on the selected automation level (the slider bar).

There are five positions for the slider bar on the Fully Automated setting of the DRS cluster. The values of the slider bar range from Conservative to Aggressive, as shown in Figure 9.48. Conservative automatically moves migrations evaluated with five stars. Any other migrations are listed on the Migrations tab and require administrator approval. If you move the slider bar from the most conservative setting one stop to the right, then all four- and five-star migrations will automatically be approved; three stars and less will wait for administrator approval. With the slider all the way over to the aggressive setting, any imbalance in the cluster that causes any recommendation will be automatically approved. Be aware that this can cause additional stress in your ESX host environment, as even a slight imbalance will trigger a migration.

DRS runs on an intelligent algorithm that is constantly being checked. Calculations for migrations can change regularly. Assume that during a period of high activity DRS makes a recommendation with three stars, and the automation level is set so three-star migrations need manual approval but the recommendation is not noticed (or an administrator is not even in the office).

An hour later, the virtual machines that caused the three-star migration in the first place have settled down and are now operating normally. At this point the Migrations tab no longer reflects the migration recommendation. The recommendation has since been withdrawn. This behavior occurs because if the migration was still listed, an administrator might approve it and cause an imbalance where one did not exist.

Earlier we mentioned that five-star migrations had little to do with load on the cluster. The first function that causes a five-star migration recommendation is when you put a host into Maintenance Mode, as shown in Figure 9.51.

FIGURE 9.51
An ESX Server host put into Maintenance Mode cannot power on new virtual machines or be a target for VMotion.

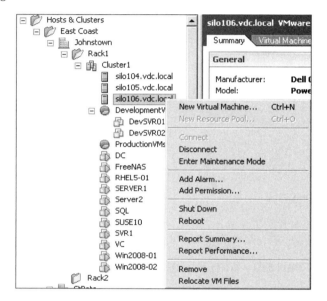

Maintenance Mode is a setting on a host that allows virtual machines currently hosted on it to continue to run, but does not permit new virtual machines to be launched on that host either manually or via a VMotion or DRS migration. Additionally, when a host belonging to an automated DRS cluster is placed into Maintenance Mode, all of the virtual machines currently running on that host receive a five-star migration recommendation, which causes all virtual machines on that host to be migrated to other hosts (assuming they meet the requirements for VMotion).

The second item that will cause a five-star migration recommendation is when two virtual machines defined in an anti-affinity rule are run on the same host, or when two virtual machines defined in an affinity rule are run on different hosts. This leads us to a discussion of DRS rules.

⊕ **Real World Scenario**

A QUICK REVIEW OF DRS CLUSTER PERFORMANCE

Monitoring the detailed performance of a cluster is an important task for any virtual infrastructure administrator. Particularly, monitoring the CPU and memory activity of the whole cluster as well as the respective resource utilization of the virtual machines within the cluster. The summary tab of the details pane for a cluster object includes a pair of bar graphs that can provide administrators with a quick performance snapshot of a DRS Cluster.

The top chart in the VMware DRS Cluster Distribution snapshot reflects the CPU and memory utilization of the hosts in the cluster. The bottom chart reflects the percentage of entitled resources that have been delivered to a virtual machine by the ESX Server host on which it runs. In English, the top chart shows how hard the ESX Server hosts are working while the bottom chart shows if the virtual machines are getting the resources they require.

The figure shown below identifies that 2 of the three ESX Server hosts are using between 0 and 10% of their memory and the third host is using between 30% and 40% of its memory. It also shows that all three hosts are able to deliver the resources required by the virtual machines running on each respective host.

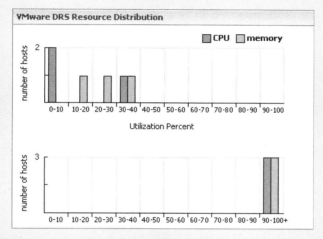

For the resource utilization-conscious virtual infrastructure admin, note that the best looking charts would show all bars toward the left hand side of the top chart and all bars toward right hand side of the bottom chart. This would identify that the ESX Server hosts are not working too hard but the virtual machines are getting all the resources they require.

By keeping an eye on these summary graphs, administrators will have a good indication of when it is time to dig deeper into cluster performance or perhaps even make a decision about growing the cluster by adding more hosts. For example, if the bars on the top chart began creeping into the 40% to 50% or 50% to 60% range, but the bottom chart still showed 90% to 100%, an administrator would know that the time to add a new host is coming soon. This type of display would indicate that all current virtual machines are getting the resources they require but the host is utilizing up to 60% of its resources.

DRS Rules

An administrator creates DRS rules to control how DRS decides which virtual machines should be combined with which other virtual machines, or which virtual machines should be kept separate by the DRS process. Consider the rules page shown in Figure 9.52.

Consider an environment with two mail server virtual machines. In all likelihood, administrators would not want both mail servers to reside on the same ESX Server host. At the same time, administrators would want a web application server and the back-end database server to reside on the same hosts. That might be a combination that should always be together to ensure rapid response times between them. These two scenarios could be serviced very well with DRS rules.

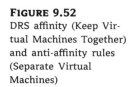

FIGURE 9.52
DRS affinity (Keep Virtual Machines Together) and anti-affinity rules (Separate Virtual Machines)

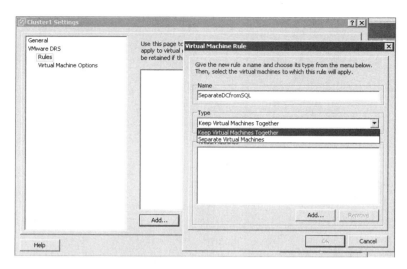

Perform the following steps to create a DRS anti-affinity rule:

1. Right-click the DRS cluster where the rules need to exist and select the Edit Settings option.

2. Click the Rules option.

3. Type a name for the rule and select the type of rule to create:

    ◆ For anti-affinity rules, select the Separate Virtual Machines option.

    ◆ For affinity rules, select the Keep Virtual Machines Together option.

4. Click the Add button to include the necessary virtual machines to the rule, as shown in Figure 9.53.

5. Click OK.

6. Review the new rule configuration, as shown in Figure 9.54.

7. Click OK.

With DRS rules, it is possible to create fallible rules, such as building a "Separate virtual machines" rule that has three virtual machines in it on a DRS cluster that only has two hosts. In this situation, VirtualCenter will generate report warnings because DRS cannot satisfy the requirements of the rule.

Rules can be temporarily disabled by clearing the check box next to the rule, as shown in Figure 9.55.

Although most virtual machines should be allowed to take advantage of the DRS balancing act, there will likely be enterprise-critical virtual machines that administrators are adamant about not being VMotion candidates. However, the virtual machines should remain in the cluster to take advantage of the High Availability (HA) feature. In other words, virtual machines will take part in HA but not DRS despite the fact that both features are enabled on the cluster. As shown in Figure 9.56, virtual machines in a cluster can be configured with individual DRS compatibility levels.

FIGURE 9.53
Adding virtual machines
to a DRS rule

FIGURE 9.54
A completed DRS rule

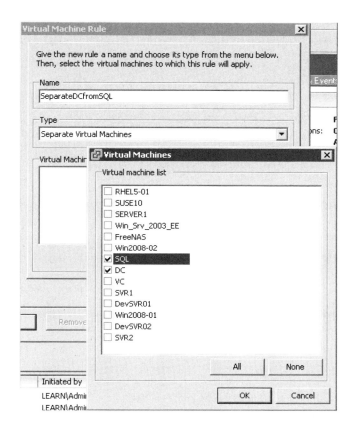

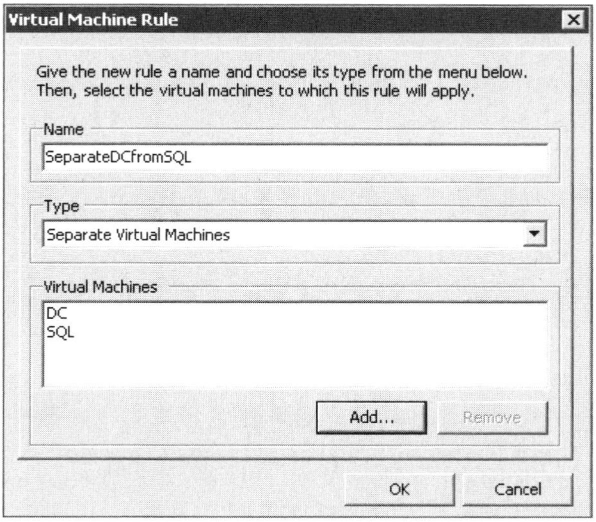

FIGURE 9.55
Temporarily disabling a
DRS rule

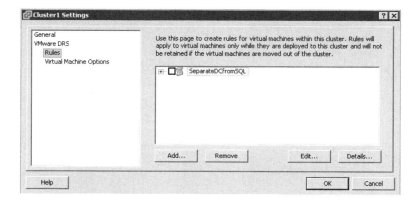

FIGURE 9.56
Virtual machine options
for a DRS cluster

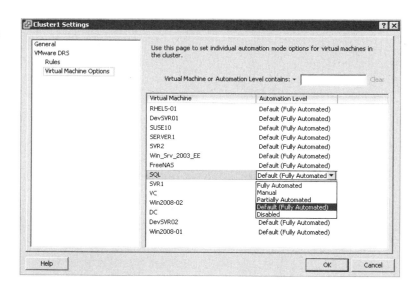

This dialog box lists the virtual machines that are part of the cluster and their default automation level. In this case, all virtual machines are set at Fully Automated because that's how the automation level of the cluster was set. The administrator can then selectively choose virtual machines that are not going to be acted upon by DRS in the same way as the rest in the cluster. The automation levels available include:

◆ Fully Automated

◆ Manual

◆ Partially Automated

◆ Disabled

◆ Default (inherited from the cluster setting)

The first three options work as discussed in this chapter. The Disabled option turns off DRS, including the automatic host selection at startup and the migration recommendations. The default option configures the virtual machine to accept the automation level set at the cluster.

AT LEAST BE OPEN TO CHANGE

Even if a virtual machine or several virtual machines have been chosen not to participate in the automation of DRS, it is best not to set virtual machines to the Disabled option since recommendations will not be provided. It is possible that a four- or five-star recommendation could be provided that suggests moving a virtual machine an administrator thought was best on specific host. Yet the migration might suggest a different host. For this reason, the Manual option is better. At least be open to the possibility that a virtual machine might perform better on a different host.

VI3 provides a number of tools for administrators to make their lives easier as long as the tools are understood and set up properly. It might also be prudent to monitor the activities of these tools to see if a change to the configuration might be warranted over time as your environment grows.

The Bottom Line

Manage virtual machine memory.   The VMkernel is active and aggressive in its management of memory utilization across the virtual machines.

   Master It   A virtual machine needs to be guaranteed 1GB of RAM.

   Master It   A virtual machine should never exceed 2GB of physical memory.

Manage virtual machine CPU allocation.   The VMkernel works actively to monitor, schedule, and migrate data across CPUs.

   Master It   A virtual machine must be guaranteed 1000MHz of CPU.

Create and manage resource pools.   Resource pools portion CPU and memory from a host or cluster to establish resource limits for pools of virtual machines.

   Master It   A resource pool needs to be able to exceed its reservation to provide for additional resource guarantees to virtual machines within the pool.

Configure and execute VMotion.   VMotion technology is a unique feature of VMware Infrastructure 3 (VI3) that allows a running virtual machine to be moved between hosts.

   Master It   Identify the virtual machine requirement for VMotion.

   Master It   Identify the ESX Server host requirements for VMotion.

   Master It   Five ESX Server hosts need to be grouped together for the purpose of enabling the Distributed Resource Scheduler (DRS) feature of VI3.

Configure and manage Distributed Resource Scheduling (DRS).   DRS builds off the success and efficiency of VMotion by offering an automated VMotion based on an algorithm that analyzes system workloads across all ESX Server nodes in a cluster.

Master It A DRS cluster should determine on which ESX Server host a virtual machine runs when the virtual machine is powered, but it should only recommend migrations for VMotion.

Master It A DRS cluster should determine on which ESX Server host a virtual machine runs when the virtual machine is powered on, and it should also manage where it runs for best performance. A VMotion should only occur if a recommendation is determined to be a four- or five-star recommendation.

Master It Two virtual machines running a web application and a back-end database should be kept together on an ESX Server host at all times. If one should be the target of a VMotion migration, the other should be as well.

Master It Two virtual machines with database applications should never run on the same ESX Server host.

Chapter 10

High Availability and Business Continuity

Once your servers are installed, storage is provisioned, virtual networking is pinging, and virtual machines are running, it is time come to define the strategies to put into place a virtual infrastructure that provides high availability and business continuity. The deployment of a virtual infrastructure opens many new doors for disaster-recovery planning. The virtual infrastructure administrator will lead the charge into a new era of ideologies and methodologies for ensuring that business continues as efficiently as possible in the face of corrupted data, failed servers, or even lost data centers.

In this chapter you will learn to:

Cluster virtual machines with Microsoft Clustering Services (MSCS)

Implement and manage VMware High Availability (HA)

Back up virtual machines with VMware Consolidated Backup (VCB)

Restore virtual machines with VMware Consolidated Backup (VCB)

Clustering Virtual Machines

When critical services and applications call for the highest levels of availability, many network administrators turn to Microsoft Cluster Services (MSCS). Microsoft Windows Server 2003 supports network load-balancing clusters and server clusters depending on the version of Windows Server 2003 installed on the server.

Microsoft Clustering

The network load-balancing (NLB) configuration involves an aggregation of servers that balances the requests for applications or services. In a typical NLB cluster, all nodes are active participants in the cluster and are consistently responding to requests for services. NLB clusters are most commonly deployed as a means of providing enhanced performance and availability. NLB clusters are best suited for scenarios involving Internet Information Services (IIS), virtual private networking, and Internet Security and Acceleration (ISA) Server, to name a few. Figure 10.1 details the architecture of an NLB cluster.

FIGURE 10.1
An NLB cluster can contain up to 32 active nodes that distribute traffic equally across each node. The NLB software allows the nodes to share a common name and IP address that is referenced by clients.

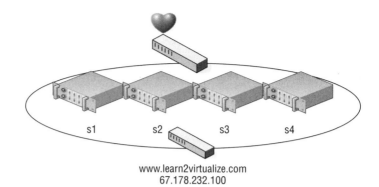

www.learn2virtualize.com
67.178.232.100

NLB SUPPORT FROM VMWARE

As of this writing, VMware does not support the use of NLB clusters across virtual machines. This is not to say it cannot be configured, or that it will not work; however, it is not a VMware-supported configuration.

Unlike NLB clusters, server clusters are used solely for the sake of availability. Server clusters do not provide performance enhancements outside of high availability. In a typical server cluster, multiple nodes are configured to be able to own a service or application resource, but only one node owns the resource at a given time. Server clusters are most often used for applications like Microsoft Exchange, Microsoft SQL Server, and DHCP services, which each share a need for a common datastore. The common datastore houses the information accessible by the node that is online and currently owns the resource, as well as the other possible owners that could assume ownership in the event of failure. Each node requires at least two network connections: one for the production network and one for the cluster service heartbeat between nodes. Figure 10.2 details the structure of a server cluster.

The different versions of Windows Server 2003 offer various levels of support for NLB and server clusters. Table 10.1 outlines the cluster support available in each version of Windows Server 2003.

WINDOWS CLUSTERING STORAGE ARCHITECTURES

Server clusters built on Windows Server 2003 can only support up to eight nodes when using a fibre channel-switched fabric. Storage architectures that use SCSI disks as direct attached storage or that use a fibre channel-arbitrated loop result in a maximum of only two nodes in a server cluster. Clustering virtual machines in ESX Server utilizes a simulated SCSI shared storage connection and is therefore limited to only two-node clustering. In addition, the clustered virtual machine solution uses only SCSI-2 reservations, not SCSI-3 reservations, and supports only the SCSI miniport drivers, not the STORPort drivers.

FIGURE 10.2
Server clusters are best suited for applications and services like SQL Server, Exchange Server, DHCP, etc., that use a common data set.

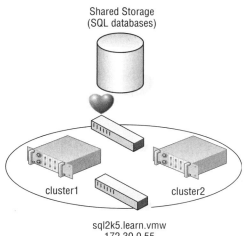

Shared Storage
(SQL databases)

cluster1   cluster2

sql2k5.learn.vmw
172.30.0.55

TABLE 10.1: Windows Server 2003 Clustering Support

OPERATING SYSTEM	NETWORK LOAD BALANCING (NLB)	SERVER CLUSTER
Windows Server 2003 Web Edition	Yes (up to 32 nodes)	No
Windows Server 2003 Standard Edition	Yes (up to 32 nodes)	No
Windows Server 2003 Enterprise Edition	Yes (up to 32 nodes)	Yes (up to 8 nodes in fibre channel switch fabric)
Windows Server 2003 Datacenter Edition	Yes (up to 32 nodes)	Yes (up to 8 nodes in fibre channel switch fabric)

MSCS, when constructed properly, provides automatic failover of services and applications hosted across multiple cluster nodes. When multiple nodes are configured as a cluster for a service or application resource, only one node owns the resource at any given time. When the current resource owner experiences failure, causing a loss in the heartbeat between the cluster nodes, another node assumes ownership of the resource to allow continued access with minimal data loss. To configure multiple Windows Server 2003 nodes into a Microsoft cluster, the following requirements must be met:

◆ Nodes must be running either Windows Server 2003 Enterprise Edition or Datacenter Edition.

◆ All nodes should have access to the same storage device(s).

◆ All nodes should have two similarly connected and configured network adapters: one for the production network and one for the heartbeat network.

◆ All nodes should have Microsoft Cluster Services installed.

Virtual Machine Clustering Scenarios

The clustering of Windows Server 2003 virtual machines using Microsoft Cluster Services (MSCS) can be done in one of three different configurations:

Cluster-in-a-Box   The clustering of two virtual machines that exist in the same ESX Server host.

Cluster-Across-Boxes   The clustering of two virtual machines that are running on different ESX Server hosts.

Physical-to-Virtual Clustering   The clustering of a physical server and a virtual machine that is running on an ESX Server host.

Clustering has long been considered an advanced technology implemented only by those with high technical skills in implementing and managing high-availability environments. While this might be more rumor than truth, it is certainly a more complex solution once the virtual machine solution is blended into the deployment.

While you may achieve results setting up clustered virtual machines, you may not receive support for your clustered solution if you violate any of the clustering restrictions put forth by VMware. The following list summarizes the dos and don'ts of clustering virtual machines as published by VMware:

◆ Only 32-bit virtual machines with a boot disk on local storage can be configured as nodes in a server cluster.

◆ Only two-node clustering is allowed.

◆ Virtual machines configured as cluster nodes must use the LSI Logic SCSI adapter and the vmxnet network adapter.

◆ Virtual machines in a clustered configuration cannot be connected to a switch configured with a NIC team.

◆ Virtual machines in a clustered configuration are not valid candidates for VMotion, nor can they be part of a DRS or HA cluster.

◆ ESX Servers hosts that run virtual machines that are part of a server cluster cannot be configured to perform a boot from SAN.

◆ ESX Server hosts that run virtual machines that are part of a server cluster cannot have both QLogic and Emulex HBAs.

Cluster-in-a-Box

The cluster-in-a-box scenario involves configuring two virtual machines hosted by the same ESX Server as nodes in a server cluster. The shared disks of the server cluster can exist as .vmdk files stored on local VMFS volumes. Figure 10.3 details the configuration of a cluster-in-a-box scenario.

After reviewing the diagram of a cluster-in-a-box configuration, you might wonder why you would want to deploy such a thing. The truth is, you wouldn't want to deploy cluster in a box because it still maintains a single point of failure. With both virtual machines running on the same host, if that host fails, both virtual machines fail. This architecture contradicts the very reason for creating failover clusters. A cluster-in-a-box still contains a single point of failure that can result in downtime of the clustered application. If the ESX Server hosting the two-node cluster-in-a-box fails, then both nodes are lost and a failover does not occur. This setup might, and I use *might* loosely, be used only to "play" with clustering services or to test clustering services and configurations. But ultimately, even for testing, it is best to use the cluster-across-boxes to get a better understanding of how this might be deployed in a production scenario.

FIGURE 10.3

A cluster-in-a-box con- figuration does not pro- vide protection against a single point of fail- ure. Therefore, it is not a common or sug- gested form of deploying Microsoft server clusters in virtual machines.

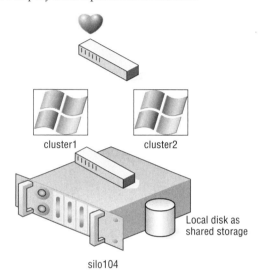

cluster1   cluster2

Local disk as shared storage

silo104

CLUSTER-IN-A-BOX

As suggested in the first part of this chapter, server clusters are deployed for high availability. High availability is not achieved using a cluster-in-a-box, and therefore this configuration should be avoided for any type of critical production applications and services.

Cluster-Across-Boxes

While the cluster-in-a-box scenario is more of an experimental or education tool for clustering, the cluster-across-boxes configuration provides a solid solution for critical virtual machines with stringent uptime requirements — for example, the enterprise-level servers and services like SQL Server and Exchange Server that are heavily relied on by the bulk of the end-user community. The cluster-across-boxes scenario, as the name applies, draws its high availability from the fact that the two nodes in the cluster are managed on different ESX Server hosts. In the event that one of the hosts fails, the second node of the cluster will assume ownership of the cluster group, and its resources and the service or application will continue responding to client requests.

The cluster-across-boxes configuration requires that virtual machines have access to the same shared storage, which must reside on a storage device external to the ESX Server hosts where the virtual machines run. The virtual hard drives that make up the operating system volume of the cluster nodes can be a standard VMDK implementation; however, the drives used as the shared storage must be set up as a special kind of drive called a raw device mapping. The raw device mapping is a feature that allows a virtual machine to establish direct access to a LUN on a SAN device.

RAW DEVICE MAPPINGS (RDMs)

A raw device mapping (RDM) is not direct access to a LUN, nor is it a normal virtual hard disk file. An RDM is a blend between the two. When adding a new disk to a virtual machine, as you will soon see, the Add Hardware Wizard presents the Raw Device Mappings as an option on the Select a Disk page. This page defines the RDM as having the ability to give a virtual machine direct access to the SAN, thereby allowing SAN management. I know this seems like a contradiction to the opening statement of this sidebar; however, we're getting to the part that oddly enough makes both statements true.

By selecting an RDM for a new disk, you're forced to select a compatibility mode for the RDM. An RDM can be configured in either Physical Compatibility mode or Virtual Compatibility mode. The Physical Compatibility mode option allows the virtual machine to have direct raw LUN access. The Virtual Compatibility mode, however, is the hybrid configuration that allows raw LUN access but only through a VMDK file acting as a proxy. The image shown here details the architecture of using an RDM in Virtual Compatibility mode:

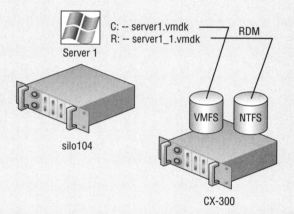

So why choose one over the other if both are ultimately providing raw LUN access? Since the RDM in Virtual Compatibility mode uses a VMDK proxy file, it offers the advantage of allowing snapshots to be taken. By using the Virtual Compatibility mode, you will gain the ability to use snapshots on top of the raw LUN access in addition to any SAN-level snapshot or mirroring software. Or, of course, in the absence of SAN-level software, the VMware snapshot feature can certainly be a valuable tool. The decision to use Physical Compatibility or Virtual Compatibility is predicated solely on the opportunity and/or need to use VMware snapshot technology.

A cluster-across-boxes requires a more complex setup than the cluster-in-a-box scenario. When clustering across boxes, all proper communication between virtual machines and all proper communication from virtual machines and storage devices must be configured properly. Figure 10.4 provides details on the setup of a two-node virtual machine cluster-across-boxes using Windows Server 2003 guest operating systems.

Perform the following steps to configure Microsoft Cluster Services across virtual machines on separate ESX Server hosts.

FIGURE 10.4
A Microsoft cluster built on virtual machines residing on separate ESX hosts requires shared storage access from each virtual machine using a raw device mapping (RDM).

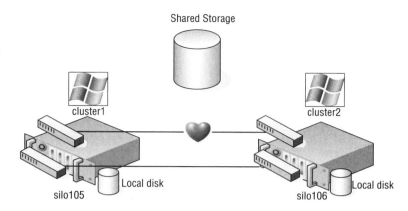

CREATING THE FIRST CLUSTER NODE

To create the first cluster node, follow these steps:

1. Create a virtual machine that is a member of a Windows Active Directory domain.

2. Right-click the new virtual machine and select the Edit Settings option.

3. Click the Add button and select the Hard Disk option.

4. Select the Raw Device Mappings radio button option, as shown in Figure 10.5, and then click the Next button.

FIGURE 10.5
Raw device mappings allow virtual machines to have direct LUN access.

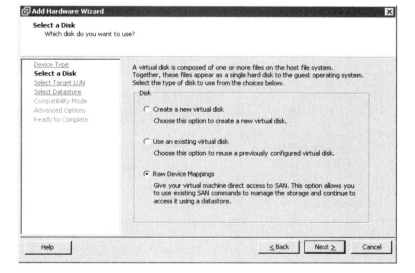

5. Select the appropriate target LUN from the list of available targets, as shown in Figure 10.6.

6. Select the datastore location, shown in Figure 10.7, where the VMDK proxy file should be stored, and then click the Next button.

FIGURE 10.6
The list of available targets includes only the LUNs not formatted as VMFS.

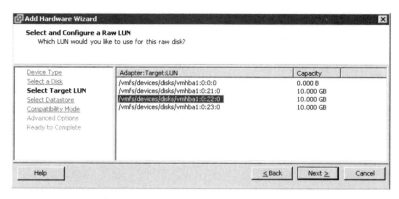

FIGURE 10.7
By default the VMDK file that points to the LUN is stored in the same location as the existing virtual machine files.

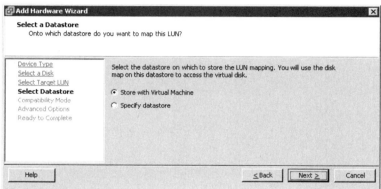

7. Select the Virtual radio button option to allow VMware snapshot functionality for the raw device mapping, as shown in Figure 10.8. Then click Next.

FIGURE 10.8
The Virtual Compatibility mode enables VMware snapshot functionality for RDMs. The physical mode allows raw LUN access but without VMware snapshots.

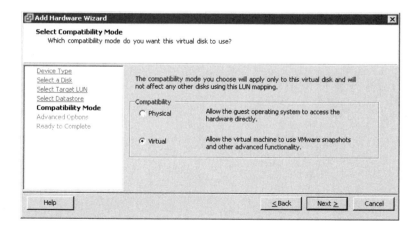

8. Select the virtual device node to which the RDM should be connected, as shown in Figure 10.9. Then click Next.

FIGURE 10.9
The virtual device node for the additional RDMs in a cluster node must be on a different SCSI node.

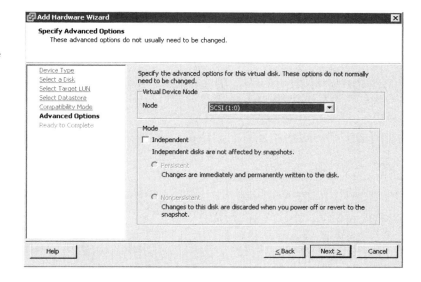

SCSI NODES FOR RDMs

RDMs used for shared storage in a Microsoft server cluster must be configured on a SCSI node that is different from the SCSI to which the hard disk is connected that holds the operating system. For example, if the operating system's virtual hard drive is configured to use the SCSI0 node, then the RDM should use the SCSI1 node.

9. Click the Finish button.

10. Right-click the virtual machine and select the Edit Settings option.

11. Select the new SCSI controller that was added as a result of adding the RDMs on a separate SCSI controller.

12. Select the Virtual radio button option under the SCSI Bus Sharing options, as shown in Figure 10.10.

13. Repeat steps 2 through 9 to configure additional RDMs for shared storage locations needed by nodes of a Microsoft server cluster.

14. Configure the virtual machine with two network adapters. Connect one network adapter to the production network and connect the other network adapter to the network used for heartbeat communications between nodes. Figure 10.11 shows a cluster node with two network adapters configured.

NICs IN A CLUSTER

Because of PCI addressing issues, all RDMs should be added prior to configuring the additional network adapters. If the NICs are configured first, you may be required to revisit the network adapter configuration after the RDMs are added to the cluster node.

FIGURE 10.10
The SCSI bus sharing for the new SCSI adapter must be set to Virtual to support running a virtual machine as a node in a Microsoft server cluster.

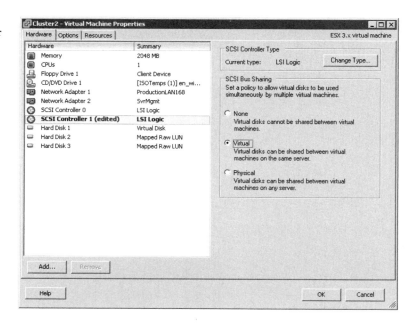

FIGURE 10.11
A node in a Microsoft server cluster requires at least two network adapters. One adapter must be able to communicate on the production network, and the second adapter is configured for internal cluster heartbeat communication.

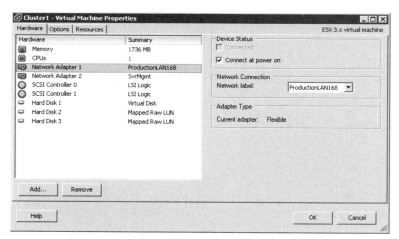

15. Power on the first node of the cluster, and assign valid IP addresses to the network adapters configured for the production and heartbeat networks. Then format the additional drives and assign drive letters, as shown in Figure 10.12.

16. Shut down the first cluster node.

17. In the VirtualCenter inventory, select the ESX Server host where the first cluster node is configured and then select the Configuration tab.

18. Select Advanced Settings from the Software menu.

FIGURE 10.12
The RDMs presented to
the first cluster node are
formatted and assigned
drive letters.

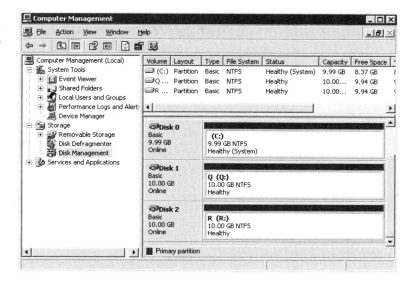

19. In the Advanced Settings dialog box, configure the following options, as shown in
Figure 10.13:

◆ Set the Disk.ResetOnFailure option to 1.

◆ Set the Disk.UseLunReset option to 1.

◆ Set the Disk.UseDeviceReset option to 0.

FIGURE 10.13
ESX Server hosts with
virtual machines config-
ured as cluster nodes
require changes to
be made to several
advanced disk config-
uration settings.

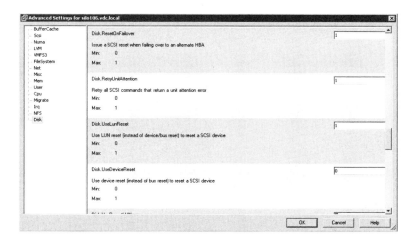

20. Proceed to the next section to configure the second cluster node and the respective ESX
Server host.

CREATING THE SECOND CLUSTER NODE

To create the second cluster node, follow these steps:

1. Create a second virtual machine that is a member of the same Active Directory domain as the first cluster node.

2. Add the same RDMs to the second cluster node using the same SCSI node values. For example, if the first node used SCSI 1:0 for the first RDM and SCSI 1:1 for the second RDM, then configure the second node to use the same configuration. As in the first cluster node configuration, add all RDMs to the virtual machine before moving on to step 3 to configure the network adapters. Don't forget to edit the SCSI bus sharing configuration for the new SCSI adapter.

3. Configure the second node with an identical network adapter configuration.

4. Verify that the hard drives corresponding to the RDMs can be seen in Disk Manager. At this point the drives will show as a status of Healthy but drive letters will not be assigned.

5. Power off the second node.

6. Edit the advanced disk settings for the ESX Server host with the second cluster node.

CREATING THE MANAGEMENT CLUSTER

To create the management cluster, follow these steps:

1. If you have the authority, create a new user account that belongs to the same Windows Active Directory domain as the two cluster nodes. The account does not need to be granted any special group memberships at this time.

2. Power on the first node of the cluster and log in as a user with administrative credentials.

3. Click Start ➤ Programs ➤ Administrative Tools, and select the Cluster Administrator console.

4. Select the Create new cluster option from the Open Connection to Cluster dialog box, as shown in Figure 10.14. Click OK.

FIGURE 10.14
The first cluster created is used to manage the nodes of the cluster.

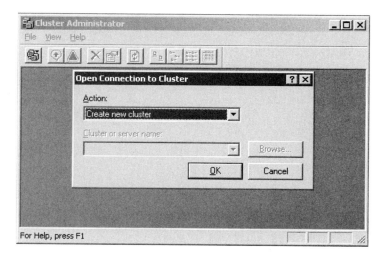

5. Provide a unique name for the name of the cluster, as shown in Figure 10.15. Ensure that it does not match the name of any existing computers on the network.

FIGURE 10.15
Configuring a Microsoft server cluster is heavily based on domain membership and the cluster name. The name provided to the cluster must be unique within the domain to which it belongs.

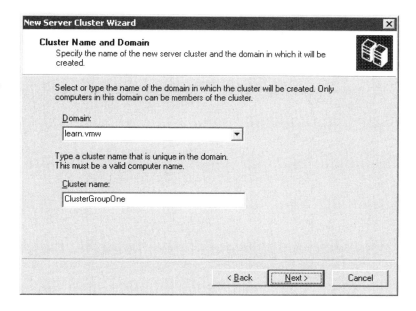

6. As shown in Figure 10.16, the next step is to execute the cluster feasibility analysis to check for all cluster-capable resources. Then click Next.

FIGURE 10.16
The cluster analysis portion of the cluster configuration wizard identifies that all cluster-capable resources are available.

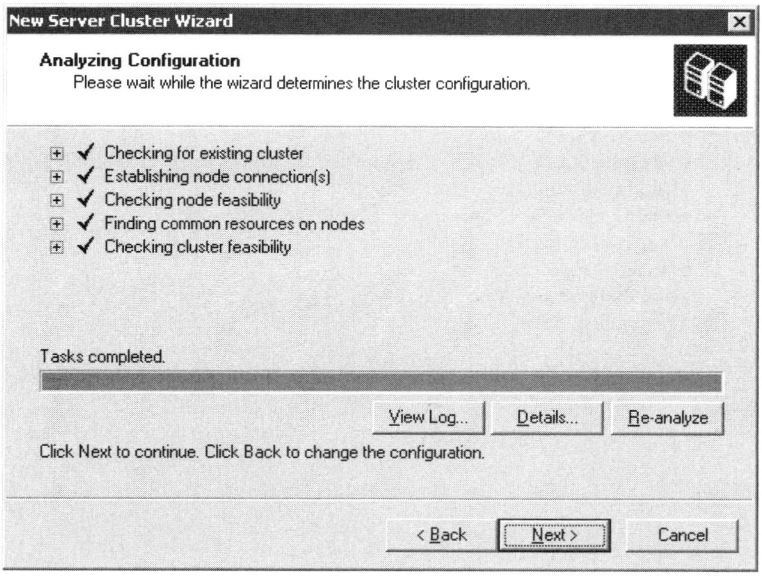

7. Provide an IP address for cluster management. As shown in Figure 10.17, the IP address configured for cluster management should be an IP address that is accessible from the network adapters configured on the production network. Click Next.

FIGURE 10.17
The IP address provided for cluster management should be unique and accessible from the production network.

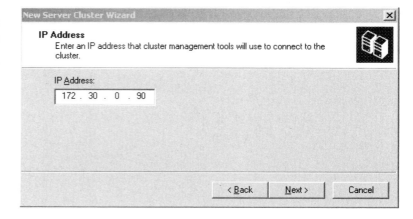

CLUSTER MANAGEMENT

To access and manage a Microsoft cluster, create a Host (A) record in the zone that corresponds to the domain to which the cluster nodes belong.

---

8. Provide the account information for the cluster service user account created in step 1 of the "Creating the Management Cluster" section. Note that the Cluster Service Account page of the New Server Cluster Wizard, shown in Figure 10.18, acknowledges that the account specified will be granted membership in the local administrators group on each cluster node. Therefore, do not share the cluster service password with users who should not have administrative capabilities. Click Next.

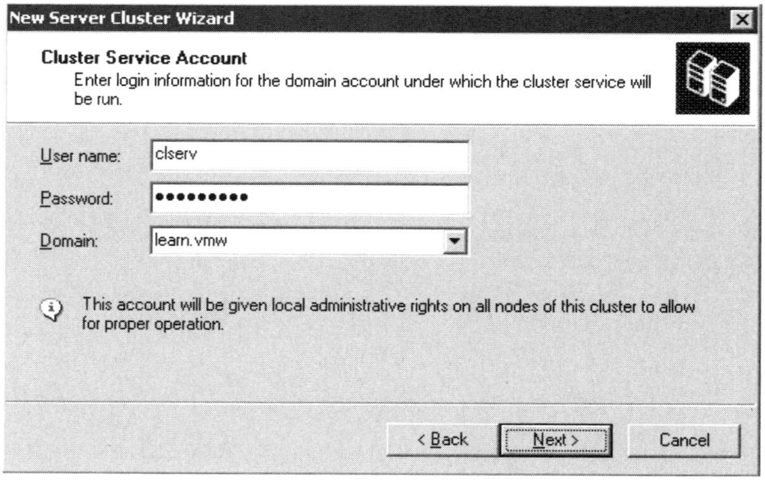

FIGURE 10.18
The cluster service account must be a domain account and will be granted local administrator rights on each cluster node.

New Server Cluster Wizard

Cluster Service Account
Enter login information for the domain account under which the cluster service will be run.

User name: clserv

Password: ●●●●●●●●●

Domain: learn.vmw

(i) This account will be given local administrative rights on all nodes of this cluster to allow for proper operation.

< Back   Next >   Cancel

9. At the completion of creating the cluster timeline, shown in Figure 10.19, click Next.

FIGURE 10.19
The cluster installation timeline provides a running report of the items configured as part of the installation process.

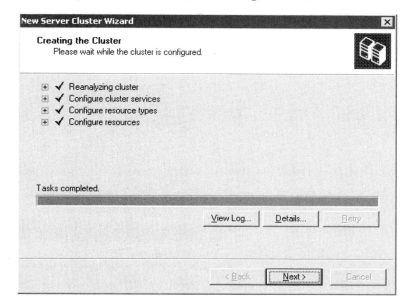

10. Continue to review the Cluster Administrator snap-in and review the new management cluster that was created, shown in Figure 10.20.

FIGURE 10.20
The completion of the initial cluster management creation wizard will result in a Cluster Group and all associated cluster resources.

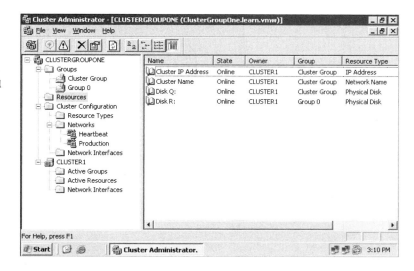

ADDING THE SECOND NODE TO THE MANAGEMENT CLUSTER

To add the second node to the management cluster, follow these steps:

1. Leave the first node powered on and power on the second node.

2. Right-click the name of the cluster, select the New option, and then click the Node option, as shown in Figure 10.21.

FIGURE 10.21
Once the management cluster is complete, an additional node can be added.

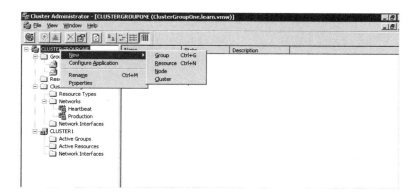

3. Specify the name of the node to be added to the cluster and then click Next, as shown in Figure 10.22.

FIGURE 10.22
You can type the name of the second node into the text box or find it using the Browse button.

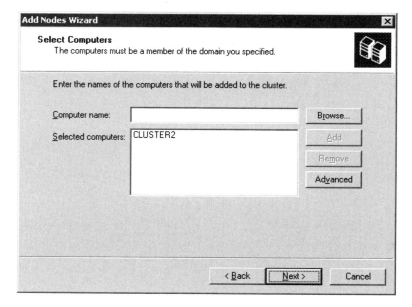

4. Once the cluster feasibility check has completed (see Figure 10.23), click the Next button.

FEASIBILITY STALL

If the feasibility check stalls and reports a 0x00138f error stating that a cluster resource cannot be found, the installation will continue to run. This is a known issue with the Windows Server 2003 cluster configuration. If you allow the installation to continue, it will eventually complete and function as expected. For more information visit http://support.microsoft.com/kb/909968.

5. Proceed to review the Cluster Administrator identifying that two nodes now exist within the new cluster.

FIGURE 10.23
A feasibility check is executed against each potential node to validate the hardware configuration that supports the appropriate shared resources and network configuration parameters.

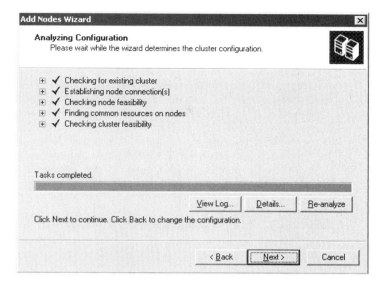

At this point the management cluster is complete; from here, application and service clusters can be configured. Some applications like Microsoft SQL Server 2005 and Microsoft Exchange Server 2007 are not only cluster-aware applications but also allow for the creation of a server cluster as part of the standard installation wizard. Other cluster-aware applications and services can be configured into a cluster using the cluster administrator.

Physical-to-Virtual Clustering

The last type of clustering scenario to discuss is the physical-to-virtual clustering configuration. As you may have guessed, this involves building a cluster with two nodes where one node is a physical machine and the other node is a virtual machine. Figure 10.24 details the setup of a two-node physical-to-virtual cluster.

FIGURE 10.24
Clustering physical machines with virtual machine counterparts can be a cost-effective way of providing high availability.

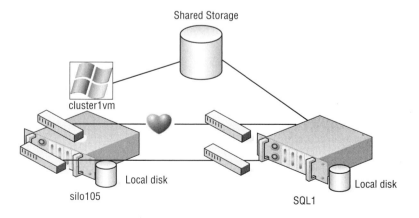

The constraints surrounding the construction of a physical-to-virtual cluster are identical to those noted in the previous configuration. Likewise, the steps to configure the virtual machine acting as a node in the physical-to-virtual cluster are identical to the steps outlined in the previous section. The virtual machine must have access to all the same storage locations as the physical machine. The virtual machine must also have access to the same pair of networks used by the physical machine for production and heartbeat communication, respectively.

The advantage to implementing a physical-to-virtual cluster is the resulting high availability with reduced financial outlay. Physical-to-virtual clustering, due to the two-node limitation of virtual machine clustering, ends up as an N+1 clustered solution, where N is the number of physical servers in the environment plus one additional physical server to host the virtual machines. In each case, each physical-virtual machine cluster creates a failover pair. With the scope of the cluster design limited to a failover pair, the most important design aspect in a physical-to-virtual cluster is the scale of the host running ESX Server. As you may have figured, the more powerful the ESX Server, the more failover incidents it can handle. A more powerful ESX Server will scale better to handle multiple physical host failures, whereas a less powerful ESX Server might only handle a single physical host failure before performance levels experience a noticeable decline.

VMware High Availability (HA)

High availability has been an industry buzzword that has stood the test of time. The need and/or desire for high availability is often a significant component to network infrastructure design. Within the scope of ESX Server, VMware High Availability (HA) is a component of the VI3 Enterprise product that provides for automatic failover of virtual machines. But — and it's a big *but* at this point in time — HA does not provide high availability in the traditional sense of the term. Commonly, the term HA means automatic failover of a service or application to another server.

Understanding HA

The VMware HA feature provides an automatic restart of the virtual machines that were running on an ESX Server host at the time it became unavailable, shown in Figure 10.25.

FIGURE 10.25
VMware HA provides an automatic restart of virtual machines that were running on an ESX Server host when it failed.

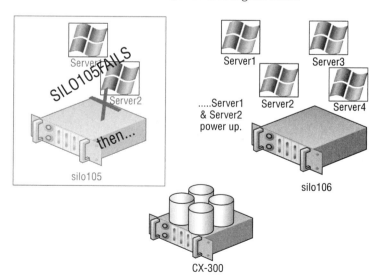

In the case of VMware HA, there is still a period of downtime when a server fails. Unfortunately, the duration of the downtime is not a value that can be calculated because it is unknown ahead of time how long it will take to boot a series of virtual machines. From this you can gather that, at this point in time, VMware HA does not provide the same level of high availability as found in a Microsoft server cluster solution. When a failover occurs between ESX Server hosts as a result of the HA feature, there is potential for data loss as a result of the virtual machine that was immediately powered off when the server failed and then brought back up minutes later on another server.

HA: WITHIN, BUT NOT BETWEEN, SITES

A requisite of HA is that each node in the HA cluster must have access to the same SAN LUNs. This requirement prevents HA from being able to failover between ESX Server hosts in different locations unless both locations have been configured to have access to the *same* storage devices. It is not acceptable just to have the data in LUNs the same due to SAN-replication software. Mirroring data from a LUN on a SAN in one location to a LUN on a SAN in a hot site is not conducive to allowing HA (VMotion or DRS).

In the VMware HA scenario, two or more ESX Server hosts are configured in a cluster. Remember, a VMware cluster represents a logical aggregation of CPU and memory resources, as shown in Figure 10.26. By editing the cluster settings, the VMware HA feature can be enabled for a cluster. The HA cluster then determines the number of hosts failures it must support.

FIGURE 10.26
A VMware ESX Server cluster logically aggregates the CPU and memory resources from all nodes in the cluster.

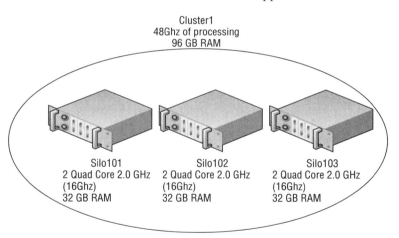

Cluster1
48Ghz of processing
96 GB RAM

Silo101
2 Quad Core 2.0 GHz
(16Ghz)
32 GB RAM

Silo102
2 Quad Core 2.0 GHz
(16Ghz)
32 GB RAM

Silo103
2 Quad Core 2.0 GHz
(16Ghz)
32 GB RAM

When ESX Server hosts are configured into a VMware HA cluster, they receive all the cluster information. VirtualCenter informs each node in the HA cluster about the cluster configuration.

HA AND VIRTUALCENTER

While VirtualCenter is most certainly required to enable and manage VMware HA, it is not required to execute HA. VirtualCenter is a tool that notifies each VMware HA-cluster node about the HA configuration. Once the nodes have been updated with the information about the cluster, VirtualCenter no longer maintains a persistent connection with each node. Each node continues to function as a member of the HA cluster independent of its communication status with VirtualCenter.

When an ESX Server host is added to a VMware HA cluster, a set of HA specific components are installed on the ESX Server. These components, shown in Figure 10.27, include:

◆ Automatic Availability Manager (AAM)

◆ VMap

◆ vpxa

FIGURE 10.27
Adding an ESX Server host to an HA cluster automatically installs the AAM, VMap, and possibly the vpxa components on the host.

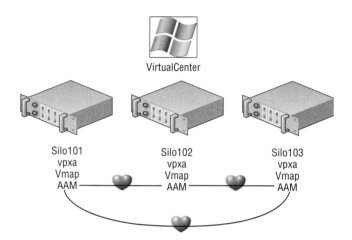

The AAM, effectively the engine for HA, is a Legato-based component that keeps an internal database of the other nodes in the cluster. The AAM is responsible for the intracluster heartbeat used to identify available and unavailable nodes. Each node in the cluster establishes a heartbeat with each of the other nodes over the Service Console network. As a best practice, you should provide redundancy to the AAM heartbeat by establishing the Service Console port group on a virtual switch with an underlying NIC team. Though the Service Console could be multihomed and have an AAM heartbeat over two different networks, this configuration is not as reliable as the NIC team. The AAM is extremely sensitive to hostname resolution; the inability to resolve names will most certainly result in an inability to execute HA. When problems arise with HA functionality, look first at hostname resolution. Having said that, during HA troubleshooting, you should identify the answers to questions like:

◆ Is the DNS server configuration correct?

◆ Is the DNS server available?

◆ If DNS is on a remote subnet, is the default gateway correct and functional?

◆ Does the /etc/hosts file have bad entries in it?

◆ Does the /etc/resolv.conf have the right search suffix?

◆ Does the /etc/resolv.conf have the right DNS server?

ADDING A HOST TO VIRTUALCENTER

When a new host is added into the VirtualCenter inventory, the host must be added by its hostname or the HA will not function properly. As just noted, HA is heavily reliant on successful name resolution. ESX Server hosts should not be added to the VirtualCenter inventory using IP addresses.

The AAM on each ESX Server host keeps an internal database of the other hosts belonging to the cluster. All hosts in a cluster are considered either a primary host or a secondary host. However, only one ESX Server in the cluster is considered the primary host at a given time, with all others considered secondary hosts. The primary host functions as the source of information for all new hosts and defaults to the first host added to the cluster. If the primary host experiences failure, the HA cluster will continue to function. In fact, in the event of primary host failure, one of the secondary hosts will move up to the status of primary host. The process of promoting secondary hosts to primary is limited to four other hosts. Only five hosts could assume the role of primary host in an HA cluster.

While the AAM is busy managing the intranode communications, the vpxa service manages the HA components. The vpxa service communicates to the AAM through a third component called the vMap.

Configuring HA

Before we detail how to set up and configure the HA feature, let's review the requirements of HA. To implement HA, all of the following requirements should be met:

◆ All hosts in an HA cluster must have access to the same shared storage locations used by all virtual machines on the cluster. This includes any fibre channel, iSCSI, and NFS datastores used by virtual machines.

◆ All hosts in an HA cluster should have an identical virtual networking configuration. If a new switch is added to one host, the same new switch should be added to all hosts in the cluster.

◆ All hosts in an HA cluster must resolve the other hosts using DNS names.

A TEST FOR HA

An easy and simple test for identifying HA capability for a virtual machine is to perform a VMotion. The requirements of VMotion are actually more stringent than those for performing an HA failover, though some of the requirements are identical. In short, if a virtual machine can successfully perform a VMotion across the hosts in a cluster, then it is safe to assume that HA will be able to power on that virtual machine from any of the hosts. To perform a full test of a virtual machine on a cluster with four nodes, perform a VMotion from node 1 to node 2, node 2 to node 3, node 3 to node 4, and finally node 4 back to node 1. If it works, then you have passed the test!

First and foremost, to configure HA a cluster must be created. Once the cluster is created, you can enable and configure HA. Figure 10.28 shows a cluster enabled for HA.

FIGURE 10.28
A cluster of ESX Server hosts can be configured with HA and DRS. The features are not mutually exclusive and can work together to provide availability and performance optimization.

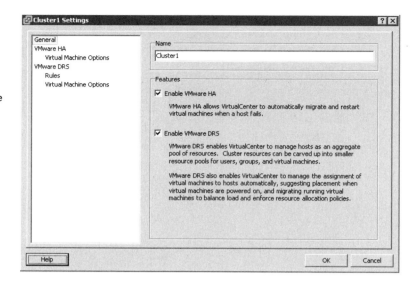

Configuring an HA cluster revolves around three different settings:

◆ Host failures allowed

◆ Admission control

◆ Virtual machine options

The configuration option for the number of host failures to allow, shown in Figure 10.29, is a critical setting. It directly influences the number of virtual machines that can run in the cluster before the cluster is in jeopardy of being unable to support an unexpected host failure.

FIGURE 10.29
The number of host failures allowed dictates the amount of spare capacity that must be retained for use in recovering virtual machines after failure.

Real World Scenario

HA CONFIGURATION FAILURE

It is not uncommon for a host in a cluster to fail during the configuration of HA. Remember the stress we put on DNS earlier in the chapter. Well, if DNS is not set correctly, you will find that the host cannot be configured for HA. Take, for example, a cluster with three nodes being configured as an HA cluster to support two-node failure. Enabling HA forces a configuration of each node in the cluster. The image here shows an HA cluster where one of the nodes, Silo104, has thrown an error related to the HA agent and is unable to complete the HA configuration:

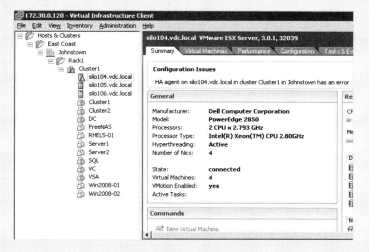

In this example, because the cluster was attempting to allow for two-node failure and there are only two nodes successfully configured, this would be impossible. The cluster in this case is now warning that there are insufficient resources to satisfy the HA failover level. Naturally, with only two nodes we cannot cover two-node failure. The image here shows an error on the cluster due to the failure in Silo104:

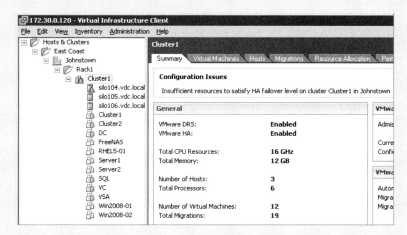

In the tasks pane of the graphic, you may have noticed that Silo105 and Silo106 both completed the HA configuration successfully. This provides evidence that the problem is probably isolated to Silo104. Reviewing the Tasks & Events tab to get more detail on the error reveals exactly that. The next image shows that the error was caused by an inability to resolve a name. This confirms the suspicion that the error is with DNS.

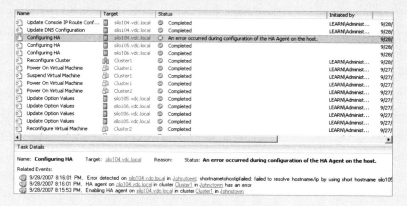

Perform the following steps to review or edit the DNS server for an ESX Server:

1. Use the Virtual Infrastructure (VI) Client to connect to a VirtualCenter server.

2. Click the name of the host in the inventory tree on the left.

3. Click the Configuration tab in the details pane on the right.

4. Click DNS and Routing from the Advanced menu.

5. If needed, edit the DNS server, as shown in the image here, to a server that can resolve the other nodes in the HA cluster:

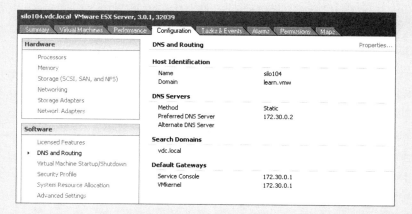

Although they should not be edited on a regular basis, you can also check the /etc/hosts and /etc/resolv.conf files, which should contain static lists of hostnames to IP addresses or the DNS search domain and name servers, respectively. This image offers a quick look at the information inside the /etc/hosts and /etc/resolv.conf files. These tools can be valuable for troubleshooting name resolution.

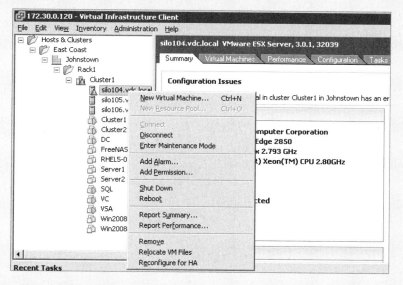

Once the DNS server, /etc/hosts, or /etc/resolv.conf has been corrected, the host with the failure can be reconfigured for HA. It's not necessary to remove the HA configuration from the cluster and then re-enable it. The image here shows the right-click context menu of Silo104, where it can be reconfigured for HA now that the name resolution problem has been fixed.

Upon completion of the configuration of the final node, the errors at the host and cluster levels will be removed, the cluster will be configured as desired, and the error regarding the inability to satisfy the failover level will disappear.

To explain the workings of HA and the differences in the configuration settings, let's look at implementation scenarios. For example, consider five ESX Server hosts named Silo101 through Silo105. All five hosts belong to an HA cluster configured to support single-host failure. Each node in the cluster is equally configured with 12GB of RAM. If each node runs eight virtual machines with 1GB of memory allocated to each virtual machine, then 8GB of unused memory across four hosts is needed to support a single-host failure. The 12GB of memory on each host minus 8GB for virtual machines leaves 4GB of memory per host. Figure 10.30 shows our five-node cluster in normal operating mode.

FIGURE 10.30
A five-node cluster configured to allow single-host failure.

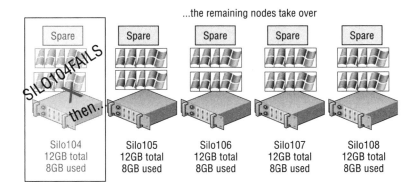

Let's assume that service console and virtual machine overhead consume 1GB of memory, leaving 3GB of memory per host. If Silo101 fails, the remaining four hosts will each have 3GB of memory to contribute to running the virtual machines orphaned by the failure. The 8GB of virtual machines will then be powered on across the remaining four hosts that collectively have 12GB of memory to spare. In this case, the configuration supported the failover. Figure 10.31 shows our five-node cluster down to four after the failure of Silo101. Assume in this same scenario that Silo101 and Silo102 both experience failure. That leaves 16GB of virtual machines to cover across only three hosts with 3GB of memory to spare? In this case, the cluster is deficient and not all of the orphaned virtual machines will be restarted.

FIGURE 10.31
A five-node cluster configured to allow single-host failure is deficient in resources to support a second failed node.

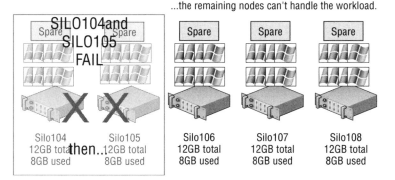

PRIMARY HOST LIMIT

In the previous section introducing the HA feature, we mentioned that the Automated Availability Manager (AAM) caps the number of primary hosts at five. This limitation translates into a maximum of four host failures allowed in a cluster.

The admission control setting goes hand in hand with the Number of host failures allowed setting. There are two possible settings for admission control:

♦ Do not power on virtual machines if they violate availability constraints (known as strict admission control).

♦ Allow virtual machines to be powered on even if they violate availability constraints (known as guaranteed admission control).

In the previous example, virtual machines would not power on when Silo102 experienced failure because by default an HA cluster is configured to use strict admission control. Figure 10.32 shows an HA cluster configured to use the default setting of strict admission control.

FIGURE 10.32
Strict admission control for an HA cluster prioritizes resource balance and fairness over resource availability.

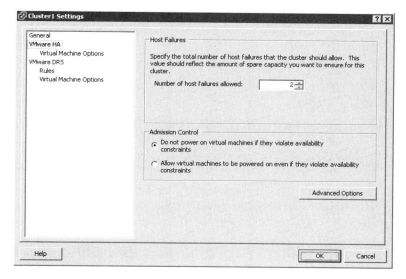

With strict admission control, the cluster will reach a point at which it will no longer start virtual machines. Figure 10.33 shows a cluster configured for two-node failover. A virtual machine with more than 3GB of memory reserved is powering on, and the resulting error is posted stating that insufficient resources are available to satisfy the configured HA level.

FIGURE 10.33
Strict admission control imposes a limit at which no more virtual machines can be powered on because the HA level would be jeopardized.

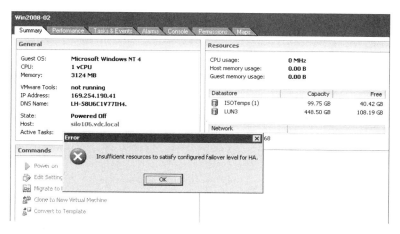

If the admission control setting of the cluster is changed from strict admission control to guaranteed admission control, then virtual machines will power on even in the event that the HA failover level is jeopardized. Figure 10.34 shows a cluster reconfigured to use guaranteed admission control.

FIGURE 10.34
Guaranteed admission control reflects the idea that when failure occurs, availability is more important than resource fairness and balance.

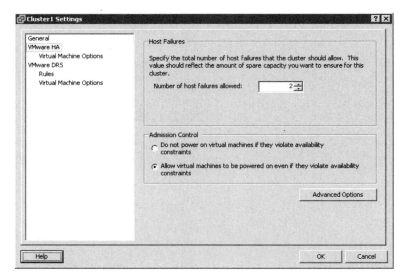

With that same cluster now configured with guaranteed admission control, the virtual machine with more than 3GB of memory can now successfully power on. In Figure 10.35, the virtual machine has successfully powered on despite the large memory use and lack of available unused resources to achieve the proper HA failover.

FIGURE 10.35
Guaranteed admission control allows resource consumption beyond the levels required to maintain spare resources for use in the event of a server failure.

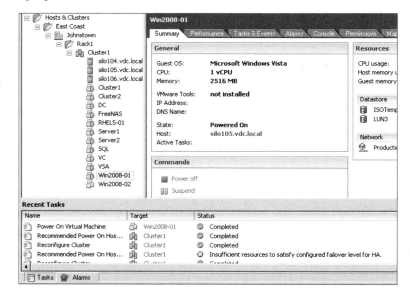

OVERCOMMITMENT IN AN HA CLUSTER

When the admission control setting is set to allow virtual machines to be powered on even if they violate availability constraints, you could find yourself in a position where there is more physical memory allocated to virtual machines than actually exists. This situation, called overcommitment, can lead to poor performance on virtual machines that become forced to page information from fast RAM out to the slower disk based swap file.

HA RESTART PRIORITY

Not all virtual machines are equal. There are some that are more important or more critical and that require higher priority when ensuring availability. When an ESX Server host experiences failure and the remaining cluster nodes are tasked with bringing virtual machines back on line, they have a finite amount of resources to fill before there are no more resources to allocate to virtual machines that need to be powered on. Rather than leave the important virtual machines to chance, an HA cluster allows for the prioritization of virtual machines. The restart priority options for virtual machines in an HA cluster include Low, Medium, High, and Disabled. For those virtual machines that should be brought up first, the restart priority should be set to High. For those virtual machines that should be brought up if resources are available, the restart priority can be set to Medium and/or Low. For those virtual machines that will not be missed for a period of time and should not be brought on line during the period of reduced resource availability, the restart priority should be set to Disabled. Figure 10.36 shows an example of virtual machines with various restart priorities configured to reflect their importance. The diagram details a configuration where virtual machines like domain controllers, database servers, and cluster nodes are assigned higher restart priority.

FIGURE 10.36
Restart priorities help minimize the downtime for more important virtual machines.

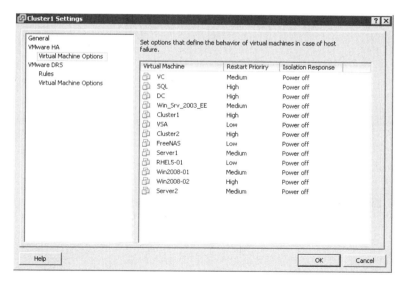

The restart priority is only put into place for the virtual machines running on the ESX Server host that experienced an unexpected failure. Virtual machines running on hosts that have not failed are not affected by the restart priority. It is possible then that virtual machines configured with a restart priority of High may not be powered on by the HA feature due to limited resources, which are in part due to lower-priority virtual machines that continue to run. For example, as shown in Figure 10.37, Silo101 hosts five virtual machines with a priority of High and five other virtual machines with priority values of Medium and Low. Meanwhile, Silo102 and Silo103 each hold ten virtual machines, but of the 20 virtual machines between them, only four are considered of high priority. When Silo101 fails, Silo102 and Silo103 will begin powering the virtual machines with a high priority. However, assume there were only enough resources to power on four of the five virtual machines with high priority. That leaves a high-priority virtual machine powered off while all other virtual machines of medium and low priority continue to run on Silo102 and Silo103.

FIGURE 10.37
High-priority virtual machines from a failed ESX Server host may not be powered on because of a lack of resources — resources consumed by virtual machines with a lower priority that are running on the other hosts in an HA cluster.

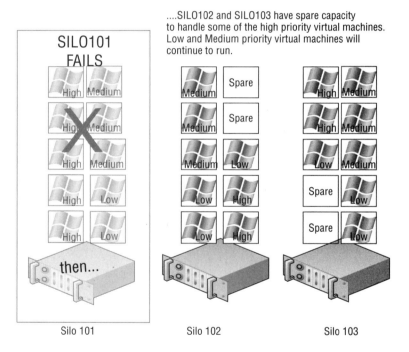

At this point in the VI3 product suite, you can still manually remedy this imbalance. Any disaster-recovery plan in a virtual environment built on VI3 should include a contingency plan that identifies virtual machines to be powered off to make resources available for those virtual machines with higher priority as a result of the network services they provide. If the budget allows, construct the HA cluster to ensure that there are ample resources to cover the needs of the critical virtual machines, even in times of reduced computing capacity.

HA ISOLATION RESPONSE

Previously, we introduced the Automated Availability Manager (AAM) and its role in conducting the heartbeat that occurs among all the nodes in the HA cluster. The heartbeat among the nodes in the cluster identifies the presence of each node to the other nodes in the cluster. When a heartbeat is no longer presented from a node in the HA cluster, the other cluster nodes spring into action to power on all the virtual machines that the missing node was running.

But what if the node with the missing heartbeat was not really missing? What if the heartbeat was missing but the node was still running? And what if the node with the missing heartbeat is still locking the virtual machine files on SAN LUN, thereby preventing the other nodes from powering on the virtual machines?

Let's look at two particular examples of a situation VMware refers to as a split-brained HA cluster. Let's assume there are three nodes in an HA cluster: Silo101, Silo102, and Silo103. Each node is configured with a single virtual switch for VMotion, and a second virtual switch consisting of a Service Console port and a virtual machines port group, as shown in Figure 10.38.

FIGURE 10.38
ESX Server hosts in an HA cluster using a single virtual switch for Service Console and virtual machine communication.

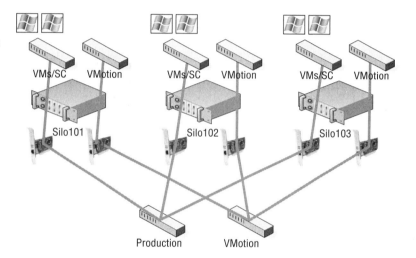

To continue with the example, suppose that an administrator mistakenly unplugs the Silo101 Service Console network cable. When each of the nodes identifies a missing heartbeat from another node, the discovery process begins. After 15 seconds of missing heartbeats, each node then pings an address called the isolation response address. By default this address is the default gateway IP address configured for the Service Console. If the ping attempt receives a reply, the node considers itself valid and continues as normal. If a host does not receive a response, as Silo101 wouldn't, it considers itself in isolation mode. At this point, the node will identify the cluster's Isolation Response configuration, which will guide the host to either power off the existing virtual machines it is hosting or leave them powered on. This isolation response value, shown in Figure 10.39, is set on a per-virtual machine basis. So what should you do? Power off the existing virtual machine? Or leave it powered on?

The answer to this question is highly dependent on the virtual and physical network infrastructures in place. In our example, the Service Console and virtual machines are connected to the same virtual switch bound to a single network adapter. In this case, when the cable for the Service Console was unplugged, communication to the Service Console and every virtual machine on that computer was lost. The solution, then, should be to power off the virtual machines. By doing so, the other nodes in the cluster will identify the releases on the locks and begin to power on the virtual machines that were not otherwise included.

FIGURE 10.39
The Isolation Response identifies the action to occur when an ESX Server host determines it is offline but powered on.

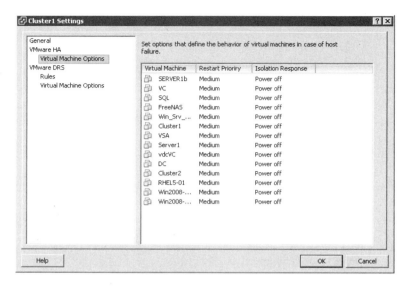

In the next example, we have the same scenario but a different infrastructure, so we don't need to worry about powering off virtual machines in a split-brain situation. Figure 10.40 diagrams a virtual networking architecture in which the Service Console, VMotion, and virtual machines all communicate through individual virtual switches bound to different physical network adapters. In this case, if the network cable connecting the Service Console is removed, the heartbeat will once again be missing; however, the virtual machines will be unaffected since they reside on a different network that is still passing communications between the virtual and physical networks.

FIGURE 10.40
Redundancy in the physical infrastructure with isolation of virtual machines from the Service Console in the virtual infrastructure provides greater flexibility for isolation response.

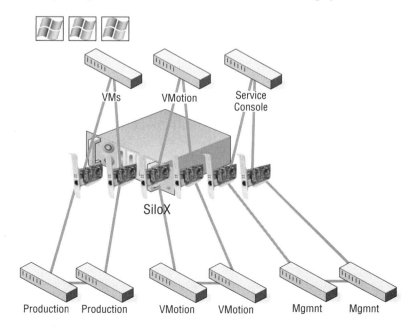

Figure 10.41 shows the isolation response setting of Leave powered on, which would accompany an infrastructure built with redundancy at the virtual and physical network levels.

FIGURE 10.41

The option to leave virtual machines running when a host is isolated should only be set when the virtual and the physical networking infrastructures support high availability.

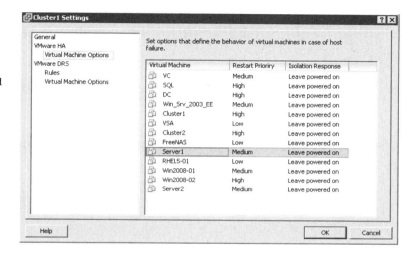

Real World Scenario

CONFIGURING THE ISOLATION RESPONSE ADDRESS

In some highly secure virtual environments, Service Console access is limited to a single, nonrouted management network. In some cases, the security plan calls for the elimination of a default gateway on the Service Console port configuration. The idea is to lock the Service Console onto the local subnet, thus preventing any type of remote network access. The disadvantage, as you might have guessed, is that without a default gateway IP address configured for the Service Console, there is no isolation address to ping as a determination of isolation status.

It is possible, however, to customize the isolation response address for scenarios just like this. The IP address can be any IP address, but should be an IP address that is not going to be unavailable or taken from the network at any time.

Perform the following steps to define a custom isolation response address:

1. Use the VI Client to connect to a VirtualCenter server.

2. Right-click on an existing cluster and select the Edit Settings option.

3. Click the VMware HA node.

4. Click the Advanced Options button.

5. Type **das.isolationaddress** in the Option column in the Advanced Options (HA) dialog box.

6. Type the IP address to be used as the isolation response address for ESX Server hosts that miss the AAM heartbeat. The following image shows a sample configuration in which the servers will ping the IP address 172.30.0.2:

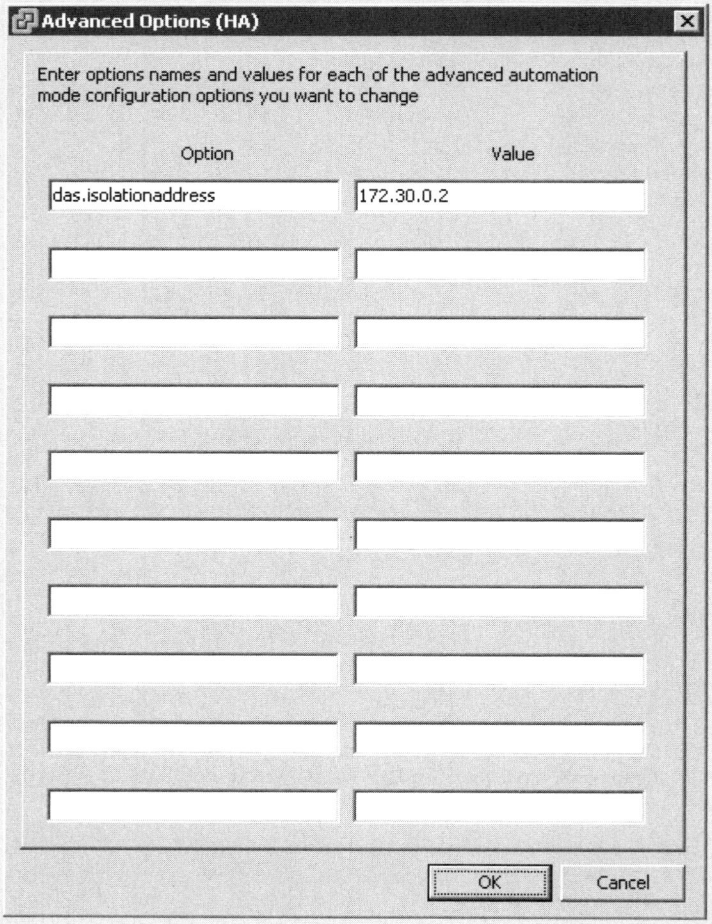

7. Click the OK button twice.

This interface can also be configured with the following options:

◆ das.isolationaddress1: To specify the first address to try.

◆ das.isolationaddress2: To specify the second address to try.

◆ das.defaultfailoverhost: To identify the preferred host to fail over to.

◆ das.failuredetectiontime: Used to change the amount of time required for failover detection.

To support a redundant HA architecture, it is best to ensure that the Service Console port is sitting atop a NIC team where each physical NIC bound to the virtual switch is connected to a different physical switch.

Backing Up with VMware Consolidated Backup (VCB)

Virtual machines are no less likely to lose data, become corrupted, or fail the way their physical counterparts might. And though some may argue against that point, it is most certainly the best way for you to look at virtual machines. With this school of thought, you might be jeopardizing the infrastructure with overconfidence in virtual machine stability. It's better to be safe than sorry. When it comes to virtual machine backup planning, VMware suggests three different methods you can use to support your disaster recovery/business continuity plan. The three methods include:

◆ Using backup agents inside the virtual machine.

◆ Using VCB to perform virtual machine backups.

◆ Using VCB to perform file-level backups (Windows guests only).

VMware Consolidated Backup (VCB) is VMware's first entry into the backup space. (For those of you who have worked with ESX 2, I am not counting the vmsnap.pl and vmres.pl as attempts to provide a backup product). VCB is a framework for backing up that integrates easily into a handful of third-party products. Although VCB can be used on its own, it lacks some of the nice features third-party backup products bring to the table. These include features like cataloging backups, scheduling capability, and media management backups. For this reason, I recommend that you use the VCB framework in conjunction with third-party products that have been tested.

More than likely, none of the three methods listed will suffice if used alone. As this chapter provides more details about each of the methods, you'll see how a solid backup strategy is based on using several of these methods in a complementary fashion.

Using Backup Agents in a Virtual Machine

Oh so many years ago when virtualization was not even a spot on your IT roadmap, you were backing up your physical servers according to some kind of business need. For most organizations, the solution involved the purchase, installation, configuration, and execution of third-party backup agents on the operating systems running on physical hardware. Now that you have jumped onto the cutting edge of technology by leading the server consolidation charge into a virtual IT infrastructure, you can still back up using the same traditional methods. Virtual machines like physical machines are targets for third-party backup tools. The downside to this time-tested model is the need to continue paying for the licenses needed to perform backups across all servers. As shown in Figure 10.42, you'll need a license for every virtual machine you wish to back up: 100 virtual machines = 100 licenses. Some vendors allow for a single ESX Server license that permits an unlimited number of agent licenses to be installed on virtual machines on that host.

In this case, virtualization has not lowered total ownership costs and the return on investment has not changed with regard to the fiscal accountability to the third-party backup company. So perhaps this is not the best avenue down which you should travel. With that being said, let's look at other options that rely heavily on the virtualized aspect of the guest operating system. These options include:

◆ Using VCB for full virtual machine backups.

◆ Using VCB for single VMDK backups.

◆ Using VCB for file-level backups.

FIGURE 10.42
Using third-party backup agents inside a virtual machine does not take advantage of virtualization. Virtual machines are treated just like their physical counterparts for the sake of a disaster recovery or business continuity plan.

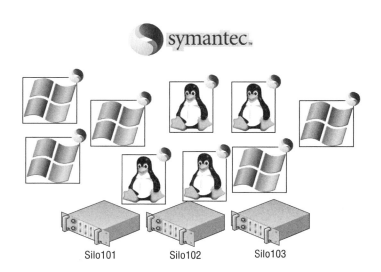

Silo101   Silo102   Silo103

Using VCB for Full Virtual Machine Backups

As we mentioned briefly in the opening section, VCB is a framework for backup that integrates with third-party backup software. It is a series of scripts that performs online, LAN-free backups of virtual machines or virtual machine files.

VCB FOR FIBRE CHANNEL ... AND ISCSI TOO!

When first released, VCB was offered as a fibre channel–only solution; VMware did not support VCB used over an iSCSI storage network. The latest release of VCB offers support for use with iSCSI storage.

The requirements for VCB 1.1 include:

◆ A physical server running Windows Server 2003 Service Pack 1.

    ◆ If using Windows Server 2003 Standard Edition, the VCB server must be configured not to automatically assign drive letters using `diskpart` to execute `automount disable` and `automount scrub`.

♦ Network connectivity for access to VirtualCenter.

♦ Fibre channel HBA with access to all SAN LUNs where virtual machine files are stored.

♦ Installation of the third-party software prior to installing and configuring VCB.

VCB on Fibre Channel Without Multipathing

The VCB proxy requires a fibre channel HBA to communicate with fibre channel SAN LUNs regarding backup processes. VCB does not, however, support multiple HBAs or multipathing software like EMC PowerPath. Insert only one fibre channel HBA into a VCB proxy.

Figure 10.43 looks at the VCB components and architecture.

FIGURE 10.43
A VCB deployment relies on several communication mediums, including network access to VirtualCenter and fibre channel access to all necessary SAN LUNs.

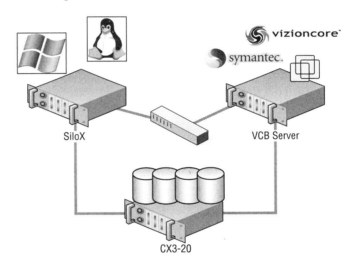

VMware regularly tests third-party support for VCB, and, as a result, the list of supported backup products continues to change. As of this writing, the following products were listed as backup products for which VMware provides integration scripts:

♦ EMC NetWorker

♦ Symantec Backup Exec

♦ Tivoli Storage Manager

♦ Veritas NetBackup

In addition to these four products, VMware lists the following products as having created integrations to allow their products to capitalize on the VCB framework:

♦ Vizioncore vRanger Pro, formerly ESXRanger Pro

♦ Certificate Associates (CA) BrightStor ARCServe

- ◆ CommVault Galaxy

- ◆ EMC Avamar

- ◆ HP Data Protector versions 5.5 and 6

Be sure to regularly visit VMware's website to download and review the PDF at `http://www` `.vmware.com/pdf/vi3_backup_guide.pdf`.

Although considered a framework for backup, VCB can actually be used as a backup product. However, it lacks the nice scheduling and graphical interface features of third-party products like Vizioncore vRanger Pro. Two of the more common VCB commands, shown in Figures 10.44 and 10.45, are:

- ◆ vcbVmName: This command enumerates the various ways a virtual machine can be referenced in the vcbMounter. Here's an example:

```
vcbVmName -h 172.30.0.120 -u administrator -p Sybex!!
   -s ipaddr:172.30.0.24
```

  where

  - ◆ `-h <VirtualCenter Server name or IP address>`

  - ◆ `-u <VirtualCenter username>`

  - ◆ `-p <VirtualCenter user password>`

  - ◆ `-s ipaddr: <IP address of virtual machine to backup>`

- ◆ vcbMounter:

  - ◆ `-h <VirtualCenter Server name or IP address>`

  - ◆ `-u <VirtualCenter username>`

  - ◆ `-p <VirtualCenter user password>`

  - ◆ `-a <name | ipaddr | moref | uuid>: <attribute value>`

  - ◆ `-t [fullvm | file]`

  - ◆ `-r <Backup directory on VCB proxy>`

VCB PROXY BACKUP DIRECTORY

When specifying the VCB backup directory using the `-r` parameter, do not specify an existing folder. For example, if a backup directory `E:\VCBBackups` already exists and a new backup should be stored in a subdirectory named Server1, then specify the subdirectory *without* creating it first. In this case, the `-r` parameter might read as follows:

`-r E:\VCBBackups\Server1`

The vcbMounter will create the new directory as needed. If the directory is created first, an error will be thrown at the beginning of the backup process. The error will state that the directory already exists.

FIGURE 10.44

The vcbVmName command enumerates the various virtual machine identifiers that can be used when running the VCB command.

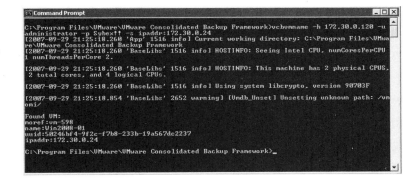

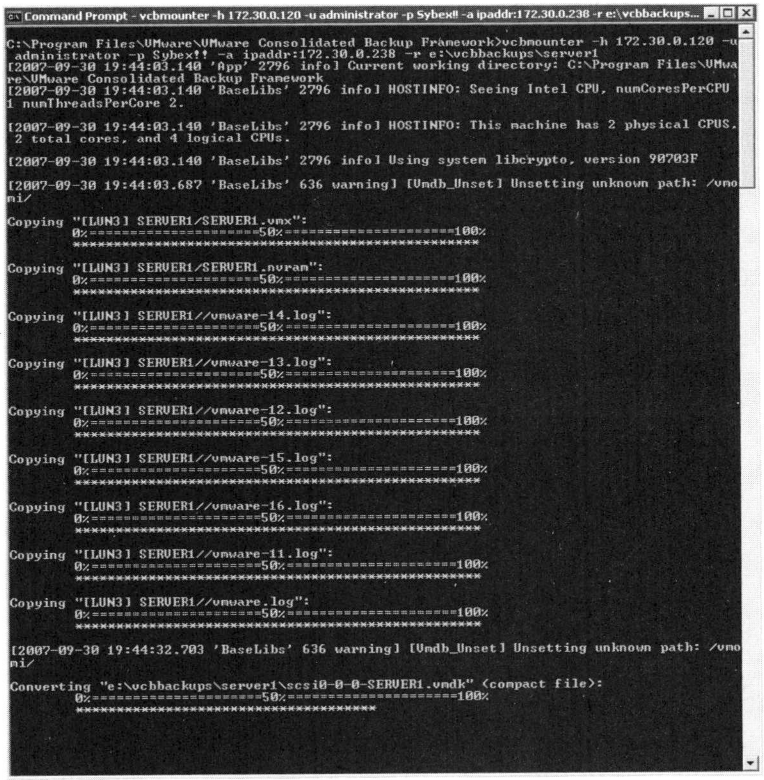

FIGURE 10.45

The vcbMounter command can be used to perform full virtual machines backups or file-level backups for Windows virtual machines.

When VCB performs a full backup of a virtual machine, it engages the VMware snapshot functionality to quiesce the file system and perform the backup. Remember that snapshots are not complete copies of data. Instead, a snapshot is the creation of a differencing file (or redo log) to which all changes are written. When the vcbMounter command is used, a snapshot is taken of the virtual machine, as shown in Figure 10.46.

FIGURE 10.46
The snapshots created by VCB can be viewed in the snapshot manager of a virtual machine.

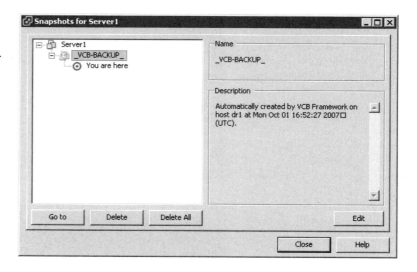

Any writes that occur during the backup are done to the differencing file. Meanwhile, VCB is busy making a copy of the VMDK, which is now read-only for the duration of the backup job. Figure 10.47 details the full virtual machine backup process. Once the backup job is completed, the snapshot is deleted, forcing all writes that occurred to the differencing file to be written to the virtual machine disk file.

FIGURE 10.47
Performing a full virtual machine backup utilizes the VMware snapshot functionality, which ensures that an online backup is correct as of that point in time.

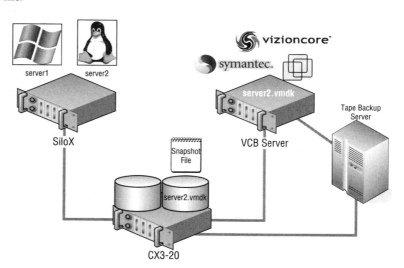

SNAPSHOTS AND VMFS LOCKING

Snapshots grow by default in 16MB increments, and for the duration of time it takes to grow a snapshot, a lock is held on the VMFS volume so the respective metadata can be updated to reflect the change in the snapshot. For this reason, do not instantiate a snapshot for many virtual machines at once. Although the lock is held only for the update to the metadata, the more virtual machines trying at the same time, the greater the chance of contention on the VMFS metadata. From an IT standpoint, this factor should drive your backup strategy to perform backups of many virtual machines only if the virtual machine files have been located on separate VMFS volumes.

Perform the following steps to perform a full virtual machine backup using VCB:

1. Log in to the backup proxy where VCB is installed.

2. Open a command prompt and change directories to the C:\Program Files\VMware\VMware Consolidated Backup Framework directory.

3. Use the vcbVmName tool to enumerate virtual machine identifiers. At the command prompt, type:

   ```
   vcbVmName <IP or name of VirtualCenter> -u <username>
      -p <password> -s ipaddr:<IP address of virtual
      machine to backup>
   ```

4. From the results of running the vcbVmName tool, select which identifier to use (moref, name, uuid, or ipaddr) in the vcbMounter command.

5. At the command prompt, type:

   ```
   VcbMounter -h <IP or name of VirtualCenter> -u
      <username> -p <password> -a ipaddr:<IP address of
      virtual machine to backup> -t fullvm -r <VCB proxy
      backup directory>
   ```

   Once the backup is complete, a list of the files can be reviewed in the directory provided in the backup script. Figure 10.48 shows the files created as part of the completed full backup of a virtual machine named Server1.

FIGURE 10.48
A full virtual machine backup using VCB creates a directory of files that include a configuration file (VMX), log files, and virtual machine hard drives (VMDK), among others.

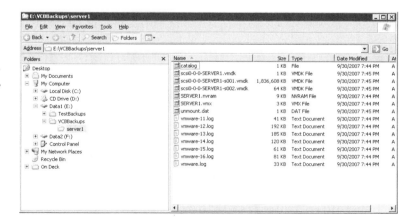

Redundant Paths

Let's look at an example of a VCB backup proxy with a single QLogic fibre channel HBA that is connected to a single fibre channel switch connected to two storage processors on the storage device. This configuration results in two different paths being available to the VCB server. The image here shows that a VCB server with a single HBA will find LUNs twice because of the redundancy at the storage-processor level:

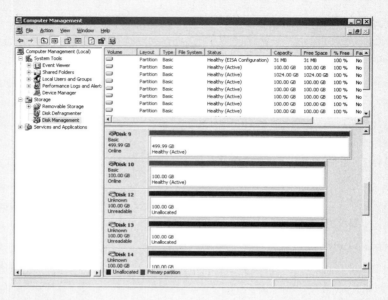

When Disk Management shows this configuration for the older versions of VCB, it presents a problem that causes every backup attempt to fail. For the pre-VCB 1.0.3 versions, the LUNs identified as Unknown and Unreadable must be disabled in Disk Management. The option to disable is located on the properties of a LUN. The following image displays the General tab of LUN properties from Disk Management where a path to a LUN can be disabled. To remove the redundant unused paths from Computer Management, the Device Usage drop-down list should be set to Do not use this device (disable).

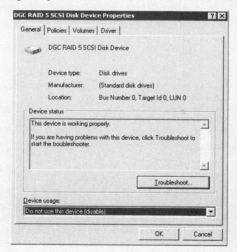

With redundant paths disabled, this will, of course, present a problem when a LUN trespasses to another storage processor. This requires a path to the LUN that is likely disabled.

Using VCB for Single VMDK Backups

Sometimes a full backup is just too much: too much data that hasn't changed, or too much data that is backed up more regularly and isn't needed again. For example, what if just the operating system drive needs to be backed up, not all the user data stored on other virtual machine disk files? A full backup would back up everything. For those situations, VCB provides a means of performing single virtual machine disk backups.

Perform the following steps for a single VMDK backup:

1. Log in to the backup proxy where VCB is installed.

2. Open a command prompt and change directories to the C:\Program Files\VMware\VMware Consolidated Backup Framework directory.

3. Use the vcbVmName tool to enumerate virtual machine identifiers. At the command prompt, type:

```
vcbVmName <IP or name of VirtualCenter> -u <username>
   -p <password> -s ipaddr:<IP address of virtual
   machine to backup>
```

4. From the results of running the vcbVmName command, note the moref value of the virtual machine.

5. Use the following command to create a snapshot of the virtual machine:

```
vcbSnapshot -h <IP or name of VirtualCenter> -u
   <username> -p <password> -c <moref value of
   virtual machine> <name of snapshot>
```

6. Note the snapshot ID (SsiDd) from the results of step 5.

7. Enumerate the disks within the snapshot using the vcbSnapshot command:

```
vcbSnapshot -h <IP or name of VirtualCenter> -u
   <username> -p <password> -l <moref value of
   virtual machine> <snapshot ID>
```

8. Change to the backup directory of the virtual machine and export the desired VMDK using the vcbExport command:

```
vcbExport -d <name of new VMDK copy> -s <name of
   existing VMDK>
```

9. Remove the snapshot by once again using the vcbSnapshot command:

```
vcbSnapshot -h <IP or name of VirtualCenter> -u
   <username> -p <password> -d <moref value of
   virtual machine> <snapshot ID>
```

Using VCB for File-Level Backups

For Windows virtual machines, and *only* for Windows virtual machines, VCB offers file-level backups. A file-level backup is an excellent complement to the full virtual machine or the single VMDK backup discussed in the previous sections. For example, suppose you built a virtual machine using two virtual disks: one for the operating system and one for the custom user data. The operating system's virtual disk will not change often with the exception of the second Tuesday of each month when new patches are released. So that virtual disk does not need consistent and regular backups. On the other hand, the virtual disk that stores user data might be updated quite frequently. To get the best of both worlds and implement an efficient backup strategy, you need to do a single VMDK backup (for the OS) and file-level backup (for the data).

Perform the following steps to conduct a file-level backup using VCB:

1. Log in to the backup proxy where VCB is installed.

2. Open a command prompt and change directories to C:\Program Files\VMware\VMware Consolidated Backup Framework.

3. Use the vcbVmName tool to enumerate virtual machine identifiers. At the command prompt, type:

```
vcbVmName <IP or name of VirtualCenter> -u <username>
   -p <password> -s ipaddr:<IP address of virtual
   machine to backup>
```

4. From the results of running the vcbVmName tool, select which identifier to use (moref, name, uuid, or ipaddr) in the vcbMounter command.

5. As shown in Figure 10.49, type the following at the command prompt:

```
VcbMounter -h <IP or name of VirtualCenter> -u
   <username> -p <password> -s ipaddr:<IP address of
   virtual machine to backup> -t file -r <VCB proxy
   backup directory>
```

6. Browse to the mounted directory to back up the required files and folders.

7. After the file- or folder-level backup is complete, use the following command, shown in Figure 10.50, to remove the mount point:

```
mountvm -u <path to mount point>
```

8. Exit the command prompt.

FIGURE 10.49
A file- or folder-level backup begins with mounting the virtual machine drives as directories under a mount point on the VCB server.

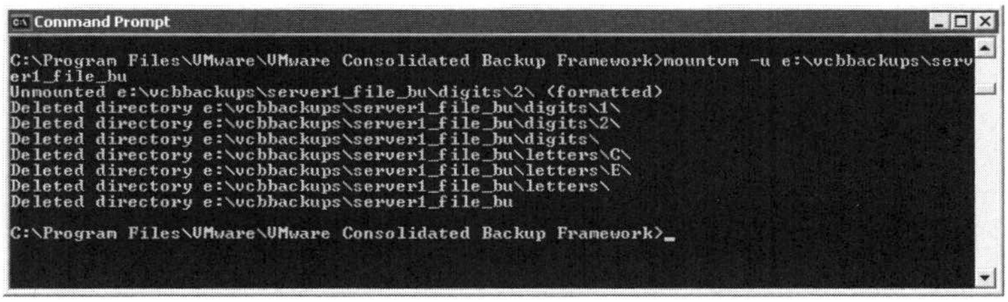

FIGURE 10.50
After performing a file- or folder-level backup using the vcbMounter command, the mount point must be removed using the mountvm command.

STICKY SNAPSHOTS

If a snapshot refuses to delete when the mountvm -u command is issued, it can always be deleted from the snapshot manager user interface, which is accessible through the VI Client.

Real World Scenario

VCB WITH THIRD-PARTY PRODUCTS

Once you have mastered the VCB framework by understanding the VCB mounter commands and the way that VCB works, then working with VCB and third-party products is an easy transition. The third-party products simply call upon the VCB framework to perform the vcbmounter command. All the while the process is wrapped up nicely inside the GUI of the third-party product. This allows for scheduling the backups through backup jobs.

Let's look at an example with Symantec Backup Exec 11d. Once the 11d product is installed, followed by the installation of VCB, a set of integration scripts can be extracted from VCB to support the Backup Exec installation. When a backup job is created in Backup Exec 11d, a pre-backup script runs (which calls vcbmounter to create the snapshot and mount the VMDKs), and once the backup job completes, a post-backup script runs to unmount the VMDKs. During the period of time that VMDKs are mounted into the file system, the Backup Exec product has access to the mounted VMDKs in order to back them up to disk or tape, as specified in the backup job. See the following sample scripts, which perform a full virtual machine backup of a virtual machine with the IP address 192.168.4.1.

First, the pre-backup script example:

```
"C:\Program Files\VMware\VMware Consolidated Backup
    Framework\backupexec\pre-backup.bat" Server1_FullVM 192.168.4.1-fullvm
```

Now, the post-backup script example:

```
"C:\Program Files\VMware\VMware Consolidated Backup
    Framework\backupexec\post-backup.bat" Server1_FullVM 192.168.1.10-fullVM
```

Notice that there is no reference to vcbmounter or the parameters required to run the command. Behind the scenes the pre-backup.bat and post-backup.bat files are reading a configuration file named config.js to pull defaults for some of the parameters for vcbmounter and then using the information given in the lines shown earlier. When vcbmounter extracts the virtual machine files to the file system of the VCB proxy, the files will be found in a folder named 192.168.4.1-fullvm in a directory specified in the configuration file. A portion of the configuration file is shown here. Note that the file identifies the directory to mount the backups to (F:\\mnt) as well as the VirtualCenter server to connect to (vc01.vlearn.vmw) and the credentials to be used (administrator /Password1):

```
/*
 * Generic configuration file for VMware Consolidated Backup (VCB).
 */

/*
 * Directory where all the VM backup jobs are supposed to reside in.
```

```
 * For each backup job, a directory with a unique name derived from the
 * backup type and the VM name will be created here.
 * If omitted, BACKUPROOT defaults to c:\\mnt.
 *
 * Make sure this directory exists before attempting any VM backups.
 */
BACKUPROOT="F:\\mnt";/*
 * URL that is used by "mountvm" to obtain the block list for a
 * disk image that is to be mounted on the backup proxy.
 *
 * Specifying this option is mandatory. There is no default
 * value.
 */
HOST="vc01.learn.vmw";
/*
 * Port for communicating with all the VC SDK services.
 * Defaults to 902
 */
// PORT="902";

/*
 * Username/password used for authentication against the mountvm server.
 * Specifying these options is mandatory.
 */
USERNAME="administrator";
PASSWORD="Password1";
```

The combination of the configuration file with the parameters passed at the time of execution results in a successful mount and copy of the virtual machine disk files followed by an unmount.

Depending on the size of the virtual machines to be backed up, it might be more feasible to back up to disk and then create a second backup job to take the virtual machine backups to a tape device.

Restoring with VMware Consolidated Backup (VCB)

Restoring data in a virtual environment can take many forms. If using VCB in combination with an approved third-party backup application, there are three specific types of restores that can be defined. These restore types include:

Centralized Restore   One backup agent on the VCB proxy.

Decentralized Restore   Several backup agents installed around the network, but not every system has one.

Self-Service Restore   Each virtual machine contains a backup agent.

Why are we discussing backup agents in the restore section? Remember, the number of backup agents purchased directly influences the virtual machines that can also be restored directly.

No matter how you implant the whole backup/restore process, you must understand that it's either "pay me now or pay me later." Something that is easier to back up is often more difficult to restore. On the flip side, something that is the most difficult to back up is often easier to restore. Figure 10.51 shows the difference between the centralized restore and the self-service restore.

FIGURE 10.51
Backup agents are not just for backup. They also allow restore capability. The number of backup agents purchased and installed directly affects the recovery plan.

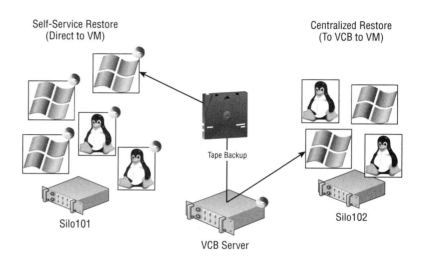

SELF-SERVICE RESTORE IS ALWAYS QUICKER

If you are looking for a restore solution focused solely on speed of restore and administrative effort, then the self-service restore method is ideal. Of course, the price is a bit heftier than its counterparts because an agent is required in the virtual machine. A centralized restore methodology would require two touches on the data to be restored. The first touch gets the data from backup media to the VCB proxy server, and the second touch gets the data from the VCB proxy server back into the virtual machine. The latter happens via standard Server Message Block (SMB) or Common Internet File System (CIFS) traffic in a Windows environment. This is a literal *servername**sharename* copy of the data back to the virtual machine where the data exists.

Perhaps the best solution is to find a happy, solid relationship between the self-service restore and the centralized restore methods. This way you can reduce (not necessarily minimize) the number of backup agents, while still allowing critical virtual machines to have data restored immediately.

To demonstrate a restore of a full virtual machine backup, let's continue with the earlier examples. Server1 at this point has a full backup created. Figure 10.52 shows that Server1 has now been deleted and is gone.

Restoring a Full Virtual Machine Backup

When bad things happen, such as the deletion or corruption of a virtual machine, a restore from a full virtual machine backup will return the environment to the point in time when the backup was taken.

FIGURE 10.52
A server from the inventory is missing and a search through the datastores does not locate the virtual machine disk files.

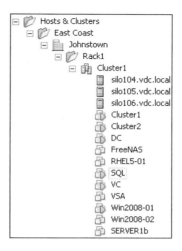

Perform the following steps on a virtual machine from a full virtual machine backup:

1. Connect to the VCB proxy and use FastSCP, shown in Figure 10.53, or WinSCP to establish a secure copy protocol session with the remote host. Shown in Figure 10.53, the data from the E:\VCBBackups\Server1 folder can be copied into a temporary directory in the service console. The temporary directory houses all of the virtual machine files from the backup of the original virtual machine.

FIGURE 10.53
The FastSCP utility, as the name proclaims, offers a fast, secure copy protocol application to move files back and forth between Windows and ESX.

2. Upon completion of the restore to a temporary location process, verify the existence of the files by navigating to the shared site, as shown in Figure 10.54. Use `Putty.exe` to connect to the Service Console and navigate to the temporary directory where the backup files are stored. Then use the `ls` command to list all the files in the temporary directory.

FIGURE 10.54
Virtual machine files needed for the restore are located in the temporary directory specified in the command.

```
root@silo105:/vmfs/volumes/LUN23 (1)/server1
[root@silo105 volumes]# cd /vmfs/volumes/"LUN23 (1)"/server1
[root@silo105 server1]# ls
catalog                        SERVER1.nvram   vmware-12.log  vmware-16.log
scsi0-0-0-SERVER1-s001.vmdk    SERVER1.vmx     vmware-13.log  vmware.log
scsi0-0-0-SERVER1-s002.vmdk    unmount.dat     vmware-14.log
scsi0-0-0-SERVER1.vmdk         vmware-11.log   vmware-15.log
[root@silo105 server1]#
```

3. From a command prompt, type the following:

```
vcbRestore -h 172.30.0.120 -u administrator -p
   Sybex123 -s <path to temp directory>
```

Figure 10.55 shows the virtual machine restore process.

4. Upon completion of the restore from the temporary location process, verify the existence of the files by navigating to datastore or by quickly glancing at the tree view of VirtualCenter.

FIGURE 10.55
Virtual machine restore times are highly dependent on the size of the virtual machine and the number of writes to it.

Restoring a Single File from a Full Virtual Machine Backup

Problems in the datacenter are not always as catastrophic as losing an entire virtual machine because of corruption or deletion. In fact, it is probably more common to experience minor issues like corrupted or deleted files. A full virtual machine backup does not have to be restored as a full virtual machine. Using the `mountvm` tool, it is possible to mount a virtual machine hard drive into the file system of the backup proxy (VCB) server. Once the hard drive is mounted, it can be browsed the same as any other directory on the server.

PUTTING FILES INTO A VMDK

Files cannot be put directly into a VMDK. Restoring files directly to a virtual machine requires a backup agent installed on the virtual machine.

Let's say that a virtual machine named Server1 has a full backup that has been completed. An administrator deletes a file named FILE TO RECOVER.txt that was on the desktop of his/her profile on Server1 and now needs to recover the file. (No, it's not in the Recycle Bin anymore.) Using the mountvm command, the VMDK backup of Server1 can be mounted into the file system of the VCB proxy server and the file can be recovered. Figure 10.56 shows the mountvm command used to mount a backup VMDK named scsi0-0-0-server1.vmdk into a mount point named server1_restore_dir off the root of the E drive. Figure 10.56 also shows the Windows Explorer application drilled into the mounted VMDK.

FIGURE 10.56

The mountvm command allows a VMDK backup file to be mounted into the VCB proxy server file system, where it can be browsed in search of files or folders to be recovered.

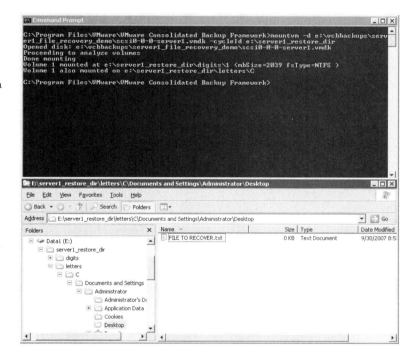

Perform the following steps to conduct a single file restore from a full virtual machine backup:

1. Log in to the VCB proxy and navigate to the directory holding the backup files for the virtual machine that includes the missing file.

2. Browse the backup directory and note the name of the VMDK to mount to the VCB file system.

3. Open a command prompt and change to the C:\Program Files\VMware\VMware Consolidated Backup Framework directory.

4. Type the following command:

```
mountvm -d <name of VMDK to mount> -cycleId <name of
    mount point>
```

5. Browse the file system of the VCB proxy server to find the new mount point. The new mount point will contain a subdirectory named `Letters` followed by a directory for the drive letter of the VMDK that has been mounted. These directories can now be browsed and manipulated as needed to recover the missing file.

6. Once the file or folder recovery is complete, type the following command:

```
mountvm -u <mount point name>
```

7. Close the command prompt window.

Real World Scenario

USER DATA BACKUPS IN WINDOWS

Although VCB offers the functionality to mount the virtual machine hard drives for file- or folder-level recovery, I recommend that you back up your custom user data drives and directories on a more regular basis than a full virtual machine backup. In addition to the methods discussed here like the file- and folder-level backups with VCB or third-party backup software like Vizioncore vRanger Pro, there are also tools like Shadow Copies of Shared Folders that are native to the Windows operating system.

Shadow Copies of Shared Folders builds off the Volume Shadow Services available in Windows Server 2003 and later. It offers scheduled online backups to changes in files that reside in shared folders. The frequency of the schedule determines the number of previous versions that will exist up to the maximum of 63. The value in complementing a VCB and Vizioncore backup strategy with shadow copies is in the restore ease. Ideally, with shadow copies enabled, users can be trained on how to recover deletions and corruptions without involving the IT staff. Only when the previous version is no longer in the list of available restores will the IT staff need to get involved with a single file restore. And for the enterprise-level shadow copy deployment, Microsoft has recently released the System Center Data Protection Manager (SCDPM). SCDPM is a shadow copy on steroids, which is used to provide online frequent backups of files and folders across the entire network.

For more information on Shadow Copies of Shared Folders, visit Microsoft's website at http://www .microsoft.com/windowsserver2003/techinfo/overview/scr.mspx.

For more information on System Center Data Protection Manager, visit Microsoft's website at http://www.microsoft.com/systemcenter/dpm/default.mspx.

Restoring VCB Backups with VMware Converter Enterprise

Perhaps one of the best new features of VirtualCenter 2.5 is the integration of the VMware Converter Enterprise. But to add to its benefit, VMware extended the functionality of the VMware Converter to allow it to perform restores of backups that were made using VMware Consolidated Backup. Figure 10.57 shows the VMware Converter Import Wizard option .

Figure 10.58 shows the files that are part of the VCB backup, including the required VMX file that must be referenced. During the import process, shown in Figure 10.59, you will need to provide the UNC path to the VMX file for the virtual machine to be restored.

FIGURE 10.57
The VMware Converter Import Wizard greatly simplifies the procedure for restoring VCB backups.

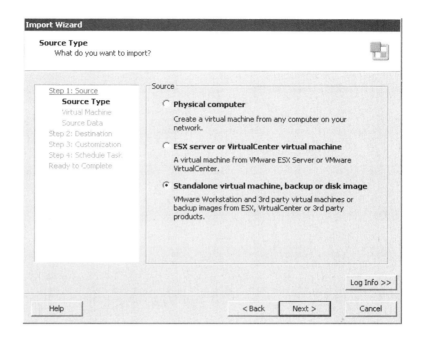

FIGURE 10.58
The VCB backup files include a VMX file with all the data about the virtual machine.

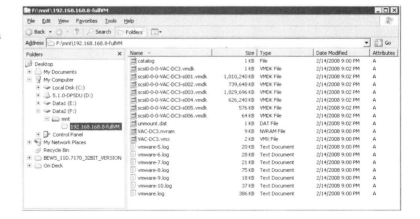

FIGURE 10.59
The VMware Converter Import Wizard requires a UNC path that references the VMX file of the virtual machine to be restored.

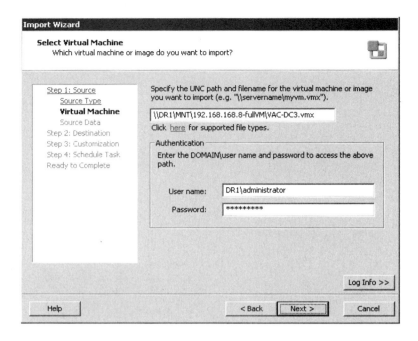

The examples shown in the previous two figures show the configuration for a backup server named DR1 with a folder that has been shared as MNT. Therefore the appropriate path for the VMX file of the virtual machine to be restored would be \\DR1\MNT\192.168.168.8-fullVM\ VAC-DC3.vmx. The remaining steps of the Import Wizard are identical to those outlined in Chapter 7.

This particular feature alone makes VirtualCenter 2.5 an invaluable tool for building a responsive disaster recovery and business continuity plan.

The Bottom Line

Cluster virtual machines with Microsoft Clustering Services (MSCS)   Clustering virtual machines provides a means of creating an infrastructure that supports high availability for individual virtual machines.

> **Master It**   A critical network service requires minimal downtime. You need to design a failover solution for the virtual machine that hosts the network service. Your solution should provide the least amount of service outage while utilizing existing hardware and software platforms.

Implement and manage VMware High Availability (HA).   VMware HA enabled on clusters of ESX Servers allows virtual machines from a failed ESX Server host to be restarted on another host. This feature offers reduced downtime and eliminates administrative effort as a response to a failed server situation.

> **Master It**   Domain controller, mail servers, and database servers must be the first virtual machines to restart in the event of server failure.

Master It In the event of server failure, you do not want virtual machines to be prevented from being powered on because of excessive resource contention.

Master It Virtual machines used for testing purposes should not be powered on by cluster nodes if they were running on the ESX Sever host that failed.

Master It Your virtual infrastructure includes redundancy at each level, including switches and NICs. Service Console ports, VMkernel ports, and virtual machine port groups exist on separate virtual switches. You need to ensure that virtual machines continue to run even if the Service Console loses network connectivity.

Back up virtual machines with VMware Consolidated Backup (VCB). VCB is a framework upon which third-party backup solutions can be constructed to perform full virtual machine and file-level backups. While the framework can be used on its own, it lacks any type of automation feature or the ability to write directly to tape.

Master It You need to design a data-recovery plan. The company purchased licenses for VMware Consolidated Backup. You must determine how VCB can accomplish your backup goals. What types of backups does VCB support?

Master It You need to implement VCB as part of a regularly scheduled backup job.

Restore virtual machines with VMware Consolidated Backup (VCB). The VCB framework encompasses not just the backup processes but also restore capabilities. Tools included with VCB allow backups of full virtual machines, individual VMDK files, or specific files from within the virtual machine operating system. In addition, VMware Enterprise Converter offers the simplest restore procedure with its support for restoring VCB backups.

Master It You need to minimize the financial impact of implementing a backup strategy for your virtual infrastructure.

Master It You need to minimize the amount of time required to restore data to any of the virtual machines in your environment.

Master It You have a full virtual machine backup of a system named Server1. A user deletes a file that is included on the last backup of Server1. You need to recover the file.

Master It You need to quickly restore a VCB backup of a virtual machine. The backup is stored in a shared folder named VMBackups on a server named Backup1. The name of the virtual machine is Server17.

Chapter 11

Monitoring Virtual Infrastructure Performance

The monitoring of a virtual infrastructure should be a combination of proactive benchmarking and reactive alarm-based actions. VirtualCenter provides both methods to help the administrator keep tabs on each of the virtual machines and hosts as well as the hierarchical objects in the inventory. Using both methods will ensure that the administrator will not be caught unaware of performance issues or lack of capacity.

VirtualCenter provides some exciting new features for monitoring your virtual machines and hosts. The new and improved Performance tab has updated graphs and more options for customization. The Datacenter, Folder, Cluster, and ESX Server objects have Virtual Machines tabs to give the administrator an at-a-glance view of how the virtual machines are running.

In this chapter you will learn to:

Create an alarm

Work with graphs

Customize host and virtual machine graphs for CPU, Memory, Network, and Disk

Save a graph

Creating Host and Virtual Machine Alarms

The Performance tab provides a robust mechanism for creating graphs that depict the actual resource consumption over time for a given host or virtual machine. The graphs provide historical information and can be used for trend analysis. VirtualCenter provides many objects and counters to analyze the performance of a single virtual machine or host for a selected interval. The Virtual Machines tab provides information on a virtual machine's CPU and memory consumption, as shown in Figure 11.1.

In addition to the graphs and high-level information tabs, the administrator can create alarms for virtual machines or hosts based on predefined triggers provided with VirtualCenter. These alarms can monitor resource consumption or the state of the virtual machine and alert the administrator when certain conditions have been met, such as high resource usage or even low resource usage. These alarms can then provide an action that informs the administrator of the condition by e-mail or SNMP trap. An action can also automatically run a script or provide other means to correct the problem the virtual machine or host may be experiencing.

FIGURE 11.1

The Virtual Machines tab of a Cluster object offers a quick look at virtual machine CPU and memory usage.

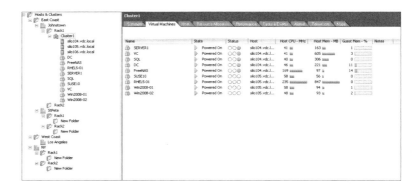

The creation of alarms to alert the administrator of a specific condition is not new in VirtualCenter. But the addition of new triggers, conditions, and actions gives the alarms more usefulness than in previous editions. As you can see in Figure 11.2, the alarms that come with VirtualCenter are defined at the topmost object, Hosts & Clusters.

FIGURE 11.2

Default alarms for hosts and virtual machines are created at the Hosts & Clusters inventory object.

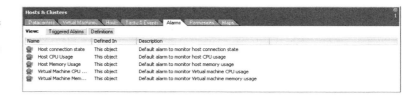

The default alarms are generic in nature and are set to provide identification of host or virtual machine CPU and memory consumption that exceeds 75% and 90% thresholds. These alarms will also identify a change in the state of the host or virtual machine. In most cases, virtual machines won't require alarms with thresholds with such high values as they are usually low-utilization applications. And while the host alarms might get to those levels in times of a server outage, a good virtualization architecture will prevent such high utilization on a consistent basis.

Since the default alarms are likely too generic for your administrative needs, creating your own alarms is often necessary. An administrator may want to watch a specific virtual machine to see if it drops below a certain threshold. A service-level agreement (SLA) for this virtual machine may specify that consumption not drop below 20% CPU utilization to meet its obligations. Also, let's say that this virtual machine normally runs around 30% CPU utilization when the application is running hot. The administrator could set a virtual machine alarm with a trigger for CPU and a condition of Is Below to 25% to send the administrator an e-mail warning that the virtual machine has dropped below 25%. The alarm can also be set to e-mail the administrator if the virtual machine drops below 20%, and, in this case, the e-mail would alert the administrator so corrective action could be taken.

Figure 11.2 shows the Alarms dialog box used to configure the triggers, thresholds, and actions of an alarm. The dialog box includes two buttons near the top-left portion: Triggered Alarms and Definitions. Any alarm(s) currently triggered display for this inventory object when you click the Triggered Alarms button. Clicking the Definitions button switches the view to show any alarms that have been created or inherited for this inventory object. Speaking of inheritance, if you create an alarm on a datacenter, folder, cluster, or resource pool, the alarm will be inherited by all child objects below it. In some cases, this is what you want, but in other cases, the alarm may be specific to a particular virtual machine or host. In such cases the alarm will be created directly on that object and therefore not inherited. Figure 11.3 shows the configuration of a trigger and thresholds for an alarm.

FIGURE 11.3
A sample alarm showing a virtual machine CPU alarm definition with an Is Below condition, a % Warning of 25%, and % Alert of 20%.

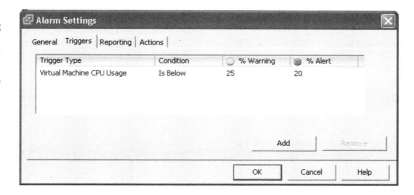

Perform the following steps to create an alarm:

1. Click to select a particular object in the inventory, such as a virtual machine, host, resource pool, cluster, folder, or datacenter. Then select the Alarms tab, and right-click in the blank area of the Definitions pane, as shown in Figure 11.4, and choose New Alarm.

FIGURE 11.4
The starting point for a new alarm.

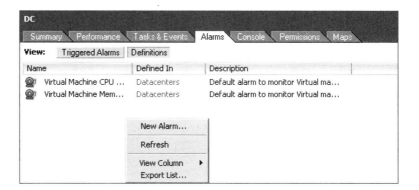

2. In the Alarm Settings dialog box, specify whether this will be a host-based alarm or a virtual machine-based alarm. In either case, most of the setup will be the same.

3. On the General tab, select the alarm type and then choose a trigger priority of either Red or Green, as shown in Figure 11.5. The red and green alarm notifications are simply visual cues of changes. They are arbitrary but can represent a good change (green) or a bad change (red).

FIGURE 11.5
On the General tab, you specify an alarm name, alarm type, and trigger priority.

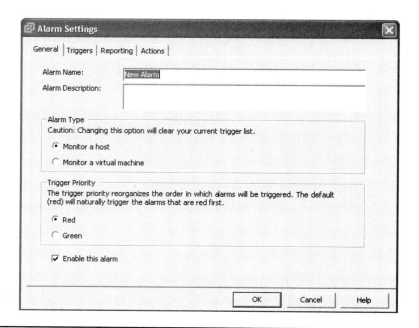

RED LIGHT, YELLOW LIGHT, GREEN LIGHT

Most alarms are of the red variety when it comes to the Trigger Priority setting. But occasionally the administrator wants to know when a virtual machine hits a warning level or when a virtual machine returns to a green condition. The yellow warnings allow administrators to catch potential problems before they reach unacceptable levels that result in performance declines. For instance, a virtual machine that kicks off a batch job during the day goes red when the job starts, and when the batch is done the virtual machine goes back to green and alerts the administrator that the job has completed.

4. If this alarm goes immediately into service, select the Enable This Alarm option.

5. Click the Triggers tab.

6. A trigger, show in Figure 11.6, provides a way to specify a particular condition or threshold to monitor. There are five possible triggers for an alarm:

◆ Host or Virtual Machine CPU Usage

◆ Host or Virtual Machine Memory Usage

◆ Host or Virtual Machine Network Usage

◆ Host or Virtual Machine Disk Usage

◆ Host or Virtual Machine State

FIGURE 11.6
Selecting a trigger for either a virtual machine or a host.

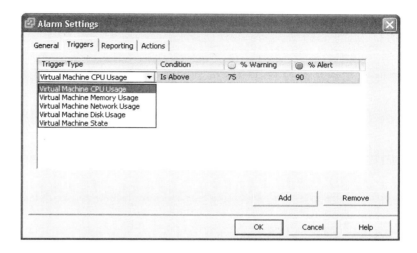

7. Once you choose a trigger type, you must specify a condition. There are only two conditions — Is Above and Is Below — for the Usage alarms. For the State alarms, Is Equal To or Not Equal To are your only choices. If the trigger type was the state of a host or virtual machine, then setting the condition to Is Equal To could provide an alert if the virtual machine was powered off, as shown in Figure 11.7.

FIGURE 11.7
Setting a trigger type of Virtual Machine State with a condition of Is Equal To, a warning of None, and an alert of Powered Off.

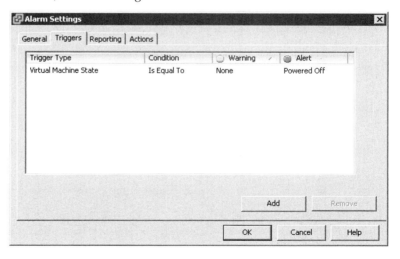

Real World Scenario

CAUTION: COUNTER VALUES WILL VARY!

The Is Above condition is selected most often for identifying a virtual machine or host that is over a certain threshold. The administrator decides what that threshold should be and what is considered abnormal behavior (or at least interesting enough behavior to be monitored). For the most part, monitoring across ESX Server hosts will be consistent. For example, administrators will define a threshold that is worthy of being notified about and configure an alarm across all hosts for monitoring that counter. However, when looking at the more granular virtual machine monitoring, it might be more difficult to come up with a single baseline that works for all virtual machines. Specifically, think about enterprise applications that must perform well for extended periods of time. For these types of scenarios, administrators would want custom alarms for earlier notifications of performance problems. This way, as opposed to reacting to a problem, administrators can be proactive in trying to prevent problems from occurring.

For virtual machines with similar functions like domain controllers and DNS servers, it might be possible to establish baselines and thresholds covering all such infrastructure servers. In the end, the beauty of the monitoring tools lies in the flexibility to be as customized and as granular as needed for each virtual infrastructure.

8. Next, provide the warning and alert thresholds required to monitor for specific usage conditions. The values for these two variables vary and depend on the type and resource tendencies of the application, SLA, or other abnormal or interesting behavior, as shown in Figure 11.8.

FIGURE 11.8
Setting warning and alert thresholds for an alarm.

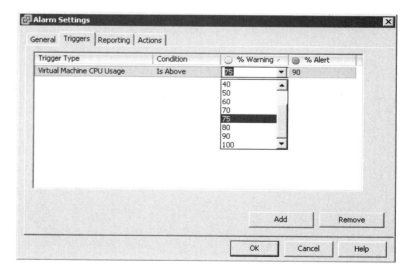

9. After you've set these four variables on the Triggers tab, it's on to the Reporting tab, as shown in Figure 11.9.

I KNOW ALREADY!

The Reporting tab is new to this version of VirtualCenter. This tab gives the administrator greater flexibility in defining how often an alarm sends an e-mail or a SNMP trap or some other action. The Tolerance section provides a way to set the percentage of change before the second alarm is sent out. If the original alarm was set to send an e-mail after an initial trigger threshold of 50%, and if the Tolerance field was set to 10%, then the second e-mail would be sent if the threshold had changed to 55%. This allows the administrator to monitor escalating events or to prevent receiving another e-mail for the same persistent but unvarying condition.

The Frequency section allows the administrator to define how much time should elapse before another e-mail or SNMP trap is sent out. An example of where this may be helpful is if a virtual machine's CPU shoots up to over 75% and the administrator knows this is normal for this virtual machine given the nature of what it was designed to do. If the condition lasted longer than what was considered normal for that virtual machine, another e-mail will be sent after so many seconds have elapsed (which could turn into minutes if a very high value is used).

Both of these Reporting features can be used simultaneously or individually to give the administrator greater precision.

FIGURE 11.9
The Reporting tab, which contains Tolerance and Frequency settings.

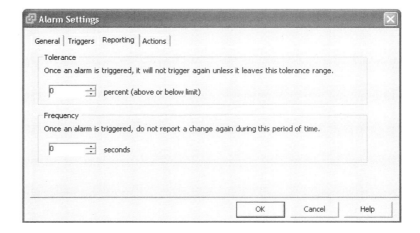

10. Click the Actions tab.

11. The reason for having the alarm is to monitor defined conditions and alert administrators, perhaps via e-mail as shown in Figure 11.10, so they can take any necessary administrative action. Administrators can also configure alarms to be proactive in trying to solve any problems by allowing the alarm to respond one of the predefined ways or by running a script that provides an infinite variety of actions. The precise action depends on whether the object being monitored is a host or a virtual machine. If it is a host, the possible actions are:

◆ Send a notification e-mail

◆ Send a notification trap

◆ Run a script

If the object being monitored is a virtual machine, then the possible actions are:

◆ Send a notification e-mail

◆ Send a notification trap

◆ Run a script

◆ Power on a virtual machine

◆ Power off a virtual machine

◆ Suspend a virtual machine

◆ Reset a virtual machine

FIGURE 11.10
An example of sending an e-mail if the alarm is triggered.

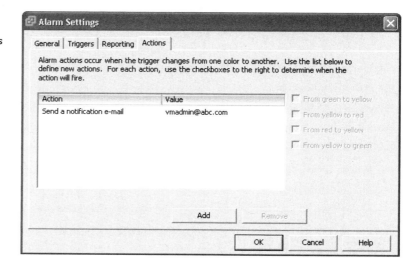

ALARM SCRIPTS

If the action to be taken involves running a script, understand that the script runs on the VirtualCenter server and may consume significant resources. On the Actions tab, under the Action column, choose Run a Script. You must then supply a value. The syntax for calling the script is `c:\fixmyvm.vbs` {*targetName*} {*alarmName*} and must be passed as one string. The *targetName* is the host or virtual machine name; the *alarmName* is the name of the alarm.

Each action is tied to a change in condition or conditions that are listed to the right of the actions as checkboxes:

◆ From Green to Yellow

◆ From Yellow to Red

◆ From Red to Yellow

◆ From Yellow to Green

12. Once you've configured all the tabs, click OK.

13. To have VirtualCenter send an e-mail for a triggered host or virtual machine alarm, provide the recipient's e-mail address (see Figure 11.11). VirtualCenter must also be configured with an SMTP server to send any e-mails. Normally, the setup of the SMTP server and the SNMP management receiver(s) would be established ahead of time. To configure the SMTP server, from the main VI Client screen choose the Administration menu, then VirtualCenter Management Server Configuration. Click on Mail in the list on the left, and then supply the SMTP server and the Sender Account so that when you receive an e-mail, you know it came from the VirtualCenter server, such as VI3alarms@learn2virtualize.com. To have VirtualCenter send an SNMP trap, follow the same procedure but click on SNMP in the VirtualCenter Management Server Configuration dialog box on the left and specify one to four management receivers to monitor for traps.

FIGURE 11.11
Setting up the SMTP server to send e-mails on behalf of the alarms on the VirtualCenter server.

Once the four tabs have been configured, click OK and your alarm will be added to the list for that object. You can have more than one alarm for an object. As with any new alarm, testing its functionality is crucial to make sure you get the desired results. If the alarm needs editing, right-click the alarm from the list and choose Edit Settings to make the necessary modifications. Or, if the alarm is no longer needed, right-click the alarm and choose Remove to delete the alarm.

Performance Graph Details and *esxtop*

VirtualCenter has many new and updated features for creating and analyzing graphs. Without these graphs, analyzing the performance of a virtual machine would be nearly impossible. Installing agents inside a virtual machine will not provide accurate details about the server's behavior or resource consumption. The reason for this is elementary: a virtual machine is only configured with virtual devices. Only the VMkernel knows the exact amount of resource consumption for any of those devices since it acts as the translator between the virtual hardware and the physical hardware. In most virtual infrastructures, the virtual machines' virtual devices can outnumber the actual physical hardware devices, necessitating complex sharing and scheduling abilities in the VMkernel.

By clicking the Performance tab for a host or virtual machine, you can learn a wealth of information. The default view for either a host or a virtual machine is CPU consumption. But before we analyze the consumption, we need to get to know the performance graphs and legends.

Performance Graphs

Starting from the top and working our way down, on the top left you'll see the host or virtual machine being monitored. Just below the tabs, the type of chart and its interval appears. The graph above is a real-time graph that shows what has occurred in the last hour. It updates every 20 seconds. You can change the interval and resource being monitored by clicking the Change Chart Options link. At the top right, we see the Refresh icon, the Save icon, and the Tear-off icon. The Refresh icon is self-explanatory, but the next two will bear some explanation a little later.

On each side of the graph are units of measure. In Figure 11.12, the counters selected are measured in Percent and MHz. Depending on the counters chosen, there may be only one unit of measurement, but no more than two. Next, on the horizontal axis, is the Time interval. Below that, the Performance Chart Legend provides color-coded keys to help the user find a specific object or item of interest. This area also breaks down the graph into the object being measured, the measurement being used, the units of measure, and the Latest, Maximum, Minimum, and Average measurements recorded for that object.

FIGURE 11.12
A Performance graph for a single virtual machine.

Hovering the mouse over the graph at a particular recorded interval of interest displays the data points at that specific moment in time, as shown in Figure 11.13.

Another nice feature of the graphs is the ability to emphasize a specific object so that it is easier to pick out this object from the other objects. By clicking the specific key at the bottom, the key and its color representing a specific object will be emphasized while the other keys and their respective colors become lighter and less visible, as shown in Figure 11.14.

FIGURE 11.13
Hovering the mouse over a specific data point on the graph will display specific measurements for that particular point in time.

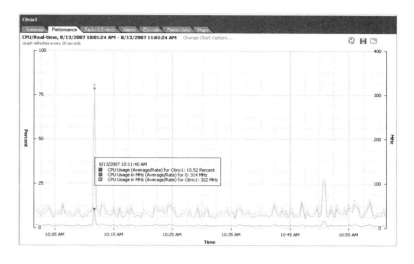

FIGURE 11.14
By clicking on a specific key in the Performance Chart Legend, that key will be emphasized while the other keys become less visible.

If the current graph does not reveal the data you were looking to find, click Change Chart Options at the top of the Performance chart to open a dialog box, shown in Figure 11.15, which lets you select from among many counters across the various physical hardware components.

On the left, you can choose which resource (CPU, Disk, Memory, Network, or System) to monitor or analyze. By selecting one of these options, you then have a choice of intervals to look at. Real-time will show you what has occurred in the last hour. The others are self-explanatory. For trend analysis, having all of these interval options allows you to choose exactly which interval you need. If these intervals are still not precise enough, you can create a custom interval c by selecting the Custom option under any of the available Chart Options, as shown in Figure 11.16.

FIGURE 11.15
The Customize Performance Chart dialog box has many options.

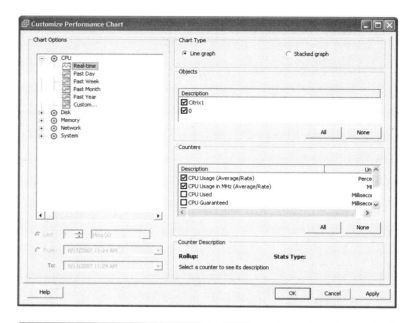

FIGURE 11.16
Setting a custom interval is easy. Here, the user only wants to look at the last six hours of data.

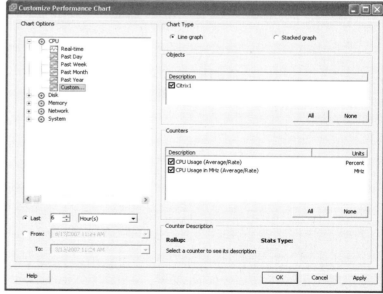

Many times, you want to look at what is happening now or what happened in the last hour for a host or a virtual machine. The Real-time interval gives the best view. This view also gives you access to certain counters for each resource type for a given host or virtual machine that are not available in the other views. If a particular counter is new to you, click on it to highlight the counter. At the bottom of the dialog box, in a section called Rollup, you'll see a description of the counter. For a host, the objects that can be monitored are the host as a whole and the individual physical devices. For the host chart option CPU, the objects and counters breakdown is shown in Figure 11.17.

FIGURE 11.17
A host's CPU objects and counters.

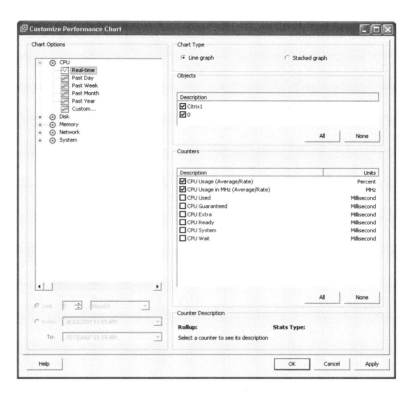

VIEWING OBJECTS AND COUNTERS

To get a clear view of all the objects and counters in the Customize Performance Chart dialog box, you have to stretch the dialog box at the top or the bottom to lengthen it. This makes all of the counters visible. Sadly, there is no way to increase the length of the Objects section to see all of them, so scrolling is necessary.

For a host chart option Disk, the objects and counters are shown in Figure 11.18. The devices being monitored reflect the vmhba paths used by the VMkernel to access the disks associated with the virtual machine. Remember that the vmhba paths that are defined can use any of three types of controllers: a local SCSI controller, a fibre channel, or an iSCSI controller (if the controller is based on the iSCSI software initiator, the device name will be vmhba32).

NO NAS MONITORING OBJECTS

NAS cannot be monitored because the connection to NAS is not local SCSI, fibre channel, or iSCSI. Even if the ESX Server is configured to use NAS, that storage medium has no object listing or counters since all of the counters seem to be based on block storage only.

FIGURE 11.18
A host's Disk objects and counters.

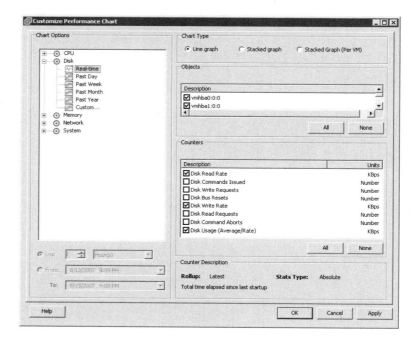

For a host chart option Memory, the objects and counters are shown in Figure 11.19. In this case, there is only one object, the host itself.

For a host chart option of Network, shown in Figure 11.20, notice the objects are the host itself and any vmnic devices used by the VMkernel. If you have a particular virtual switch you want to monitor, find out which vmnic(s) are associated with that vSwitch by switching your view in the VI Client to the Configuration tab of the ESX host and then selecting Networking in the Hardware section.

For a host chart option System, the objects and counters are shown in Figure 11.21. There are several objects for the host with this chart option. This allows the administrator to see how many physical CPU cycles are being consumed by certain processes like vmware-authd or drivers. Be aware that many of the objects may not have any data associated with them.

For a virtual machine, the objects that can be monitored are the virtual machine as a whole and the individual virtual devices. For a virtual machine chart option CPU, the objects and counters breakdown is shown in Figure 11.22. Notice that the virtual device is the virtual processor 0, not the physical processor 0. If the virtual machine was configured with more than one processor, they would increment by one — 0, 1, 2, 3, etc.

FIGURE 11.19
A host's Memory objects
and counters.

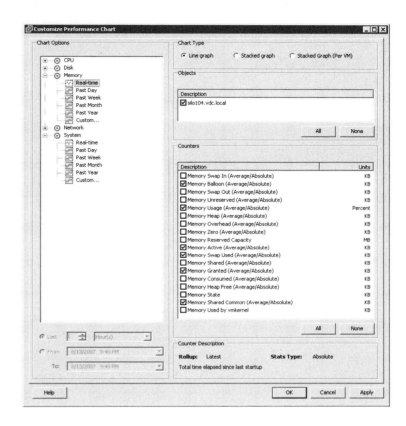

FIGURE 11.20
A host's Network objects
and counters.

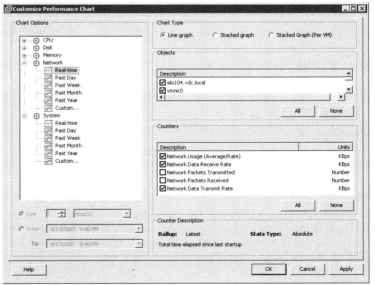

FIGURE 11.21
A host's System objects and counters.

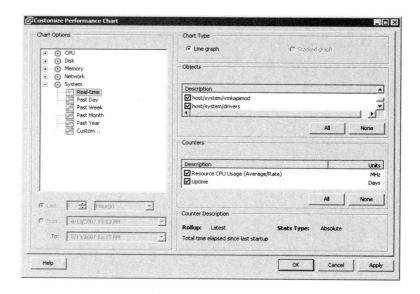

FIGURE 11.22
A virtual machine's CPU objects and counters.

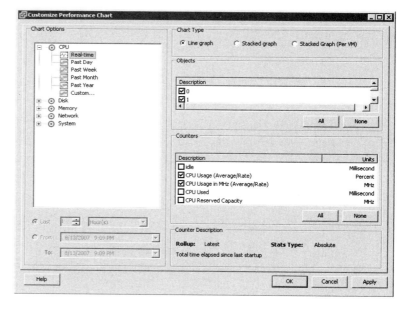

For a virtual machine chart option Disk, the objects and counters breakdown is shown in Figure 11.23. Notice the virtual device is described as vmhba40:0:0, which corresponds to a VMkernel storage device, in this case, an iSCSI software initiator.

For a virtual machine chart option Memory, the objects and counters breakdown is shown in Figure 11.24. The only object is the virtual machine itself, but there are several counters.

FIGURE 11.23
A virtual machine's Disk
objects and counters.

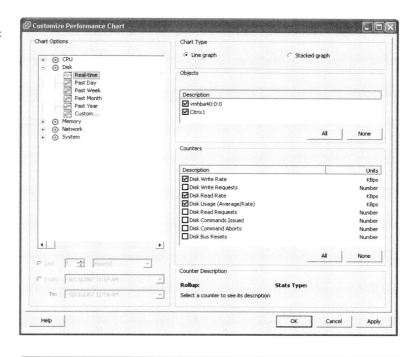

FIGURE 11.24
A virtual machine's
Memory objects and
counters.

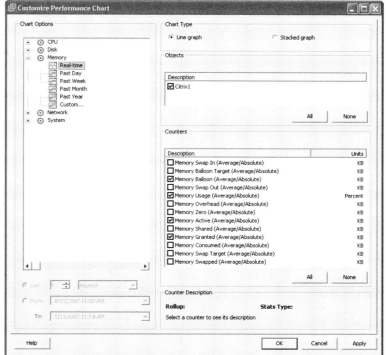

For a virtual machine chart option Network, the objects and counters breakdown is shown in Figure 11.25. Notice that the virtual network device is described as 4000. If the virtual machine had two or more network adapters, they would be incremented by one for each — for example, 4001, 4002, 4003, 4004.

FIGURE 11.25
A virtual machine's Network objects and counters.

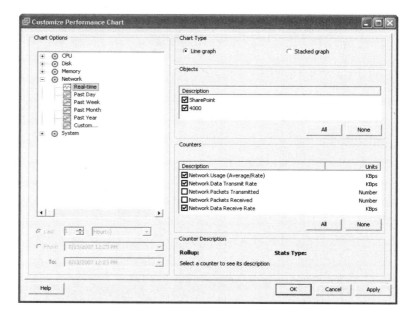

For a virtual machine chart option System, the object is the virtual machine itself, with counters of Heartbeat and Uptime, as shown in Figure 11.26.

Once you have selected the options you need for your graph, click OK.

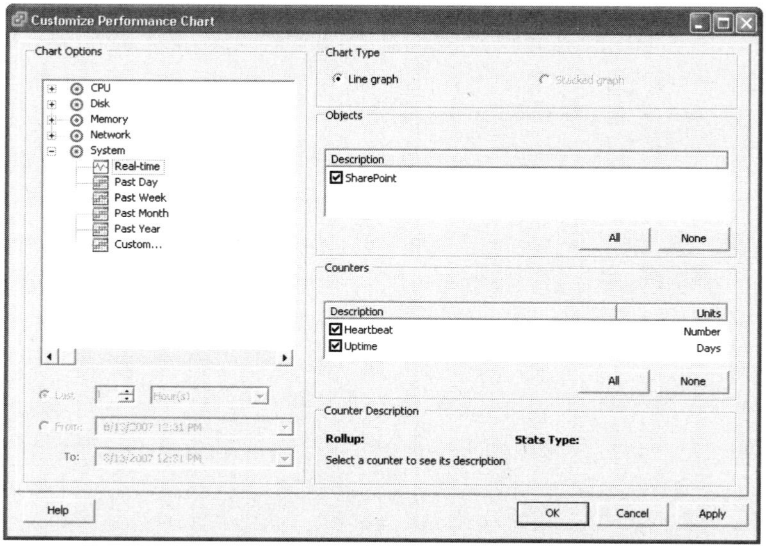

FIGURE 11.26
A virtual machine's System objects and counters.

Now that we are back to the graph, the Save icon in the top-right corner saves the graph into an Excel-formatted file. In the Time section of the Export Performance dialog box shown in Figure 11.27, choose the currently displayed interval or a different time frame.

Next, in the Chart Options section, select the type of graph to be saved: Line Graph or Stacked Graph. Figure 11.28 shows an example of a line graph.

FIGURE 11.27
Saving a Performance graph. Be sure to select the interval and chart options you want. Also, you have a choice of the chart type and size.

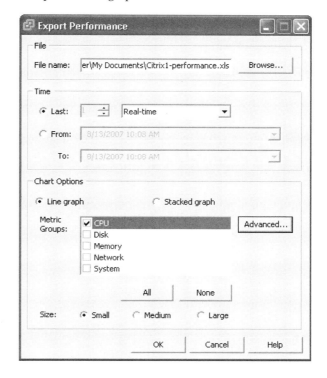

FIGURE 11.28
An example of the line graph for a virtual machine.

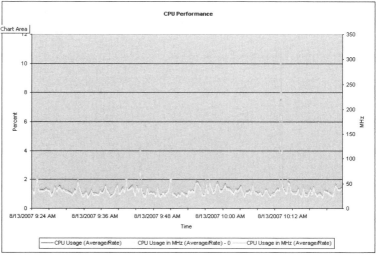

A stacked graph of the same data looks as shown in Figure 11.29.

FIGURE 11.29
An example of a stacked graph for a virtual machine — same data, just a different view.

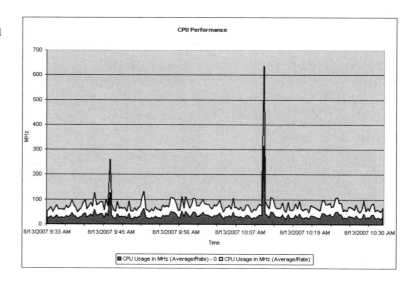

Stacked graphs are useful when looking at several virtual machines on the same host. When they are stacked on top of one another, it gives an aggregate usage, with colors to distinguish between them. This allows you to identify the busiest virtual machine or the one that represents the largest load on the server. Also, you can click the Advanced button to select or deselect specific counters to be saved as part of the Excel graph.

Here's another nice feature: click the Popup Chart icon to display the graph in a new window. This lets you easily compare this host or virtual machine with another host or virtual machine, as shown in Figure 11.30.

FIGURE 11.30
An example of the Popup Chart feature.

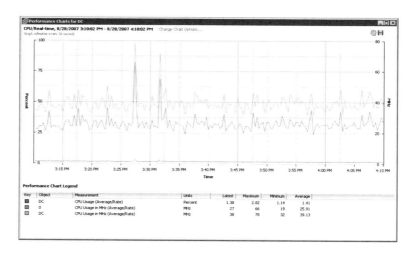

esxtop

Virtual machine performance can also be monitored using a command-line tool named `esxtop`. A great reason to use `esxtop` is the immediate feedback it gives you after you've made an adjustment to a virtual machine. The `esxtop` command is not new, but it does include some new features and capabilities. All four resource types (CPU, Disk, Memory, and Network) can be monitored for a particular ESX host.

With the new and improved `esxtop` we can look at two counters, CPU Used and Ready Time. We can also see these counters in the virtual machine graphs, but with this tool they are calculated as percentages. If virtual machines are running on the same host, we can easily compare the virtual machines as they are identifiable by name, unlike in previous versions. If they run on two different hosts, then a direct comparison is harder without opening two different `ssh` client sessions. Even then, the virtual machines are not in direct competition, so an apples-to-apples comparison may be difficult. In Figure 11.31, `esxtop` is monitoring the CPU usage of several virtual machines running on the same host, which is the default view. The amount of processor time being used, %USED, and the amount of time not getting scheduled, %RDY, are listed for each virtual machine. If we increase a virtual machine's reservation or shares, we'll see a corresponding change in these two fields, as %USED will increase its percentage and %RDY will decrease. If you look at one of the other screens for a different resource, just press C to bring it back to the CPU resource screen.

FIGURE 11.31
The command-line tool esxtop showing CPU statistics for several virtual machines and VMkernel processes.

ESXTOP

Remember, `esxtop` only shows a single ESX host. In a virtual infrastructure where VMotion, DRS, and HA have been deployed, virtual machines may move around often. Making reservation or share changes while the virtual machine is currently on one ESX Server may not have the desired consequences if the virtual machine is moved to another server and the mix of virtual machines on that server represents different performance loads.

To monitor memory usage, press M. This gives you real-time statistics about the ESX Server's memory usage in the top portion and the virtual machines' memory usage in the lower section, as shown in Figure 11.32.

To monitor network statistics about the vmnics, individual virtual machines, or VMkernel ports used for iSCSI, VMotion, and NFS, press N. The columns showing network usage, as shown in Figure 11.33, include packets transmitted and received and megabytes transmitted and received for each vmnic or port. Also shown in the DNAME column are the vSwitches and, to the left, what is plugged into them, including virtual machines, VMkernel, and service console ports. If a particular virtual machine is monopolizing the vSwitch, you can look at the amount of network traffic on a specific switch and the individual ports to see which virtual machine is the culprit.

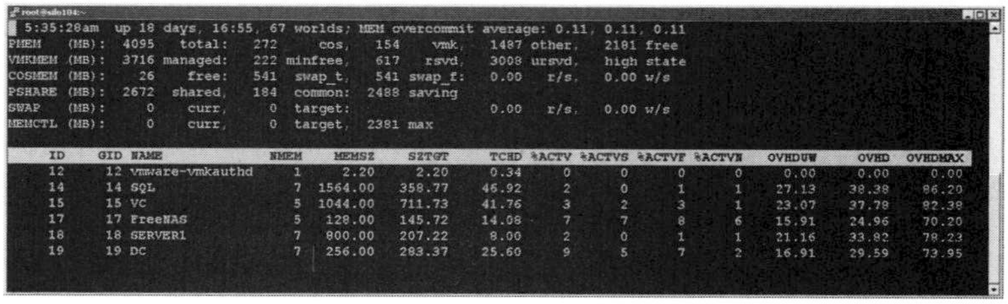

FIGURE 11.32
Using esxtop to display memory usage on a single ESX host.

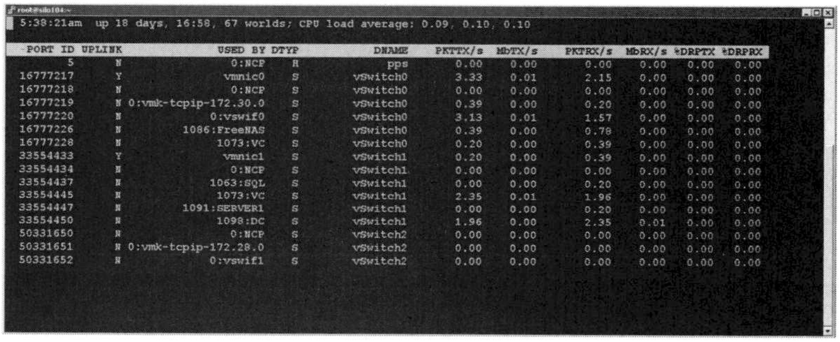

FIGURE 11.33
Using esxtop to display network statistics on an ESX Server.

To monitor disk I/O statistics about each of the SCSI controllers, press D. The output of disk I/O monitoring with esxtop is shown in Figure 11.34. The columns on the far left are most often used to determine disk loads. Those columns show loads based on reads and writes per second and megabytes read and written per second. Another important column is the NVMS, which shows how many virtual machines are sharing the same controller. If an application in one of the virtual machines is sluggish, it's easy to see using this column how many other virtual machines it may be competing with.

FIGURE 11.34
Using esxtop to display controller I/O statistics.

Another great feature of esxtop is the ability to capture performance data for a short period of time and then play back that data. Using the command vm-support, you can set an interval and duration for the capture.

Perform these steps to capture data to be played back on esxtop:

1. While logged in as root or after switching to root user, change your working directory to /tmp by issuing the command **cd /tmp**.

2. Issue the command **vm-support -S -i 10 -d 180**. This creates an `esxtop` snapshot, capturing data every ten seconds, for the duration of 180 seconds, as shown in Figure 11.35.

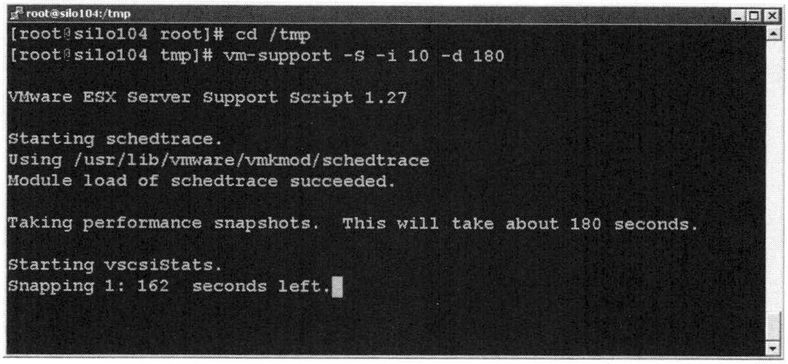

FIGURE 11.35
Capturing data for esxtop.

```
 root@silo104:/tmp                                                    _□×
[root@silo104 root]# cd /tmp
[root@silo104 tmp]# vm-support -S -i 10 -d 180

VMware ESX Server Support Script 1.27

Starting schedtrace.
Using /usr/lib/vmware/vmkmod/schedtrace
Module load of schedtrace succeeded.

Taking performance snapshots.  This will take about 180 seconds.

Starting vscsiStats.
Snapping 1: 162  seconds left.█
```

3. The resulting file is a tarball and is gzipped. It must be extracted with the command `tar -xzf esx*.tgz`. This will create a `vm-support` directory that will be called in the next command.

4. Run **esxtop-R /vm-support*** to replay the data for analysis, as shown in Figure 11.36.

FIGURE 11.36
Replaying the data in esxtop.

Monitoring Host and Virtual Machine CPU Usage

When monitoring a virtual machine, it's always a good starting point to keep an eye on CPU consumption. Many virtual machines started out in life as underperforming physical servers. One of VMware's most successful sales pitches is being able to take all those lackluster physical boxes that are not busy and convert them to virtual machines. Thus, a server starts life physical, but then goes through a midlife crisis and converts to the religion of virtualization. Once converted, virtual infrastructure managers tend to think of these new converts as simple, lackluster, and low-utilization servers with nothing to worry over or monitor. The truth, though, is quite the opposite.

When the server was physical, it had an entire box to itself. Now it must share its resources with many other siblings. In aggregate, they represent quite a load and if some or many of them become somewhat busy, they fight with each other for the finite capabilities of the ESX Server they run on. Of course, they don't know they are fighting, but the VMkernel tries to placate them. Virtual CPUs need to be scheduled, and it does a remarkable job given that there are more virtual machines than physical processors most of the time. But in every virtual infrastructure manager's life, there comes a day when one virtual machine becomes unhappy. Usually it sends a surrogate, the application owner, to tell the manager that this server was a lot happier when it was physical. But since the conversion, life has not been the same. It is now time for the manager to convert to the religion of virtual machine monitoring and figure out what is making this virtual machine so unhappy. Thankfully, VMware Infrastructure 3 (VI3) has all the tools to make such monitoring and analysis very easy.

Let's begin with a hypothetical scenario. A help desk ticket has been submitted indicating that an application owner isn't getting the expected level of performance on a particular server, which in this case is a virtual machine. A virtual infrastructure manager needs to delve deeper into the problem, asking as many questions as necessary to discover what the application owner needs to be happy. Some performance issues are subjective, meaning some users may complain about the slowness of their applications, but they have no objective benchmark for such a claim. Other times, this is reflected in a specific benchmark, such as the number of transactions by a database server or throughput for a web server. In this case, our issue revolves around benchmarking CPU usage, so our application is CPU-processing intensive when it does its job.

ASSESSMENTS, EXPECTATIONS, AND ADJUSTMENTS

If an assessment was done prior to virtualizing a server, there may be hard numbers to look at to give some details as to what was expected with regard to minimum performance or service-level agreement (SLA). If not, the virtual infrastructure manager needs to work with the application's owner to make more CPU resources available to the unhappy virtual machine when needed.

VirtualCenter's graphs, which we have explored in great detail, are the best way to analyze usage, both short- and long-term. The great thing about the graphs is that they can tell a story about how the virtual machine has performed in the last hour, day, week, month, or even year. Maybe the help desk ticket describes a slowness issue in the last hour. As Figure 11.37 shows, we can look at the virtual machine's ability to work for the last hour.

Perform these steps to create a CPU graph:

1. Connect to the VirtualCenter server or an individual ESX Server host with the VI Client.

2. In the inventory tree, click on a virtual machine. This shows you the Summary tab. Click the Performance tab, as shown in Figure 11.37.

3. Click the Change Chart Options link.

4. Under Chart Options, click on the Network bulls-eye or the + sign, as shown in Figure 11.38. This view allows you to select the objects and counters that will provide the most relevant information. Real-time CPU graphs have a lot of counters, but usually only a few are used for any one graph. In this case, we'll use CPU Usage in MHz (Average/Rate) and CPU Ready to see how much physical processor is being used and how long on average it's taking the virtual machine to be scheduled on a physical processor.

FIGURE 11.37
The Performance tab is your starting point.

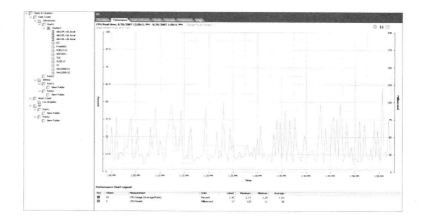

FIGURE 11.38
The default resource for a virtual machine is CPU.

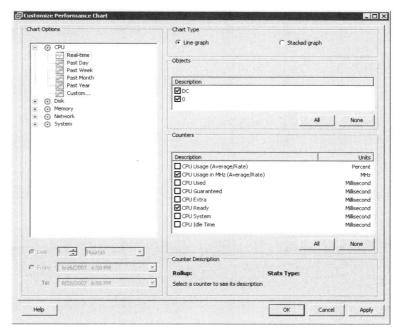

CPU READY

CPU Ready is a special counter only available using the Real-time interval. A virtual machine waiting many thousands of milliseconds to be scheduled on a processor may indicate that the ESX Server is overloaded, a resource pool has too tight a limit, the virtual machine has too few CPU shares, or, if no one is complaining, nothing at all. Be sure to work with the server or application owner to determine an acceptable amount of CPU Ready for any CPU-intensive virtual machine.

5. Select those relevant objects and counters to provide the information needed, as shown in Figure 11.39. Then, choose the chart type and click OK.

FIGURE 11.39
The graph shows the virtual machine's CPU consumption and how long, in milliseconds, it takes to schedule the virtual machine on a physical processor.

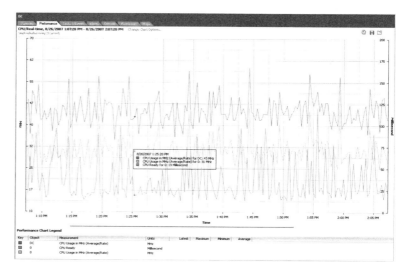

Monitoring a host's overall CPU usage is fairly straightforward. Keep in mind that other factors usually come into play when looking at spare CPU capacity. Add-ons such as VMotion, DRS, and HA directly impact whether there is enough spare capacity on a server or a cluster of servers. With ESX 3.x, the Service Console will usually not be as competitive for processor 0 since there are fewer processes to consume CPU time. Agents installed on the Service Console will have some impact, again on processor 0.

SERVICE CONSOLE STUCK ON 0

The Service Console, as noted, uses processor 0. But note that it will *only* use processor 0. The Service Console does not get migrated to other processors even in the face of heavy contention.

Follow these steps to create a real-time graph for a host's CPU usage:

1. Connect to the VirtualCenter server or an individual ESX Server host with the VI Client.

2. In the inventory tree, click on a host. This shows you the Summary tab. Click the Performance tab, as shown in Figure 11.40.

3. Click the Change Chart Options link.

4. Under Chart Options, click on the Network bull's-eye or the + sign, as shown in Figure 11.41. The objects to choose from are the physical, hyper-threaded, or core processors. There are two often-used counters in this customization dialog box: CPU Usage (Average/Rate) and CPU Reserved Capacity. Both are used to see how an individual ESX

Server is being utilized. CPU Usage shows actual usage, and CPU Reserved Capacity shows how much usage is left.

FIGURE 11.40
The Performance tab is the central focus of obtaining information about virtual machine or host performance levels.

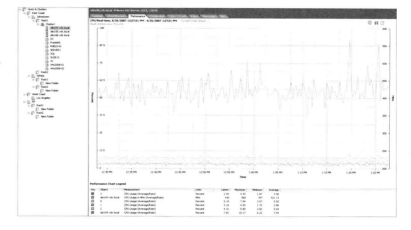

FIGURE 11.41
Looking at host processor usage and spare capacity.

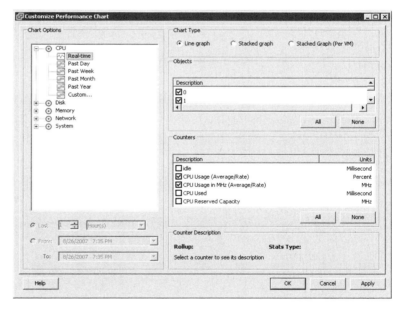

CPU RESERVED CAPACITY

The CPU Reserved Capacity counter can be used to monitor spare capacity for a single ESX Server. However, if DRS has been enabled, the Resource Allocation tab for the Cluster inventory object is more relevant since it shows cluster usage and spare capacity at a glance for all servers in a cluster.

5. Select those relevant objects and counters to provide the information required, as shown in Figure 11.42. If necessary, choose the chart type. Click OK.

FIGURE 11.42
This graph displays the host's overall usage and reserve capacity.

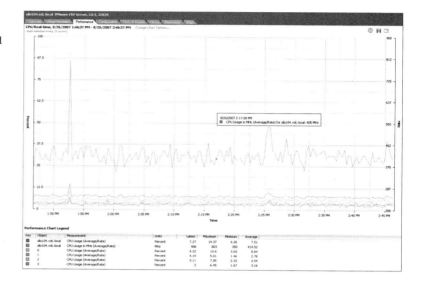

VMKERNEL BALANCING ACT

Always remember that on an oversubscribed ESX Server, the VMkernel will load balance the virtual machines based on current loads, reservations, and shares represented on individual virtual machines and/or resource pools.

By looking at the Resource Allocation tab for a Cluster or Resource Pool inventory object, we can get a picture of how CPU resources are being used for the entire pool (see Figure 11.43). This high-level method of looking at resource usage is useful for analyzing overall infrastructure utilization. This tab does a good job of adjusting individual virtual machine or resource pool reservations, limits, and/or shares without editing each object independently.

FIGURE 11.43
This tab displays the cluster's overall usage and reserve capacity.

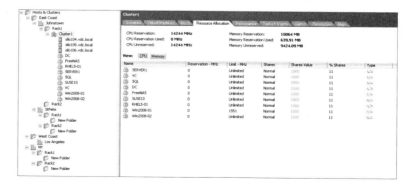

Monitoring Host and Virtual Machine Memory Usage

Monitoring memory usage, whether on a host or a virtual machine, can be challenging. The monitoring itself is not difficult; it's the availability of the physical resource that can be a challenge. Of the four resources, memory can be oversubscribed without much effort. Depending on the physical form-factor chosen to host ESX Server 3.x, running out of physical RAM is easy to do. Although the blade form-factor creates a very dense consolidation effort, the blades sometimes are constrained by the amount of physical memory and network adapters that can be installed. But even with other regular form-factors, having enough memory installed comes down to how much the physical server can accommodate and your budget.

Many virtual machines do not need a great deal of memory to do their jobs effectively. If an assessment has been done prior to consolidation efforts, the amount of memory being used by any one server can be identified up front. Once the server has been converted, editing the virtual machines settings to a value more in tune with its actual usage can be achieved. This allows you to consolidate more servers onto fewer hosts. But what if the server is new to the organization and does not have a track record? What amount of memory should the virtual machine be configured with? Should you use the application's vendor recommendation? Should you start low and increase later? Or start high and reduce later?

PRE-ESX SERVER BASELINE: SCENARIO 1

If the server was first deployed as a physical server with a given role, there might be some record of usage before being converted into an ESX Server. Many times physical servers are purchased with more memory than what the application needs or uses. This may be done due to hardware vendor inducements during purchasing, or standardization on a specific hardware model and build within an organization. Or it could be a case of memory inflation, where a customer goes by the application vendor's recommendations. These recommendations can be inflated to make sure the hardware will not be an issue when it comes to performance.

VMware provides a service, Capacity Planner, that assesses the physical server's resource usage prior to conversion. Even with other products or tools, assessing a physical server's memory usage during peak intervals is relatively easy. Once the physical server has been converted, the virtual machine can be configured with a new limit that reflects actual usage and not a guess. Some servers respond well in this scenario. Others start well enough, but over time increase their memory usage. This is where using VirtualCenter's graphs can be very helpful. Since the charts can be modified to reflect long-term trends and usage, it is easy to identify a virtual machine that has an increased need for more memory or, in some cases, the reverse.

NEW SERVERS: SCENARIO 2

The second scenario is harder to predict. A new server with no track record leaves much to the discretion of the virtual infrastructure manager. Using the application vendor's recommendation may be the best start for the virtual machine. Once the virtual machine has been live for some period of time, VirtualCenter's graphs can help determine what the actual usage is over a particular time frame and make adjustments accordingly.

Perform these steps to create a real-time graph for a virtual machine's memory usage:

1. Connect to the VirtualCenter server or an individual ESX Server host with the VI Client.

2. In the inventory tree, click on a virtual machine. This shows you the Summary tab. Click the Performance tab, as shown in Figure 11.44.

FIGURE 11.44
The Performance tab can be altered from the default CPU monitoring to support custom charting needs.

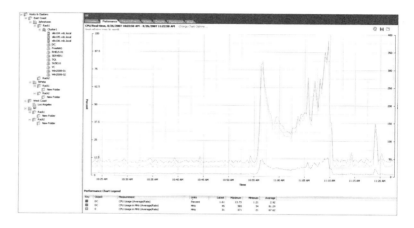

3. Click the Change Chart Options link.

4. Under Chart Options, click on the Network bull's-eye or the + sign. This view allows you to select the objects and counters that provide the most relevant information, as shown in Figure 11.45. Real-time memory graphs have a lot of counters, but usually only a few are used for any one graph. In this case, we'll use Memory Usage (Average/Absolute), Memory Overhead (Average/Absolute), and Memory Consumed (Average/Granted) to get a clear picture of memory utilization as it relates to host consumption and relative to what the virtual machine was configured with.

5. In Figure 11.46, the graph shows virtual machine memory consumption. Many times, you may like to know how much overhead is associated with a virtual machine or how much memory the virtual machine is using compared to what it was configured with. Choose the chart type and click OK.

When monitoring a host server's memory usage, overall utilization is important to watch. As explained earlier in this chapter, creating alarms to alert you when certain conditions arise is one way of monitoring your hosts. In addition to alarms, occasionally looking at host graphs as they pertain to memory usage will give you some perspective as to what is normal on your servers and what is abnormal or weird. There are even more counters to choose from when customizing your graphs, but, again, you will usually select just a few for any one graph.

Perform these steps to create a real-time graph for a host's memory usage:

1. Connect to the VirtualCenter server or an individual ESX Server host with the VI Client.

2. In the inventory tree, click on a virtual machine. This shows you the Summary tab. Click the Performance tab, as shown in Figure 11.47.

FIGURE 11.45
Selecting objects and
counters to monitor
memory usage for a
virtual machine.

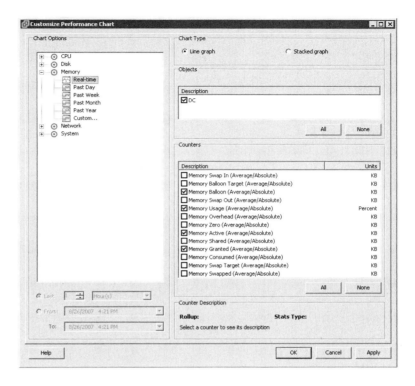

FIGURE 11.46
Select those relevant
objects and counters
to provide the infor-
mation needed.

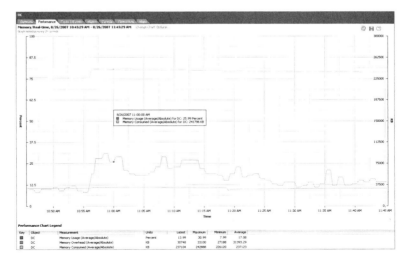

3. Click the Change Chart Options link.

4. Under Chart Options, click on the Network bull's-eye or the + sign. This view allows you to select the objects and counters that provide the most relevant information, as shown in Figure 11.48. Real-time memory graphs have a lot of counters, but usually only a few are

used for any one graph. In this case, we'll use Memory Usage (Average/Absolute), Memory Overhead (Average/Absolute), Memory Active (Average/Absolute), Memory Consumed (Average/Granted), and Memory Used by VMkernel to get a clear picture of memory utilization as it relates to the host.

FIGURE 11.47
The Performance tab for a host defaults to monitoring information about CPU usage on the entire host.

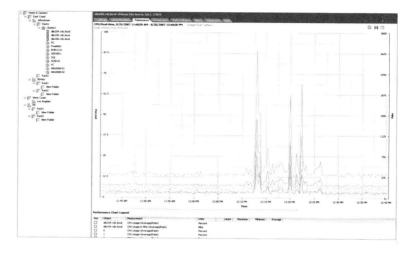

FIGURE 11.48
Setting up the memory options for a host's memory graph.

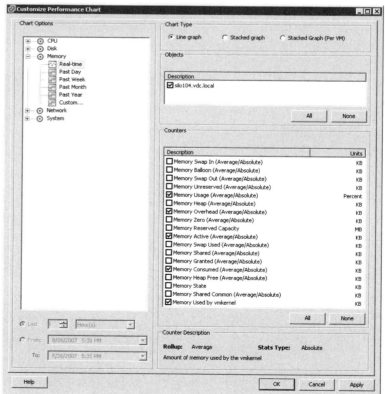

COUNTERS, COUNTERS, AND MORE COUNTERS

As with virtual machines, there are a plethora of counters that can be utilized with a host for monitoring memory usage. Which ones you select will depend on what you're looking for. Straight memory usage monitoring is common, but don't forget that there are other counters that could be helpful, such as Ballooning, Unreserved, VMkernel Swap, and Shared, just to name a few. The ability to assemble the appropriate counters for finding the right information comes with experience and depends on what is being monitored.

5. The graph, shown in Figure 11.49, shows host overhead and virtual machine memory consumption. Many times, you may like to know how much overhead is associated with a virtual machine or how much memory the virtual machine is using compared to what it was configured with. Click OK.

FIGURE 11.49
Select those relevant objects and counters to provide the information needed. If necessary, choose the chart type.

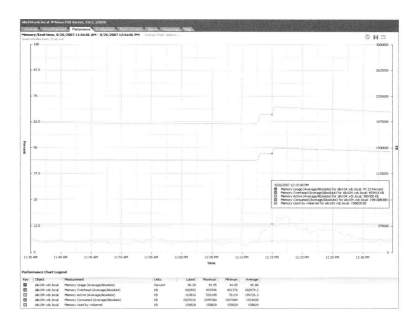

Monitoring Host and Virtual Machine Network Usage

VirtualCenter's graphs provide a wonderful tool for measuring a virtual machine's or a host's network usage.

Monitoring network usage requires a slightly different approach than monitoring CPU or memory. With either CPU or memory, reservations, limits, and shares can dictate how much of these two resources can be consumed by any one virtual machine. Network usage cannot be constrained by any of those mechanisms. Since virtual machines plug into a virtual machine port group, which is part of a vSwitch on a single host, how the virtual machine interacts with the vSwitch can be manipulated by the virtual switch's or port group's policy. For instance, if the administrator needs to restrict a virtual machine's overall network output, Traffic Shaping can be configured on the vSwitch, but more likely on the port group, to restrict the virtual machine to a specific amount of outbound bandwidth. There is no way to restrict virtual machine inbound bandwidth on the ESX Server.

VIRTUAL MACHINE ISOLATION

Certain virtual machines may indeed need to be limited to a specific amount of outbound bandwidth. Servers such as FTP, file and print, web and proxy servers, or any server whose main function is to act as a file repository or connection broker may need to be limited or traffic shaped to an amount of bandwidth that allows it to meet its service target, but not to monopolize the host it runs on. Isolating any of these virtual machines to a vSwitch of its own is more likely a better solution, but requires it the appropriate hardware configuration.

You can measure a virtual machine's or a host's output or reception of network traffic using the graphs in VirtualCenter. The graphs can provide accurate information on the actual usage, or ample information that a particular virtual machine is monopolizing a virtual switch, especially using the Stacked Graph chart type. Figure 11.50 shows a virtual machine's network utilization.

FIGURE 11.50
An example of a virtual machine's network usage.

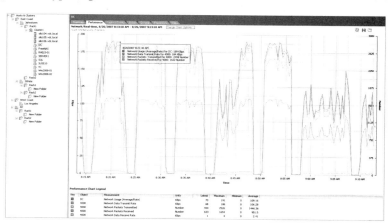

Perform the following steps to create a real-time graph for a virtual machine's transmitted network usage:

1. Connect to the VirtualCenter server or an individual ESX Server host with the VI Client.

2. In the inventory tree, click on a virtual machine. This shows you the Summary tab. Click the Performance tab, shown in Figure 11.51.

3. Click the Change Chart Options link.

4. Under Chart Options, click on the Network bull's-eye or the + sign.

5. By selecting the Real-time option on the left, you can then choose which objects and counters on the right you want to monitor. In this example, let's say you want to monitor

a virtual machine's outbound bandwidth. Select the 4000 counter and then select Network Data Transmit Rate and Network Packets Transmitted (see Figure 11.52). These two counters will give you a great window into how much network bandwidth this particular virtual machine is consuming in the outbound direction. Click OK.

FIGURE 11.51
To begin customizing a Network graph, click the Performance tab.

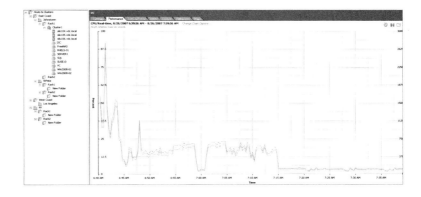

FIGURE 11.52
Changing the graph view to network-related information.

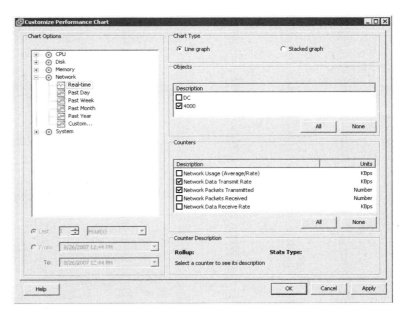

6. The Network Data Transmit Rate is in kilobytes/second and its unit of measurement is shown on the left as KBps. The Network Packets Transmitted represents the number of packets being transmitted. The unit of measurement is Number and appears on the right. By hovering your mouse over any data point in the graph, you can find out how much bandwidth is being consumed or how many packets are being transmitted, as shown in Figure 11.53.

FIGURE 11.53
This graph shows real-time outbound network usage using the mouse pointer to show a specific data point.

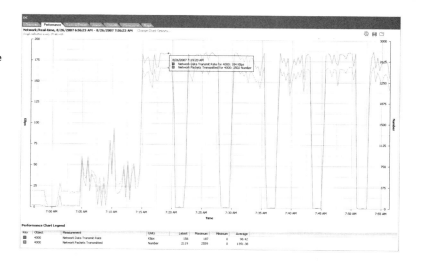

When looking at historical network data usage for a virtual machine, there is only one object, the virtual machine, and one counter that can be used, Network Usage (Average/Rate). This counter will show average aggregated usage, both received and transmitted, in KBps (see Figures 11.54 and 11.55).

FIGURE 11.54
Choosing the chart option Past Day, the object virtual machine, and the counter Network Usage (Average/Rate).

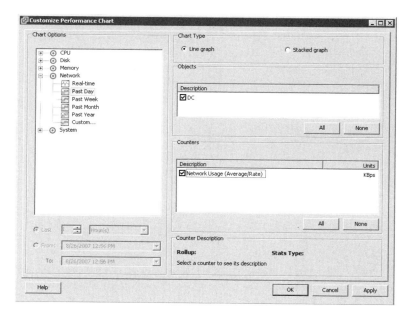

Follow these steps to create a real-time graph for a host's transmitted network usage:

1. Connect to the VirtualCenter server or an individual ESX Server host with the VI Client.

FIGURE 11.55
Graph showing this virtual machine's network usage for the past day.

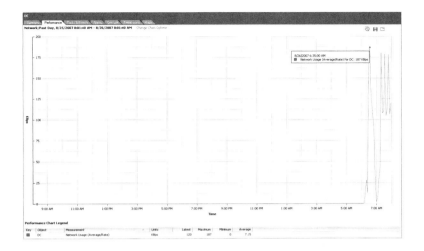

2. In the inventory tree, click on an ESX host. This will show you the Summary tab in the Details section on the right. Select the Performance tab, shown in Figure 11.56.

FIGURE 11.56
Changing to the Performance tab for a host.

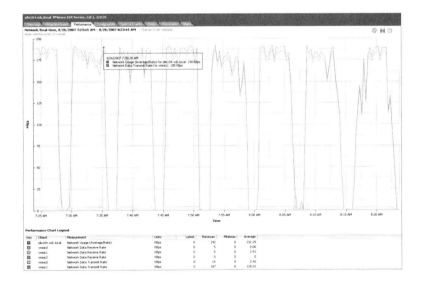

3. Click the Change Chart Options link.

4. Under Chart Options, click on the Network bull's-eye or the + sign, shown in Figure 11.57.

5. By selecting the Real-time option on the left, you can then choose which objects and counters on the right you want to monitor. In this example, let's say you want to monitor a host's outbound bandwidth per vmnic. Select the vmnics objects and then select Network Data Transmit Rate and Network Packets Transmitted (see Figure 11.58). Click OK.

FIGURE 11.57
Setting up a graph to show a host's network usage.

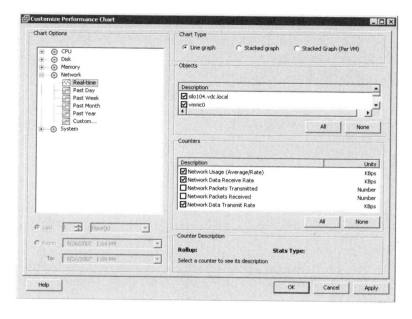

FIGURE 11.58
Choosing specific vmnics provides a way to see overall network traffic for a virtual switch or NIC team.

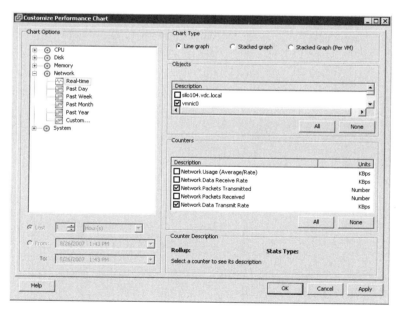

6. Very much like the earlier example for a virtual machine, these two counters will give you a window into how much network activity is occurring on this particular host in the outbound direction for each vmnic. This is especially relevant if you want to see different rates of usage for each physical network interface, which, by definition, represents different virtual switches or NIC teams. An example of network monitoring using the Performance tab is shown in Figure 11.59.

FIGURE 11.59
Graph displaying transmission data for all vmnics on the ESX host.

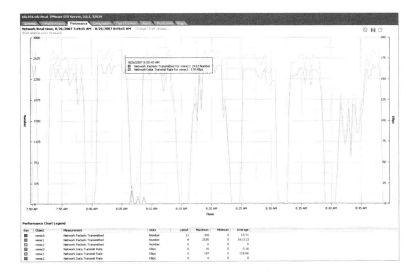

What if you wanted to see which virtual machine was producing the most network activity on an ESX host? Change the graph to display the virtual machines as objects by choosing the Stacked Graph (Per VM) chart type. This allows the administrator to select all or only those virtual machines to monitor for network activity. Be aware, though, that the only counter available with a stacked graph is Network Usage (Average/Usage). See Figures 11.60 and 11.61.

FIGURE 11.60
Choosing a Stacked Graph chart type allows you to make quick comparisons between the virtual machines running on an ESX host.

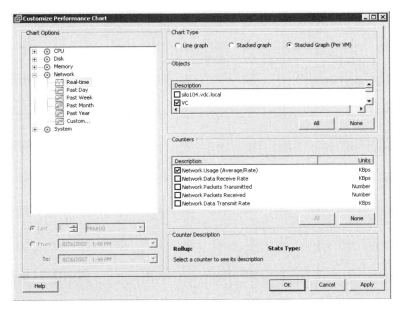

FIGURE 11.61
Here is a stacked graph comparing each virtual machine and showing aggregate usage of all virtual machines running on a specific ESX host. This graph emphasizes the DC virtual machine.

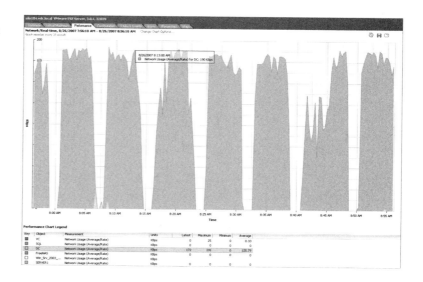

Monitoring Host and Virtual Machine Disk Usage

Monitoring a host's controller or virtual machine's virtual disk usage is similar in scope to monitoring network usage. This resource, which represents a controller or the storing of a virtual machine's virtual disk on a type of supported storage, isn't restricted by CPU or memory mechanisms like reservations, limits, or shares. The only way to restrict a virtual machine's disk activity is to assign shares on the individual virtual machine, which in turn may have to compete with other virtual machines running from the same storage volume. VirtualCenter's graphs come to our aid again in showing actual usage for both ESX hosts and virtual machines.

Using the graph in Figure 11.62, we can monitor a host's overall controller activity. This view doesn't allow us to see why the activity is occurring or which virtual machine is generating the activity, but if we are looking for a particular host with suspicious disk I/O activity, this is a starting point.

FIGURE 11.62
VirtualCenter graphs can report on host or virtual machine performance.

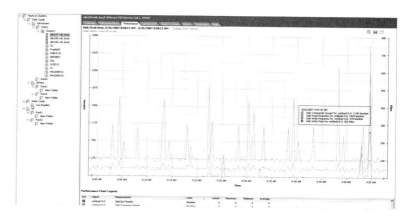

Perform these steps to create a host graph showing disk controller utilization:

1. Connect to the VirtualCenter server or an individual ESX Server host with the VI Client.

2. In the inventory tree, click on an ESX host. This shows you the Summary tab in the Details section on the right. Select the Performance tab.

3. Click the Change Chart Options link.

4. Under Chart Options, click on the Disk bull's-eye or the + sign, shown in Figure 11.63. Chart Options allows you to choose the interval of time to monitor. For this example, we chose Real-time, which shows Disk activity for the last hour.

FIGURE 11.63
Creating a real-time graph for monitoring host controller utilization.

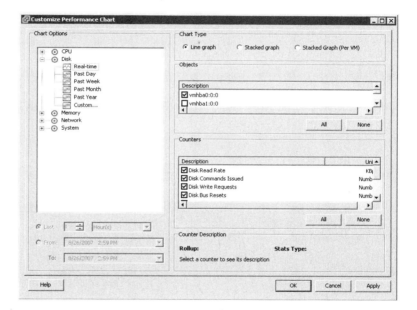

5. Selecting an object or objects, in this case a controller, and a counter or counters lets you monitor for activity that is interesting or necessary to meet service levels. In the custom chart selection shown in Figure 11.64, selecting the objects vmhba0:0:0 and silo104.vdc.local, then selecting counters Disk Read Rate, Disk Write Rate, and Disk Usage (Average/Rate) will give an overall view of the activity for controller 0.

6. In reviewing the graph in Figure 11.65, we discover that the host isn't generating much Read activity, except for one spike around 9:55 AM. Write activity isn't much either and the Disk Usage counter is showing a low pattern of activity, which aggregates the data for both Read and Write.

Host disk I/O is in a controller context, but we can switch to a Stacked Graph view (see Figure 11.66) that allows us to see each virtual machine's activity stacked on top of one another to see their aggregate usage as well.

FIGURE 11.64
Setting up the objects
and counters for a
real-time graph for a
specific controller.

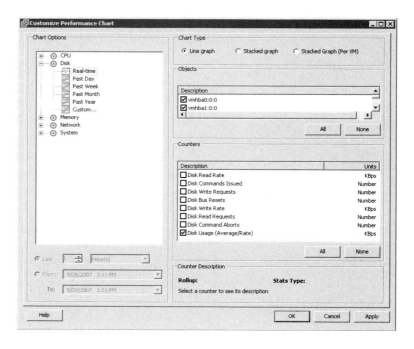

FIGURE 11.65
Controller usage graph
for vmhba0:0:0.

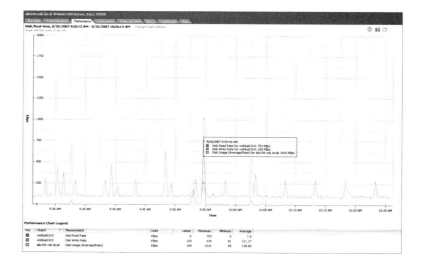

FIGURE 11.66
Switching to
Stacked Graph
per-virtual-machine
view lets us make quick
comparisons or find a
virtual machine that is
monopolizing its vol-
ume. This particular
graph shows very little
disk activity for either
virtual machine.

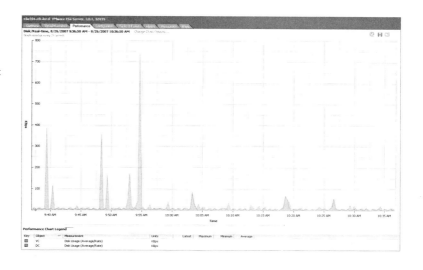

STACKED VIEWS

A stacked view is very helpful in identifying whether one particular virtual machine is monopolizing
a volume. Whichever virtual machine has the tallest stack in the comparison may be degrading the
performance of other virtual machines' virtual disks.

Now let's switch to the virtual machine view. Looking at individual virtual machines for insight
into their disk utilization can lead to some useful conclusions. File and print virtual machines, or
any server that provides print queues or database services, will generate some disk-related I/O
that needs to be monitored. In some cases, if the virtual machine is generating too much I/O, it
may degrade the performance of other virtual machines running out of the same volume. Let's
take a look at a virtual machine's graph.

Perform these steps to create a virtual machine graph showing real-time disk controller
utilization:

1. Connect to the VirtualCenter server or an individual ESX Server host with the VI Client.

2. In the inventory tree, click on an ESX host. This shows you the Summary tab in the Details
   section on the right. Select the Performance tab.

3. Click the Change Chart Options link.

4. Under Chart Options, click on the Disk bull's-eye or the + sign, as shown in Figure 11.67.

5. Using the graph objects vmhba0:0:0 and the virtual machine name, plus the counters of Disk
   Read, Disk Write, and Disk Usage (Average/Rate) counters, we can produce an informative
   picture of this virtual machine's disk I/O behavior. This virtual machine is busy at work
   generating reads and writes for its application. Does the graph show enough I/O to meet
   a service-level agreement or does this virtual machine need some help? The graphs allow
   administrators to make informed decisions, usually working with the application owners,
   so that any adjustments to improve I/O will lead to happy virtual machine owners.

FIGURE 11.67
Setting up the graph for a single virtual machine.

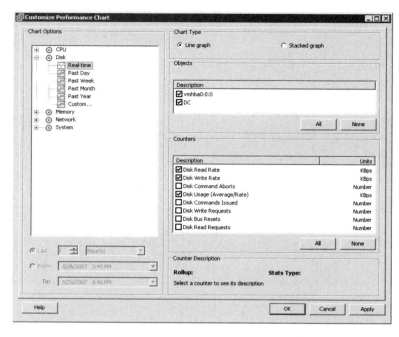

FIGURE 11.68
A virtual machine disk usage graph can help you decide if you need to make adjustments.

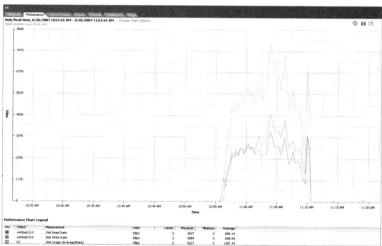

The graph in Figure 11.68 shows real disk I/O that may indicate that a virtual machine is performing its duties well. In addition, by looking at longer intervals of time to gain a historical perspective it may show that the virtual machine has become busier or fallen off its regular output and is therefore not meeting expectations. If the amount of I/O is just slightly impaired, then adjusting the virtual machine's shares may be a way to prioritize its disk I/O ahead of other virtual machines sharing the volume. The administrator may be forced to move the virtual machine's virtual disk(s) to another volume or LUN if share adjustments don't achieve the required results.

The Bottom Line

Create an alarm

Work with graphs

Customize host and virtual machine graphs for CPU, Memory, Network, and Disk

Save a graph

Create an alarm. Creating host and virtual machine alarms is a proactive way to be alerted to abnormal behavior for all four resource groups or state changes. Alarms can be applied to a single host or virtual machine or a group of either object in the VirtualCenter hierarchy.

Master It Creating host and virtual machine alarms.

Work with graphs Creating and working with Performance graphs is the best way to monitor what is currently happening in your virtual infrastructure. Maybe more important, though, is a graph's ability to analyze trends in the performance of your hosts and virtual machines. Graphs can be saved and archived or printed for justifying purchase decisions or showing before-and-after comparisons after adjustments have been made to either hosts or virtual machines.

Master It Creating graphs for hosts and virtual machines.

Master It Using `esxtop` to monitor resources on a single ESX host.

Customizing Host and Virtual Machine Graphs for CPU, Memory, Disk, and Network Adapters.

Master It Use the graphs to monitor CPU usage regularly for hosts and the virtual machines.

Master It Create graphs showing host memory usage using the various objects, counters, and chart types.

Master It Create graphs showing virtual machine memory usage using the various objects, counters, and chart types.

Master It Create graphs showing host and virtual machine network usage using the various objects, counters, and chart types.

Master It Create graphs showing host and virtual machine usage using the various objects, counters, and chart types.

Save a graph Graphs can be saved as evidence, I mean justification, as to why new hardware is required.

Master It You need to provide a graph to upper management in support of your proposal for two new servers to be configured as ESX Server hosts.

Chapter 12

Securing a Virtual Infrastructure

On a scale of 1 to 10 in importance, security always rates close to a 10 in setting up and securing an ESX Server. As VMware has increased the capabilities and features that come with their products, those same products and features must fit within the security policies with which other servers must comply. Most of the time, ESX and VirtualCenter servers fit easily and nicely within those security policies, but sometimes it is hard to do so. As of VMware Infrastructure 3 (VI3), the task to make VI3 conform to a company's security policies has become easier.

Much of the security access for VI3 revolves around the user accounts used to log into VirtualCenter and the ESX Service Console. VirtualCenter uses Windows accounts, usually Active Directory accounts, to assign roles and permissions to inventory objects, such as datacenters, clusters, resource pools, and virtual machines. ESX Server user accounts are local accounts and are usually for administrative purposes only. How these local accounts are used or allowed to perform certain actions is the focus of this chapter.

In this chapter you will learn to:

- ◆ Create and apply roles and permissions in VirtualCenter

- ◆ Create users on the ESX Service Console

- ◆ Use Kerberos authentication on ESX Server

- ◆ Enable and disable services on the firewall

- ◆ Audit and monitor important files

- ◆ Manage updates and patches with VMware Update Manager

User Access to VirtualCenter and ESX Server

With VirtualCenter's inherent Windows architecture, it can rely on and utilize the user and group infrastructure of Active Directory for logging into VirtualCenter. VirtualCenter has no functionality to manage Windows users or groups. The administrator can pull in any user or group that is locally on the Windows server that VirtualCenter is installed on or from the domain. Once the user has been identified and added, a role can be selected that best fits the requirements of that user. Once the user logs into VirtualCenter using the Virtual Infrastructure (VI) Client, the console only shows what the user is allowed to see and only provides specific functionality that corresponds with that user's role (see Figures 12.1 and 12.2).

FIGURE 12.1
An example of a user having logged into VirtualCenter and being shown an "Administrator" view of the inventory

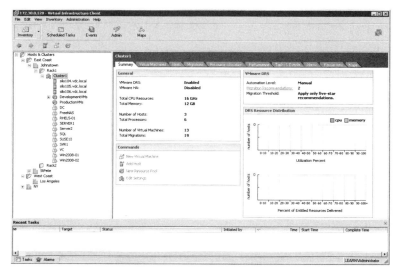

FIGURE 12.2
An example of a user having logged into VirtualCenter and being shown a "VM Administrator" view on a specific resource pool

Perform the following steps to assign a user account and role to a VirtualCenter inventory object:

1. Log into VirtualCenter with the VI Client with the Administrator role (see Figure 12.3).

2. Right-click on the inventory object to which you wish to add a permission and select Add Permission, as shown in Figure 12.4.

3. In the Assign Permissions dialog box, click the Add button to open the Select Users dialog box (see Figure 12.5).

4. Make a selection from the Domains drop-down list, and select the user or group, as shown in Figure 12.6. Click Add, then OK.

FIGURE 12.3
Logging in with an
account that can assign
permissions

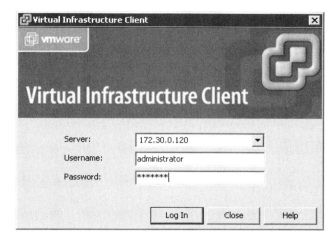

FIGURE 12.4
Select the inventory
object for the new
permission.

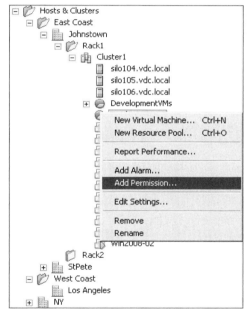

5. Select the appropriate role from the Assigned Role drop-down list, as shown in Figure 12.7. Choose a role that best fits the user's job function. If one of the predefined roles does not fit, create and use a custom role. Click OK when you're done.

6. The completed permission appears on the Permissions tab for that inventory object, as shown in Figure 12.8.

By default, ESX Server still relies on a local user and group accounts model. But with the advent of VirtualCenter's centralized management role, most activities are funneled through

VirtualCenter, using Windows accounts that have been assigned a role, which have then been assigned to an inventory object. This combination of Windows account, role, and inventory object creates a permission that allows (or disallows) the user to perform certain functions. Since the user doesn't log into the ESX Server directly, this minimizes the need for many local user accounts on the ESX Server and thus provides better security. Alas, there still is a need, however small or infrequent, for local accounts on an ESX Server used primarily for administration.

FIGURE 12.5
Beginning the process of adding a user

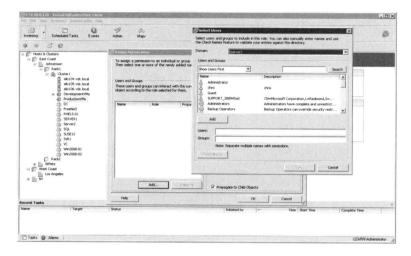

FIGURE 12.6
Choose a domain, user, or group, then click Add and OK.

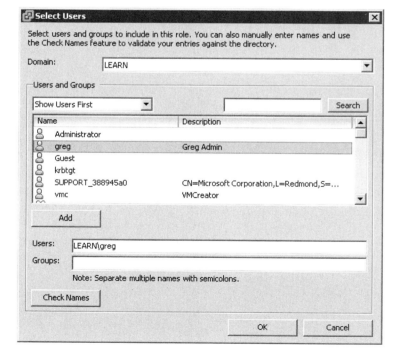

FIGURE 12.7
Choosing a role for the
new user

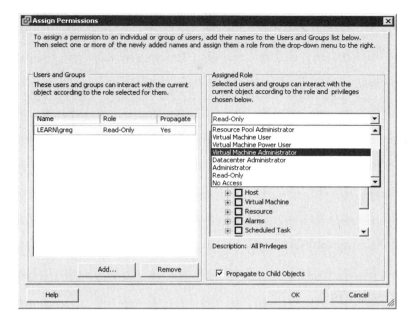

FIGURE 12.8
A new role has been
created that best fits the
user's job function.

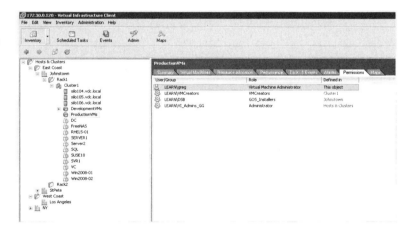

TO VC OR NOT TO VC

The best way to administer your virtual infrastructure is to connect the VI Client to the VirtualCenter server. Although you can connect the VI Client to an ESX Server directly, you lose a great deal of functionality. If you didn't purchase VirtualCenter, you may have to connect to the ESX Server(s). In such instances, you'd have to create user accounts locally on the ESX Server for virtual machine administration.

When using VirtualCenter to access your virtual infrastructure, the administrator or user is usually only creating a task and not directly interfacing with the ESX Servers or the virtual machines. Say for instance, Shane, an administrator, wants to create a new virtual machine. He first needs a proper role, such as "VM Administrator" on an inventory object, to accomplish such a feat (see Figure 12.9).

FIGURE 12.9
Having the proper role to accomplish your task is the starting point when using VirtualCenter.

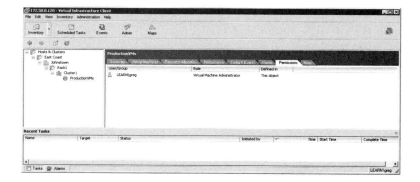

As shown in Figure 12.9, Shane has been assigned the VM Administrator role on the ProductionVMs resource pool. This role gives him what he needs to create, modify, and monitor virtual machines for that pool. But, does Shane's user account have direct access to the ESX Servers when he's logged into VirtualCenter? No, and in fact, a proxy account is used to communicate Shane's tasks to the appropriate ESX Server. This account, vpxuser, is the only account that VirtualCenter stores and tracks in its back-end database as shown in Figure 12.10.

FIGURE 12.10
An ESX Server host managed by Virtual-Center has a vpxuser account created for communication between the host and VC.

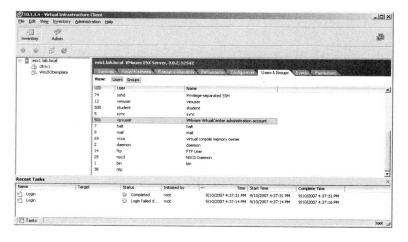

Any time VirtualCenter polls an ESX Server or an administrator creates a task that needs to be communicated to an ESX Server, the account vpxuser is used.

VPXUSER SECURITY

The vpxuser account and password are stored in the VirtualCenter database and on the ESX Servers. It is used to communicate from a VirtualCenter server to an ESX Server. The vpxuser password consists of 32 (randomly selected) characters, is encrypted using SHA1 on an ESX Server, and is obfuscated on VirtualCenter. Each vpxuser password is unique to the ESX Server being managed by VirtualCenter.

No direct administrator intervention is warranted or advised for this account as this will break VirtualCenter functions needing this account. The account and password are never used by humans, nor do they have shell access on an ESX Server. Thus, it isn't necessary to manage this account or include it with normal administrative and regular user account security policies.

If folders are used to organize these objects, or if the inventory view is changed to Virtual Machines and Templates, as shown in Figure 12.6, folders can be used to organize the virtual machines and templates, irrespective of the Host and Clusters inventory objects. Thus, you can assign roles to those folders that are related to virtual machine administration. It is best to use one view or the other when assigning virtual machine–centric roles to avoid conflicts in permissions. Since VirtualCenter presents the administrator with the Hosts and Clusters view by default, many administrators use this view for virtual machines. A good habit is to switch to Virtual Machines and Templates whenever you are assigning user roles to a virtual machine or a group of virtual machines in a folder.

So, when is it appropriate to log into an ESX Server on the Service Console? Not very often for almost all everyday administrative tasks. There are times, however, when an administrator has to troubleshoot a problem or set up or monitor specific processes on the ESX Server that cannot be managed with VirtualCenter. A good example is setting up the NTP service so the ESX Server can synchronize its time with a trusted time source. Although the administrator can open the firewall with the VI Client connected to VirtualCenter for a given ESX Server, the actual service is enabled locally on the Service Console.

In most cases, the number and the frequency of use of local user accounts on an ESX Server have diminished considerably. Usually, two or three accounts are all that is needed for access to the Service Console. Why two or three? The best reason to have at least two accounts is in case one of the user accounts is unavailable for situations like user vacations, sickness, or accidents. Having fewer accounts also makes auditing much easier in those high-security environments that require auditing of administrative accounts. The following steps show one way to create local user accounts:

1. Log into the ESX Server Service Console with the root account.

2. Type **useradd** *username* at the command prompt.

3. Type **passwd** *username* to set an initial password.

4. Type the password twice as shown in Figure 12.11.

FIGURE 12.11
Creating a new user account and setting the initial password

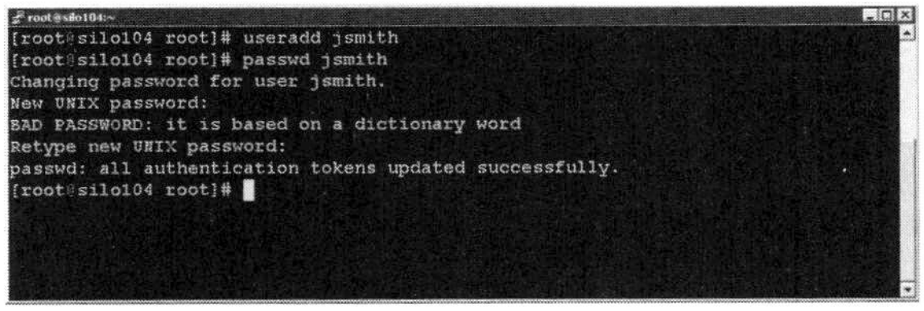

5. Open a new ssh session and test the user account and password as shown in Figure 12.12.

FIGURE 12.12
Testing the new user
account

```
jsmith@silo104:~
login as: jsmith
jsmith@172.30.0.104's password:
Last login: Mon Sep 10 15:08:34 2007 from 192.168.2.105
[jsmith@silo104 jsmith]$
```

You can also log into the ESX Server with the VI Client and create users using the Users and Groups tab. Be careful when creating passwords with this client, as many special characters are not passed through the interface properly. Once the accounts have been created, limit their access to specific tools and client services if needed, as you'll see in the next section.

SERVICE CONSOLE USER PASSWORDS

Avoid using any kind of special characters for Service Console user passwords. These characters can cause problems when managing a server from the command line.

Managing Client Access to ESX Server

Starting with VI3, root can no longer log into an ESX Server with a ssh client. This provides better security for the root account, which should be protected at all costs. In previous versions of ESX Server, the root account could log into the Service Console via a remote ssh client session. This provided an avenue to brute-force the root password. The file that defines this policy is sshd_config, located in the /etc/ssh directory, and the attribute that allows or disallows remote root logins is PermitRootLogin. Keeping this attribute set to No is considered a best practice.

For those times when logging into ESX Servers directly is required, limit access to only certain individuals or client computers to help lock down these incoming client connections. These restrictions allow easier compliance with security access policies and can be audited to prove such compliance.

There are two good ways to restrict access to remote client access services. One is to limit the number of user accounts allowed to log on. As discussed earlier, there isn't much need to create and maintain several user accounts locally on an ESX Server. For those times when direct ESX Server access is needed, say with ssh, modify the sshd_config file to allow or to deny specific users. An argument against this technique is that there should only be administrative accounts on the server, so all of them would probably need ssh access and there's no reason to add them to sshd_config.

Perform the following steps to limit ssh connections to specific users:

1. Log into the Service Console as root.

2. If the user accounts have not been created, create them using useradd.

3. Change the working directory to /etc/ssh.

4. Make a copy of the sshd_config file as shown in Figure 12.13.

FIGURE 12.13
Always create a copy of
the original file before
making edits.

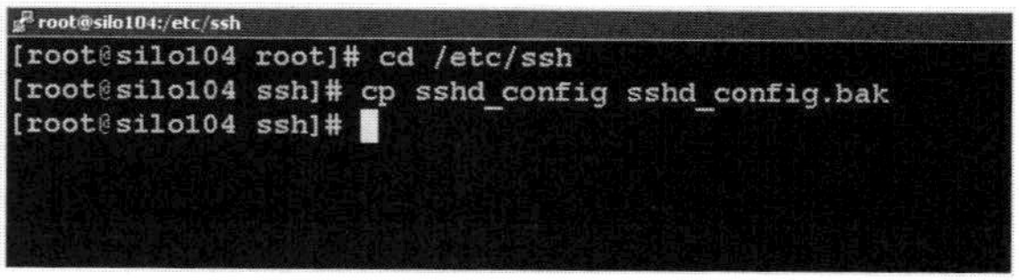

```
root@silo104:/etc/ssh
[root@silo104 root]# cd /etc/ssh
[root@silo104 ssh]# cp sshd_config sshd_config.bak
[root@silo104 ssh]#
```

5. Edit the sshd_config file with vi or nano by adding the AllowUsers attribute and the users. Be sure to separate the user accounts with spaces as shown in Figure 12.14.

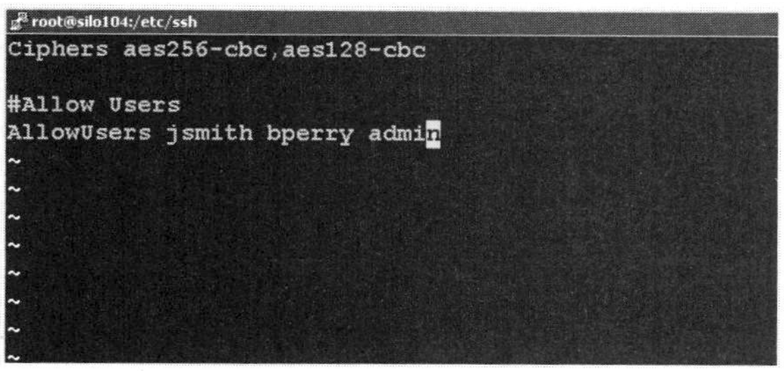

FIGURE 12.14
Adding the attribute
AllowUsers and the
user accounts that will
use ssh to remotely
access the ESX Server

6. Save the sshd_config file.

7. Restart the sshd service as shown in Figure 12.15.

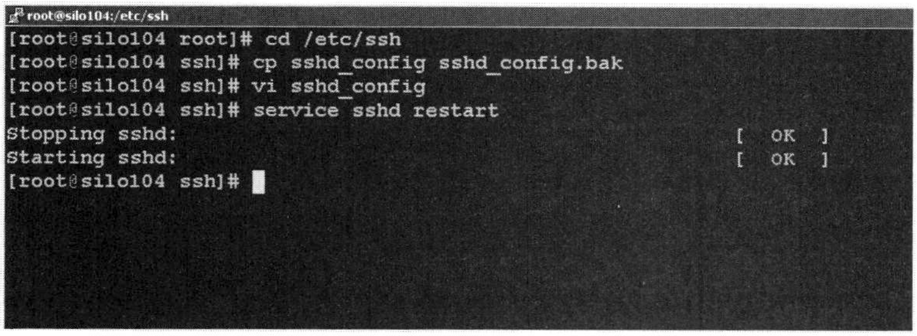

FIGURE 12.15
For the edited
sshd_config file
to have an impact,
you must restart the
sshd service.

8. Test the new sshd_config file by trying to log on with an unspecified account as shown in Figure 12.16.

FIGURE 12.16
Testing the new users
and a bogus user for
access with ssh

SSH ACCESS

When using the AllowUser attribute with the sshd_config file, and after only creating the necessary user accounts for administrative purposes, you do not have to specify the DenyUsers attribute. By implicit denial, any other accounts created but not listed in the AllowUsers section are unable to log in remotely with ssh.

User accounts created using the VI Client can be granted shell access by clicking the Allow Shell Access option in the Create User wizard.

Another way to limit access to ESX client services such as `ssh` and `vmware-authd` (the process that controls VI Client connections) is to use TCP wrappers. TCP wrappers can restrict specific hosts from connecting to the ESX Server. TCP wrappers are transparent to the underlying services, and there's no need to restart those services when changes have been made to the `/etc/hosts.allow` or `/etc/hosts.deny` file (these files are used to allow or deny certain host connections). The syntax for defining the hosts allowed to connect and those that can't is very flexible. Some examples of the syntax for allowing a specific host to connect are as follows:

```
sshd:192.168.31.42:allow
sshd:host1.abc.com:allow
sshd:192.168.31.0/24:allow
```

Once the administrator has defined which hosts are allowed to connect, the follow-up is to deny all other hosts. You add this line (or lines) to the `/etc/hosts.deny` file, or you can consolidate all of the rules in `/etc/hosts.allow`. Here are some examples of the syntax for denying a specific host or hosts to connect:

```
vmware-authd:192.168.40.33:deny
vmware-authd:host2.abc.com:deny
vmware-authd:All:deny
```

HOSTS.ALLOW AND HOSTS.DENY RULES

Be careful when arranging the order of your rules; the first rule matched to a host becomes the policy, even if there is another rule further down that also matches the policy.

Perform the following steps to limit host connections to `ssh` or `vmware-authd`:

1. Log into the Service Console as `root`.

2. Change the working directory to `/etc`.

3. Make a copy of the `hosts.allow` file as shown in Figure 12.17.

FIGURE 12.17
Making a copy of
hosts.allow to save
the original con-
figuration

4. Edit `hosts.allow` with `vi` or `nano` to include only those hosts that should have access and to restrict all others as shown in Figure 12.18. Remember, you can consolidate your entries into one file, but be careful of their order.

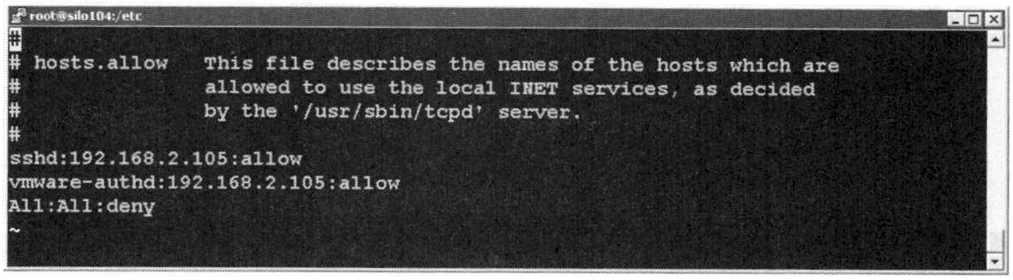

FIGURE 12.18
Editing the
hosts.allow file

5. Save the file.

6. Test the host connections to make sure only those hosts specified have access and all others do not, as shown in Figure 12.19.

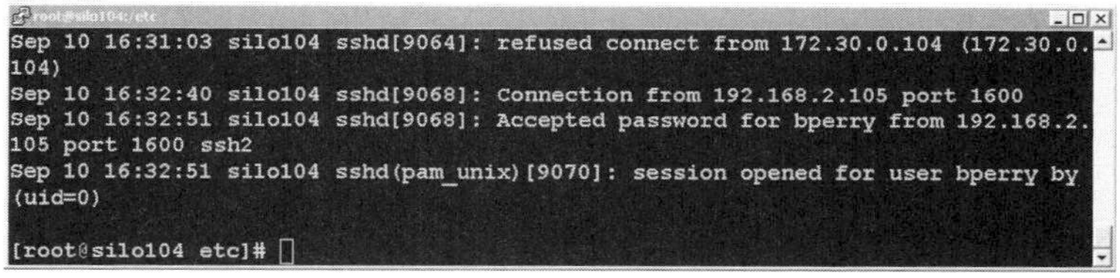

FIGURE 12.19
Looking at
/var/log/messages,
we can see the refused
connection from
172.30.0.104, but an
accepted connection
from 192.160.2.105.

Managing and Configuring the Service Console Firewall

The configuration of the ESX Server's firewall is one area that VMware has made very easy. The firewall is based on IP tables, a firewall technology readily available on most Linux distributions. Working with IP tables is not for the uninitiated. But, with the esxcfg-firewall command-line utility, creating only those firewall rules necessary for proper ESX functionality is easy.

The default setup for the Service Console firewall is very secure. For both incoming and outgoing connections, only those ports necessary for management of the virtual machines and the ESX Server are open. This default mode of operation is High security. The other two modes of operation are Medium, which doesn't block outgoing ports, and Low, which doesn't block ingoing or outgoing ports. Some default ports open when using High are:

◆ 902 — VI Client connections

◆ 903 — Virtual Machine desktop connection

◆ 80/443 — Web browser connections

◆ 22 — ssh client connections

◆ 27000/27010 — License Server, if the ESX Server is managed by VirtualCenter

As shown in Figure 12.20, there are several other ports, having mostly to do with Common Information Model (CIM). CIM allows monitoring of many aspects of the hardware and storage of an ESX Server.

FIGURE 12.20
Ports open on a default
installation of ESX 3.X

When you consider opening a new port, you can use the VI Client connected to VirtualCenter or the Service Console command `esxcfg-firewall`. Most of the time it is easy to open predefined ports with the VI Client, but in some cases, you might need to open a port for a lesser-known service or process, such as monitoring agents.

SERVICE CONSOLE FIREWALL SERVICES

ESX server has an XML file, `/etc/vmware/firewall/services.xml`, that defines those services used most often on an ESX Server and that are shown in the VI Client in the Security Profile. VMware does not support editing this file to add your own services.

Monitoring the firewall's configuration is an important step in auditing access to an ESX Server. As shown in Figure 12.20, using the VI Client is one way to monitor currently open ports on the firewall. In some cases, though, newly opened ports will not show up using the V I Client. The best way to audit currently open ports and the services using them is to use `esxcfg-firewall` `-q`. This listing is always accurate if user access has been restricted, as demonstrated earlier in this chapter.

Perform these steps to audit the current firewall settings:

1. Log into the Service Console as root.

2. Type the command **esxcfg-firewall -q** as shown in Figure 12.21.

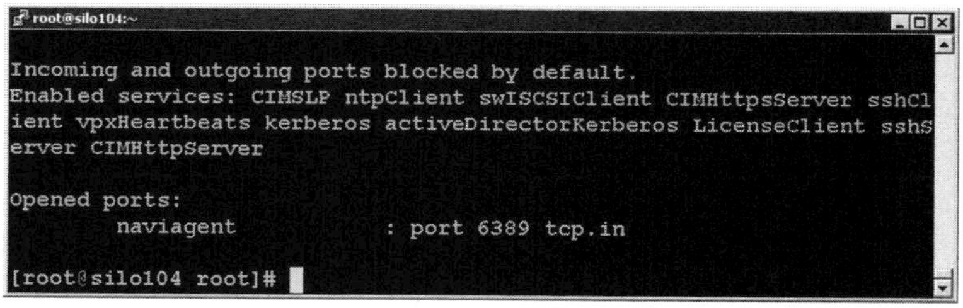

FIGURE 12.21
Auditing the Service
Console firewall

```
root@silo104:~                                                    _□×
Incoming and outgoing ports blocked by default.
Enabled services: CIMSLP ntpClient swISCSIClient CIMHttpsServer sshCl
ient vpxHeartbeats kerberos activeDirectorKerberos LicenseClient sshS
erver CIMHttpServer

Opened ports:
        naviagent               : port 6389 tcp.in

[root@silo104 root]#
```

3. Check that the server is blocking incoming and outgoing ports (High security). Check that only needed services ports have been enabled, and check that only necessary ports for added agents have been opened.

Use the `esxcfg-firewall` command to open ports defined in the `services.xml` file or those not listed in the profile.

Follow these steps to enable the firewall for locally defined services:

1. Log into the Service Console as root.

2. Type the command **esxcfg-firewall -s** to list possible services.

3. Once the service name has been located, type **esxcfg-firewall -q** *service_name* to check the firewall's port status.

4. Type **esxcfg-firewall -e** *service_name* to enable the firewall port.

5. Type **esxcfg-firewall -q** *service_name* to verify the port status as shown in Figure 12.22.

FIGURE 12.22
Enabling a firewall port for a predefined service

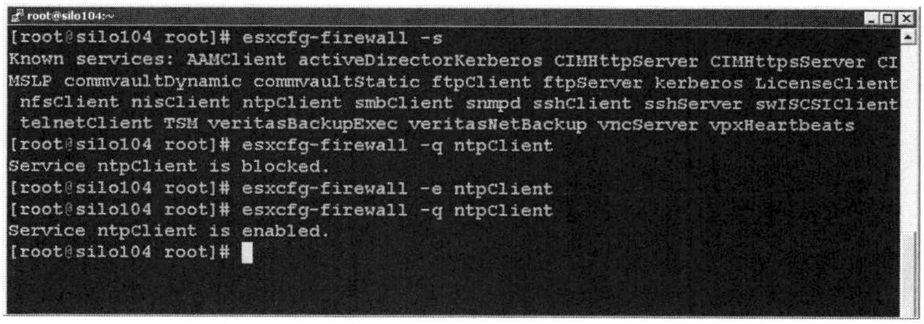

If you need to open a port for an agent or other third-party application not listed in `services.xml`, the `esxcfg-firewall` command still does that job, but the administrator has to know exactly what the agent or application needs. One example, the Dell OpenManage Server Agent, needs a specific port open to communicate with the OpenManage Web Administrative console. The command `esxcfg-firewall -o 1311,tcp,in,OpenManageRequest` opens the needed port. Breaking down the command:

◆ `-o` opens the port (`-c` would close the port).

◆ `1311` is the port to be opened.

◆ `tcp` is the protocol to be used.

◆ `in` specifies incoming traffic.

◆ `OpenManageRequest` is the name of the agent or service.

Perform the following steps to open a port for an agent or application not included in the default firewall services list:

1. Log into the Service Console as root.

2. Type **esxcfg-firewall -o** *port*,**tcp** or **udp**,**in** or **out**,*name* as shown in Figure 12.23.

FIGURE 12.23
Enabling a firewall
port for an unlisted
service or agent

```
root@silo104:~
[root@silo104 root]# esxcfg-firewall -o 1311,tcp,in,OpenManageRequest
[root@silo104 root]#
```

3. Type **esxcfg-firewall -q** to verify the status of the port as shown in Figure 12.24.

FIGURE 12.24
Verifying the status of
the newly opened port

```
root@silo104:~                                                          _□×
Incoming and outgoing ports blocked by default.
Enabled services: CIMSLP ntpClient swISCSIClient CIMHttpsServer vpxHeartbeats Li
censeClient sshServer CIMHttpServer

Opened ports:
        OpenManageRequest    : port 1311 tcp.in
        naviagent            : port 6389 tcp.in

[root@silo104 root]#
```

Once the firewall changes have been made, you still have to install the agent or application
and test your connectivity. If at some point you want to close a port that is no longer needed,
esxcfg-firewall does the trick.

Perform the following steps to limit ssh connections to specific users:

1. Log into the Service Console as root.

2. Type **esxcfg-firewall -q** to check the status and port number as shown in Figure 12.25.

FIGURE 12.25
Verifying the status of
the port to be closed

```
root@silo104:~                                                          _□×
Incoming and outgoing ports blocked by default.
Enabled services: CIMSLP ntpClient swISCSIClient CIMHttpsServer vpxHeartbeats Li
censeClient sshServer CIMHttpServer

Opened ports:
        OpenManageRequest    : port 1311 tcp.in
        naviagent            : port 6389 tcp.in

[root@silo104 root]#
```

3. Type **esxcfg-firewall -c** *port*, **tcp** or **udp**, **in** or **out**, *name* as shown in Figure 12.26.

FIGURE 12.26
Closing the firewall
port for an unlisted
service or agent

```
root@silo104:~                                                          _□×
Incoming and outgoing ports blocked by default.
Enabled services: CIMSLP ntpClient swISCSIClient CIMHttpsServer vpxHeartbeats Li
censeClient sshServer CIMHttpServer

Opened ports:
        OpenManageRequest    : port 1311 tcp.in
        naviagent            : port 6389 tcp.in

[root@silo104 root]# esxcfg-firewall -c 1311,tcp,in,OpenManageRequest
[root@silo104 root]#
```

4. Verify that the port is closed as shown in Figure 12.27.

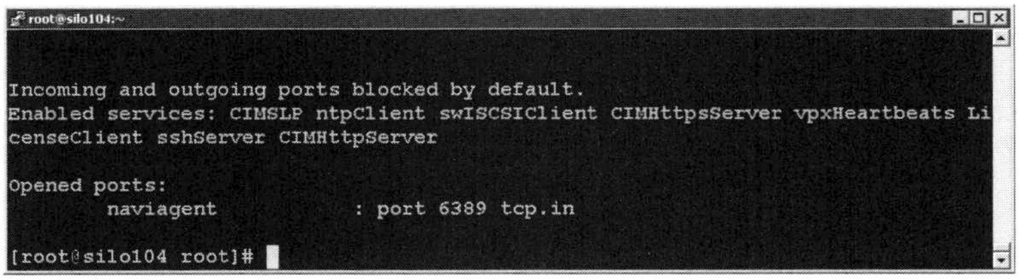

FIGURE 12.27
Confirming the closing
of the firewall port

```
root@silo104:~                                                          _□×
Incoming and outgoing ports blocked by default.
Enabled services: CIMSLP ntpClient swISCSIClient CIMHttpsServer vpxHeartbeats Li
censeClient sshServer CIMHttpServer

Opened ports:
        naviagent                : port 6389 tcp.in

[root@silo104 root]#
```

Kerberos Authentication for ESX Server

ESX Servers, by default, use local users and groups to assign permissions to directories and files. With VI3, there is no longer a need for large numbers of these local accounts. But, even in enterprise datacenters, two or three accounts are needed for those rare instances when a task cannot be accomplished through VirtualCenter. Some examples of these instances are:

◆ VirtualCenter is not available or is down.

◆ You are troubleshooting ESX Server boot and configuration problems.

◆ You are setting up specific services that weren't set up during the basic installation, such as NTP.

◆ You are auditing the ESX Server configuration and remote access by comparing archived files with live versions of the same files.

This list is not exhaustive, but does give some insight into why logging locally into an ESX Server is sometimes necessary. With a few changes to the underlying authentication module, user accounts can be authenticated against Active Directory (AD). This allows for a consistent way to apply security polices as they relate to user management by allowing AD administrators to set policies on password complexity, expiration, and user account changes at an AD level, bypassing local ESX Server setup.

SERVICE CONSOLE USER ACCOUNTS

Even with AD integration, user accounts must be created locally on the ESX Server. When creating those accounts, make sure the names for those accounts match the names in Active Directory. By default, there is no mechanism for reconciling local ESX accounts with AD users. If a user is deleted in AD, you must manually delete the user on the ESX Server.

The easiest way to implement AD authentication is to use the `esxcfg-auth` tool. This valuable tool can be used to set local user security policies, such as password complexity, reuse, and length. In this case, `esxcfg-auth` hands over the authentication process to AD by modifying the krb5.conf file, creating the kdc.conf file, and modifying the pam.d file so that VI Client and ssh connections use Kerberos authentication.

Perform the following steps to set up Active Directory authentication:

1. Log into the Service Console as root.

2. Issue the following command as shown in Figure 12.28:

```
# esxcfg-auth --enablead --addomain domain_name --addc domain_name
```

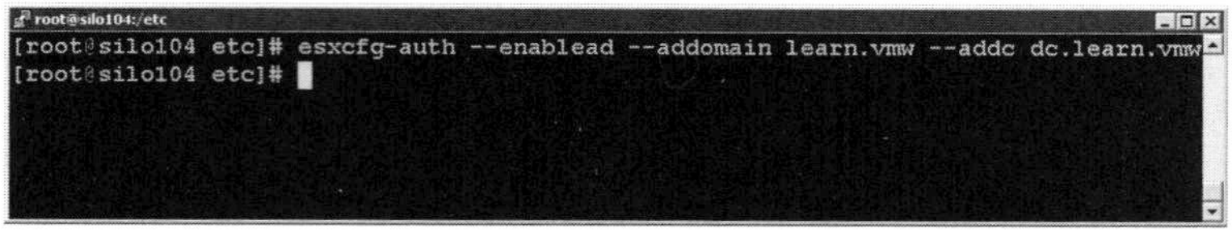

FIGURE 12.28
The first authentica-
tion attempt by the ESX
Server is handled by
Active Directory.

ACCESSING LOCAL AND REMOTE DOMAIN CONTROLLERS

In this example, the assumption is that a local domain controller will handle the authentication. In some cases, if there is a firewall between the ESX servers and the domain controller, the ports listed in krb5.conf may need to be opened. Also, Active Directory DNS should return the local domain controller for this operation. Although you can specify a domain controller in the above command, it's better to just name the domain and let DNS sort out the local DC.

3. Check the krb5.conf file to see if the necessary changes have been made as shown in Figure 12.29.

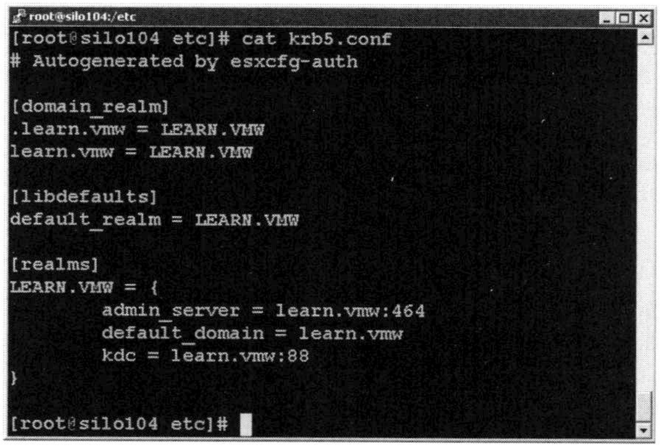

FIGURE 12.29
Double-check the file
to be sure the correct
information was added.

4. Create only the necessary administrative user accounts that match existing Active Directory accounts. Do not set the passwords for these accounts as shown in Figures 12.30 and 12.31.

FIGURE 12.30
Check the existing
user account in Active
Directory.

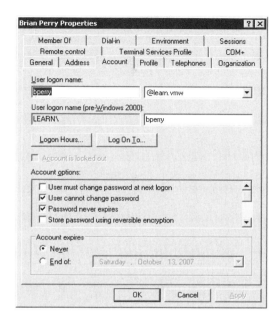

FIGURE 12.31
Create the local Ser-
vice Console account
that matches the
name in AD.

5. Log in with one of the administrative accounts as shown in Figure 12.32.

FIGURE 12.32
Log in with a local
account to check that
Active Directory authen-
ticated the user.

6. Check the logs to see if the process is working without errors as shown in Figure 12.33.

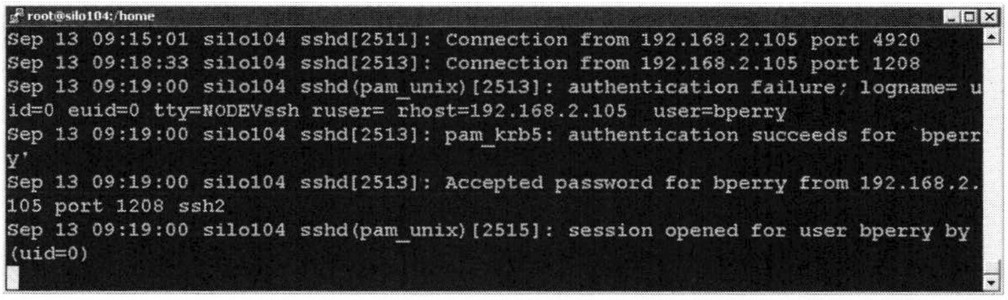

FIGURE 12.33
Review the system logs
for any errors with
the Kerberos authen-
tication process.

Auditing and Monitoring Important Files

There are several files on an ESX Server that tell a lot about the server and how it was configured. Thankfully, with VI3, the job of tracking your ESX Server's configuration has become much easier with the advent of the VI Client. In many instances, though, auditing and monitoring several files directly from the Service Console is warranted because they are stored on the ESX Server itself.

Why do you need to audit these files on a regular basis? For starters, good security on any server begins with knowing how the server is configured. If the configuration has changed, unbeknownst to the administrator, then any security-related decisions could be flawed. Worse, if the change is significant, your virtual machines could suffer or someone who doesn't have your best interests in mind could sabotage your hosting platform. That person won't take down one server — they'll take down many servers.

The files that we'll cover in this section deal with how the server is configured and ultimately set up to provide certain services. VMware provides a tool to make the collection of these files easy. As a matter of fact, you can use either the VI Client or the Service Console command vm-support. This command is usually used to troubleshoot problems with your ESX Server, but you can also use this command to audit and to monitor the same server.

VM-SUPPORT AS DOCUMENTATION

One way to document any changes to the ESX Server's configuration is to run vm-support any time a change has been made. In this way, all changes can be tracked over time and compared with specific setups. In a security audit, using the output from this command is vital to comply with regulatory guidelines for server documentation. By running vm-support at least once a month, you also capture logs files and other critical files for archive purposes.

Let's look at what you can collect using the Service Console. You'll need to log in as root to run vm-support. Figure 12.34 shows that we ran the command vm-support and shows the resulting file. As a good practice, use the /tmp directory as the temporary location for the support files.

FIGURE 12.34
After running the vm-support command, check to see the end result.

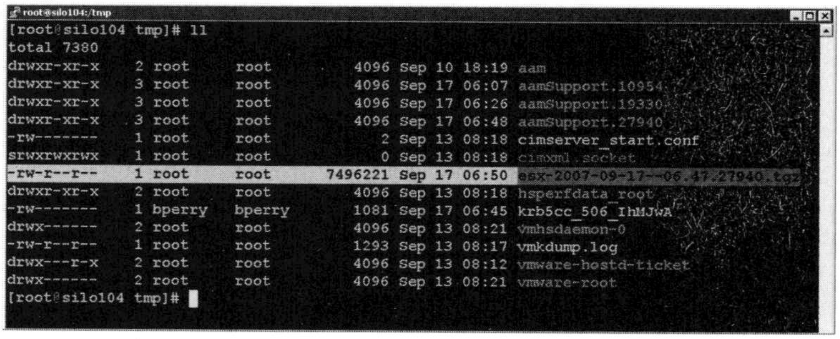

After creating the `.tgz` file, you can copy the file to an archive location, preferably on another server, or extract the file in the current directory.

Perform the following steps to run the `vm-support` command and extract the files into a temporary directory:

1. Log into the Service Console as root.

2. Switch to the `/tmp` directory.

3. Run the `vm-support` command as shown in Figures 12.35 and 12.36.

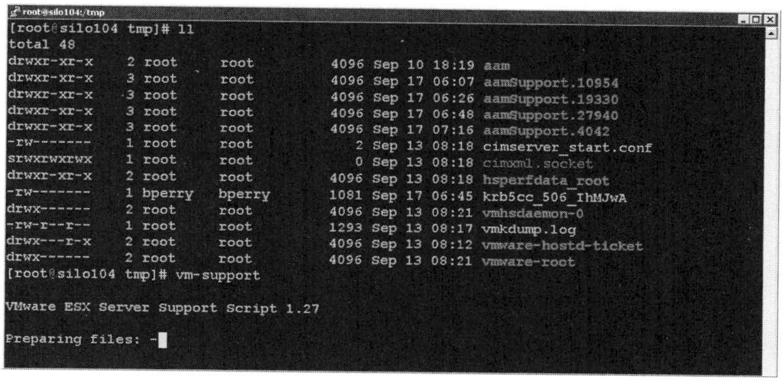

FIGURE 12.35
The `vm-support` command collects diagnostic data about the server configuration.

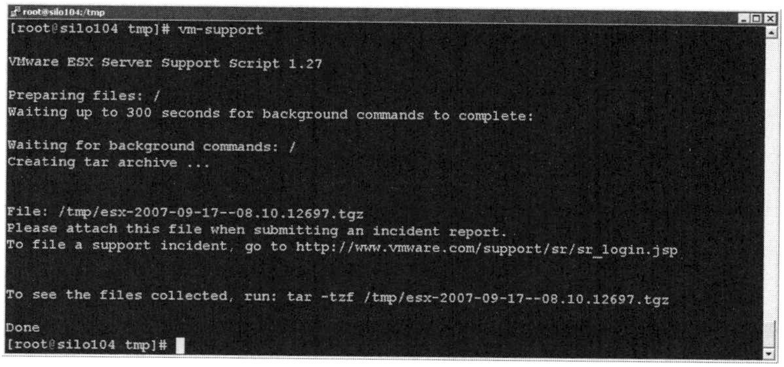

FIGURE 12.36
Running the `vm-support` command

4. Extract the resulting `.tgz` file as shown in Figure 12.37.

FIGURE 12.37
Extracting the `.tgz` file for analysis

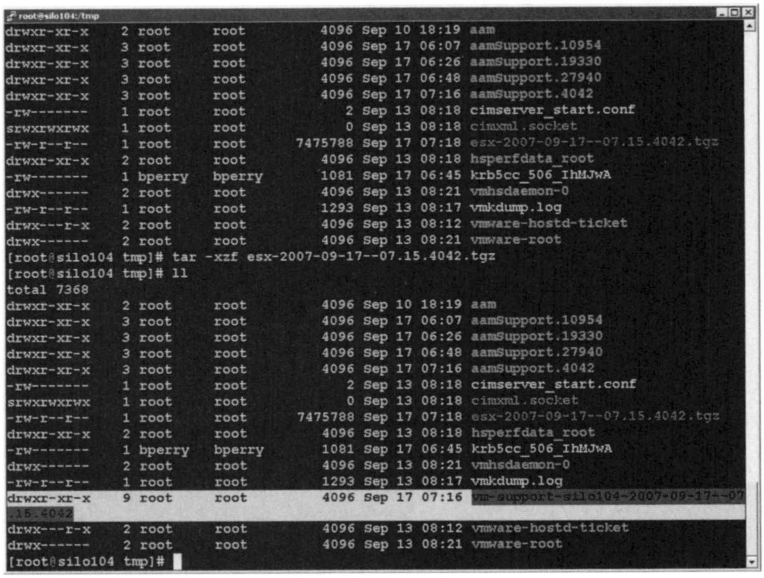

This method captures many files, but one in particular of great importance for auditing is `/etc/vmware/esx.conf`. This is important, as any changes to the overall configuration of the ESX Server are documented in this file, and we can see the time when it was last changed as shown in Figure 12.38.

FIGURE 12.38
Auditing `esx.conf` is very important.

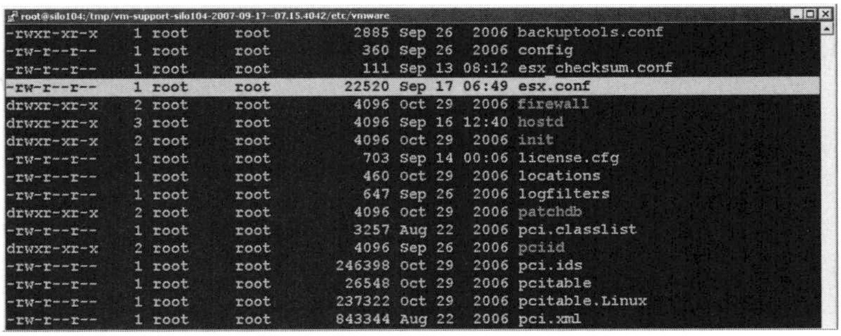

In this case, the file has a timestamp of September 17, 06:49a.m. If we compare this output with the current file, the outputs should match if there hasn't been a scheduled maintenance on the server. But in Figure 12.39, we see that the timestamp on the file has changed. The live file has a timestamp of September 17, 07:35a.m.

FIGURE 12.39
Comparing a live file to one captured with `vm-support`

```
root@silo104:/etc/vmware
[root@silo104 vmware]# cd /etc/vmware
[root@silo104 vmware]# ll
total 2472
-rwxr-xr-x    1 root     root      2885 Sep 26  2006 backuptools.conf
-rw-r--r--    1 root     root       360 Sep 26  2006 config
-rw-r--r--    1 root     root       111 Sep 13 08:12 esx checksum.conf
-rw-r--r--    1 root     root     22555 Sep 17 07:35 esx.conf
drwxr-xr-x    2 root     root      4096 Oct 29  2006 firewall
drwxr-xr-x    3 root     root      4096 Sep 16 12:40 hostd
drwxr-xr-x    2 root     root      4096 Oct 29  2006 init
-rw-r--r--    1 root     root       703 Sep 14 00:06 license.cfg
-rw-r--r--    1 root     root       460 Oct 29  2006 locations
-rw-r--r--    1 root     root       647 Sep 26  2006 logfilters
drwxr-xr-x    2 root     root      4096 Oct 29  2006 patchdb
-rw-r--r--    1 root     root      3257 Aug 22  2006 pci.classlist
drwxr-xr-x    2 root     root      4096 Sep 26  2006 pciid
```

Since the timestamps do not match, how could we compare the captured file, using `vm-support`, with the current version? Using a Linux command known as `diff`, we can compare two files to see if any changes have occurred as shown in Figure 12.40.

FIGURE 12.40
After auditing `esx.conf`, we saw it had changed. Using `diff`, we can easily see what was changed.

```
root@silo104:/etc/vmware
[root@silo104 vmware]# diff /etc/vmware/esx.conf /tmp/vm-support-silo104-2007-09-17--07.1
5.4042/etc/vmware/esx.conf
297d296
< /firewall/services/vncServer = "1"
[root@silo104 vmware]#
```

Someone has changed the firewall to allow a VNC server to run on the ESX Server's Service Console. Many times, though, you will discover changes to the network configuration, storage, or even services that have been implemented due to changes on the firewall to allow the traffic in or out. The techniques we've discussed give you an easy way to monitor and to audit changes to files on the ESX Server. Scripting these steps is not difficult and would make the process even faster, especially if you have dozens of ESX Servers to audit.

VMware Update Manager

VMware Update Manager is a VirtualCenter 2.5 plug-in that offers an automated patch management solution for ESX Server 3.5 and 3i hosts and virtual machines running Windows or Linux. The Update Manager scans hosts and virtual machines and compares them against administrator-defined security baselines to determine if patches are missing. The update process is DRS aware and works in a non-disruptive manner to prevent downtime.

To get started with the VMware Update Manager the plug-in must be installed and enabled from the Plugins menu in VirtualCenter 2.5 as shown in Figure 12.41.

FIGURE 12.41
VMware Update Manager plugin is installed from the Plugins menu in VirtualCenter 2.5.

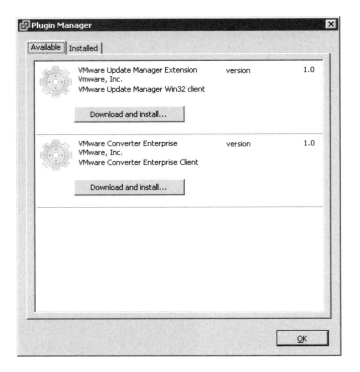

PLUGIN INSTALLATION

The installation of plugins is required on each system where the VI Client is being used to connect to VirtualCenter 2.5.

Once the plugin has been installed it will need to be enabled as shown in Figure 12.42.

◆ Once the plug-in is installed and enabled, baselines need to be established. The baselines provide a comparable standard against which an ESX Server host or virtual machine is measured to determine its level of compliance. VirtualCenter 2.5 provides the following default baselines shown in Figure 12.43. Non-critical Virtual Machine Updates

◆ Non-critical Host Updates

◆ Critical Virtual Machine Updates

◆ Critical Host Updates

Creating a custom baseline allows administrators to pick and choose the updates to be delivered. For example, suppose that you wanted to push out all critical and non-critical host and virtual machine updates. A custom baseline can be created for all updates.

FIGURE 12.42
VMware Update
Manager plug-in must
be enabled after
installation.

FIGURE 12.43
Default baselines
for VMware Update
Manager.

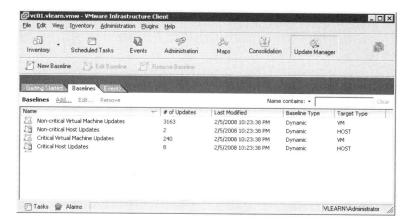

Perform the following steps to create a custom baseline.

1. Use the VI Client to connect to VirtualCenter 2.5.

2. Click the Update Manager icon from the menu bar of VirtualCenter.

3. From the Getting Started tab, click the Create a new baseline link. Alternately, you could select the baselines tab and click Add or click the New Baseline.

4. The New Baseline Wizard starts as shown in Figure 12.44.

FIGURE 12.44
Custom baselines can be established for hosts and virtual machines.

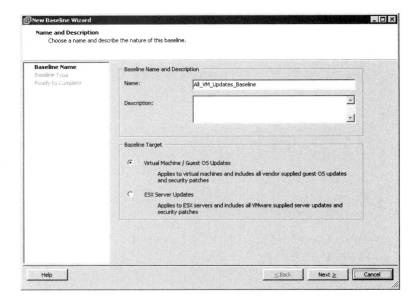

5. Type in a name for the custom baseline and select the Virtual Machine / Guest OS Updates or ESX Server Updates radio button.

6. Click the Next button.

7. Select the baseline type:

◆ Fixed: allows for the selection of specific updates. Selecting this option adds a step in the wizard that allows for the selection of updates to be delivered as part of the baseline.

◆ Dynamic: allows the baseline to be populated automatically with critical, non-critical, or all updates.

8. Select Add or Remove Specific Updates from this Baseline to customize the list of updates and click the Next button. Selecting this option adds another step in the wizard that allows for the selection of updates to be excluded shown in Figure 12.45. If not selecting this option click the Next button to proceed.

9. Click the Finish button.

FIGURE 12.45
Updates can be excluded
from baselines.

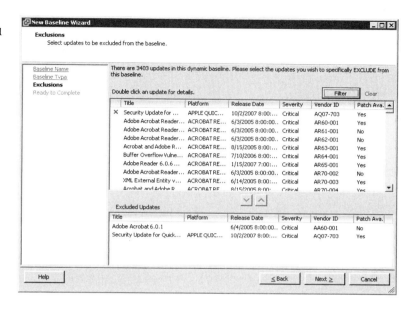

Once the appropriate baselines have been configured they can be applied to hosts and virtual machines. Baselines can be attached at various levels in the hierarchy. For example, a baseline for host updates can be applied at the cluster level to affect all servers in the cluster as shown in Figure 12.46. Or baselines can be applied at a more granular level by attaching them directly to a host.

FIGURE 12.46
Baselines for host
updates can be applied
at higher levels, like a
cluster, to affect multi-
ple hosts.

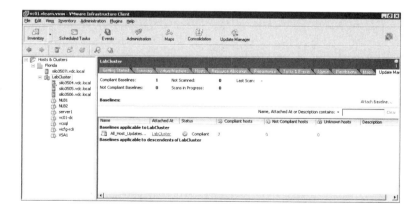

The Update Manager tab identifies the number of hosts that are compliant, non-compliant, or unknown. By clicking on the number value shown in each column, as shown in Figure 12.47, more details can be obtained about the respective hosts. In this particular case silo3504.vdc.local and silo3506.vdc.local are compliant, leaving silo3505.vdc.local as the lone host in an unknown status.

FIGURE 12.47
VMware Update Manager makes it easy to identify compliant and non-compliant systems.

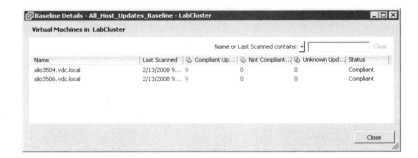

From the Update Manager tab at the cluster level you can instantiate a remediation by right-clicking the appropriate baseline and selecting the Remediate option. Otherwise you could navigate to the Update Manager tab for the individual host or hosts that need remediation and perform the update on a host-by-host basis. Selecting the Remediate option will start the Remediate wizard shown in Figure 12.48

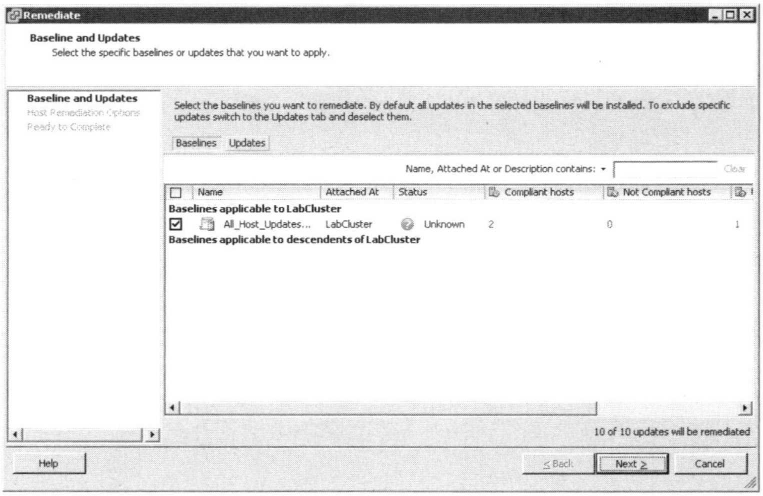

FIGURE 12.48
Use the Remediation option to install all the updates that are missing according to the defined and attached baseline.

The remediation wizard will provide the option for performing the remediation immediately or scheduled for a later date and time. In order to perform the remediation (install the updates) the host must be put into maintenance mode. Remember that maintenance mode requires all virtual machines to be powered off, suspended, or VMotion'ed off to another host. Therefore the remediation wizard offers the ability to configure failure options as shown in Figure 12.49. The failure options include the response, the retry delay, and the number of retries. Failure response includes a drop-down list with the following options:

◆ Fail Task

◆ Retry

◆ Power off virtual machines and retry

◆ Suspend virtual machines and retry

DRS AND UPDATE MANAGER

Since the Update Manager requires a host in maintenance mode, this is yet another good reason to set DRS to a fully automated state. This would allow virtual machines to be relocated via VMotion to another host in order to proceed with the remediation of the ESX Server host. Otherwise you may find that the host sits in the Enter Maintenance Mode state until administrative action is taken to power off, suspend, or move the running virtual machines.

FIGURE 12.49
Immediate or scheduled remediation of an ESX Server host requires the host to be in maintenance mode.

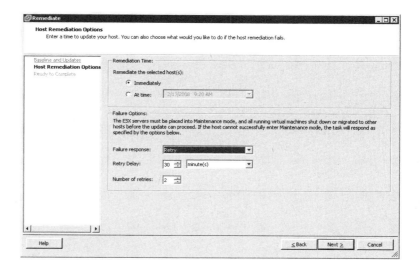

Once the host has been put into maintenance mode the update process will begin and the Tasks pane will show each of the successive update installations as shown in Figure 12.50. Upon completion of all the updates the host will be rebooted and brought out of maintenance, where virtual machines can then be powered on or relocated back to the host.

Thus far in looking at Update Manager we have seen how host updates are managed through the Hosts & Clusters view in VirtualCenter 2.5. The updates for virtual machines are very similar but are best managed from the Virtual Machines & Templates view. This facilitates managing the updates for virtual machines that are organized into folder structures in the VirtualCenter inventory. The procedure for applying virtual machine patches is nearly identical to the process as discussed for ESX Server host. As shown in Figure 12.51, the remediation wizard for virtual machines allows for distinct schedules for virtual machines in various states; powered on, powered off, or suspended.

FIGURE 12.50
Host updates are installed while in maintenance mode and then the host is rebooted and brought out of maintenance mode.

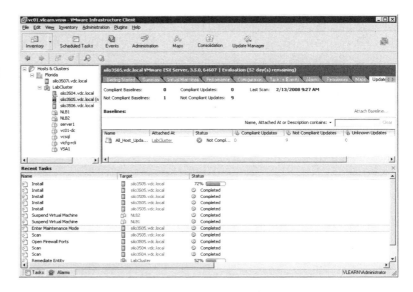

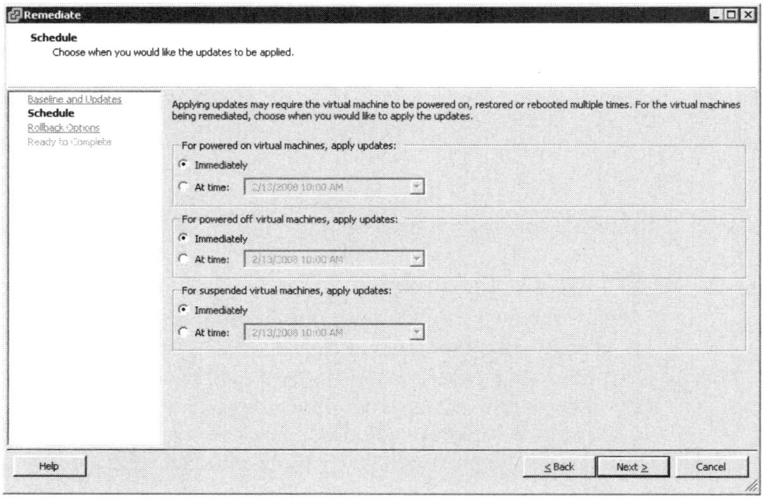

FIGURE 12.51
Virtual Machines in different states can be scheduled for different remediation times.

Perhaps the best feature of virtual machine updates is that VMware has included, by default, the creation of a snapshot prior to the installation of the updates, thereby providing a rollback option. As shown in Figure 12.52, the remediation wizard allows the administrator to define the length of time that the snapshot should be maintained, because as you may know and as stated in the wizard, snapshots can reduce virtual machine performance and hinder VMotion. Ideally the snapshot should be kept only for a duration of time long enough to ensure the system is still functioning normally and then it should be removed.

FIGURE 12.52
Snapshots taken prior to virtual machine remediation are maintained for a definable period of time.

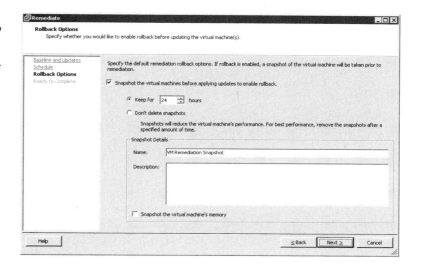

As the remediation process proceeds, the Tasks pane will identify the entity undergoing remediation as well as the hosts that are managing the virtual machines that are being updated.

The VMware Update Manager provides is a simple tool with significant impact on the virtual infrastructure. Whether you use the tool for updating virtual machines in place of the native Microsoft tools is up to you, but most certainly its use case for updating ESX Server hosts is indisputable. The simplicity of the tool coupled with its existing and seamless integration with VirtualCenter means that patch management for ESX Server hosts can be done in a matter of the few minutes it takes to create a baseline and perform remediation.

The Bottom Line

Create and apply roles and permissions in VirtualCenter Creating host and virtual machine alarms is a proactive way to be alerted to abnormal behavior for all four resource groups or state changes. Alarms can be applied to a single host, a virtual machine, or a group of either object in the VirtualCenter hierarchy.

Master It Company security policy dictates that access to VirtualCenter requires users to only be granted the rights necessary to perform their jobs.

Master It Create ESX Server user accounts.

Create users on the ESX Service Console Restricting which users and hosts can connect to an ESX Server is one of the most important security steps you can implement.

Master It Company security policy dictates that direct access to the Service Console must be restricted.

Master It Configure TCP wrappers to restrict host access to the Service Console.

Enable and disable services on the firewall The Service Console firewall is locked down by default for only those ports needed to provide management for virtualization. There are times when other ports will need to be opened using `esxcfg-firewall`.

Master It A security inspection requires an audit of the existing Service Console firewall configuration.

Master It Open the firewall for specific services or agents.

Use Kerberos authentication on ESX Server Kerberos authentication allows for Active Directory authentication of local ESX Server user accounts. This simplifies account management and centralizes user account security policies.

Master It Direct authentication to ESX Server hosts should be secured using an existing Active Directory infrastructure.

Audit and monitor important files Changes to Service Console files should be audited and monitored on a regular basis.

Master It A server failure results in a call to VMware support. The technician requests that you send information about your environment for further review.

Manage updates and patches with VMware Update Manager VMware Update Manager provides an integrated and easy-to- use utility for managing ESX Server host and virtual machine updates.

Master It You have just installed ESX 3.5 on seven new Dell Poweredge 2950 servers into a DRS/HA cluster. No virtual machines exist. You need to apply all updates immediately.

Master It Two days ago you added a new Dell Poweredge R900 server named silo3507 .vdc.local to a partially automated DRS/HA cluster. There are six virtual machines running on silo3507. You need to apply critical updates to silo3507.

Master It You have ten virtual machines that serve as domain controllers. You want to install all of the latest Windows updates on all ten virtual machines using VMware Update Manager. The installation of updates should not affect production during business hours of 9:00 AM to 5:00 PM. You want a 24-hour window of opportunity to remove the update.

Chapter 13

Configuring and Managing ESXi

ESXi is a revolutionary advancement to the architecture of ESX. In this chapter, we'll explain the new ESXi architecture, and how to configure and manage it.

In this chapter you will learn to:

◆ Understand the architecture of ESXi

◆ Deploy ESXi Installable

◆ Deploy ESXi Embedded

◆ Manage ESXi

Understanding ESXi Architecture

In earlier chapters of this book, we introduced you to the architecture of the ESX Server product designed by VMware. As a review, remember that when you install ESX Server 3.5 you are installing two components, VMkernel and Service Console, that are used for virtualization and management, respectively. The VMkernel is the hypervisor that provides resource allocation to virtual machines, and the Service Console is the Linux-based operating system that manages the VMkernel and the virtual machines it services.

ESXi presents a revolutionary alteration to the architecture of ESX. How? The ESXi product is a hypervisor that no longer relies on the Service Console operating system. In fact, the Service Console operating system that ESX Server 3.5 relied on is completely removed in ESXi. Figure 13.1 shows a comparison of the two architectures.

FIGURE 13.1
The elimination of the Service Console in ESXi presents a dramatic change in the VMware-based virtualization architecture.

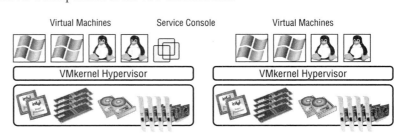

ESXi is a hypervisor-only deployment in the form the VMkernel as a 32 MB footprint with all the logic to continue its primary function of managing virtual machines access to physical resources. Because there is only a 32 MB footprint dedicated to providing resource management, this system can be deployed with less concern for local security. In other versions of VMware's hypervisor, including ESX 3.5, the Service Console is the one element of the system that is vulnerable to security issues; thus it needs security patches and updates from the manufacturer. Invariably, when an organization shifts to a new product, especially one as profound as VI3, there will be hesitation because of the unknown risks and security vulnerabilities. However, ESXi arms enterprise architects with a tool that minimizes the installation architecture, thus making the shift to VI3 an easier sell to those responsible for ensuring the security and safety of a company's information system.

THE FUTURE OF VIRTUALIZATION

I am hoping that you have picked up on my excitement about ESXi. I am excited that ESXi will significantly reduce the security profiling to be performed in all my future virtualization consultations and endeavors. However, I am even more excited at the thought of ESXi as the beginning of a revolution. I see the hypervisor becoming a commodity in IT space as many companies try to bring hypervisors to market. As this commoditization takes place, it will be the tools around the hypervisor that will become the differentiating factor. And in today's market, despite the fact that other companies may market the release of a hypervisor, unquestionably the company making and breaking all the rules in the virtualization marketplace is and will continue to be VMware.

ESXi will be available in two different formats:

◆ ESXi Installable

◆ ESXi Embedded

With such a small footprint, ESXi is easy to install. In fact, with ESXi Embedded, you can order server systems preconfigured with ESXi. This enables you to receive, rack, power on, and configure the system within minutes. The ESXi Installable will require slightly more effort, but in both cases you will save a lot of time deploying new hardware into the infrastructure. In fact, once the server is racked, cabled, and loaded, you can break the deployment into four easy steps:

1. Power on the server and boot to the thin virtualization of ESXi.

2. Reconfigure the root password.

3. (If necessary) Configure a static IP address, subnet mask, default gateway, and DNS server.

4. Add the new hypervisor into VirtualCenter and add virtual switches.

If the new system running ESXi is added to an existing DRS cluster inside of VirtualCenter, it will automatically become a target hypervisor for the workload distribution of the cluster. In effect, this concept of building thin virtualization directly into the hardware platform so it is accessible right out of the box is creating a plug-and-play virtual infrastructure where hardware can easily be added and removed as required.

Regardless of the format deployed, the feature sets will be the same. Although ESXi can be installed and managed as its own server at a less expensive licensing cost, it will lack the enterprise functionality mentioned throughout the book — features like VMotion, High Availability (HA), and Distributed Resource Scheduler (DRS). At the time of this writing, in looking at the VMware product line including VI3, you will find the following:

◆ ESXi includes:

- ◆ Hypervisor functionality (VMkernel)
- ◆ Virtual Machine File System (VMFS)
- ◆ Virtual SMP

◆ VI Foundation includes:

- ◆ Hypervisor functionality (VMkernel) with ESX 3.5 or 3i
- ◆ Virtual Machine File System (VMFS)
- ◆ Virtual SMP
- ◆ Virtual Center Agent
- ◆ VMware Update Manager
- ◆ VMware Consolidate Backup

◆ VI Standard includes:

- ◆ Hypervisor functionality (VMkernel) with ESX 3.5 or 3i
- ◆ Virtual Machine File System (VMFS)
- ◆ Virtual SMP
- ◆ Virtual Center Agent
- ◆ VMware Update Manager
- ◆ VMware Consolidate Backup (VCB)
- ◆ VMware High Availability (HA)

◆ VI Enterprise includes:

- ◆ Hypervisor functionality (VMkernel) with ESX 3.5 or 3i
- ◆ Virtual Machine File System (VMFS)
- ◆ Virtual SMP
- ◆ Virtual Center Agent
- ◆ VMware Update Manager
- ◆ VMware Consolidate Backup (VCB)
- ◆ VMware High Availability (HA)
- ◆ VMotion
- ◆ Storage VMotion
- ◆ Distributed Resource Scheduler (DRS)

Real World Scenario

ESX1 AND THE V1 PRODUCTS

While any of the license versions will support ESXi, VirtualCenter is a mandatory component for the implementation of VMotion, DRS, and HA. You may find documentation that states ESXi does not support these features. That documentation is true only in the situation where ESXi is deployed without the VirtualCenter component. As noted in Chapter 2, there is a cost for the VirtualCenter license as well. I recommend including either the Gold or Platinum support plans from VMware.

In addition to the necessary processor and memory hardware, VMware suggests the following minimum hardware requirements to install and configure ESXi:

◆ At least one Broadcom 570x or Intel Pro/1000 Ethernet adapter.

◆ A compatible SCSI adapter, fibre channel adapter, iSCSI host bus adapter, or internal RAID controller

◆ Access to a local disk or shared storage for virtual machines.

These are, of course, minimum requirements, and much can be done to enhance the performance of the ESXi host, including:

Increasing Memory   Greater amounts of memory provide for larger capacity for virtualization.

Increasing the Number of Network Adapters   The more Gigabit Ethernet adapters available in a server, the more flexible and robust the virtual networking architecture can be.

Adding Multiple Multicore Processors   Multicore processors provide enhanced virtualization capability without incurring additional licensing costs.

ESX1 AND THE HCL

As noted several times throughout this book, you should always consult the VMware compatibility guides to identify hardware compatibility for your version of VMware. ESXi is no different. Check the compatibility guides at http://www.vmware.com before buying any components to add to your virtual infrastructure.

Deploying ESXi Installable

The installation of ESXi Installable begins by ensuring that the computer system is configured to boot from the CD-ROM drive. To do this, insert the ESXi Installable installation CD into the drive and power on the system. The installation files can be downloaded from VMware's website at http://www.vmware.com/downloads. The installation files for ESXi are listed separately from ESX Server 3.5. Once the server is powered on and boots from the CD, the VMware VMvisor Boot Menu will display, as shown in Figure 13.2. To make changes to the installation parameters, press the Tab key. The default parameters will show beneath the boot menu.

FIGURE 13.2
Installing ESXi Installable to local drives requires downloading the appropriate disk image (.iso) from VMware.

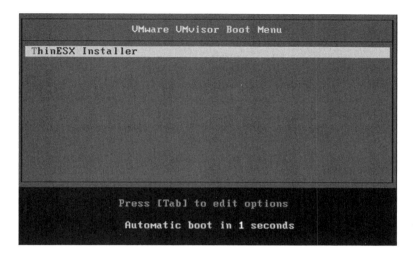

Once you accept the license agreement, you will have the opportunity to select the hard drive onto which you wish to install ESXi. The available logical disks will be listed as shown in Figure 13.3. The ESXi Installable requires local hard drives to be available for the installation. The local hard drives can be Serial ATA (SATA), SCSI, or Serial Attached SCSI (SAS) as long as they are connected to a controller that is listed on the ESXi compatibility guide. The size of the hard drives is irrelevant since enterprise deployments of VI3 will most commonly place all virtual machines, templates, and ISOs on a shared storage device. Keep that in mind when you are in the process of identifying hardware specifications for new servers that you intend to use as thin virtualization clients with ESXi Installable. Do not incur the expenses of large disk arrays for the local storage on ESXi hosts. The smallest hard drives available in a RAID1 configuration will provide ample room and redundancy for the installation of ESXi.

FIGURE 13.3
ESXi can be installed on SATA, SCSI, or SAS drives.

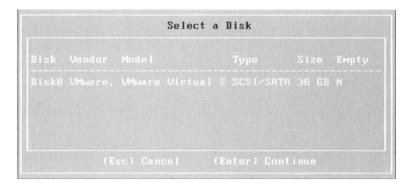

If the disk you select for the installation has existing data, you will receive a warning message about the data being overwritten with the new installation, as shown in Figure 13.4. Always be sure that answering yes to this prompt does not erase any critical data.

Once the installation process begins, it takes only a few minutes to load the thin hypervisor. Upon completion, the server will require a reboot and is configured by default to obtain an IP address via DHCP. Later in this chapter we'll discuss how to configure and manage ESXi.

FIGURE 13.4
Disks with existing data will be overwritten during the ESXi installation procedure.

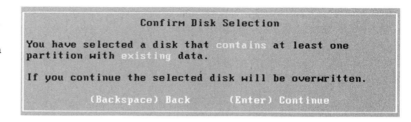

Perform the following steps to install ESXi:

1. Insert the ESXi Installable installation CD into the physical CD-ROM drive.

2. Boot the computer from the installation CD.

3. Allow the three-second Automatic boot timer to expire before beginning the installation of the ThinESX Installer option selected on the VMware VMvisor Boot Menu.

4. The setup process will load the VMware ISO and VMkernel components, as shown in Figure 13.5.

FIGURE 13.5
The VMware ISO will load the VMkernel components to begin the installation.

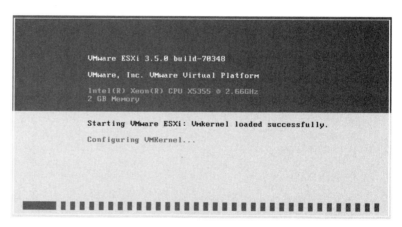

5. Once the components are loaded and the Welcome to the VMware ESXi 3.5.0 Installation screen is displayed, as shown in Figure 13.6, press Enter to perform the installation.

6. Press the F11 key to accept the license agreement and to continue the installation.

7. Select the appropriate disk onto which you will install ESXi and press the Enter key to continue.

8. If you receive a warning about existing data, press Enter to continue only after verifying that the data loss will not be of concern.

9. Press the F11 key to install.

FIGURE 13.6
Installing ESXi on a local disk.

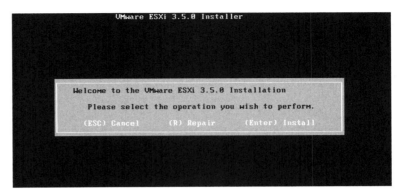

Deploying ESXi Embedded

ESXi Embedded refers to the original equipment manufacturer (OEM) installation of ESXi onto a persistent storage device inside the qualified hardware. This is an exciting option that will save administrators the time of performing any type of installation. The embedded hypervisor truly allows for the plug-and-play hardware-type atmosphere. You can see that major server manufacturers are banking on this idea because their server designs include an internal USB port. Perhaps eventually the ESXi hypervisor will move from USB flash drive on an internal port to some type of flash memory built right onto the motherboard.

ESXi ON INTERNAL USB

At the time of this writing, there were no manufacturers selling the ESXi embedded. However, there were reports of agreements with major vendors like Dell and HP that each company would have several products available in Q2 of 2008. In my work with the good folks at Dell, they assured me it was coming soon but that further tests and design work had to be completed to ensure the security of the USB flash device on the internal port. Dell, like other manufacturers, puts all server designs through rigorous tests, including earthquake tests. Until they are confident that the products will withstand these rigorous tests, they have opted not to simply place a USB flash disk inside the system without some type of locking mechanism to ensure its placement. Perhaps a solution will have been devised by the time the book is published.

The installation files for ESXi Embedded are not available for public download; however, ESXi is available for download. It is suggested that only the OEMs will have access to the files necessary for building the persistent storage devices with the thin hypervisor installed. In best estimation, OEMs will be provided with a .dd file or an image file that can be extracted to the storage devices. For those who have been given access to the .dd file, it is possible to use dd.exe or WinImage to extract the installation files to a USB flash drive. The result is a bootable image of ESXi embedded onto the device.

When you purchase a system with ESXi Embedded, you only need to rack the server, connect the networking cables, and power on. The ESXi embedded on the persistent storage will obtain an IP address from a DHCP server to provide immediate access via console, VI Client, or VirtualCenter.

The server set to run ESXi Embedded must be configured to boot from the appropriate device. Take, for example, a Dell server with a USB flash drive with ESXi Embedded connected to an internal (or external) USB port. To run the thin hypervisor, the server must be configured to boot from the USB device. Figure 13.7 shows the BIOS of a Dell PowerEdge server.

FIGURE 13.7
To run the thin hypervisor of ESXi Embedded, the server must be configured to boot from the persistent storage device.

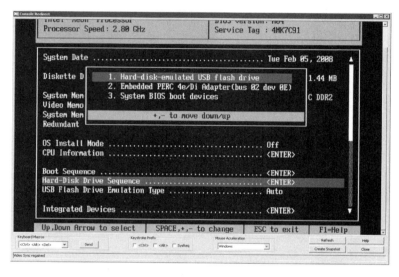

While this is just an example of using ESXi Embedded, the ideas and principles will be the same even when the system manufacturers finally get around to shipping the product.

DELL AND ESXI

Based on my conversations and work with Dell in writing this chapter, Dell will add an internal USB connection in the next generation of the Dell PowerEdge server line.

At the time of this writing, ESXi Embedded was still not an option for purchase from the Dell website. Again, according to Dell the release of the product as an embedded feature will not occur until Dell has completed a period of rigorous testing that ensures system functionality and performance in even the harshest of conditions.

Managing ESXi

ESXi can be managed in several ways, including from the local console, VirtualCenter, VI Client, or a remote command-line interface. VirtualCenter will be the most common choice in order to have the opportunity to manage a mixture of ESX Server 3.5 versions within the same VirtualCenter.

ESXi Console

Once the ESXi installation is complete or if your new ESXi Embedded server has just arrived, you can use the local console to perform some limited configuration of the host. Each of the following sections details the ESXi management tasks available from the console.

CONFIGURE ROOT PASSWORD

By pressing the F2 key, you'll be offered the Customize System screen where configuration takes place. The first option in the list is the Configure Root Password option, shown in Figure 13.8. Pressing the Enter key will open the Configure Root Password box, shown in Figure 13.9.

FIGURE 13.8
ESXi provides a simple-to-use interface for customizing the installation.

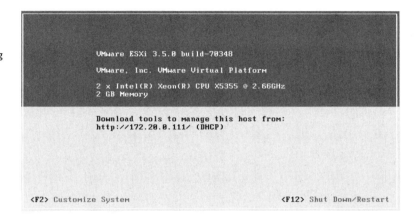

FIGURE 13.9
Change the root password upon first boot of the ESXi thin hypervisor.

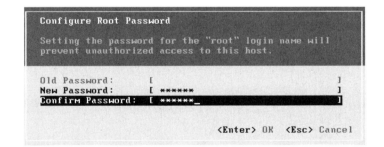

CONFIGURE LOCKDOWN MODE

ESXi includes a configuration option that allows administrators to prevent direct access to an ESXi host via the VI Client application under the context of the root user. Access directly to the system using the VI Client is still permissible with nonroot user accounts. If no other accounts except the root exist, then the only way to manage the server would be remotely from VirtualCenter or the Remote Command-Line Interface (RCLI). Figures 13.10 and 13.11 show the Configure Lockdown Mode option and the enabling of the option.

FIGURE 13.10
Lockdown mode prevents root user access to the system via the VI Client.

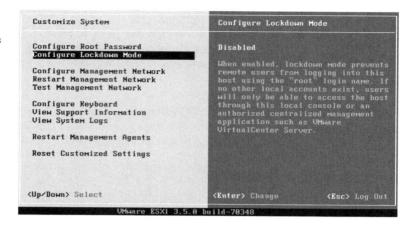

FIGURE 13.11
Lockdown mode can be enabled and disabled as needed to support server management.

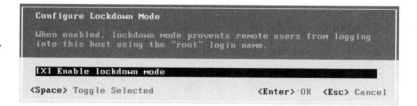

CONFIGURE MANAGEMENT NETWORK

Selecting the Configure Network Management option, shown in Figure 13.12, offers a set of options for configuring network communications like physical NIC assignment, IP address, subnet mask, DNS, and so forth.

FIGURE 13.12
The network communication parameters of an ESXi host can be altered as part of the post-installation configuration.

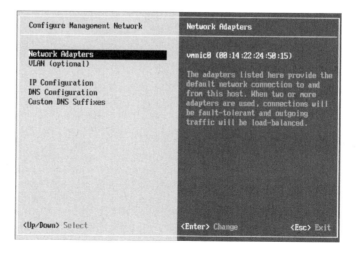

The Configure Network Management option provides a submenu for each of the following:

Network Adapters   As shown in Figure 13.13, the Network Adapters screen allows you to select which network adapter in the computer should be used for host management. Multiple adapters can be selected for providing redundancy and load balancing to the host management traffic.

FIGURE 13.13
One or more network adapters can be selected for the host's default management network.

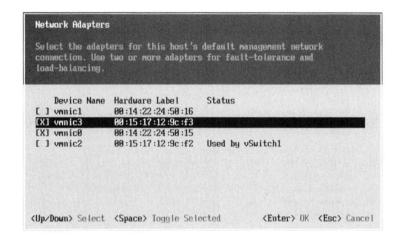

VLAN   As shown in Figure 13.14, VLAN configuration is possible on ESXi. VLANs are used to segment off the management traffic when a single physical network is used for multiple data transmission types. The configuration window accepts VLAN IDs in the range of 1 to 4094, or use 4095 for access to all VLANs.

FIGURE 13.14
VLANs can provide traffic segmentation for the host's management network.

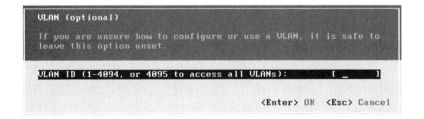

IP Configuration   As shown in Figure 13.15, IP Configuration allows for the configuration of a static IP address, a subnet mask, and a default gateway. The default is for the host to obtain an IP address via DHCP. It is always best to provide enterprise servers, especially ESX Server hosts, with a static IP address.

DNS Configuration   As shown in Figure 13.16, DNS Configuration allows for the configuration of primary and alternate DNS servers as well as the hostname for the ESXi host. As with ESX Server 3.5, hostname resolution is an important part of the host's functionality. Therefore, a corresponding Host (A) record should be created in DNS with the name of each ESXi host referencing the IP address as assigned in the IP Configuration page.

FIGURE 13.15
ESXi hosts can be configured with static IP address information or remain set to the default of obtaining an IP address from DHCP.

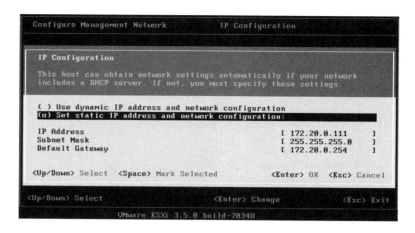

FIGURE 13.16
ESXi hosts can be configured with multiple DNS servers and a unique hostname to be referenced by other servers in the VirtualCenter inventory.

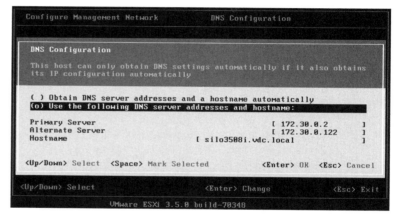

Custom DNS Suffixes As shown in Figure 13.17, Custom DNS Suffixes allows for the configuration of DNS suffixes that are appended when a host uses short, unqualified names. Multiple suffixes can be listed by separating each suffix with a space. For example, if the DNS suffixes include vdc.local, learn.vmw, and vdc.vmw, and the host references the unqualified name of Silo108, the suffixes will be appended until a name can be resolved. The first name tried will be silo108.vdc.local, followed by silo108.learn.vmw if no response is returned from the first suffix attempt, followed by silo108.vdc.vmw if no response is returned from either of the first two suffix attempts.

FIGURE 13.17
DNS suffixes allow hosts to reference other systems using short, unqualified names.

ESXi AND DHCP

If an ESXi host is connected to a physical network that does not have a DHCP server to deliver, the server will assign itself the IP address of 169.254.0.1 with a 255.255.0.0 subnet mask.

RESTART MANAGEMENT NETWORK

The option to restart the management network forces a DHCP lease renewal. If the ESXi host is configured to obtain an IP address via DHCP, this option could force a change in the IP address, resulting in loss of access to the host because the DNS entry for the host would retain the old IP address configuration. For this reason alone, it is a good idea, and strongly suggested, that ESX Server hosts be manually configured with static IP address information. Since ESX Servers do not perform a dynamic update of DNS records, administrators will need to carefully manage the Host (A) records of each ESX Server to ensure they are accurate in the event of an IP address change.

TEST MANAGEMENT NETWORK

The Test Management Network option in the Customize System menu list is an excellent troubleshooting utility. It can be used to test IP connectivity and name resolution. The option uses the ping utility against the default gateway, the primary DNS server, and the alternate DNS server. In addition, it will attempt to resolve your hostname. Figures 13.18 and 13.19 show the test configuration and the test operation.

FIGURE 13.18
ESXi has a built-in utility for troubleshooting IP connectivity and name resolution.

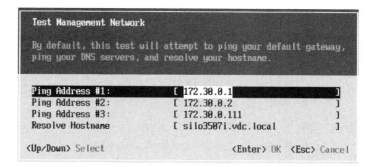

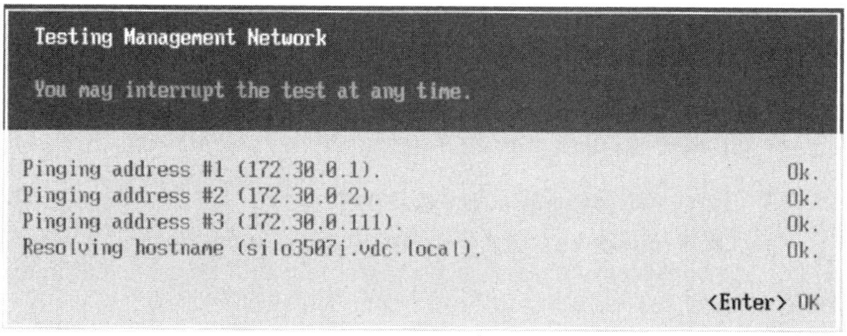

FIGURE 13.19
Using the Test Management Network can be extremely helpful in determining if problems stem from host configuration issues or external configuration issues.

This tool will be helpful when you are having problems connecting to an ESXi host, as it allows you to rule out internal configuration issues. As you have probably seen, the configuration of ESXi is minimal already, so this tool will help you identify local versus external configuration issues. In the case when all tests came back with an OK status, it would be more likely that any type of connectivity problem is coming from an external configuration problem, not a problem with the ESXi host upon which this test was performed. The test results identify that IP connectivity is good, the DNS server is responding, and that name resolution for the local host hostname is working.

Configure Keyboard

As the name suggests, this option allows for the configuration of the keyboard. The options include:

◆ Default

◆ French

◆ German

◆ Japanese

◆ Russian

View Support Information

The View Support Information option provides information about:

◆ Serial number

◆ License serial number

◆ SSL Thumbprint (SHA1)

View System Logs

The View System Logs option provides a look at several logs, including:

◆ Messages (press 1)

◆ Config (press 2)

◆ Management agent (hostd) (press 3)

◆ VirtualCenter agent (vpxa) (press 4)

Once you have selected a particular log to view, press the H key to get help on how to navigate through the logs. As shown in Figure 13.20, the logs (hostd is shown) are plain text and human-readable logs but certainly require some experience in going through them. The value in these logs is in knowing how to get to them and how to navigate them to troubleshoot when problems arise. It is unlikely that you will regularly visit these logs on a voluntary basis.

Restart Management Agents

This option, as the name suggests, allows for restarting the management agents (hostd) that govern the remote management and control of the ESXi thin hypervisor. Executing a restart of hostd will cause a temporary loss of access to the hypervisor.

Reset Customized Settings

This option reverts back to all defaults that exist just after the installation of ESXi. This includes resetting IP configuration and the root password and the unregistering of virtual machines.

s
[2008-02-05 11:54:07.868 'VersionValidator' 16384 info] Management restriction c
hecks enabled
[2008-02-05 11:54:07.868 'Solo' 16384 info] Plugin started
[2008-02-05 11:54:07.868 'HttpSvc' 16384 info] Http Service started: Server UNIX
(/var/run/vmware/proxy-webserver)
[2008-02-05 11:54:07.868 'DebugBrowser' 16384 info] Http Service started: Server
UNIX(/var/run/vmware/proxy-mob)
[2008-02-05 11:54:07.868 'Statssvc' 16384 info] Starting statssvc plugin
[2008-02-05 11:54:07.869 'SupportsvcPlugin' 16384 info] PlmCollector initialized
[2008-02-05 11:54:07.869 'SupportsvcPlugin' 16384 info] Starting regular Collect
or
[2008-02-05 11:54:07.869 'SupportsvcPlugin' 16384 info] Plugin started
[2008-02-05 11:54:07.869 'VcsvcPlugin' 16384 info] Plugin started
[2008-02-05 11:54:07.869 'VdisksvcPlugin' 16384 info] Plugin started
[2008-02-05 11:54:07.871 'Vimsvc' 16384 info] Started vimsvc plugin
[2008-02-05 11:54:07.871 'Vmsvc' 16384 info] VMServices Plugin started
[2008-02-05 11:54:07.871 'App' 16384 info] Closing stdout and stderr.
[2008-02-05 11:54:07.871 'App' 16384 info] Product state has been set: esx, VMwa
re ESX Server
[2008-02-05 11:54:07.871 'App' 16384 info]
[2008-02-05 11:54:07.872 'App' 16384 warning] Error logging contents of Map File
: FileIO error: Could not find file : /proc/self/maps
[2008-02-05 11:54:07.872 'Memory checker' 16384 info] Check resources every 0 se
<Q> Quit </> RegExp Search <H> Help

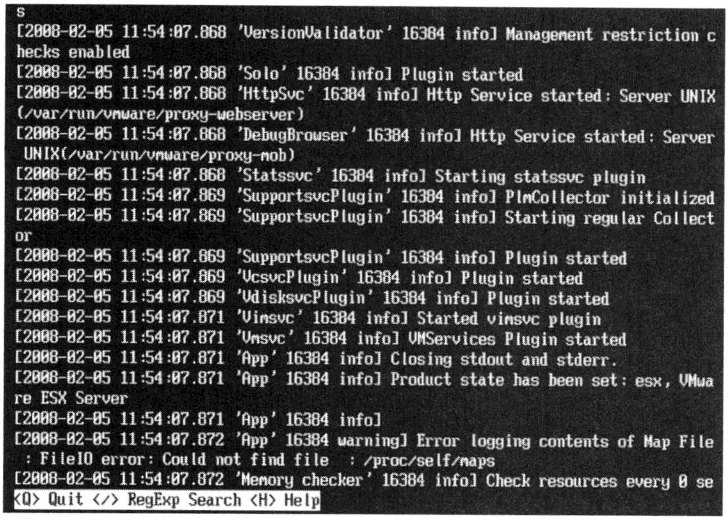

FIGURE 13.20
Logs on ESXi are accessible and can be reviewed for troubleshooting or maintenance.

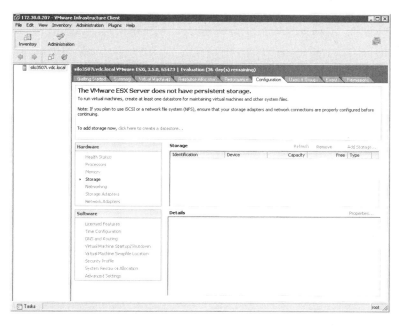

VI Client

Once your initial configuration from the console is completed, your management tasks will shift to using the more user-friendly VI Client. The VI Client can be used to connect directly to an ESXi host, as shown in Figure 13.21, but the more common method will be to connect through VirtualCenter (coming up next).

172.30.0.207 - VMware Infrastructure Client
File Edit View Inventory Administration Plugins Help
Inventory
Administration
silo3507i.vdc.local
silo3507i.vdc.local VMware ESXi, 3.5.0, 65423 | Evaluation (36 day(s) remaining)
Configuration
The VMware ESX Server does not have persistent storage.
To run virtual machines, create at least one datastore for maintaining virtual machines and other system files.
Note: If you plan to use iSCSI or a network file system (NFS), ensure that your storage adapters and network connections are properly configured before continuing.
To add storage now, click here to create a datastore...
Hardware
Storage
Software
Storage
Identification
Device
Capacity
Free
Type
Details
Tasks
root

FIGURE 13.21
The VI Client can be used to connect directly to an ESXi host.

Notice in Figure 13.21 that the host is presented with a configuration issue stating that the ESX Server does not have persistent storage. If a server is set up to run the ESXi Embedded version but still contains local hard drives, remember that the local drives are not used during the installation procedure and remain empty. The server in Figure 13.21 is running ESXi Embedded. In Figure 13.22, the VI Client is connected to a server running ESXi Installable and does not show that error. You can see in the figure that a local storage device is configured. Remember in the previous section, on deploying ESXi Installable, that the installation process required the selection of a hard disk. Therefore, a storage device is already configured.

FIGURE 13.22
ESXi Installable hosts have storage devices configured as part of the installation process.

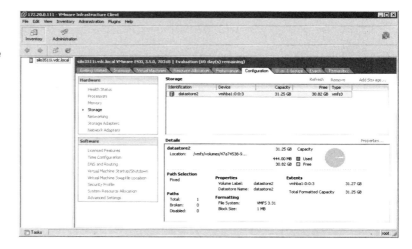

VI CLIENT TO HOST OR VI CLIENT TO VIRTUALCENTER

While the VI Client will be used predominantly for connecting to VirtualCenter and managing hosts from a centralized interface, it is important to note that connecting through VirtualCenter does not provide the Users & Groups tab that allows for the creation of local users and groups on the ESX host.

VirtualCenter 2.5

As noted in the previous section, VI Client connections to VirtualCenter will be the most common means of managing an ESXi host. All in all, your management of an ESXi host should be no different than the management of an ESX Server 3.5 host. The architectures may differ, but together in the same datacenters and clusters they will act no differently. Figure 13.23 displays the Hosts tab of a datacenter in the VirtualCenter inventory. With the exception of the naming scheme, it is not possible to tell which server is running the ESXi product as opposed to ESX Server 3.5.

One distinct difference that can be seen when managing an ESXi host is the existence of the Health Status option from the Hardware menu on the Configuration tab. Figure 13.24 shows the hardware monitoring data that is discovered as part of the health status of an ESXi host.

Once added to a VirtualCenter inventory, an ESXi host is capable of all the same enterprise features of VMotion, DRS, and HA. These thin hypervisor hosts are susceptible to all the feature constraints as any other host. Networking requirements, storage requirements, and so forth must all be met to support these features.

FIGURE 13.23
ESXi hosts are managed right alongside the ESX Server 3.5 hosts in VirtualCenter.

FIGURE 13.24
ESXi hosts have an additional menu item for monitoring the hardware health status.

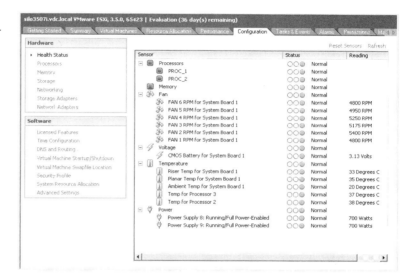

Remote Command-Line Interface (RCLI)

With no console operating system to connect to, ESXi would seem to be limited in its management capability. However, for those environments with many servers whose administrators refuse to perform tasks repeatedly through the VI Client, VMware now provides a remote command-line interface for host management. This tool is available in two formats:

◆ Remote CLI installable package for installation on Windows or Linux

◆ Remote CLI virtual machine appliance

Both tools can be downloaded from the VMware website. The Remote CLIs support a long list of commands for managing ESX Server hosts. The tools are based on the VMware Infrastructure (VI) Perl Toolkit, which relies on Perl and a few other libraries.

CLI AND SCRIPTING

Before we go any further with the command-line tools and scripting, I want to be sure that you are aware of the various security concerns and implications. All of these commands will require the submission of a user name and password. Depending on how you implement the command, the password might be presented on the screen in clear text or it might be stored in a file in clear text. As you look at configuring ESX Server, hosts using scripts and command-line tools ensure that you have adopted the appropriate security methods to prevent improper uses, ranging from determining passwords to high-level accounts. For example, if you create configuration files, limit the permissions (even read permissions) to ensure that unauthorized users cannot read the files and thereby discover passwords to elevated accounts.

In addition to these security concerns, let me address another issue for those who might be new to the idea of scripting. *You do not have to do this.* While it is certainly true that scripting can save time, keep in mind that it is only true for those who have achieved a high level of proficiency in the scripting methods and only in those environments with a significant number of hosts to manage. The remaining portions of this chapter will most likely come across as a time-consuming effort for those unfamiliar with scripting technologies. So maybe you are asking yourself, "When should I use scripting?" The answer varies, but you can apply some common sense to the situation by considering the following:

◆   What would be the length of your learning curve to perform scripting versus just performing the task through the VI Client? If you only have a handful of hosts, it might be quicker to use the VI Client than it would be to figure out how to script from the ground up.

◆   How often will you be performing this task? If you have ten hosts with six network adapters that are all used in virtual switches and there is no intention of adding more adapters and configuring more virtual switches, then creating a script to add virtual switches to the ten hosts would be a waste of time. On top of that, if you are only adding one or two new ESX Server hosts per year, it might be less administratively cumbersome to manually configure each new server with the necessary virtual switches. On the other hand, if you were adding one or two new ESX Server hosts per week, then generating a script to create virtual switches might make the learning curve worth it.

In conclusion, I know that many of you who are getting into virtualization management and have long been Windows administrators may not be experts in the realm of scripting, especially in Perl. So understand that scripting is an option that is beneficial in some, but not necessarily all, cases. It is up to you to decide whether to learn to script or whether to use the graphical tools, even if they do incur extra time. VMware has done an excellent job in structuring the VI3 suite of products around the idea that scripting is an option, not a mandate.

For each of the remote CLI commands, the following options are available as part of the command execution:

--config   Specifies the location of the configuration to be used, which must be a location accessible from the current directory. The equivalent variable used in a configuration file is VI_CONFIG.

--password   Specifies the password for use in combination with the --username parameter. If the username and password are not specified in the execution string, you will be prompted for them. The equivalent variable used in a configuration file is VI_PASSWORD.

--portnumber   Used to specify the port used to connect to the ESX Server host. The default port is 443. The equivalent variable used in a configuration file is VI_PORTNUMBER.

--protocol   Used to specify the protocol used to connect to the ESX Server host. The default protocol is HTTPS. The equivalent variable used in a configuration file is VI_PROTOCOL.

--server   Used to identify the server against which the command should be run. The default is the localhost. The equivalent variable used in a configuration file is VI_SERVER.

--servicepath   Used to identify the service path to connect to the ESX Server host. The default is /sdk/webService. The equivalent variable used in a configuration file is VI_SERVICEPATH.

--sessionfile   Used to reference a saved session file. The equivalent variable used in a configuration file is VI_SESSIONFILE.

--url   Used to connect to the VI SDK specified in the URL. The equivalent variable used in a configuration file is VI_URL.

--username   Used to specify the username for the authentication context. If the username and password are not specified, you will be prompted for them. The equivalent variable used in a configuration file is VI_USERNAME.

--verbose   Used to provide more detail in the debugging information. The equivalent variable used in a configuration file is VI_VERBOSE.

--version   Used to display version information.

USING --*HELP*

For any of the commands listed below, you can type the command followed by --help to get a look at the parameters that can be passed in.

Here is a list of commands with explanations and samples:

resxtop   This command provides real-time monitoring of ESX CPU, memory, disk, and network adapter utilization. To run resxtop on an ESX host with an IP address of 172.30.0.105, use the following command:

```
resxtop -server 172.30.0.105 -username root
```

Once the tool is running, use the C, M, D, and N keys to switch between CPU, memory, disk, and network counters, respectively. Figures 13.25 and 13.26 show the resxtop output for CPU and memory.

FIGURE 13.25
The resxtop Remote CLI command provides CPU utilization data.

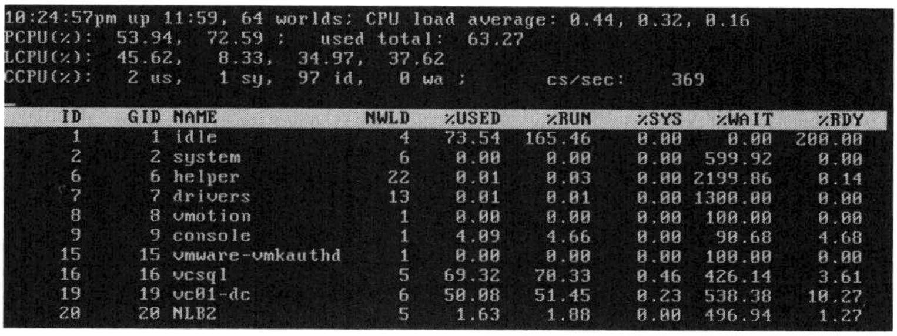

```
10:24:57pm up 11:59, 64 worlds; CPU load average: 0.44, 0.32, 0.16
PCPU(%):  53.94,  72.59 ;   used total:  63.27
LCPU(%):  45.62,   8.33,  34.97,  37.62
CCPU(%):   2 us,   1 sy,  97 id,   0 wa ;       cs/sec:     369

   ID   GID NAME            NWLD   %USED   %RUN   %SYS    %WAIT   %RDY
    1     1 idle               4   73.54 165.46   0.00     0.00 200.00
    2     2 system             6    0.00   0.00   0.00   599.92   0.00
    6     6 helper            22    0.01   0.03   0.00  2199.86   0.14
    7     7 drivers           13    0.01   0.01   0.00  1300.00   0.00
    8     8 vmotion            1    0.00   0.00   0.00   100.00   0.00
    9     9 console            1    4.89   4.66   0.00    90.68   4.68
   15    15 vmware-vmkauthd    1    0.00   0.00   0.00   100.00   0.00
   16    16 vcsql              5   69.32  70.33   0.46   426.14   3.61
   19    19 vc01-dc            6   50.08  51.45   0.23   538.38  10.27
   20    20 NLB2               5    1.63   1.88   0.00   496.94   1.27
```

svmotion   This command performs the storage migration process of moving the disk files of a virtual machine to a different LUN.

vicfg-advcfg   This option is not recommended for customer use. This command is typically used only under the guidance of VMware technical support.

FIGURE 13.26
Pressing the M key
makes resxtop dis-
play data regarding
memory utilization.

```
 2:20:12pm up 6 days  3:24, 134 worlds; MEM overcommit avg: 0.00, 0.00, 0.00
PMEM   /MB:   6141   total:    314    vmk,    480 other,    5346 free
VMKMEM/MB:   5944 managed:    356 minfree,    901 rsvd,    4888 ursvd, high state
PSHARE/MB:    205 shared,     67 common:    138 saving
SWAP   /MB:      0   curr,      0 target:                 0.00 r/s,    0.00 w/s
MEMCTL/MB:      0   curr,      0 target,    819 max

   GID NAME             NWLD      MEMSZ       SZTGT       TCHD %ACTV %ACTVS %ACTVF %A
    14 init.1063           1       4.06        4.06        0.55     0      0      0
   106 busybox.1149        1       4.06        4.06        0.56     0      0      0
   108 vmklogger.1151      1       3.56        3.56        0.48     0      0      0
   298 busybox.1350        1       4.09        4.09        0.62     0      0      0
   303 busybox.1355        1       4.06        4.06        0.58     0      0      0
   312 sh.1364             1       4.18        4.18        0.63     0      0      0
   322 hostd.1374         15      84.10       84.10       58.49     0      0      0
   333 slpd.1385           1       4.02        4.02        0.89     0      0      0
   345 sfcbd.1400          1       7.28        7.28        2.09     0      0      0
   347 sfcbd.1402          1       7.24        7.24        2.26     0      0      0
   348 sfcbd.1403          1       7.24        7.24        1.80     0      0      0
   359 wsmand.1414         3       8.70        8.70        1.40     0      0      0
   365 sh.1422             1       4.18        4.18        0.61     0      0      0
   395 sh.1452             1       4.18        4.18        0.63     0      0      0
   404 sfcbd.1461          1       7.49        7.49        2.96     0      0      0
   406 sfcbd.1463          2       9.45        9.45        3.36     0      0      0
   410 vpxa.1469          22      60.05       60.05       27.81     0      0      0
```

vicfg-cfgbackup   This tool allows for the backup and restore of the configuration data of an ESXi host.

vicfg-dumppart   This tool allows for querying, setting, and scanning the diagnostic data "dumps" of an ESX Server host.

vicfg-mpath   This tool allows for the configuration of multipathing settings for fibre channel or iSCSI LUNs.

vicfg-nas   This tool provides settings and parameters for managing NFS access for your ESX Server host. For example, the following syntax adds a NAS datastore named NFSDS to a server named silo107.vdc.local. The NFS server is named nfs1.vdc.local and has a directory named /iso that is shared:

```
vicfg-nas --server silo107.vdc.local --username root
   --password -a -o nfs1.vdc.local -s /iso NFSDS
```

vicfg-nics   This tool provides management of physical network adapters. Figure 13.27 shows a simple listing of all network adapters on a server with an IP address of 172.30.01 using the following syntax:

```
vicfg-nics --server 172.30.0.105 --username root --list
```

FIGURE 13.27
The vicfg-nics tool
can identify details
about network adapters.

vicfg-ntp   This command allows for the configuration of NTP servers for the 3i hosts.

vicfg-rescan   This command executes a remote HBA rescan.

vicfg-route   This command allows for setting the IP address of the default gateway for the VMkernel.

vicfg-snmp This command allows for the configuration of SNMP for ESX Server hosts.

vicfg-syslog This command allows for the specification of the remote syslog server for an ESX Server host.

vicfg-vmhbadevs This command provides information regarding the LUNs available to an ESX Server host.

vicfg-vmknic This command allows for the configuration of VMkernel network adapters.

vicfg-vswitch This command allows for adding, removing, and modifying virtual switches and virtual switch properties. Review the following examples. Keep in mind that the parameters of --server and --username (and then a password) would be required to run the commands against a remote host.

To add a new virtual switch named vSwitch3:

```
vicfg-vswitch --add vSwitch3
```

To add a new port group named TestVMs to vSwitch3:

```
vicfg-vswitch --add-pg="TestVMs" vSwitch3
```

To list all the virtual switches:

```
vicfg-vswitch -l
```

vihostupdate This command allows for the management of software updates on an ESXi host. It provides the necessary parameters for applying software updates and monitoring installed updates.

ESX UPDATES

While the command-line tool might be attractive to the hard-core command-line junkie types, software updates and patch monitoring are best performed using the new VMware Update Manager that is built into VirtualCenter 2.5.

---

vifs This command allows copying, removing, getting, and putting on files and directories.

vmkfstools This command allows for the creation and manipulation of file systems (VMFS), virtual disks (VMDK), logical volumes, and physical storage devices.

All of these commands can be combined with the use of a configuration file to simplify the scripting syntax. A configuration file is a file accessible by the system where the remote command line is being generated (Windows host, Linux host, or virtual appliance) that allows for commonly used parameters to be stored in a file and then referenced as part of the CLI command execution. A configuration file for a host named silo101.vdc.local would include information as shown here:

```
VI_SERVER=silo101.vdc.local
VI_USERNAME= root
VI_PASSWORD = learnvmware
```

This configuration file is then called in during the execution of the command as shown in the following syntax. This command would create an NFS datastore named NFS_ISOs on the host `silo101.vdc.local` that points to an `/iso` directory on an NFS server named `nfsserver .learn.vmw`:

```
vicfg-nas --config <path to config file> -a -o
    nfsserver.learn.vmw -s /iso NFS_ISOs
```

The Bottom Line

Understand the architecture of ESXi.   ESXi presents a radical change not just to the virtualization world but to the system manufacturers that want to be part of virtualization evolution. By removing the local management component, the Service Console, ESXi presents a thin yet highly functional hypervisor on which virtual machines can run. But don't mistake thin for meaning not as feature rich. ESXi supports all the same enterprise features of VMotion, DRS, and HA that have made VMware ESX the number-one choice for the foundation of virtualization platforms around the world.

> **Master It**   You manage a datacenter that experiences rapid growth. You need to identify a way to introduce new hardware resources into the virtual infrastructure with minimal administrative effort and maximum security.

Deploy ESXi Installable.   ESXi Installable provides existing VI3 licensees with the ability to shift their infrastructures to the new thin hypervisor architecture. The installation files can be downloaded as part of the existing license agreement without any penalty or additional cost. ESXi Installable installs onto local disk drives.

> **Master It**   You manage a datacenter with five existing ESX Server 3.5 hosts. You wish to restructure the datacenter to use the thin hypervisor architecture of ESXi.

Deploy ESXi Embedded.   ESXi Embedded, like ESXi Installable, is a thin hypervisor architecture with no reliance on a console operating system; however, the hypervisor runs from an embedded storage module on the host. System manufacturers like Dell offer next-generation products that include internal storage functionality for running ESXi Embedded.

> **Master It**   You want to construct a virtual infrastructure on physical servers without local storage devices. You want the CPU and memory of each server to be allocated to a VMware cluster for supporting HA and DRS.

Manage ESXi.   Managing ESXi can be done using the console of the system, the VI Client connected directly to the server, the VI Client connected to VirtualCenter, or from a command line using the remote CLI tools. The remote CLI tools can be deployed on a Windows host, Linux host, or from within a downloadable virtual appliance. All are available from the VMware website.

> **Master It**   You have deployed four servers running ESXi. You need to configure them into a cluster that supports DRS and HA.

> **Master It**   You have 30 ESXi hosts to which you need to add a new virtual switch. Your administrative desktop runs Windows XP Professional.

Appendix A

The Bottom Line

Each of The Bottom Line sections in the chapters suggest exercises to deepen skills and understanding. Sometimes there is only one possible solution, but often you are encouraged to use your skills and creativity to create something that builds on what you know and lets you explore one of many possible solutions.

Chapter 1: Introducing VMware Infrastructure 3

Identify the role of each product in the VI3 suite. Now that you've been introduced to the products included in the VMware Infrastructure 3 suite, we can begin discussing the technical details, best practices, and how-tos that will make your life as a virtual infrastructure administrator a whole lot easier. This chapter has shown that each of the products in the VI3 suite plays an integral part in the overall process of creating, managing, and maintaining a virtual enterprise. Figure 1.9 highlights the VI3 product suite and how it integrates and interoperates to provide a robust set of tools upon which a scalable, reliable, and redundant virtual enterprise can be built.

The next chapter will begin a start-to-finish look at designing, implementing, managing, monitoring, and troubleshooting a virtual enterprise built on VI3. I'll dive into much greater detail on each of the products I introduced in this chapter. This introduction should provide you with a solid foundation so we can discuss the different products beginning with the next chapter. You can use this introduction as a reference throughout the remaining chapters if you want to refresh your base knowledge for each of the products in the suite.

Master It You want to centralize the management of ESX Server hosts and all virtual machines.

Solution Install VMware VirtualCenter Server and add each host to the VirtualCenter inventory.

Master It You want to minimize the occurrence of system downtime during periods of planned maintenance.

Solution Implement VMware VMotion for the hot migration of running virtual machines.

Master It You want to provide an automated method of maintaining fairness and balance of resource utilization.

Solution Implement a cluster of ESX Server hosts and enable the Distributed Resource Scheduler (DRS) feature.

Master It You want to provide an automated restart of virtual machines when an ESX Server fails.

Solution   Implement a cluster of ESX Server hosts and enable the High Availability (HA) feature.

Master It   You want to institute a method of providing disaster recovery and business continuity in the event of virtual machine failure.

Solution   Install VMware Consolidated Backup with a supported third-party backup application. Construct a backup plan based on company policy.

FIGURE 1.9
The products in the VMware Infrastructure suite work together to provide a scalable, robust, and reliable framework for creating, managing, and monitoring a virtual enterprise.

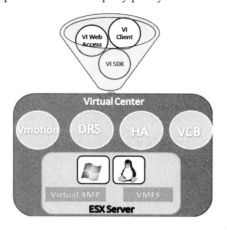

Chapter 2: Planning and Installing ESX Server

Understand ESX Server compatibility requirements.   ESX Server has tight restrictions with regard to supported hardware. VMware is the only company that provides hardware drivers for the VMware-supported hardware. The compatibility lists provided by VMware are living documents that will continue to change as new hardware is approved.

Master It   You want to reconfigure an existing physical server as an ESX Server host.

Solution   Review the ESX Server Systems Compatibility Guide to identify if the existing server is compatible with ESX Server.

Plan an ESX Server deployment.   A great deal of detailed planning and projecting is required to deploy a scalable virtual infrastructure.

Master It   Your company wants to achieve the greatest ROI while maintaining high performance and availability levels. You need to produce a report that details the virtual infrastructure hardware specifications and costs.

Solution   For the greatest ROI, the server specifications for each ESX Server host should maximize the number of cores per slot as well as the speed of each core. Physical memory should be maximized to provide ample room for current, future, and failover virtual machines.

Install ESX Server.   ESX Server is a fairly straightforward installation process with only one or two details to pay close attention to.

Master It   You need to reinstall ESX Server and want to be sure that inadvertent data loss cannot occur. The ESX Server will boot from local disks.

Solution   Disconnect the new ESX Server from the storage area networks to prevent the discovery of existing LUNs that might contain data.

Perform postinstallation configuration.   Once the installation of ESX Server is complete the configuration can be tweaked to meet the needs of the organization.

Master It   After installing ESX Server, the web-based management page is returning a "page not found" error.

Solution   Use the `esxcfg-nics` and `esxcfg-vswitch` commands to identify and edit the Service Console NIC association.

Master It   Your department heads have defined a company policy mandating the installation of antivirus software into the Service Console. Additional software might be installed at a later date.

Solution   Adjust the amount of RAM allocated to the Service Console. Increase it to the maximum value of 800MB.

Install the Virtual Infrastructure Client (VI Client).   The Virtual Infrastructure Client is a flexible management tool that allows management of an ESX Server host directly or by connecting to a VirtualCenter installation.

Master It   You want to manage the ESX Server hosts from your administrative workstation.

Solution   Install the VI Server host home page or the VirtualCenter home page.

Chapter 3: Creating and Managing Virtual Networks

Identify the components of virtual networking.   Virtual networking is made up of a combination of relationships that exist between the logical networking components created in the VMkernel of ESX Server and the physical network devices. The virtual machines are configured on vSwitches bound to physical network adapters that are connected to physical switches.

Create virtual switches and virtual switch port groups.   Virtual switches, ports, and port groups are the cornerstone of the virtual networking architecture. These virtual components provide the tools for connecting to the physical network components to allow communication between the virtual and physical environments.

Master It   Virtual machines need to communicate with physical servers on the production network.

Solution   Create a vSwitch with a virtual machine port group. Associate the vSwitch with a physical network adapter connected to a physical switch used for the production network.

Master It   Service console communication must occur on a dedicated management network.

Solution   Create a vSwitch with a Service Console port, assigning it a valid IP address for the management network. Associate the vSwitch with a physical network adapter connected to a physical switch for the management network.

Master It   A dedicated network has been implemented to support VMotion.

Solution Create a vSwitch with a VMkernel port, assigning it a valid IP address for the VMotion network. Associate the vSwitch with a physical network adapter connected to a physical switch for the VMotion network.

Master It A dedicated storage network has been implemented to support communication to iSCSI and NFS storage devices.

Solution Create a vSwitch with a VMkernel port, assigning it a valid IP address for the storage network. Associate the vSwitch with a physical network adapter connected to a physical switch for the storage network.

Create and manage NIC teams. NIC teams offer the opportunity for redundancy and load balancing of network traffic. NIC teams offer three load-balancing policies: port-based, source MAC-based, and IP hash-based load balancing.

Master It Virtual machines with one virtual network adapter must be capable of using multiple physical network adapters when connecting to multiple network destinations.

Solution Create a NIC team set to use the IP hash-based load balancing policy.

Master It A vSwitch configured with a NIC team needs to experience failback when a physical network adapter is repaired after failover.

Solution Configure the virtual switch Rolling Failover policy to No or create an explicit Failover Order.

Master It Bandwidth available on multiple physical network adapters must be accessible to a single virtual network adapter on a virtual machine.

Solution Connect the virtual machine to a vSwitch with a NIC team using multiple physical network adapters connected to the same physical switch. Configure the physical switch for link aggregation in static (manual) mode and configure the vSwitch to use the IP hash-based failover policy.

Master It Discovery time after a failover event on a NIC team needs to be minimized to prevent unnecessary delays.

Solution Configure the virtual switch's Notify Switches setting to Yes.

Create and manage virtual LANs (VLANs). The use of vLANs in a virtual networking architecture offers security, scalability, and communication efficiency.

Master It A vSwitch needs to be configured with two vLANs named VLAN101 and VLAN102.

Solution Create two virtual machine port groups with the appropriate VLAN IDs in the port group configuration.

Master It A vSwitch is configured with vLANs identical to those configured on the physical switch to which it is connected; however, traffic between the two switches is not functioning.

Solution Configure the physical switch port to which the vSwitch is connected as a trunk port.

Configure virtual switch security policies. Virtual switch security comes in a tight little package that includes three specific security settings that deal with identifying and processing traffic through a virtual switch. Promiscuous Mode, MAC Address Changes, and Forged Transmits each provides a securable vSwitch architecture, which ensures that only the right systems are sending and receiving traffic as expected.

Master It   A virtual machine with an installed intrusion detection system (IDS) needs to "sniff" the traffic passing through a vSwitch but the vSwitch is not configured to allow virtual machines to identify all traffic on the switch. You need to allow the functionality of the IDS while minimizing the security impact on the network.

Solution   Create a virtual machine port group on the switch. Set the Promiscuous Mode option to Accept and configure the virtual machine to use the new virtual machine port group.

Master It   An administrator of a Windows Server 2003 computer has changed the IP address of the guest operating system from the properties of the network adapter. The administrator now states that the Windows Server 2003 computer cannot communicate with requesting clients. You identify that the virtual machine port group to which the virtual machine is connected does not permit the vSwitch to send traffic when the effective and initial MAC addresses do not match.

Solution   On the virtual machine port group, set the Forged Transmits option to Accept.

Chapter 4: Creating and Managing Storage Devices

Differentiate among the various storage options available to VI3.   The storage options available for VMware Infrastructure 3 offer a wide range of performance and cost options. From the high-speed, high-cost fibre channel solution to the efficient, cost-effective iSCSI solution, to the slower, yet cheaper NAS/NFS, each solution has a place in any organization on a mission to virtualize.

Master It   Identify the characteristics of each storage technology and which VI3 features each supports.

Solution   Fibre channel, iSCSI, and NAS/NFS all allow for VMotion, DRS, and HA. Fibre channel is traditionally more expensive than iSCSI, which is more expensive than NAS/NFS.
Fibre channel and iSCSI storage support a boot from SAN configuration for ESX Server. Only fibre channel SANs support virtual machines configured as part of Microsoft Server Cluster.

Design a storage area network for VI3.   Once you've selected a storage technology, begin with the implementation of a dedicated storage network to optimize the transfer of storage traffic. A dedicated network for an iSCSI or NAS/NFS deployment will isolate the storage traffic from the e-mail, Internet, and file transfer traffic of the standard corporate LAN. From there, the LUN design for a fibre channel or iSCSI storage solution will work itself out in the form of the adaptive approach, predictive approach, or a hybrid of the two.

Master It   Identify use cases for the adaptive and predictive LUN design schemes.

Solution   The adaptive scheme is good for non-disk-intensive virtual machines and for minimizing administrative overhead. The predictive scheme involves more administrative effort for designing and creating the LUN strategy but offers a better performance opportunity for the VM.

Configure and manage fibre channel and iSCSI storage networks. Deploying a fibre channel SAN involves the development of a zoning and LUN masking strategy that ensures data security across ESX Server hosts while still providing for the needs of VMotion, HA, and DRS. The nodes in the fibre channel infrastructure are identified by 64-bit unique addresses called World Wide Names (WWNs). The iSCSI storage solution continues to use IP and MAC addresses for node identification and communication. ESX Server hosts use a four-part naming structure for accessing pools of storage on a SAN. Communication to an iSCSI storage device requires that both the Service Console and the VMkernel be able to communicate with the device.

Master It Identify the SAN LUNs that have been available to an ESX Server host.

Solution Use the Rescan link from the Storage node of the Configuration tab.

Configure and manage NAS storage. NAS storage offers a cheap solution for providing a shared storage pool for ESX Server hosts. Since the ESX Server host connects under the context of root, the NFS server must be configured with the no_root_squash parameter. A VMkernel port with access to the NAS server is required for an ESX Server host to function.

Master It Identify the ESX Server and NFS server requirements for using a NAS/NFS device.

Solution Configure the ESX Server with a VMkernel port. Configure the shared directory on the NFS server using the rw, no_root_squash, and sync parameters.

Create and manage VMFS volumes. VMFS is the proprietary, highly efficient file system used by ESX Server hosts for storing virtual machine files, ISO files, and templates. VMFS volumes can be extended to overcome the 2TB limitation, but the file sizes within the VMFS volume still keep a maximum of 2TB. VMFS is managed through the VI Client or from a series of command-line tools, including vmkfstools and esxcfg-vmhbadevs.

Master It Increase the size of a VMFS volume.

Solution Use the datastore properties page to add a non-VMFS LUN as an extent in the existing datastore.

Master It Balance the I/O of an ESX Server to use all existing hardware.

Solution Use the datastore properties page to manually set the active paths to each LUN so that all HBAs in the local ESX Server host are being utilized.

Chapter 5: Installing and Configuring VirtualCenter 2.0

Understand the features and role of VirtualCenter. If ESX Server 3.0 is the heart and soul of the virtual infrastructure, then VirtualCenter is the equivalent of the brain that keeps it all moving. VirtualCenter keeps the management capabilities within a defined framework and allows for controlled, detailed delegation of permissions assignment to meet a company's management needs. Access control strategies maintain the principle of least privilege, while VMotion and DRS maintain performance levels and resource fairness.

The VirtualCenter inventory will be a living entity in your virtual world; it will change regularly in response to the changing demands of the network and the consistently changing management practices of today's IT environments. There is no single way to design or implement a

VirtualCenter inventory, just as there is no single design implementation that will stand the test of time. Be open to change and to utilizing the dynamic nature of VirtualCenter to allow your infrastructure to be flexible, scalable, and secure.

Install and configure a VirtualCenter database.   VirtualCenter can use Oracle, SQL Server, or MSDE as its back-end database platform. Production environments will not be supported unless running on Oracle or SQL Server, reserving MSDE for nonproduction, demonstration, or evaluation purposes.

> **Master It**   Configure a SQL Server 2000 database to support VirtualCenter.
>
> **Solution**   Provide the SQL authenticated user account with membership in the db_owner database role for the VirtualCenter database.
>
> **Master It**   Configure a SQL 2005 database to support VirtualCenter.
>
> **Solution**   Provide the SQL authenticated user account with membership in the db_owner database role for the MSDB database and configure the account as the owner of the Virtual-Center database.

Install and configure a VirtualCenter Server.   VirtualCenter and the VirtualCenter License Server should be installed on the same server. For web access to VirtualCenter, the Apache Tomcat service can be installed and enabled.

Use VirtualCenter topology maps.   VirtualCenter topology maps offer a graphical display of the relationships that exist between hosts, virtual machines, datastores, and networks.

Plan a VirtualCenter deployment.   The VirtualCenter application is a proxy that acts on the ESX Server hosts that are in the inventory. Ensuring availability of the VirtualCenter application requires planning the redundancy and availability of the backend VirtualCenter database.

Chapter 6: Creating and Managing Virtual Machines

While company policy should ultimately drive virtual machine creation, there are best practices that can be followed to ensure performance and ease management. Virtual machines should always start as single virtual CPU systems with a minimum of two hard drives for separating the operating system from the user data.

Install a guest operating system.   Installing a guest operating system on a set of virtual machine hardware is similar to an installation on physical hardware and requires the same licensing considerations.

Install the VMware Tools.   The VMware Tools provide valuable additions to virtual machines and, although they are not installed by default, they should not be treated as an optional component. The VMware Tools install drivers and features for better memory management, optimized SCSI drivers, and enhanced video and mouse, among other benefits.

> **Master It**   Install the VMware Tools into a guest operating system.
>
> **Solution**   Use the Inventory menu to select the Install VMware Tools option.

Manage and modify a virtual machine.   A running virtual machine is limited in its modifications. Only a hard disk can be added to a running virtual machine, but CD/DVD-ROM drives, floppy drives, and network adapters can all be configured while the virtual machine is in a powered-on state.

Master It   Add a new network adapter to a virtual machine.

Solution   Turn off the virtual machine, and add the new network adapter through the virtual machine settings.

Master It   Add a new hard drive to a virtual machine.

Solution   Add the new hard drive through the virtual machine settings.

Create templates and deploy virtual machines.   Templates save administrators a great deal of time when deploying new virtual machines. Not only will templates reduce deployment times, but they also help reduce mistakes for new machines.

Master It   Prepare VirtualCenter for guest operating system customizations.

Solution   Extract the `sysprep.exe` and `setupcl.exe` files from the Windows Server 2003 CD to the directory `C:\Documents and Settings\All Users\Application Data\VMware\ VMware VirtualCenter\sysprep\svr2003`. Or use older versions of `sysprep` extracted to the appropriate subdirectory on the VirtualCenter server.

Chapter 7: Migrating and Importing Virtual Machines

Use the VirtualCenter 2.5 Consolidation feature.   The Consolidation feature of VirtualCenter 2.5 offers a simplified utility for creating a consolidation plan for small- and medium-sized businesses.

Master It   Your company has 27 physical servers that it has identified as virtualization candidates. You need to provide a documented effort for determining which systems are ideal candidates and where on the four-node cluster the virtual machine should run.

Solution   Use the VirtualCenter 2.5 Consolidation feature to monitor resource utilization on the 27 hosts. Once the confidence level is high, review the consolidation plan to see which servers are good candidates for virtual machines and which ESX Server hosts are best for running the converted system.

Perform physical-to-virtual migrations of running computers.   A hot migration, or hot clone, is the conversion of a running computer into a virtual machine. The hot cloning process is ideal for systems with relatively static data sets to ensure time-consistent conversions of the target computer.

Master It   Your company's business hours are 8:00 ~AM to 6:00 ~PM. There are four physical servers that function as domain controllers. You want to convert three of them to virtual machines running in your new three-node ESX Server cluster.

Solution   Perform a hot clone of the three domain controllers during nonbusiness hours. Once the conversion is complete, power off the physical computers and power on the virtual machines.

Master It   You have an existing virtual machine that has a 10GB C drive with only 1MB of space remaining. You need to provide an additional 20GB of space to the C drive.

Solution   Use the VMware Converter to perform a virtual-to-virtual migration. During the migration process, add 20GB of space to the C:\volume of the new virtual machine. After the migration, decommission the old virtual machine.

Perform physical-to-virtual migrations of computers that are powered off. A cold migration, or cold clone, is the conversion of a computer into a virtual machine while booted from the VMware Converter boot CD. The cold cloning process is ideal for systems that rely on frequently changing data sets, since the data cannot be modified during the conversion process.

Master It Your company has a computer that runs Microsoft SQL Server 2005. The IT staff has identified the system as a good target for becoming a virtual machine. You need to plan the conversion of the SQL Server 2005 computer into a virtual machine.

Solution Schedule a planned outage during nonbusiness hours to perform a cold clone of the SQL Server 2005 computer.

Import virtual appliances. The ability to import virtual appliances is a new feature of VirtualCenter 2.5. Appliances can be pulled directly from VMware or can be imported from a local file or URL.

Master It You need to deploy the remote command-line management tool as a virtual appliance in your VirtualCenter 2.5 inventory.

Solution Use the Import Virtual Appliance feature to import the virtual machine directly from the VMware website.

Chapter 8: Configuring and Managing Virtual Infrastructure Access Controls

Manage and maintain ESX Server permissions. Grant permissions to an ESX Server host with caution. Ideally, the number of individuals who have the ability to connect directly to an ESX Server host should be minimized.

Master It A group of administrators needs the ability to connect directly to an ESX Server host to perform management tasks.

Solution Create Service Console user accounts for each administrator who requires direct access.

Manage and maintain VirtualCenter permissions. The VirtualCenter permissions model builds off Windows-based user accounts and provides a great degree of flexibility, thus allowing virtual infrastructure administrators to maintain the principle of least privilege.

Master It Domain administrators from a Windows Active Directory domain should not be able to manage the virtual infrastructure.

Solution Create a new group in Active Directory and assign the new group the Administrator role at the Hosts & Clusters level in VirtualCenter. Remove the local Administrators group permission.

Master It Users with Windows-based groups need varying levels of access to the VirtualCenter inventory.

Solution Assign the Windows group to the appropriate VirtualCenter roles and assign the permission at the appropriate VirtualCenter inventory object.

Master It   A default VirtualCenter role provides too much permission for a new user who needs access to VirtualCenter objects.

Solution   Create a custom VirtualCenter role and assign the appropriate privileges.

Manage virtual machines using the web console.   The web console utility is solely for the management of virtual machines. It is a great tool for allowing virtual machine administrators management capabilities without using the full VI Client. Like the VI Client, however, the web console is an excellent means for connecting to a virtual machine when traditional in-band management tools are not available.

Master It   You need to access a virtual machine but the corporate firewall does not permit traffic on nonstandard ports.

Solution   Use the web access utility to connect to VirtualCenter and establish a remote console session.

Master It   You need to send a Windows administrator a link that will provide access to a virtual machine console. The administrator wants to establish this link as an Internet Explorer favorite.

Solution   Generate a remote console URL by connecting to the web access utility of VirtualCenter.

Chapter 9: Managing and Monitoring Resource Access

Manage virtual machine memory.   The VMkernel is active and aggressive in its management of memory utilization across the virtual machines.

Master It   A virtual machine needs to be guaranteed 1GB of RAM.

Solution   Configure the virtual machine with a 1GB reservation.

Master It   A virtual machine should never exceed 2GB of physical memory.

Solution   Configure the virtual machine with a 2GB limit.

Manage virtual machine CPU allocation.   The VMkernel works actively to monitor, schedule, and migrate data across CPUs.

Master It   A virtual machine must be guaranteed 1000MHz of CPU.

Solution   Configure the virtual machine with 1000MHz of CPU.

Create and manage resource pools.   Resource pools portion CPU and memory from a host or cluster to establish resource limits for pools of virtual machines.

Master It   A resource pool needs to be able to exceed its reservation to provide for additional resource guarantees to virtual machines within the pool.

Solution   Configure the resource pool with an expandable reservation.

Configure and execute VMotion.   VMotion technology is a unique feature of VMware Infrastructure 3 (VI3) that allows a running virtual machine to be moved between hosts.

Master It   Identify the virtual machine requirement for VMotion.

Solution   Virtual machines cannot be connected to a CD-ROM or floppy image on a nonshared datastore.

Virtual machines cannot be connected to an internal-only virtual switch.

Virtual machines cannot be part of a Microsoft Server Cluster.

Virtual machines cannot be configured with CPU affinity.

Master It   Identify the ESX Server host requirements for VMotion.

Solution   Both ESX Server hosts must have access to the same storage devices (fibre channel, iSCSI, and NAS devices).

Both ESX Server hosts must have exactly the same labeled virtual switches that provide access to the same physical networks configured with the same IP subnets.

Both ESX Server hosts must have compatible CPUs (CPU family, CPU vendor, SSE instructions, VT configuration, NX/XD configuration).

Both ESX Server hosts must have access to the same VMotion network.

Create and manage clusters.

Master It   Five ESX Server hosts need to be grouped together for the purpose of enabling the Distributed Resource Scheduler (DRS) feature of VI3.

Solution   Create a cluster object in the VirtualCenter inventory and enable DRS on the cluster.

Configure and manage Distributed Resource Scheduling (DRS).   DRS builds off the success and efficiency of VMotion by offering an automated VMotion based on an algorithm that analyzes system workloads across all ESX Server nodes in a cluster.

Master It   A DRS cluster should determine on which ESX Server host a virtual machine runs when the virtual machine is powered, but it should only recommend migrations for VMotion.

Solution   Configure the DRS cluster to use the Partially Automated setting.

Master It   A DRS cluster should determine on which ESX Server host a virtual machine runs when the virtual machine is powered on, and it should also manage where it runs for best performance. A VMotion should only occur if a recommendation is determined to be a four- or five-star recommendation.

Solution   Configure the DRS cluster to use the Fully Automated setting with the moderately conservative setting.

Master It   Two virtual machines running a web application and a back-end database should be kept together on an ESX Server host at all times. If one should be the target of a VMotion migration, the other should be as well.

Solution   Configure both virtual machines in an affinity rule that keeps the virtual machines together.

Master It   Two virtual machines with database applications should never run on the same ESX Server host.

Solution   Configure the virtual machines in an anti-affinity rule that separates the virtual machines.

Chapter 10: High Availability and Business Continuity

Cluster virtual machines with Microsoft Clustering Services (MSCS)   Clustering virtual machines provides a means of creating an infrastructure that supports high availability for individual virtual machines.

Master It   A critical network service requires minimal downtime. You need to design a failover solution for the virtual machine that hosts the network service. Your solution should provide the least amount of service outage while utilizing existing hardware and software platforms.

Solution   Configure two virtual machines in a cluster-across-boxes. Use raw device mappings (RDMs) for the shared storage device required by the cluster nodes.

Implement and manage VMware High Availability (HA).   VMware HA enabled on clusters of ESX Servers allows virtual machines from a failed ESX Server host to be restarted on another host. This features offers reduced downtime and eliminates administrative effort as a response to a failed server situation.

Master It   Domain controller, mail servers, and database servers must be the first virtual machines to restart in the event of server failure.

Solution   Configure a restart priority of High for each of the virtual machines hosting the domain controller, mail server, or database server role.

Master It   In the event of server failure, you do not want virtual machines to be prevented from being powered on because of excessive resource contention.

Solution   Configure the HA cluster to use guaranteed admission control.

Master It   Virtual machines used for testing purposes should not be powered on by cluster nodes if they were running on the ESX Sever host that failed.

Solution   Configure the testing virtual machines with a per–virtual machine setting that disables the HA restart.

Master It   Your virtual infrastructure includes redundancy at each level, including switches and NICs. Service Console ports, VMkernel ports, and virtual machine port groups exist on separate virtual switches. You need to ensure that virtual machines continue to run even if the Service Console loses network connectivity.

Solution   Configure each virtual machine with an isolation response that leaves them powered on.

Back up virtual machines with VMware Consolidated Backup (VCB).   VCB is a framework upon which third-party backup solutions can be constructed to perform full virtual machine and file level backups. While the framework can be used on its own, it lacks any type of automation feature or the ability to write directly to tape.

Master It   You need to design a data-recovery plan. The company purchased licenses for VMware Consolidated Backup. You must determine how VCB can accomplish your backup goals. What types of backups does VCB support?

Solution   VCB allows full virtual machine backups for any guest operating system. VCB allows single VMDK backups for any guest operating system. It allows file- and folder-level backups of Windows guest operating systems only.

Master It   You need to implement VCB as part of a regularly scheduled backup job.

Solution   Review the VCB compatibility guide to determine which third-party backup tools have VCB integration modules.

Restore virtual machines with VMware Consolidated Backup (VCB).   The VCB framework encompasses not just the backup processes but also restore capabilities. Tools included with VCB allow backups of full virtual machines, individual VMDK files, or specific files from within the virtual machine operating system. In addition VMware Enterprise Converter offers the simplest restore procedure, with its support for restoring VCB backups.

Master It   You need to minimize the financial impact of implementing a backup strategy for your virtual infrastructure.

Solution   Implement a single backup agent on the VCB proxy. Use the VCB proxy for all backup and restore tasks.

Master It   You need to minimize the amount of time required to restore data to any of the virtual machines in your environment.

Solution   Install a backup agent inside of each virtual machine. Perform restores directly into the virtual machine.

Master It   You have a full virtual machine backup of a system named Server1. A user deletes a file that is included on the last backup of Server1. You need to recover the file.

Solution   Mount the full virtual machine backup into the file system of the VCB proxy server. Copy the file from the mount point. Remove the mount point.

Master It   You need to quickly restore a VCB backup of a virtual machine. The backup is stored in a shared folder named `VMBackups` on a server named Backup1. The name of the virtual machine is Server17.

Solution   Use the VMware Converter Enterprise Import Wizard to restore from `\\Backup1\VMBackups\Server17.vmx`.

Chapter 11: Monitoring Virtual Infrastructure Performance

Create an alarm.   Creating host and virtual machine alarms is a proactive way to be alerted to abnormal behavior for all four resource groups or state changes. Alarms can be applied to a single host or virtual machine or a group of either object in the VirtualCenter hierarchy.

Master it   Creating host and virtual machine alarms.

Solution   There are many variations to alarms. Be sure to monitor only what is necessary to respond to problems or to alert service-level issues.

Work with graphs   Creating and working with Performance graphs is the best way to monitor what is currently happening in your virtual infrastructure. Maybe more importantly, though, is a graph's ability to analyze trends in the performance of your hosts and virtual machines. Graphs can be saved and archived or printed for justifying purchase decisions or showing Before and After comparisons after adjustments have been made to either hosts or virtual machines.

Master It   Creating graphs for hosts and virtual machines.

Solution   Know your graph options, chart types, objects, and counters to get the most out of them. Practice their use every day to become familiar with their subtleties.

Master It   Using `esxtop` to monitor resources on a single ESX host.

Solution   Use the four letters C, M, N, and D on your keyboard to change your resource views.

Master It   Use the graphs to monitor CPU usage regularly for hosts and the virtual machines.

Solution   Use Change Chart Options to customize your graphs to zero in on problems. Allow the graphs to be your guide when making decisions about capacity or service-level agreements. When monitoring virtual machines, be sure to use the counter CPU Ready to provide some insight on a virtual machine's ability to be scheduled.

Master It   Create graphs showing host memory usage using the various objects, counters, and chart types.

Solution   Use Change Chart Options to customize your graphs to look specifically for host memory bottlenecks such as ballooning and swap usage.

Master It   Create graphs showing virtual machine memory usage using the various objects, counters, and chart types.

Solution   Use Change Chart Options to customize your graphs to look for virtual machine problems such as configuring a virtual machine with too little or too much memory.

Master It   Create graphs showing host and virtual machine network usage using the various objects, counters, and chart types.

Solution   Monitoring for overall virtual machine network activity can be achieved by using those vmnic objects that correspond with the appropriate vSwitch the virtual machines are connected to. Use the graphs to make decisions about traffic shaping and nic-teaming.

Master It   Create graphs showing host and virtual machine usage using the various objects, counters, and chart types.

Solution   The Disk Usage counter for both host and virtual machine graphs will be the most often used. Use the longer intervals to spot trends in disk I/O behaviors.

Save a graph.   Saving graphics provides evidence of the occurrence of an event and justification for adding more hardware to the virtual infrastructure.

Master It   You need to provide a graph to upper management in support of your proposal for 2 new servers to be configured as ESX Server hosts.

Solution   Use the Performance tab for hosts and virtual machines to save charts any hardware device that is identified as a bottleneck that causes problems or will lead to a contention issue.

Chapter 12: Securing a Virtual Infrastructure

Create and apply roles and permissions in VirtualCenter.   Creating host and virtual machine alarms is a proactive way to be alerted to abnormal behavior for all four resource groups or state changes. Alarms can be applied to a single host, a virtual machine, or a group of either object in the VirtualCenter hierarchy.

> **Master It**   Company security policy dictates that access to VirtualCenter requires users to only be granted the rights necessary to perform their jobs.
>
> **Solution**   There are several predefined roles, and roles can be created to fit particular job requirements. Assign roles to the lowest object in the inventory that allows users to do their job.
>
> **Master It**   Create ESX Server user accounts.
>
> **Solution**   You have two options for creating local users accounts on ESX Server: using command line and using the VI Client.

Create users on the ESX Service Console.   Restricting which users and hosts can connect to an ESX Server is one of the most important security steps you can implement.

> **Master It**   Company security policy dictates that direct access to the Service Console must be restricted.
>
> **Solution**   Configure sshd_config with AllowUsers to specify the users who are allowed to log in to the Service Console.
>
> **Master It**   Configure TCP wrappers to restrict host access to the Service Console.
>
> **Solution**   Edit hosts.allow to specify which hosts are allowed to connect to the Service Console.

Enable and disable services on the firewall.   The Service Console firewall is locked down by default for only those ports needed to provide management for virtualization. There are times when other ports will need to be opened using esxcfg-firewall.

> **Master It**   A security inspection requires an audit of the existing Service Console firewall configuration.
>
> **Solution**   Use esxcfg-firewall -q to audit your ESX Server's current firewall setup.
>
> **Master It**   Open the firewall for specific services or agents.
>
> **Solution**   Use esxcfg-firewall -e *service_name* to enable firewall access to specific services. Use esxcfg-firewall -o to open lesser-known ports for services or agents.

Use Kerberos authentication on ESX Server.   Kerberos authentication allows for Active Directory authentication of local ESX Server user accounts. This simplifies account management and centralizes user account security policies.

> **Master It**   Direct authentication to ESX Server hosts should be secured using an existing Active Directory infrastructure.
>
> **Solution**   Use esxcfg-auth to implement Kerberos authentication.

Audit and monitor important files. Changes to Service Console files should be audited and monitored on a regular basis.

Master It A server failure results in a call to VMware support. The technician requests that you send information about your environment for further review.

Solution Create and extract the vm-support file. Send the file to the technician.

Manage updates and patches with VMware Update Manager VMware Update Manager provides an integrated and easy-to-use utility for managing ESX Server host and virtual machine updates.

Master It You have just installed ESX 3.5 on seven new Dell Poweredge 2950 servers into a DRS/HA cluster. No virtual machines exist. You need to apply all updates immediately.

Solution Create a custom baseline for all updates, attach the baseline at the cluster level, and perform an immediate remediation.

Master It Two days ago you added a new Dell Poweredge R900 server named silo3507 .vdc.local to a partially automated DRS/HA cluster. There are six virtual machines running on silo3507. You need to apply critical updates to silo3507.

Solution Attach the critical updates baseline to silo3507 and perform an immediate remediation. Either alter the failure options to power off or suspend virtual machines or manually relocate virtual machines off of silo3507 to allow it to enter maintenance mode and begin remediation.

Master It You have ten virtual machines that serve as domain controllers. You want to install all of the latest Windows updates on all ten virtual machines using VMware Update Manager. The installation of updates should not affect production during business hours of 9:00 AM to 5:00 PM. You want a 24-hour window of opportunity to remove the update.

Solution Use the Virtual Machines & Templates view to create a folder to hold the ten virtual machines. Create a baseline that includes all updates and attach the baseline at the folder level. Schedule a remediation to happen during non-business hours. Configure VMware Update Manager to maintain the rollback snapshot for a period of 24 hours.

Chapter 13: Configuring and Managing ESXi

Understand the architecture of ESXi. ESXi presents a radical change not just to the virtualization world but to the system manufacturers that want to be part of virtualization evolution. By removing the local management component, the Service Console, ESXi presents a thin yet highly functional hypervisor on which virtual machines can run. But don't mistake thin for meaning not as feature-rich. ESXi supports all the same enterprise features of VMotion, DRS, and HA that have made VMware ESX the number one choice for the foundation of virtualization platforms around the world.

Master It You manage a datacenter that experiences rapid growth. You need to identify a way to introduce new hardware resources into the virtual infrastructure with minimal administrative effort and maximum security.

Solution Build a VI3 solution on top of ESXi. Take advantage of the "plug-and-play" nature of the solution, its minimal footprint design, and its enhanced security through Service Console elimination.

Deploy ESXi Installable.   ESXi Installable provides existing VI3 licensees with the ability to shift their infrastructure to the new thin hypervisor architecture. The installation files can be downloaded as part of the existing license agreement without any penalty or additional cost. ESXi Installable installs onto local disk drives.

Master It   You manage a datacenter with five existing ESX Server 3.5 hosts. You wish to restructure the datacenter to use the thin hypervisor architecture of ESXi.

Solution   Download the ESXi Installable installation files from `http://www.vmware.com/downloads`. Burn the ISO image to a CD and perform the installation on local disks.

Deploy ESXi Embedded.   ESXi Embedded, like ESXi Installable, is a thin hypervisor architecture with no reliance on a console operating system; however, the hypervisor runs from an embedded storage module on the host. System manufacturers like Dell offer next-generation products that include internal storage functionality for running ESXi Embedded.

Master It   You want to construct a virtual infrastructure on physical servers without local storage devices. You want the CPU and memory of each server to be allocated to a VMware cluster for supporting HA and DRS.

Solution   Purchase new server hardware that includes support for an internal, on-board storage module with ESXi Embedded preinstalled on the server.

Manage ESXi.   Managing ESXi can be done using the console of the system, the VI Client connected directly to the server, the VI Client connected to VirtualCenter, or from a command line using the remote CLI tools. The remote CLI tools can be deployed on a Windows host, Linux host, or from within a downloadable virtual appliance. All are available from the VMware website.

Master It   You have deployed four servers running ESXi. You need to configure them into a cluster that supports DRS and HA.

Solution   Use the VI Client to connect to a VirtualCenter 2.5 server and add each of the hosts into a cluster. Enable the cluster for DRS and HA.

Master It   You have 30 ESXi hosts to which you need to add a new virtual switch. Your administrative desktop runs Windows XP Professional.

Solution   Download the remote CLI tools for Windows. Install the tools and create a script that adds the virtual switch using the `vicfg-vswitch` command.

Appendix B

Common Linux and ESX Commands

Navigating the Service Console command line and performing management, configuration, and troubleshooting tasks is an important skill set for virtual infrastructure administrators.

This appendix discusses the following topics: navigating and managing the Service Console, managing disks and files in the Service Console, and using `esxcfg`, a management tool from VMware.

Navigating, Managing, and Monitoring through the Service Console

First and foremost, getting around the service console is a critical skill for troubleshooting and managing ESX Server hosts when the traditional graphical tools are not available. The following commands are some of the common and basic commands for moving around a Linux-based operating system.

cd   Used to change directories.

Example: #cd /vmfs/volumes

ls   Used to list files and folders in the current directory.

Example: #ls

ls -l   Used to list files and folders in a long format with rights and owners.

ls -s   Used to list files and folders in a short format.

ls -R   Used to list files and folders with the ability to scroll.

whoami   Used to identify the effective user.

who am i   Used to identify the currently logged-on user.

logout   Used to log out the current user.

reboot   Used to reboot a system.

adduser   Used to add a new user.

Example: useradd newaccount

passwd   Used to update a user account password.

Example: passwd newaccount

Managing Directories, Files, and Disks in the Service Console

Without a graphical interface to use creating, managing, and deleting files and directories will have to be done in the console session. The following commands provide basic instruction on moving, copying, creating, and deleting files and directories.

mv Used to move or rename files.

Example 1: `mv oldfile newfile`

Example 2: `mv file1 /newfolder/file1`

cp Used to copy directories or files. Can be used to rename a file during the copy process.

-`f` to force the copy

-`p` to copy the permissions

Example 1: `cp file1 /newdocs/file1`

Example 2: `cp file1 /newdocs/file2`

rm Used to remove files and directories.

-`f` to force the removal

Example: `rm -f /olddirectory`

rmdir Used to remove empty directories.

Example: `rmdir`

touch Used to create a new file or change file access and modification time.

Example: `touch mynewfile.txt`

fdisk Used to manage disk partitions.

mount Used to mount CD-ROM or floppy drives.

Example: `mount /mnt/cdrom`

Using *esxcfg*

In addition to the standard Linux commands covered thus far VMware has implemented a specific set of commands directed toward ESX-specific tasks. The following list of commands show how to manage various components of the ESX Server configuration.

esxcfg-auth Used to configure an ESX Server host to support network-based authentication methods (e.g., Active Directory [AD]).

`--enablead` to configure Service Console for AD authentication

`--addomain` to set the domain the Service Console will authenticate against

`--addc` to set the domain controller to authenticate against for AD authentication

`--usecrack` to enable the `pam_cracklib` for managing password complexity

esxcfg-firewall Used to query, enable, and disable services on the Service Console firewall.

`-q` to query the current firewall settings

`-q` *servicename* to query the status of a specific service

`-q` `incoming/outgoing` to query the status of incoming and outgoing ports

`--blockIncoming` to block all incoming connections on ports not required for system function

`--blockOutgoing` to block all outgoing connections on ports not required for system function

`--allowIncoming` to allow incoming connections on all ports

`--allowOutgoing` to allow outgoing connections on all ports

`--e` *servicename* to enable a specific service

`--d` *servicename* to disable a specific service

esxcfg-info   Used to review the hardware information for Service Console and VMKernel.

`-w` to print hardware information

`-s` to print storage and disk information

`-n` to print network information

esxcfg-mpath   Used to view and configure the multipathing settings for an ESX Server host's fibre channel or iSCSI storage devices.

`-p` to set the policy for mru (most recently used), fixed, or rr (round-robin)

`-P` to define a path to operate on

`-s` with "on" or "off" to enable or disale a specific path

`-f` to set a specified path as the preferred

esxcfg-nas   Used to configure NAS storage on ESX Server.

`-l` to list all NAS

`-a` to add a new NAS datastore on a specified host

`-o` to provide the name of the NAS host

`-s` to provide the name of the NAS share

`-delete` to delete a NAS datastore

esxcfg-nics   Used to obtain information about and configure the physical network adapters installed in an ESX Server host.

`-s` to set the speed of a card to 10, 100, 1000, or 10,000.

`-d` to set the duplex to half or full

esxcfg-route   Used to configure the default gateway for the VMkernel.

esxcfg-swiscsi   Used to configure the software iSCSI component of ESX Server.

`-e` to enable software iSCSI

-d to disable software iSCSI

-q to query if software iSCSI is enabled

-s to scan for new LUNs using software iSCSI

esxcfg-vmhbadevs   Used to obtain information about the LUNs available to the ESX Server.

-m to print the VMFS UUID if formatted as VMFS

esxcfg-vmknic   Used to configure the VMkernel NIC.

-a to add a VMkernel port group

-d to delete a VMKernel

-e to enable the VMkernel NIC

-D to disable the VMkernel port

-i to set the IP address of the VMkernel NIC

-n to set the network mask for the IP of the call

esxcfg-vswif   Used to set the parameters of the Service Console

-a to add a Service Console NIC (this option is predicated on having IP information and port group names)

-d to delete a the Service Console NIC

-e to enable the Service Console NIC

-D to disable the Service Console NIC

-p to set the port group name for the Service Console NIC

-i to set the IP address to be used for the Service Console NIC

-n to set the network mask of for the Service Console NIC

esxcfg-vswitch   Used to add, remove, or modify a virtual switch.

-a to add a new virtual switch

-d to delete a new virtual switch

-l to list all existing virtual switches

-L to unlink a network adapter from a hosting provider

-U to link a network adapter

-v to set the vLAN ID for a port group

-A to add a new port group

-D to delete a port group

-C to query for the existence of a port group name

Using *vicfg*

The latest updates to the VI3 product suite, ESX Server 3.5, ESXi, and VirtualCenter 2.5 have also brought about the introduction of a new set of command line tools in the vicfg. The commands are similar to the esxcfg commands but are more directly dedicated to remote host management functions using the new remote command line interface tool available from VMware.

vicfgvicfg-nas   Used to manipulate NAS/NFS.

--add or -a to add a new NAS file system

--delete or -d to delete a NAS file system

--help to display help text

--nasserver or -o followed by <n_host> to add the hostname of the new NAS file system

--share or -s used with -a to provide the name of the directory that is exported on the NAS device

--vihost or -h followed by <host> to direct the command to a particular ESX Server host

vicfg-vmhbadevs   Used to discover information about available LUNs.

--help to display help text

--query or -q to print the output in 2.6 compatibility mode

--vihost or -h followed by <host> to direct the command to a particular ESX Server host

--vmfs or -m to print the VMFS UUID in addition to the HBA and /dev names for LUNs that are formatted as VMFS

vicfg-mpath   Used to manipulate multipathing.

--help to display help text

--bulk or -b to show all LUNs and paths in parsable format

--detailed or -d to show all information about a LUN, including its globally unique name

--hbas or -a to print the list of HBAs that can be identified by a unique ID

--list or --l to list all LUNs on the system and the paths to each LUN

--lun or -L followed by <lun> to specify the LUN to use in the operations command (this option is not used by itself)

--path or -P followed by <path> to specify the path to use in the operations command (this option is not used by itself)

--policy or -p followed by [mru | fixed] to set the policy for a given LUN (the option for round-robin (rr) can be used but is still experimental)

--preferred or -f to set the specified path (--path) as the preferred path

`--query` or `-q` to query a LUN for information

`--state` or `-s` followed by `on` or `off` to enable or disable a given path

`--vihost` or `-h` followed by `<host>` to direct the command to a particular ESX Server host

vicfg-rescan   Used to perform a rescan for discovering new LUNs.

`--help` to display help text

`--vihost` or `-h` followed by `<host>` to direct the command to a particular ESX Server host

`<VMkernel_SCSI_adapter_name>` to provide the name of the adapter to rescan (i.e., vmhba1)

vicfg-dumppart   Used to query, set, and scan diagnostic partitions on ESXi.

`--activate` or `-a` to activate the configured diagnostic partition (performs the same as `--set`)

`--deactivate` or `-d` to deactivate the currently active diagnostic partition

`--find` or `-f` to find all diagnostic partitions

`--get-active` or `-t` to get the active diagnostic partition for the system

`--get-config` or `-c` to get the configured diagnostic partition for the system

`--list` or `-l` to list all partitions on the system that can act as a diagnostic partition

`--set` or `-s` followed by `<vmhbaw:x:y:z>` to set the active and configured diagnostic partition

`--vihost` or `-h` followed by `<host>` to direct the command to a particular ESX Server host

vicfg-nics   Used to report on and manage physical network adapters.

`--help` to display help text

`--auto` or `-a` to set the given adapter to autonegotiate the speed and duplex settings

`--duplex` or `-d` followed by `[full | half]` `<nic>` to set the duplex value for a given NIC

`--speed` or `-s` followed by `<speed><nic>` to set the speed value for a given NIC

`--list` or `-l` to list the physical adapters in the system

`--vihost` or `-h` followed by `<host>` to direct the command to a particular ESX Server host

vicfg-vmknic   Used to configure virtual network adapters.

`--help` to display help text

`--add` or `-a` to add a virtual network adapter to the system (an IP address and port group name must be specified)

`--del` or `-d` followed by `<port_group>` to delete the virtual network adapter on the specified port group

`--ip` or `-i` followed by `[<IP address>| DHCP]` to set the virtual network adapter to a given IP address or to obtain an address from a DHCP server

`--list` or `-l` to list virtual network adapters on the system

`--netmask` or `-n` followed by `<netmask>` to set the network mask for the assigned IP address

`--vihost` or `-h` followed by `<host>` to direct the command to a particular ESX Server host

vicfg-vswitch   Used to configure virtual switches.

`--help` to display help text

`--add` or `-a` followed by `<vswitch_name>` to add a new virtual switch

`--add-pg` or `-A` followed by `<portgroup> <switch>` to add a port group to the specified switch

`--check` or `-c` followed by `<virtual_switch>` to check for the existence of a virtual switch

`--check-pg` or `-C` followed by `<port_group>` to check for the existence of a port group

`--delete` or `-d` followed by `<vswitch_name>` to delete the specified virtual switch (this command will not work if any of the virtual switch ports are in use)

`--del-pg` or `-D` followed by `<portgroup>` to delete the specified port group (this command will not work if the port group is in use)

`--link` or `-L` followed by `<pnic>` to add a physical adapter to a virtual switch

`--list` or `-l` to list all virtual switches and port groups

`--mtu` or `-m` to set the maximum transmission unit (MTU) of the virtual switch

`--pg` or `-p` followed by `<port_group>` to provide the name of a port group when using the `--vlan` option (use the ALL parameter to set VLAN IDs on all port groups of a virtual switch)

`--vlan` or `-v` to set the VLAN ID for a specific port group (using the parameter 0 disables all VLAN IDs; using `--vlan` requires the `--pg` option)

`--vihost` or `-h` followed by `<host>` to direct the command to a particular ESX Server host

vicfg-route   Used to configure the default route for VMkernel ports.

`--help` to display help text

`--vihost` or `-h` followed by `<host>` to direct the command to a particular ESX Server host

`<gateway>` to specify the default gateway to be used by the VMkernel

vicfg-ntp   Used to configure NTP settings.

`--help` to display help text

`--add` or `-a` followed by `<server>` to add an NTP server

`--delete` or `-d` followed by `<server>` to delete an NTP server

`--list` or `-l` to list the configured NTP servers

`--vihost` or `-h` followed by `<host>` to direct the command to a particular ESX Server host

Appendix C

Third-Party Virtualization Tools

The virtualization sector of information technology, led by VMware Infrastructure 3, is relatively new and despite its infancy it has quickly matured and found its way into more than 90% of the data centers among the world's largest companies. With this type of corporate penetration it is not a surprise that many software companies are beginning to build custom applications to complement VI3 deployments. This appendix aims to introduce to some of the early tools that are available in helping manage, optimize, secure, and recover the assets in your virtual environment.

Disaster-Recovery and Business-Continuity Tools

Perhaps the largest area of virtual infrastructure support with third-party virtualization tools is the disaster-recovery and business-continuity segment of the market. The virtualization tools listed here are several of the best tools available with regard to ease of use, functionality, and cost.

vRanger Pro

vRanger Pro, previously known as ESXRanger, is one of the most recognized backup solutions in virtualization environments. Developed by Vizioncore Inc., vRanger Pro is a Windows-based application that simplifies performing online backups and restoring virtual machines. The easy-to-use Windows-based graphical user interface (GUI) eliminates scripting for IT administrators, so no specialized knowledge is necessary to deploy a reliable backup strategy. vRanger Pro runs on a centralized Windows host and can run using the standard Windows scheduler, thus further eliminating the need for complex scripting. The GUI offers a Startup wizard and VirtualCenter integration for ease of operation, as well as compression options to save storage space. vRanger Pro compresses virtual machine disk files (VMDK) before sending them to the chosen destination target server, such as the local VMFS, a Linux server, or a Windows server. NAS, SAN, Novell, UNC, and mapped drives are also supported if they are accessible to the Windows host. vRanger Pro provides full-image restore to any VMware ESX Server without needing to know the prior configurations. It also reduces or eliminates the need to create manual installations and configurations to the backup image. Restores are efficiently relocated, and they run quickly because the images are compressed and all configurations are included. For Windows guests, file-level restores are available to provide an advanced file level of protection.

vRanger Pro uses the included VSS drivers to leverage Microsoft's Volume Shadow Copy Service technology to pause application writes. The VSS feature enables quiescing for supported databases to provide "transactionally consistent" backup images that can be used to recover the application as well as the image.

In an effort to reduce time and space for virtual machine backups, vRanger Pro includes a differential backups technology that captures only the changes that have occurred since the last successful full backup image. Backup administrators have the flexibility of designing retention policies to support the corporate disaster-recovery plan and the space available for the backup files.

vRanger Pro includes a P2V-DR module to provide the functionality of rapidly and frequently converting physical machines into virtual machines as part of a disaster-recovery strategy. This module functions as an agentless deployment and without the need to reboot the source computer.

The application also captures details about how long a particular backup process will take, allowing you to plan for the next backup window. In addition, users can record IP addresses, compression ratios, and the virtual machines' locations on the various LUNs. Details about backups and VMs are stored in the repository and can be accessed for reporting and analysis.

Unlike traditional backup agents, vRanger Pro runs outside the guest operating system, and can be integrated with VMware VirtualCenter for efficient backup management. The backups can be offloaded from the host leveraging integration with VMware VCB. vRanger Pro recognizes the VMotion feature and is aware when a virtual machine is migrated to a new host. This allows vRanger Pro to follow virtual machines from host to host to perform regularly scheduled backups even after the virtual machines have moved.

vReplicator

vReplicator, previously known as esxReplicator, is a host-level image replication solution for VMware infrastructure. Also developed by Vizioncore Inc., vReplicator is a Windows-based application that enables companies to leverage virtualization technology to keep applications running day in and day out all year round by replicating entire virtual machines, including configuration settings, patches to the OS, the application and the data, and all other OS-level changes.

vReplicator selectively replicates virtual machines from many hosts to one host, as well as to dissimilar hardware platforms. In physical server environments, disaster-recovery solutions are expensive and difficult to deploy and maintain because they require redundant, overbuilt standby servers that are typically dormant and underutilized until a portion of the production environment becomes unavailable. Virtualization eliminates the expense of overbuilding by allowing higher utilization of existing servers. vReplicator offers a strategic and bandwidth-conscious approach to replication: it enables full virtual machines to be selectively and cost-effectively replicated without agents, and with full flexibility to complement the existing server environment, while reducing the financial impact of the overall solution.

vReplicator selectively replicates individual virtual machines selected by the virtual infrastructure administrator. This eliminates the maintenance, network traffic, and hardware and software expenses of replicating all the LUNs from a SAN. Because vReplicator works from a centralized server, installation components are not needed on either the source or the target virtual machines.

vReplicator operates from a centralized server and does not need to be installed on either the source or the target virtual machines, which eliminates the licensing costs, management, and maintenance involved with agent-based solutions. vReplicator provides a Setup wizard for the configuration of replication jobs. The solution can be configured for direct communication between the vReplicator server, the source, and the destination hosts, or it can be configured to leverage VirtualCenter. Replication job settings include replication intervals, the destination server, and the target datastore. Status information is available in the GUI to determine the duration of replication processes as well as to verify successful replications. Performance statistics are available to determine the workload on a host and the impact of replication on the virtualized environment. These statistics are helpful in determining the limitations of the host and the performance requirements for replication. vReplicator is integrated with VirtualCenter to provide a recognizable hierarchy of virtual machines and the respective hosts involved in replication. This integration with

VirtualCenter allows the solution to be VMotion and DRS aware so replication jobs continue even after the virtual machines have moved.

The initial synchronization for vReplicator leverages proven Vizioncore technology for the initial copy of the source virtual machine. After the initial synchronization, a differential engine sends only changes to the destination host and applies them to the closed target virtual machine. The replication engine of vReplicator is a Windows service that resides on the server where vReplicator has been installed. This reduces the impact on the underlying virtualization platform implementation by offloading the work to the dedicated vReplicator server. vReplicator validates the differential information needed to perform live replication without interruption to the virtual machine. The differential engine checks for changes to VMDKs as a catalyst for performing block-level replication. To prevent problems in the replication and recovery process, vReplicator copies changed blocks to the target system before applying them. By copying the blocks before writing them into the replicated virtual machine files, vReplicator ensures that if any problems arise during the process the original blocks can be written back to the target. Ultimately this logic prevents the need to recopy the entire VMDK.

esXpress

esXpress is a virtual infrastructure backup solution created by PHD Technologies. The latest version as of this writing, esXpress v3.1, is a unique solution that involves the use of a small, low-impact virtual machine called a virtual backup appliance (VBA) that provides a sophisticated backup technology to a VMware virtual infrastructure. Although the product sits inside a dedicated virtual machine, the backup destinations include all of the following storage targets:

◆ FTP

◆ SSH

◆ CIFS/SMB (Windows file shares)

◆ iSCSI (VMFS)

◆ Fibre channel (VMFS)

esXpress installs a GUI helper virtual machine that provides for the configuration of the backup process but once configured is not required for the execution of the backups. The product is licensed and installed on a per-host basis. Uniquely it is not licensed per socket or per core, and therefore does not penalize you for having a well-stocked set of equipment for your virtual infrastructure. This also means that esXpress will scale with your hardware without any additional costs. Today your server might have two quad-core processors, but the future might see an upgrade to four quad-core processors. Such a change will not incur any additional costs for the esXpress deployment. And it gets better; PHD does not charge you for licenses for esXpress installations on ESX Server hosts that will only serve as restore targets. The licenses come in four different types: free, LE, Pro, and Enterprise. The differences in the licenses revolve around the number of simultaneous backups, bandwidth throttling, and full versus differential backup capability.

Once configured, when a backup job is instantiated esXpress will perform a consistency check across the VMX, VMSD, VirtualCenter, and datastore. Pending a successful consistency check, it will take a snapshot and create a VBA to manage the backup process. The number of simultaneous VBAs a host can support is based on the number of cores in the physical server (and of course the license purchased). A server with eight processor cores can spawn eight VBA virtual machines, each responsible for the backup of an individual virtual machine. Upon completion of the backup, the VBA is deleted from disk. As backups are completed, new VBAs will be spawned to continue the process of backing up all the desired virtual machines.

The backup procedure of esXpress is completely integrated into VirtualCenter, thus eliminating the need to use any other interface or software application. However, for those times when access to VirtualCenter just isn't possible, a console session (or SSH session via `putty.exe`) can be used to configure, manage, and administer the backup processes. esXpress adds features like compression and encryption to provide enhanced efficiency and encryption to its product.

By default, esXpress performs full backups on the first day of the month and complements that with a differential backup every other day. The differential feature allows for the efficient use of space for storing backups.

Perhaps one of the most unsung features in esXpress is the ability to replicate backup data to alternate locations. By including a replication technology in the product, esXpress offers a true disaster-recovery solution that provides administrators with an easy off-site recovery process. Using the replication feature to send backups to another VMFS datastore in another location means that virtual machines can be powered on in the remote location when disaster occurs.

In all, esXpress offers a unique product with a great level of functionality.

Acronis True Image Echo Enterprise

Acronis True Image Echo Enterprise has long been a leading disaster-recovery tool for physical servers. Acronis now extends its reach into creating image-level backups of virtual machines. With support for both Linux and Windows 32-bit and 64-bit virtual machines, True Image Echo Enterprise covers most of the guest operating systems installed into virtual machines in VMware Infrastructure 3 (VI3) deployment. The Acronis True Image Echo Enterprise product includes many new features for simplifying the backup and restore process. Among these features are:

◆ Direct to DVD

◆ Image mounting for modifying without restoring

◆ Image verification and validation

◆ Acronis Universal Restore

After an unplanned system crash, True Image Echo Enterprise Server allows administrators to perform a full system restore, a bare-metal restore, or a simple restore of individual files and folders in a matter of minutes from a centralized management console. Complete system restoration with the Acronis Universal Restore feature can be executed to an existing virtual machine, a new virtual machine, or even a physical box with different hardware. When troubleshooting a problem requires re-creating the issue on a physical server, True Image Echo Enterprise makes this an easy task.

Double-Take for VMware Infrastructure

Double-Take for VMware Infrastructure provides virtual machine protection by offering replication services for virtual machine files. The Double-Take for VMware Infrastructure product installs on a single Windows server in the network environment and allows multiple virtual machines to be protected from a centralized management console.

Double-Take for VMware Infrastructure sits comfortably in the realm of products dedicated to easing the disaster recovery and business continuity for organizations with a VMware virtual infrastructure. Double-Take for VMware Infrastructure captures changes at defined intervals, keeping the target virtual disk up to date and ready for failover, recovery, and backup at any time.

When a production server outage occurs, the replicated virtual machine can be started on the target server with the latest replicated data. The virtual machine will be consistent as of the last successful replication procedure. Replication is supported between any type of storage supported by the VMware ESX Server, including direct attached SCSI, fibre channel or iSCSI SANs, and NAS/NFS.

The concept of whole virtual machine protection resonates from the idea that a replica of the entire virtual machine is created, including operating system, applications, and all relevant patches, as part of the copy process. Like some of the other products in this category, Double-Take has the advantage of being an agentless utility that understands the VMware VMotion feature and provides a centralized interface for managing the backups and restores.

No "agent" software is required on the ESX Server, or within any protected VM, so protection scenarios are easily managed and rapidly deployed. Double-Take for VMware Infrastructure needs to be installed only once, and multiple protection scenarios can be launched. This approach aggregates resource consumption by VM protection so it can be easily monitored and managed at the VMware enterprise level.

Setting up a VM protection scenario is easy with a directed step-by-step workflow that guides the user through the process. With just a few mouse clicks, and in less than a minute, a VM protection scenario can be created and deployed.

The Double-Take for VMware Infrastructure management interface leverages the logical groupings and hierarchies available in VMware VirtualCenter. This makes it possible for an administrator to easily navigate through configured virtual machines to select them for management and protection by Double-Take for VMware Infrastructure.

Double-Take for VMware Infrastructure provides options for compressing the replicated files, providing flexible trade-offs between host system resource consumption and network bandwidth usage. This product provides flexibility to configure the frequency of change replication based on either the amount of change or the time that has elapsed since the last replication window.

Monitoring and Reporting

Several tools are available for monitoring and reporting a virtual infrastructure that provide great complements to the native tools in VI3. These tools work seamlessly to provide detailed data about hosts and virtual machines.

vCharter

vCharter, previously known as esxCharter, is a Windows-based application developed by Vizioncore Inc. vCharter is a data-collection engine installed on a central Windows server that connects to each ESX Server host on a user-defined interval to collect data about ESX Server hosts and virtual machines. vCharter is a comprehensive tool for monitoring real-time metrics regarding a VMware infrastructure deployment. It is capable of delivering both real-time and historical performance data. The vCharter user interface offers the performance view for an entire virtualized environment, including the ability to drill down for a more granular look at specific objects in the inventory, such as containers, hosts, or virtual machines. With all of the detailed capabilities and the "At a Glance" and "Top Five" views, vCharter provides either a deep or a shallow look at the performance of the virtual infrastructure.

Reports from vCharter can be constructed on-demand or can be delivered via e-mail on a scheduled basis. In addition to the e-mail functionality for sending custom reports, vCharter can be configured to send e-mails regarding performance thresholds.

Perhaps the most unique feature of vCharter is its ability to track resource costs associated with virtual machines in an effort to provide chargeback data. For hosting providers or IT departments that bill internal departments, the vCharter chargeback functionality provides an easy way to monitor virtual machine and host costs for accurate client billing.

Overall, vCharter takes an impressive step forward in comparison to the native monitoring tools found in the VI Client. With added functionality and enhanced detail, vCharter will provide all of the data administrators could need about the performance of their virtual infrastructure.

Veeam Monitor

Veeam Monitor is a Windows-centric utility focused on three aspects of the virtual infrastructure:

◆ Monitoring

◆ Alerting

◆ Capacity planning

Veeam Monitor is at its best in environments that include a VirtualCenter server that centrally manages the VI3 deployment. Smaller environments that do not use VirtualCenter can still use Veeam Monitor but will not experience the full functionality of the tool.

The Veeam Monitor monitoring process details the performance statistics of resource pools, clusters, or individual hosts and virtual machines. Administrators can get a high-level overview of virtual infrastructure performance, or they can dive into details to discover system bottlenecks that are causing performance issues.

All the data gathered from Veeam Monitor is consolidated into a SQL Server database, making it available for some of the other features in Veeam Monitor: trending and capacity planning. All of the historical data saved in the SQL Server database can be used to identify trends in resource utilization and plan for future growth.

The data-collection process of Veeam Monitor includes an alerting component that allows administrators to stay on top of performance at all times. Veeam Monitor also integrates with leading monitoring tools like CA Unicenter, IBM Tivoli, and HP OpenView.

When deployed correctly, Veeam Monitor arms administrators with a powerful tool for being proactive about system performance and bottleneck identification.

Veeam Reporter

Veeam Reporter is in a class of its own when it comes to VI3 reporting. Whereas Veeam Monitor is focused on performance metrics, Veeam Reporter is focused on:

◆ Discovery

◆ Documentation

◆ Analysis

The SQL stored data captured by Veeam Reporter is designed to provide easy-to-use documentation about the virtual infrastructure. The tool can be used to analyze the environment and report the information in Microsoft Visio, Microsoft Word, Microsoft Excel, or Adobe Acrobat (PDF) formats. This output provides one of the most sought-after yet never-accomplished feats in the world of IT management: documentation.

The content within these various file formats is just as flexible and deep. Veeam Reporter can gather information regarding:

◆ Network architecture, including virtual switches, ESX Server hosts, and virtual machines.

◆ Storage devices, including details of local and SAN-based storage and the virtual machine files stored within. In addition, Veeam Reporter provides metrics on storage capacity, limits, and utilization for the entire datastore or the virtual machines residing in the respective datastore.

◆ Resource pool configuration, including CPU and memory allocations.

◆ A full VI3 inventory for complete documentation of the virtual infrastructure.

Of all the tools, Veeam Reporter provides a level of functionality that is unparalleled by any other product in its category. It is unique in its offering and will most certainly save administrators a great deal of time and headaches in documenting and managing the growth of the virtual infrastructure.

Management, Operations, and Configuration

Most of the early software products developed for a virtual infrastructure focused on supporting the backup and the restore of virtual machines for business continuity and disaster recovery. A growing number of applications focus on supporting the management of the ESX Server hosts or the virtual machines. In some cases, even some traditional Windows-based applications have become even more useful when used inside the virtual infrastructure.

Acronis Disc Director

Disc Director is an application composed of partition, boot managers, and hard disk data editing tools developed by Acronis Inc. This tool has been around for some time now, and its use in a virtual machine makes it an excellent application to have handy when managing a virtual infrastructure. Disk Director can perform online disk configuration changes in physical computers as well as in virtual machines. Some of the more useful features for virtual machines include the ability to:

◆ Resize, move, split, and merge partitions without data loss or destruction.

◆ Convert partitions to other file systems without data loss.

◆ Copy (move) partition contents.

◆ Delete partitions.

◆ Recover hard disk partitions that were accidentally deleted or damaged due to a hardware or a software error.

◆ Format, label, assign letters, hide and unhide partitions, set active partitions, and perform additional disk management operations.

◆ Boot installed operating systems from any hard disk partition.

◆ Boot installed operating systems from under Windows.

◆ Recover boot records, files and folders structure, find lost clusters, remove viruses, and so forth.

Disk Director provides an advantage when extending Windows disk drives for virtual machines because the extension of the disk can be performed without any downtime regardless of which disk partitions are being altered. Acronis Disk Director is a great tool to have in your repertoire, especially now that a VMDK can be extended right through the properties of the virtual machine.

Veeam Configurator

Throughout this book we have shown how many tasks can be completed using the VI Client GUI as well as the command line. And while the command line can be powerful and ultimately save time, a learning curve is involved that often makes administrators shy away from the command line. Veeam Configurator provides a centralized GUI for managing a portion of the ESX Server configuration settings for multiple ESX Server hosts.

Veeam Configurator is made up of modules, called Experts, that eliminate the need to know scripting. The latest version of Veeam Configurator is version 1.5 and includes the following six Experts:

RootAccess Expert   Allows for enabling or disabling of root access via SSH.

TimeSync Expert   Allows for NTP configuration across multiple ESX Server hosts.

AddUser Expert   Facilitates creating additional Service Console user accounts on one or more hosts simultaneously.

PatchLevel Expert   Provides reporting on the current patch level for all ESX Server hosts.

EsxDiag Expert   Collects diagnostic data across multiple ESX Server hosts, including TCP and DNS information, Service Console configuration, NTP settings, and failed services.

CustomScript Expert   Allows for executing custom scripts on multiple ESX Server hosts at the same time. This is an excellent way to allow limited scripting knowledge to have a big impact.

Veeam Configurator can be a big timesaver for the administrator responsible for multiple ESX Server hosts. Whether from three hosts to thirty hosts, Veeam Configurator allows for customizations and scripts to be executed in a centralized location.

Veeam FastSCP

Veeam FastSCP is a free tool that provides file copy and management features. Using FastSCP you can copy files from a Windows system to an ESX Server system or vice versa, as well as copy files within or between ESX Server systems. Imagine you want to copy ISO files to a SAN LUN accessible by an ESX server host, or perhaps you want to make a copy of the entire directory where a virtual machine's files are stored. Veeam FastSCP is the perfect fit. If your backup strategy involves VCB, then FastSCP might be the tool of choice for copying restored virtual machine files back into an ESX-accessible directory to perform the `vcbRestore` command.

With its FastSCP product, Veeam has identified and solved the major problems with providing data transfer to and from ESX Server hosts. Whereas FTP lacked security and SCP lacked efficiency, FastSCP provides efficient and secure data transfer.

The interface for FastSCP is comfortable and easy to use and with a price tag of $0 this is definitely a tool you'll want to install.

WinSCP

WinSCP (Windows Secure Copy) is an open source free Secure Shell File Transfer Protocol (SFTP) client and FTP client for Windows. WinSCP provides two program interfaces:

Norton Commander Interface The first interface is based on Norton Commander (and similar file managers). The interface displays two panels: a local folder structure in the left panel and a remote folder structure in the right panel.

Explorer-like Interface The second interface is similar to Windows Explorer in that you will only see the remote folder structure. To transfer files, perform a drag-and-drop operation between the WinSCP window and the Windows Explorer window.

WinSCP, like FastSCP, is used for file management services between and within ESX Server hosts. Unfortunately, this tool is significantly outperformed by FastSCP, but it has for a long time been a staple for ESX Server administrators.

FabulaTech USB over Network

One of the most significant features in today's IT world that has been eliminated from the virtual machines running on ESX Server 3.5 is the support for USB devices. For some administrators, access to USB devices is a critical component. The FabulaTech USB over Network product offers an excellent solution for USB access for virtual machines.

USB over Network allows USB devices to be connected to a physical computer and then mapped into virtual machines over the standard TCP/IP network. For example, suppose that a virtual machine needs access to a high-speed scanner that connects via USB. With USB over Network, the scanner can be connected to a physical computer somewhere on the network and then mapped into the virtual machine. The physical computer where the scanner is connected would use the USB over Network Server and the virtual machine would be installed with the USB over Network Client. The solution ends up presenting the high-speed scanner to the virtual machine as if it were truly a local device.

Lost Creations viplugins

On the smaller scale, but high up on the functionality scale are the products created by a company named Lost Creations. From their web site at www.lostcreations.com (or www.viplugins.com) you will find some very useful plugins for VirtualCenter. Among their available plugins you will find:

◆ SVMotion 0.4.4 — This VI plugin, perhaps the most useful of all, allows VMware administrators to invoke storage VMotion (SVMotion) events from within VirtualCenter. The first release of Storage VMotion, available at the time of writing, required a command line execution using the svmotion.pl utility.

◆ Add Port Groups 0.1.0 — This plugin facilitates managing virtual networks across multiple ESX Server hosts. It allows for the creation of multiple port groups (the vSwitch must exist) of any type on a number of ESX servers and virtual switches at once, thus eliminating the need to recreate on a host-by-host basis.

◆ RDP 1.0.1 — This tool builds Remote Desktop access directly into the Virtual Infrastructure client connection. The right-click context menu of a virtual machine includes an option to initiate an RDP session.

◆ Console 0.1.5 — This plugin adds a console tab to the details pane of an ESX Server host. Similar to the console tab natively available for virtual machine this plugin adds direct console access to an ESX Server from within the Virtual Infrastructure client.

◆ Invoke 0.1.7 — This plugin provides a high level of customization by allowing an administrator to invoke third-party applications from within the Virtual Infrastructure client connection. It can even pass the existing session cookie to the third-party application. This opens up the VI Client to a new world of integration with perl, Java, or .NET applications.

Appendix D

VMware Infrastructure 3 Best Practices

This appendix serves as an overview of the many design, deployment, management, and monitoring concepts discussed throughout the book. It can be used as a quick reference for any phase of your virtual infrastructure deployment. The appendix is also meant as a review of the material we covered, with a focus on the concepts of VMware Infrastructure 3 (VI3) that are commonly discussed in the world of virtualization management. By reviewing the appendix, you can gauge your level of fluency with the concepts we've discussed. If you're unsure of any of the best practices outlined here, you can revisit the various sections of the book for more details about that particular best practice.

Installation Best Practices

The following best practice suggestions are derived from the full details outlined in Chapters 2 and 13.

- Review your architecture needs to determine if ESX Server 3.5 or ESXi is the right foundation for your virtual infrastructure. Identify the answers to questions like:
    - Do I have a need for the console operating system?
    - Do I have a need to minimize the footprint on the physical server?
    - Do I want to install any third-party applications that require the service console?
- Always consult the ESX Server compatibility guides before purchasing any new hardware. Even if you are successful at installing on unsupported hardware, be aware that using hardware not listed on the compatibility guides will force any support calls to end abruptly. Ensure that you review the appropriate compatibility guide for the product you have chosen to install.
- Plan the Service Console management methods before installing. Identify the answers to questions like:
    - Will the Service Console be on a dedicated management network or on the same network as virtual machines?
    - Will I be using VLANs or physical hardware to segment the Service Console?
    - How will I provide redundancy for the Service Console communication?

◆ If you're installing ESX Server 3.5, construct a Service Console security plan. Ensure limited access to the Service Console by minimizing the number of administrators with local user accounts or knowledge of the root password.

◆ Create user accounts for each administrative user who requires direct access to an ESX Server host.

◆ Establish strong user account policies in the Service Console by integrating ESX Server with Active Directory or by deploying a Linux-based security module.

◆ Establish growth projections and plan the ESX Server partition strategy accordingly.

 ◆ Increase /root partition size to provide ample room for growth and/or the installation of third-party applications. If the root of the file system runs out of space, there will most certainly be issues to address.

 ◆ Increase /swap partition size to address any projected increases in the amount of RAM provided to the Service Console. The /swap should be twice the amount of RAM that will be allocated to the Service Console.

 ◆ Change /var/log to /var and increase partition size to provide ample room for logs and the ESX Server patch management process that writes to the /var directory during the process.

◆ Unless performing a boot from SAN, detach ESX Server hosts from the external storage devices to prevent overwriting existing data. At minimum, don't present LUNs to a new ESX Server host until the installation is complete.

◆ When reinstalling ESX Server on a physical server, be careful not to initiate LUNs with existing data. Once again, disconnecting a host from the SAN during the reinstall process will eliminate the threat of erasing data.

◆ Configure a time synchronization strategy that synchronizes all ESX Server hosts with the same external time server.

◆ Ensure the security of console access by guaranteeing the physical security of the box. If the server is configured with a remote console adapter, like the Dell Remote Access Controller (DRAC), ensure the default password has been changed and that the DRAC network is not readily accessible to other network segments.

Virtual Networking Best Practices

The configuration details regarding the virtual networking best practices shown here can be found in Chapter 3.

◆ Plan the virtual-to-physical networking integration.

◆ Maximize the number of physical network adapters (Ethernet ports) to provide flexibility in the virtual networking architecture.

◆ Separate Service Console, iSCSI, NAS, VMotion, and virtual machine traffic across different physical networks pending the availability of network adapters or use a VLAN architecture to segment the traffic.

◆ Create virtual switches with VLAN IDs to provide security, segmentation, and scalability to the virtual switching architecture.

◆ Construct a virtual networking security policy for virtual switches, ports, and port groups.

◆ Create port groups for security, traffic shaping, or VLAN tagging.

◆ For optimal security, configure the virtual switch properties with the following settings:

    ◆ Promiscuous mode: Reject

    ◆ MAC Address Changes: Reject

    ◆ Forged Transmits: Reject

◆ Avoid VLAN tags used by common third-party hardware devices, like VLAN0. Virtual switches do not support the native VLAN as physical switches do.

◆ Define traffic shaping to reduce the outbound bandwidth available either to the virtual machines that do not require full access to the bandwidth of the physical adapter or to the virtual machines that inappropriately monopolize bandwidth. Weigh the options of micro-managing virtual machine bandwidth against the configuration of NIC teams with the installation of additional network adapters.

◆ Construct NIC teams on a physical adapter connected to separate bus architectures. For example, use one onboard network adapter in combination with an adapter from an expansion card. Do *not* use two adapters from the same expansion card in the same NIC team or two onboard adapters in the same NIC team.

◆ To eliminate a single point of failure at the physical switch, connect network adapters in a NIC team to separate physical switches that belong to the same broadcast domain.

◆ Consider creating a NIC team for the service console. Otherwise, consider providing multiple vswif ports on different networks for redundant Service Console access.

◆ Construct a dedicated Gigabit LAN for VMotion. Ideally, all physical network adapters in the server offer gigabit speeds.

◆ Create separate networks for test and production virtual machines.

Storage Management Best Practices

The configuration details regarding the virtual networking best practices shown here can be found in Chapter 4.

◆ When booting from SAN, mask each bootable LUN to be seen only by the ESX Server booting from that LUN.

◆ Build a dedicated and isolated storage network for iSCSI SAN storage to isolate and secure iSCSI storage-related traffic.

◆ Build a dedicated and isolated storage network for NAS/NFS storage to isolate and secure NAS/NFS storage-related traffic.

◆ Perform all masking at the storage device, not at the ESX Server host.

◆ Separate disk-intensive virtual machines on different LUNs carved from separate physical disks.

◆ Provide individual zoning configurations for each ESX Server host.

◆ Allow the SAN administrators to manage LUN sizes. VMFS extents might help immediate needs, but might lead to loss of data in the event that an extent becomes corrupted or damaged.

◆ Spread the storage communication workload across the available hardware devices. For example, if the ESX Server host has two fibre channel adapters, ensure that the VMkernel is not sending all traffic through one adapter while the other remains dormant.

◆ Use separate storage locations for test virtual machines and production virtual machines.

◆ Build LUNs in sizes that are easy to manage yet can host multiple virtual machines. For example create 300GB or 400GB LUNs to host 5 or 6 virtual machines. Be prepared to use storage VMotion to move disk intensive virtual machines.

◆ Use storage VMotion to eliminate down time when needing to migrate a virtual machine between datastores.

◆ Use Raw Device Mappings (RDMs) for Microsoft Clustering scenarios or to provide virtual machines with access to existing LUNs that contain data on NTFS formatted storage.

◆ Implement a solid change management practice for the deployment of new LUNs. Identify a standard sized LUN and stray from the standard only when the situation calls for it.

VirtualCenter Best Practices

The configuration details regarding the virtual networking best practices shown here can be found in Chapters 5 and 8.

◆ Uninstall IIS prior to installing VirtualCenter Server.

◆ Use the Service applet in the Windows Control Panel to configure the VMware VirtualCenter Server Service for autorestart.

◆ Design a strong high availability solution for the VirtualCenter database server (i.e., Microsoft Clustering or consistent database backups).

◆ To install VirtualCenter 2.5 with a SQL Server 2005 back-end database requires a SQL Server authenticated user account with membership in the db_owner database role and ownership of the VirtualCenter database. Once the installation of VC 2.5 is complete, the db_owner database role membership can (and should) be removed.

◆ Carefully monitor the transaction logs of the VirtualCenter database. To eliminate transaction log growth, configure SQL Server databases in Simple Recovery mode. For maximum recoverability, configure SQL Server database in Full Recovery mode.

◆ Configure VirtualCenter in an active/passive server cluster with Microsoft Clustering Services for high availability, or install VirtualCenter into a virtual machine and perform a copy of the virtual machine at regular intervals.

◆ Create a VirtualCenter hierarchy to support your management model. If your organization manages resources by location, then create management objects (datacenters, clusters, folders) based on location. On the other hand, if your organization manages by department, then create objects accordingly. In most organizations the VirtualCenter hierarchy will reflect a hybrid approach that combines location, department, server function, server type, and so forth.

◆ Apply the principle of least privilege to permissions assignment policies in VirtualCenter. Employees who use VirtualCenter as a common management tool should be granted only the permissions required to perform their job.

◆ Use Windows groups in the VirtualCenter security model. Assigning Windows groups to a VirtualCenter role that is assigned privileges and permissions will facilitate the application of similar settings in the future. For example, create a Windows group called DomainControllerAdmins that is a member of the VC role called DCAdmins, which has the privilege to power on and power off and has been granted the permission on a folder containing all domain controller virtual machines. When a new user is hired to administer the domain controller virtual machines, the user can simply be added to the DomainControllerAdmins Windows group and will inherit all the necessary permissions.

◆ Identify a systematic approach to LUN creation and management. Identify either the adaptive or the predictive scheme as the LUN management process. Keep in mind that your overall storage management may involve a combination of larger LUNs with several virtual machine files and smaller LUNs for individual virtual machine files.

◆ Configure DRS to perform VMotion based on comfort level. Some VMotion will be necessary to ensure balance and fairness of resource allocation.

◆ Disable the automated VMotion for critical virtual machines that you do not wish to be VMotion candidates based on the DRS algorithm.

◆ If the DRS algorithm suggests a VMotion migration of four or five stars, it is in the best interest of the system to apply the recommendation. The algorithm takes into account many factors for offering recommendations that result in increased system performance.

Virtual Machine Best Practices

The configuration details regarding the virtual networking best practices shown here can be found in Chapters 6 and 7.

◆ Construct virtual machines with separate drives for operating systems and user data. Place each of the virtual SCSI hard drives on separate virtual SCSI adapters.

◆ Always install VMware Tools to provide the optimized SCSI drivers, enhanced virtual NIC drives, and support for quiescing the file system during the VMware snapshot process.

◆ Use the VMware tools to complement the Windows Time Services to synchronize the time on a virtual machine. The Windows server functioning as the PDC emulator operations master should be configured to synchronize time with the same time server used by the ESX Server hosts.

◆ Avoid special characters and spaces in the display names of virtual machines. Create virtual machine display names with the same rules you apply when providing DNS hostnames.

◆ During a physical-to-virtual migration, adjust the size of the hard drives to prevent excess storage consumption of the target datastore.

◆ After a physical-to-virtual migration, reduce the amount of memory to a more appropriate level. In most physical server environments, the amount of RAM is drastically overallocated. In virtual environments, resource allocation must be carefully considered.

◆ After a physical-to-virtual migration, reduce the number of CPUs to one. Increase only as needed by the virtual machine. Additional virtual CPUs can cause unwanted contention with the scheduling of multiple vCPUs onto pCPUs. The number of vCPUs in a virtual machine should be less than the number of pCPUs in the server to prevent the virtual machine from consuming all pCPUs.

◆ Maintain virtual machine templates for several different operating system installations. For example, create and maintain templates for Windows Server 2003, Windows Server 2003 Service Pack 1, Windows Server 2003 Service Pack 2, Windows Server 2008, and so forth.

◆ When templates are brought online, place them onto isolated networks away from access by standard end users.

◆ Use CPU and memory reservations to guarantee resources to critical virtual machines and use share values to guarantee appropriate resources to critical virtual machines during periods of increased contention.

Disaster Recovery and Business Continuity Best Practices

The configuration details regarding the virtual networking best practices shown here can be found in Chapter 10.

◆ Implement Microsoft Clustering Services to achieve high availability of individual virtual machines. Note that versions of ESX Server prior to 3.5 were certified for support of Microsoft server clusters in virtual machines. As of this writing, the recertification process for clustering in a virtual machine was not complete. Please refer to the VMware website for updated information about supported technologies.

◆ Implement VMware High Availability (HA) to provide automatic restart of virtual machines residing on an ESX Server that fails.

◆ Use strict admission control for HA clusters unless virtual machine performance is not as important as simply having the virtual machine powered on.

◆ Prioritize virtual machines for startup after server failure. Prepare a contingency plan for powering off unnecessary virtual machines in the event of server failure, resulting in reduced computing power.

◆ Implement a backup strategy that involves a blend of full virtual machine backups with file level backups.

◆ Purchase enough backup agents to ensure minimal recovery times for servers with critical production data. Schedule the backups to ensure that recovery times are appropriate for the data type. For example, for data with greater value and a requirement for quicker restore, backups should be scheduled more often than usual.

◆ Do not use virtual machine snapshots as long-term solutions to disaster recovery or business continuity. Snapshots are meant as a temporary means of providing an easy rollback feature and are used primarily for short term recovery purposes.

◆ Back up data as often as needed as determined by a written business continuity/disaster recovery plan. More critical data should be backed up more often to prevent less data loss in the event of disaster.

◆ Test the full and virtual machine backups regularly by restoring to a test or development network.

◆ Store a copy of virtual machine backups in an off-site location. Otherwise, use tools to perform virtual machine replication to distant datacenters. Virtualization offers significant advantages in the realm of disaster recovery because virtual machines are encapsulated into a discrete set of files.

◆ Purchase licenses for Windows Server 2003 Datacenter to achieve a greater return on investment and achieve less stringent VMotion restrictions. Datacenter licenses allow for the installation of an unlimited number of virtual machines per ESX Server host.

VI3 Monitoring and Troubleshooting Best Practices

The following best practices will help you troubleshoot a problematic VI3 deployment.

◆ Monitor virtual machine performance with a combination of tools inside the virtual machine and tools in VI3. For example, use Task Manager inside of a virtual machine and the performance reports from VirtualCenter to monitor CPU utilization and to identify bottlenecks.

◆ Regularly review the levels of CPUReady and Ballooning in the performance charts provided by VirtualCenter. Abnormally high values of either counter would indicate an issue with CPU or memory, respectively.

◆ Create virtual machine benchmarks as a standard of comparison when changes are made.

◆ Create e-mail-based performance alarms for key virtual machines. Allow administrators to be notified of system problems for virtual machines that provide core network services such as mail, databases, and authentication.

◆ Identify the root of any problem, then attempt fixes based on monitoring results, feature dependencies, and the company's documented change management process. For example, if VMware HA is not failing over properly, review the DNS configuration for the affected hosts since HA relies on name resolution across ESX Server hosts.

◆ Engage in a systematic approach to identifying and fixing problems with ESX Server hosts and virtual machines.

Index